A Practical Guide to

GST Audits and Certification

A Practical Guide to GST Audits and Certification

Second Edition

CA Madhukar N Hiregange, B.Com., FCA, DISA, Passed CISA

Shri B.S.V. Murthy, Bachelor in Science, LL.B, IRS (Retd)

CA Mahadev R, B.Com., FCA

CA Ravi Kumar Somani, B.Com., ACA

Technical Reviewer: **CA Yogesh Virmani**

BLOOMSBURY

NEW DELHI • LONDON • OXFORD • NEW YORK • SYDNEY

First published in India 2018

ISBN 978-93-89165-26-5

10 9 8 7 6 5 4 3 2 1

Bloomsbury Publishing India Pvt. Ltd
DDA Complex, LSC Building No.4
Second Floor, Pocket C–6 & 7, Vasant Kunj
New Delhi 110070
Phone: +91-11-40574957, 40574954
www.bloomsbury.com
CIN: U22130DL2012PTC232353

To provide feedback, please mail at professionalbooks@bloomsbury.com

Printed and bound in India by Rajkamal Electric Press, Kundli

To find out more about our authors and books visit www.bloomsbury.com/in/academic/accounting-tax-law
Here you will find extracts, author interviews, details of forthcoming events and the option to sign up for our newsletters.

About the authors

CA Madhukar N Hiregange [B.Com., FCA, DISA, Passed CISA], is a senior partner at Hiregange & Associates. He has jointly authored 22 books on Central Excise, Service Tax, Karnataka VAT and Excise/Service Tax Audit, IDT - IPCC Study Material, Central Sales Tax, GST - A Primer-2 Editions, GST Classification & Exemption 2017, Compendium of Issues and Solutions in GST – March 2018/ May 2019 and GST Tariff – October 2018. He is also working on 3 sectoral books on GST, slated to be published in August 2019. He is constantly active in spreading awareness about Indirect Taxes through seminars, articles, pdicai. org, linkedin, facebook, youtube, caclubindia.com & hiregangeacademy.com, etc. He has also been a Central Council Member, ICAI, for the term 2010-13 & 2106-19, with a vision of enhancing the credibility of the profession and strengthening the professional in practice and employment. He has also served as Chairman of the Indirect Tax Committee, for the year 2012 and term 2016-19, with the privilege of leading a wonderful and contributing team for 4 years.

He is actively involved in efforts to make the indirect taxation simple, certain and fair, and also in creating an awareness of the potential of knowledge in the field of indirect taxes in India.

He is Managing Trustee of the Empower Education Foundation and is interested in the education of lesser privileged. He firmly believes in "Value-Based Practice and Life".

Shri BSV Murthy, [B.Sc., LLB, IRS (Retd)], after graduation joined Indian Revenue Service in 1979. During his career, he has been a part of:

- The project steering committee for development of risk management system in Customs,
- The committees set up for considering refund system, staffing in Central Excise etc.;
- The team which developed an audit manual in collaboration with Revenue Canada;
- The Indian delegation to Sri Lanka and Nepal.

He received the *Presidential award* for distinguished service record in the year 2005. During his career, he got exposure to all the areas of indirect taxes and for 7 years from 2008, he served as a member of the Customs, Excise and Service Tax

Appellate Tribunal and got retired from services in the year 2015. He continues to be active in the professional consultancy after retirement.

CA Mahadev.R [B. Com., FCA], [B.Com., FCA]

is a partner at Hiregange & Associates, Bangalore. He has been involved in advising clients across different manufacturing and service industries, on various issues under indirect taxes including reviews under GST, for ensuring better compliance.

He has assisted many renowned authors of books on Central Excise Made Simple, Practical guide to Service tax etc. and a co-authored a book on 'Goods and Service Tax', published by Himalaya Publishing House, for B.com students. He is also an active contributor of articles to Karnataka State Chartered Accountants Association (KSCAA) journal, GST Law Times etc.

CA Ravi Kumar Somani [B.Com., ACA], is a partner at Hiregange & Associates, Pune. He has been involved in performing indirect tax reviews across varied sectors and guiding clients on contracts structuring, workable business models, transactional structuring, developing systems and processes for compliance under Indirect Taxes.

He has authored a book on Indirect Taxes 'Self study guide to Indirect Taxes', published by Asia Law House. He is a faculty at ICAI and has given lectures at various professional forums on Service Tax and GST. He is also an active contributor of articles in GST Law Times, MCCIA, Newsletter of Pune Branch of ICAI and on other professional forums.

Technical reviewer

CA Yogesh Virmani, presently working in PricewaterhouseCoopers Pvt. Ltd. (PwC) as a Director. Yogesh has over 11 years of experience in the field of indirect taxation.

Yogesh has been actively involved in advising holistic and business oriented solutions to corporates from an indirect tax perspective. He frequently interacts with various tax authorities on matters relating to indirect taxation.

Preface

GST in India has now completed two years of tumultuous existence with frequent major changes coming in the way of clear understanding of the mixed unique law. The passing of the GST in consensus with all the States is no mean achievement, though it led to a dilution in the implementation of pure and pristine principles of this value-added tax. The push to make the law simple has also led to many unsavoury practices of the past resurfacing.

The audit function is recognised as an essential part of the economy of any country. Today it leverages the rapidly changing technology to provide credibility and assurance to stakeholders ranging from the general public, investors, shareholders, lenders, regulators and other users of financial statements. We added 2 chapters of value, one being on the Customs audit, which has some link to the GST audit and can be a complimentary service. Further a chapter on year-end activities, useful for the audit of the year 2018-19.

The main objective of this book is to enable one with knowledge of the GST law, to be able to comply with the presently complex law and elaborate procedures as well as for the professionals to review and certify. The role of voluntary concurrent review being of value to the industry and trade has been underlined throughout this book. The incidental objective sought is prevention and mitigation of disputes and consequent corruption which has been the bane of the earlier indirect tax laws in India.

A taxpayer has to comply with this complex law, which places added responsibility on a taxpayer for compliance by the suppliers, which is unfair but has to be complied till the new returns are in place. Even in the case of bonafide errors by either the taxpayer or by the officers, the limitation to raise demands is four and half years, which can be extended to six and half years, in case of deliberate evasion, with a very high-interest rate on tax determined and penalties. There is a famous proverb "knowledge is power". In line with that, for a taxpayer, expert knowledge of GST law is essential for due compliance with laws and avoiding huge costs/penalties. Alternatively, he may also opt for GST consultancy and compliance audits by professionals, which are more likely.

This book would be particularly useful for the Chartered Accountants and Management Accountants who have been specified as the professionals to certify the reconciliation and to taxpayers who want to put in their own efforts. It would also be useful for other professionals i.e. Advocates, Tax consultants and to the individuals handling Finance, Accounts & Taxation portfolio in the industry. The book should also be a useful guide for the GST Revenue officers of the Centre, State and the Directorate of Revenue Intelligence.

The different types of audits and methodology of conducting them by professionals have been discussed using the technical standards. The mandatory audit above the threshold is notified which covers all interpretational facets of GST. Working knowledge would not be sufficient for the certification. Audit and reconciliation skills would be necessary for compliance. The annual return is to be filed by June 30th 2019. The form, as well as some of the utilities, have been provided on the GST Portal. The Form GSTR 9C is still to be open up, which indicates that the possibility of further extension exists. Chapter 21 of the book provides a detailed analysis of the Form GSTR 9 annual return. Chapter 22 similarly provides detailed guidance to the auditor on the reconciliation statement and certification.

The effort is focused on collating relevant aspects of audit in the GST regime. This would be a vital tool to eliminate errors in the initial period of lack of awareness and detect/prevent revenue leakages. It would also further the Government's initiative of being less intrusive in line, with making India as the preferred location for investment by ensuring "ease of doing business". This exercise would be an independent check and balance against errors and frauds.

We are grateful for the noble profession of Chartered Accountancy which has provided us more than we dreamt of in terms of being able to contribute to making indirect tax laws in India simple, fair and transparent. We have relied on the extensive material developed by the Indirect Tax Committee, ICAI and its pronouncements which has enhanced the effort.

We would like to place our special acknowledgements to Shri K.S. Ravishankar who has been a guide for ethical practice under whom many ethical practitioners have grown. Special acknowledgements to CA Subba Reddy, CA Lakshmi GK and other staff of Hiregange & Associates for contributing to the research and collation of the first publication.

We would like to thank our respective families for their patience and co-operation in giving time in the evenings and holidays to enable this academic pursuit. We appreciate the proactive support from the publishers Bloomsbury in bringing out this pioneering publication on GST audit.

The encouraging response of reader prompted us to review, improve the quality and utility of the book. We would be glad to have readers provide their valuable open feedback on improvements in the next edition.

CA Madhukar N Hiregange
Shri B.S.V. Murthy, Advocate
CA Mahadev R
CA Ravi Kumar Somani

Contents at a glance

PART 5
CONDUCT OF AUDIT – AREAS OF FOCUS

PART 6
FILING OF ANNUAL RETURN

PART 7
MANDATORY CERTIFICATION – RECONCILIATION STATEMENT

PART 8
CUSTOMS AUDIT, YEAR-END ACTION POINTS AND OTHER CERTIFICATIONS

Table of contents

PART 2
FUNDAMENTAL CONCEPTS OF AUDIT

PART 3
AUDIT PROCESS, METHODOLOGY & APPROACH

PART 4
AUDIT STANDARDS, ACCOUNTING STANDARDS AND GUIDANCE NOTE

PART 5
CONDUCT OF AUDIT – AREAS OF FOCUS

PART 6
FILING OF ANNUAL RETURN

PART 7
MANDATORY CERTIFICATION – RECONCILIATION STATEMENT

PART 8
CUSTOMS AUDIT, YEAR-END ACTION POINTS AND OTHER CERTIFICATIONS

How to use the book?

1. This book is divided into 8 parts in order of need of understanding of audit process ending with the appendices. Readers may find value by going through the relevant parts of this book.
2. The first part deals with the overview of GST audit- opportunities and advantages;
3. The second part deals with audit concepts and the role of the auditor;
4. The third part is audit methodology and processes;
5. The fourth part has the details of technical standards needed to do a professional audit;
6. The fifth part has discussions on how GST audit can be done;
7. The sixth part has discussions on understanding and tips to fill annual return (GSTR-9); Table by table discussion provided.
8. The seventh part provides detailed discussions on mandatory certification of reconciliation statement (GSTR-9C); Table by table discussion provided with analysis.
9. The eighth part covers chapters on audit under customs, year-end action points for taxpayers for better compliance, and other certifications under GST.
10. The last part has appendices which contain the important definitions, extracts of important provisions, standards on auditing, notified formats of GSTR-9 and GSTR-9C and important formats useful for audits such as engagement letter, acceptance letter etc.
11. Online Link http://bit.ly/GSTAudit provides for Free Online Updates and other important information.

How to use the book?

List of abbreviations and terms used

Sl. No.	Abbreviation	Terms / Description
1	AAS	Auditing and Assurance Standard
2	AASB	Auditing and Assurance Standards Board
3	ACA	Association Of Chartered Accountants
4	ACCA	Association of Chartered Certified Association
5	ACL	Audit Command Language
6	AFT	Aviation Turbine Fuel
7	AG	Auditor General
8	ALP	Arms' Length Price
9	AOA	Articles of Association
10	AOP	Association of Person
11	AT	Adjusted Turnover
12	ATI	Adjusted Taxable Income
13	B2B	Business To Business
14	B2C	Business To Customer
15	BCP	Business Continuity Planning
16	BCD	Basic Custom Duty
17	BOE	Bills of Exchange
18	BRC	Bank Realization Certificate
19	BTP	Bio-Technology Park
20	C&AG	Comptroller and Auditor General
21	C&F	Cost and Freight
22	CA	Chartered Accountant
23	CAAT	Computer Aided Audit Tools
24	CARO	Companies (Auditor's Report) Order
25	CBEC	Central Board of Excise and Customs
26	CBIC	Central Board of Indirect taxes and Customs
27	CCIT	Chief Commissioner of Income Tax
28	CE	Central Excise
29	CENVAT	Central Value Added Tax
30	CEO	Chief Executive Officer

Sl. No.	Abbreviation	Terms / Description
31	CFO	Chief Financial Officer
32	CG	Central Government
33	CGST	Central Goods and Services Tax
34	CISA	Certified Information Systems Auditor
35	CIT	Commissioner of Income Tax
36	CMA	Cost and Management Accounting
37	COA	Chart of Accounts
38	COP	Certificate of Practice
39	CST	Central Sales Tax
40	CTA	Custom Tariff Act
41	CTR	Current Transaction Report
42	CVD	Countervailing Duty
43	DC	Delivery Challan
44	DGFT	Directorate General of Foreign Trade
45	DISA	Diploma Course on Systems security and Audit
46	DSA	Direct Selling Agent
47	DSC	Digital Signature Certificate
48	DTA	Domestic Tariff Area
49	ECO	E-Commerce Operator
50	EGM	Export General Manifest
51	EHTP	Electronics Hardware Technology Park
52	EOU	Export Oriented Unit
53	EPCG	Export Promotion Capital Goods
54	EPZ	Export Processing Zone
55	ERP	Enterprise Resource Planning
56	EU-VAT	European Union Value Added Tax
57	EVC	Electronic Verification Code
58	FAQ	Frequently Asked Question
59	FCA	Fellow Chartered Accountants
60	FEMA	Foreign Exchange and Management Act
61	FIRC	Foreign Inward Remittance Certificate
62	FMCG	Fast Moving Consumer Goods
63	FOC	Free of Cost

Sl. No.	Abbreviation	Terms / Description
64	FTP	Foreign Trade Policy
65	FY	Financial Year
66	GAAP	Generally Accepted Accounting Principles
67	GL	General Ledger
68	GST	Goods and Services Tax
69	GSTIN	Goods and Service Tax Identification Number
70	GSTN	Goods and Service Tax Network
71	GSTR	Goods and Services Tax Return
72	GTA	Goods Transportation Agency
73	HO	Head Office
74	HOD	Head of Department
75	HSD	High Speed Diesel
76	HSN	Harmonized System of Nomenclature
77	IAPC	International Auditing Practices Committee
78	ICAI	Institute of Chartered Accountants of India
79	ICD	Inland Container Depot
80	ICES	Indian Customs EDI System
81	ICQ	Internal Control Questionnaire
82	ICWAI	Institute of Cost and Works Accountant of India
83	IDT	Indirect Taxes
84	IESBAC	International Ethics Standard Board of Accountants
85	IFAC	International Federation of Accountants
86	IFRS	International Financial Reporting Standards
87	IGAAP	Indian Generally Accepted Accounting Principles
88	IGST	Integrated Goods and Services Tax
89	IPC	Indian Penal Code
90	IPSAS	International Public Sector Accounting Standards
91	IRS	Indian Revenue Services
92	ISA	International Standards on Auditing
93	ISD	Input Service Distributor
94	IT	Information Technology
95	ITC	Input Tax Credit
96	ITR	Income Tax Return

Sl. No.	Abbreviation	Terms / Description
97	JW	Job Work /Job Worker
98	KYC	Know Your Client
99	LLB	Bachelor of Law
100	LLP	Limited Liability Partnership
101	LUT	Letter of Undertaking
102	MCA	Ministry of Corporate Affairs
103	MEIS	Merchandise Exports from India Scheme
104	MIS	Management Information System
105	MOA	Memorandum of Association
106	NACAS	National Advisory Committee on Accounting Standards
107	NBFC	Non-Banking Financial Company
108	NFRA	National Financial Reporting Authority
109	OIDAR	Online Information Database Access and Retrieval
110	OPC	One Person Company
111	OTP	One Time Password
112	P&L	Profit and Loss account
113	PAN	Permanent Account Number
114	PCAOB	Public Company Accounting Oversight Board
115	PFY	Previous Financial Year
116	POS	Place of Supply
117	PSU	Public Sector Unit
118	RBI	Reserve Bank of India
119	RC	Reverse Charge
120	RCM	Reverse Charge Mechanism
121	SA	Standards on Auditing
122	SAC	Services Accounting Code
123	SAD	Special Additional Duty
124	SAE	Standards on Assurance Engagements
125	SC	Supreme Court
126	SCN	Show Cause Notice
127	SEBI	Securities Exchange Boards of India
128	SEIS	Service Exports from India Scheme
129	SEZ	Special Economic Zones

Sl. No.	Abbreviation	Terms / Description
130	SGST	State Goods and Services Tax
131	SIA	Standards on Internal Auditing
132	SME	Small and Medium Enterprises
133	SOP	Standard Operating Procedure
134	SQC	Standard on Quality Control
135	SRE	Standard on Review Engagements
136	SRS	Standards on Related Services
137	ST	Service Tax
138	STP	Software Technology Park
139	TCS	Tax Collection at Source
140	TDS	Tax Deduction at Source
141	The CA Act	The Chartered Accountants Act, 1949
142	TOS	Time of Supply
143	TRAN	Transitional Form
144	TV	Transaction Value
145	UIN	Unique Identification Number
146	UN	United Nations
147	UQC	Unit Quantity Code
148	URD	Unregistered Dealer
149	UT	Union Territory
150	UTGST	Union Territory Goods and Service Tax

Chapter 1

Basic Concepts of GST Law

1.1 BACKGROUND

India has had a number of taxes introduced at various points of time. Under indirect taxes we have had central excise, central sales tax, value added tax, service tax, luxury tax, entertainment tax, betting and gambling tax, entry tax in States and many more. Each of these taxes was administered by State or the Centre or both. They had different threshold exemption, taxed different activities/events, their own classification entries, valuation principles, demand, recovery mechanisms and procedures, which made it difficult for doing business. There were also many changes in each year making the multiple laws uncertain and unreliable. The foreign direct investment which is a life line for any developing economy is dependent on "*ease of doing business*". India improved its ranking to 77th among 190 countries this year.*[1] Tax reforms in the form of introduction of GST helped to improve this rating.

The Government as a part of 40 years old unfinished agenda of implementing value added tax in India merged 11 indirect taxes of the Centre and States. This was done in a unique consensus approach (give and take) to get all States on board which lead to the pristine principles of an ideal GST to be diluted quite substantially with many aspects of the erstwhile sales tax (VAT) getting into this new law. Statutes relating to the Goods and Service Tax have been implemented with effect from 1st July, 2017 after constitutional amendment in 2016.[2] Basic customs duty on goods imported into India is not part of the GST as it is used to regulate the imports into India.[3] Some transactions/products like electricity, 5 petroleum products, stamp duty, liquor have been kept out of GST in line with the States' demand and considerations of possible fall in gross revenue. Some of them may over period of time be merged depending on the comfort of the State revenues. Presently feasibility of including 5 petroleum products for the purpose of levy of GST is being examined which does not require any constitutional amendment and only requires the GST Council to recommend after the Centre and States agree. However, revenue concerns of the Centre and State in the light of

---

1 As per World Bank, Jan 2019.

2 The Constitution Amendment Bill of 2014 was passed on 14th July 2016.

3 A special chapter on Customs Audit (Chapter-23) along with the audit to be conducted by revenue is added in this book.

lower collection of GST and less than expected growth in direct tax may lead to postponement.

The main objectives of GST are:

- Enlarge the tax base now that India is moving towards being a developed economy,
- Encourage the parallel economy to join the mainstream which presently contributes less or not at all to the tax collections,
- Avoid the cascading impact of multiple levies. i.e. tax on tax making goods and services competitive,
- Reduce the multiplicity of taxes on transactions and lead to a common market,
- Reduce the cost of compliance for Government/assessee and
- Reduce the interface between the tax payer and the administrators by using information technology.

The experience in the last 24 months on the total collections has been reasonable though the economy continues to grow at about 7% per annum. GST has helped the direct tax collections to clock a 16% growth in 2017-19 to some extent. The GST collection post March 2018 has been up a bit less than the expected level even though the number of registrants has increased by more than 60% to 135 Lakhs. Assessees in the parallel economy have joined the mainstream to some extent and are registered. The recent months of filing of annual return has seen increase beyond 1 Lakh crores and with the audits next 2 months may also be so.

The recent move of enhancing the threshold exemption to Rs. 40 lakhs for goods in most States*[4] and composition to Rs.150 lakhs would lead to significant downward impact on the expected collections in 2019-20.

The majority of these registered persons may not be paying significant part of the tax due. Some maybe availing excess credits, under invoicing, part invoicing when dealing with the customers in the unorganised stream. They may be awaiting the final decision on reverse charge from unregistered suppliers as well as the unfolding of the matching procedures. The GST technology infrastructure was pushed through without the normal user testing and frequent amendments have been a feature of the GSTN. The ill effects of the big bang reforms with reverse charge on procurements from unregistered suppliers (now limited to few sectors to be notified) and credit matching (onus shifted to the supplier other than in exceptional cases) instead of a graded implementation has led to many compromises with frequent amendments and government is unable to implement GST effectively even today. The education of the tax officers which was taken up

---

4 See note in end of this chapter for applicability of different limits for goods and services State wise.

in earnest in the start has been subsequently ignored to a great extent. It appears that the linking of examination and officer's promotion to understanding is the only way to teach this new law.

The trade/industry is coming to grips with nuances of this new law slowly. The filling of the annual returns, reconciliation and audit exercise would underline the need to know this law in depth.

The improvements in the past year and half are as under:

(1) The simplification of the return filing process by introducing GSTR 3B in 2017 has allowed the business to business part of the economy to transact business and file returns. The further simplification from April 2019 should make it easier and fair for the small and medium entrepreneurs with shifting non-compliance liability primarily to the supplier.

(2) Technology which had to cope with law being amended frequently with capacity building and expanding the IT infrastructure is able to manage billions of transactions. The anomalies in the network not being in line with the law or rules are being resolved regularly. Some glitches are still there even in the annual return (Form-9) [though it was revised in 2019] and Audit form 9C.

(3) The larger tax payers have found the advantage of this single tax and have embraced it fully with their vendors. They are hoping that the rough edges are resolved as soon as possible.

(4) The Government is expressing its concern on the collections which are a bit below expectation and very happy with the increased registration which indicates the firm movement towards compliance by the SME sector.

(5) The annual return (Form-9) and GST audit (Form- 9C) have been notified and assessees have started the compliance with the assistance of the professionals. One of the main objectives this year is to identify and correct the transitionary errors as well as errors due to lack of understanding of the law.

Those expected in the coming months could be as under:

(1) The final decision on limiting of the RCM levy on unregistered procurement [not applicable till end of September 2019. Amendment made in the provisions to apply this provision only to notified class of persons]

(2) Continue to broaden the base which has shown remarkable growth in the starting.

(3) Correct/clarify the several restrictions, practical issues and drafting lacunae [before the GST Council].

(4) Amend the credit matching mechanism with invoice uploaded by the supplier being the important check point.

(5) To win back the trust of the tax payer with simpler business friendly law.

(6) To put IT based identification of tax leakage areas and identifying the errant tax evader post September 2019. This would necessitate issue of enquiry letter and confirmation of answers. In case of no replies or inadequate replies the need of hearing and possible demand under a show cause notice could be started.

(7) Put in place the simpler version of regular returns.

1.2 SCHEME OF GST

1.2.1 Levy

The levy of GST under section 9 of the CGST Act and section 5 of IGST Act is on supply of goods or services or both within the State and outside the State respectively. It appears that the "supply" as well as the "goods and/or service or both" are equally important.

It has also been fastened on the receiver of the specified goods and services for few activities. Further, procurements from unregistered suppliers are also planned to be covered (presently suspended up to 30th September 2019) in a limited manner for some specified sectors to provide a level playing field to the Indian tax compliant supplier as well as the tax compliant receiver. This is called the reverse charge. The fundamental principle here was that every supply over a period of time would be liable to GST either by the supplier or the receiver. This objective has been diluted at present with the increase in the limits for threshold as well as composition.

Initially it was expected that the rate of tax between services and goods would be only one. However, now that we have a number of rates and classification of goods and services. This added to the special valuation methods add to the number of effective impact of rates. The special rates without input tax credit implemented for the hotel and real estate industry could distort the basic principle of GST.

The exemptions to goods and services have also been provided to a limited extent. Identifying the activity as a supply or goods or services is also needed as the time of supply and place of supply would determine payment of IGST or CGST (UTGST) and the principles to be followed for goods and services to determine the same are different. It would also determine whether tax is leviable on exports or imports.

1.2.1.1 Supply

Supply has been defined to include all the activities which were hitherto covered in the 11 State and Central taxes which have been subsumed in GST. This very wide definition is normally applicable only if activity is in furtherance of business and with a consideration. The wide definition of "business" means that almost all activities are covered including the activities by Government and supplies to Government unless specifically excluded and one may have to be very careful in taking a view that it is not a business. It means that all hither to untaxed sectors like the education, medical, religious and charitable could be liable for part of their activities.

1.2.1.2 Supply with Consideration

The normal supply includes agreeing to supply goods or services in the course of business. It specifically includes: sale, transfer, barter, exchange, license, rental, lease and disposal.

It also specifically includes import of services for a consideration whether or not the activity is a business. Therefore imports on personal account would be liable with liability on either the provider (OIDAR) or the importer.

1.2.1.3 Supply without Consideration

Schedule I provides the details of activities which are considered to be liable even though there has been no consideration. They are:

- ITC availed business assets being transferred even if transfer is permanent. This would include those assets out of credits availed in the earlier regime as the credit would have been carried forward or utilised. The receiver would be eligible for credit.
- Supply made between distinct persons (same PAN- different registrations) which means that stock transfers of goods would also be liable. Similarly the supply of services between the branches and offices with different registration (normally in different States) are liable from 1st July 2017. The deputation of employees may not be taxable as there is an employee employer relationship and thus cannot be considered as a manpower supply. Supreme Court confirmed this in service tax which could apply in GST.[5]
- Supply between related persons in the course of business. Services to employees are also considered as being between related persons. Therefore supplies which are not part of their gross emoluments would also be liable.

---

5 CCE Vs Nissin Brake I P Ltd – 2019 –TIOL- 151-SC -ST

- Import of services from related parties or from any of their other establishments outside India.
- Supply of goods by agent to principal or vice versa when agent is working on behalf of the principal.

1.2.1.4 Activities/Transactions Deemed to Goods or Services

The single rate for goods services in India may not be possible in the foreseeable future, till we are a developed economy with nobody under the poverty line. The differences between goods and services in the present law are as follows:

- rate of tax
- place of supply
- time of supply
- input tax credit to some extent.

In the earlier indirect tax regime there were disputes on activities and transactions whether goods or services. The State and the Centre would be concurrently taxing the same transaction. In GST this has been mitigated to some extent now in Sch-II which sets out which would be goods and which services. These are as under:

i. Any transfer of title in goods at time of supply (normal sale),

ii. Any transfer of title in goods in future is a supply of goods (hire purchase, rent to own, closed end leasing),

iii. Any transfer of right in goods or undivided share in goods would be a supply of services, (computer or equipment hired out for a day or a year),

iv. Any lease, tenancy, easement (right to enter), license to occupy land is a service,

v. Any lease or letting out of building (residential/commercial) wholly or partly is a service,

vi. Any treatment or process on another persons' goods is a service,

vii. Any permanent transfer or disposal of business asset is a supply of goods (used motor car given to partner, under construction property given to joint venture partner, merger)

viii. Any temporary transfer or use of business asset including private (non business use) would be a service (letting out the factory or plug and play facility),

ix. Where a taxable person ceases to do business any goods which are part of the business shall be deemed to be supply of goods unless:

    a. the business is continued to be carried on by a representative (heir- designated person) or

    b. business is transferred as a going concern.

x. Some specific activities considered to be services are: renting of immovable property; construction of complex, civil structure except where consideration is received after issuance of completion certificate; temporary transfer or right to us of intellectual property rights; development, design, programing, customisation, adaptation, enhancement, implementation of information technology software; agreeing to obligation to refrain or tolerate or do an act; and transfer of right to use goods.

xi. Composite works contract or supply of food or drink (other than alcohol) by way of or part of service would be a service.

xii. Supply of goods by an unincorporated association or body of persons to a member would be a supply of goods.

Supply included vide sec 7(1)(d) which read- "the activities to be treated as supply of goods or supply of services as referred to in Sch II". However, w.e.f. 1st July 2017*[6] retrospective amendment made and sec 7(1A) inserted to clarify that only if an activity or transaction is a supply as set out in sec 7(1) then only Sch II has to be referred.

1.2.1.5 Activities not supply of Services or Goods

Supply excludes certain activities which are not supply of goods or services as per Sch- III:

These activities are as under:

- Services by employee to employer
- Services by court or tribunal
- Services by MLAs, MPs and persons who hold posts in bodies established by Central or State Government.
- Sale of land and sale of building other than those under construction.
- Actionable claims other than lottery, betting and gambling.
- Gifts from employer to employee not exceeding Rs. 50,000 (provided in Sch I) in a financial year.
- Supply of goods from a place in the non-taxable territory to another place in the non-taxable territory [global trade] without such goods entering into India.
- Supply of warehoused goods [as provided in the Customs Act] to any person before clearance for home consumption.

---

6 Central Goods and Services Tax (Amendment) Act, 2018, vide Notification No. 31 OF 2018, dated 30.08.2019.

- Supply of goods by the consignee to any other person, by endorsement of documents of title to the goods, after the goods have been dispatched from the port of origin located outside India but before clearance for home consumption (commonly referred to as 'high sea sales').

1.2.1.6 Reverse Charge Mechanism

In the economy of India we have had a large number of the goods and services being provided by the unorganised trade/industry supplying to the final consumer as well as the trade and industry. Tax liability in case of specified services like specified services by the Government, goods transport agent service, sponsorship service, legal services, service from outside India etc. under section 9(3). This provision is a carry forward from the service tax regime. These procurements do not have any exemption and one has to register from day one if receiving them even if one is within the threshold limit of Rs.10/20/40 lakhs. Composition dealers would also be liable for payment under reverse charge.

In general there are some suppliers of goods and services who may be small and below the threshold limit of Rs. 20/10 Lakhs [w.e.f. 1.04.2019- Rs 40 Lakhs]. In addition there are those who have been avoiding the tax by not raising invoices, under invoicing and are keeping themselves under the limit by having multiple businesses. Therefore one more levy on receipts from unregistered suppliers by registered persons had been imposed under sections 9 (4) of the CGST Act and 5(4) of the IGST Act. This levy has been postponed due to the resistance and adverse impact on many SMEs in the initial period.[7] Many SMEs do not have proper accounting policies traditionally and business is done on trust. Since they need to be competitive they do not invest on record keeping to the extent they should be doing. The income tax for many unorganised sectors needs to be calculated based only on the gross turnover with a percentage of deemed income less some specified deductions. In the present system where a SME supplier does not pay the tax or file the return and disappears, the receiver has to repay the credit availed along with interest. This anomaly has been corrected from July 2019*[8] where the primary responsibility would be of the supplier other than in exceptional circumstances of abetting or disappearance of the supplier.

---

7 Imposed from 1st July till 13th October. From that date onwards it is kept in abeyance now till 30th September 2019.

8 As of now but may be postponed. However the new returns have the complexity of HSN wise reporting which could be challenging.

1.2.1.7 Small Supplier Exemption

The registration is exempted to those who supply goods or services below an aggregate value of Rs.20 Lakhs per year*[9]. A smaller limit of Rs.10 Lakhs has been fixed for the Special Category States. This exemption however is not available for the following:

(1) One who is liable for reverse charge under section 9 (3) of CGST or 5(3) of IGST for specified services,

(2) One who is liable for reverse charge under section 9 (4) of CGST or 5(4) of IGST for any supplies form unregistered suppliers (kept in abeyance till 31st September 2019),

(3) Involves in e- commerce business through an e commerce operator,

(4) Engages as a casual taxable person or non-resident person making taxable supplies,

(5) Online data base service provider outside India,

(6) Person who is required to deduct tax,

(7) Person who does interstate supply of goods (interstate supply of services is allowed within the exemption)

(8) Agent of a principal and

(9) Any person notified by Government.

1.2.1.8 Composition

In India due to the large number of entrepreneurs being uneducated or operating in unorganised sectors like man power supply, construction, hotels and small traders, States came up with alternative tax collection mechanisms which did not need maintenance of complete or proper accounting records. These schemes however were used by many whose turnover was in 100s of crores. In some States there was no limit fixed due to graft/compromises made.

In GST also considering that such real smaller players are in large numbers, a scheme of lower payment of tax has been implemented. The tax rates are: traders - 1%, Specified manufacturers - 1% and Suppliers of food & beverages- 5%. This is available up to Rs. 1 Crore*[10] subject to the following conditions:

(1) Person having business in different States needs to be separately registered in all of them. (In other words, a person cannot be in composition in one registration and outside in another registration). The aggregate turnover from all locations should not exceed Rs. 1.5 crore,

---

9 Enhanced to Rs. 40 lakhs for goods we.f. April 2019 in most States. Some States have chosen not to increase the limit. *See* note in end of chapter.

10 Enhanced to Rs.1.50 crores w.e.f April 2019.

(2) Service providers cannot opt for this scheme except those engaged in the supply of food and beverages, (outdoor caterer/hotel etc.). In case of other services, the value of service should not exceed 10% of other turnover (manufacturing/trading) in the state in previous financial year or Rs.5 lakh.

(3) No input tax credit is available to such person,

(4) Such person cannot collect the composition tax from the recipient[11],

(5) Composition dealer cannot have any stock which are procured from outside state/imported in hand before opting for composition,

(6) Person who makes any supply of goods through an Electronic Commerce Operator cannot opt for the scheme and

(7) Person who is a manufacturer of such goods as may be notified on the recommendation of the Council cannot opt for the scheme. Ice cream, pan masala and tobacco products under chapter 24 are notified till date.

The disadvantage of the composition scheme when one is an intermediary is that the ITC is not availed and there is a tax outflow. The receiver cannot avail credit. Therefore the composition scheme is not beneficial to those in B2B activity but to only those who supply to the final consumer [B2C].

1.2.1.9 Special Small Supplier Scheme

Smaller service providers normally provide service to the unregistered entities who may not be able to avail the ITC. They were many exemptions which they were enjoying and importantly centralized registration in the earlier regime. Some of the benefits are not available in GST as there is a considered effort to expand the base. Further in GST they need to go for multiple registrations and there is increased compliance. The rate of 18%, with hardly any input tax credit, was leading to service providers creating multiple firms.

Notification 2/2019, G.S.R. 189E, dated 7th March, 2019, was put in place for the service providers who had less than Rs. 50 lakhs of supplies*[12] in the year 2018-19 to pay 3% CGST + 3 % SGST*[13]. The conditions for this are as under:

i. They shall not make exempt supplies,

ii. They should have no interstate supplies,

iii. They are nor a casual or non resident taxable persons.

---

11 Industry has represented that the composition tax charged should be available as credit to the receiver to be fair to the dealer and also avoid cascading to that extent.

12 Aggregate turnover will include exempt, except- extended deposits/loans/advances where consideration is interest or discount.

13 State laws expected to follow the Central.

iv. They do not do business through the e-commerce.

v. They shall not collect the GST from customers.

Note: This exemption is not available to ice cream, pan masala and tobacco products under chapter 24.

1.2.2 Inter and Intra State supply

The intra-State supply is where the location of the supplier and the place of supply of goods or services or both are within the State. Inter-state supply would be when location of the supplier and the place of supply of are in different States or Union Territories. Relevant sections to determine the place of supply are sections 12 or 13 of the IGST Act.

The applicability of types of GST in normal transactions can be seen in table below:

Type of Transaction	Type of Tax
Supply of goods, or of services, or both within the State (Same transaction would suffer both types of tax)	SGST or UTGST of respective State
	CGST
Supply of goods, or of services, or both in course of inter-State trade or commerce	IGST
Supply of goods, or of services, or both in course of import into the territory of India	IGST

1.2.3 Valuation

Valuation disputes in the past were frequent in central excise and started in service tax and less in VAT. However most of the issues in excise got resolved as the law developed. In service tax few disputes arose due to subjectivity and lack of comparison which are reaching finality at the apex court this year. In VAT transaction valuation was much simpler and only issues of evasion used to come up. Many States restricted the credit when goods were sold below the cost.

In GST surprisingly the valuation principles under central excise for goods and service tax for services have been adopted with market value concept of customs added with alternatives when not possible.

The transaction value is to be adopted where the supplier and recipient are **not related** and the price is the **sole consideration**. (Section 15) This value needs to be adjusted for aspects which impact the price. The transaction value would include:

- taxes paid other than GST,
- amounts incurred by the receiver which are in relation to the supply,

- incidental expenses including packing , commission etc. charged by the supplier,
- interest or late fee or penalty for delayed payment of consideration,
- subsidies directly linked to the price other than Central/State subsidies.

The Transaction Value (TV) would exclude:

- the discount which is given before or at the time of the supply and
- that which is known at the time of supply (target, quantity discount). Where the TV is not determinable then one would have to refer to the GST Rules 27 to 35. Government has also reserved the right to specify valuation methods. The list of related persons has also been provided.

1.2.4 Valuation Rules (Rule 27- 35)

The valuation rules prescribe different methods for different types of transactions making an attempt to arrive at a fair price (not tainted by relationships and other advantages). Important ones are as under:

1.2.4.1 Normal Method to arrive – Adjusted Transaction Value (Rule 27)

(i) When consideration is not wholly in money then the open market value of the supply would be considered. Open Market Value (OMV) could be said to be comparable untainted value at the same time.

(ii) Where the OMV is not possible to get the above value then the value received in money and the money value of other consideration. Example of this could be as under:

- Amortised value of capital goods supplied free of cost (cost/possible usage)
- Advances impacting the price (Advance for machinery/working capital). The bank interest saved by the supplier,
- The value of the component supplied free of cost for incorporation.
- Reasonable means to arrive at the advantage can be used.

(iii) Where the (ii) above is not possible then the value of goods or services which are akin. This value may require to be adjusted for realities and maybe subjective.

(iv) Where the (iii) above is not possible then value would be 110% of the cost of production or provision of service. (Rule 30)

(v) Where the (iv) above is also not possible then any reasonable means consistent with the above principles. (Rule 31) In this case the judicial developments in central excise in most cases and service tax in a few cases would provide guidance.

1.2.4.2 Pure Agent Supply (Rule 33)

There are times when the contract could be for supply of some services but could also involve supply of services or goods from other third parties.

Pure agent is one who:

- enters into an agreement to be an agent to incur costs or expenditure while providing the service contracted for,
- does not hold title to the goods or services supplied to the recipient,
- does not use such goods or services for himself or for provision of service to the recipient, and
- receives only the actual amount incurred (no margin).

The conditions for excluding value of supply are as under:

(i) the supplier acts as an agent of the recipient for the supply and payment both received and made on behalf of the recipient,

(ii) the payments made to third parties is separately indicated in invoice of such pure agent,

(iii) the above supplies are in addition to services provided on own account.

Examples of such transactions could be as under:

A Custom House Agent who arranges import may pay port charges, terminal handling charges rent of plot, pay the customs duties, etc. in addition to his services of providing liaison and co-ordination.

A Chartered Accountant/Company Secretary or Cost and Management Accountant may pay the ROC fees on behalf of the client in addition to his professional charges

Note: It may be preferable that the invoice for such deduction is in the name of the clients.

1.2.4.3 Valuation of supply to distinct person (branches/division) or related person (Rule 28)

In this case the valuation to distinct/related persons could be the open market value, if not available value of goods or services of like kind and quality and if that is also not possible 110% of cost (rule 30) or reasonable method (rule 31)

Further an option of supplier charging 90% of the price charged by the recipient may also find favour.

A major relaxation is that where the credit is eligible to the recipient*[14], the value declared in the invoice shall be deemed to be the open market value. It is suggested that this relaxation be tempered with reasonableness to avoid disputes.

However where the supply is to a distinct person who is not eligible for the credit (due to supplying exempt goods/services) then the OMV or other alternatives from Rule 27 to 33 are to be used.

1.2.4.4 Valuation of supply through agent (Rule 29)

In this case on option has been provided for the supply of goods either way of going for the open market value or 90% of the price charged for supply to unrelated parties. If this is not possible then to follow 110% of cost (rule 30) or reasonable method (rule 31).

1.2.4.5 Specific Valuation Methods (Rule 32- Optional)

(i) For exchange of foreign exchange the value shall be the difference between buying and selling rate as declared by RBI.

If not available then 1% of the value of Indian rupees received or paid.

Further an yearly option to value at 1% of the gross currency exchanged up to Rs. 1 Lakh (subject to minimum of Rs 250- If less then 25,000), if more then Rs1,000 + ½ % between 1- 10 Lakhs, if more then 5,000 + 1/10%of amount exceeding 10 lakhs subject to maximum of Rs 60,000/-

(ii) For air travel – 5% of basic fare for domestic or 10% for international fare. Basic fare is the fare used for paying commission in the normal course.

(iii) For life insurance business the value would be arrived at after deducting the investment allocation and where not determinable as in a single premium policy 10% deemed to be value. In all other cases it would be 5% of the 1st premium and 12.5% of the subsequent premiums.

(iv) Resale of second hand goods by person in that business would be the value calculated as the difference between the purchase and sale price. If the difference is negative, no tax need be paid.

(v) For physical or digital vouchers value would be the redemption value (in most cases the face value).

In some cases the tax payer may have charged one consolidated price inclusive of tax. This is also called cum tax value. In such cases the value would be determined as under:

Rate is 18% IGST then = 100x100/118 = 84.47.

---

14 The full credit should be available which means that there cannot be any exempt or non taxable supplies from that distinct entity/State.

It is expected that some of the disputes which existed for goods and service valuation would continue in the GST regime and many settled position of law may be revisited unless a comprehensive circular on old settled cases as relevant to GST is issued.

1.2.5 Input Tax Credit (ITC)

The principle of set off is that the GST paid at the earlier stage on supplies received (capital goods, inputs, input services) is allowed as a deduction from the tax payable. In normal businesses the eligible credits are reduced from the cost of procurement/purchases at the stage of first accounting. In most businesses the margins would be less than the eligible credit which may be as high as 10-17 % whereas margin would be only 1-8%.

In the earlier regime only in central excise and service tax among the central levies the set off was available. VAT input tax credit was allowed for the procurement within the State. The service provider was unable to get the VAT credit and the traders the service tax credit. Most of the dealers did not get registered under central excise to enable them to pass on the duty of excise or the additional duty of customs (CVD) or the special additional duty (SAD) when they imported or dealt with imported goods. There were some indirect taxes where credit was not available for adjustment and payment of net amount. That is to say the whole tax as applicable was payable as under:

(1) Basic Customs Duties

(2) Luxury tax

(3) Betting & Gambling tax

(4) Octroi/Local body tax/Entry tax

(5) Entertainment tax

There were some taxes which were not available for credit at all even in VAT or central excise/service tax as under:

(1) Basic Customs Duty/anti-dumping duty/safeguard duty

(2) Central Sales Tax (whether or not against the "C Form")

(3) Luxury tax

(4) Octroi/Local body tax/Entry tax (In some States this was adjustable to the VAT)

(5) Betting & Gambling tax

(6) Entertainment tax

(7) Special Additional Duty (SAD) credit was not available to trader. However there was a system of refund to be claimed from Customs after goods are sold on payment of VAT due to the fact that the SAD was in lieu of VAT/CST and credit was not available.

Now in GST the ITC has been expanded partially since there is major indirect tax other than GST in business other than stamp duty. Credit is available unless restricted. To this extent the taxes on taxes is also avoided to some extent other than barred credits and non-taxable activity.

However where no GST is paid then credit would not be available. The excluded activities where GST is not applicable as on date are:

(a) Electricity presently a State subject.

(b) Taxes on immovable property also a State subject.

(c) 5 Petroleum Products which are substantially used in businesses: Petrol, Diesel, Aviation Fuel, Natural Gas, Petroleum crude are subjects to Excise duty as well as VAT[15].

(d) Liquor presently also State subject

These would cascade and tax on tax would continue to this extent.

The industry would like that the GST be imposed on all the above as the taxes paid on expenditure in furtherance of business on the above activities are quite substantial. Presently the credit lost in the above could be more than Rs.4 Lakhs crores for FY 2018-19. In the past IDT regime also this credit was not available but moving to GST it should have been included to reduce the tax on tax leading to cascading. Some States have been asking for these to be included under the GST net.

The eligibility of adjustment or utilisation of the credit of IGST/CGST & SGST of one State needs to be understood.

The State GST would be eligible for credit for that State which is logical. Credit would also be available for payment of the GST in that State. The State GST would also be available for payment of IGST.

The CGST collected in a State would be available for credit and for adjustment when paying the Central GST. Central GST as understood collected by a State would not be available for CGST of another State. For a multi-state tax payer the CGST of Karnataka may not be usable in Bihar for payment of CGST. However similar to SGST, the CGST in a State can be used for payment of IGST.

IGST can be utilised for adjustment and payment of IGST, CGST or SGST in that State. It means that IGST credit is preferable to either SGST or CGST.

Insertion of sec 49A postulates that the order of utilisation for CGST would be 1st CGST and then IGST and similarly for SGST. For this purpose, IGST credit was required to be utilized first towards these payments. This resulted in unnecessary accumulation of credits under single head. Rule 88A was introduced effective

15 Government is examining whether petroleum products could be included in the GST. Maybe in the next budget of 2019.

from April 2019 allowing utilization of IGST first for IGST payment and then remaining balance for payment of any other type of GST.

There is a restriction on order of utilisation which needs to be kept in mind.

IGST – Used first for IGST then if balance available for CGST or SGST, any order.

CGST of State – Used for CGST in that State first and if balance is there then for payment of IGST. If the balance is available then it can be carried forward.[16]

SGST of State – Used for SGST in that State first and if balance is there then for payment of IGST. If balance is available then it can be carried forward.

1.2.5.1 Eligibility

GST was expected to completely remove cascading of multi point duty as well as restrictions built over a period of time. In the earlier regimes the CENVAT Credit as well as VAT ITC was restricted for several items. Credits in GST are more liberal but still have a number of restrictions.

The GST credit is available subject to conditions as under:

(1) Buyer/Recipient is having a tax invoice or other tax paying document which has been uploaded by the supplier,

(2) Buyer/Recipient has received the supply or goods or services,

(3) Tax has been paid on such supply[17] (by the supplier)

(4) Return is to be furnished by the receiver,

(5) He is to pay the supplier within 180 days. If not, credit and interest thereon would be added to his output liability.[18] Credit of tax available on full payment at any later date.

(6) In regard to capital goods where depreciation is claimed on the GST credit availed, the credit is not available.*[19]

(7) The time limit for credit is the due date for filing of the return of September of next financial year or furnishing of the annual return whichever is earlier.

---

16 There is a demand from industry that at least CGST of one State can be used for CGST of another State.

17 The non-compliance by the supplier is subject to action against him. Making the buyer liable for that is unreasonable and therefore in the amendment in August 2018 it has been proposed to make the supplier responsible in normal circumstances.

18 This again is quite unreasonable and Government should not invade the business decision. The major defaulters in making payment in time is the Government and the PSUs.

19 If however at a later date, the depreciation is offered for income tax then the ITC would not be reversible.

The law also provides for enabling credit of input tax and restrictively capital goods credit in case of various special circumstances such as a composition dealer, a small trader or one who is exempt becoming taxable, one who has taken registration, on the basis of a certificate from a chartered accountant etc. subject to conditions. GST is a procedural law and requires compliance of the rules as prescribed. The vigilant only would be able to avail optimum due credit and avoid interest costs.

1.2.5.2 Blocked

We examine the continuing restriction under section 17(5) of CGST Act briefly as under:

(i) Motor Vehicles for transportation of persons having approved seating capacity of not more than 13 persons*[20] (including driver). Exceptions where credit would be available are:

- if used for making taxable supplies (only for such service providers) of: further supply (distributor/lessors of MV); transportation of passengers (bus operators, cab operator) or for imparting training (driving, flying etc.)

Note: The conveyances for transportation of goods could cover cars, buses, boats, airplanes etc. The industries who could claim the credit for transportation of goods could be the transportation/logistic industry, construction industry, mining, manufacturing, catering etc. In the past they may not have availed the credit or only part credit.

Changes have been made in section 17(5) now to allow credit on vehicles with seating capacity of more than 13 persons which could cover buses as well. The credit of lease/rent/hiring of motor vehicles and other credits related to motor vehicles like insurance, repair etc. pertaining to motor vehicles with seating capacity of 13 or less though used in furtherance of business has been restricted after the amendments.

The word 'conveyances' has been removed and separate restriction provided for vessels and aircraft with exception when used for further supply, transportation of passengers and imparting training on navigating or flying. Credit is available if used for transportation of goods.

(ii) Works contract for immovable property other than plant and machinery[21] or where the service is used further for works contract.

---

20 No restrictions if motor vehicle, vessel or aircraft used for transportation of goods

21 The inputs used in the foundation and structures forming part of the plant and machinery classified with the plant would be eligible.

(iii) Goods and services for construction of immovable property other than plant and machinery for himself. This means that a builder cannot avail the credit for GST paid to a contractor for a building meant for renting or manufacture of taxable goods. However if the contractor/developer is selling the property (before completion) then he can avail the credits of goods or services used.

(iv) Membership of a club, health or fitness centres are barred even if used for furtherance for business.

(v) Travel benefits to employees on vacation such as leave or home travel concession

(vi) Food, beverages, outdoor catering, beauty treatment, health services, cosmetic/plastic surgery unless used for making a further supply in the same category or as an element of composite/mixed supply.

(vii) Rent a cab, life insurance and health insurance unless used for making an outward supply or the Central/State Govt. notifies that it is obligatory for employer to provide. Recently, amendments have been made to allow credit on any services or goods which are obligatory for the employer to provide. This way credit on food/outdoor catering could also be taken by tax payers when such facility is provided as per the statutory obligation. This would be effective on notified date.

(viii) Goods or services used for personal consumption.

(ix) Goods lost, stolen, destroyed, written off or disposed of by way of free gift or free samples.

The above provisions are subject to different interpretations and have been hotly disputed with most issues being in favor of the tax payer in the past in earlier CENVAT regime. Auditors may refer to a good analytical commentary for more clarity and specifics.[22]

The person who has opted for composition would not be eligible for any credit till he opts out at which time he would be eligible for credit of the stocks in hand. The non-resident dealer who imports goods can utilize the credit of such goods if eligible otherwise.

The person who receives a notice consequent to evasion (sec 74) or transports goods liable to GST (sec 129) without payment of tax or such goods are confiscated (sec130) shall not be eligible for ITC. This is particularly a very harsh

---

22 The background material on GST of April 2019 of the Institute of Chartered Accountants of India. idtc@icai.in to understand the compliances as well as the benefits.

The seizure of goods/conveyances due to E-way bill clerical mistakes even by complaint assessees is an example.

provision in the light of the complexity, frequently changing law and quasi-judicial orders with total revenue bias.

Note: The credit should only be denied to a person who uses goods or services for personal/private use. In all other ITC used in furtherance of business, denials are unreasonable and do not move to a seamless credit system. There could be many genuine cases where due to lack of knowledge of the complex provision one makes an error. Further the evader would be liable for stringent penalties, interest @24% and further action of prosecution. The denial of credit could close the trade or business which should not be the intention of any tax law. This is especially true when even the senior tax officers openly share their lack of knowledge of this new law after more than 21 months.

1.2.5.3 Apportionment

The assessee may be having non- taxable or exempt supplies or use the goods for non- business purposes or a combination. In such cases he would be eligible for only credit to the extent used for taxable and zero rated (direct exports and SEZ) supplies. This would be as per the rules in this regard.

The value of exempt supplies would include supplies on which recipient is liable to pay under reverse charge[23] value of securities[24], sale of land, sale of completed building[25]. This provision has the potential to create thousands of disputes once verification starts.

Rule 42 (for calculating the reversal) does not work on the basis of ITC not available for activities on which tax has not been paid. It has the potential to be used for tax planning and for the unwary lead to huge denial of ITC. This has been the case in the residential/commercial construction activities till 1.4.2019.

For banking, financial institution or a non-banking financial company an option of avail 50% of the eligible ITC on capital goods, inputs and input services is available. One can opt for it once a year. This 50% would not apply for transactions within the entity where GST has been paid.

1.2.5.4 Is ITC a Right or Concession?

In the VAT regime with monthly deductions allowed, the ITC was more of a concession. Courts also held to that effect. In CENVAT applicable to central excise as well as service tax, it was more in the nature of a right. In the GST regime one of the basic reasons for implementation was said to be to avoid

---

23 This is wholly unreasonable as credit is not availed by the supplier at all. ITC would not be used for receiving goods or services.

24 Investments will give income automatically and services used would be minimal and specific services not eligible.

25 Similarly sale of land or building in cities the common services would be minimal and specific services not eligible.

cascading impact of multipoint taxes. However in the drafting of the provisions we observe that most of the restrictions have been routed through the Act and where not explicit it is subject to "as maybe prescribed" which is again part of the law.

However, it is expected that over a period of time, the provisions which are unreasonable could be read down by the court itself. One may have to await the development of the law for this. One way of complying with the law could be to avail doubtful credits and reverse the same under protest with acknowledged communication to the jurisdictional revenue office. This would ensure that as and when the law develops, one could avail the credit and the time limitation could be overcome.

1.2.6 Classification

Classification means categorizing products and services into chapter headings under chapters to ensure that there is uniformity across the States in India as well as with the world at large. GST as in case of customs and excise has followed the Harmonised System of Nomenclature (HSN) but listed in form of schedules as was done under VAT. VAT was never an advanced or well drafted law.[26]

Any mistake in classification especially at a lower rate could be catastrophic for the business as the differential tax with interest and penalty may be in multiples of the net profit earned. Demands would also be made after efflux of time which means that the profit after tax and after distribution would not be sufficient to pay the differential tax. Consequently the capital or investment itself can be eroded. The denial of credit if intent to evade is upheld could lead to instant bankruptcy.[27] Killing the goose that lays the golden egg is an old saying which would apply here.

There have been continuous and regular changes to the rates in the 1st year which were decided without much application of mind. Hopefully a final list would be made available by September 2019 which would be the rate applicable from 1st July 2017 itself to avoid further confusion as Government is rectifying incorrect classification/fitment.[28]

1.2.6.1 Classification Principles

We have a number of rates in GST due to the federal structure and varied culture, economic disparity and nature of our people. The broad list of GST rates as per the given schedule is as follows:

---

26 The classification in schedules with chapter headings coming in all schedules is confusing. The HSN format maybe adopted. Till date no rates have been made retrospective.

27 When interest, penalty and possible prosecution exists, not allowing credit is a draconian provision.

28 Many dealers/service providers have not followed unreasonable classification. Some have not even invoiced. Since the fault is of poor drafting, the retrospective amendment for rates should be announced for all changes till 31st march 2018.

Rates for Goods

- **5%** in respect of goods specified in Schedule I,
- **12%** in respect of goods specified in Schedule II,
- **18%** in respect of goods specified in Schedule III,
- **28%** in respect of goods specified in Schedule IV,
- **3%** in respect of goods specified in Schedule V,
- **0.25%** in respect of goods specified in Schedule VI.

Additionally some cesses have also been set out for few products.

Rates for Services

- **5%** - Rent a cab, job work relating to textiles, restaurant services, transport of passengers, GTA service, print media advertisement etc.
- **12%** - Accommodation where tariff is between Rs.1000 to Rs.2500/-, Business class air travel etc.
- **18%** - General Rate – all services not covered in other rates including specified construction services.
- **28%** - Luxurious hotels, gambling, amusement park entry etc.

Note: There have been a number of changes in rates due to some good classification practices not having been followed. Government says that it would over time rationalise them after making proper fitment. This exercise was done in central excise by having only 1 basic rate in the last decade. In FY 2019-2020, it is expected that some rationalisation would be done but a single rate may not be possible in a federal country which is developing and has substantial population below the poverty line.

Rates under Composition

- 1% in case of traders, manufacturers and affordable residential apartments without ITC w.e.f 1.4.19.
- 5% in case of Suppliers of food and beverages service (Restaurant etc.) and residential apartment (other than affordable) without ITC w.e.f. 1.4.19.

Note: It may also be noted that in the first few year a number of changes are expected. The changed rate would be applicable from the date of notification. Change would be only prospective unless made applicable retrospectively which for the changes made till date has not been done.

This means that if one makes an error of classifying at a higher rate he would not be competitive and if lower, then the exposure to demand with interest and penalty exists. In B2B transaction where the recipient is eligible for GST credit one may choose to err on the side of revenue. The language used in section 16(2) allows this since the credit of tax charged is allowed as credit and not the tax paid or payable.

The understanding of the product or service in terms of the agreement, usage, how perceived in the trade, how advertised could give one an idea of the item and general understanding on where it needs to be classified. However in GST one would have to refer to the various schedules set out to identify where the product/service would be appropriately classified.

The schedules mentioned have enumerated the description of goods and refer to the Customs Tariff Act. There are also general rules of interpretation set out in sequence which need to be applied. They are as under:

(1) As per the titles, terms of heading and description in the schedule (read with the section/chapter notes)

(2) Unfinished or incomplete goods classified as respective goods

(3) Mixtures as per dominant item of mixture

(4) Specific description prevails over general

(5) Mixtures of different material as per material which gives the essential characteristics

(6) If all above is not possible, then as per heading, which appears last in all schedules.

The classification under the Customs Tariff is based on the Harmonised System of Nomenclature which can be a valuable guide as it is more descriptive. The earlier customs and central excise law has a history of classification disputes. These case laws may provide a good direction when there is a doubt.

The practitioner would require referring to a good commentary as well as an updated comprehensive commodity wise classification book to be able to advise appropriately

1.2.6.2 How to Classify under Appropriate Rate?

Notification 01/2017, central tax, dated 28.06.2017, provides that the goods have to be classified based on the rules for the interpretation of the Custom Tariff Act 1975 (CTA), including section notes and chapter notes and the explanatory notes. The assessee should first understand the various facets of the product/service and should classify under CTA using the HSN number.

Further, in case of services, separate annexure has provided "scheme of classification of services" based on which the assessee has to classify the service and ascertain the applicable rates.

The stages and steps involved in reaching the appropriate classification are as under:

Stage I: Preliminary Examination

(1) The understanding of the activity or transaction as per the supplier and trade is the first step. Where the activity is of technical nature the technical or

scientific meaning is to be understood. If there is any difficulty then only the dictionary meaning or ISI specifications may be examined. The end or predominant use could also be a good indicator.*[29]

(2) The next aspect would be to determine whether the supply is of goods or services keeping in mind Schedule II (deemed goods or deemed service) and Schedule III (activities not services or goods).

(3) In case of combination of goods or services or both applying the understanding of composite, non-composite and mixed supply to determine what are activities for which the classifications is to be determined.

(4) The domain knowledge of the global, Indian and specific local area understanding of the activity could be indicative.

(5) It may also be important to be aware whether the GST paid is available as input tax credit and what is the customer's product as end use also helps in some cases.

(6) The normal name/nomenclature in the trade and purchase order/contract*[30] could be the start point. This can be matched with the notified rate schedule.

(7) The same exercise can be done for the product/service in the customs tariff. The section notes and chapter notes to the Schedule to be read and applied.

(8) On completing the above steps if there is no doubt/ambiguity, the classification arrived at could be final.

Stage II: Detailed Study (in case of doubt/ambiguity)

(9) The reference shall be made to the rules for interpretation of the customs tariff:

(a) In case of the unfinished or incomplete goods, ascertain if the unfinished product has the essential characteristics of the finished product, if yes; apply that classification to the unfinished product.

(b) If the classification is not ascertained as per point (a) mentioned above, find out the heading, which is more specific to the nature of product. This is an important rule which is practically applied in most cases.

(c) If the classification is still unclear, ascertain which material gives the article its essential characteristics and use that classification.

---

29 Since the GST tariff is based on the HSN, google search of the product or service may indicate a tariff classification which can be confirmed.

30 A number of tax payers get into a dispute position due to the contracts/work orders/purchase orders not being clear on classification.

(10) The competitors and different customers classification could confirm to a limited extent the classification arrived at by the assessee.

(11) There may still be cases of doubts or alternative classifications. The non-statutory principles of functional use, judicial precedents in customs and the Central Excise (for goods) and Finance Act, 1994 (in relation to service) etc. will have to be applied.

Stage III: Choosing the Rate applicable

(12) Examine whether any exemption or concession for the goods or services is specified.

(13) It may be examined whether the exemption is conditional or unconditional. If unconditional then the assessee has no choice but to claim the exemption.

(14) If notification is conditional then assessee has to ensure conditions are complied with/compliable in full or substantially.

(15) The supplier should as far as possible, provide the tariff nomenclature along with the description of the goods as it is to be invoiced to the customer.

The GST classification has undergone a number of changes and further changes are expected in the next year or so to get a stable fitment for all products and services. The assessee needs to be conservative in such cases. The recommended way forward in such cases is as under:

(a) Represent to the GST Council on own or through the Industry the factual background of the goods or services providing the justification for a particular classification. If the rate is not fair then reasons for rate change may also be sought.

(b) This representation may also be made to the CBIC and the relevant State GST Commissioners.

(c) Making the representation concurrently through the association would be advisable.

(d) If there is a lack of response simultaneously go for an advance ruling.*[31] If satisfied with finding all the classification is frozen. In case there is no clarity emerging or matter not taken up by authorities the assessee can approach the High Court for relief.

(e) Feasibility of opting for provisional assessment also could be considered.*[32]

---

31 Advance rulings till date have not provided confidence on their judiciousness and revenue bias is very clear.

32 In the past it was observed that the closure was taking decades.

1.2.7 Exemption

Exemptions under GST have been grudgingly given which is the right way to go about as far as goods are concerned. In services the earlier exemptions in service tax have been trimmed. The broad basing of taxation has been achieved to some extent. However quite a lot of fine tuning is required to avoid disputes. The provision that one cannot opt for payment of GST in case of doubt for unconditional exemption is quite inappropriate as GST is not a settled law. If one errs in favour of revenue one may be penalised.[33] The best practice is to read the exemption strictly to see if one is eligible for the benefit. Once eligible if there are purely procedural requirements then one can be liberal. A good practice is to write to the jurisdictional GST officers seeking a confirmation to have a defense to ensure that one is within the limitation period in case of denial of credit in future.

Under all tax laws exemptions are to be read strictly and all conditions thereto should be satisfied. Some exemptions are conditional. The exemption which is unconditional is to be compulsorily availed. No option to pay erring on the side of revenue (as was done in central excise till 2005) is provided though this is a new law which is unfair to the tax payer when the law is not simple and unambiguous. In central excise which was a developed law this restriction was inserted in 2005. In service tax which was a developing law which was 23 years old this type of provision was not there. In case of doubt on applicability of ST, assessees were allowed to pay ST and avail credit. The goods which are exempted are set out in schedule – I – notification 1/17 and services which are exempted have been set out in Notification 12/17 dt. 28.6.17 as amended from time to time. Unconditional exemptions have to be compulsorily claimed and payment of GST on exempt supplies may lead to denial of full credit on the transaction. This is a very conservative view and would be safe to follow.

Experts opine that there could be occasions when there is a doubt about availability of exemption*[34]. Then availing exemption also would be risky. In view of the law allowing the input tax credit of the tax charged, there is no risk for the person who is availing the credit. The risk for the person charging the tax would be imposition of penalty only since tax has already been paid and cannot be forcibly refunded.

The entrepreneur or the consultant may be tempted to start with the nil or lower rate which may not be the proper procedure to be followed. The product or service should be first understood and classified without reference to the rates. Fitment into the description is paramount. Then the rates and alternative classification examined for the appropriate classification and finally eligibility for exemption.

33 On count of no liability there no credit one may face denial of credit for 6 years which could destroy the business.

34 The doubt could be disclosed on record by way of RPAD to the jurisdictional GST officer as a measure of caution.

There are very few exemptions in GST as compared to the erstwhile VAT, service tax and central excise laws. In the present classification many challenges are observed in the Nil vs 5% rate; and the 18% vs 28% rate. It would depend on the product/service being in intermediary stage (less issues as credit available to next stage) and it being a final product/service (more issues as consumer is only interested in the final price). The continued exercise to fit the proper rate is ongoing.

1.2.8 In case of choice - Whether to claim exemption?

In earlier laws i.e. in Central Excise, State Value Added Tax and Service Tax, the government was issuing conditional notification and unconditional notification. Presently, in GST there are two exemptions issued for supply of goods 02/2017 Central tax dated 28.06.2017, and supply of service 12/2017 Central tax dated 28.06.2017. In both the cases assessee has to opt for exemption.

However there are exceptions. For a restaurant, the government has issued a notification which is conditional notification where restaurant opts for 5% GST without input tax credit and in other cases respective rates i.e. 12%, 18% or 28%. Similarly for Goods Transport Agent either 5% under reverse charge to specified person liable to pay the freight or forward charge of 12% with Input tax credit for GTA.

This may be a challenge when there is an exemption available which is not clear. Assessees who choose to opt for payment as a measure of caution where the exemption is clear and unambiguous may not be protected.

However when there is a conditional exemption one can choose. This choice should depend on the receiver's profile i.e. whether he can avail the credit or not and whether he is an exporter/SEZ who has to go for a refund.

1.2.9 Place of Supply

Place of Supply (POS) has the twin objective of confirming whether a transaction is deemed to be in India or Outside India as well as determine the State/Union Territory in which the levy accrues. The POS under GST generally follows the destination principle. However to take care of international best practices as well as practical issues to ensure that the States get their dues, some exceptions are there in goods and bit more in services.

An honest mistake can be costly as one may pay GST on reverse charge when not liable or not pay when liable while importing services. In case of export the same mistake can be made. Paying IGST to wrong State or in place of Local SGST + CGST may also lead to demands and simultaneous refund necessity which would block funds.[35]. If the mistake is detected after 2 years, there can be no refund

[35] Industry would be relieved if the adjustment can be done in the back end by the technological means.

claim for the tax paid but for demanding the tax not paid, there would be still one and a half years available.

The POS for goods would depend on the location of the supplier as well as where is the place of supply. If in the same State then it would be an intra-state supply (State GST + CGST) and if not then interstate supply (IGST). Pertinent sections in CGST = 10-14; and in IGST= 12 & 13.

1.2.10 Time of Supply (TOS)

The time of supply triggers the levy of GST. The law provides that the TOS would be the earliest of payment, delivery of goods/provision of services, invoicing. Court have opined that the most important activity is supply and if there is a conflict then that time may prevail. Some differences have been carved out when dealing with relatives and differing commercial transactions. Some of those specified are as under:

Reverse Charge – 60 days from date of issue of invoice or date of payment. If with related parties then date of recording of supply.

Vouchers – Where supply is identifiable along with the rate – then date of issue of voucher. If not then the date of redemption.

Interest, late fee or penalty for delay in payment – On receipt of amount.

In case of non-recording- When return filed or payment made (may be post an audit or investigation)

1.2.11 Job Work/Repair

The job work route is followed to a large extent to ensure concentration on core competencies, lower costs, as they are specialised and quality enhancement. Job work is understood as working on goods supplied by the principal. There may be situations where some material is also added by the job worker. Where job worker adds substantial material, the transaction may not be called a job work and it may be advisable to supply on payment of tax and get back on payment of tax. Job worker in this case may need to be registered and avail the credit. Section 143 enables supply of goods for job work without Payment of GST. There are time limits for receipt back for inputs, capital gods except for moulds, dies, jigs and fixture. When not received back they would be deemed to have been supplied as on the date of initial supply.

The practical business aspects of directly receiving the inputs, capital goods etc., direct supply to customer after the processing, supply to other job workers have been enabled. Scrap and waste may be supplied back or disposed of by the job worker on payment of appropriate taxes.

Repairs may be covered herein but not specifically covered.

The common practice of having vendors involved in contract manufacturing is not job work. Manufacturing by loan licensee system followed in pharmaceutical industry also is not job work but independent manufacture and supply of goods.

1.2.12 Tax Collection at Source: E-Commerce Operator (ECO)

The proliferation of internet and purchase through it in India has been tremendous. Supplies of goods and services using software has been growing exponentially and these transactions need to be taxed in India. There are different types of transactions as under:

(a) ECO provides a platform and supplier supplies goods or services directly to the buyer. ECO will get a commission on the amount of transaction.

(b) ECO supplies the goods or services to the buyer directly or indirectly and payment is made online to the ECO. If direct then ECO is a regular supplier. If not then he would be an operator.

(c) ECO delivers and collects food, merchandise etc. Here if considered an agent then under GST law, the tax needs to be paid either by the supplier or the ECO.

(d) There could be many variants of the above.

The intermediary software platform on which the buyer and seller meet and complete a transaction has now been made liable to register if he has a presence in India. The ECO who is not having a presence in India would have to have a representative in India who would need to register. The primary responsibility for payment of GST remains with the supplier.

Under section 52, the ECO would have to deduct 1% or less from the supplier payment and pay the same to the revenue as Tax Collection at Source. This would help the revenue to track those who transact on these sites.

Considering the many facets of such business including the extra territorial jurisdiction and feasibility of monitoring this provision had been put on hold up to 30.9.2018. From 1st October 2018 the ECO would have to comply with this provision.*[36]

1.2.13 Tax Deduction at Source: Specified Recipients

The local VAT laws had provided that procurement by public sector units, Government concerns and at times even larger companies would be subjected to a deduction of Tax at Source akin to the TDS under Income Tax. This amount of VAT would be available as a payment proof for the dealers who provided works

---

36 The understanding of this sector and the various ways in which business is done are changing day to day. It is advisable to refer to a good sectoral commentary specific to e-commerce.

contract services and in some cases even on goods supplied. The deductor was required to remit the tax to the State Government and file a return to enable the dealer to be able to take a set off of the tax already paid. There has been large scale non-compliance by the deductors in the past.

Under GST, section 51 provides similarly that a department of Central/State government, local authority, Governmental agencies or notified persons shall deduct tax at 1% and pay to Government along with an electronic statement of outward supplies. In the present GST regime there does not seem to be any reason for this provision to be made applicable. This has been made applicable from 1st October 2018 to all those who are specified. The compliance in the past where under VAT they were to deduct and file returns was not satisfactory in majority of cases as it is made applicable to mainly the Government entities.

1.2.14 Demand, Interest & Penalties

The tax may at times not be paid, underpaid, credit may not be reversed or partially reversed, refunds may be excess claimed due to inadvertence, lack of knowledge or intentionally. The tax payer who identifies the non/short payments etc. could *suo moto* pay with interest and disclose in his returns. Show cause notice means a notice issued by the proper officer asking an individual or group of people to explain or to "show cause" in writing as to why the tax should not be demanded and penal action should not be taken against the individual or group of people involved in certain incidents, misconducts or wrong doing.

Section 73 sets out the time limit for order to be 3 years form the due date of furnishing annual return or from date of erroneous refund. The show cause notice is required to be issued at least 3 months earlier. In cases of fraud, misstatement, suppression leading to short or nonpayment or excess credit or erroneous refund then the period for notice within 5 years of the time limit for the order. The show cause notice is required to be issued at least 6 months earlier. There are other offences specified for transportation and dealing in goods/services without payment of GST. Since the provisions of demand and recovery are especially harsh, tax compliant assessees may opt for voluntary review of their compliances or get the annual audit of GST done concurrently to avoid interest and penalties.

In case of disagreement with the allegations raised in the SCN, the tax payer has an option to file a reply against the notice and there is no statutory time limit prescribed for the same. However, it should get concluded within the time prescribed above. While replying the notice the assessee should keep the following points in mind.

(a) Provide brief facts about the company, whether the company is a manufacturer, trader or service provider.

(b) Facts of the case i.e. issue raised by the department, documents relied upon by the department.

(c) Reply to the issue raised by the department by providing details of transaction, documents relied upon by the assessee, legal provisions, circular, notification and case law if any.

The detailed reply should be submitted to the department along with relied upon documents to the department to support the case.

1.2.15 Personal Hearing

The personal hearing is a proceeding before the authority/court or other decision-making body, to explain the case in person and plead for dropping/setting aside the notice/order. Without giving opportunity to the assessee the department can't come to conclusion or pass on order against the assessee. Personal hearing is a right of assessee and following the principles of natural justice, it is compulsory to hear the assessee in person before passing any order. After submission of reply to the show cause notice, the department would go through the reply and give opportunity to appear before the respective authority. The assessee/authorised representative, on the day of hearing has to appear before the respective authority and present the details of the case and submit additional documents like any case law or any other relevant documents along with summary of case (Synopsis). The proper officer/authority after hearing the assessee/authorised representative would pass on appropriate order which may be favourable/against the assessee.

The GST law provides very little time to the taxpayers to defend themselves against the show cause notice. In the case of show cause notices within the normal period of limitation, the time available for submission of reply to the notice and completion of the process of personal hearing and issue of a speaking order is only three months and in the case of notices involving extended period, the total period available is only six months. The departmental officers would be having sufficient time since the notices are issued by the Department and requisite study can be done in advance whereas an assessee has to prepare detailed reply and in view of the legal provisions relating to additional evidence in the GST law, at the original adjudication stage, a proper defense is essential. It is hoped that these provisions will undergo changes by the time the notices start getting issued and adjudication processes start.*[37]

The amount would be recovered by way of voluntary payment or from monies owed to the assessee (bank/NBFC), by selling goods belonging to assessee, from other persons who owe money, as arrears of land revenue through the District Collector or through the magistrate as fine.

---

37 In budget speech by the Finance Minister the way forward to resolve all these disputes would be online with the need for physical presence being limited. However time will tell whether this is practical or the administrators would enable this wonderful vision.

1.2.16 Appeals and Revision

The option of appeal is available to any person who is aggrieved by the decision or order passed by the adjudicating authority. 'Any person' may be assessee or department. The appeal should be filed before 'Appellate Authority' or 'Appellate Tribunal' based on the monetary limit or the adjudicating authority that passed the order.

The law also gives the power of revision to the revisional authority who on the basis of report from Commissioner of State tax or on his own motion can call for the records. He may after examination, take up revision of the order by issuing show cause notice if he finds the order prejudicial to revenue, illegal or improper. Revision cannot be taken up on the same issue, if an appeal has been filed on that issue and before six months of the order. However he has 3 years to take up revision. He can enhance the tax demand or penalty after hearing the party.

The law gives two advantages to the revenue. The first is six months' time to file appeal and the second is revision.

The appeal before appellate authority/tribunal is required to be filed within three months from the date on which the order is communicated and appellate authority has power to condone one month of delay in filing the appeal, if sufficient cause is proved. Further pre-deposit is required to be paid before filing the appeal to appellate authority:

(a) In case of admitted liability – Entire tax, interest, fee, penalty or any other amount is required to be deposited.

(b) Any other liability – sum equal to 10% of the remaining amount of tax in dispute is to be deposited. This is subject to maximum amount of Rs.25 Crore.

The pre-deposit to be paid before filing the appeal to appellate tribunal is:

(a) In case of admitted liability – Entire tax, interest, fee, penalty or any other amount is required to be deposited.

(b) In other liability – sum equal to 20% of the remaining amount of tax in dispute in addition to the amount deposited while filing appeal to appellate authority is to be deposited. This is subject to maximum amount of Rs.50 crores.

(c) The appeal before appellant tribunal is required to be filed within three months. However the tribunal has the power to condone the delay up to three months if there are valid grounds.

Any person, aggrieved by any order of the appellate tribunal has an option to file the appeal before the High Court or the Supreme Court if there is a question of law to be considered by following the procedure prescribed therein.

The resolution of notice is open to challenge by the revenue (in case order in favour of assessee) or by the assessee himself in case of adverse orders. The first appeal would lie to the Commissioner Appeals and next to the appellate tribunal. The final fact finding authority is the tribunal.

In case of question of law the High Court may hear the appeal. The final authority is the Supreme Court where any order passed by the tribunal (Regional or National bench) could be heard on questions of law.

Note: The fact that majority of the disputes are in favour of the tax payer in the past, indicates that the need to pre- deposit 30% of the tax and wait for years for final decision of the tribunal makes this provision draconian for tax compliant assessees. It was known to result in unethical practices by some tax officers in the past, which may continue in this regime.

1.2.17 Any alternative to litigation?

Even in the case of a genuine dispute arising because of bona fide belief on the part of the tax payer and mistake on the part of the department, if the assessee likes the dispute to be resolved by dispute resolution mechanism, if the original adjudicating authority does not agree with him and confirms the demand, he would be liable to tax, interest and 10% penalty. This coupled with pre-deposit requirements which require 10% of tax to be deposited to take the matter to the appellate tribunal, would make litigation a very costly proposition.

Wherever taxpayer gets a hint of litigation relating to valuation/ classification /availability of exemption, it may be advisable to seek provisional assessment. In the case of provisional assessment, if allowed, proper officer has to decide the issue within six months and there will be no penalty and only interest would be payable. For issue of show cause notice, department has 4 years and six months whereas in the case of provisional assessment, the dispute gets resolved faster.

1.2.18 Transitional Provisions

The fact that GST was applicable from 1st July required many provisions for enabling continuation of business without impacting or stopping them. The main provisions in transition are briefly explained as under:

(1) Migration of existing tax payers: All those having a valid PAN were provided a provisional registration and after additional information provided a final registration. Those who did not provide the information got the provisional registration cancelled.

(2) Carry forward of CENVAT by those registered earlier under central excise or service tax as well as ITC under VAT: The compliance under these laws by the unorganised and smaller assessees was quite poor and many made mistakes while filing their form (tran-1). There were also technical glitches. The Government has given time up to 25th December, 2018 in cases where technical glitches were the

reasons for non-filing. Courts have interfered and for those who did not file due to issues in uploading have been allowed to file again. This is only with the revenue officers' satisfaction and therefore leads to graft.

(3) Balance of capital goods CENVAT credit: This has also been enabled to the extent of credit not carried forward.

(4) Credit on stocks: The stocks in hand with a trader, manufacturer or service provider would be available as inputs, semi-finished goods or finished goods. The tax involved in these goods would be eligible for credit subject to conditions. Two schemes were provided for those who had invoices and those not in possession. Large number of SME have not claimed it (trans-1) and it is understood that many have claimed it excessively.*[38]

(5) Transition provisions were also there for goods or services in transit, Input Service Distributor balance, centralised service providers, job work, price revisions, refunds, goods on which TDS was deducted under the VAT law etc.

The transitional provisions and their compliance have been done with bye passes due to system restrictions and lack of knowledge on the part of the majority of assessees. Many disputes are expected and Courts have ruled to enable many such unfair restrictions. However many rulings are not in favour as on date.

The cautious tax compliant assessee may get a compliance of transition done in depth to avoid demands in years to come as also claim justified credit carry forward which may have been missed. The window for missed credit has closed on 20th April 2019 for 2017-18. Now the only possibility is to avail the ITC missed for any reason in the May 2019 onwards is to include in GSTR 3B return and reverse it under protest and file the protest letter with the revenue.*[39] In the future if any restrictive provisions are found illegal or arbitrary or are section 16/ 17 is read down and credit becomes eligible, one can avail the credit without the time limits being applicable.

1.2.19 Other Miscellaneous Provisions

Some important provisions have been discussed hereunder briefly:

(1) Advance Ruling: The facility for getting a written clarity for goods or services or both on aspects of: applicability of GST; classification;

---

38 For the construction projects the doubt on availing excise duty credits for the inputs already consumed in the building whether can be considered a semi finished goods is not clear. However if the amount outstanding on incomplete projects is liable to GST, then what is being taxed is not an immovable property. Consequently ITC on embedded inputs should be available.

39 Please see Chapter 17 in end for procedure to pay under protest.

applicability of notification (including exemption); determination of time and value; admissibility of ITC; whether one requires registration. The facility would not be available to determine place of supply. The experience till date does not inspire confidence with settled law being unsettled as well as contrary judgments.

(2) Anti-Profiteering: This provision is addressed to those who profiteer (excessive margins/profits) taking advantage of reduction in tax rates or get higher input tax credit. The consumer should apply for relief. It may not have any significant impact and is applicable only for another year unless provisions get extended. It has been successful when there has been a reduction in rate of consumer supplies. The tax payer confirms in Form 9 that there is no case of anti profiteering.

1.3 STATE-WISE THRESHOLD LIMITS FOR OBTAINING REGISTRATION FOR DIFFERENT CATEGORY OF SUPPLIERS MAKING SUPPLY IN SUCH STATES W.E.F. 1ST APRIL 2019

I. Supplier exclusively engaged in the supply of goods[40] other than ice cream and other edible ice, whether or not containing cocoa; Pan masala; Tobacco and manufactured tobacco substitutes.

Threshold limit	States under threshold limit
Rs. 10 lacs	***Special category States:*** Manipur, Mizoram, Nagaland, Tripura.
Rs. 20 lacs	***Special category States***[41]: Arunachal Pradesh, Meghalaya, Sikkim, Uttarakhand.
	Union territory: Puducherry.
	Other States: Telengana.
Rs. 40 lacs	***Special category States:*** Assam. Himachal Pradesh, Jammu & Kashmir.
	Union territory: Andaman & Nicobar Islands, Chandigarh, Dadra & Nagar Haveli, Daman & Diu, Delhi, Lakshadweep.
	Other States: Andhra Pradesh, Bihar, Chhattisgarh, Goa, Gujarat, Haryana, Jharkhand, Karnataka, Kerala, Madhya Pradesh, Maharashtra, Orissa, Punjab, Rajasthan, Tamil Nadu, Uttar Pradesh, West Bengal.

40 Vide Notification No. 10/2019-Central Tax dated 7th March, 2019 **w.e.f. 01.04.2019.**

41 Inserted by the CGST (Amdt.) Act, 2018 (31 of 2018), dt.30-08-2018, **w.e.f.01-02-2019** vide Notification No. 02/2019 – Central Tax, dt. 29-01-2019.

II. Supplier engaged in supply of goods & services

Threshold limit	States under threshold limit
Rs. 10 lacs	***Special category States:*** Manipur, Mizoram, Nagaland, Tripura.
Rs. 20 lacs	***Special category States***[42]: Arunachal Pradesh, Assam, Himachal Pradesh, Jammu & Kashmir[43], Meghalaya, Sikkim, Uttarakhand.
	Union territory: Andaman & Nicobar Islands, Chandigarh, Dadra & Nagar Haveli, Daman & Diu, Delhi, Lakshadweep, Puducherry.
	Other States: Andhra Pradesh, Bihar, Chhattisgarh, Goa, Gujarat, Haryana, Jharkhand, Karnataka, Kerala, Madhya Pradesh, Maharashtra, Orissa, Punjab, Rajasthan, Tamil Nadu, Telengana, Uttar Pradesh, West Bengal.

42 Inserted by the CGST (Amdt.) Act, 2018 (31 of 2018), dt.30-08-2018, **w.e.f.01-02-2019** vide Notification No. 02/2019 – Central Tax, dt. 29-01-2019.

43 Inserted by the CGST (Extension to J&K) Act, 2017 (26 of 2017), dt. 23-08-2017, **w.r.e.f. 08-07-2017**.

Chapter 2

Stepwise Important Procedures at a Glance

2.1 WHEN TO REGISTER?

Every supplier would be liable to be registered under this Act in the State other than special category States if his turnover in a financial year exceeds twenty lakh rupees (Rs.40 lakhs w.e.f. 1.4.19 for goods in many States*[1])from where he makes a taxable supply of goods or service or both. The limit for registration in the special category States is Rs. 10 lakhs (In some cases Rs. 20 lakhs). If there are many locations and also in these special States then the threshold limit would be Rs. 10/20 lakhs.

Registration enables credit and also comes with requirement of compliances such as maintaining proper books and filing returns etc.

The following persons have to compulsorily register under GST Act irrespective of whether the turnover exceeds prescribed limits or not:

(a) The person making interstate taxable supply other than the supply of service.

(b) Casual taxable person making taxable supply.

(c) Person who is required to pay tax under reverse charge.

(d) Person who is required to pay tax under sub-section (5) of section 9.

(e) Non-resident taxable person making taxable supply.

(f) Person who is required to deduct TDS under section 51.

(g) Supply of goods or service on behalf of another taxable person whether as an agent or otherwise.

(h) Input service distributor.

(i) A person who supplies through electronic commerce operator who is required to collect tax at source under section 52.

(j) Electronic commerce operator.

---

1 A note on the various exemptions available is provided at the end of the Earlier Chapter on basic concepts of GST.

(k) The person supplying OIDAR services from place outside India to a person in India.

(l) Such other person as notified by the government.

Note 1: Notification 10/2017 of Integrated tax dated 13th October 2017 provides an exemption to the person making the interstate supply of taxable service from obtaining registration if his turnover does not exceed Rs. 20/10 lakhs as the case may be.

Note 2: Notification 65/2017 of Central tax dated 15th November 2017 provides an exemption to the person making the supply of services other than services specified in 9(5) through e-commerce operator from obtaining registration, if his turnover does not exceed Rs. 20/10 lakhs as the case may be.

Note 3: Notification 07/2017 of Integrated tax dated 14th September 2017 provides exemption to persons engaged in job work activity making interstate supply of services from obtaining registration, other than person liable to be registered under section 22(1) and making supply of service in relation to goods mentioned in SI 151 in annexure to Rule 138 of CGST rules.

Note 4: Notification 31/2018 of Central tax dated 9th August 2018 specifies the person who did not file the complete FORM GST REG-26 till 31st December 2017 but received only a Provisional Identification Number (PIN) may apply for GSTIN by following the procedure prescribed in the said notification.

Note 5: Notification 05/2017 of Central tax dated 19th June 2017 provides exemption to persons engaged in making supplies of taxable goods or services or both, wherein the total tax is required to be paid by the recipient under reverse charge as per sub-section (3) of section 9 of CGST Act, 2017 from obtaining registration.

Note 6: Notification 10/2019 of Central tax dated 7th March 2019 provides an exemption from obtaining registration to the persons engaged exclusive supply of goods and whose turnover does not exceed Rs 40 lakhs with few exceptions w.e.f. 1st April 2019..

2.2 CHOICE AVAILABLE - WHETHER TO REGISTER?

A person who makes a taxable supply of goods or service or both and whose turnover does not exceed Rs.40, 20 or 10 lakhs as applicable, has the option to voluntarily register under GST. Once the person opts for registration he has to comply with the Act and rules relating to maintenance of records, invoicing, returns, audit etc. The advantages of voluntary registration could be as under:

(i) Assessee can collect taxes and claim input tax credit, thereby making him competitive in taxable Business to Business (B2B) activities (buyers who are registered would prefer to do business with a registered person),

(ii) The capital goods credit can be availed,

(iii) The receiver can avail the credit of tax charged,

(iv) Exempted or normal buyers would not like to comply on behalf of supplier under the Reverse charge mechanism under Sec 9(4) as and when made applicable.

(v) Assessee can engage in interstate trade if registered.

(vi) Smaller suppliers within Rs.50 Lakhs in previous year can opt for the 6% scheme in which ITC can be taken and clients can avail the credit.

There could be a few situations where the threshold exemption could be beneficial. The small supplier who is supplying to the small-scale sector (customers below threshold, composition suppliers, exempted suppliers, or to consumer (B2C) may not get any financial benefit by getting registered.)

2.3 HOW TO REGISTER UNDER GST?

The registration number is based on the PAN of the registrant. If the assessee is in Karnataka, the registration number would begin with the State code i.e. 29 then PAN of the assessee and check digit, the total would be 15 digits. In the State, he can obtain only one registration. However, he has option to obtain more than one registration in the State if he has more than one business by treating each business as a separate business vertical.

The assessee has to follow the following procedure to register under GST.
www.gst.gov.in

↓

Select - Taxpayers – (Normal/TDS/TCS/ISD) – **REGISTER NOW**

↓

Following details to be provided
Select -Taxpayer/GST Practitioner/Tax deductor/non-resident taxable person

↓

State/UT and Place

↓

Legal Name of the business

↓

PAN & Email-id & Mobile No

Once details are provided on GST Portal, the system would validate PAN with income tax database, Email Id, and mobile number by sending OTP to mobile and email id.

Once mobile and email id are validated, the system would provide TRN (Temporary reference number) which is valid for 15 days within which the assessee has to upload all the required details on the portal and submit the application. After uploading all the documents it has to be verified and submitted using DSC (Digital Signature) in case of company/LLP/Society etc in any other case EVC or DSC.

2.4 CASUAL TAXABLE PERSON AND NON-RESIDENT TAXABLE PERSON

Any person who occasionally carries out any transaction in the State, where he is not having a place of business is treated as a casual taxable person in that State. Similarly, if such person comes from outside India and is not having any place of business in India, then he is referred to as a non-resident taxable person.

They would also need to take registration in the State, where they supply goods or services or both. They are required to apply for registration 5 days before commencement of business in that State. Other aspects are as follows:

The registration is valid for 90 days, in case if any earlier date is specified in the application then it is valid till then. The 90 days period can be extended by the proper officer. Tax liability for such period has to be estimated and deposited in advance during submission of application. If extension is sought, the additional tax liability is to be paid on estimation. The amount deposited would be credited to electronic cash ledger and such an amount can be utilised for payment of tax liability.

2.5 DISPLAY OF REGISTRATION CERTIFICATE

Every registered person shall display his registration certificate in a prominent location at his principal place of business and at every additional place of business.

The registered person is also required to display his GSTIN number on the name board exhibited at the entry of the principal place of business and at every additional place of business.-

2.6 AMENDMENT OF REGISTRATION

If there is any change in any of the particulars furnished in the application of registration, the taxpayer is required to submit the application in FORM GST REG-14 within 15 days of such change along with documents (if any).

In case of following changes in the registration certificate, approval of the proper officer is required and proper officer issues order in FORM GST REG-15,

(a) where the change relates to, -

(i) legal name of business;

(ii) address of the principal place of business or any additional place(s) of business; or

(iii) addition, deletion or retirement of partners or directors, Karta, Managing Committee, Board of Trustees, Chief Executive Officer or equivalent, responsible for the day to day affairs of the business,

(b) If change relates to any particulars other than those specified above, the certificate of registration shall be amended upon submission of the application in FORM GST REG-14.

2.7 CANCELLATION OF REGISTRATION

The officer on his own or on receiving an application from a registered person may cancel the registration, under following circumstances.

- The business has been transferred/discontinued/amalgamated/De-merged/disposed off.
- Change in the constitution of business.
- No longer liable to be registered other than a person registered on a voluntary basis.

During pendency of proceedings, the registration may be suspended temporarily. Officer may cancel the registration including retrospectively under following circumstances, after giving the opportunity of being heard:

- Contravened the provision of Act or Rule,
- Registration of a composition dealer who has not filed 3 consecutive returns,
- A registered person, other than composition dealer who has not filed 6 consecutive returns,
- A person who has voluntarily registered, but has not commenced the business within 6 months from the date of registration.
- Registration obtained by fraud, wilful misstatement or suppression of facts.

The cancellation of registration would not limit any liability of the person to pay tax. Even in these circumstances, the registration may be suspendered temporarily.

Every registered person whose registration has been cancelled has to file final return within three months of date of cancellation or date of order of cancellation, whichever is later.

2.8 HOW TO VALUE THE SUPPLY?

Normally, GST is to be paid on the 'Transaction Value' that is the actual price of supply as set out in the invoice unless it is between related persons or where the price is not the sole consideration for sale. Section 15 of the CGST Act deals with the value of taxable supply.

The value of supply would include:

- Any taxes, duties, cesses, fees, and charges levied under any law for the time being in force other than GST.
- Any amount that the supplier is liable to pay, in relation to such supply but which has been incurred by the recipient of the supply and not included in the price actually paid or payable for the goods or services or both.
- Incidental expenses, including commission and packing, charged by the supplier to the recipient of a supply and any amount charged for anything done by the supplier in respect of the supply of goods or services or both at the time of, or before delivery of the goods or supply of the services;
- Interest or late fee or penalty for delayed payment of any consideration for any supply; and
- Subsidies directly linked to the price excluding subsidies provided by the Central government and State governments.

The amount of subsidy would be included in the value of supply of the supplier who receives the subsidy.

The value of supply would not include:

- Discount available before or at the time of the supply provided such discount has been duly recorded in the invoice issued in respect of such supply (same invoice); and
- After the supply has been affected, if:
    - such discount is established in terms of an agreement entered into at or before the time of such supply and specifically linked to relevant invoices; and
    - input tax credit as is attributable to the discount on the basis of a document issued by the supplier has been reversed by the recipient of the supply.

In case the transaction value is not ascertainable as explained above, the reference to be made to CGST Rules, 2017 related to valuation aspect. In following circumstances, CGST rules w.r.t valuation is required to be referred:

- In case price is not the sole consideration,
- In case the supply of goods or services or both are between related party.
- In case the consideration is received partly in money and partly in kind.
- Supply of principal and agent, which is considered as deemed supply as per schedule I.

In all the above situations, one is required to examine the CGST rules relevant to valuation. Rule 27 to Rule 35 provides valuation rules in the CGST Rules, 2017 which covers different scenarios including special valuation in case of sale of used goods, money exchange services, air ticket booking and conditions for pure agent deductions.

2.9 HOW TO MOVE GOODS?

A registered taxable person has to raise a tax invoice to move goods, along with an e-way bill initially interstate and now in all States. Other than supply, a taxable person should raise delivery challan for transfer of goods along with the e-way bill.

For the provision of service, the assessee has to raise tax invoice after completion of provision of service within 30 days. In the case of banking company/financial institution/non-banking financial company, the time period becomes forty five days from the date of supply of services.

The invoice to be raised in triplicate, 1st copy is for Buyer, 2nd copy for the transporter and third copy for the supplier. In case of supply of service, there should be 2 copies with original for the receiver of service and duplicate is for the service supplier.

2.10 HOW TO MATCH AND AVAIL THE CREDIT?

A person registered under GST can avail ITC, of tax paid on the supply of goods or services used or intended to be used in the course or furtherance of business subject to restrictions.

(1) According to Rule 36 of the CGST Rules, 2017 documents required for availing Input Tax credit are:

  (a) Invoice issued by the supplier of goods and services or both in accordance with the Tax invoice provisions as per section 31 of CGST Act.

(b) Tax invoice issued by the recipient who is liable to pay tax on reverse charge basis as per section 9(3) and as per section 9(4) of the CGST Act, 2017

(c) Debit note issued by the supplier as per provisions of section 34 of the CGST Act, 2017

(d) Bill of entry or any other documents prescribed under the Customs Act, 1962 for assessment of IGST on Imports.

(e) Input service Distributor Invoice or credit note or any other documents issued by an ISD dealer.

2.11 CONDITIONS FOR CREDIT

(a) Input tax credit would be available only if all particulars as provided in Rule 46 are available on the invoice and relevant information is furnished in form GSTR-2 of the recipient. Presently GSTR-2 reporting has been suspended and new system of uploading outward supply invoices is proposed which would be the basis for claiming the input tax credit.

(b) Vide notification 39/2018 Central tax dated 04th September 2018 inserted proviso to Rule 36 of CGST Rules, 2017. According to the said rule, if document issued under section 31 contains details of:

- the amount of tax charged,
- description of goods or services,
- total value of supply of goods or services or both,
- GSTIN of the supplier and recipient and
- place of supply in case of inter-State supply,

Then input tax credit may be availed by the recipient (registered person) This amendment maybe understood as clarificatory and therefore applicable retrospectively.

(c) Input tax credit would not be availed, in respect of any tax paid pursuance of any order, where demand is confirmed on account of any fraud, wilful miss-statement or suppression of facts and tax paid on seizure of goods or conveyance due to incomplete E-way bill.

(d) The registered person must be in possession of tax invoice, he should have received goods and services or both. The exception is when goods are delivered by the supplier to other person based on the direction of recipient. The exception is also provided for services recently.

(e) The supplier must have paid tax to the government either by way of electronic credit ledger or through utilization of input tax credit admissible for such supply.

(f) In case goods are received in installments, after receipt of last lot or installment.

(g) In case, a registered person has claimed depreciation on tax component of the cost of capital goods, and Plant and machinery, Input tax credit on the said tax component shall not be allowed.

(h) Appropriate disclosure of credits in monthly return is also important.

(i) The registered person would not be eligible for taking Input tax credit in case of any invoice/debit notes for the supply of goods or services or both after the due date of filing return for September following the end of financial year or furnishing of annual return, whichever is earlier.

2.12 HOW TO DO JOB WORK?

Job work is defined to mean treatment or process undertaken by one person on goods belonging to another person. Where the receiver is adding components or substantial material to the goods sent on job work by the principal, the transaction would still be a job work. However Third party contract manufacturer manufacture is not job worker.

Job work can be done by the same entity between distinct persons (located in different States or business vertical)

In GST regime the supply attracts the tax. The goods can alternatively be sent on a supply invoice with GST (this would not be job work) without transfer of ownership. Job worker can avail the credit, process the material and send back under an invoice with GST.

The principal may under intimation and subject to conditions send and receive back taxable goods without payment of GST to a job worker as provided in sec 143. He can also send to any of his own places of business or other job workers for further processing or, for supplying such goods on payment of GST or for export. The principal also has the option to directly supply the raw material or even the final processed products to end customers on payment of GST or export from the premises of job worker itself, subject to fulfillment of applicable conditions. The goods sent for job work have to be received back within one year for inputs, three years for capital goods other than moulds and dies. Jigs and fixtures or tools are not required to be received back.

The stock movement and reconciliation of goods sent on job work and received back is important. Compliances to be noted are:

- If inputs/capital goods sent for job-work are not received back by the principal within 1 year or 3 years (for capital goods) it would be deemed that such inputs were supplied by the principal to the job-worker on the day when the said inputs were sent out. (interest cost)

- If the job-worker or the principal is registered then either of them may supply the scrap or waste on payment of tax. Both entities may retain evidence of GST payment.
- The details of following challans issued and received during the quarter would be furnished in FORM GST ITC-04 on or before the 25th day of the month succeeding the said quarter:-
    - Goods dispatched to a job worker
    - Goods received from a job worker
    - Goods sent from one job worker to another job worker.
    - Goods supplied from job worker.

Further, vide notification no. 7/2017-IGST dated 14.09.2017 exempts the job workers engaged in making the inter-State supply of services to a registered person from obtaining registration under GST Act.

The goods can be sent for job work by raising delivery challan along with e-way bill. Further, e-way bill is compulsory to send the goods for job work.

2.13 PROCEDURE FOR DISTRIBUTION OF ITC

The input service distributor (ISD) shall distribute the input tax credit in accordance with the provisions of section 20 of CGST Act, 2017 read with Rule 39 of CGST Rules, 2017. The ITC can be distributed as follows:

(a) The ITC available in the month **shall** be distributed in the same month and details shall be filed in GSTR-6 return.

(b) The ISD shall distribute separately the eligible and ineligible input tax credit.

(c) The credit of tax paid on input services attributable to a recipient of credit shall be distributed only to that recipient

(d) The credit of tax paid on input services attributable to more than one recipient of credit, shall be distributed pro rata basis based on the turnover in the state.

(e) If ISD receives any credit note, the tax involved in such credit note is also required to be distributed to the recipient/s of credit for reduction at their end.

(f) ISD credit would be eligible for the recipient subject to restrictions in the ITC provisions.

2.14 HOW TO RAISE INVOICE?

Invoice is an important part of GST. Sec 31 sets out the timing to raise the invoice in case of goods and services, continuous supply and revised invoice. The other documents for advance, reverse charge, exception to issue of tax invoice for exempted supplies and composition are also specified.

There is no specific format prescribed in the law for raising an invoice. However the law prescribes the contents in tax invoice as under:

(a) *Name, address and Goods and Services Tax Identification Number of the supplier.*

(b) A consecutive serial number not exceeding sixteen characters, in one or multiple series, containing alphabets or numerals or special characters-hyphen or dash and slash symbolized as "-" and "/" respectively, and any combination thereof, unique for a financial year.

(c) Date of its issue.

(d) *Name, address and Goods and Services Tax Identification Number or Unique Identity Number, if registered, of the recipient.*

(e) Name and address of the recipient and the address of delivery, along with the name of the State and its code, if such recipient is un-registered and where the value of the taxable supply is fifty thousand rupees or more.

(f) Name and address of the recipient and the address of delivery, along with the name of the State and its code, if such recipient is un-registered and where the value of the taxable supply is less than fifty thousand rupees and the recipient requests that such details be recorded in the tax invoice.

(g) Harmonised System of Nomenclature code for goods or services.

(h) *Description of goods or services.*

(i) Quantity in case of goods and unit or Unique Quantity Code thereof.

(j) *Total value of supply of goods or services or both.*

(k) Taxable value of the supply of goods or services or both.

(l) Discount or abatement, if any.

(m) Rate of tax (central tax, State tax, integrated tax, Union territory tax or cess).

(n) *Amount of tax charged in respect of taxable goods or services (central tax, State tax, integrated tax, Union territory tax or cess).* GST law does not allow all inclusive price.

(o) *Place of supply along with the name of the State, in the case of a supply in the course of inter-State trade or commerce.*

(p) Address of delivery where the same is different from the place of supply.

(q) Whether the tax is payable on reverse charge basis; and

(r) Signature or digital signature of the supplier or his authorised representative.

Notification 39/18 dt 4.9.18 has relaxed the conditions wherein only the 5 details underlined above are sufficient for making it valid.

A few optional exclusions of a. to r. above have been provided for insurers, banking and financial institutions and non-banking financial Companies, goods transport agents and passenger transport. It is important to note that where the invoice does not have the details prescribed it could be said to be defective and penalty for non- compliance is possible.

2.15 HOW TO RAISE DEBIT NOTE/CREDIT NOTE?

Debit Notes or Credit Notes are issued when there is a variation in the price and the amount payable by the receiver (buyer) increases or decreases after the invoice is issued.

When the amount payable by the buyer to seller decreases –There can be a change in the value of goods after the goods are delivered and invoice issued by the seller. This can be due to a return of goods or due to the bad quality of the goods delivered, short supply etc. The seller issues a Credit Note as a response or acknowledgment to the debit note.

When the amount payable by the buyer to seller increases - When the value of invoice increases, due to extra goods being delivered or the goods already delivered have been charged at a lower price, a debit note is required to be issued. The Debit Note, in this case, is issued by the seller to the buyer.

The tax liability would be adjusted but no reduction in output tax liability of the supplier would be permitted if the incidence of tax and interest on such supply has been passed on to any other person.

In business there may be a need to avoid the credit note with GST to avoid cumbersome compliances. This would not have any impact where the buyer is availing the credit and pays GST in cash on his value addition. The requirement of separate credit note in respect of each invoice is being done away with amendment to Section 34 which could provide relief in case of large number of transactions involved. However this important ease has not still been enabled in the GST portal. The linkage may be necessary to confirm that the discount is eligible for deductions from the value.

The registered person would not issue credit note in relation to supply of goods or services after the due date for filing return for September following end of financial year or furnishing annual return, whichever is earlier. However there is no time limit specified to issue debit notes.

2.16 EXPORT/SEZ SUPPLY

Exports and supply to SEZ are called as zero-rated whereby no tax is payable subject to following the procedure contained in the rules. The benefit of availment of input tax and refund of accumulated credit would be available in two ways:

(i) With payment of taxes utilising the credit

(ii) Without payment of tax

2.16.1 Procedure for export with payment of IGST

(1) The assessee has to raise tax invoice mentioning GST rate and the tax amount payable. In case of direct exports, a commercial invoice could be raised for issue to customer abroad. Refund of IGST can be claimed by assessee based on tax invoice.

(2) Ensure that the details such as invoice reference, value, HSN, rate of tax are appropriately captured in shipping bill/bill of export as well. Shipping bill/bill of export would be deemed to be the application form.

(3) In case of export of services, a separate application to be made in form GST RFD-01.

(4) The person claiming refund of IGST paid on export of goods should ensure that he has not received the supplies on which suppliers have claimed benefit of concession/exemption such as advance authorization, EOU, merchant exports/EPCG schemes.

(5) Details of exports to be uploaded in table 6A of GSTR-1 as well as GSTR-3B return.

(6) Based on the details uploaded, the officers would correlate the EGM details with customs database and process the refund.

(7) Correct bank account details must be provided for credit of refund amounts.

(8) Later the department may verify the eligibility of credit and call for other required documents to process the refund.

(9) The tax invoice issued for export or SEZ supplies have to carry an endorsement "Supply meant for export/supply to SEZ unit or SEZ developer for authorised operations on payment of IGST".

2.16.2 Procedure for export without payment of IGST

(1) The assessee has to obtain the letter of undertaking (LUT) by making online application on GST portal. Such LUT would expire on 31st March and requires renewal from 1st April every year.*[2] After obtaining LUT, he can

2 As clarified by circular 8/8/17 dt. 4.10.17.

supply the goods or services to SEZ unit/for direct exports without payment of IGST.

(2) The assessee has to raise tax invoice without mentioning GST.

(3) Application should be made in form GST RFD-11 along with requisite documents.

(4) Provide the details of exports and SEZ supplies in form GSTR-3B and GSTR-1.

(5) Co-relate the EGM details with customs database.

(6) The tax invoice issued for export or SEZ supplies has to carry an endorsement "Supply meant for export/supply to SEZ unit or SEZ developer for authorised operations under LUT or bond without payment of IGST".

2.17 DEEMED EXPORTS

In terms of section 147 of the CGST Act, 2017, the government has notified few supplies as deemed exports where goods supplied does not leave India and consideration for such supply is received either in Indian rupees or in any convertible foreign exchange, if such goods are manufactured in India. This includes supplies against advance authorization, EPCG scheme, supplies to EOUs and gold supply to a specified bank under advance authorization scheme. The procedure to be followed in this regard as per GST circular no.14/14/2017 dated 6th November 2017 is as follows:

(i) The recipient EOU/EHTP/STP/BTP unit has to give prior intimation in a prescribed proforma in "Form 'A" bearing a running serial number containing the goods to be procured, as pre-approved by the Development Commissioner and the details of the supplier before such deemed export supplies are made. The said intimation has to be given to the registered supplier, the jurisdictional GST officer in charge of such registered supplier and its jurisdictional GST officer.

(ii) The registered supplier thereafter would supply goods under tax invoice to the recipient EOU/EHTP/STP/BTP unit.

(iii) On receipt of such supplies, the EOU/EHTP/STP/BTP unit needs to endorse the tax invoice and send a copy of the endorsed tax invoice to the registered supplier, the jurisdictional GST officer in charge of such registered supplier and its jurisdictional GST officer.

(iv) The endorsed tax invoice would be considered as proof of deemed export supplies by the registered person to EOU/EHTP/STP/BTP unit.

(v) The recipient EOU/EHTP/STP/BTP unit has to maintain records of such deemed export supplies in digital form, based upon data elements contained in "Form-B". The software for maintenance of digital records shall incorporate the feature of audit trail. While the data elements contained in the Form-B are mandatory, the recipient units will be free to add or continue with any additional data fields, as per their commercial requirements. All recipient units are required to enter data accurately and immediately upon the goods being received in, utilized by or removed from the said unit. The digital records should be kept updated, accurate, complete and available at the said unit at all times for verification by the proper officer, whenever required. A digital copy of Form ' B containing transactions for the month, shall be provided to the jurisdictional GST officer, each month (by the 10th of month) in a CD or Pen drive, as convenient to the said unit. Form A and B could be taken from referred to circular.

2.18 SUPPLY OF GOODS TO MERCHANT EXPORTER

Supply of goods by a registered person to another registered person would be subject to concessional GST rate of 0.1% in case of inter-State supplies and 0.1% (CGST & SGST put together) in case of intra-State supplies subject to fulfilment of following conditions:

(i) the registered supplier shall supply the goods to the registered recipient on a tax invoice;

(ii) the registered recipient shall export the said goods within a period of ninety days from the date of issue of a tax invoice by the registered supplier;

(iii) the registered recipient shall indicate the Goods and Services Tax Identification Number of the registered supplier and the tax invoice number issued by the registered supplier in respect of the said goods in the shipping bill or bill of export, as the case may be;

(iv) the registered recipient shall be registered with an Export Promotion Council or a Commodity Board recognised by the Department of Commerce;

(v) the registered recipient shall place an order on registered supplier for procuring goods at concessional rate and a copy of the same shall also be provided to the jurisdictional tax officer of the registered supplier;

(vi) the registered recipient shall move the said goods from place of registered supplier'

(a) directly to the Port, Inland Container Deport, Airport or Land Customs Station from where the said goods are to be exported; or

(b) directly to a registered warehouse from where the said goods shall be move to the Port, Inland Container Deport, Airport or Land Customs Station from where the said goods are to be exported;

(vii) if the registered recipient intends to aggregate supplies from multiple registered suppliers and then export, the goods from each registered supplier shall move to a registered warehouse and after aggregation, the registered recipient shall move goods to the Port, Inland Container Deport, Airport or Land Customs Station from where they shall be exported;

(viii) in case of situation referred to in condition (vii), the registered recipient shall endorse receipt of goods on the tax invoice and also obtain acknowledgement of receipt of goods in the registered warehouse from the warehouse operator and the endorsed tax invoice and the acknowledgment of the warehouse operator shall be provided to the registered supplier as well as to the jurisdictional tax officer of such supplier; and

(ix) when goods have been exported, the registered recipient shall provide copy of shipping bill or bill of export containing details of Goods and Services Tax Identification Number (GSTIN) and tax invoice of the registered supplier along with proof of export general manifest or export report having been filed to the registered supplier as well as jurisdictional tax officer of such supplier.

2.19 WHAT RECORDS TO MAINTAIN?

The registered person should keep and maintain true and correct, accurate accounts/records at his principal place of business. These would cover:

(i) Production and Manufacture of goods;

(ii) Inward and outward supply of goods or services or both;

(iii) Stock of goods;

(iv) Input tax credit availed;

(v) Output tax payable and paid;

(vi) Separate account of advances received, paid and adjustments made thereto;

(vii) Names and complete addresses of suppliers and recipients of goods or services or both;

(i) Monthly production details in the case of manufacturers and

(ii) Such other particulars as may be prescribed

In case more than one place of business is specified in the certificate of registration, the accounts relating to each place of business would be kept at such place of business. The accounts and records may be kept and maintained in the electronic form as prescribed.

2.20 HOW TO PAY TAXES?

In GST the tax has to be paid online. The payment of tax is necessary where the ITC is not sufficient for a particular month. The payment of tax should be made on monthly basis on the supply/advance received/RCM payment etc. by 20th of subsequent month. The composition dealer has to file on or before 18th of the quarter ending.

2.21 HOW TO CALCULATE INTEREST?

Tax would be payable as determined either by the assessee himself or as consequent to adjudication resulting in a non-levy, wrong levy, short levy, wrong classification or availment of ineligible credit. Interest would be payable from the due date until the date of payment of the said tax. The rate at which interest is to be calculated is presently 18% per annum and should be computed based on the number of days of delay. It may be noted that when GSTR3 B is not filed, the interest would be on gross tax amount and not net of ITC.*[3]

If a taxable person makes undue or excess claim of ITC or undue or excess reduction in output tax liability would pay an interest not exceeding 24% on undue or excess claim or undue or excess reduction in terms of Section 42 (10) and Section 43(10). One argument is that the interest under this section cannot be levied as the system of GSTR-2 and GSTR-3 are suspended presently.

If a refund is sanctioned and not paid within 60 days from the date of receipt of the application, the government has to pay interest at 6%. In case of order received from adjudicating authority or appellate authority or appellate tribunal or Court which has attained finality, the interest would be 9%.

2.22 VOLUNTARY PAYMENT UNDER DRC-03

The taxpayer can make voluntary payments which have not been made while filing GST returns. The DRC-03 can also be used for payment of tax before issue of notice under section 73 or 74 of CGST Act, 2017 or make payment within 30 days from the date of issue of notice.

---

3 This is unfair and Government is not allowed to collect tax which is not due under Article 365 of the Constitution. However, the Telangana HC in the case of Mega Cabs in 2019 has confirmed this view. Expert opine that this may not be intention of the law and this aspect may see more challenge.

2.23 PAYMENT OF TAX AND OTHER AMOUNTS IN INSTALMENTS

The taxpayer can make an application to the Commissioner under section 80 of CGST Act, 2017 to seek extension of time to pay any amount due under the act or pay the amount due in instalment.

The taxpayer is required to file the application in FORM GST DRC-20 seeking extension of time for payment of taxes or any other amount due under the act or for allowing payment of such dues in instalments.

After considering request, the Commissioner has to issue an order in FORM GST DRC-21 allowing the taxpayer further time or to make payment in instalments.

2.24 HOW TO CLAIM REFUND?

Refund claim is to be filed under section 54, within a period of 2 years from the relevant date to the assistant/deputy commissioner. Claiming a refund of any balance in the electronic cash ledger should be in accordance with sec 49(6). A specialised agency of the UN organisation or any multilateral financial institution and organisation notified under the united nations, consulate or embassy of foreign countries or any other person or class of persons entitled to a refund of tax paid by it on inward supplies of goods or services or both may make an application for a refund before the expiry of six months from the last date of the quarter in which such supply is received.

Refund claim can be filed for exports, supply to SEZ, Supply to EOU/EHTP/BTP/STP and inverted tax structure. It should be ensured that the duty burden was not passed on to the customer as that would lead to the denial of the refund under the principle of unjust enrichment. It should also be noted that the burden to prove that tax burden has not been passed on is on the claimant. If passed then refund would not be admissible. For procedure, the topic on exports/SEZ supply could be referred.

2.25 HOW TO FILE RETURN?

A taxable person has a legal obligation to declare his tax liability and credits availed during the period covered under return, to furnish details about the taxes paid, to disclose such other aspects as may be applicable as per return format and file the correct and complete return within the stipulated time frame.

GST is a self-assessed destination-based taxation system. The submission and processing of return is an important link between the taxpayer & tax administration. It is an important tool for:

- compliance verification program of tax administration;
- to declare tax liability for a given period;
- a mode for transfer of information to tax administration;

- providing necessary inputs for taking policy decision;
- management of audit and anti-evasion programs of tax administration;
- finalization of the tax liabilities of the taxpayer within the stipulated period of limitation.

It is very important that the data input in the returns is verified for correctness and appropriateness, reconciled, complete, not duplicated. Many tax payers are not giving due time and simply upload/get uploaded incorrect, invalid, unreconciled data. The portal is a computer wherein the garbage in would give garbage out result. It is ideal that a checklist for preparation of the 3B as well as GSTR-1 be followed.

Persons who are required to file returns in GST regime are supplier of goods/service, input service distributor, composition dealer, casual taxable person, person deducting TDS, e-commerce operators, non-resident taxable person, composition dealer etc. Various returns to be filed by under GST are as follows:

Persons required to file	Periodicity	Form of return	Due date
All registered persons other than specified	Monthly	GSTR-3B	20th of subsequent month
– All registered persons other than specified	Monthly	GSTR-1	11th of subsequent month
– If less than 1.5 crore aggregate turnover	Quarterly	GSTR-1	11th day after end of quarter
Composition dealers	Quarterly	GSTR-4	18th day after end of quarter
Non-resident taxable persons	Monthly	GSTR-5	20th of subsequent month
Input service distributor	Monthly	GSTR-6	13th of subsequent month
Annual return	Yearly	GSTR-9/9A	31st December after end of financial year

Return statements like GSTR-2 and GSTR-3 are suspended and new system of return filing is being proposed.

2.26 PROPOSED GST RETURNS

The provision of returns in the unorganised business has a number of challenges. The provision u/s 16 requiring the recipient to pay the tax if tax not paid or return is not filed by supplier. This seems to impose an impractical compliance by the buyer for errors of his vendors. This and need for simplification of returns led to this new provision to be put in place from 1st July 2019.

Every registered person based on preceding FY turnover and type of transactions has to select the type of return to be filed as mentioned below.

- NORMAL monthly (Form RET-01): Mandatory for turnover in preceding FY > Rs. 5 crore and turnover < Rs. 5 crore has the option to select which type of return to be filed. GST liability to be paid monthly.
- NORMAL quarterly (Form RET-01): Turnover in preceding FY < Rs. 5 crores. GST liability to be paid monthly.
- SAHAJ quarterly (Form RET-02): Turnover in preceding FY < Rs. 5 crores and only B2C supplies and taxes to be paid under reverse charge, NIL and exempt supplies. GST liability to be paid monthly.
- SUGAM quarterly (Form RET-03): Turnover in preceding FY < Rs. 5 crores and only B2B, B2C supplies and taxes to be paid under reverse charge, NIL and exempt supplies. GST liability to be paid monthly.

Every registered person needs to file the following two annexures in addition to returns mentioned above:

- Form GST ANX-1: Annexure of outward supplies, imports and inward supplies attracting reverse charge.
- Form GST ANX-2: Details of auto-drafted inward supplies.

2.27 HOW TO GET READY FOR AUDIT?

Audit means scrutiny and verification of documents, events and processes in order to verify facts and to draw conclusions regarding the correctness of recording of facts and the efficiency of a system under study. When department issues notice for audit, for the activity carried out by the assessee, the assessee has to keep the records properly and provide the reconciliation between the books and returns. Though in GST all the details would be uploaded i.e. sales, advance, credit note and debit note, sales return, supplementary invoice, purchases, import details and the department can verify the details online, but the physical documents have to be verified by visiting premises and checking whether the details are uploaded properly, whether the invoices are properly available with the assessee.

The assessee has to keep the documents properly and fill the profile shared by the department to be submitted to the department. It is important to attend the officers by a knowledgeable person who is reasonably good in GST law. The visitor register could also be updated with details of officers visiting the business premises for audit purpose. This could be useful in proving that department has knowledge of certain information which could reduce the tax/penalty.

2.28 CORRESPONDENCE WITH DEPARTMENT

In earlier tax laws correspondence with the department was largely manual. Any issues faced by the assessee, the assessee had to write a letter and visit the department for submission of a letter and obtain acknowledgment for future reference. Where the letter was not accepted by the department, most of the assessee were sending the letters by registered post/speed post with acknowledgment due. Initially while discussing GST, the government has promised that the GST would be fully automated and would be done electronically with the help of technology. There would not be any interaction between assessee and officers in GST era, everything should be done through online from registration, return, refund, reply to notices etc. However the information technology systems were not put in place after due validation and many manual and face to face situations have been suggested to solve the day to day issues of the tax payers. Over a period of time it is expected most normal transactions would be online including the refund.

2.29 HOW TO DEAL WITH VISITS FROM REVENUE?

The departmental officers from the jurisdictional range or division may visit the manufacturers, traders or service providers in terms of Rule 139 of CGST Rules, 2017 read with section 67 of the CGST Act, 2017. The officer who visit the premises for inspection, search etc., should have authorisation from the proper officer not below the rank of Joint Commissioner.

Section 71 empowers any officer not below the rank of Deputy Commissioner to have access to business premises for audit, scrutiny, verification and checks to safeguard revenue. This is with a notice of 15 days normally.

It is expected that this power is not exercised routinely and only done when there is a valid reason.*[4]

The procedure to deal with the officers who come for search is as follows:

(a) The identity card of the officer may be asked by the security at the gate.

(b) Ask the officers including the sub-ordinate officers to make entry in the visitors register including the time of visit.

---

4 In many States the State GST officers and at times the Central officers are on fishing expedition and coercing the tax payer who may not have access to good advice to pay tax with interest and penalty without following the due process of law.

(c) If officer refuses to sign in the visitors register, the same may be intimated to the senior officer.

(d) Check whether the authorisation is provided to the proper officer in FORM GST INS-01.

(e) Every visit may be followed up by sending minutes of the meeting to the jurisdictional officer as well as visiting officer by way of official mail/RPAD or speed post.

The procedure in case of audit or verification would start with an intimation. One could get ready with the needed information as set out in the section. The audit/ verification would culminate in observation being shared and if agreed could be paid with interest or reversed after taking expert confirmation.

2.30 HOW TO DEAL WITH INSPECTION DURING MOVEMENT?

The need to have an inspection of goods while in transit has arosen due to some tax evasive practices as under:

- Supply and consequent movement without invoices
- Supply and consequent movement on understated or over stated quantities.
- Multiple supplies with only 1 invoice
- Non registration though over the threshold limit
- Not opting for regular scheme when under compostion scheme.
- Tracking of goods movement by using technology such as google or Radio frequency identification device [RFID] fixed to conveyances. Section 68 enjoins on the transporter carrying any consignment of goods to carry documents prescribed as well as devices as prescribed *[5] This has become the main check after abolishing of check posts. This enables the inspection of goods while being transported for which e-way bill provisions have been put in place. There are some products exempted like LPG and jewellery and some value limits. The respective States have specified different rules. However for interstate movement it is uniform across India.

The assessee who moves goods should be very clear to comply in detail and not miss out making full entries. The tax compliant may also face the same treatment as those who evade in case of any seizure of conveyance until the rating system is

5 such as invoice, bill, delivery challan, vehicle fitted with Radio Frequency Identification device (RFID), google for start, stop, destination identification etc.

in place.*[6] It is understood that the data mining and collation would help in unearthing those who are out of the mainstream.

2.31 HOW TO RESPOND TO A SUMMONS

The Director General of Anti-profiteering or an officer authorised by him, has the power to issue summon to any person whose attendance is necessary to give evidence or produce documents or any other thing under section 70 of CGST Act, 2017. (Rule 132)

(a) The produce to be followed when the summons is issued: The issue of summon being a judicial proceedings, cannot be ignored

(b) Summons should be read carefully. Sometimes summons would require documents or information to be given. In such cases appearance may not be necessary. In case of doubt clarifications can be sought before appearance. The party on whom the summon is issued is required to appear before the authority.

(c) The person on whom the summon is issued should give answers to the questions asked by the proper officer.

(d) If the proper officer records the statement, it needs to be taken care whether the proper officer is recording the statement provided properly. [not dictated].

(e) The favourable parts of statement not recorded can be sent by RPAD/SP as soon as possible if felt relevant.

(f) The person should request for the photocopy of the statement recorded from the proper officer.

(g) If high handed tactics are used, the statement is advisable to be retracted within a day or two with sharing with the higher officer and the Commissioner of GST. Copy of such retraction should always be sent to the investigating officer also.

2.32 PROCEDURE TO RELEASE THE SEIZED GOODS

The goods seized by the proper officer during the visit, inspection or search of the premises may be released on a provisional basis upon execution of bond for the value of goods in FORM GST INS-04 and furnish the security in form of bank guarantee equivalent to the amount of applicable tax, interest and penalty payable as per Rule 140 of CGST Rules, 2017.

The security shall be encashed if the person fails to produce the goods when it is required.

6 Rating system may take another 2 years to be in place.

2.33 TAX DEDUCTED AT SOURCE

The following category of persons have to deduct TDS at the rate of 2% (1% CGST & 1% SGST) from the payment made to supplier of taxable goods or services when the total value of supply under a contract exceeds Rs. 2.5 lakh.

a) Department or an establishment of CG/SG.

b) Local authority.

c) Governmental agencies.

d) Authority or board, set up by an act of parliament or state legislature.

e) Authority or board, established by any govt. with 51% or more participation by way of equity or control.

f) Society established under CG/SG/local authorities.

g) Public sector undertakings.

The deductor needs to file TDS return in form GSTR 7 and make payment within 10 days after the end of month in which such deduction made and also to be issue TDS certificate to the deductee.

The amount deducted would be credited to electronic cash ledger of deductee and same may use for set off his output tax liability.

Note 1: In terms of notification 50/2018 of Central tax dated 13th September 2018, government on recommendation of council notified the persons mentioned in (**d** to **g)** above to deduct TDS.

Note 2: In terms of notification 73/2018 of Central Tax dated 31st December 2018, TDS need not to be deducted for supply of goods or services which take place between one person to another person specified above.

Note: This method of collecting tax in VAT has led to many disputes due to the non-compliance by the person who deducts and could lead to increase in cost by 2%.

2.34 COLLECTION OF TAX AT SOURCE

The e-commerce business is growing at leaps and bounds. There is a possibility that the suppliers of goods or services may not be registered even though they are liable. It is also possible that there may be elements of undervaluation in these transactions. To bring transparency to these transactions this provision has been put in place.

Every electronic commerce operator, not being an agent, have to collect an amount calculated at 1% (0.5% CGST & 0.5% SGST for intra state and 1% IGST for interstate supplies), of the net value of taxable supplies made through it by other suppliers where the consideration with respect to such supplies is to be collected by the operator.

Net value of taxable supplies means aggregate value of taxable supplies of goods or services other than 9(5) made during month by all registered persons through operator reduced by aggregate value of taxable supplies returned to supplier during the month.

Every electronic commerce operator needs to file TCS return in form GSTR 8 and make payment within 10 days after the end of month in which such collection made.

The supplier who has supplied the goods or services or both through the operator shall claim credit in his electronic cash ledger of the amount collected and reflected in the return.

Note 1: Notification 52/2018 of Central Tax dated 20th September 2018, notified the 0.5% CGST would be collected by the electronic commerce operator as tax collected at source.

2.35 CONCLUSION

This chapter covers in brief the procedural compliances. The importance of compliance of prescribed procedures which are directly linked to the provisions of the Act cannot be undermined in GST. It is also a need for the GST audit where the auditor would have to comment on other compliances as part of his report. A commentary on the procedures as a ready referencer would definitely ensure better compliance.

Chapter 3

Professional Opportunities in GST

3.1 BACKGROUND

The total indirect tax revenue (Centre and State) in 2017-18 was about Rs. 20 lakh crores. The Government is estimating it to be around Rs. 23 lakh crores for the year 2018-19. This includes Rs. 14 lakh crores from GST and Rs. 9 lakh crores from Customs, VAT and Excise Duty on 5 petroleum products, tobacco and liquor. The number of registered tax payers has increased by more than 85% from 75 lakhs since the time of VAT, Central Excise and Service Tax to 130 lakhs in GST. This is a major achievement inspite of the dampening impact of demonetization and recent global tariff wars. This figure includes those taxpayers also who were not and are not filing the returns. The era of rewarding the honest entrepreneur appears to have started albeit slowly.

It is estimated that in many sectors like steel, cement, plastic, real estate sector, textiles, jewellery, some consumer products today, about 30% of the manufacturers/ processors, distributors, retail traders, service providers including contractors/man power suppliers have not opted to register. This is inspite of the fact that they are required to be registered. In fact in many cases they avoid to do business with those registered or those who issue invoices with tax!! Such players could be below the threshold limit which for goods has been enhanced now to Rs. 40 lakhs in most States. Many of them on record only trade in exempted products. There is still a significant part of unorganised trade which is off records. They are part of the "grey/ parallel economy". It is also a cause of concern that those who are outside the threshold are under the Composition Option. In GST unlike in Central Excise the possibility of 100s of registration under threshold or composition within same family and group exists.

The ones who claim either exemption (including threshold) or composition break the credit chain and could also stop the payment of tax on the value added at later stages. The last mile to consumer where the margin is the maximum may end up with that value added being out of tax totally even for products which are manufactured by the organised sector.

The compliance focus of Central Board of Indirect Taxes (CBIC) and GST Council at present is only on Business to Business (B2B) segment. The business to consumer part may get attention start in 2020. Some of the amendments provisions and proposals on way forward shared by the CBIC which would generally impact the trade/ industry/ service provider are:

(i) The revival/extension of the reverse charge for procurements from select unregistered suppliers of goods and services may be in place by October 2019. This would force many who have opted for multiple enterprises, under invoicing to join the compliant stream.

(ii) The capturing of the reverse charge mechanism already in place which had a low compliance in service tax regime. The SMEs as well as the exporters were not compliant to a great degree.

(iii) The limited matching of tax paid by supplier to credit availed by recipient would bolster/safeguard the revenue to some extent. However this may require notices to all by revenue which may start by end of 2019. Well run businesses have automated the process of internal vendor wise matching of transactions to avoid disputes in the future. It also helps them to recover, raise a debit note or not pay errant suppliers.

(iv) The comparison of the total value in e-way bills under an aadhar number (for the unregistered) or with the value declared in return, if filed.*[1]

(v) Data analysis on "value of procurements" versus "value of supplies" is being collated.

(vi) The business of fake bills and circular trading is going on to a moderate extent. Focus on such errant suppliers using information technology is apparently partially successful. However the consequent demand on the buyers of such bills may not be followed up adequately. This would also reduce substantially once the liability shifts to the supplier once the need to upload is put in place by 1st September 2019[2].

(vii) The practice of selling goods to one and giving the bill to another, however, seems to be continuing unabated especially in the unorganised sector which could include steel, sand, jelly, brick, steel, cement manufacturers/ suppliers. The procurement through agents where they supply goods from one and bill from another is also continuing. The analysis of ratios in similar/ same industry and audits by professionals and revenue could correct this errant practice to some extent.

1 This data is being collected as and when e-way bill is generated.

2 The date has been extended from April 19 to July and now September.

(viii) Large numbers of notices based on irregular patterns in value and tax credit and vendor information are expected in the second half of 2019. These measures may bring down the evasion substantially.*[3]

(ix) The active, collaborative working of the GST/Income Tax administration and GSTN as soon as possible, with quick action, may bring some more errant evaders to the mainstream of tax compliance. This would lead to increase in both taxes

These measures may lead to tax evaders as well as errant small suppliers in retail or service segment in FMCG, real estate, textile, jewellery and other industry to come on board to seek registration and be tax compliant. This would help to ensure that honest taxpayers are able to flourish in their businesses.

Small dealers, manufacturers and service providers making B2B supplies, who do not wish to stop/ reduce their services to the registered trade, industry or businesses are voluntarily registering to ensure that their clients get the benefit of input tax credit available to them. Larger entities are also mandating the procurement only from registered suppliers. This would make them competitive and grow on the longer term.

Those who are making mainly B2C supplies i.e. directly selling to the consumers would like to avail the eligible threshold limit of exemption up to Rs. 20/ 40 lakhs or opt for composition scheme up to Rs. 100/ 150 lakhs for goods and services and Rs. 50 lakhs for services at concessional rate of 6%.

It has also been observed that a number of small taxpayers i.e. manufacturers and retailers have resorted to registering multiple enterprises so that they can continue to procure from unregistered taxpayers and would end up paying only 1% of their gross outward supplies. These tactics are adopted normally within the family or within associate group entities. The tax administrators know this fact, but they may be strengthening devices to capture such miscreants. In course of time, it is expected that the limits could be reduced or clubbing of concerns based on certain parameters would be put in place by way of amendment in law. The increase in the number of transactions falling under reverse charge is an on-going exercise in identified sectors. The recent scheme for real estate of 1/ 5% without ITC but having a condition of 80% from registered suppliers is an example. However the habit could continue to be a cause of concern.

3.2 PROFESSIONAL'S ADVANTAGE

The knowledge of accounting, costing, direct and indirect tax laws, company law and certain allied commercial laws like The Indian Contract Act, 1872, Companies Act etc. makes the professionals fairly comprehensive legal and tax practitioners.

---

3 The soft pedalling on the non-compliance due to portal issues and complications in the law at present may end in July 2019.

This coupled with the experience from understanding businesses through conduct of audits, providing opinions, preparation/ certification of financial statements, representing before financial, tax and appellate authorities provides Chartered Accountants an edge with a deeper understanding of nature of business enabling them to resolve issues.

The cost accountants also have the above advantage to some extent, having deeper costing knowledge.

The total number of professionals who are aware of basics of GST could exceed 200,000 as on date. Those with in depth knowledge required for conducting a value added review/ audit and consultancy as on date may be only around 35,000. The extent of continued education and certificate courses (including online) conducted by the Regulatory bodies like the ICAI would augment this number with time.

The non-qualified consultants who outnumber the qualified professionals today operating in indirect tax area are finding that the scope of being an intermediary between the client and the tax administrators is disappearing day by day. They would need to equip themselves not only with higher level of legal knowledge but with the understanding of the accounting, specifically in the digital environment and learning of audit techniques. If they do not do so , their clients may be move over to knowledgeable professionals after the tax payer is exposed to a number of demands starting off in the second half of 2019 or in later years.

The professionals earlier practicing in VAT, Service Tax and Excise/ Customs would find it easier to understand the GST which is a mixed bag of all these laws. However, there would be a bit of unlearning the erstwhile principles and concepts wherever there is a change under the GST law. In the present GST Act and Rules, 2017, we may witness that numerous provisions have been borrowed from VAT, Service Tax, Central Excise and Customs. The GST law was intended to be simple and clear but as it stands today, it is very cumbersome and it may not be conceivable for SMEs to comply without professional assistance. In addition to the above, the professional services are also required on account of reconciliation and audit work as contained under the provisions of GST law to be completed within the specified period of time.

The authors are of the view that the professional services would be *sine-quo-non* to comply with the provisions of GST law, for enterprises having aggregate turnover above a reasonable level, say Rs. 10 crores per annum. The major chunk of professional services would be diverted towards Chartered Accountants and other professionals. It may entail the challenge of having adequate number of knowledgeable Chartered Accountants or professionals to serve. The other professionals like advocates, CMA's, CS's etc. may also fulfil the requirements to the extent of their professional acumen of the GST law. The tax authorities, time and again have asserted that the CA professionals have always proved to be pioneers keeping themselves abreast with the contemporary law and their presentation skills before various administrative and judicial authorities. It makes sense that CA professionals must increase their knowledge and skill and take advantage of the opportunity to conduct independent GST audit and provide value added GST review and consultancy services within the frame work of law. The competent and honest tax officers would also prefer the professional due to his capability of studying and updating the ever changing GST law.

3.3 PROFESSIONAL'S ROLE

The canvas of compliance and advisory work under the contemporary law is very large in this period. The advent of GST has been considered as a historical shift from the erstwhile multiplicity of laws where none of the practitioners could cater to the needs of the industry to ensure compliance under different laws. The GST law has provided a once in a life time opportunity, to provide services in the form of handholding to the industry to comply and to boost their businesses.

Specific contributions by the professionals could be:

(i) Providing consultancy and opinion on classification and rates applicable for the goods and services using the Harmonised System of Nomenclature (HSN) as well as the interpretative rules laid down in First Schedule to Customs Tariff Act and Scheme of Classification annexed with the notification.

(ii) Industry wise services may also gain importance. One example could be in relation to the on-going projects by the builders, to assist them to come out of the dilemma whether to choose to continue the time tested prevailing scheme of taxation with the benefit of claim of ITC or switch to the hotchpotch of the new tariff i.e. @5% or 1% where all ITC claims are barred. The reversal of ITC for those who are opting for the new scheme appears to be unworkable as on date for the SMEs in the industry.

To assist builders who are in the new scheme - fulfilling condition laid down under the law that they should at least maintain 80% of their inward supplies from registered vendors, else, to comply with the liability to pay RCM on the shortfall.

Another example could be compliances specific to job work which is used by manufacturers quite frequently. Special provisions for compliance in jewellery sector can be used to avoid demands which can lead to closure.

(iii) Advising on availability of exemptions contained in the notifications and ensuring that the conditions, if any, for availing exemptions are complied with. This would be of paramount importance for the taxpayers supplying to entities enjoying exemption on Central/ State Government works

(iv) Developing analytical inferences entailing benefits to the taxpayers adopting the theory of optimisation where across the chain benefits of ITC would be analysed and reasoned decisions would be given to both inward vendors and outward customers. This would assist in framing procurement and competitive pricing policies for the taxpayer.

(v) To examine the areas where representation services (for change in law) can be given to business communities, where they feel hardships in complying with the provisions of law or they wish to redress any unfairness in the policy of the Government. This would be possible specifically when the tax gatherers and GST Council are vigilant not only to listen but are ready to mitigate hardships of the tax payer.

(vi) The professionals having in depth knowledge of the taxation system both under direct and indirect taxes can impart services to SMEs by sharing their knowledge, in as much as, doing impact analysis of various statutory GST levies and exemptions available to them.

(viii) The large business houses have been actively utilising the professional services in the GST field from impact studies in 2016-17 (based on model law) to now reconcile and audit their accounts as per the statutory requirements. Their focus is on ensuring their eligible ITC claim, the enjoyment of exemptions and the proper valuation. Businesses are aware that this is the right time to lay a strong foundation to mitigate disputes in times to come. It would then provide stable path for their growth and safeguard their margins.

(ix) The multi facet team of professionals can not only educate the businesses in the field of taxation but can also suggest better ways how to integrate their accounting resources by adopting innovative technologies in the form of ERP etc. and that aligned to GST law and rules.

(x) To create efficiencies by advising the top management to opt for the wheel and spoke options where they are having multiple locations. It may benefit the businesses not only as a cost savings but availing optimum input credits as well.

xi) The professionals can assist in managing and analysing large data of businesses with the help of contemporary analytical automated tools, software, internal control systems etc. This would improve the GST compliances by automating reconciliations, payment of taxes and filing of accurate returns. Choosing of the right tools (may be free) or need to customise and testing are the professional's strength.

(xii) It may be seen that in spite of all efforts made by the law makers to make the GST law to be simple, it has finally turned to be a very challenging law. It has lengthy provisions, full of complexity and interpretational issues which consequent to representations being made have led to too many amendments and issuance of circulars. This means that there is a need for regular workshops, specific trainings and imparting knowledge not only at all levels of management but to the vendors and customers at large. The knowledgeable and certified professionals can assist the large business houses in this knowledge and skilling of the workforce.

(xiii) The industry/business runs on various contracts entered into with employees, vendors, service providers, customers and other stakeholders. These contracts are in in terms of the Contract Act, 1872. Contracts may be oral or written but safety could be in the written ones which can have evidentiary value. The GST law provides specific treatment for composite and mixed supplies. There is also a non-composite supply which has not been specifically enumerated. The mistakes in this can have far reaching tax consequences. A professional with legal strength can bring clarity by creating well-thought-out/drafted agreements to plan taxes in a safe manner.

(xiv) The professionals can update businesses even in those areas where unfair provisions have been made but the same are made moving by law makers and create value to them. For example, the claim of ITC for the financial year 2017-18 was not allowed initially beyond September 2018 returns. This was extended to March 2019 returns but with condition that the credits are reflected in 2A.

(xv) The professionals can play an important role to reconcile inward and outward supplies furnished by a taxpayer in its GST returns with that declared by him in his audited financial statements. This requires knowledge of the accounting standards, the professional capabilities to understand and suggest appropriate method to recognise revenue as well as understanding of direct and indirect tax statutes. The movement of goods made otherwise than supplies through e-way bills like goods sent on job-work or goods sent on approval basis may require a thorough analysis whether such supplies could be termed as taxable supplies as per GST law. It may help taxpayers to pay their due taxes, avoid seizures with consequential demands and litigation and bring about cost optimisation.

(xvi) Many professionals have specialisation in information technology/data analytics and some even have hand on consulting skills in ERP environment. These skills could ensure that the client would get his IT integrated and would be able to comply with the complex needs of GST compliance.

(xvii) The professionals can share the knowledge and information through newsletters, webcasts, video conferencing facilities in their offices, wherefrom they can impart online training and consultation services across various locations of clients business houses. Such advisory services may be extended through web portals, chat boats, word file updates, audio & video files and through webinars. Such services can be imparted for a specific business or for general stakeholders at large.

(xviii) More than 200,000 professionals are imparting compliance services under GST to various taxpayers making it possible to claim their ITC, pay tax dues, file their returns or to claim refunds on periodical basis.

(xix) The demand of professional services would increase with the passage of time in the field of dispute resolution. The number of disputes post September 2019 is bound to be substantial. The definition of supply, claim of ITC, valuation, classification, place of supply, exemption, the sky high rates of mandatory interest on defaults and other interpretational issues are giving almost a clear signal that there would be a tussle between the taxpayers and the tax gatherers in all the time to come.

(xx) The larger taxpayers may be seeking professional services on regular basis to set their ITC claims through reconciliation between their books of accounts and data received in FORM GSTR-2A. Also, there may be cases where vendors may be non-compliant while filing their return, auditors may review all such possible claims, including reversal and re-claim of credits as the case may be.

(xxi) Once the law and the compliances simplifies in the times to come, the need of professional services in internal audit would be in high.

(xxii) The professionals have always played a significant role by making available various claims of the taxpayers under various statutes. Claim of refunds, duty drawbacks, budgetary supports, subsidies, benefits of export schemes such as advance authorisation, EPCG, MEIS, SEIS etc. are some examples where professional impart services not only in the determination but in following up and ensuring receipt.

(xxiii) The GST law has created numerous certification opportunities not only in the field of audit, special audit but also in the field of claim of various ITCs e.g. section 18(1) and while claiming refund under section 54 of the Act.

(xxiv) The provisions of anti-profiteering as contained under section 171 of the CGST Act may lead to disputes and demands. The businesses need to frame pricing policies where the GST law allows more ITC and/ or their output tax liability has been decreased.

(xxv) The mandatory GST reconciliation and audit by professional CAs for the year 2018-19 would be a year for the professionals to demonstrate their independence and integrity. This job, if done diligently, would prove that they are competent and knowledgeable and assure to the revenue department that there is no need of invasive investigation or audit by tax officers.

(xxvi) It is true that if one can avoid a dispute in tax it is economically much better. Therefore, a preventive exercise of early correction/ disclosure could avoid or mitigate the disputes allowing clients to concentrate on their core activities. One of the preventive exercises the businesses can take is to consult professionals when they receive letters from the department involving large amount of tax or recurring issues involving tax liability. Professional advice taken at the initial stage, can help in ensuring that no mistakes are made in defence. Quite often businesses think that if the differential tax is paid with interest, there may be no litigation; this should never be taken for granted.

3.4 TYPES OF SERVICES

The professionals can now widen their horizons to provide the following types of services under broad heads such as:

(i) Review/ Audit/ Certification
(ii) Consultancy/ Advisory Services
(iii) Assistance/ Compliance
(iv) Dispute Resolution
(v) Teaching/Training
(vi) Due diligence
(vii) Drafting
(viii) Other Services

3.4.1 Review/ Audit/ Certification

(a) General health check can be understood to be an internal audit of GST, done at the behest of the management. It may also have to be conducted for each unit in different States or within State which is registered separately as a distinct person. It could be done by the internal professionals or through hiring external professionals to achieve greater degree of independence. The objective could be to give assurance as to the compliance of the law, optimization of available benefits, streamlining of the processes and procedures including building internal controls, adopted for indirect tax compliance and validation of documentations. Large business organisations may be more inclined to get the internal audit done specifically for their major vendors to augment their ITCs.

(b) The professionals may undertake review of specific business affairs as per management's insight of areas which are weak and areas which may require improvement. Such reviews also depend on where the organisation is facing/ expected to face challenge or dispute. To illustrate few such areas could be eligibility of ITC, classification, availability of exemptions, valuation of a transaction, job work procedures, e-way bill requirements, zero rated supplies, deemed exports, exports, EOU compliances, SEZ compliances contract manufacturer, audit for the statutory auditor and more.

(c) The GST law provides for audit by department when there is a suspicion that there is undervaluation or excessive tax credits. The Comptroller and Audit General Office could also conduct audits of bigger tax payers on a regular basis. [may be much less than in the erstwhile indirect tax laws]. In the past these audits were dreaded and tax compliant assesses would get a review (pre-audit) done before such audits.

(d) The annual return in FORM GSTR-9 has been notified. This form would apply to all tax payers. The contents of the form, indicates that it is not easy to fill up.

(e) The inclusion of mandatory reconciliation in FORM GSTR-9C for taxpayers having aggregate turnover above a specified limit, of audited financial statements with the annual return in FORM GSTR-9 and submission of relevant statements under section 35(5) is expected to be a major check to be put in place similar to the tax audit under Income Tax. The number of tax payers who may be covered in the reconciliation could exceed 25 lakhs due to the fact that State-wise/ GSTIN-wise audit would be needed. These audits should be completed prior to the specified date.

The advantages of audit to the stakeholders like taxpayers, revenue authorities, the consumers at large as well as the professionals are numerous. These exercises as per the experience of the authors in the past have always been a substantial value added assignment for the tax payer. In such assignments the professionals are perceived to be a profit centre even though they would be independent.

3.4.2 Consultancy/ Advisory services

The tax payer would like to come to a professional because of many reasons. To name a few: clarification of doubts, understanding what to be included what to be excluded in a bundle of supplies, confirmation of understanding, bidding for a big project, transaction structuring, to validate another's opinion, get a solution to a GST business problem, avoid a dispute, confirm an advantage, ITC, concessional rate, convince the tax authority of stand, resolve his vendor's or customer's doubts, answer the enquiry from the department, date of rate or other changes in law etc.

This service could be given as and when required. In our country this is very common and most times given orally across the table or over phone. In this time of unclear law, this mode may not be advisable to both parties. It would be advisable to record the query or at least the answer in writing as there may be some gap in the communication and actual implementation. Professionals may like to revisit the law before confirming. If stakes are big, then an elaborate study of the facts, understanding the issues involved could end with a considered written opinion. Communication by email, is suggested. The written opinions as per the authors should contain the facts clearly, the queries, the reasoning and the final opinion or suggestion on way forward. GST being a developing law, a conservative approach is advisable.

Many taxpayers who are tax compliant (mainly corporates) prefer retainership arrangements where the professionals know the business, who may visit and understand the business well, and then communicate with designated officers. This service would have the advantage of online information share and early identification and resolution of the issues.

The retainership service if coupled with a quarterly visit and limited review of major aspects can also identify the areas needing larger attention. This service may over a period of two years be reviewed, if necessary.

There are a number of compliances under Company Law, Income Tax, Insolvency & Bankruptcy code etc. which may need limited advisory services to be plugged in.

3.4.3 Assistance/ Compliance Services

The compliance has been and even today is the most sought after service. The illustrative type of services could be: record keeping, invoicing, liability confirmation, ITC confirmation/ reconciliation, payment of GST, return filing, uploading, rectifying mistakes made in transition, invoicing, credit availment, refund, registration (including amendments, cancellation), replies to differences between FORM GSTR-3B and FORM GSTR-2A or FORM GSTR-3B and FORM GSTR-1, etc.

It should be kept in mind that at occasion the tax payer may not be clear of what he needs. Therefore, all such assignments with limitation and management role need to be communicated and confirmed before taking up the work. There would also be documented mail trail as well as working notes for each assignment. It is also preferable that all routine jobs have short checklists in place to provide quality services. Monitoring of these activities and validating the solution/ working is also a necessary part of this service.

This is the most under rated service in India with no defined scope while more than 300,000 service providers provide service in this space.

3.4.4 Dispute Resolution

The indirect laws in the past have been a hotbed of disputes due to law being complex, frequent changes, issue of FAQs, circulars, contrary advance rulings, inherent tax reduction attitude of the businesses, adventurous consultants, poor invoicing/ record keeping, lack of reconciliation or confirmation procedure for compliance, some trigger happy tax officers, governments attitude of appealing each and every issue and escalating to the Apex Court etc. For this sector anti-profiteering could be an additional area.

The total pending disputes in Indirect Tax as on date under earlier law having tax involving would be around Rs.1,50,000 Crores. It has also been observed that the success rate for revenue in the past was not more than 15%. Even, as on date the resolution of old disputes has not been focused on. In fact, the last one year has seen the disputes in VAT, Service Tax and Central Excise being resurrected by way of closing old files, conduct of audit for the past etc. This in itself can keep the advocates and other professionals engaged for next 5 years at the least.

In GST the interface with the tax officers has been minimum except for areas of refunds/ e- way bill errors, as it is still to be automated. The GST law is expected to end the scrutiny and inspector/ audit raj. The notice, replies, hearing, appeals would all be online in the ensuing years.

The GST law had been hurriedly drafted and is an amalgam of the old laws. The GST Council regularly meets to iron out the rough edges and in the past 21 months we have seen more than 500 Notifications, countless Circulars, FAQs, tweets etc. In the time to come this pace of amending notifications, circulars etc. may decline. Till then there would be a major challenge of keeping updated by all.

Therefore, till this new law stabilises, it is expected that there would be substantial disputes. The illustrative list of areas of concern are: threshold turnover, composition scheme, change in effective rates, audit limit, place of supply, time of supply, input tax credit (especially reversals), type of supply (composite, non-composite or mixed), classification, exemption, valuation, job-work, input service distributor, cross-charge billing amongst distinct persons, etc.

The general lack of awareness and also the existence of the grey economy have led to substantial leakages of revenue in the past 21 months. The Directorate General of GST Intelligence (DGGSTI) may conduct enquiry, raids to detect and record GST evasion. Professionals with in depth knowledge would be able to guide such tax payers to comply with the law and assist them taking such investigations to the logical ends.

In all disputes, it is imperative that the facts and grounds to disprove the allegations may be communicated before the authorities in reply to the very first notice. The submission of different facts at later stages of time especially at the appellate stages is frowned on. Before the Tribunal the advocates have gradually been conceding ground to other professionals who have specialised in indirect taxes. In GST the understanding of the financials and accounting may provide an edge to the CA professionals over the members of the Bar Councils. Professionals who study LLB may find themselves in an advantageous position to argue effectively and even in later years argue the cases in the High Court and Supreme Court. The knowledge of allied laws and pleading skills would make a professional much more respected. This further coupled with humility would give better results.

It is a fact that in India the trade and industry pays more for resolving the problems rather than preventing them as it is a trend throughout the developed world.

3.4.5 Teaching/ Training

India is a vast country and GST is a historic self drafted law passed in consensus of all States and centre. The law today as compared to the model GST law or the law which was put in place in July 2017 is quite different. It is expected that the total number of executives in companies, professionals and those interested in trade and industry who need a working knowledge in GST is more than a million. The students of professional courses, commerce stream and management schools, tax officers, accountants/ compliance personnel's and those directly related to marketing, procurement and finance, who need to understand this dynamic law would not be less than 5 to 8 million. There is an urgent need for knowledgeable faculties and trainers. Unlike in the past, this area of teaching and training now has also become quite remunerative whether to the students or to the trade and industry. It would also be a contribution to the country in smoothly ushering in this new law and making it a complete success.

3.4.6 Due diligence

Sometimes the businesses aggressively plan their organisational growth and structure by opting to merge, de-merge, amalgamate and buy or make decisions. Such planning may not be within the framework of different laws which can be fatal. Due diligence focuses on 'the rule of law' which would safeguard enterprises. Businesses may not normally be aware of such detailed or specific compliances. In case of mergers, demergers, takeovers, sale of projects or entities a number of compliances would needs to be confirmed. This may require analysis of the returns and verification of the transactions. This is to ensure that there are no hidden liabilities, evaluation of pending disputes, compliances up to date closing balances of ITC etc. are logical and valid.

3.4.7 Drafting

The unorganised part of the industry is significant. However, the agreements/ contracts entered into for supply, service, joint development, sale of under construction, sale complete properties etc. are normally poorly drafted. While entering into such agreements the treatment of GST is either ignored or not done with proper application of mind. The practice of "cut- paste" of old agreements can lead to situation where the written words are different to what is intended to be achieved in such agreements. In case of any verification/ audit etc. the agreements would form the basis of demand, if any. This could lead to avoidable disputes.

Further, in joint development agreements or joint ventures or tendering for Governmental orders, the need for clarity on liability for tax, should be precise and clear to avoid future disputes. An example could be "GST as applicable". Whether it is Gross GST or Net GST after ITC deduction? No specific clause on GST but some general clause on applicable taxes being there. The treatment of tax deducted at source and need for recouping if compliance not done by deductor is at times missing or unclear.

The system of raising of purchase or work orders with clause that tax needs to be paid and returns filed by the supplier is important as credit would need to be reversed for non compliance by supplier. The need of the hour is to comply with the provisions of law to avail the required ITC credit.

In case of purchase orders having "Bill to Ship to" concept the proper mention of the address and GSTIN of the third party may be required to be seen to enable input tax credit being ensured. If the receiver of the goods and not the billed one has to avail credit, the billed receiver may have to issue an invoice. Such subtle requirements may escape attention resulting in significant losses.

Even, in tax inclusive contracts, the perusal of GST documents should clearly ensure that GST is separately shown so that credit becomes eligible for the customer.

3.4.8 Project and transaction structuring

It is said that in the matter of tax the vigilant is rewarded. In India knowledge of the different laws and different practices prevalent coupled with an ability to look into the future for the final possible judicial view on aspects where law is not clear is very important. The experience of consulting for some time in indirect laws as well as regulations could provide some insights while planning to optimise the tax or cost of tax. This is more true for the SME sector due to the fact that there is an unfair restriction of the ITC even if building used for business. Case in point is the GST payable on factory building or commercial renting without credit for the inputs or inputs services. The law however provides for the ITC on plant and machinery used in furtherance of business. Knowledge helps when we see that sometimes judicial view taken holds that even buildings can be considered as plant.

There are a few concessions where the ITC is not available like the supply of food/beverages and residential buildings. In the procurement of inputs especially in the cases where there is no ITC available the choice of vendors can make a difference. The use of own labour versus the manpower supplier could make a difference. The service providers opting for the 6% rate instead of 18% would also make a difference. The use of transportation exemption by the registered service providers could avoid the RCM on the same. The overall cost of the taxes in the project could be bought down with smart and safe tax planning.

The projects where these is an outgo on GST, the optimisation of ITC by examining each major component to see whether any credit is lost could be value additive. Some examples could be procurement of vehicles for transportation, breaking up the plant and machinery setting up from building and availment of the ITC on the vehicles, spares, insurance and parts.

3.4.9 Others

There are a number of laws and regulations which are complementary to GST and many which are at variance. The knowledge of these laws would enable service in a more comprehensive, safer and compliant manner. Some of these could laws be as under:

A. **Companies Act: This may be useful in case of identifying the related persons. Further the reporting of state of affairs in the audited financials are critical for compliance in GST as the figures need to be reconciled with the returns filed, reconciliation done and audit report provided.**

B. Indian Contract Act: All understanding in trade and industry are based on agreements/ contract be it a work/ purchase order or service agreements. The understanding of who is an agent is important under gst.

C. Indian Evidence Act: The basis of transactions are facts, whether relevant, whether duly supported by documents. Important that it is all pervasive and applicable whether it is to do with the taxes payable or the credits availed. All transactions need to be evidenced. The admission of electronic records with or without digital signature can make a difference.

D. Indian Penal Code: The checks and balances in every tax law include search, seizure, arrest and prosecution. GST law needs officers to follow the IPC as well as the CRPC.

E. General Clauses Act: This law can be relied on where there are no specific definitions in the GST act or rules. Examples could be immovable property, financial year etc. Aspects such as when the law would become operative, computation of time etc. are some clarity which can be got by referring to this law.

F. Customs Act: There are some upscale projects where the imported tiles, fittings etc are commonly used. In such cases the need to understand the various alternative methods of import could reduce the net duty being paid.

G. Foreign Trade Policy: India is now a global player and has a large amount of imports and exports. The various economic options are laid down in the FTP which could reduce the cost of imports as well as bring in additional benefits for exporters.

H. The State Stamp Act: This is paid for registration of property and the accepted practices are to be understood. There appears to be a lot of divergence in the practices across different States in India. Two examples are: as regards timing of registration (completed- semi finished stage or at stage of pure land), valuation (at guidance value/ market value). The fact that this is a State subject is also important.

I. Income Tax: There is a liability to pay income tax on earning whether in real estate business or otherwise. All assessees including individuals are liable for capital gains. There are some exemptions and other aspects which can minimise the income tax. Therefore planning for income tax while making any investments in real estate or going for a home is important.

J. Insolvency & Bankruptcy Code: The code includes the evaluation of the status and dues and liabilities in indirect taxes would be important to be arrived at correctly. Further at the time of disposal of the business assets payment of GST would be relevant.

K. Arbitration: The real estate sector sees a number of disputes due to the widespread practice of focus on oral understandings. It is surprising that even when reduced in writing the agreement may not capture the actual understanding. This may need to be arbitrated.

L. Standards: The accounting standards play a major role in the proper classification of the projects whether into land, land and building, plant and machinery, aspects of capitalisation etc. In valuation the cost accounting standards would be important.

M. Specific to Industry/ Type: There could be laws which are specific to particular industry such as Real Estate Development and Regulation Act(RERA).

3.5 CONCLUSION

The new levy of GST is bound to come up with obvious challenges due to the law not being drafted well, too many laws impacting this sector, frequent amendments to rates and low awareness of the impact. There could also be many different interpretations, existence of advance rulings, circulars which need to be resolved. The extent of making use of the opportunities would largely depend on understanding of the laws and preparedness for what is not covered in the law. The development of different skill sets may also be important to choose the service area a professional concentrates on. Professionals may find collaboration necessary with other professionals with adequate knowledge of GST or other laws to be able to complete their assignments with due care.

Professionals may take a cue from the words of Abraham Lincoln – *"Give me six hours to chop down a tree and I will spend the first four sharpening the axe"*.

Chapter 4

Importance of Audits

System of audits is very critical and significant to ensure one safeguards ones assets and works effectively/efficiently. Consequently it limits exposure of demands in future due to non-compliance of GST Act and Rules. In the self-assessment regime the trust reposed on the tax payer, comes with the liability to pay heavy interest and penalties even for bona fide errors. The general notion of industry that indirect tax laws are very complicated and not understandable has been furthered in GST due to the innumerable amendments and lack of clarity from the tax administrators.

Further for the unorganised sector with many lakhs of smaller entrepreneurs, it is worse as they may not be able to get professional advice and in the past non-compliance for a few was the way of life. The nature of GST as a law depending substantially more on the information technology rather than the connection to tax officers which provides less scope for non detection are hard realties which need to be stressed.

The need for regular accounting as a means of growth in future are directions which the professional may have to emphasise. The understanding that evasion may be much more difficult and would result in future closure possibilities is slowly dawning. The mantra now is that "*all who earn, need to pay due taxes*".

In this background, a non-intrusive and independent GST audit would play a vital role in understanding of GST law better. Further through the increased detection of non-compliance, non-payment of taxes, incorrect availment of tax credits, wrong refunds etc. entrepreneurs would find compliance more cost effective and have the advantage of growing their business with less risk. GST audit would have many advantages for major stakeholders such as industry, government and society in general.

Non-compliances under GST could prove to be very expensive for the tax payer considering the limitation period for demands has been increased considerably when compared to central excise or service tax law. The period for demand and recovery in case of tax not paid, short payment of tax, erroneous refund or wrong input tax claim for a financial year is 3 years from due date of filing annual return for such financial year which could effectively be 3 years 9 months. In case of fraud or any wilful-misstatement or suppression of facts to evade tax, then period of demand is 5 years from due date of filing annual return for financial year which could effectively be 5 years 9 months. The interest @18% for short payment of tax and for availing and utilising of ITC @24% over years can be almost equal to the demand. Mandatory penalty payable would be 15%.

In addition to this there is a requirement of depositing 10% of disputable amount with the 1st appellate authority and 20% at the 2nd appellate stage (over all 30%) in case of demands. This would have huge impact on cash flow of the assessee as the customer at a later point of time may not be agreeable to pay the differential tax. The tax compliant assesses may not like to have avoidable disputes, which means their compliance levels need to be high. It is known that the cost of dispute resolution is both time consuming as well as expensive in the legal system prevalent in India today. In case of valuation in mergers, demergers, take over, the absence of disputes is a definite advantage for higher valuation.

4.1 TO INDUSTRY/AUDITEE

(1) **Time saving:** In today's world of compliance, most of the tax/finance executives of the organization have to face multiple challenges from highly standardized compliance processes, legal policy changes, accounting standards/IFRS adoption etc. It may entail consulting with the experts in different disciplines since many are interconnected. These activities would take away substantial time and effort of finance and accounting professionals of an organization. The introduction of GST has avoided the compliance under multiple laws which has been welcomed by the organised and tax compliant. However, GST has kept on getting more complicated. The tax treatment has changed for the trader, service provider or manufacturer with accountability and transparency increased. The effort needed for compliance is also more regular and substantially increased.

Review of compliance by professionals on regular basis internally would be important. Professionals with GST expertise are few. Organizations could hire tax audit professionals in line for concurrent /internal audit. The mandatory audit consequently would be of much better quality, smoother and would require less time due to concurrent verification.

(2) **Value addition:** GST audit could give value additive advantage as a well trained professional could guide on tax planning, cost control, proper claim of credits, avoiding payment of interest/penalty by ensuring proper compliance. The audit exercise should not be looked as cost by the auditee as this would give cost and tax advantages for auditees in the initial few years.

(3) **Creates Awareness:** GST audit enables auditee and concerned personnel in procurement and supply chain to be aware of the law as it stands and recent changes and developments in the legal aspects, procedures, tax rates, exemptions, concessions etc. Such awareness could bring innovative ideas, new thought processes to auditee to develop business as well as optimise the tax payment.

(4) **Better Tax Compliance:** The annual return is to be certified that it is true and correct; nothing has been concealed and in case of reduction in output

tax liability the benefit thereon has been /will be passed by the authorised person of tax payer. This is an onerous responsibility on management. GST audit helps in claiming accurate Input tax credits, calculations for correct refunds, tax liability, calculations of Interests/late fees in case of delayed payment of taxes. This also alerts auditee in any case of wrong payment of tax, mismatches. Due to this better compliance is possible by way of implementation of preventive and corrective controls and processes. Rectification of errors could also be faster saving interest. The GSTR3B and GSTR 1 are to be reconciled on monthly or quarterly basis and then only the annual return is to be filed. Failure to do so would automatically lead to automated queries which could take more time and effort to resolve.

(5) **Long term competitive advantages:** Due to other advantages such as better tax compliance, cost reduction, there would be competitive advantage for auditee. In GST law, there is going to be a system of GST compliance ratings for assesses based on compliance. A proper GST audit could also ensure better GST compliance rating which can be one of the parameter for winning new orders from customers. This would also be one of the factors to determine the periodicity of the audits by the department and C & A G's audit. Such rating could also have impact on the availment of bank loans, procurement from suppliers and general comfort of the customers.

(6) **Cross organizational awareness:** Better audit practices in GST would bring cross organizational (functional division like stores, sales and purchases) awareness which could be with respect to aspects such as production practices, stock transfers, stock planning, and marketing approach. A professional having experience in audit of similar business could share the advantage with other auditees as well.[1]

(7) **Facilitate better preparation of financial Statements:** Financial statements could be helpful for an auditor conducting the GST audit as the due date for GST audit would be after finalization of financial statements. However, GST audit which is taken up on concurrent basis could facilitate early correction as well as better preparation of financial Statements giving correct picture on GST compliance.

(8) **Attracts Investments:** Investors would have confidence to invest in those organizations which have better GST compliance ratings and minimum or no disputes with the government. A clean GST audit report could also be important in attracting new investments for business development and provide comfort to vendors, customers and other stakeholders.

---

1 The auditor should ensure that confidential information of other clients is not revealed while sharing the best practices.

(9) **Helps to assess performance of key personnel:** Outcome of GST audit which could be either by tax department or tax professional would throw light on performance of key personnel in GST compliances. It also enables the management to take key decisions in this regard especially regarding cost reduction and alternative tax optimization.

4.2 TO THE GOVERNMENT

(1) **Helps to detect, prevent and correct frauds and errors:** Our country has witnessed many cases of errors of negligence due to not understanding of the law and few cases of frauds in taxation. It is the foremost responsibility of the Government to ensure that cases of errors are detected, corrected and prevented. This would also have the impact of making frauds difficult in GST.

(2) **Increased Revenue flows:** Independent, professional audit of GST records and accounts and other documents by competent professionals would help in enhanced compliance with GST law. This helps in better revenue flows to the government which has been confirmed in income tax.

(3) **Better Compliance:** The audits under GST would ensure that assesses are aware of tax provisions and development resulting in better tax compliance by them, their vendors and customers. As compliance improve so will the revenue as we have seen for the month of October 2018 and March 2019 where it has crossed Rs.1 Lakh crores. This could lead to reduction in tax rates and enabling free flow of ITC over time as promised several times by the Finance Minister.

(4) **Lesser cost:** System of mandatory audit by professional auditors has already resulted in lesser tax administration cost for Government. In earlier indirect tax laws, there was no statutory audit requirement from professionals in various laws such as central excise, service tax etc. Tax payers are more likely to comply with suggestions of independent professionals and are not uncomfortable with them as it is being done for many laws. It is fact that the professional would also point out the areas where benefits available under the law are to be taken.

(5) **Improvement of financial practices and reporting:** A proper GST tax audit would ensure better reporting and disclosure practices from tax payers. This could be helpful to government in making important decisions by data mining and identification of those not in the mainstream.

(6) **Helps the Government to identify loopholes in tax system:** Every major new law in India has loopholes unknown to government at the time of introduction due to poor initial drafting and GST was worse since done in a hurry and with a number of compromises with the States. Some of the amendments have also opened up new interpretation which may result in

lower taxes. Tax payers could always find new routes for tax planning (within the framework of law). They would use law to their advantage. Mandatory GST audit, special audits from professional could help the government to understand the specific weakness in the tax system. Subsequently they could amend law to make it fool-proof and meet the objectives of GST.

4.3 TO CONSUMERS

(1) **Ensures uniform transparent tax costs/rates:** Efficient audit system could result in plugging the revenue leakage and lead to better tax collections. With increased tax revenues, Government would be able to reduce the mean tax rate. The Government is also attempting to have fewer and uniform tax rates like in developed countries which, is difficult due to the federal structure of India. Consumption could also increase with lower uniform tax rates in society due to lower cost of goods/services.

(2) **Helps society to identify credible and prompt brands/organizations:** GST audits would ensure better compliances with better ratings. Consumers would be in a position to identify the credible organizations and good tax compliant brands. It has helped in identifying a few cases of anti-profiteering as on date.

(3) **Spending of Government on essentials increases:** GST audit would lead to increased tax revenues for the year 2020-21 for sure. With increase in tax revenues, the government can allocate more funds for essential projects to help final deserving low income consumers and citizens.

(4) **Brings transparency to tax system:** The tax charged in the invoice is the tax collected by Government. This transparency gives confidence to the consumer. The increased tax revenues would create trust among general public and new businesses could get started providing more employment opportunities in the society. GST audit would discourage unorganized businesses and force them to be more disciplined. This would aid those who do by having better growth.

ANNEXURE – 1 - CHART ON SOURCES OF GST LAW/RULES

Relevance of Earlier Indirect Tax Laws in GST

The GST law has been a mixture of the present indirect tax laws to a great extent. The old law had settled position for many issues. Auditors may find knowing where the provisions were adapted from may find the earlier law as well as the Court decisions in that regard useful. The reference to the provisions, development of provision, decided judicial decisions available in the old law could be referred in case of doubts or disputes.

Topics	VAT	CE	ST	Others
Definitions	Many	Many	Many	Yes
Levy	Yes	Yes	Yes	No
Composition	Yes	No	No	No
E- Commerce	No	No	Yes	No
Time of Supply- Goods	Partial	Removal	No	No
TOS- Services	No	No	Partial	No
POS – Goods	No	Removal	Partial	Customs
POS- Services	No	No	POS Rules	EU- VAT
RCM- Goods	URD Purchases	No	No	Customs
RCM- Services	X	X	RCM	EU- VAT
Tax Credit	Yes	Yes	Yes	No
ITC Reversal	No	Yes	Yes	No
Registration	Yes	No	No	No
Classification- Goods	No	CE Tariff	No	Customs
Classification- Services	No	No	Partial	No
Exemption – Goods	No	CE Tariff	No	Yes
Exemption- Services	No	No	Some directly copied	No
Valuation Goods	Transaction Value partly	CE Valuation Rules	No	Customs
Valuation Services	No	No	ST Valuation Rules	No
Job Work	No	Yes	No	No

Topics	VAT	CE	ST	Others
Audit- Professional	Yes (in most States)	No	No	No
Audit- Revenue	Yes	Yes	Yes	No
Demand	No	Yes	Yes	No

Common difficulties carried forward from Indirect Taxation

The above chart indicates a number of principles have been borrowed from the earlier indirect tax laws. Some of the important aspects which favour the tax collection mechanism but are not in line with the business ease as well as some which can lead to substantial leakage of revenue and encourage evasion could be as under:

(1) GST is a far more complex law than any of the erstwhile laws as it is an amalgam of all. The checks and balances to collect tax early and fully with unreasonable compliances are expected to lead to large scale non compliances. The resistance to filing of the GSTR-1 even today (only 80% have filed for the year 2017-18) The statistics of 2018-19 being Rs 1-2 Lakh crores short is not encouraging. This supports the view that not much has changed as well as the deep rooted decades of evasion by select trade/service sectors continues. Government may be forced to take sustained and regular interception of vehicles, enquiries and searches to get its message that evasion would not be tolerated clear in latter part of years 2019 and 2020.

Once most suppliers are in the mainstream of compliance then, it is expected that the draconian aspects of the present law would be revisited.

(2) The levy being attracted on registration is from the VAT laws. This is creating a number of issues in regard to the procurement from the unregistered suppliers. Those outside the net would close that business and start new ones to avoid losing on the input taxes which are substantially more than the margins in trade. Setting up of multiple entities for claiming the enhanced exemption of Rs.40 lakhs as well as opting for composition is expected to be a common method of reducing taxes in this year.

(3) The concept of composite, non-composite and mixed supply is from the service tax concept of "naturally bundled or not". The interpretation being subjective would see a number of disputes going up to the apex court. The amounts involved could also be in 10,000 crores or above.

(4) Threshold exemption of Rs. 20/40 lakhs is a via media of the Rs. 150 lakhs under central excise, Rs. 10 lakhs in service tax and lower in VAT. This higher threshold with the common practice of several PAN based files in every family may find many leakages in the Business to Consumer [B2C]

segment in goods. It could also be prevalent in the last leg of the supply chain which has the maximum margin available.

(5) The composition scheme is mainly from VAT which was a much abused scheme with high level of corruption. The increased threshold of Rs.150 lakhs and multiple PAN based files as above could see much higher leakages as the threshold here is quite high. This appears to be a common trend in some FMCG as well as the pharma products today.

(6) The tax on advances has been from the service tax regime introduced in 2011. This method which is against all business and accounting norms has witnessed in 7 years only partial compliance in service tax and bound to result in large scale non-compliance in GST in this regard.

(7) The place of supply is based on the EU VAT law to some extent for goods and for services the earlier service tax- place of provision of services rules. The impact is not limited to import and export but between each of the States and Union Territories. Unless an automatic adjustment is provided, demands and refund method suggested is unworkable for SMEs today.

(8) The impact on incorrect credit due to mistakes of the vendors or tax payer's unskilled staff can lead to unintended losses.

(9) The sequence of tax adjustment between IGST, CGST and SGST should be totally interchangeable. The recent changes may restrict the free ITC usage. Ideally this adjustment should be done is the backend*[2]

(10) The valuation provisions have primarily been adapted from central excise unfortunately for both goods and services. The services have a bit of service tax concepts adapted. In payment of GST on the transfer of goods or services to the same company in different States is mandatory. This would also lead to disputes in the future as the provision of declared value being accepted if credit is available at the other end would be used commonly and lead to many allegations of non compliances. The knee jerk amendments and clarifications presently being followed for many issues being raised could lead to reinventing the fairly settled valuation issues.

(11) The enabling of the input tax credit across trading and manufacture/service and reduction in some restrictions has reduced the cascading. However the continuing restrictions, lower rates without ITC, and very complex method of reversing credit would again be a major challenge to the SMEs.

(12) Treatment of availed input tax credit on par with utilized input tax credit is not fair to the assessees. When there is no revenue loss penalising for a

---

2 The recent insertion of Rule 88A, 49A & B in the Central Goods and Services Tax Rules, 2017, could lead to accumulation of credit in CGST or SGST for businesses which have more supplies within the State.

procedural error is not good law. Further this has seen litigation in the central excise regime which would again add to the pendencies on courts.

(13) The need to file all returns electronically through the GST portal today is a nightmare with corrections difficult and even uploading of real transaction not enabled. The new return formats are to be in place from September 2019. Even after 2 years formats are not frozen in advance. To overcome the lack of updation, many tax payers and consultants are adopting short cuts (whether in line with the law or not) to ensure filing is complete. This would without doubt lead to disputes in times to come in 100,000s. The cost of incorrect uploading would be demands in later period along with 18/24% interest and mandatory penalty.

(14) The certification by the tax payer that what is declared is correct may be impossibility as human errors would invariably be there. It appears that the government has forgotten that the main business of the businessman is creating wealth and not doing complicated accounting many of which flies in the face of reason.

The GST law in bits and pieces is an improvement over the VAT law and also to some extent the service tax provisions. However as a whole the law is much more complicated than any of the earlier laws. This dilution maybe due to the consensus approach adopted as well as over dependence on the executive which has resulted in a law which is loaded against the tax compliant and honest tax payer. The changes in year 2019 seen till date may also have political overtones but post election, it is expected that reforms would be taken up in real earnest.

Chapter 5

Introduction to Audit-General

5.1 INTRODUCTION

The word *'audit'* means 'to hear'. There were times when manual book-keeping was not prevalent. Auditors used to hear the accounts read out for them and check that the organisation's personnel were not negligent or fraudulent. Today businesses have evolved to complex structures.

Today's technologically advanced times is posing more challenges for the audit community. They need to stay current, relevant and develop a knack of being watchful of things beyond and beneath what's visible while empathising with the business needs and also adding value to the organisation. Needless to say that the auditing profession has grown with academics identifying an audit society, professionals learning, pursuing it as a career path. The stakeholders including government getting audit performed either on voluntary or on a mandatory basis.

Today, auditing is a measure that provides a third party assurance that the subject matter is free from material misstatements. The result of an audit is that stakeholders (including investors, vendors, customers, funders etc.) would effectively evaluate and have more confidence and credibility in/on the financials. Audit also improves the efficiency and effectiveness of risk management, control, and the governance process in an organisation.

5.2 AUDIT IN THE PAST - A BRIEF BACKDROP

Auditing is as old as accounting. Auditing existed long back from 4th century BC, where the ancient Egyptians and Babylonians had auditing systems for checking movement in and out of storehouses, including oral "audit reports", resulting in the term "auditor" (from audire, to hear in Latin). It was in use in all ancient countries such as Mesopotamia, Greece, Egypt. Rome, U.K. and India. The Vedas contain the reference to accounts and auditing.

India is an ancient country and one of the well-known works pertaining to this era is "*Artha Shasthra*" written by *Vishnugupta Kautilya* popularly known as the '*Chanakya'*. *Arthshasthra* has detailed rules for accounting and auditing of public finances. Broadly, *Kautilya's Arthshastra* covered accounting principles and standards, role and responsibilities of accountants and auditors, the methodology of accounting, auditing and fraud risk management, and the role of ethics in managing financial activities.

Kautilya suggested good salaries to accountants and auditors as high income would keep them ethical. Accountants would be more prone to commit fraud if they earned very little. The fascinating part of *Kautilya's* approach was that he recognized the conflict of interest between finance and auditing functions. He categorically stated that the head of finance and head of audit should independently and separately report to the king. He recognized the possibility of collusion between the two. Even today, in India, in the government, the C&AG and Ministry of Finance are two separate functions. However, in the corporate world in few companies, chief audit executive reports to the CFO rather than the CEO. *Kautilya* believed character reflected personal values of individual and ethical values learning must commence from childhood. He proposed measures to build an ethical climate in the kingdom. However, he was practical and recognized the potential of corruption.

5.3 LEGISLATIVE BACKGROUND OF AUDIT IN INDIA

The East India Company which was the forerunner of the British government in India felt the need for the proper accounting system and auditing when their business expanded in India. Audit and accounts department was set up by the British in 1858 in India.

The new companies act enacted in the year 1913, which specified books of accounts to be maintained and formal qualification to act as an auditor. A Certificate from the government was issued in order to act as auditor.

It made the audit of company accounts compulsory with the increase in the size of the companies and the volume of transactions, the main objective of audit shifted to ascertaining whether the accounts were true and fair rather than true and correct. [Tax authorities have however insisted on true and correct] Hence the emphasis was not on arithmetical accuracy but on a fair representation of the financial efforts.

In the year 1948, just after independence in 1947, an expert committee was created to look into the matter. They recommended that a separate autonomous association of accountants should be formed to regulate the profession. This was accepted the recommendation and passed the Chartered Accountants Act in 1949. a statutory body was established.

In July, 2002, the Auditing Practices Committee has been converted into an Auditing and Assurance Standards Board by the Council of the Institute, Later, w.e.f. April 1, 2008, the nomenclature of AASs under the authority of the Council is collectively known as the Engagement Standards and Quality Control Standards which include the following:

- Standards on Auditing (SA's);
- Standards on Review engagements (SRE's);
- Standards on Assurance Engagements (SAEs);

- Standards on Related Services (SRSs);
- Standard on Quality Control.

Apart from private accountants, the Constitution of India (Articles 148 to 151) mandated the Comptroller and Auditor General of India (C&AG) as a government's arm of the audit which possesses considerable authority, dignity and independence. C&AG is to ensure the accountability of administration to legislature both at the Centre and at the States.

Dr. B.R. Ambedkar placed the auditing profession as beyond Judiciary while he said that "I am of the opinion that this dignitary or officer is probably the most important officer of the Constitution of India. He is the one man who is going to see that expenses voted by Parliament are not exceeded, or varied from what has been laid down by Parliament in what is called the Appropriation Act. If this functionary is to carry out the duties - and his duties, I submit are far more important than the duties of the judiciary."

5.4 DEVELOPMENT OF THE AUDIT PROFESSION IN INDIA

The original objective of auditing was to detect, prevent and correct errors and frauds. However, the aspect of auditing evolved and grew rapidly after the industrial revolution in the 18th century with the growth of the joint stock companies the ownership and management became separate. The shareholders who were the owners needed a report from an independent expert on the authenticity of accounts of the company managed by the board of directors who were the employees. The objective of audit shifted and audit was expected to ascertain whether the accounts were transparent, understandable, in line with the standards of accounting and provide a true and fair view while also detect, prevent and correct errors and frauds.

Today, various audits carried out in India can be broadly classified into statutory audit and internal audit. Mandatory audits requirement is specified under various statutes i.e. presently Companies act, 2013 require every company to get its books of accounts audited, Income tax act mandates the auditing of taxes for certain class of tax payers, similarly there is a requirement of concurrent audits in Banks, Environmental & Energy audits in factories, C&AG audits for Government companies and public sector undertakings etc. Similarly, stock audits, due diligence reviews, risk based control audits, enterprise risk managements, taxation reviews etc. are a few internal/management audits being performed for the last decade.

It can be said that auditing has come a long way from mere hearing of accounts to the specific area, need, statute based audits being performed in a complex business environment using various audit tools and techniques in the computerised environment.

5.5 MEANING OF AUDIT

An audit is a systematic and independent examination of books, accounts, statutory records, documents, vouchers and other relevant information of an organization to ascertain how far the financial statements, as well as non-financial disclosures, present a true and fair view of the concern. It also attempts to ensure that the books of accounts are properly maintained by the concern as required by law.

SA 200 issued by ICAI defines the term auditing means "an audit is an independent examination of financial information of an entity, whether profit oriented or not and irrespective of its size or legal form, when such examination is conducted with a view to express an opinion thereof."

CGST Act, 2017 defines the term audit means "examination of books of records, returns and other documents maintained or furnished by the registered person under this act or the rules made thereunder or under any other law for the time being in force to verify:

- The correctness of turnover declared, taxes paid, refund claimed and input tax credit availed and
- To assess his compliance with the provisions of this act or the rules made thereunder."

Audit could be said to be limited to a certain extent in GST.

Therefore, various features of audit can be as under:

(a) Audit is a systematic and scientific examination of the books of accounts, documents, records etc. of a business;

(b) It is undertaken by an independent person or body of persons who are duly qualified for the job expected to do the job as per the relevant standards.

(c) Audit is a verification of the vouchers, documents, information and results shown by the profit and loss account and the state of affairs as shown by the balance sheet.

(d) The auditor has to inspect, compare, reconcile, check, review, scrutinize the vouchers//account statements supporting the transactions and examine correspondence, minute books of shareholders, directors, Memorandum of Association and Articles of association etc., in the course of completion of the audit using various audit tools and techniques.

(e) It is a critical review of the processes, systems and associated internal controls therein.

(f) In accounting function, the auditor has to satisfy himself with the authenticity of the financial statements and report that they exhibit a true and fair view of the state of affairs of the concern.

(g) In statute audits, the auditors need to satisfy the compliance to the statute and report the non-compliances.

5.6 AUDIT DISTINGUISHED FROM CERTIFICATION, INSPECTION, INVESTIGATION AND INQUIRY

Audit is different from Certification, Inspection, Investigation and inquiry in reference to meaning, objective, scope etc.

"Certification" is related to confirmation of the accuracy of the facts stated therein without any estimate or opinion.

"Inspection" is checking documents, records, facilities, and any other resources to verify factual position vis-à-vis certain set of standards. It is act of examining something, often closely.

"Investigation" implies a systematic and in - depth examination or inquiry to establish a fact or to evaluate a specific situation.

"Inquiry" is any process that has the aim of augmenting knowledge, resolving doubt, or solving a problem.

To brief the difference of all above terms refer to following table:

Basis of Difference	Audit	Certification	Inspection
Objective	Audit is to verify whether financial statements display a true and fair view of the state of affairs and the working results of the entity.	Confirms the correctness & accuracy of contents of the certificate based on the books of accounts.	Inspection is to verify whether the fact to be confirmed as per Standards as applicable.
Scope	Scope is wide and in case of statutory audit the scope of work is determined by relevant provisions of law.	Scope is more specific to the subject matter.	Specific to the area of inspection.
Periodicity	The audit is carried on either quarterly, half yearly or yearly.	No periodicity.	May differ from weekly, monthly, or specific dates

Basis of Difference	Audit	Certification	Inspection
Principles	Compliance with Generally Accepted Accounting Principles (GAAP), Audit Procedures and disclosure requirements.	Principles may be as per Acts or Regulations	May vary based on policies of different entities.
Person Performing Work	Depends on the type of Audit it may be done by Chartered Accountant or by other auditors.	Authorised Person as per relevant laws or rules.	Appointed Person who is authorised.
Legal Obligation	Depends on mandate of relevant statue or not.	By Specific law or otherwise as per need.	Based on laid down process and policies without any legal obligation.
Appointing Authority	Statutory Audit - Auditor is appointed by Members (Shareholders) Others - Generally with the management.	By the person who requires.	By person who requires

Difference between Investigation and Inquiry is as under:

Basis of Difference	Investigation	Inquiry
Objective	Examine the activities in detail to establish an allegation or fact.	Confirm the occurrence of event.
Scope	It covers examination and inquiry into the matter. The outcome of the same is not certain.	It is limited but it can be expanded
Periodicity	May cover longer periods.	Not fixed as it is very flexible.
Principles	It is analytical in nature, observing, collecting and evaluating facts/evidence.	As per the suitability of the situation.

Basis of Difference	Investigation	Inquiry
Person Performing Work	Person having strong domain and prior experience in the subject matter.	Eligible, qualified as per scope.
Legal Obligation	Maybe as per any Act or regulation.	May not be as per Act or regulation.
Appointing Authority	By authority who believes that investigation is necessary.	Any person who believes that inquiry is necessary.

5.7 EVIDENCE LAW AND AUDIT

Evidence is information, whether obtained from audit procedures or other sources that are used by the auditor in arriving at the conclusions on which the auditor's opinion is based. Audit evidence is used to provide a factual basis for audit opinions, conclusions and recommendations.

The importance of evidence is also provided in the Indian Evidence Act, 1872 which states that evidences are fundamental in civil as well as in criminal cases to establish or conclude upon the authenticity. Four key questions govern in the relevance of drawing conclusion i.e.

- What is the evidence given of?
- How the evidence is given?
- On whom does the burden of proof lies? and
- What is the conclusion of the evaluation of the evidence so provided?

Therefore, the matter in respect of which the evidence is drawn, how it is available, who would prove it, are all important in evaluating the evidence in drawing the conclusions.

The auditor needs to possess necessary evidence to support his opinion or report. Evidence is cumulative in nature and is primarily obtained from audit procedures undertaken and recorded performed during the course of the audit.

SA 500 (Audit Evidence) explains what constitutes audit evidence in an audit of financial statements, and deals with the auditor's responsibility to design and perform audit procedures to obtain sufficient appropriate audit evidence to be able to draw reasonable conclusions. Evidence can be obtained by performing various audit procedures which include inspection, observation, confirmation, recalculation, re-performance and analytical procedures.

The way in which any procedure is performed and the manner in which the evidence is obtained and the source from where the evidence is obtained determines its reliability. Factors which may govern the reliability of audit evidence are as under:

- Internal evidence more reliable when internal control is effective.
- External evidence is more reliable than internal evidence.
- Written evidence is more reliable.
- Original documents are more reliable.

Sufficient audit evidence means quantum of audit evidence obtained by the auditor and its appropriateness. Auditor decides to obtain more audit evidence when there are chances of risk of material misstatement as per the auditor's assessment. Its reliability, depends upon the source and nature of audit evidence. The quantum of evidence depends upon the quality of evidence.

[See appendix for Standard]

5.8 REGULATORY AUTHORITIES FOR AUDITS IN INDIA

The ICAI regulates the audit function and provides regulatory framework in the form of standards, guidelines and in respect of audit are as under:

5.8.1 Quality Review Board of ICAI

Quality Review is the formal inspection of the service. Quality Review is one of the methods of quality Control. The 'Board' performs the following functions u/s 28B of the Chartered Accountants Act, 1949 as under:

(a) To make recommendations to the Council with regard to the quality of services provided by the members of the Institute;

(b) To review the quality of services provided by the members of the Institute including audit services; and

(c) To guide the members of the Institute to improve the quality of services and adherence to the various statutory and other regulatory requirements.

5.8.2 Peer Review

The term 'peer' means a person of similar standing. The term "peer review" would mean review of the work done by a professional, by another member of the same profession with similar standing.

This is being used by all accountancy bodies as a tool for enhancing the quality of services being rendered by professional accountants.

Main objective of peer review are as under:

(1) To ensure that in carrying out the assurance service assignments, the members of the Institute comply with Technical, Professional and Ethical Standards including other regulatory requirements thereto, and

(2) To ensure that such a member (Practice Unit) has in place proper system (including documentation system) to amply demonstrate the quality of assurance services

The review shall focus on:

(1) Compliance with technical Standards;

(2) Quality of Reporting;

(3) Office Systems and procedures with regard to compliance of attestation service systems and procedures;

(4) Training Programs for Staff (including Article and Audit Clerks) concerned with attestation functions, including appropriate infrastructure.

Note: *Similar to the ICAI, the Institute of Cost and Management Accountants of India also regulates the assurance functions of their members. The relevant standards as well as guidance notes of both the institutes have been provided in the Appendix. Further, the list of publications which could provide a good reference have also been listed.*

Chapter 6

Types of Audit

6.1 INTRODUCTION

Today, audit is more risk-based and controls driven for determining the coverage of substantive verification. In some larger concerns, ERP is used where using audit tools so that 100% verification can be done. Further, based on the type and purpose of the audit the extent of risk assessment may vary.

Broadly, various types of audits are as under:

6.1.1 Financial Audit

Financial audits typically focus on financial controls as they relate to reporting. These audits focus on accounting controls present in the general ledger or sub-ledger systems. Auditing of financial statements is mainly done by the external auditors. Internal Audit compliments the work that is performed by the external auditors on the financial statements.

6.1.2 Operational Audit

Operational audits focus on the review and assessment of business processes. The activities of the business processes may result in a direct or indirect financial impact on the organization. Operational Audit primarily focuses on operations but can extend the scope to other administrative and support functions including accounting procedures that can impact the financial reporting.

6.1.3 Statutory/Compliance Audit

Compliance audits review the level of compliance with internal policies or external regulatory requirements. For instance, a GST audit or an Income tax audit is a compliance audit, emerging due to the statutory requirement of the respective Act. However, a compliance audit can also be management-initiated audit i.e. without any statutory requirement to perform the same under any law.

6.1.4 Information Systems Audit

Audits of Information Systems look at the overall infrastructure and network of the organization and the controls that relate to the security of the network and the systems that are maintained in support of the goals of the organization. It also includes technical operations, data center operations, project management procedures, and application controls.

6.2 VARIOUS STATUTORY AUDITS IN INDIA

In India, statutory audits are Companies Audit, Bank audit, Audit of insurance companies, Environmental audit, Energy audits, etc. In taxation statutes an audit under Income Tax Act, 1961 which has various provisions requiring a compulsory audit. Similarly, in the Indirect taxes, the audit was already prevalent under some of the local State VAT Acts and a mechanism of departmental audit and special audits was built-in under the provisions of erstwhile Central Excise and Service Tax laws. Further, with the introduction of Goods and services tax laws, the government has incorporated various audit requirements including an audit by the independent professionals.

6.2.1 Companies Act, 2013

Audit under Companies Act is a proper and accurate compilation of financial information of a corporate and its disclosure, in a manner that is standardized and understood by stakeholders, is central to the credibility of the corporates and soundness of investment decisions by the investors. The preparation of financial information and its audit, therefore, needs to be regulated through law with stringent penalties for non-observance. Sections 139 to 147 under Chapter X of the Companies Act, 2013 contain provisions regarding audit and auditors. In the audit report, the auditors must state, besides other things, whether the financial statements represent a true and fair view of the state of the company's affairs as at the end of the Financial Year.

6.2.2 Internal Audit

Internal audit is an independent management function, which involves a continuous and critical appraisal of the functioning of an entity with a view to suggest improvements thereto and add value to and strengthen the overall governance mechanism of the entity, including the entity's strategic risk management and internal control system. In simple terms, it was, and is, a way of ensuring businesses and public sector organizations use their resources efficiently and apply processes consistently. As per section 138 of the Indian Companies Act, 2013 read with Rule 13 of Companies (Accounts) Rules, 2014, certain class of companies are required to appoint Internal Auditors.

6.2.3 Bank Audit

The statutory audit of banks forms an integral and important part of the control mechanism of the regulators, like RBI. It provides the stakeholders including the Regulators, a comfort with regard to the credibility of the financial information that a bank generates at every year-end. Given the nature, scope and volume of transactions undertaken by banks in India, coupled with their geographical spread and the various regulatory directions to which they are subject, an audit of the financial statements of banks indeed becomes very challenging for the auditors.

6.2.4 Energy Audit

An energy audit is an inspection survey and an analysis of energy flows for energy conservation in a building. It may include a process or system to reduce the amount of energy input into the system without negatively affecting the output. In commercial and industrial real estate, an energy audit is the first step in identifying opportunities to reduce energy expense and carbon footprint. In India, The Bureau of Energy Efficiency, Ministry of Power, came up with a scheme known as Perform Achieve and Trade (PAT). Through this scheme, energy audit became mandatory for certain class of companies to reduce their specific energy consumption. The detailed energy audit conducted by an accredited energy auditor is indeed referred to as Mandatory Energy Audit.

6.2.5 Environmental Audits

Environmental audit can be defined as a basic management tool comprising of a systematic, documented, periodic and objective evaluation of how well environmental organizations, management systems, and equipment are performing. India is the first country in the world to make environmental audits compulsory. The Government of India, by its gazette notification, [No. GSR 329 (E)] of March 13, 1992, made it mandatory for all industries to provide annual environmental audit reports of their operations, beginning with 1992-93. This required industries to provide details of water, raw materials, and energy resources used, and the products and wastes generated by them. These audit reports were to be submitted to the concerned State Pollution Control Boards or before September 30 every year. The aim of the audit is to facilitate management control of environmental practices and to enable the company to assess compliance with its policies including meeting regulatory requirements.

6.2.6 Forensic Audit

A forensic audit, also known as forensic accounting, refers to the application of accounting methods for detection and gathering evidence of frauds, embezzlement, or any other such white-collar crimes. It is the application of accounting skills to legal questions. As of now, it has taken up an important role in both public and private organizations, especially in advanced economies. It is a new area, but in recent years, banks, Insurance Companies and even police have increased taking help of forensic accountants. The increase in white collar crimes and the difficulties faced by law enforcement agencies in uncovering fraud have also contributed to the growth of the profession.

6.2.7 Tax Audit under Income Tax Act, 1961

Income tax law also mandates an audit called 'Tax Audit'. As the name itself suggests, a Tax audit is an examination/review of accounts of any business/profession carried out by the taxpayer from an income tax viewpoint.

6.2.8 Audit under GST Act

With the completion of almost two years since the introduction of GST, it is critical to start focusing on various compliances such as input and output reconciliations, preparation and filing of annual return and GST audit certification. All of these compliances would form an important basis for the first audit/scrutiny/assessment under the GST law. The law prescribes multiple audits conducted by the authorities, an external auditor appointed by the authorities or audit certification by a person appointed by the company. GST law envisages mainly three types of audits as briefly explained below:

6.2.8.1 Audit by CA/CMA

In this case, the audit is performed by a chartered accountant or a cost accountant. Every registered person whose aggregate turnover during a financial year exceeds two crore rupees has to get his accounts audited by a Chartered Accountant or a Cost Accountant and furnish a copy of audited annual accounts and a reconciliation statement, duly certified, in FORM GSTR-9C.

6.2.8.2 Departmental Audit

In this case, the Commissioner or any officer authorised by him, can undertake the audit of any registered person for such period, at such frequency and in such manner as may be prescribed.

6.2.8.3 Special Audit

In this case, a registered person can be directed to get his records including books of account examined and audited by a chartered accountant or a cost accountant during any stage of scrutiny, inquiry, investigation or any other proceedings depending upon the complexity of the case.

6.3 STATUTORY AUDIT/CERTIFICATION IN GST

Section 35(5) of the Goods and Service Tax Act, 2017 read with rule 80(3) of the GST Rules provides that every registered person whose turnover during a financial year exceeds Rs. 2 crores shall get his accounts audited by a chartered accountant or a cost accountant and submit a copy of the audited annual accounts, the reconciliation statement under section 44(2) and such other documents in such form and manner as may be prescribed.

Further, section 44(2) of Goods and Service Tax, 2017 states that every registered person who is required to get his accounts audited in accordance with the provisions of section 35(5) shall furnish, electronically the following:

(i) Annual Return under section 44(1) of the CGST Act, 2017;

(ii) Audited Annual Accounts;

(iii) Reconciliation Statement;

(iv) Such other particulars as may be prescribed.

Detailed explanation about this type of audit is explained in the subsequent chapters.

6.4 MANAGEMENT REVIEWS IN GST

Management review is not mandated in the statute but conducted at the behest of the management. It has variants such as of operational audit which is a voluntary appraisal activity undertaken by an organization to provide assurance over the effectiveness of internal controls, risk management, and governance to facilitate the achievement of organizational objectives. Internal audit can be performed by employees of the organization or by the professionals independent of the organization who reports to the management.

Unlike an external audit, whose scope is primarily restricted to matters that concern the financial statements, the scope of work of an internal audit can be very broad and can encompass any matters which can affect the achievement of organizational objectives. It could also be restricted by the management. Internal audit is centred around certain key activities which include:

- Examining the effectiveness of internal controls and strengthening the same with the various preventive, detective and corrective controls.
- Monitoring compliance with laws and regulations
- Reviewing and verifying where necessary the financial and operating information
- Evaluating risk management policies and procedures of the company
- Examining the operations/process for their effectiveness and efficiency.
- Various internal audits and management reviews that businesses can undertake from the standpoint of Goods and Services Tax can be as under:

6.4.1 Complete health check reviews

GST health check reviews can be conducted on the periodical basis covering all functions having GST impact. This could include sales, procurements, inventory, finance, etc. Such reviews would be also helpful for GST mandatory statutory audit and more importantly, it provides management with the comfort on the level of compliance in the organization. This exercise is also value additive where various benefits available in the law are also identified on a timely basis. Broadly, this would cover the following:

- Review of GST outward supplies, tax rates applied, concessions, and exemptions claimed, fulfilment of related conditions, export benefits claimed, etc.
- Review of GST input tax credits claimed to assess eligibility, ineligibility, completeness, documentation for credits, transitional credits carry forward, etc.
- Review of procedural compliances including GST registrations obtained, payment of taxes, filing of returns, disclosure of ITC & outward supplies in returns, movement of goods for job work, carry forward of credits, etc.
- Review of reverse charge compliance by reviewing the expense ledgers on a sampling basis, payments made, availment of re-credit after payment, eligibility of such credits, rate and abatements if any claimed including documentation.

6.4.2 Area-specific reviews

Management can decide to conduct area-specific reviews as per the need and requirement of the organization. Various areas that can be reviewed on the specific basis from GST point of view can be sales, procurements, IT, ERP/systems, exports & refunds, ITC credits, reverse charge, compliance and documentation, agreements/contracts, disputes & litigation management, etc. Areas specific reviews are very niche and specific, its coverage is more in-depth and it helps management in streamlining and strengthening the specific business process being reviewed.

6.4.3 Due Diligence reviews

In business restructuring deals, tax due diligence of the buyer side is required. This may be required to be done voluntarily by the buyer or based on specific direction by the seller. The review is intended to highlight the tax exposure which may carry on to the new entity. This becomes more critical in cases where the entity is exposed to multiple indirect tax laws. The review identifies areas of non-compliance current or in long term, potential risks and even threats, changes required if any in the terms of the contract and also suggest alternative structuring strategy to optimise tax incidence.

6.4.4 Systems and processes reviews

Indirect tax systems impact almost all financial transaction of business. This necessitates having a proper control system to manage tax function at transaction levels. The businesses have now become system driven where human interference is reduced to very minimal. The complex business structure coupled with system automation requires flawless tax system inbuilt as a robust system in all the business processes. Therefore, this review assists management in identifying the risks and gaps at various levels of GST compliance and the possible threat if the same remains unaddressed. The review helps management in incorporating various preventive, and corrective controls at various levels of a business process and it helps in streamlining and strengthening the entire business process cycle from its inception to the end which eventually cuts down the chances of mistakes, errors and frauds thereby improving the overall compliance matrix.

6.4.5 IT/ERP systems review

Various compliances in GST are automated and are to be performed electronically in a digital manner in so much so that large businesses have and are in the process of automating the entire transactional chain in a manner that the manual tasks and the risks associated therewith are cut down. More reliance is placed on the results thrown out of the IT systems or the ERP modules and any error in the initial configuration/set up and the walkthrough in which the results are used can have larger consequences. Therefore businesses get the audit of the IT/ERP systems done by CISA/DISA qualified professionals which not only helps in weeding out such errors and also provides additional ways and means of automation.

6.4.6 Follow up Review

These are reviews conducted months after an internal or external audit report has been issued. They are designed to evaluate corrective action that has been taken on the audit issues reported in the original report. The purpose of a follow-up review is to revisit past audits recommendations and management's action plan to determine if corrective actions were taken and are working, or if situations have changed to warrant different actions.

6.4.7 Investigative Review

This is a review that takes place as a result of a report of unusual or suspicious activity on the part of an individual or a department. It is usually focused on specific aspects of the work of a department or individual. Investigations are conducted to determine the extent of loss, assess weaknesses in controls, and make recommendations for corrective actions.

Chapter 7

Audits under GST Law

7.1 INTRODUCTION

GST law mainly functions under the principles of self-assessment whereby the taxpayer assesses the tax liability and discharges the same. GST is a transactional tax where the tax is normally only on business activities though tax is sometime payable on deemed supplies (schedule I). The taxpayers create checks and balances at the time of recording of the transaction itself so that the tax is properly calculated, reported and paid after availing the input tax credit set-offs. The assessment of the tax is challenging in the business environment where the responsibility of initial capturing these details is on the junior accountants who may not be very knowledgeable in GST. Therefore, in order to have a confirmation and certainity about the GST calculations, reconciliations, disclosures and other compliances, a system of audits in a fair, transparent, independent and systematic manner is required.

7.2 VARIOUS AUDITS UNDER GST

A system of audit under the GST act is multi-facet wherein apart from the audit by independent professionals, the law also provides for the regular audit by the departmental officers and a mechanism of a special audit by revenue. This can be understood hereunder:

1. **Audit by professionals:** Section 35(5) of the GST Act, 2017 provides for audit to be conducted by CA/CMA if the turnover during the financial year exceeds Rs.2 Crores.
2. **Audit by Tax authorities:** Section 65 of the GST Act, 2017 provides for audit to be conducted by the commissioner or any officer authorised by him by way of a general or a specific order at such frequency and in such manner as may be prescribed.
3. **Special Audit:** Section 66 of the GST Act, 2017 provides for Special Audit is required to be conducted by a chartered accountant or a cost accountant as may be nominated by the Commissioner.

It is important to note that all the above audits are not mutually exclusive and an assessee may undergo one or more of them on a periodic basis. We would now discuss each one of these audits in detail.

7.3 AUDIT BY PROFESSIONALS

Section 35(5) of the Goods and Service Tax Act, 2017 read with rule 80(3) of the GST rules provides that every registered person whose turnover during a financial year exceeds Rs. 2 crores shall get his accounts audited by a chartered accountant or a cost accountant and submit a copy of the audited annual accounts, the reconciliation statement under section 44(2) and such other documents in such form and manner as may be prescribed.

Further, section 44(2) of Goods and Service Tax, 2017 states that every registered person who is required to get his accounts audited in accordance with the provisions of section 35(5) shall furnish, electronically the following:

(i) Annual Return under section 44(1) of the CGST Act, 2017;

(ii) Audited Annual Accounts;

(iii) Reconciliation Statement;

(iv) Such other particulars as may be prescribed.

7.3.1 Annual Return

Annual return is required to be submitted in form GSTR 9 and the same must be furnished on or before the thirty-first day of December following the end of each financial year. Similarly, it is required to be submitted in form GSTR 9A for persons covered under the composition scheme. The annual return is a summation or consolidation of various periodic returns filed i.e. GSTR 1 (i.e. details of outward supplies) and GSTR 3B (i.e. details of inward supplies). However, the assessee can declare in the Annual Returns the details of the additional tax liability which has not been earlier declared and any additional tax liability arising therefrom can be paid through Form DRC 03. It must be noted that Input Tax Credit cannot be directly availed in the Annual Returns. Such credits have to be availed in the monthly returns to be filed in form GSTR 3B.

Consequence of failure to submit the annual return

Section 47(2) provides that in case of failure to submit the annual return within the specified time, a late fee would be leviable @ Rs. 100 per day during which such failure continues subject to a maximum of a quarter percent of the turnover in the State/UT. There is no specific penalty prescribed in the GST Law for not getting the accounts audited by a Chartered Accountant or a Cost Accountant. Therefore, in terms of section 125 of the CGST Act, 2017 he may be subjected to a general penalty up to Rs.25,000/-.

7.3.2 Reconciliation Statement

The annual return is prepared based on the audited annual accounts whereas the other periodic GST returns are prepared based on the various transactions recorded prior to final auditing. There is a possibility that the details as declared in the audited financial statements in respect of outward supplies i.e. Turnover/sales or inward supplies i.e. expenses/credits may have difference with that of the details as submitted in the annual returns filed and therefore one needs to submit the reconciliation statement in Form GSTR 9C to reconcile the difference in value of supplies as declared in the audited financial statements vis-à-vis the annual return as furnished for the financial year.

Here it is important to note that declaration of the details of outward supplies missed out and consequent payment of taxes or adjustment of the taxes paid by issuing credit notes etc. needs to be done only before the end of September of the following financial year and above aspects to the extent not corrected would end up becoming a permanent reconciliation difference and needs to be disclosed in Form GSTR 9C. Further, the reconciliation process in case of entities having multiple registrations in multiple States/UTs would be a daunting task as reliable audited annual accounts must be made available separately to the auditors state wise. The adverse consequences of non-reconciliation will have to be taken as per the provisions of the law since no rectification is possible.

While preparing the reconciliation statement, special attention must be given to transactions not appearing in the financial accounts for ex: stock transfers, free samples, gifts, transactions with related parties, etc. This would be very important and critical aspect in the entire reconciliation activity and most importantly, it would be difficult to comment to what extent the auditor can take shelter under the principle that things not bypassing the books of accounts, cannot be called upon to have caused any professional negligence if not dug out in the normal course of the audit since the responsibility is cast upon to state that the details submitted thereon is True and Correct".

Further, it is important to note that the reconciliation statement needs to be prepared based on the Annual returns and the information as being representative of the audited financial statements for the respective GSTIN i.e. for each state. It is important that the assessee's have these details available through the accounting module a reconciliation statement can be prepared between the accounts audited and the annual return. Further, in case where the assessee's have multiple GST No's in the same state then the accounting must be done in such manner and the accounting module must provide the information such that the customized financial statements that are representative of the audited financial statements can be made available for each GSTIN within the state.

Certificate Vs. Report: Since the format for the audit report/certificate is also not yet notified, it is not clear as to whether it would be in the nature of an audit report like the statutory audit report or a tax audit report, or a certificate as in the case of VAT audits. If it is in the nature of a certificate, then the responsibility of the GST auditor would be substantially higher.

Para 2.2 of the 'Guidance Note on Audit Report and certificates for Special Purpose' issued by the ICAI notes the difference between the term 'certificate' and 'report' as under:

- "A Certificate is a written confirmation of the accuracy of facts stated therein and does not involve any estimate or the opinion;"
- "A Report, on the other hand, is a formal statement usually made after an enquiry, examination or review of specified matters under report and includes the reporting auditor's opinion thereon".

Thus, where a certificate is issued, the Chartered Accountant would be responsible for the factual accuracy of what is stated therein. In case of a report, he is responsible for ensuring that the report is based on the factual data, true and fair (or in some cases true and correct) to the best of his belief, knowledge, and information furnished to him. The relevant standards are provided in the Appendix.

7.4 IMPORTANT POINTS TO BE NOTED

7.4.1 Key points for CA's to be noted while accepting the appointment as a GST Auditor

Section 2(1)(b) of the CA Act, 1948 defines the term 'Chartered Accountant' to mean a person who is a member of the Institute. Section 2(2) provides that a member would be deemed to be in practice if he engages himself, for a consideration, in the specified activities, which includes inter alia audit. Section 6 inter alia provides that a member cannot practice without obtaining Certificate of Practice Thus, only a member of ICAI having a Certificate of Practice (COP), or a firm of Chartered Accountants can take up the GST Audit. Additionally, a Chartered Accountant must bear in mind the following:

- Member in part-time practice (including an employee having a COP) is not entitled to perform attest function. (242nd Council Meeting Resolution);
- Member having a substantial interest in an assessee cannot take up its audit. (Clause 4 of Part I of the Second Schedule of the Chartered Accountants Act, 1949 ("the CA Act") read with Appendix 9 of CA Regulations 1988);
- In case of Joint Audits, all the auditors would have to sign the audit report. If the auditors have a different opinion, then they should issue separate audit reports.
- Member responsible for writing/maintenance of books of account of an assessee should not take up its audit (Clause (4) of Part I of the Second Schedule to the CA Act);

- Member not to accept the audit of a person to whom he is indebted for more than Rs. 10,000/- (Chapter X of ICAI Guidelines);
- Member not to charge professional fees based on a percentage of profit or which are contingent upon the finding or the result of the professional employment. (Clause 10 of part I of the First Schedule to the CA Act);
- Internal auditor of an assessee cannot be appointed as his tax auditor (281st Council Meeting Resolution).
- In case of joint audits, all the auditors would have to sign the audit report and should issue separate reports where they have different opinions. (Ref SA 299).
- The restrictions applicable for appointment of a statutory auditor where the fee for other services are more than the statutory audit fee, in case of specified entities, are not applicable GST auditors (Chapter IX of ICAI Guidelines).
- An assessee may have GST registrations in more than one State. In such cases, the assessee may appoint a single/multiple auditor(s) for the distinct registrations under the same PAN. It is possible that accounts and records that are kept in different States may be in the local language of that State. In such cases, it is suggested that the auditor should not accept the audit of accounts written in a language which he/his staff do not understand. The code of conduct under both the regulatory Acts are provided in the Appendix.

7.4.2 Some of the best practices to be adopted for GST audit

The evaluation of the internal control *vis-a-vis* GST would indicate the areas to be focused. This could be done by verifying:

(a) Internal Control questionnaire must be designed and used in the course of audit in order to understand the various systems and controls and accordingly an auditor can decide the extent of the reliance that can be placed and the substantive procedures that have to be performed in the course of conduct of GST audit.

(b) Auditor can place higher reliance over systems, processes and controls by performing a detailed Information system audit or a GST internal audit on a periodic basis or use the work of the other auditors performed if any, in this regard.

(c) A proper audit plan must be designed and implemented so that the audit is conducted smoothly as per the desired objective.

(d) The use of generalised audit software/tools including excel macros can be a very effective aid to the GST audit which can reduce the time to be taken for audit and give better assurance on the overall audit procedures.

(e) The auditor must prepare and follow a thorough audit program and a checklist as a tool to ensure coverage and manner in which the audit is to be performed.

(f) Reconciliation of the books of account or reports from the ERP's to the returns is imperative.

7.5 AUDIT BY DEPARTMENT - SECTION 65 OF THE CGST/SGST ACT

Tax liability on the supply of goods or services or both is computed by a registered person under the self-assessment scheme of the Act. In order to ensure whether the tax liability has been correctly computed and discharged by the registered person, it becomes essential for the department to conduct an audit of records maintained by the person. The Commissioner or an officer authorised by him may undertake an audit of any registered person by issuing a general order or a special order.

Generally, the department would have a Director General of Audit who supervises the audit functions. Separate audit commissionerate would be constituted who would plan, delegate and administer the audit. The audit of the assessee is carried out through visits by 'audit groups' which consist of Superintendents and Inspectors. The audit groups prepare the assessee master file, collect the relevant information and documents, Desk review shall be done before forming the audit plan. As planned, the audit would be conducted and corrections and improvements would be suggested to the assessee.

The draft audit report would be discussed and communicated to the assessee and with the details of spot recoveries and willingness of the assessee to accept the demand etc. the same would be placed before the monitoring committee. If the assessee does not accept the audit para or pay under protest, the adjudication process would be initiated by the Jurisdictional GST Officer.

7.6 DEPARTMENTAL AUDIT UNDER GST

Section 65 authorizes the conduct of audit by the Commissioner or any other officer authorised by him of the transactions of the registered persons only. The Commissioner may issue a general order or a specific order, to authorize officers to conduct such an audit. As per rule 101(1), the period of audit under section 65(1) shall be a financial year or multiples thereof. Thus, Audit cannot be conducted for a part of the financial year in normal circumstances. Period to be covered under the Audit can be a single financial year or two financial years or three and so on.

The frequency and manner for conducting such audit are yet to be prescribed.

The audit would be conducted at the place of business of the registered person or office of tax authorities. Intimation of audit is to be issued to the taxable person at least 15 days in advance in accordance with rule 101(2) in **Form GST ADT-01** and the audit is to be completed within 3 months from the date of commencement of audit, which may be extended by the Commissioner, where required, by a further period not exceeding 6 months. The Commissioner needs to record reasons in writing for grant of any such extension.

The expression "commencement of audit" would mean the date on which the records and other documents, called for by the tax authorities, are made available by the registered person or the actual institution of audit at the place of business, whichever is later.

During the course of the audit, the authorized officer may require the registered person to afford him the necessary facility to verify the books of account and also to furnish the required information and render assistance for timely completion of the audit.

As per rule 101(3), the proper officer authorised to conduct an audit of the 'records' and the 'books of account' of the registered person would, with the assistance of the team of officers and officials accompanying him, verify:

(a) the documents on the basis of which the books of account are maintained

(b) the returns and statements furnished under the provisions of the Act

(c) the correctness of the turnover, exemptions, and deductions claimed

(d) the correctness of the rate of tax applied in respect of the supply of goods or services or both

(e) the correctness of input tax credit availed and utilised,

(f) the correctness of refund claimed

(g) other relevant issues and

(h) record the observations in his audit notes

The provisions of section 65(5) casts an obligation on the registered person to afford necessary facility for verification of books and records, render assistance for timely completion of audit and furnish information and statements.

On completion, information is required to be provided to the registered person including the findings during the audit as per section 65(6) read with rule 101(5) in **FORM GST ADT-02** within thirty days of the conclusion of the audit.

In cases where tax liability is identified during the audit or input tax credit wrongly availed or utilized by the auditee, the procedure laid down under section 73 or 74 is to be followed. An audit cannot conclude automatically resulting in a demand. Independent application of mind is necessary for a valid demand to be raised.

7.7 DEPARTMENTAL AUDIT VIS-À-VIS AUDIT BY PROFESSIONAL

This book was to cover detailed intricacies of the departmental audit as envisaged in section 65 along with the statutory audit contemplated in section 35 of the CGST Act. However, in the absence of detailed guideline about the departmental audit, it was felt that it would be appropriate to cover the said audit after the Government comes out with the details of the type of audit, records to be verified, and details to be reconciled and the format of the report.

Why an independent audit comprehensive is preferable before the conduct of statutory/departmental audit?

Presently, there is a need for an audit to be performed both by the professionals and also the revenue officers to be less intrusive but ensure a check on revenue leakage. Audits would be conducted on larger assessees over Rs. 2 Crores. The departmental audit would be done on a sample basis and not akin to the almost 100% audit or scrutiny in the past. The focus of government on ensuring ease of doing business has led to the annual return format, reconciliation and statements accompanying to be attempted to be made as simple as possible which is a challenge. Further, the departmental audit would also be using the details in the reconciliation report and the report for the purpose of departmental audit. Various reasons as to how the audit by the department and by the professionals complement each other is explained below:

- It is not enough if the intention is to be compliant, an assessee has to be either knowledgeable or take professional help.
- Provisions relating to demands, adjudication, appeals and revision, inspections, search and seizure, confiscation, etc. in the GST regime are quite harsh and therefore even an assessee intending to be fully compliant can make mistakes and even bona fide mistakes attract penalty in the GST regime and the provisions relating to transportation are also quite harsh.
- Selection of assessee for departmental audit would be on scientific and other parameters. Compliance rating and reconciliation audit report can be expected to be an important part of the process of selection. Unlike the previous indirect tax regime, the GST law gives 4 and half years to issue show cause notice and therefore even if the audit happens after four years even mistaken omissions/commissions resulting in short/non-payment of tax would get covered and tax will have to be paid back with very high rate of interest and if the assessee disputes the stand of the department, penalty also gets attracted.
- Several accounts and records have been prescribed. However, there is no harm in maintaining as many records as possible so that while maintaining the records, compliance with legal provisions is also

ensured. It is necessary to see whether the maintenance of records and accounts take care of compliance with law and procedures.

- This audit of GST records would give the management an idea about the level of knowledge of law and quality of records and accounts.
- It prepares them for the intense scrutiny with an intention to find areas of non-compliance by the departmental audit as and when it takes place.
- It also creates confidence in the minds of the persons handling the GST related work.

What is the difference between a statutory audit by chartered accountant/cost accountant and departmental audit?

- Points that are paid attention in the departmental audit are
  - Compliance with law;
  - Payment of correct tax to the government;
  - Availment of the correct input tax credit;
  - Special efforts to find omissions and commissions.

In India professionals like chartered accountants and advocates are not supposed to solicit business or advertise. Therefore an assessee has to choose competent professionals or firms to look into their accounts and records and confirm that he has complied with the legal provisions.

7.8 SPECIAL AUDIT - SECTION 66 OF THE CGST/SGST ACT

Special audits provide a lawful and legal way for the GST officers to take the assistance of other professionals i.e. a chartered accountant or cost accountant to determine tax liabilities in complex issues/cases. The professional expertise of a chartered accountant or cost accountant would be of great significance in ensuring that the interest of revenue is safeguarded at all times.

If at any stage of scrutiny, enquiry, investigation or any other proceedings before him, any officer not below the rank of Assistant Commissioner, having regard to the nature and complexity of the case and the interest of revenue, is of the opinion that the value has not been correctly declared or the credit availed is not within the normal limits, he may, with the prior approval of the Commissioner, direct such registered person by a communication in writing to get his records including books of account examined and audited by a chartered accountant or a cost accountant as may be nominated by the Commissioner.

The Chartered Accountant or Cost Accountant nominated by the Commissioner would, within a period of 90 days from the date of his nomination, furnish the Audit Report to the Assistant Commissioner on whose direction audit is conducted. However, the aforesaid period of 90 days may be extended by the

Assistant Commissioner on his own motion, or on an application made by the registered person or the Chartered Accountant or Cost Accountant nominated by the Commissioner, for material and sufficient reason.

It is also worth highlighting here that even if the accounts and records of the registered person are audited under any other provisions of the CGST Act/SGST Act or any other law in force [such as Companies Act, 2013 or Income Tax Act, 1961], the said registered person would be required to get his records audited by a Special Auditor. Thus, provisions of Special Audit have an Overriding Effect on other Audit provisions of the CGST Act/SGST Act or of any other Act.

The Registered Person would be given an opportunity of being heard where any material gathered on the basis of Special Audit under the CGST Act/SGST Act is proposed to be used against him in any proceedings under the Act as per the Principle of Natural Justice.

The expenses of examination and audit of records of the Registered Person by the Special Auditor [including the remuneration of the Special Auditor] would be determined and paid by the Commissioner. And the aforesaid determination of expenses would be final which means that no appeal can be filed to any Authority against such determination

It is also essential to note that if special audit of the records and documents of the registered person results in detection of tax not paid or short paid or tax erroneously refunded, or input tax credit wrongly availed or utilized by him, the proper officer may proceed to initiate action under section 73 or section 74 of the CGST Act/SGST Act.

7.9 PROCEDURE OF ORDERING SPECIAL AUDIT AND SUBMISSION OF SPECIAL AUDIT REPORT

Rule 102 of the CGST/SGST Rules, 2017 provides that where special audit is required to be conducted under section 66 of CGST and SGST Act, the officer referred to in the said section would issue a direction in form GST ADT-03 to the registered person to get his records audited by the chartered accountant or cost accountant specified in the said direction. On the conclusion of special audit, the registered person would be informed of the findings of the special audit in form GST ADT-04.

Chapter 8

Roles, powers, duties and liabilities of Auditor

8.1 INTRODUCTION

It is important for an auditor to understand his role, powers, duties and liabilities before accepting any audit assignment. They differ based on the type or nature of audit and objective of the person appointing. Some assignments may limit, others may expand the scope beyond the statutory need. The powers and responsibilities can be understood by going through the legal provisions in GST, accounting and auditing standards and guidance note issued by Institute of Chartered Accountants of India. In this chapter, we discuss few aspects which have bearing on different GST audit assignments.

8.2 ROLE OF AN AUDITOR

The role of an auditor undertaking statutory audits under GST law is now getting clearer. The certification requirement as per form 9C is more to ensure correct reporting of outward & inward supply details including credits and tax payment between audited financial statements and annual return. It would be important that though the statutory annual audit appointment is done by the entity, the purpose and objective of the assignment which would include identification and prevention of errors or credibility to the books and returns filed are to be kept in mind. There are a few pronouncements of Courts defining the role of an auditor in statutory audit under Companies Act. The general role of an auditor is to examine the financial records and accounts maintained by an entity and validate/confirm the true financial position. The Supreme Court in case of *Institute of Chartered Accountants of India vs. P.K.Mukherjee (1968) 38 Comp.Cas.628:AIR 1968 SC 1104* has held that "*He is expected to play the role of watch-dog on behalf of shareholders of company*". In GST audit, the role of an auditor would be to provide correct picture on GST compliance of any entity considering requirements of GST. In case of special audits wherein the auditor has been appointed by the tax department, his role would include conducting the audit on specified area and issue of the report within the agreed time. These audits are only ordered in the cases where there is some doubt on the extent of input tax credit or value of the supplies.

The role of the auditor who undertakes GST audits on behalf of the management would be defined by the scope of work and limitations placed by management. In this case, the obligation is only to the client. However, auditor may like to disassociate and not continue the audit assignments wherein tax evasion is taking place.

8.3 POWERS AND DUTIES OF AN AUDITOR

Audit under GST law is mandatory for all registered persons with specified turnover. The powers and duties of an auditor are not specifically stated for an auditor appointed to undertake audit under section 35(5) of GST Act. Section 143 of the Companies Act 2013 has discussion on powers and duties of an auditor which though cannot be said to be powers and duties under GST audit as well. Duties under GST audit could involve the following:

(i) Audit of annual accounts (maybe under Companies Act or other laws). However, where audit is not required under other laws, the annual financial audit may have to be done specifically to comply with GST audit under Section 35(5).

(ii) Reconciliation statement filing in form GSTR-9C which would reconcile the annual returns information with annual financial statement's information.

(iii) Other particulars relating to various aspects of GST as maybe relevant to arrive at the accuracy of the tax payable, paid, credit availed, refund claim and other compliances.

(iv) Reporting the observations, discrepancies and limitations, if any.

(v) Maintenance of working papers and information shared by the auditee ensuring confidentiality.

(vi) Undertaking the audit in accordance with relevant auditing and accounting standards.

Few of the aspects to be noted are as follows:

(1) Auditor of a company should have access to books of account, vouchers and entitled to get information and explanation as he may consider necessary for the performance of his duties. Even in GST audit, auditor should get access to all information which would have impact under GST to perform his duties. For the purpose of GST, audit includes examination of records, returns and other documents maintained or furnished by the registered person under GST Act or GST rules or any other law to verify correctness of:

- turnover declared,
- taxes paid,
- refund claimed
- input tax credit availed and

to assess other compliances. Therefore, access to books need not be restricted to only to GST records.

(2) Auditor needs to report to the members of the company on the accounts examined by him and on every financial statement/books of accounts.

(3) Auditor should comply with auditing and accounting standards. This would be relevant to GST audit as well. Chapter 11 and 12 of this book could be referred to understand the relevant standards of accounting and auditing.

Other than the above, as an auditor it is his duty to report all his observations, comments about non-compliance, short comings and deficiencies in the other particulars audit report based on his verification.

8.4 SPECIAL AUDIT UNDER GST

Indirect tax laws under service tax or central excise had provisions for conducting special audits in special circumstances to protect the interest of the exchequer. The audits were conducted by the professionals based on direction from tax department with formats prescribed by them. This was not widely used as the professional fees was paid by the revenue department. The fees was not commensurate with the time and effort and undue delays and questioning led by the Commissioners at times led to the more knowledgeable and experts in indirect taxes avoiding this audit.

Even in GST law, an officer is not below the rank of assistant commissioner can order for special audit under section 66 of the CGST Act 2017. Such audit could be ordered in special circumstances such as wrong valuation, wrong credit claim which is observed by him during any stage of scrutiny, inquiry, investigation or any other proceedings before him having regard to nature and complexity of case and interest of revenue. The auditor who has been appointed to conduct the audit would get his remuneration fixed by commissioner.

The officer/s, chartered accountant or cost accountant nominated under section 66 of the Act would have right to get access to following records for scrutiny or audit:

(i) Records prepared or maintained by the registered person and declared to the proper officer in such manner as may be prescribed;

(ii) Trial balance or its equivalent;

(iii) Statements of annual financial accounts, duly audited, wherever required;

(iv) Cost audit report, if any, under section 148 of the Companies Act, 2013;

(v) Income-tax audit report, if any, under section 44AB of the Income-tax Act, 1961; and

(vi) any other relevant record.

In this scenario, it is important to ascertain if such auditor appointed would become a public servant as he would be appointed to conduct audit to protect interest of revenue and get remuneration from government. Section 21 of Indian Penal Code (IPC) denotes few persons as public servants. The list includes every person in service or pay of government or remunerated by fees or commission for performance of any public duty by the government. Protecting the interest of revenue could be treated as public duty. Therefore, such special auditor could also be governed by the IPC.

IPC has penal provisions for public servants on acts such framing of incorrect document, making any false entry or making any statement having false statement, issue or signing of false certificates. Such persons could be punished with imprisonment or fine or both when such acts are proved intentional. Therefore, professionals who accept the special audit should take extra care to ensure that there are no false facts or statements in the audit report issued.

8.5 POWERS OF DEPARTMENTAL AUDITORS

Section 65 of the CGST Act 2017 gives certain powers to tax authorities with respect to audit. They are as follows:

(a) Commissioner or any officer authorized by such GST commissioner could undertake the audit in GST law on by issue of a prior notice.

(b) An audit can be completed within 3 months. If needed, it could be extended by another 6 months.

(c) Such auditors should get the necessary facility to verify books of account and get all necessary information to complete the audit in time.

(d) The proper officer can initiate action under section 73 or Section 74 on registered person in case of detection of any non-compliance with respect to tax payments or credits during the audit.

Apart from above, the authorized officers have right to access any place of business of a registered person to inspect books of account, documents, computers, computer programs, computer software whether installed in a computer or otherwise and such other things officers may require for carrying out any audit, scrutiny, verification and checks as may be necessary to safeguard the interest of revenue.

The officer/s would have right to get access to records for scrutiny or audit as stated in case of section 66 above.

8.6 PENALTIES/PUNISHMENT FOR NOT FURNISHING INFORMATION

It is important for the auditee to know about his roles and responsibilities as well during the audit. In case of audit under section 35(5), the auditee would have to furnish all the information and records necessary for conduct and issue of audit report. Otherwise, such auditor could complete the audit only with few reservations or limitations which would not serve the purpose. This may even prevent the auditor from issuing the audit certificate leading to audit by revenue as well as penal consequences.

In case of audit conducted by department under section 65 or special audit conducted by professional under section 66 of the CGST Act 2017, the auditee should furnish the necessary information for conduct of audit. Otherwise, penal provisions as per Section 122 gets attracted wherein the minimum penalty for non-furnishing of any information sought by officer is Rs.20,000/-including penalty under SGST law.

It would be of interest to note that the penal provisions could also get attracted in terms of IPC as such departmental officers or professional auditor appointed are public servants. Auditor appointed by the entity could bring these provisions to the notice of his client so that such client could take extra care during audit by department. The relevant IPC sections which could get triggered in case auditee prevents the departmental audit could be:

(a) Omission to produce document [Section 175] – Any person who is legally bound to produce any document including electronic record to any public servant intentionally would be liable for punishment of simple imprisonment for a term which may extend to one month, or with fine which may extend to five hundred rupees, or with both.

(b) Furnishing false information [Section 177] – Any person who is legally bound to furnish information on any subject to any public servant, furnishes any information as true which he knows or has reason to believe to be false would be liable to be punished with simple imprisonment for a term which may extend to six months, or with fine which may extend to one thousand rupees, or with both.

(c) Obstructing public servant in discharge of public functions [Section 186] – Any person who voluntarily obstructs any public servant in the discharge of his public functions would be liable to be punished with imprisonment of either description for a term which may extend to three months, or with fine which may extend to five hundred rupees, or with both. Therefore, if the auditee obstructs the auditor, he could be in trouble.

8.7 PENALTY FOR FAILURE TO GET BOOKS AUDITED

Audit of annual returns under earlier central laws such as central excise and service tax was not mandatory. Most of the State VAT laws had provision for mandatory audit of books of account by a chartered accountant or cost accountant or other specified persons. Non-compliance led to penal provisions being invoked and triggered investigation.

Section 122 of the CGST Act consist list of offences which would be liable for penalty. The list does not cover any penalty for non-filing of audit report. Therefore, non-submission of audit report could attract general penalty up to Rs.25,000/- under section 125 of the CGST Act. Equivalent penalty could be levied even under SGST law as well. Once GST compliance rating could also get affected when introduced for non-filing of audit report.

In terms of Section 74 (1) of the CGST Act allows the officer to issue show cause notice in case it appears to him that GST has not been paid or short paid or erroneously refunded or where input tax credit has been wrongly availed or utilised by reason of fraud, or any wilful-misstatement or suppression of facts to evade tax. In such cases, notice has to be issued at least six months before adjudication order is to be passed. According to section 74(10), order has to be passed within a period of 5 years from due date of furnishing the annual return for the financial year to which tax relates. Penalty could be levied equal to tax amount. If audit report has been filed, it would be easy for the assessee to substantiate that there is no suppression of facts.

Once it is proved that there was no suppression of facts, there would be lesser penalty including limitation period of 3 years from the due date of furnishing the annual return as against 5 years.

8.8 REASONABLE CARE

The professional appointed for an audit assignment should take due care and apply reasonable skill. Absence of care or skill in a professional engagement could end up in inviting penalty provisions for the auditor. In the case of GST audits, the law being new, adequate knowledge of the provisions of GST Acts and rules would be important. According to clause 7 of Part I of Schedule II to the Chartered Accountants Act 1949, a chartered accountant would be held guilty of misconduct if he does not exercise due diligence or is grossly negligent in the conduct of his professional duties.

Diligence means careful or persistence work or effort. Professional appointed should be careful and skilled enough to perform the GST audit. He should have updated knowledge of applicable legislations in this regard. He should be aware of the applicable technical and professional standards. Significance of due care and skill is well contained in one of the passages quoted from the judgement of the Karnataka High Court in a disciplinary case of *B. Shantaram Rao.* which is provided below:

> *"It is the duty of an auditor to bring to bear on the work he has to perform that skill, care and caution which a reasonably competent, careful, and cautious auditor would use. What is reasonable skill, care and caution must depend on the particular circumstances of each case. An auditor is not bound to be a detective, or, as was said, to approach his work with suspicion or with a foregone conclusion that there is something wrong. He is a watch-dog but not a blood-hound. If there is anything calculated to excite suspicion he should probe it to the bottom; but in the absence of anything of that kind he is only bound to be reasonably cautious and careful."*

It should not happen that the auditor completes the GST audit without applying sufficient skill and care. There are few incidents of auditors signing the audit certificates without even verifying the documents and records. Such incidents could tarnish the image of the profession as well as reduce the reliance on such audits by revenue. There are judicial pronouncements of the courts wherein the professional were held negligent. Few of them provided below:

(a) Chartered Accountant, without examination of stock register of the firm and without examining other relevant matters connected with the certificate, issued wrong consumption certificate in respect of raw material and components. [T.S. Vaidyanatha Iyer in Re: Page 153 of Vol. V of the Disciplinary Cases and pages 211-212 of April, 1977 issue of ICAI's Newsletter - Judgement delivered on 27th January, 1977]

(b) Chartered Accountant had issued a fictitious certificate of purchase turnover of books to a firm. [The Joint Chief Controller of Imports & Exports vs. B.K. Nagraj - Page 645 of Vol. VI(1) of Disciplinary cases - judgement dated 10th January, 1991)

(c) Chartered Accountant failed to report various violations of the Companies Act, 1956 in his report on the audit of the accounts of the Company. [Registrar of Companies, Bangalore, Karnataka vs. S.R. Bhandary – Page 351 of Vol. VIII – 1 – 21(6) of Disciplinary Cases – Judgement delivered dated 17th December, 2003)

8.9 PROFESSIONAL MISCONDUCT BY AUDITOR - DISCIPLINARY JURISDICTION

GST law as such does not have any provision for penalizing the auditor for any professional misconduct. Section 158 of the CGST Act specifies that the public servant who could be a departmental officer should not disclose details of returns or accounts or any statement obtained under the Act other than for criminal proceedings. However, there are few exceptions to this rule.

Any of the details obtained which would be relevant for any inquiry into a misconduct charge in connection with any proceedings under GST Act against a practicing advocate, a tax practitioner, a practicing cost accountant, a practicing chartered accountant, a practicing company secretary could be provided by a public servant to authority empowered to take disciplinary action against the members practicing the profession of a legal practitioner, a cost accountant, a chartered accountant or a company secretary, as the case may be. From this we could infer that the respective governing bodies of professionals only could take disciplinary action against auditors in case of misconduct. However, the revenue authorities or the Commissioner who appoints the auditors could complain to the professionals' body in case he is of the opinion that the audit has not been conducted properly.

8.10 TECHNICAL GUIDE OF ICAI

In GST, the audit/certification under section 35(5) is required in case of a tax payer whose value of turnover exceed Rs. 2 crores per annum. Similar limit in Income tax provisions as well. Professionals could refer to the *'Technical Guide on Annual return and GST audit'* of ICAI released in October 2018 which covers the important aspects of annual return and conduct of audit under GST law. This technical guide can be referred to understand and get awareness about the audit and annual return. It could also be a protection to prove that the professional has used due care while conducting the audit.

Chapter 9

Audit Report and Certificate

9.1 INTRODUCTION

The auditor who has been appointed for the audit assignment would be required to issue either audit report or audit certificate. VAT laws with mandatory audit provisions had different audit report formats. However, the special audit provisions under central excise or service tax law did not prescribe any format. In GST regime, a registered person whose aggregate turnover in a financial year exceeds two crore rupees needs to get his accounts audited as specified under in section 35(5). A chartered or a cost accountant could also take up special audit on behalf of the department.

9.2 FORMAT OF AUDIT REPORT UNDER SECTION 35(5) AND SPECIAL AUDIT

A person liable for mandatory audit under section 35(5) has to submit a copy of audited annual accounts and a reconciliation statement which should be certified in Form GSTR-9C. The form needs to be filed electronically or through a facilitation centre which would be notified by the commissioner. The auditor appointed is expected to certify that he has examined the books of accounts which include a balance sheet, profit & loss account, cash flow statement in addition to certification on agreement/not in agreement of books of account with those books which are maintained at the principal place of business including additional place of business. The observations, including qualifications if any need to be reported. The auditor should also report that all documents/records/accounts as required under GST law have been maintained or not. If the certification under section 35(5) is being done by the auditor who has not audited books of accounts, there is no need to report on the agreement of books of accounts with books maintained at books of account. It would be sufficient to mention the details of the auditor who has done the audit.

In case of a professional who has been appointed for special audit under section 66, the findings are to be reported to the appointing authority. Like earlier laws of central excise and service tax, even in GST law, there is no specified format for issue of the special audit report. The professional is free to submit his observations in the desired format. Subsequently, the observations in a special audit would be reported by the department to the auditee in Form ADT-04.

9.3 MANNER OF PERFORMANCE OF SPECIAL AUDIT NOT TO BE SPECIFIED BY OFFICERS

For a specified purpose such as the audit of credits claimed or valuation of supplies made, a cost or chartered accountant could be appointed by the department. However, such auditor cannot be ordered for the manner in which the audit is to be undertaken. Integrity and independence are the basic characteristics of a professional. Independence of a professional cannot be influenced by the order of officers or in self-interest. Auditor appointed should be honest, straight forward and sincere in his approach. He should not allow prejudice or bias to override his overall objective of the assignment. Any order or instruction to the auditor with respect to the manner of performance of audit could affect the independence.

Before accepting the audit under section 66, the auditor should consider if such assignment involves any threat to his independence. When any conflict of interest/threat exists, then the auditor should take action to eliminate such threats or he should avoid accepting the assignment.

It is important to note that there is no bar or limitation to order aspects and the manner in which the reports are to be issued by the auditor. The department could also come up with a manual for such special audit just like manuals which were there in central excise and service tax provisions for EA-2000 audit.

The principles of independence would apply even for a certification assignment. No certification assignment should be undertaken by the professional when his independence is at stake.

9.4 REPORT AND CERTIFICATES DISTINGUISHED

Audit certificate provides a confirmation of correctness and accuracy of few matters whereas audit report is issued expressing the opinion on the statement of accounts. For instance, a person who wishes to come out of composition scheme and start paying regular GST would be eligible for taking ITC on stocks lying at the time of opting to pay tax. For this purpose, he needs to file a declaration about stock in terms of rule 40 of the CGST Rules, 2017. Such a declaration needs to be certified for its correctness by a chartered or cost accountant.

An auditor should understand the basic differences between the report and certificate. Following are a few important differences:

Particulars	Auditor's report	Auditor's certificate
Nature	It is an expression of opinion about the account.	It is a confirmation of correctness and accuracy about some matters.
Audit basis	The report is based on assumptions and estimations	The certificate is based on actual figures and facts.

Particulars	Auditor's report	Auditor's certificate
Criticism	There may be criticism about the report.	There is no scope of criticism about the certificate.
Advice	In the scope, there is a scope of giving constructive advice in the company.	No scope of constructive advice exists in case of a certificate.
Time of issue	After the end of each accounting year, the report is mandatory.	The certificate is not mandatory every year. It is specific to the purpose.

A professional could refer to '*Guidance Note on Tax Audit under section 44AB of the Income-tax Act, 1961*' of ICAI to understand what is expected from an auditor in case of certification of information as 'true and correct'. In addition to this 'Guidance note on reports and certificates for special purposes' of ICAI would also be useful in understanding the difference between audit report and audit certificate.

For the purpose of GSTR-9C, the auditor has to certify that according to his opinion, to best of his information and according to the examination of books of account and explanations given, particulars in the form are **true and correct** which could be subject to observations and qualifications. This requirement would put more onus on the auditor to ensure that there is reasonable assurance in what is getting reported.

"True and correct" indicates complete assurance indicating that the auditor has performed procedures as considered appropriate to reduce the risk to zero which may not be practically possible. However, he is expected to provide reasonable assurance considering materiality aspect. Due to inherent limitations such as test check, nature of the business, use of professional judgment, timings and environment, the auditor may not be able to give absolute assurance. For the purpose of GSTR-9C certification, the auditor could ensure reasonable assurance for which he has to design the process considering reporting requirement which could be understood in subsequent Chapter 10 on audit process and methodology.

9.5 OPPORTUNITY OF BEING HEARD TO THE AUDITEE AND FEW JUDGEMENTS

Section 66(4) of CGST Act 2017 provides that the registered person whose books have been subject to special audit should be given an opportunity of being heard in respect of material gathered which is proposed to be used in any proceedings against him. Such provision is based on the principle of natural justice.

Violation of natural justice results in a violation of article 14 of the Constitution of India as it denies equality before the law. Article 14, 19, 21 of the Indian Constitution lay down the cornerstone of natural justice in India. Supreme Court has held that a properly expressed and authenticated order can be challenged on the ground that condition precedent to the making of the order has not been fulfilled or the principles of natural justice have not been observed.

Supreme Court in case of ***Tin Box Co. vs. CIT (2001) 249 ITR 216 (SC)*** has held that the right is so fundamental that the failure to observe the principles of natural justice cannot be made good in an appeal. Lack of opportunity before the Assessing Officer cannot be rectified by the appellate authority by giving such an opportunity.

Here it would be relevant to discuss the observation of Rajasthan high court in case of ***Rastra Sahayak Vidyalaya Samiti vs. CCIT (2012) 246 CTR 154 (Raj).*** The high court held that the commissioner must give an opportunity to the assessee if he desires to use the evidence collected against the assessee through reports of subordinate authorities. On the facts, the court held that order passed by Chief Commissioner denying approval, relying upon certain adverse material without supplying the same to the petitioner and without allowing an opportunity of rebuttal, thereof does not fully meet the requirement of principles of natural justice.

9.6 ACTION POINTS FOR SPECIAL AUDITS AND OTHER CERTIFICATIONS

In GST law, a cost or chartered accountant certification is needed in the following circumstances:

(a) The claim of credit on stock lying in special circumstances such as the shift to the regular scheme from composition scheme, new registration on crossing the threshold limit, exempt supply becoming taxable supplies [Section 18 read with rule 40(1)(d)].

(b) Transfer of credit in case of transfer, merger, amalgamations, etc. [Section 18 read with rule 41(2)]

(c) Reversal of credit on the market value of stock [Section 29(5) read with rule 44(5)]

(d) Filing of refund claim [Section 54 read with rule 89(2)(m)]

(e) Certificate under notification of Department of Industrial Policy read with circular no.1060/9/2017-CX (Budgetary support in GST)

(f) Report to be issued for special audit [Rule 102)]

Few important action points before taking up any of the above-mentioned tasks, the cost or chartered accountant could consider following aspects:

(1) An engagement letter should be prepared detailing out the scope, terms of services and management responsibility based on the type of assignment. Even in case of special audit assignment undertaken

based on request from tax department, an engagement letter should be prepared.

(2) Team engaged in the assignment should be briefed about the scope of services.

(3) Relevant provisions of GST should be understood for undertaking the assignment.

(4) In case of certification of merger, de-merger, amalgamation, lease or transfer of business, the professional should have an understanding of legal provisions applicable as he needs to certify that even liabilities are transferred.

(5) In case of certification of refund claim as per Rule 89(2)(m), a detailed verification of financial statements, sales invoices and purchase invoices necessary to ensure that incidence of tax, interest has not been passed on to any other person.

(6) It may so happen that the professional may not be able to get complete information or data required for certification. In such cases, it is very important for him to disclose all the limitations in the notes to certificates.

(7) Before relying on the internal controls, it would be important to assess the risks involved in the systems.

(8) Critical issues to be noted and discussed with the management before certification.

(9) Depending on the nature of the assignment, a standard questionnaire and checklist should be prepared and used. This would ensure that all important aspects have been covered.

(10) Proper working papers and evidences for certified facts should be kept for future reference without fail.

(11) In case of a special audit, tests to be performed to obtain the audit evidences.

(12) Review the data and assess if all important information obtained.

(13) Depending on the nature of review in special audit, the necessary legal provisions, case laws, notifications, and circulars to be referred. The standards on auditing in the Appendix to this book may also be referred for more understanding.

Chapter 10

Audit Process and Methodology

10.1 INTRODUCTION

The designing of the audit process and understanding the audit methodology is key for the conduct of an audit. It assists the audit team in a structured approach in conduct of the audit. Absence of the process could result in losing the direction of audit and spending time on lesser important matters and not examining more important aspects. The process could include various stages such as preliminary discussion, obtaining information, desk review, risk assessment etc.

In this chapter, we discuss all important stages which could be essential for the successful conduct of the audit. It would guide the audit team which could include junior members who may not be aware of the various stages involved in an audit. It is important to note that there could be a change in the order of stages which could depend on the size of the auditee, familiarity of the auditor with the entity, assignments done in the past where these aspects may have been examined, time available for certification, information available and risks involved.

The various stages are as follows:

10.2 STAGE 1: PRELIMINARY DISCUSSION WITH MANAGEMENT

After getting engaged, while sending acceptance letter for audit, it may be advisable to send the Internal Control Questionnaire [ICQ] to the auditee for filling. Audit process would start with a preliminary discussion with the management of auditee using the ICQ. Every successful audit including GST audit would be based on sound planning and effective involvement of management and the auditor. This would help the auditor in better understanding of operations and for management, effective implementation of audit recommendations or compliance with the law would be possible.

The main purpose of preliminary discussion would be to understand the relevance of the audit, the expectation of client and scope of audit assignment including the GST law requirement. An auditor can also gather sufficient information for proper GST audit planning during this stage.

10.2.1 Techniques for gathering information

The techniques which could be used by the GST auditor for gathering information are discussed below:

(1) **Information on website and internet:** In today's world, the internet has a vast pool of information wherein a good amount of details of

the auditee, industry in which auditee operates, etc. could be obtained. Website of the industry association and auditee would also contain information which could be referred by the audit team before commencing the discussion with the management. This could also save the time of auditors and the auditee. An auditor can focus and seek such information which is not readily available with him.

(2) **Interviewing the key management personnel:** The auditor could interview the key management personnel like top management, accounts officers, finance head and other functional heads such as marketing, procurement, etc. who would have relevant information on products, services, nature of operations, branches. The auditor could also understand the organizational structure and assess the quality of the managerial personnel.

(3) **Physical visit of business premises:** The auditor may visit the business premises/branches/project sites along with key management personnel to understand the business processes. At this stage, it is possible for the auditor to get an insight into the broad internal control systems quality of the personnel on the ground level. The auditor needs to involve all his team members during the visit so that even they would get a good idea about the business.

(4) **Superficial review of compliances and financial performance:** The auditor could carry out a basic review of compliances such as one system or interconnected systems, to arrive at the liability, capturing of credits, payment of taxes and filing of GST returns within the due date. Financial performances could also be reviewed to get a fair idea on the overall performance of the business. Reasons may also be obtained for non-compliance of basic GST provisions to enable advise on compliance.

(5) **Preparation of auditee's profile:** Preparation of auditee's profile could also be a part of an audit assignment. A basic auditee's profile could be prepared before discussion with the management. Later, the profile could be updated with more information after discussing with the auditee. The profile should contain the key details about the business and activities performed along with key indicators for GST compliance, which would help him in planning for compliance and substantive tests to be performed by the audit team. The profile would also serve as a future reference to identify likely areas of risk besides saving time and effort. New team members would find all this base information as and when need and auditee may not asked the same questions repeatedly. Major contents of the profile could be as under:

- Products or services of auditee including rate, classification and exemption details

- Nature of operations generally performed
- Branches, units or site related activities being performed
- Type of transactions usually done: Intra-state, Inter-state, imports, exports
- Existence or non-existence of foreign currency payments and the purpose of such payments
- Existence or Non-Existence of foreign currency receipts and the purpose of such receipts
- Details of related parties and type of transactions
- Details of advance rulings (if any) applied
- Important accounting ratios
- Details about tax litigations pending and the updated status
- Types of registration and number of registration obtained under GST

With the introduction of GST law replacing various indirect tax laws, the way in which business is being done could have changed substantially or may need to change. At this stage, the auditor should be able to build a good relationship with the client without affecting his independence for gaining the support for his conduct of his audit. In case the audit certification under section 35(5) of the Act is being undertaken by the auditor who has conducted the audit, then all these aspects could be considered while regular audit under other law so that there is no duplication.

10.3 STAGE 2: OBTAINING INFORMATION FROM AUDITEE

For successful conducting the GST audit, obtaining sufficient and proper information from the auditee is the primary step. The information could be obtained at different stages of the audit. Basic information could be obtained during the enquiry stage and more during desk review after acceptance of the audit assignment. Internal control questionnaire could be completed and used by the auditor to understand the knowledge of the level of internal controls that are existing with the auditee. Thereafter, other information could be obtained during the actual conduct of audit which could be from the auditors or auditee's location using information technology.

Process of obtaining Information would begin with an analysis of auditee's business/industry. This can be followed up by getting other details such as financial statements, minutes of meeting filed with the registrar of companies, etc. which could be easily available, especially in case of public companies. The auditor should recognize suitable and reliable information which would enable him in meeting audit objective.

Important steps to be considered by the GST auditor while obtaining the information from the auditee could be as under:

Step 1: Preliminary knowledge of the Entity

It is important for the auditor to obtain preliminary information about the industry, nature of ownership/management, regulatory environment and operations of the auditee. This should be done before the confirmation of the audit engagement as there may be reasons for not accepting due to the risk associated with the entity.

Step 2: Follow up for information after acceptance of audit engagement

After accepting the audit engagement, more detailed information about the auditee including the tax compliances and confirmation to the answers ICQ should be obtained. To the extent possible, all information should be obtained relating to GST compliances. The auditor should perform the necessary procedures designed to identify significant changes which have taken place in the area of operations, products, services or both, the constitution of the entity and strategic process, registrations on a periodical basis.

Step 3: Interview with key management personnel and others charged with governance

The auditor should interview the key management personnel who could throw light on the information about the supplies being made and current issues. A questionnaire for each function such as sales, procurements, stores, etc. of the organization should be prepared and used by the auditor to ensure completeness.

The important information sources for the GST auditor to get information about the auditee:

(a) Going through the official website of the auditee,

(b) Information from MCA web site on payment,

(c) Incorporation documents like Memorandum and articles of associations/partnership deeds etc.,

(d) Organizational structure and hierarchy of the reporting system

(e) Discussion with statutory auditors and review of statutory audit reports and other audit reports, if any,

(f) Discussion with other auditors, legal advisors, cost accountants who had provided services to the entity,

(g) News, association publications and any other kinds of literature related to the industry of auditee to understand the issues and challenges,

(h) Other legislations and regulations that would affect the business of the entity

(i) Minutes of meetings of the board, correspondence of annual general meetings, published reports, brochures, catalogues, etc. would provide great information

(j) Sales plans, procedure manuals (standard operating procedures) of accounting, internal control systems, purchase policy, credit policy followed by the entity and

(k) Past disputes in taxation for the industry as well as the entity.

(l) Going through the internal financial systems report (prepared as per Companies Act, 2013) could help in understanding the systems including procedures being followed.

Utilization of knowledge of the entity

Understanding the business of auditee would be useful for the auditor in the following ways:

(a) Assessing the risks and identification of key focus areas for audit

(b) Understanding the transactions not appearing in the financial statements but having GST implication

(c) Planning and performing the GST audit effectively and efficiently

(d) Evaluation of the audit evidence

(e) Providing better and quality service to the client

(f) Interpretation of legal provisions would be easier if business knowledge is good

(g) Assessing the time and effort needed for the audit

(h) Planning the audit team for execution of the assignment

It is the responsibility of the auditor to ensure that the engagement team assigned to the audit engagement obtains sufficient knowledge of business to enable them to carry out the audit effectively.

10.4 STAGE 3: DESK REVIEW

The time spent in the auditees location intrudes into the auditee's productive time. To limit the time for the actual conduct of the audit at the premises of the auditee, it is suggested to make a preliminary review of available information of auditee at auditor's premises before visiting auditee's place.

Audit team could carry out the desk review on the basis of details available in the permanent audit file (if any). If not available start preparing the file. Other basic documents pertaining to the audit period could be requested by the team from auditee. It is preferable for the auditor to spend at least 30% of his total time in planning the audit including desk review.

10.4.1 Benefits of desk review under GST

- The objective of desk review under GST audit is to obtain maximum information before going to the auditee's place which would help save a lot of time and efforts even for the auditee in explaining.
- Desk review also helps in having minimum and most important interactions with the client on a visit.
- Preliminary work which need not require the audit engagement team to be present at the auditee's place can be completed under desk review itself. Major and important aspects could be discussed with experienced members in auditor's office.
- Focus areas under GST audit can be identified at the desk review stage to conduct the audit effectively.
- Audit team engaged for audit could get clarity on most issues without visiting the client's place. Potential issues could also be discussed with previous audit team in case there is a change in the audit team.
- The cost of an audit could also be significantly reduced.

10.4.2 Important information to be obtained

The following could be important information which could be obtained during the desk review:

(a) Name, address, contact details

(b) Nature of business/business verticals referring to the website, permanent audit file, other possible sources

(c) Location of business

(d) Registration certificates under various laws

(e) Description of goods/services including classification, rates, exemptions applicable

(f) Details of outward supplies involving works contracts, composite supplies, mixed supplies, and continuous supplies, if any

(g) ISD and cross charging details

(h) Type of customers, type of GST payable

(i) Major customers, major competitors, major vendors

(j) Latest financial statements

(k) Latest GST compliance returns filed including correspondences with the tax department

(l) Reconciliation statements prepared between financials and returns

(m) Refund claims filed and their status

(n) Disputes with the department and their status

(o) Major agreement copies with vendors and customers

(p) Advance rulings, if any, obtained

(q) Legal opinions, if any, obtained

(r) Other documents needed for audit to the extent possible

10.5 STAGE 4: ASSESSMENT OF AUDIT RISKS

Audit risk could be termed as the risk that the auditor gives an inappropriate audit opinion when the financial statements are materially misstated which ultimately leads to expressing an inappropriate opinion in an audit assignment. Material misstatements could be a result of improper assessments and conclusions drawn. In GST incorrect interpretation especially on rate and exemption can lead to exposure to the client which could be catastrophic for their continuity.

The auditor needs to evaluate the audit risks while formulating audit plans and substantive tests of controls for audit. The audit plan and program need to be altered on real-time basis as and when there is an assessment or detection of risks in order to mitigate the risk in some areas of suspected vulnerabilities relating to GST. The auditor should consider if information obtained from the auditee is relevant for the identification of materially substantive risks.

Auditor has to perform necessary risk assessment procedures in order to provide the basis for the analysis of the information that he has obtained from the auditee. For this purpose, the auditor should devise the auditee's profile which would include all the necessary information about business and processes carried out. This exercise provides an indication for the auditor to assess the areas of importance and possible risks involved.

It may so happen that the auditor has information about the auditee which was obtained while carrying out other assignments. However, he should ascertain if there have been any changes. If yes, he should update the information as relevant to GST audit.

Audit team members involved in the audit engagements should discuss the susceptibility of the incorrect data obtained relating to GST and the intensity of material misstatements which may affect the compliances.

10.5.1 Procedures to be followed in risk assessment

Following procedures could be followed to assess the risk involved in an audit assignment:

(a) Inquiries with the management and others within the auditee's entity who might be having information which is critical to identify the risks of any material misstatement due to frauds or errors, if any.

(b) Performing analytical procedures.

(c) Analyzing the situation through observations and inspections of variances.

10.5.2 Various type of risks

Audit risks can be categorized into inherent risks, control risks and detection risks which are discussed in subsequent paragraphs. These aspects to be discussed by the audit team to assess the risks involved in GST audit of any entity.

Audit risk = Inherent risk × Detection risk × Control risk

10.5.2.1 Inherent risks

This is a risk of probability of errors and inconsistencies in a class of transactions which are materially substantive either individually or when aggregated with other material misstatements. A financial statement would not include unrecorded transactions or omitted deemed supplies. Further the correctness of classification or under or over valuation or whether IGST to be paid or CGST + SGST of relevant State would not be apparent from the statements. Therefore the transaction laible to GST maybe omitted or incorrect which cannot be controlled. It may not be possible to get protected with the existence of internal controls when inherent risk exists. Such risks could be due to various factors which are listed after this para. Audit plan and audit strategies have to be designed after considering such risks if they exist. Global, Indian and regional understanding of business is a must to address the inherent risks. If the auditor is of the opinion that he does not have the capability or resources to take up the audits which involve such risks, he should not accept the assignment. Considering the requirement of certification under section 35(5), the auditor need not investigate any such aspects but needs to exercise due diligence. Further, due care should be taken to ensure that risks associated with reporting requirements are understood and addressed appropriately.

Examples of Inherent Risk:

(1) Complexities in the business with a rapid increase in growth in numbers or skyrocketing share prices or geographic spread.

(2) Large cash balances considering the nature of the industry.

(3) Industries dealing in products where the rate of tax is unduly large like gutka, motor vehicle spares, etc.

(4) Industries which are evasion prone like jewellery, textiles, financial services (derivatives, share market), etc.

(5) Complex undeterminable ownership of companies.

(6) Off balances sheet transactions like the recent bill discounting done by foreign branches- not reported.

(7) Top management, CFO turnover or even resignation of the statutory auditor.

(8) A spate of acquisitions, mergers, demergers with lack of clarity.

(9) A large number of special purpose vehicles and subsidiaries.

(10) Industries are dependent on imports which are volatile or prone to obsolescence.

(11) Very high debt-equity ratios indicating unhealthy leverage, low quick ratios which indicates severe financial pressures or past reports indicating doubts on continuity.

10.5.2.2 Control risks

Control risks are the risks that the material misstatements in financial transactions cannot be detected by the present internal control system in place. This means that this risk is directly related to the systems of internal control. As a preliminary measure, the auditor should evaluate the internal control structure to assess its probable effectiveness. Here the risk of a process failure may be related to the information technology in use and improper GST implementation at the time of transition with check and balances being absent. Non-integration of the GST reports to the ERP in place could be a major control risk. The auditor should understand the standard operating procedures if any (there may be none for GST transactions) and explain it to the team members as well. The team should also understand the controls and authorizations provided in the auditee's entity. In the case of GST audit and certification, it would be important for the auditor to understand the internal controls adopted to ensure GST compliance. Controls should address all important processes in place for compliance aspect such as determination of levy, rate of tax, adopting to regular changes in the law, valuation of supplies, input tax credit availment etc.

Examples could be as under:

(1) The accounting personnel in-house not having any idea of the GST provisions and procedures.

(2) The internal audit not including GST in the scope and the lack of competent monitoring senior officers/lack of chartered accountants doing any review on a periodic basis.

(3) GST entries being made in excel at the end of the month rather than at the time of recording of the transaction.

(4) Transactions recorded after the year-end.

(5) No segregation of duties unless small and proprietary organisation.

(6) No authorisation process in GST transaction recording and passing of entries.

(7) Processes not in place for detection, prevention and correction for duplicated (ITC) or missed transactions (invoices).

10.5.2.3 Detection risks

Detection risk refers to the risk that the auditor or audit team fails to detect the material misstatement. Audit procedures may not result in the appropriate conclusion. When compared to inherent risks and the control risks, the probability of detection risk relates directly to the effectiveness of audit procedures, having nothing to do with auditee's systems.

Inherent and control risks are different from detection risks as they are independent from the audit procedures. They are part of the entities business and environment. Though inherent and control risks cannot be controlled by the auditor, he can assess them and design his own substantive procedures to produce an acceptable level of his detection risks thus reducing the audit risks to the independently lower level.

Examples could be as under:

(1) GST audit accepted without understanding the scope and need to do substantial test check and use of expensive audit tools.

(2) GST audit done by untrained, unskilled juniors with inadequate knowledge of GST.

(3) Reduction in the audit procedures based on oral assurances of the management or due to inadequate compensation.

(4) Taking up the audit assignments at the last moment without any time for conducting a proper exercise.

(5) Not using a internal control questionnaire or alternative evaluating of the controls.

(6) The filling of checklists at the end of the audit instead of ongoing recording and only if audit process carried out. Not filling in these as mere documentation.

(7) Misapplication of the audit process like calculating improper /irrelevant ratios.

10.5.3 Auditor's response to the assessed risks

Assessed risks of the auditor may affect not only the types of audit procedures performed but also the actions which are required to be taken by the auditor in order to mitigate the risks. The reasons for assessments given to the risk are relevant in the determination of the nature of audit procedures to be adopted. If the assessed risk is lower because of the particular characteristics of a class of transactions without considering any related controls, then the auditor may consider only substantive analytical procedures alone. On the other hand, if the assessed risks are lower because of related controls, then auditor could intend to have less of substantive audit procedures. The use of the standards which are technical in nature could also assist in ensuring that the audit is carried out as it should be.

The other measures to mitigate the above risks could be as under:

(1) **Completeness tests:** The confirmation that all transactions are recorded. This could be done by reconciliations of delivery challans to gate record to the invoices, goods inward to the gate records to the vendor's invoices, job work sent and received records, etc. This could also be done by using short micros in excel where the entire data can be verified in minutes. We look up and other functions in excel could be used. In the case of ERPs audit tools may be necessary to confirm this. Alternatively, the reports to be pulled to excel and verification carried out.

(2) **Duplication tests:** This could also be done similar to the completeness.

(3) **Classification tests:** The major streams of outward supply and credits could be identified and the proper classification carried out. If that is not possible the process for the classification may be verified.

(4) **Valuation tests:** The major streams of outward supplies may be examined with the agreements to see if the concept of composite, mixed and non-composite supplies have been adhered to. The valuation rules if applicable especially when the supplies are to the consumer market may be concentrated on.

(5) **Data Analytics:** In case of millions of transactions the robustness of the creation of masters, management override – exception report examination, further analytics and use of regression may validate the data.(discussed in detail later)

10.6 STAGE 5: AUDIT PLAN AND AUDIT PROGRAM

10.6.1 Audit plan

Audit plan under GST includes specific guidelines to be followed while conducting a GST audit. Audit plan helps the auditor to obtain sufficient appropriate evidence for the circumstances and helps to keep costs of audit at a reasonable level while mitigating the errors. Audit Planning is necessary to conduct an audit in an efficient and timely manner. During the planning phase, audit objectives and scope are determined based on which an audit program is prepared.

The audit plan should basically aim at performing the audit with the maximum efficiency possible under the circumstances. This is possible only when the audit team is able to address contentious and core issues within a limited time frame. The audit plan should be prepared taking into account the information gathered at the earlier stages. Major audit issues and areas to be addressed during the audit along with personnel responsible for the areas is to be identified during the audit planning stage. Any audit which is not planned could lead to frustration especially when auditee's business is complex with vast transactions.

The audit plan should be more detailed covering the nature of the audit, timing and extent of audit procedures to be performed by the audit team members. The advantages that would accrue if one were to follow the audit plan are:

(1) More attention to critical and important areas of audit;

(2) Effective and efficient organization and management of the audit;

(3) Selection of team members with an appropriate level of competency and expertise to respond proactively to the anticipated and real-time risks;

(4) Proper direction and supervision of engagement team members and review of their work;

(5) Proper coordination of work done by other auditors, internal auditors, accounts officers.

10.6.2 Contents of the audit plan

After understanding the advantages of having the audit plan, it is necessary to understand the contents of the audit plan. An audit plan should include the following:

(1) Nature, timing, and extent of planned risk assessment procedures

(2) Business background

(3) Coverage and scope of work

(4) Team composition

(5) Periodicity of audit etc

10.6.3 Audit Program

Audit program can be understood as written guidelines which can also be meant as an action plan which contains the exact details of work to be done by the auditor and his team. It would contain the list of audit procedures to be performed in order to obtain appropriate evidence. The objectives of the audit program would be as follows:

(1) To assist in planning and performance of audit providing a set of instructions to the audit team.

(2) To provide evidence to support auditor's opinion/views.

(3) To provide means to control and record proper execution of audit work, review audit work.

(4) To guide in the distribution of audit work based on competency of team members.

(5) To ensure all important aspects are covered in the audit.

(6) To convey the coverage to the auditee based on which auditee could make/suggest a change in scope, if permissible.

10.6.4 Preparation of audit program

Audit program needs to be prepared considering the nature of the industry, auditing standards, GST provisions, audit risks involved, etc. In the program, the auditor needs to break up various areas to be reviewed such as outward supplies, inward supplies, GST input tax credits, export transactions, valuation, review of important contracts, etc. GST audit certification requires reconciliation of details disclosed in periodical GST annual return which is a summary of periodical returns filed by the auditee. It is important to cover reconciliation aspects as well. After accepting a GST audit, the auditor can prepare the audit program stage wise considering the various aspects to be covered at different phases. Audit program could also be shared with the auditee which would enable him to understand the scope and coverage of audit. The information obtained from the answers to the internal control questionnaire should be useful in customization of the audit program as an auditor would have got an understanding of the areas of weakness. For internal use, the auditor may also need to have a detailed audit checklist on each of the aspects of the audit program. Audit checklist need not be shared with the auditee by the auditor. However, the audit team should be aware of the purpose of the audit checklist and ensure that all the items are checked without fail during the course of the audit. For the preparation of checklist, Chapter 15, 16 and 17 could be referred.

A sample GST audit program is provided at the end of this chapter under heading 10.12.

10.7 STAGE 6: WORK AT THE OFFICE OF AUDITEE

The auditor would be required to perform verification at the office of the auditee to examine the records after obtaining necessary information in preliminary discussion with management, desk review and assessment of audit risks. Irrespective of the size of the auditee or number of transactions or activities, the auditor should make it a point to visit the office of the auditee. Forming an opinion only based on records made available without visit may not do justice to audit.

Advantages of conducting an audit at auditee's premises could be as follows:

(a) Any data, records or information needed on urgent basis could be obtained in quick time.

(b) The auditor would have the privilege of having a conversation with many of the right officers of the auditee.

(c) Many a times, clarification of issues could be provided by people involved in other operative function.

(d) Practical issues faced by auditee could be better appreciated.

(e) We remember more when we see and hear compared to reading. This would be advantageous in the conduct of an audit of other entities.

(f) Access to original documents would be available.

(g) Coordination with different departments would be easier.

Auditor and engagement team may perform the functions like examining the financial statements, interview with the operational managers, review of GST returns filed with the working statements, vouching of purchase invoices to verify the correctness of credit availed, reverse charge mechanism compliance, review of outward supply invoices to ascertain if aspects like rate of tax, classification, exemptions, valuation, type of tax, place and time of supply are proper. The chapters on **'Conduct of Audit'** (Part 5), could be a good guide on the list of items to be audited which includes even methodology of the check.

Key points to be noted while performing the verification/field work:

10.7.1 Venue

These audit procedures would be usually carried out at the premises of auditee. The head office would necessarily be covered as all the important records would be maintained there. Additional places such as godowns, branches, etc. should also be visited to understand the activities and check specific records such as stock movement records. The auditor would be able to get to know about the additional place of business from the GST registration certificate.

10.7.2 Communication and confirmation of visit

The auditor should communicate about the visit to the auditee which could be through phone or e-mails. Many times necessary documents would not be kept ready unless intimation is given earlier. The auditor should visit only after confirmation on the readiness of data, records and other information expected from the visit. It is also important for the auditor to communicate the functions or areas which he would like to cover and functional officers to be interacted with for conduct of the audit. If necessary, one visit could be made to make the auditee understand the requirements list for audit. This could save time for both.

10.7.3 Examination of the records

The chapters on **'Conduct of audit'** (Part 5), could be referred to understand various aspects to be verified. Following are the important records to be kept by the auditee for an audit of GST:

(a) Related to the production and manufacture of goods;

(b) Inward and outward supply of goods or services or both;

(c) The stock of goods;

(d) Input tax credit availed;

(e) Output tax payable and paid;

(f) Records of the consignor, consignee, and other relevant details;

(g) Accounts relating to the place of business;

(h) Delivery challans;

(i) Bill of Entry, Invoices, Bill of Supply;

(j) E-way bills;

(k) Letter of Undertakings and Bonds;

(l) Periodical returns;

(m) Job work challans and registers;

(n) Certificates obtained for the removal of goods at concessional rates.

(o) Refund claims

(p) Correspondence relating to disputes that have already arisen.

(q) Correspondence file with the department.

The list provided above is only indicative and it could vary depending upon the industry. The auditor should ensure that all the relevant records are examined. A detailed checklist could also be prepared for each of the above-listed records which could be followed by the audit team members to ensure that the important aspects are not left out. It is relevant to note that the certification does not require the auditor to verify aspects such as E-way bills or job work transactions. However, including them as part of the program could safeguard the auditee from future litigations when non-compliances are highlighted by the auditor.

10.7.4 Planning of time to be spent

In today's world, the business entities need to deal with a variety of audits under different statutes. Therefore, the auditor should not expect full-time presence of officers of an auditee for audit. Proper planning should be done at the stage of desk review and preliminary discussion. There could be a change in a number of days planned. If the volume of transactions or aspects is less than estimated, it would take lesser time and if volumes or aspects are high, then more time may be needed. This factor should be considered on the visit by the auditor. If required, the auditor could also take a break from the audit citing the reason of non-availability of complete information which could save the time of auditee as well as the auditor. Tracking status of audit team members work is also important at this stage with regular communication and guidance.

10.7.5 Auditor's responsibilities on the visit

The auditor should know his responsibilities and also communicate them to his subordinates. Few of the key responsibilities could be as follows:

(i) To act in a professional manner demonstrating qualities such as integrity, independence;

(ii) To be co-operative, willing to give accurate and competent advice to auditee;

(iii) To ensure that the team is behaving appropriately with the auditee;

(iv) To complete the audit within the agreed time. If not possible, communicate in advance to the auditee;

(v) To send a request for the necessary books, accounting records, and documents which are necessary for the purpose of GST audit well in advance;

(vi) To ensure that the rights and interests of the auditee are safeguarded in accordance with the provisions of GST law giving right and legal advice.

10.7.6 Auditee's responsibility on the visit of auditor

The auditor could also highlight the responsibilities of the auditee in his acceptance letter as well as in his visit. Few of the key responsibilities of auditee could be as follows:

(i) To be fair and honest, courteous and provide correct information for audit;

(ii) To provide proper space, access to the computers with a brief training on ERP being used (if not known to the auditor);

(iii) Providing a point of contacts for seeking information for audit;

(iv) Taking prompt action on suggestions;

(v) Involved and concerned officers available for audit queries for some fixed part of the day.

Though most of these points cannot be communicated to auditee directly, a few points could be conveyed to the auditee in the offer letter or audit engagement letter.

10.8 STAGE 7: AUDIT TOOLS AND TECHNIQUES

Audit tools and techniques serve to undertake audit engagements more efficiently. The business world is changing with technologies such as block-chain, artificial intelligence. It would be impractical to undertake an audit engagement without application of proper automated audit tools and techniques. Few of the important audit tools and techniques have been discussed in this step.

10.8.1 Audit tools

Audit tools refer to tools to identify, extract, convert, capture, store, and analyze data or information for audit purposes. There are various audit tools including computerized tools which could be used by the auditor. The common ones are as follows:

10.8.1.1 Internal control questionnaire (ICQ)

ICQ would contain a list of questions for the auditee to answer which would help the auditor to understand the various aspects of controls existing in the organization. This would also help the auditor to prepare his audit plan and audit program. Even the detective, preventive and corrective risks associated with the audit could be evaluated. The auditor may have to customise the standard ICQ depending on the nature of the industry. Questions could be answered with yes, no or not applicable. Points with "not applicable" could be ignored or given less importance while planning for the audit. The focus would be on those answered in the negative. Considering the importance of the internal controls, this book contains the detailed examination subject wise in Chapter 14, 15 and 16.

10.8.1.2 Audit program

Audit program would contain the step by step approach and areas of coverage in the audit. Auditor for the purpose of undertaking the GST audit should design the audit program considering the reporting requirements and nature of the industry. Based on the output of ICQ, the audit program could be customised to meet the requirements. Audit program could also assist the auditor in the extent of delegation of work to his juniors. The sample audit program attached at the end of this chapter could be referred by the GST auditor and modified as needed.

10.8.1.3 Audit checklist

The audit checklist covers each component of the audit program in detail. It provides further minute verification steps to be checked by the audit team. Audit checklist should be exhaustive covering all legal aspects to be verified and confirmed in the audit report. The checklist could act as a manual for the audit team to understand what to verify and how to verify. This would reduce the risk of missing out on important aspects to be verified. Answers to the checklist could be complied (answered as a yes) or not complied (answered as a no). Wherever there is non-compliance, the auditor should examine further and if non-compliance observed report them and advise the auditee to comply. The benefits which accrue could be ensured to be available and conditions thereof are confirmed. A sample audit checklist has been provided in Chapter 22. Audit checklist need not be shared with the auditee.

10.8.1.4 Computerised tools

With growing applicability of computers and information technology in the audit profession, usage of Computer-Aided Audit Tools (CAAT) is key for an auditor. Many of the organizations have moved to hundred percent computerization of all data and information. Even the tax laws in India have started allowing the assessee to maintain the records in electronic forms. If the auditor does not understand the computerisation, then it would not be possible for him to assess the risk. The timely completion of audit could be a challenge owing to the increase in a number of transactions in big organizations. As on date the majority of the auditors are not using the computer tools due to lack of knowledge in using such tools.

Business analytics consists of various techniques using operation research, statistics, artificial intelligence, information technology and management strategies used for framing business issues/problems. They are solved by collecting relevant past/current data, analyzing them using regression to create value for organisations. Auditors could use these techniques on big data to confirm features of the organisation or gain valuable insights on the running of the company. It can also be used to predict the probability of frauds. In case of doubts ongoing concern, the predictive analysis can be used to arrive at answers.

CAATs could be used in performing the GST audit including tests of general controls, 100% verification, sampling, analysis of trends, preparing ratios, comparing data with different periods, etc. CAATs allow the auditor to get access to data without dependence on the auditee, test the reliability of auditee's software, and perform checks effectively and efficiently.

CAATs may consist of package programs or purpose-written programs which are briefly discussed below:

(i) **Package programs** - These are generalized computer programs designed to perform data processing functions, such as reading data, selecting and analyzing information, performing calculations, creating data files and reporting in a format specified by the auditor. This could be used for checking aspects like uniformity in charging the rate of taxes, selection of samples, etc. The common ones are Idea, ACL, Microsoft Access and Active Data to some extent. ACL tool is very widely being used. The advantage with such type of tools is that these tools do not modify the source data and they are very powerful with the capability of accessing any data type.

(ii) **Purpose-written programs** - These programs perform audit tasks in specific circumstances. These programs may be developed by the auditor or by an outside programmer. In some cases, the auditor may use an entity's existing programs in their original or modified state because it may be more efficient than developing independent programs. These programs could be examined for suitability in conducting the GST audit.

(iii) **MS Excel** - Excel utilities are wide and well known with facilities like we look up, filter, pivot tables, what if analysis, analysis Tool Pak, solver etc. same utilities are used in normal audits. The excel utilities could be used along with the purpose written or package software programs for data analysis.

(iv) **GST audit tool:** There could be specific GST audit tools which could get developed in future considering the reporting requirements in the GST audit report format. This could save substantial time for the auditor in times to come. The auditor would be able to focus on audit than on gathering information, conversion, etc. These tools could be used along with other tools as well to ensure completeness and meet the requirement of reporting.

It is also very common for many all-purpose ERPs such as SAP, Oracle, Tally, ERPs, etc., to provide for general audit tools to analyze the data. It is important for the auditor to obtain reasonable assurance on the quality, reliability, usefulness, and security of data or information collected while using the CAAT. The GST network may provide various utilities for analysis. The auditor should test the tools before actual use in audits.

10.8.2 Auditing Techniques

Auditing techniques stand for methods adopted by the auditor to obtain the appropriate evidence while conducting the audit. If audit tools emphasize on the means through which auditing procedures to be done, auditing techniques emphasize on the manner in which auditing procedures should proceed. The auditor could refer to important standards on auditing issued by the ICAI such as SA 520 on analytical procedures and SA 530 on audit sampling to understand the various techniques through which evidences could be gathered. Few auditing techniques have been discussed below:

10.8.2.1 Analytical review procedures

Analytical review procedures could consist of systematic study and comparison of relationships between various records of GST such as sales register, purchase register, stock transfers, etc. and other books of the auditee to ascertain if there are significant fluctuations or variations from the expected relationship. Before conducting the analytical review procedures, the auditor should undertake the following:

(i) Analyse if the analytical review procedures would be effective in relation to the audit objective and quantify the degree of assurance which may be derived from such procedures. Data analytics may be used where the data set is big.

(ii) Make an estimation of the expected amounts or relationships and compare the same with actual figures. An example could be estimating the units of electricity to be consumed for the manufacture of a unit of goods and then comparing the production with actuals.

(iii) In case of any significant variations, patterns, investigate the reasons for the same.

(iv) Conclude as to whether the required degree of audit assurance has been derived from the analytical procedures followed.

Various analytical procedures are as under:

(1) **Trends**: Trend analysis could be one of the most effective methods for the comparison of data or information. Information such as sales, purchases, input tax credit, output tax liability figures could be analyzed by comparing documents such as GST periodical returns of the current period with prior period returns or industry standards.

(2) **Reasonableness**: Tests could be conducted to review the relationship of certain activities. An example could be a review of % of scrap generated with the quantity of goods produced. Another example could be a sales commission paid with total sales made. Substantial variations could be an alarm signal for the auditor.

(3) **Ratio analysis**: Ratio analysis could also be conducted by the GST auditor based on the available information and compare with the previous year figures. Some basic ratios which could be helpful for the auditor in GST audit could be as under:

(i) ITC ratio on inputs = Total ITC/Total purchase of inputs

[This could help in understanding the % of ITC being claimed against total inputs procured. The high variance could mean an excess or short claim of credit.]

(ii) ITC ratio on capital goods = Total ITC/Total purchase of capital goods

[This could help in understanding the % of ITC being claimed against total capital goods procured. High variance could mean excess or short claim of credit.]

(iii) ITC to Liability ratio = Total ITC/Total GST liability

[This could help in understanding the % of ITC being availed and utilized towards GST liability. High variance could mean ineffective utilization of ITC]

(iv) Sales return ratio= Sales return/Gross sales

[This could help in understanding the sales returns % to review adjustments made in GST liability]

10.8.2.2 Sampling technique

Sampling in an audit can be defined as the application of audit procedures to less than 100% of items within a population of audit relevance such that all sampling units have a chance of selection in order to provide the auditor with a reasonable basis on which to draw conclusions about the entire population. Unlike earlier days, selection of small sample size may not be acceptable to mitigate the risks involved. Even auditee's expectations can result in an increase in sample size to ensure minimum exposures to future demands in the form of penalty or interest. In a GST audit, the auditor is reporting on the true and correct nature of the information provided. This automatically warrants an increase in sample size though one may not be expected to check 100% transactions. Similar certification in Income Tax Audit which has been conducted for quite some time as of now.

There are various types of sampling methods such as random sampling, systematic sampling, haphazard sampling, etc. Choosing the right method using audit tools would be key for the auditor. All legal factors and reporting needs in a GST audit should be considered for the selection of samples. Selection of samples should be such that it covers all variety and types of transactions considering the nature of goods or services, time of supply, payment terms, place of supply, etc. Monetary unit selection method could be a better option which involves checking of all transactions above a fixed limit. For example, all sale transactions above Rs.2 lakh. [In value terms it would cover a substantial part of the transactions]

10.8.2.3 Inspection of documents and records

The auditor should inspect the documents and records relating to the GST and examine them along with the transactions to confirm the authenticity of the transactions, to check whether such documents are appropriate, to ensure whether such transactions are authorized and to ensure whether the transactions are proper. He should also check the controls exists to ensure recording of all inward and outward supply transactions, payment and receipts, etc.

10.8.2.4 Physical verification

Physical verification of assets could be relevant in GST audit as well. In terms of Section 16, the GST registered person would be eligible to claim the input tax credit on inputs and capital goods when they are actually received for use in business. The auditor could conduct physical verification to ensure this aspect. Alternatively, he may rely on a stock audit report undertaken recently as well.

10.8.2.5 Inquiry and confirmation

The technique of inquiry and confirmation could also be useful for the auditor in the conduct of GST auditor for a few aspects. Especially for service organizations this would be important as services are tangible and auditor may have to rely on the explanations of the auditee, agreement terms and other documents available. For more details, relevant standards available in the Appendix.

10.8.3 Blockchain technology

Blockchain is a distributed ledger containing relevant details for all transactions processed. Digital signatures or cryptography would be used to protect the validity and authenticity of these transactions processed. In this technology, the transactions are understandably recorded in an efficient and permanent manner. In the future, blockchain technology could have a substantial impact on the way the audit is being conducted. There could be less interaction with auditees as most of the information would be available for the auditor on the blockchain technology.

There could be a change in the sampling technique as with audit tools all transactions possibly could be verified. The audit process could also be faster as a certain process like third-party confirmation, waiting for statements from banks, etc. may not be needed in blockchain technology.

10.8.4 Artificial Intelligence

Artificial intelligence is a movement to imitate and human brain and learning process. Machines (robots) are configured to learn from experience. The machine can compute much faster and check millions of data sets in a few minutes. In the initial stages, domain experts can give vital knowledge inputs which machines will not forget. Today even skill refinement such as playing basketball, cleaning the room is possible through complex algorithms. The open source has many resources such a “rattle”, “python” etc. which are quite advanced and free.

The new technology would face challenges also in the beginning as this is a new technology and in countries like India, systems are not fully computerized. However, the auditor needs to update their skills in these types of new technologies which otherwise could pose a challenge to their existence. This could have an impact on the way GST audit certification needs to be done. Only time would answer these aspects.

10.9 STAGE 8: AUDIT DOCUMENTATION AND WORKING PAPERS

Audit documentation is the written record (including computerised) prepared during the audit process which forms the foundation for auditor's statements and conclusions. Audit documentation supports in reviewing the performance of the audit and also helps in the supervision of audit engagement. It is also possible to review the quality of work as such documentation becomes evidence about significant conclusions drawn by the auditor while conducting the audit.

From GST's perspective, audit documentation or working papers are documents obtained as evidences during the conduct of GST compliance audit. The working papers provide evidence that the GST auditor has gathered the necessary evidence and also that the evaluation has been done in accordance to it.

According to SA-230 standard issued by the Institute of Chartered Accountants of India (ICAI), "Working papers must include audit program, queries, the explanation given for the queries, schedules of important items like depreciation, inventories, confirmation from the third parties, certificates issued by management, banks, etc.". For GST audit also documents such as audit program, queries including explanations given, return copies, details of credit availed, sales made, etc. would be critical.

Working papers which have long-run and major impact need to be categorized and kept in the permanent file of client. Those working papers which would have an impact in the current period of audit could be kept in the current file. Permanent audit file of the auditee could have all important and basic information. This file can also be a ready reference for the subsequent audit team. It may be possible that with digitalisation, most of the audit workings including evidences could be in electronic form. In such cases, proper references/index should be available to locate the same. Proper back up on readable medium is important.

10.9.1 Purposes of Audit Documentation

The purpose of audit documentation could be any of the following aspects

(a) Evidence for the auditors to ascertain if overall objectives set by the auditor are met.

(b) Evidence to prove that audit was planned and performed in accordance with the Standards of Auditing issued by the professional bodies such as ICAI.

(c) Assist the engagement team to plan and perform the GST audit effectively.

(d) Enabling the engagement team to be responsible for their work.

(e) To preserve the records of matters which are significant for the continuance of future audits.

(f) Enabling the conduct of external inspections, peer reviews in consonance with pertinent legal, regulatory or other requirements.

10.9.2 Contents of Audit Working Papers

Audit team making note of the audit observations should be aware of the importance and contents of audit working paper. Having necessary and source of information would be key for successful completion of the audit. Any observation without documentary support could reduce the importance of it. The following could be important contents of GST audit working papers which need customization based on aspects of GST being audited:

(1) Name of the client

(2) Period covered by the audit

(3) Sources of data

(4) Audit methodology and tools used

(5) Detailed observations with important aspects such as date, amount, document references and remarks

(6) Comments of the concerned person

(7) Evidences of supervision and review of work

(8) Initials of members of staff with name who prepared the working paper and date prepared

(9) Initials of the reviewer with name, partner and date reviewed

10.9.3 Obtaining Management Representation Letters (MRL)

For the purpose of GSTR-9C certification, the auditor needs to certify that the details provided in GSTR-9C are true and correct. Considering the quantum, nature of the transaction and other limitations such as time and resources, practically it may not be possible for an auditor to check each and every transaction. There could be various information which auditor needs to rely on the management. In such a scenario, the Management Representation Letters (MRL) play a key role to safeguard the interest of the auditors. Detailed discussion on MRL is available in Chapter 22 – Mandatory certification – Reconciliation statement.

10.9.4 Other important aspects to be considered

(1) When there are any significant contracts or agreements entered with customers or vendors by the auditee, the auditor should include abstracts or copies of those contracts or agreements in the audit documentation.

(2) Discussions of significant findings or issues with management, those charged with governance, and others, including the nature of the significant findings or issues discussed should be recorded including date, name of persons involved in the discussion.

(3) Legal opinions if any obtained, notifications, circulars relied on by the auditee for GST supplies should be documented by the auditor to ascertain the eligibility and correctness.

(4) Important correspondences with the tax department should be obtained by the auditor including the status of litigations pending if any.

(5) Documentation should ensure compliance with standards on auditing.

(6) Audit documentation is not limited to documents prepared by the auditor but may include other appropriate documents such as minutes of meetings prepared by the auditee as well.

(7) Good audit documentation system would not only ensure effective audit but also save the time of auditee, partners or reviewers as well. Simple steps like the numbering of working papers, index of observations, signing of checklists, cross-referencing of working papers wherever needed could be very useful.

(8) Audit documents are the property of the auditor. However, ensuring confidentiality of the information obtained during the audit process is the primary responsibility of the auditor.

(9) Audit firms are required to establish policies and procedures for the retention of audit engagement documents. Statutes, regulations or the audit firms' quality control policies may specify a retention period of longer than five years.

Where the documents are maintained electronically, a proper backup is to be taken and kept safely. These details are taken from applicable standards, as provided in the Appendix.

10.10 STAGE 9: DRAFT REPORT AND OBTAINING MANAGEMENT COMMENTS

10.10.1 Draft GST audit report

After the conduct of audit at the premises of auditee, the auditor needs to prepare the draft audit report to obtain management comments. There is no standard draft report format. In case of GST certification audit, there is a specified format in GST Form 9C which needs to be issued by the auditor. Based on this form, the auditor could design the draft audit report format. In the case of general GST compliance reviews, the auditor can have his own format which could broadly cover the following aspects:

(i) Heading as the Draft Audit Report

(ii). Reference and scope of audit which could explain the date of offer, confirmation, coverage, sampling technique used, laws & regulations referred, and details of various auditing/accounting standards used.

(iii) Introduction paragraph which could contain basic details of auditee such as type of business, locations, registrations obtained.

(iv) Executive summary covering important points having major revenue impacts in the form of liabilities or credits. The purpose of this summary could be to draw the attention of the top management on serious issues.

(v) Discussion of observations under the following sub-headings:

  (a) Conceptual report - Issues having revenue impact such as short or increased liability, non availment or excess availment of credit, wrong rate of tax, etc. could be reported under this head.

  (b) Systems report – Issues in relation to systems which could have revenue impact in the longer run if not complied could be reported under this.

  (c) Transactions report- Issues not having a major impact, arithmetical errors could be reported under this head.

  (d) Annexures – This could have instances in support of issues reported in above headings, legal extracts, notifications, etc.

(vi) Limitation – In most of the audit assignments, the auditor would not be able to verify all the intended information which could be due to paucity of time, records not updated, the busy schedule of the client, etc. In such cases, those aspects could be reported and highlighted in the audit report.

The draft audit report prepared could be first shared with the auditee as a draft and presented to the management for any comments. This is important to ensure that the recommendations present in the draft audit report are practical from the point of view of compliances and implementation.

10.10.2 Obtaining management comments

Obtaining management comments would be key to finalize the audit report as there may be differences in understanding of few facts, wrong or incomplete explanations obtained by the auditor leading to the wrong conclusion and certain issues could have been complied (followed correctly). The auditor should present the draft audit report to the management along with necessary supporting documentary evidence to get comments and confirmation from the management.

After the meeting, the audit team should work with the auditee to achieve consensus and reach an agreement on the findings of the audit in case of differences in an independent manner. This would help in the finalisation of the report. Comments from management would consist of:

- Agreements and disagreements of the management regarding the findings made from the audit process.
- Management's views and opinions about the recommendations including the action plans suggested by the auditor.
- Decision of the management to accept or not to accept the course of action to mitigate the assessed risks by the auditor.

The auditor could communicate the following with those charged with governance:

(i) Auditor's views about significant qualitative aspects of the entity's practices relating to book-keeping of accounts and records for GST purposes, arriving at tax positions, invoices maintained, workings prepared for GST return filings and other compliances.

(ii) Auditor's opinion and his inferences about any discrepancies in the records and policies relating to valuations followed by the entity.

(iii) Significant difficulties and ambiguities faced during the process of audit.

(iv) Any written representations and confirmations needed to reach a conclusion.

(v) If the auditor has identified one or more deficiencies in the internal control system of the auditee which could have a material impact, the auditor should seek comments regarding these deficiencies on a timely basis before reaching any conclusion.

10.11 STAGE 10: PREPARATION OF FINAL AUDIT REPORT

The final audit report would be applicable for the statutory audit as well as for the management audit. It would be used by the auditee for all legal compliances as well as for presentation to the stakeholders. It is important that the report is addressed to the board in case of a management audit. The statutory audit certification has to be done in notified format of GSTR-9C. If the audit assignment includes the conduct of interim audit as a part of statutory audit, then the auditor should make it a point that the points reported are considered while certification in form GSTR-9C. Readers could refer Chapter 22 on Mandatory certification-Reconciliation Statement for understanding the detailed reporting requirement.

10.12 SAMPLE GST AUDIT PROGRAM

SAMPLE GST AUDIT PROGRAM	
Name and Address of the entity, State and Registration no.	
Contact persons	
Phone numbers	
E-mail Id	
Nature of business	
Audit team and Partner in charge	

Sl. No.	Particulars
A.	**UNDERSTANDING OF BUSINESS**
1	Peruse the website of entity and google other information available on industry as well as the business
2	Physical walk through in visit to principal place of business /head office
3	Review of audited financial statements, cashflow and gross trial balance for last 2 financial years
4	Review of product /service including advertisement material and literature
5	Review the organizational structure in India including related parties
6	Ascertaining the associated inherent, control and detection risks
7	Discussion with HODs to get clarity - challenges in business
8	Statewise Registration /Business Verticals/Additional place of business – Understanding
B.	**UNDERSTANDING THE AUTOMATION /ERP**
9	Review of automation/computerisation in the organisation covering hardware, software, physical, access controls
10	Review if the software/ERP including link to GSTN has controls /options to take care all the updated legal provisions of GST.
11	Review if there are any adverse comments in Internal Audit, Earlier GST reports and in IS audit if nay conducted
12	Review if there is a system of updating the masters /ledgers with updated information of customers, vendors etc.
11	Review of books and records maintained to ascertain if there in accordance with GST law

Sl. No.	Particulars
C.	**REVENUE /SUPPLY - GOODS /SERVICES**
12	Review of Profit of Loss account to ascertain
13	a. Exemptions /Concessions /Composition scheme opted
	b. Supply in DTA /Exports
14	c. Transactions with related parties /distinct persons according to Schedule I
	d. Special transactions such as SEZ, EOU,UN etc.
15	Review of nature of supply and implication - Composite supply /Mixed supply
	Verification of system of advance receipts to study GST impact and treatment
16	Verification of adjustments made for advance receipts with sale invoices
	Verification of treatment of sales /service return and tax adjustments
17	Verification of conditions fulfilled for deductions claimed for sale /service return, defects
	Verification of discount policy in organization and impact under GST
18	Verification of conditions fulfilled for deductions against discounts allowed
	Verification of unbilled revenues, adjustments and GST impact
19	Verification of Inter unit supplies and GST impact on such supplies - Schedule I
	Verification of benefits adopted for exports and fulfilment of conditions
20	Verification of terms of agreements entered with customers having impact on valuation
21	Verification of recoveries from employees and GST impact on such recoveries
22	Verification of rate of tax adopted for taxable supplies made
23	Verification of rates adopted in case of changes in rates in between different rates
24	Verification of sales to SEZ to ascertain if they are zero rated
25	Verification of exports made with tax payment or without tax payment
26	Verification of rebate/refunds claimed against exports
27	Verification of sales made as deemed export

Sl. No.	Particulars
28	Verification of refund claims in respect of deemed exports
29	Verification of sale of fixed assets and impact under GST
30	Verification if any goods /services liable under RCM are being provided
31	Verification if billings for support services to own branches /units are done - Schedule I
32	Verification of sales made on approval basis to ascertain GST compliance
33	Verification of sales made from exhibitions to ascertain GST compliance
34	Verification of sales made as casual taxable person in any state to ascertain GST compliance
35	Verification different sale schemes and impact in GST
36	Reconciliation of details of supplies as per annual return and books of accounts
D.	**PROCUREMENT OF GOODS AND SERVICES**
37	Review of procurement policy and system of the organization including imports
38	Review the nature of services and goods procured to ascertain GST impact
39	Verification of procurements made through different class such as registered dealer/manufacturer/service provider /unregistered dealer
40	Verification of purchase and expense invoices on sampling basis to study impact under GST with respect to taxations and credits
41	Verification of expenses liable for GST under RCM, credits in them for reimbursements etc.
42	Verification of financial ledgers where ITC are taken /not taken
43	Verification of treatment of purchase returns to study the possible impact under GST
44	Verification the foreign currency payments to ascertain RCM liability
45	Verification if goods /services are sourced at respective branches to claim credit benefit- ISD registration
46	Review of classification of goods as inputs or capital goods based on accounting
47	Review system of claiming credit and timing involved for taking credit
48	Verification of payments made within stipulated time for taking credit and reversals made if any

Sl. No.	Particulars
49	Review if invoices are addressed to goods /services receiving location
50	Verification of reconciliation of all expenses on which ITC availed been prepared and verified along with annual return
E.	**CLASSIFICATION AND VALUATION**
51	Review the system of recognising sales /services and system of invoicing customers
52	Verification of classification policy of goods/services
53	Review if schedule II to CGST considered for deemed service /goods
54	Review terms of agreement/invoices to ensure description /classification is matching
55	Verification of the rate of tax adopted
56	Review present valuation mechanism adopted for regular sales to customers, supplies to related parties, supplies without monetary consideration
57	Review free supplies if any to study GST impact
58	Review of reimbursements claimed and impact on GST valuation
59	Review if there are advance receipts and its impact on valuation
60	Review valuation adopted for supplies to agents, own branches or godowns
61	Verification of valuation principles followed in case of different sale schemes
62	Verification of valuation adopted in case of recoveries from employees such cab, canteen, telephone
63	Verification of valuation of gifts issued to related parties or others
F.	**FINANCIAL STATEMENTS REVIEW**
64	Review the shareholding pattern by investment by group companies /associated enterprises
65	Review of employee /director/partner benefits provided which could be treated as supplies and have impact under GST
66	Studying the nature of accounts maintained by the organization
67	Review of GSTIN wise books of accounts maintained and accounts related to that for disclosure in GST-9c statement
68	Review of notes to accounts to understand the transactions with related parties, accounting principles etc.

Sl. No.	Particulars
69	Review of debit notes and credit notes which are in line with GST /not in line with GST
70	Verification of adjustments on account of foreign exchange fluctuations for disclosure in GSTR-9c
71	Verification of adjustments on account of advances from customers for disclosure in GSTR-9c
72	Verification of non-operating incomes, impact in GST and disclosure in GSTR-9c
73	Reconciliation of difference between annual return and financial statements for the differences after understanding reasons from management
74	Ascertaining the taxes payable and paid along with interest implication
75	Review the income and customer ledgers, gross trial balance for credits other than payments
G.	**REVIEW OF DOCUMENTATION**
76	Verification of tax invoices issued for time of supply and place of supply on test check
77	Verification of tax invoices or bill of supply issued for disclosure compliance in GST
78	Verification of delivery challans issued for movement of goods for approval, job work etc.
79	Review of various returns filed under GST such as GSTR-1, GSTR-3B and annual return
80	Review of relevant reconciliation statements prepared
81	Review of litigations and related documents as necessary for audit certification
82	Review of various reports generated for compliance such as sales register, credit register, fixed asset register
83	Review of registration certificates and places added
84	Review of documentation at branches or additional places for compliance with GST law
85	Review of export and import documents for taxes paid, zero rate claim, credits claim
86	Review of registration certificate display compliance
87	Taking management representational letters where needed

Sl. No.	Particulars
H.	**REVIEW OF AGREEMENTS /CONTRACTS**
88	Review of agreements /contracts /orders to identify important clauses with customers or vendors which could have major impact under GST
89	Review of agreements to ascertain type of supplies being made
90	Review of agreements to understand the discount policy
91	Review of agreements to understand various sale schemes
92	Review of agreements to understand the time of supply
93	Review of agreements to understand payment terms
I.	**TAX CREDITS**
94	Review nature of expenses incurred to assess GST credits
95	Verification if there are transactions of personal nature where credits being disallowed
96	Verification of credit availment mechanism and suggest on improvement requirement
97	Verification of goods issued free of cost or as samples and GST credit impact
98	Verification of purchases for credit optimization
99	Verification of credit apportionment in case of supply of taxable and exempted supplies
100	Verification of credit availment in case of assets put partially for non-business /non-taxable use
101	Verification of documents based on which credits claimed
102	Verification of credit register and contents
103	Verification of conditions fulfilled for credit claim
104	Verification the reconciliation of the ITC prepared and disclosures made in financials and annual return
J.	**REVIEW OF PERIODICAL RETURNS**
105	Verification of GSTR-3B and GSTR-1 filed along with Annual return filed
106	Ensuring that the disclosures are made in annual return for reconciliation in GSTR-9C
107	Verification of taxes paid at different rates and disclosure
108	Verification of type of taxes paid and disclosure

Sl. No.	Particulars
109	Verification of procurement details disclosed with classification
110	Verification of interest and penalties paid along with disclosure
L.	**CERTIFICATION IN FORM GSTR-9C**
111	Quantification of tax liabilities to be discharged based on information provided by management
112	Quantification of interest liabilities to be discharged based on information provided by management
113	Quantification of wrong /ineligible credits claimed based on information provided by management
114	Reconciliation of details of sales, procurements, expenses, tax, credits between financials and GST annual return
115	Certifying as required including reporting on non-compliances, providing observations, suggestions for improvement in book keeping
116	Obtaining the Management Representation as per ICAI Guidelines

Note: *This program would have to be customised for the industry served. For instance, the program for the bank or insurance entity could be substantially different than the areas of focus covered in the above program.*

Chapter 11

ICAI's Relevant Auditing Standards

11.1 INTRODUCTION

NACAS (National Advisory Committee on Accounting Standard) set up under the Companies Act, 1956 and NFRA (National Financial Reporting Authority) set up under the Companies Act, 2013, are the bodies for the purpose of rendering advise and regulating of compliances with the standards notified in relation to accounting and auditing. Main objectives of NFRA are in addition to rendering advice to the Central Government on the formulation and lying down of accounting policies and accounting standards for adoption by companies or class of companies, regulatory powers to regulate the above issues also. ICAI formulates Auditing Standards for guidance to its members in conducting the audit of certain class of assessees. Further, the following are issued which are required to be followed by the auditors:

- Statements on Standards on Auditing
- Accounting Standards
- Guidance notes issued on auditing, taxation etc

Any deviations from statements and standards by reporting entity are required to be reported by the auditor in the report to enable the users of the financial statements to be aware of such deviations. There are 44 standards as on date and moving forward would be more. Audit is also moving into 100% verification using technology as also real time.

It is important to understand that until 100% audit is feasible, all audits only provide a reasonable assurance that what is stated is accurate. This is irrespective of the certification being "true and fair" as required under the Companies Act or "true and correct" that is required under the Income Tax or GST.

11.2 RELEVANT ICAI AUDIT STANDARDS (SAs)

SAs are prepared based on the International Standards on Auditing (ISA) issued by the International Auditing Practices Committee (IAPC) of the International Federation of Accountants (IFAC). There would be very few departures and carve outs as needed for India. SAs establish standards which are to be complied to ensure that the auditors perform their audit in accordance with the generally accepted auditing practices. For any reason, if a member is unable to perform an audit in accordance with the SAs, his report must draw attention to the material departures there from.

11.3 RELEVANCE OF SAs TO GST AUDIT

SA's are applicable to all kinds of audits whenever an independent audit is carried out and also applicable to GST audit. The relevance of SA's to GST is briefly discussed standard wise, as under:

11.3.1 SA 200 – Overall objectives of the independent auditor and conduct of audit in accordance with standards of auditing

Objective: This standard establishes the independent auditor's overall responsibilities when conducting an audit of financial statements in accordance with SAs. Specifically, it sets out the overall objectives of the independent auditor, and explains the nature and scope of an audit designed to enable the independent auditor to meet those objectives. It also explains the scope, authority and structure of the SAs, and includes requirements establishing the general responsibilities of the independent auditor applicable in all audits, including the obligation to comply with the SAs. The purpose of an audit is to enhance the degree of confidence of intended users in the financial statements. This is achieved by the expression of an opinion by the auditor on whether the financial statements are prepared, in all material respects, in accordance with an applicable financial reporting framework. An audit conducted in accordance with SAs and relevant ethical requirements enables the auditor to form that opinion. One needs to understand the various threats to independence:

- Self interest threat: Auditor having some interest in the business being audited. This could also happen when there is a huge amount outstanding to the auditor from the client.
- Self review threat: Auditor doing the accounting and filing of returns also certifying the accuracy. This is common in smaller entities in India. The regulators recently have been after the big accounting firms who through their surrogate firms also do audit and certification for their client big and small.
- Advocacy threat: Auditor involved in promoting the business of the client may have his objectivity compromised.
- Familiarity threat: Over a period of time the auditor considers that there is no / less distance between the entity.
- Intimidatory threat: Over a period of time the client gets into a position of dictating to the auditor due to errors made and accepted by the auditor or just plain aggressive behaviour.

In all these cases, it would be difficult for the auditor to exercise independence and consequently his report may not be credible or reliable.

Relevance in GST: The standard provides for the auditor's responsibility when conducting an audit. Auditor must perform the audit with integrity, objectivity, professional competence and due care, and confidentiality etc. Further, the auditor is required to maintain an attitude of professional scepticism i.e., a questioning mind, being alert to conditions which may indicate possible misstatement due to error or fraud. The auditor should ensure that he has competent staff having goods knowledge of law and procedures under GST. The audit process adopted to check the compliance under GST is to be documented and the working papers are to be retained as evidence. The GST auditor should be concerned about the GST figures that enter the financial statements / books of accounts. Hence, auditor should devise appropriate audit procedures in order to verify the accuracy and fairness of the figures and disclosures. One of the overall objectives of an auditor must be to obtain a reasonable assurance about whether the financial statements as a whole are free from material misstatement, whether due to fraud or error. This becomes important more so, when the GST auditor places reliance on the GSTIN level financial statements/ trial balance for the conduct of audit.

11.3.2 SA 210 – Agreeing the terms of audit engagement

Objective: The decision as to whether an audit engagement is to be accepted, continued or rejected is to be determined only when the basis upon which it needs to be performed has been agreed:

(1) Establishing whether pre-conditions for an audit are present;

(2) Confirming that there is a common understanding between the management and where appropriate those charged with the governance of the terms of the audit engagement.

Relevance in GST: Auditors would be performing the audit under GST for the first time in 2019 for the years 20171-8 and 2018-19. It is essential that the GST auditor clearly reduces the terms of the engagement in writing with the auditee to avoid any confusions at a later point in time. For example: Auditee may expect auditor to also draw the entire annual returns in Form GSTR 9 within the scope for GST audit. An audit engagement letter must broadly cover the following:

(1) The objective and the scope of the GST audit,

(2) The responsibilities of the auditor*[1] and the management in relation to preparation of statements required under GST and others,

---

1 Includes obtaining sufficient audit evidence, share inherent limitation of sample verification and express that it is only an expression of opinion.

(3) Reference to the expected form and reports to be issued by the auditor and

(4) Professional fees duly agreed upon and accepted,

(5) Limitation on scope etc.

All of these may not be required year after year but needed for the first time or when there is a change in the terms if there is reasonable justification.

11.3.3 SA 220 – Quality control for an audit of financial statements

Objective: This standard deals with the specific responsibilities of the auditor regarding quality control procedures for an audit of financial statements. It also addresses, where applicable, the responsibilities of the engagement quality control reviewer. This SA is to be read in conjunction with relevant ethical requirements.

Relevance in GST: A strong system of regular monitoring, direction and supervision must be exercised by the engagement manager/ partner. Further, a proper audit programme, approach and a detailed checklist can be shared with team as a guidance for smooth conduct of audit in a timely manner. The auditor must ensure that quality control procedures are implemented during the audit and audit complies with professional standards, regulatory and legal requirements. Further, the auditor needs to ensure the following:

(1) Audit work is properly delegated to those who have basic knowledge of GST, various changes therein. Also, a fair knowledge of the industry and the implication/ issues faced by the industry must be also be broadly known to those conducting the audit.

(2) Regular review of the work performed by the engagement manager,

(3) Conclusion is formed on compliance of independent requirement that apply to the audit engagement and

(4) Engagement team has capabilities and competencies to perform the audit engagement.

11.3.4 SA 230 – Audit documentation

Objective: This standard deals with the auditor's responsibility to prepare audit documentation for an audit of financial statements. It is to be adapted as necessary in the circumstances when applied to audits of other historical financial information. The specific documentation requirements of other SAs do not limit the application of this SA. Laws or regulations may establish additional documentation requirements.

Relevance in GST: The observations noted during the audit are to be documented using standardized working papers. The auditor shall document in such a way that an auditor (an individual whether internal or external to the firm who has practical audit experience) having no previous connection with the audit understands the:

(1) Nature, timing and extent of audit procedures (including test of control as well as substantive checks) performed,

(2) The results of audit procedures performed and

(3) The significant matters arising out of the audit and the conclusion reached

Working papers comprises of audit program, internal control questionnaire, audit checklist, query lists and compliance reports from the management and documents taken from auditee would form part of the working papers. System of bifurcation of working papers into permanent and temporary audit file is appreciated. For instance, in GST the entire working papers may be bifurcated into verification of Outward Supplies (Revenues), Input Taxes Credit, Reverse Charge, transitional aspects and other procedural compliances. Further, the other important files such as Offer letter, Engagement Letter, NDA, MRL, Audit Report etc, must also be properly documented and preserved.

11.3.5 SA 240 – The responsibilities relating to fraud in audit of financial statements

Objective: This standard deals with the auditor's responsibilities relating to fraud in an audit of financial statements. Specifically, it expands on how SA 315, "Identifying and Assessing the Risks of Material Misstatement Through Understanding the Entity and Its Environment," and SA 330, "The Auditor's Responses to Assessed Risks," are to be applied in relation to risks of material misstatement due to fraud.

Relevance in GST: In a tax law, there is a very thin line of difference between tax planning and tax evasion. Therefore may be cases of fraud, collusion, evasion, suppression, wilful misstatement etc. The auditor shall consider the impact of the said fraud if any, on the financial statements, tax liability and accordingly adequate reporting must be made in the audit forms to be filed. GST auditor would be responsible to identify and assess the risk of material misstatement due to fraud. Obtain adequate audit evidence for the risk identified and report appropriately to the identified or suspected fraud.

If fraud and errors are detected in the GST area, the possibility of collusion with customers, suppliers, other officials from finance, stores, marketing /sales or even with the GST officials, may be examined. The GST auditor may examine the inherent control weakness which exists in the economy, industry and more so in the reporting company and risk can be evaluated. The indications of intentional act to deceive need to be kept in mind by exercising professional scepticism.

11.3.6 SA 260 – Communication with Those Charged With Governance (TCWG)

Objective: To promote effective two-way communication between the auditor and those charged with governance.

Relevance in GST: The auditor shall communicate with TCWG:

(1) The responsibilities of auditor w.r.t financial statements,

(2) The information required from TCWG relevant to audit and

(3) The timely observations arising from audit that are significant.

It may be possible that in the course of GST audit some critical aspects may have been noted which may have a high impact. This could include any detected fraud, substantial additional tax exposure, basic non-compliances to the law. Based on assessment of the auditor, any such critical observations must be timely communicated with those charged with the governance so that timely action is taken.

11.3.7 SA 265 – Communicating deficiencies in internal control to those charged with the governance

Objective: To promote effective two-way communication between the auditor and those charged with governance.

Relevance in GST: The internal controls maintained by the reporting entity with regard to the GST procedures and operations. These preventive and corrective controls are needed for ensuring completeness of outwards supply, inwards supply, appropriateness of tax paid, tax credit availed. The focus need to be on the process of accounting of transactions, its validity, authorisation, movement reconciliation, how depicted in returns, reconciliation of GSTR 3B to GSTR-1 as well as returns to the books. The flow / process should be examined by the auditor. Any weakness identified, should be communicated to those charged to the governance so that necessary action can be taken by them.

11.3.8 SA 299 – Responsibility of the Joint Auditors

Objective: This standard lays down the principles for effective conduct of joint audit to achieve the overall objectives of the auditor as laid down in SA 200, "Overall Objectives of the Independent Auditor and the conduct of an audit in accordance with Standards on Auditing". In addition to the requirements enunciated in this standard, the joint auditors also need to comply with all the relevant requirements of other applicable standards on auditing.

Relevance in GST: A registered person can appoint two or more chartered accountants as joint auditors under GST for one GSTIN in which case the roles and responsibilities of each of the joint auditors should be clearly defined. The audit report has to be signed by all the joint auditors for one GSTIN. However, they can give their reports separately in case of disagreement. The responsibility of joint auditors under the GST laws would be the same that of audit under the Companies Act or the Income- tax Act.

There could be scenarios where auditor is appointed by the entity for each of its registrations. Here they need to have a common break up for turnover, tax ITC etc location wise duly certified by the management to start their audits.

Further, where a joint auditor comes across a matter relating to GST having an impact at the entire entity level for all of the GST registrations or the matter relating to the areas of responsibility of other joint auditors and which deserve their attention then he should communicate the same to all the other joint auditors in writing.

11.3.9 SA 300 – Planning an Audit of Financial Statements

Objective: This standard deals with the auditor's responsibility to plan an audit of financial statements in an effective manner. This SA is framed in the context of recurring audits. Additional considerations in initial audit engagements are separately identified.

Relevance in GST: Knowledge of industry and business, accounting of transactions, reporting under GST, reconciliations, internal controls of reporting entity are essential to conduct an effective audit. Based on the knowledge so gained, GST auditor has to devise an audit plan. A well-designed audit plan serves as a guide to the audit engagement team to conduct an effective audit. Further, the auditor should obtain an understanding of the significance and complexity of the CIS activities and the availability of data for use in the audit.

11.3.10 SA 315 – Identifying and assessing the risk of material misstatements through understanding the entity and its environment

Objective: This standard deals with the auditor's responsibility to identify and assess the risks of material misstatement in the financial statements, through understanding the entity and its environment, including the entity's internal control. In auditor's opinion, if any of the identified risks is a significant risk, the auditor has to obtain an understanding of the entity's control, including control activities relevant to that risk. During an audit, if the auditor obtains additional audit evidence or new information which changes the level of risk assessed then auditor should revise the assessment and modify the further planned audit procedures accordingly.

Relevance in GST: The auditor shall understand the entities environment and internal control by enquiring with:

(1) Those charged with governance,

(2) Internal audit personnel and

(3) Employees, Legal counsel, Marketing & Sales personnel.

(4) Using analytical procedure,

(5) Observation of entities operations, reports, premises, and

(6) Discussion with management and obtaining knowledge about business

This helps an auditor in identifying and assessing the risk of material misstatements. Further, the above factors become more important in GST audit since auditor would be placing a reliance on the financial statements at GSTIN level which may not be directly correlated with the signed audited financial statements. Further, various reporting of the transactions in the GST environment w.r.t the debit notes, credit notes, internal stock transfers, related party transactions, reconciliations with the returns etc. may not be properly reported and can cause a risk of material misstatements if not timely identified and addressed by the GST auditor.

11.3.11 SA 320 – Materiality in planning and performing an audit

Objective: This standard deals with the auditor's responsibility to apply the concept of materiality in planning and performing an audit of financial statements. SA 450, explains how materiality is applied in evaluating the effect of identified misstatements on the audit and of uncorrected misstatements, if any, on the financial statements.

Relevance in GST: The concept of materiality must be applied by the auditor both in planning and performing the audit, and in evaluating the effect of identified misstatements on the audit and of uncorrected misstatements, if any, on the financial statements and in forming the opinion in the auditor's report.

GST auditor should plan and perform the audit to obtain reasonable assurance as to whether the relevant GSTR 9C is free of material mis-statements. An audit includes examination on a test check basis, using the concept of materiality, evidence supporting the amounts and disclosures in Form GSTR 9C. The auditor must set materiality levels for errors/deviations that may occur in the figures of the GST affecting the financial statements. The materiality level set can be revised as the audit progresses. The audit report should contain the areas of weaknesses that effects GST compliances etc., which can result in material errors or irregularities. Immaterial errors can be ignored unless they become material due to recurrence or in combination with similar errors.

Misstatements, including omissions, are considered to be material if they, individually or in the aggregate, could reasonably be expected to influence the economic decisions of users taken on the basis of the financial statements.

Further, judgments about materiality are made in the light of surrounding circumstances, and are affected by the size or nature of a misstatement, or a combination of both.

It is important to understand that the verification needs to be more in case of certifying the "correctness" of the financial statements.

11.3.12 SA 330 – The auditors responses to assessed risks

Objective: This standard deals with the auditor's responsibility to design and implement responses to the risks of material misstatement identified and assessed by the auditor in accordance with SA 315, "Identifying and Assessing Risks of Material Misstatement Through Understanding the Entity and Its Environment" in a financial statement audit.

The objective of the auditor is to obtain sufficient appropriate audit evidence about the assessed risks of material misstatement, through designing and implementing appropriate responses to those risks.

Relevance in GST: Auditor is responsible to design and implement responses to risk assessed during the audit. The responses include:

(1) Emphasizing to the team to maintain professional scepticism

(2) Providing more supervision

(3) Assigning more experienced staff or those with specialized skills or using experts

(4) Making changes to the nature, timing and extent of audit procedures

(5) Widening the scope of audit

11.3.13 SA 402 – Audit considerations relating to an entity using a service organization

Objective: This standard deals with the user auditor's responsibility to obtain sufficient appropriate audit evidence when a user entity uses the services of one or more service organisations.

Relevance in GST: It may be possible that the work in respect of accounting including preparation and filing of GST returns is outsourced by the auditee to any third party service organization. In such a situation, the auditor has to perform the following audit procedures to obtain an understanding of the services provided by service organization:

(1) The nature of services provided by service organization and the importance of those services to the user entity

(2) The materiality of those transactions provided by service organization to the user entity

(3) The degree of interaction between the activities of service organization and user entity

(4) The nature of relationship between user entity and service organization

11.3.14 SA 450 – Evaluation of misstatements identified during the audit

Objective: This standard deals with the auditor's responsibility to evaluate the effect of identified misstatements on the audit and of uncorrected misstatements, if any, on the financial statements. SA 700 deals with the auditor's responsibility, in forming an opinion on the financial statements, to conclude whether reasonable assurance has been obtained about whether the financial statements as a whole are free from material misstatement. The auditor's conclusion required by SA 700 (Revised) takes into account the auditor's evaluation of uncorrected misstatements, if any, on the financial statements, in accordance with this SA. SA 3202 deals with the auditor's responsibility to apply the concept of materiality appropriately in planning and performing an audit of financial statement.

Relevance in GST: The auditor shall accumulate the misstatements identified during the GST audit and determine whether the audit plan and strategy requires revision based on:

i) The nature of identified misstatements and circumstances of their occurrence may indicate that the other misstatements may occur; and

ii) The aggregate of misstatements accumulated approached materiality.

11.3.15 SA 500 – Audit Evidence

Objective: This standard explains what constitutes audit evidence in an audit of financial statements, and deals with the auditor's responsibility to design and perform audit procedures to obtain sufficient appropriate audit evidence to be able to draw reasonable conclusions on which to base the auditor's opinion. This SA is applicable to all the audit evidence obtained during the course of the audit.

Relevance in GST: Various internal and external evidences needs to be obtained by the auditor in order to a reasonable conclusion. Various internal evidences may include agreement with supplier/ customers, copy of the invoice issued, working papers based on which various returns have been filed, various accounting entries passed, GL ledgers etc. Further, various external evidences would include letters/ correspondences received from the departmental. Delivery challans, supplier and customer correspondences etc. The management representation duly signed is an important indication to management on its responsibility and works as an effective safeguard to the auditor.

It is important to note that an audit does not guarantee that all material misstatements would be detected because of the following inherent limitations such as audit evidence available is persuasive than conclusive, use of professional judgment in gathering and evaluating evidence and forming conclusions based on that evidence.

11.3.16 SA 505 – External Confirmations

Objective: This standard deals with the auditor's use of external confirmation procedures to obtain audit evidence in accordance with the requirements of SA 330 and SA 500. Audit evidence is more reliable when it is obtained from independent sources outside the entity. Further, audit evidence obtained directly by the auditor is more reliable than audit evidence obtained indirectly or by inference.

Relevance in GST: Auditor can use the GSTR 2A data that is generated online by the GST portal and based on the materiality, auditor can obtain external confirmations from the vendors confirming filing of GST returns or payment of taxes etc. Further, in case the rate of tax is determined by the auditee based on the customer's PO, then confirmation of the correctness of the tax rate derived can be obtained from the customers. External confirmations can also be obtained by the auditor from the job worker to confirm that goods are returned back within the statutory time-limit. The system of confirmation of balance of the debtors/ creditors could confirm the completeness of recording where there appear to be control weaknesses.

11.3.17 SA 510 – Initial audit engagements – Opening

Objective: This standard deals with the auditor's responsibilities relating to opening balances when conducting an initial audit engagement. In addition to financial statement amounts, opening balances include matters requiring disclosure that existed at the beginning of the period, such as contingencies and commitments. When the financial statements include comparative financial information, the requirements and guidance in SA 710 also apply. SA 300 includes additional requirements and guidance regarding activities prior to starting an initial audit.

Relevance in GST: The auditor shall verify the opening balances of accounts pertaining to GST such as unutilized balances in Input Tax Credit, credits transferred through Form TRAN1 and the same can be reconciled with returns filed prior to the GST period under the erstwhile tax laws. Further, spill over transactions must be looked into by the auditor to verify correctness and completeness in the payment of taxes under the GST law as compared to the earlier laws based on the principles of Time of Supply. In case of any deviations, the risk involved in the assignment should be judged and decision should be taken regarding continuation of agreement.

11.3.18 SA 520 – Analytical procedures

Objective: This standard deals with the auditor's use of analytical procedures as substantive procedures ("substantive analytical procedures"), and as procedures near the end of the audit that assist the auditor when forming an overall conclusion on the financial statements. The use of analytical procedures as risk assessment procedures is dealt with in SA 315. SA 330 includes requirements and guidance regarding the nature, timing and extent of audit procedures in response to assessed risks; these audit procedures may include substantive analytical procedures.

Relevance in GST: In the course of performing GST audit, auditor would need to perform various analytical procedures which includes comparison of ratios such as cash to credit ratios, ITC to procurement, tax to turnover etc. Differences in various reconciliations must be analytically resolved, correctness of tax rates, timely payment of taxes, computation of interest, eligibility of credits, place of supply adopted etc. needs to be analytically verified to ensure its completeness, correctness and timeliness of various compliances.

11.3.19 SA 530 – Audit Sampling

Objective: The objective of the auditor while using audit sampling is to provide a reasonable basis for the auditor to draw conclusions about the population from which the sample is selected. The choice of the sampling method whether it is block sampling, haphazard sampling, stratified/ non stratified sampling, random sampling, cluster sampling or monetary value weighted sampling would be the choice of the auditor considering the entity. In the event that 100% verification is possible there is no need of using this standard.

It is a worrying fact that majority of auditors today use non statistical sampling which may not protect them in case of any fraud detected at later years.

Relevance in GST: The level and depth of GST audit is very high due to the need of certifying the "true and correct" nature of the statements. The auditor needs to select a sample basis and sample size considering the factors like number of transactions in the review period, different nature of transactions, risk involved (SA 315) etc. Sample selections must be done in a standardized manner ensuring the sample selected represents the whole population. Further, the following shall be documented as audit evidence:

(1) Sample selected (detailed) for verification of ITC etc.

(2) Manner in which sample is selected

(3) % of sample in whole population etc. [By ensuring coverage of 70-80% in value terms some comfort is possible]

In case of ERP based accounting, the inbuilt audit tools need to be understood, selected and used.

Having regard to the test/sample nature of an audit, there is an unavoidable risk that even some material misstatements and to a lesser extent error, if either exists, may remain undetected. An auditor is not expected to reduce the sampling risk to zero.

11.3.20 SA 550 – Related parties

Objective: This standard deals with the auditor's responsibilities regarding related party relationships and transactions when performing an audit of financial statements. Specifically, it expands on how SA 315, SA 330 and SA 240 are to be applied in relation to risks of material misstatement associated with related party relationships and transactions.

Relevance in GST: The transactions with related parties holds utmost importance in the context of GST audit. Since, the special valuation mechanism has been provided in the GST law for all related party transactions and in some cases the related party transactions are subjected to levy of GST even if no consideration is separately charged for the supply of goods or service. Further, the meaning of the term 'related parties' is wide to cover various interconnected undertakings in so much so that even employer and employees are considered as a related parties. The transactions where there is no consideration could also be a supply if with related parties. Therefore, auditor is required to identify and evaluate the transactions entered by the auditee with related parties, the levy, valuation adopted by the auditee. Further, focus must also be paid to the transactions with the distinct persons the taxation principles of which have been kept on par with the related parties.

11.3.21 SA 560 – Subsequent events

Objective: This standard deals with the auditor's responsibilities relating to subsequent events in an audit of financial statements. It does not deal with matters relating to the auditor's responsibilities for other information obtained after the date of the auditor's report, which are addressed in SA 720 (Revised) However, such other information may bring to light a subsequent event that is within the scope of this SA.

Relevance in GST: The subsequent events holds very high relevance in the context of GST audit as it is possible that certain transactions for which non-compliance is noted in FY 2017-18 or 2018-19 have been fully or partially rectified in the subsequent year. For example: In case auditee has availed any ineligible input tax credit in FY 17-18, then it may be possible that the same was later identified and reversed by the auditor in the returns filed by them in FY 2018-19. Therefore, before reporting any non-compliance on account of GST audit, it is important that the auditor also review the subsequent events to avoid incorrect and improper reporting. Further, there may be many other cases of subsequent events such as missed credits, confirmation/rejection of sale of goods sent on approval basis, GST demands raised for the past period etc, goods returned from job work after the statutory time-limit, payment not made on 180 days etc.

11.3.22 SA 580 – Written Representations

Objective: This standard deals with the auditor's responsibility to obtain written representations from management and, where appropriate, those charged with governance.

Relevance in GST: Written representation can be obtained from the management related to the oral confirmations given by them. Such written representations shall be documented as audit evidence and can be mentioned as limitations in the GST report. The matters requiring written representations is required to be judged by the auditor as the same cannot be taken as defence for all the areas. Third party evidence is more reliable as long as it is signed by the authorised person.

Further, this standard requires the auditor, at the conclusion of the audit, should obtain representation letters from management about these matters. The responses to those inquiries, the written representations, comprise the evidential matters that the auditor will rely upon in forming an opinion on the GSTR 9C or other reports and certifications. For instance, auditor needs to compile the various factors noted during the process of the audit, challenges faced, reliance placed etc. and a proper Management Representation Letter i.e. MRL must be obtained.

On a practical note this should be obtained before the signing of the auditor report.

11.3.23 SA 600 – Using the work of another auditor

Objective: When the auditor delegates work to qualified consultants or uses work performed by other auditors and experts, he would continue to be responsible for forming and expressing his opinion on the financial information. However, he would be entitled to rely on work performed by others, provided he exercises adequate skill and care and is not aware of any reason to believe that he should not have so relied. There should be enough evidence to prove adequacy of the work done by the other auditor.

Relevance in GST: GST auditor can refer to the report made by other auditor and check whether the significant findings, qualification, reservations, emphasis of matter, notes made have any impact on GST. Certification in cases where the reconciliation statement (FORM GSTR-9C) is drawn up by a person other than the person who had conducted the audit of the accounts, the GST auditor has to use the audited financial statements of company auditor for reconciliation with GSTR 9 and certification of report purpose etc.

11.3.24 SA 610 – Using the work of Internal Auditors

Objective: This standard deals with the external auditor's responsibilities if using the work of internal auditors. This includes

(a) Using the work of the internal audit function in obtaining audit evidence and

(b) Using internal auditors to provide direct assistance under the direction, supervision and review of the external auditor.

Relevance in GST: The report issued by the internal auditor can be referred to understand the key areas which requires in depth examination. Further, any weakness in the system that has impact on GST can be identified and suggestions if any can be given. Extent of reliance that the GST auditor can place on the various preventive, detective and corrective controls as highlighted by the internal auditor would determine the extent of substantive and compliance procedures that the GST auditor is expected to incorporate in the course of GST audit. Auditor must also see if there is any Information Systems audit undertaken as this would provide GST auditor with the level of reliance that can be placed on the various reports generated from the ERP system and other IT/ accounting tools.

11.3.25 SA 620 – Using the work of expert

Objective: This standard deals with the auditor's responsibilities regarding the use of an individual or organisation's work in a field of expertise other than accounting or auditing, when that work is used to assist the auditor in obtaining sufficient appropriate audit evidence.

Relevance in GST: Work of another expert can be used in forming conclusions related to GST. Owing to the volume of transactions, interpretation of data extracted from JSON or excel files, if specialised skills are needed by the auditors, they should seek help from professionals either from the auditors' staff or from another professional/expert. In case of such a professional is required, the auditors should obtain sufficient appropriate audit evidence for such help by using this standard. This may include legal opinions taken from an advocate/ other CA's etc. in understanding a term, completion certificate given by the certified chartered engineer in case of construction industry etc.

11.3.26 SA 700 – Forming an opinion and reporting on financial statements

Objective: This standard deals with the auditor's responsibility to form an opinion on the financial statements. It also deals with the form and content of the auditor's report issued as a result of an audit of financial statements.

Relevance in GST: Decision in relation to extent of reliance can be made on financial statements may be taken on referring to the opinion formed by the auditor. This can be used in determining the risk involved for performing the GST audit. Accordingly, GST auditor can report in accordance with the format notified.

Part B of GSTR 9C required GST Auditor to issue a certificate along with the reconciliation statement in Part A. It may be noted that Audit certification also requires GST auditor to confirm the examination of financials and review of books of accounts maintained. Accordingly he has to issue the audit report that the particulars given in Form No. 9C are true and correct with opinion having observations/ qualifications, if any.

11.3.27 SA 701 – Communicating Key Audit Matters in the Independent Auditor's Report

Objective: The objectives of the auditor are to determine key audit matters and, having formed an opinion on the financial statements, communicate those matters by describing them in the auditor's report. The purpose of communicating key audit matters is to enhance the communicative value of the auditor's report by providing greater transparency about the audit that was performed. It provides additional information to intended users of the financial statements to assist them in understanding those matters that, in the auditor's professional judgment, were of most significance in the audit of the financial statements of the current period.

Relevance in GST: Key audit matters are those matters that, in the auditor's professional judgment, were of most significance in the GST Audit however it may not require auditor to modify the opinion. The adequacy of the description of a key audit matter is a matter of professional judgment. Audit documentation prepared during the GST audit can also be useful to the auditor in formulating the description of a key audit matter. For example, written communications, or the auditor's documentation of oral communications, with those charged with governance and other audit documentation provides a useful basis for the auditor's communication in the GSTR 9C.

Illustration could be: Auditor observes that the ITC credit is not clearly available for cement and steel used in foundation/ structure related to the lifts and hoists in factory and office building. Management take an expert opinion and opine that it is available. ITC amount is Rs. 5 Crores and auditor feels that there could be a dispute. This matter is not required to be qualified in the audit report but maybe shared with the stakeholders in the financial audit report.

11.3.28 SA 705 – Modifications to the Opinion in the Independent Auditor's Report

Objective: This standard deals with the auditor's responsibility to issue an appropriate report in circumstances when, in forming an opinion in accordance with SA 700 (Revised), the auditor concludes that a modification to the auditor's opinion on the financial statements is necessary. This SA also deals with how the form and content of the auditor's report is affected when the auditor expresses a modified opinion.

The objective of the auditor is to express clearly an appropriately modified opinion on the financial statements that are necessary when:

(a) The auditor concludes, based on the audit evidence obtained, that the financial statements as a whole are not free from material misstatement; or

(b) The auditor is unable to obtain sufficient appropriate audit evidence to conclude that the financial statements as a whole are free from material misstatement

Relevance in GST: It may happen that while conducting GST audit, auditor is not been presented with adequate information which is necessary for completing the Audit or there is adequate information which clearly states that GST returns filed are not free from material misstatements. Auditor in such a situation shall form a modified opinion and report the same in GSTR 9C.

The auditor shall express an adverse opinion when the auditor, having obtained sufficient appropriate audit evidence, concludes that misstatements, individually or in the aggregate, are both material and pervasive to the financial statements.

The auditor shall disclaim an opinion when the auditor is unable to obtain sufficient appropriate audit evidence on which to base the opinion, and the auditor concludes that the possible effects on the financial statements of undetected misstatements, if any, could be both material and pervasive.

There are also few other standards such as SA 250, SA 501, SA 540, SA 570, SA 706, SA 710, SA 720, SA 800, SA 805, SA 810 which could be referred for the purpose of audit.

[Detailed standards provided in Appendices]

Chapter 12

ICAI's Relevant Accounting Standards

12.1 INTRODUCTION

The ICAI has issued various accounting standards for maintaining uniformity in the preparation and presentation of the accounts of various entities. Accounting standards are policy documents developed by accounting body, ICAI, in respect of presentation and disclosure of accounting transactions in the financial statements. The accounting standards reduce accounting alternatives, thereby enhancing the comparability of financial statements of different enterprises. In case of deviations from the standards, the auditor is required to disclose the same in the audit report so that the users of such statements are aware of such deviations.

Indian Accounting Standards (Ind AS) are similar to the International Financial Reporting Standards (IFRS). National Advisory Committee on Accounting Standards (NACAS) recommends these accounting standards to the Ministry of Corporate Affairs (MCA). MCA notifies the accounting standards applicable for companies in India. Till date MCA has notified 41 Ind AS. These are required to be followed by certain entities from FY 2016-17 and gradually by other entities in subsequent financial years.*[1]

12.2 RELEVANCE OF ACCOUNTING STANDARDS TO GST AUDIT

In addition to knowledge of provisions of GST law, an auditor conducting audit under GST also requires knowledge of the accounting standards and the accounting policies adopted by the registered person, which would affect the GST audit to the extent that they have a bearing on the disclosure of the balance in the financial statements. The following accounting standards can be referred for the purpose of GST audit:

12.2.1 AS 1 – Disclosure of Accounting Policies (Ind AS 1)

AS 1 deals with disclosure of significant accounting policies followed in the preparation and presentation of financial statements. A fundamental accounting assumption in any financial statement is based on going concern, consistency and

1 The ICAI has uploaded entire Ind AS on its web site which should be followed by those who prepare and verify the accounts.

accrual system concepts. Under Ind AS, excise duty was included in the revenue, since it is a (manufacture) production-based tax. GST is not included in revenue, because it is levied at the time of sales. GST is a destination-based tax, which is levied at the point of supply. Hence, it is likely that revenue would not be presented including GST. For the first three months of 2017-18 revenue would be presented at Gross for Excise Less Excise Duty paid, and for the subsequent period it would be shown only Net, which would bring some distortion in reading of the numbers for the users and also comparative for the previous years would be different. As stated above, consistency in the disclosure is the key to any accounting policy. In this context it is to be noted that that the various tax treatment and disclosures such as grouping of credits in current assets, tax payable in current liabilities, passing of accounting entries pertaining to reverse charge at each transactional level, timely passing of utilisation entries and most importantly the balance of input tax credits as shown in the financial statements must match with that as appearing in the electronic credit ledger. Clear accounting policies in respect of disclosure of taxation must be laid out and the same must be consistently followed.

12.2.2 AS 2 – Valuation of Inventories (Ind AS 2)

A primary issue in accounting for inventories is the determination of the value at which inventories are carried in the financial statements until the related revenues are recognised. This standard deals with the determination of such value, including the ascertainment of cost of inventories and any write-down thereof to net realisable value. Inventories are to be valued at cost after reduction of input tax credits, which are later adjusted with output tax liability payable to the taxing authorities. Hence, the value of inventory does not include, input tax credit of GST paid on purchases.

Valuation of inventory may require inclusion of GST paid on procurement, in cases where input tax credit is restricted. Certain instances where input tax credit is not available are:

- Services/goods used for personal purposes;
- Restricted credits u/s 17(5) of the CGST Act;
- Goods/services used for exempted supply.

Thus, there should be an evaluative process to determine which credit is eligible and which one becomes part of the cost of inventory, as per the applicable accounting standard. Transitional credit taken on stocks can be a determinative factor of the inventory valuation, since many companies do not have a mechanism for valuation of inventory in the middle of the year i.e. June 30, 2017, when the GST was implemented, therefore a proper certification from the professional as to the valuation of the inventory needs to be done, on the basis of which the transitional credit could be availed, more so for the goods reported as in WIP stage. This is an important aspect since it evidence the basis on which the credits were taken in the transitional stage, which would attract many eyeballs if proper records/ documentation is not in place, resultantly which could also invite unnecessary litigation. Further, in case where any credits earlier availed has been later reversed in the subsequent financial year, either *suo-motu* or in the course of audit, then the impact of such reversal on the inventory valuation must be looked at.

12.2.3 AS 3 – Cash Flow Statements (Ind AS 7)

Information of the cash flows of an enterprise is useful in providing users of financial statements a basis to assess the ability of the enterprise to generate cash and cash equivalents and the need of the enterprise to utilise those cash flows. The economic decisions which are to be taken by the users, require an evaluation of the ability of an enterprise to generate cash and cash equivalents, and the timing and certainty of their generation.

Cash Flow Statement reflects various sources of generation of cash flows and its utilization during the financial year. In general, GST is required to be paid on all supplies for which consideration is received/receivable. Hence, sources of cash generation could be helpful in determining whether the entity has discharged GST on all taxable supplies or any transaction has been missed to be reported under GST.

12.2.4 AS 4 – Contingencies and Events occurring after the Balance Sheet Date (Ind AS 10)

Events which occur between the balance sheet date and the date on which the financial statements are approved, may indicate the need for adjustments to assets and liabilities as at the balance sheet date or may require disclosure.

Adjustments to assets and liabilities are required for events occurring after the balance sheet date that provide additional information materially affecting the determination of the amounts relating to conditions existing at the balance sheet date. For example, an adjustment may be made for a loss on a trade receivable account which is confirmed by the insolvency of a customer which occurs after the balance sheet date.

In case of goods sent to job worker before balance sheet date and not received/sold directly subsequently, within specified period (inputs within 1 year and capital goods within 3 years), the input tax credit availed on the same is required to be paid. In this scenario, disclosure is to be given by way of a foot note in the financial statements. Sale on approval basis etc. Further, accounting effect must also be given for reversal of credits on account of payments not made to vendors within 180 days which comes to the knowledge later in the subsequent financial year, for reversal/ reclaim or finalization in the computation of the common credits provisionally reversed earlier. There may be many other transactions which would have an impact on accounting in the financial year but which are known subsequent to the end of the financial year.

12.2.5 AS 5 – Net profit or Loss for the Period, Prior Period Items and Changes in Accounting Policies (Ind AS 8)

The objective of this standard is to prescribe the classification and disclosure of certain items in the statement of profit and loss so that all enterprises prepare and present such a statement on a uniform basis. This enhances the comparability of the financial statements of an enterprise over time and with the financial statements of other enterprises. Accordingly, this standard requires the classification and disclosure of extraordinary and prior period items, and the disclosure of certain items within profit or loss from ordinary activities. It also specifies the accounting treatment for changes in accounting estimates and the disclosures to be made in the financial statements regarding changes in accounting policies. In case where the GST is expensed-off (i.e., credit is not availed) at the time of accounting invoice, availment as credit is possible subsequently according to this standard. Effectively, profit increases to this extent in the current period, where input tax credit for the input received in the previous year is availed in the subsequent year. In all cases where the transitional credits that were expensed off in the past have been availed, separate reporting for the same is needed. Further, any tax liability of the past is known in the current financial year which has a substantial impact on the net profits/ losses, then same must be separately reported.

12.2.6 AS 7 – Accounting for Construction Contracts (Ind AS 11)

The objective of this standard is to prescribe the accounting treatment of revenue and costs associated with construction contracts. The nature of the activity undertaken in construction contracts, the date at which the contract activity is entered into and the date when the activity is completed usually fall into different accounting periods. Therefore, the primary issue in accounting for construction contracts is the allocation of contract revenue and contract costs to the accounting periods in which construction work is performed. This standard uses the recognition criteria established in the framework for the preparation and presentation of financial statements to determine when contract revenue and contract costs should be recognised as revenue and expenses in the statement of profit and loss. It also provides practical guidance on the application of these criteria.

GST law provides for the separate tax treatment for long term contracts of supply of goods or services under the concept of 'Continuous supply of goods/ services', and accordingly the time of supply is suitably adjusted to collect the taxes at various events agreed upon as milestone of payments with the customers in a staggered manner, upto the point of completion of the contract. This diverse treatment of disclosures of revenue in the books as per this standard and payment of taxes based on the principles of time of supply puts substantial onus on the GST auditor to properly gauge the reasons of differences, reconcile and report the same in Form GSTR 9C.

12.2.7 AS 9 – Revenue Recognition (Ind AS 18)

The GST component collected from customers does not form part of turnover that is disclosed in Profit or Loss statement. Income received or receivable in or in relation to supply requires discharge of GST.

The concept of time of supply (i.e. invoice raised or payment made whichever is earlier) will decide when revenue will be recognised under GST and liability to be discharged, which might lead to a situation wherein GST would be paid on the agreement as per the date of invoice, but the revenue would not be recognized in the books because the customer may not have obtained benefits from the agreement yet.

GST would be required to be discharged on such supplies, but would not be recognised as revenue in the financial statement. As per Schedule I of the CGST Act- GST is leviable on certain transactions even if such transactions are made without consideration - like supply of goods from principal to agent, disposal of business assets, supplies to related parties etc. Under Ind AS transactions without any consideration would not form a part of the financial statements and would be treated as a non-balance sheet item / off-Balance sheet item.

Sale of Goods: Time of sale shall be construed when the seller has transferred the property in the goods to the buyer for a consideration. The transfer of property in goods, in most cases, results in, or coincides with, the transfer of significant risks and rewards of ownership to the buyer. However, there may be situations where the transfer of property in goods does not coincide with the transfer of significant risks and rewards of ownership. Revenue in such situations is recognized at the time of transfer of significant risks and rewards of ownership to the buyer.

Rendering of Services: Revenue from service transactions is usually recognized when the service is performed, either by the proportionate completion method or by the completed service contract method.

(a) Proportionate completion method— Performance consists of the execution of more than one act. Revenue is recognized proportionately by reference to the performance of each act. For all practical purposes, when services are provided by an indeterminate number of acts over a specific period of time, revenue is recognized on a straight-line basis over the specific period unless there is evidence that some other better method better represents the pattern of performance.

(b) Completed service contract method—Performance consists of the execution of a single action. Alternatively, services performed in more than a single act, and the services yet to be performed, are significant in relation to the transaction taken as a whole, such performance could not be deemed to be completed until the execution of those actions. The completed service contract method is relevant to these patterns of performance and accordingly revenue is recognized when the sole or final act takes place and the service becomes chargeable.

Further, valuation of contracts under Ind AS might differ in certain aspects from the GST Laws. For example, the contract value may not include any duties and taxes paid which is refundable, interest on delayed payment, expenditure incurred by the recipient etc. These differences might lead to differences in valuation of contracts. Accounting and financial reporting is one such aspect which needs to be analysed carefully.

Transitional provisions under GST: The transitional provisions in section 142(1) of the CGST Act, state that a registered person under the GST would be required to raise a tax invoice for the goods returned by him to the supplier, if such goods were bought by him in the pre-GST regime. Thus, a registered tax payer under the GST would be obligated to raise a tax invoice and the same would form a part of his turnover under the GST laws. However, as per the Ind AS while reporting it in the financial statements it would be treated as a reduction from purchases and not as turnover.

12.2.8 AS 10 – Property, Plant and Equipment (Ind AS 16)

The objective of this standard is to prescribe the accounting treatment for property, plant and equipment so that users of the financial statements can discern information about investment made by an enterprise in its property, plant and equipment and the changes in such investment. The principal issues in accounting for property, plant and equipment are the recognition of the assets, the determination of their carrying amounts and the depreciation charges and impairment losses to be recognised in relation to them.

The amount capitalized to asset does not include creditable taxes i.e., GST paid on capital assets can be availed, provided the same is not capitalized and depreciation is not claimed on the same. In nutshell, ITC shall not be allowed on the tax component of the cost of capital goods, if depreciation on such tax component has been claimed under the Income Tax Act, 1961. Further, the cost of fixed asset comprises of its purchase price including import duties and other non - refundable taxes or levies and any directly attributable cost of bringing the asset to its working condition for its intended use. Administration and other general overhead expenses are usually excluded from the cost of fixed assets because they do not relate to a specific fixed asset. However, in some circumstances, such expenses as are specifically attributable to the construction of a project or to the acquisition of a fixed asset or bringing it to its working condition, may be included as part of the cost of the construction project or as part of the cost of the fixed asset. Many tax compliant companies ensure that the civil, electrical, structures used in the foundation related to the plant and machinery is capitalised as P&M. This enables ITC credit on cement, steel etc. used for erection.

12.2.9 AS11 – The effects of changes in foreign exchange rates

An enterprise may carry on activities involving foreign exchange in two ways. It may have transactions in foreign currencies or it may have foreign operations. In order to include foreign currency transactions and foreign operations in the financial statements of an enterprise, transactions must be expressed in the enterprise's reporting currency and the financial statements of foreign operations must be translated into the enterprise's reporting currency.

This standard prescribes the foreign exchange rate to be used in case of transactions in foreign currencies. However, foreign éxchange conversion rate to be considered for GST is prescribed in valuation rules. Accordingly, the rate to be used is as:

(1) In case of supply of goods – as notified by CBIC.

(2) In case of supply of services – as per generally accepted accounting standards.

Different exchange rates may be applied for supply of goods for paying tax under the GST regime and in accounting valuation. This can be one of the reasons for turnover differences in GSTR 9C between financial statements and GSTR 9. A comparative statement for difference in foreign exchange as per Rule 34 of the CGST Rules and AS11 should be made, and difference in turnovers because of difference in foreign exchange rates would be reported in GSTR 9C. The difference between the exchange rate as per CBIC and that finally realised would not be having any impact in either form 9 or 9C.

12.2.10 AS 12 – Accounting for Government Grants (Ind AS 20)

This standard deals with accounting for Government grants. Government grants are sometimes called by other names such as subsidies, reimbursements, cash incentives, duty drawbacks, etc. The Government provides subsidies to certain industries /projects, in the prices charged for supply.

Section 15(2)(e) of the CGST Act, 2017 the value of supply shall include subsidies directly linked to the price excluding subsidies provided by the Central Government and State Governments. By this it may be inferred that Government Grants would not be treated as revenue for the purpose of GST.

12.2.11 AS 18 – Related Party Disclosures(Ind AS 24)

The objective of this standard is to establish requirements for disclosure of:

(a) related party relationships; and

(b) transactions between a reporting enterprise and its related parties.

This standard should be applied in reporting related party relationships and transactions between a reporting enterprise and its related parties. The requirements of this standard apply to the financial statements of each reporting enterprise as also to consolidated financial statements presented by a holding company.

Related party as per the Accounting Standard 18 and as defined under the valuation provision under the GST may not be the same. However, the GST auditor can refer notes to accounts to identify possible related party transactions from valuation perspective. The auditor may check whether auditee has carried out transactions with the related party as per the valuation rule 28 or not. Further, the valuation to be adopted is open market value (except where recipient unit is eligible to avail input tax credit) as per GST valuation provisions.

The transactions with related parties have importance in the context of GST audit. Since, the special valuation mechanism has been provided in the GST law for all related party transactions and in some cases the related party transactions are subjected to levy of GST even if no consideration is separately charged. Further, the meaning of the term 'related parties' is wide to cover various interconnected undertakings in so much so that even employer and employees are considered as a related parties. Therefore, auditor is required to identify and evaluate the transactions entered by the auditee with related parties, the levy, valuation adopted by the auditee. Further, focus must also be paid to the transactions with the distinct persons the taxation principles of which have been kept on par with the related parties.

12.2.12 AS 29 – Provisions, contingent liabilities and assets (Ind AS 37)

The objective of this standard is to ensure that appropriate recognition criteria and measurement bases are applied to provisions and contingent liabilities and that sufficient information is disclosed in the notes to the financial statements to enable users to understand their nature, timing and amount. The objective of this standard is also to lay down appropriate accounting for contingent assets.

A contingent liability is a present obligation with uncertainties about either the probability of outflow of resources or the amount of the outflows, and possible obligations whose existence is uncertain. A contingent asset is a possible asset whose existence is uncertain.

Auditor is duty bound to understand the possible outcome of various litigations and pending refund claims of the entity and accordingly based on the communication with the legal counsels handling such cases. A reasonable view of the possible outcome of such cases must be arrived at and in case the possible outcome of such litigation is not favourable, then appropriate reporting of the same as contingent liabilities must be made in the audited financial statements.

12.2.13 AS 24 – Discontinuing operations

Disclosure of discontinuing operations is to be included in financial statements. Transfer of business assets is a deemed supply and GST is to be paid on the same.

12.3 CONCLUSION

The following of the auditing as well as the accounting standards by the professional conducting the annual audit would improve quality of the audit and its effectiveness. More importantly it can add value in terms of ITC and act as a safeguard to the auditor.

Chapter 13

Draft – Ethical issues and guidance for audit under Section 35(5) of CGST Act, 2017

The Institute of Chartered Accountant of India (ICAI) is working on a guidance note on ethical standards in conduct of the reconciliation statement and its certification, which touches on the basic principles to be followed, precautions to be taken in assignment including the important ethical standards to be considered during GST audit assignment.

Please refer Appendix 22 at the end of the book.

Chapter 14

Internal Control

14.1 INTRODUCTION

In any organisation, internal controls play a very important role in the management of the organisation. Internal control ensures accountability, responsibility and is an effective and systematic management tool to use resources optimally. The internal controls include:

(i) "Control Environment" which includes the factors such as structure and method of assigning responsibility and authority, operating style, integrity, ethical values etc.

(ii) "Control Activities" which means the policies and procedures in order to achieve the specific objectives of the management in addition to the control environment.

Implementing an Internal control is the primary duty of the management and auditors could advise on improvement. The knowledge of GST and allied laws should be an essential precondition which would apply to the auditor.

The internal control questionnaire [ICQ], especially for compliance with the developing GST law (which may be modified with the amendments in the first year or so) can be a useful tool. This would indicate the overall as well as area wise checks and balances in place.

14.2 ANSWERS GIVEN TO THE QUESTIONS

This answering of the ICQ provides a better picture of the likely compliance with the GST statute by the assessee. The Lack of control or ineffective internal control would indicate to the management that appropriate remedial action is needed. The strong control could lead to limited sample checks.

Documentation (capture, tagging, reference, and storage) has assumed greater importance now with the increased use of ever-changing information technology.

Standards on Internal Audit (SIA) – 12 "Internal Control Evaluation" issued by the Institute of Chartered Accountants of India provides the standards and guidance on the procedures to be followed by the internal auditor in evaluating the system of internal control in an entity and for communicating weakness therein to those charged with governance.

The auditor should obtain an understanding of the internal control procedures sufficient to develop an audit plan. In order to obtain the understanding of internal control procedure, the auditor may provide an internal control questionnaire to the management before the commencement of the audit. He may examine the available answers and with the help of management fill in those which are not answered. Filling this at a later date or during the conduct of audit is not a good practice. The answers which are negative may need to be examined in depth further. There would be a need to do more substantive verification in areas of weaknesses identified to be included in the audit plan.

Further, the standard provides that while evaluating the internal control the auditor should consider the following aspects:

(1) Ascertain the mission statement, goals and objectives of the entity;

(2) Assess the entity level risk;

(3) Assess the activity level/process level risks;

(4) Prepare the business control sheet for each significant activity in each department/function and ascertain the documentation maintained and the effectiveness of the controls;

(5) Prioritize the activities which are most critical for the success of each department/function;

(6) Ascertain the area where there are no controls or inadequate controls from the business control sheets. This process is called "control gap" analysis.

In order to evaluate the effectiveness of the internal control system in the organisation the process of "Test of Controls" has to be performed. Tests of control normally include –

(i) Inspection of documents and events to gain evidence whether the internal controls are operating properly;

(ii) Inquiries and observations on internal control where there is no audit trail and ascertain the who actually performs such control rather than who is supposed to be;

(iii) Re-perform the internal control to ensure that the control is properly operated in the organisation;

(iv) Test the controls in operating of the computerised applications, software in the organisation.

Further, during the course of the audit, it would be seen whether the answers to the question given, or noted in the discussion actually reflect the reality in the organisation or not. If not, Auditor would indicate what the consequences that may follow are and what kind of remedial actions would be required. For this purpose, "SA-315 - Identifying and Assessing the Risk of Material Misstatement through

Understanding the Entity and its Environment" which deals with the responsibility of the Auditor to identify and assess the risk through understanding the entity and its environment, including the internal control, can be taken for consideration. A proper review of internal control and remedial action to rectify defects or omissions would ensure that management is aware of the legal consequences of areas where the action is not taken and the risks involved.

In this chapter, questions asked in the questionnaire have been reproduced. The background, as well as the legal provisions/significance wherever relevant, have been discussed in the initial chapter on overview of GST. The approach for verification of each aspect has been provided in the chapter on the conduct of the audit.

14.3 GST QUESTIONNAIRE

1. **Standard operating procedure**

   (i) Does the organisation have a standard operating procedure for overall management and operation (including the taxation)? Does it have a separate portion setting out the operating procedure as regards implementation /compliance of GST?

2. **Transitional Procedures**

   (i) Have all the premises of the organisation been migrated to GST and obtained the registration certificate within the prescribed time limit?

   (ii) Has the management analysed the options/schemes i.e. composition scheme, exemption notifications etc. for getting registered under GST?

   (iii) Has the organisation carried forward its closing credit (as per Service Tax, Excise Duty, and VAT) through Tran – 1?

   (iv) Is the carried forward credit eligible to be carried forward for utilisation under GST?

   (v) Has the organisation taken care pertaining to transactions of sale of goods on approval basis made during the previous law regime?

3. **Authorised person**

   (i) Has the organisation assigned specific responsibilities and defined roles of different persons/officers who have competence and knowledge in relation to GST?

   (ii) Has the management intimated the Department the name and designation of the authorised person/s for dealing with the Department?

(iii) If yes, is the person/s authorised empowered to take decisions regarding tax liabilities if disputes arise?

(iv) If not, has the management specified who exactly will have to take decisions with regard to issues arising in GST which has financial implications?

(v) Is there any monetary limit based norm for taking decisions in relation to issues with financial implications?

4. Correspondence with the department

(i) Does the management have a proper system of correspondence management wherein responsibility for receipt of correspondence, reaching the correspondence to the concerned person and ensuring that concerned person/s responds in time is monitored?

(ii) Does the organisation have a proper system of documenting i.e. registers/files etc. the communication with/by the department along with the postal covers of the correspondence received from the department? What is the system to ensure that notices received through GST network are acted upon on the Internet or manually within the deadline?

5. Vendor management - Review of contracts

(i) Does the entity have regular running contracts with vendors?

(ii) Is there a mechanism or a system to ensure that such contracts are examined with reference to the provisions of GST law?

(iii) Are there supplies without contracts and outward supplies are effected based on internal policy? (Examine some representative current contracts for study as well as the policy document. Materiality could be used in selection.)

(iv) Does the internal control system of the organisation ensure that while contracts are entered into or renewed, following aspects are considered to ensure compliance with GST law and the advantages or disadvantages for the organisation?

(a) Composite supply or mixed supply, Classification.

(b) The rate of tax. (Time of supply)

(c) Place of supply.

(d) Value.

(e) Free supply.

(f) Any advance.

(g) Penalty or interest charged for late payment.

(h) Escalation clause.

(i) Payment terms.

6. Composite supply or mixed supply and Classification

(i) Is there a system to ensure that any new supply of goods or services or both is correctly identified as a composite supply or mixed supply?

(ii) Has the classification been done on the basis of rules for interpretation of the First Schedule of the Customs Tariff Act, 1975? Does the system ensure that classification is done in accordance with law, rules and industry practice?

(iii) Whenever there is a change in the rate of tax made, is there a system to check whether such a change has an impact on any mixed supply of the organisation?

(iv) When there is no clarity as regards classification and eligibility for exemption under a notification does it seek written advice?

(v) Does the management follow the practice of payment of the higher rate of tax pending clarification or take the risk and pay the lower amount of tax pending clarification?

(vi) Has the management obtained any Advance Ruling pertaining to classification of any supply as either composite or mixed supply?

7. The rate of tax

(i) Does the organisation have a system to verify the correctness of the rate of tax payable to outward supplies as well as inward supplies (RCM) by checking the classification, relevant notification?

(ii) Is there a system to ensure that whenever there is a change in the rate of tax, there is a person responsible in the organisation to check whether there is any change in respect of supplies made/received by the organisation?

8. Place of supply

(i) Has the organisation determined the place of supply of goods or services or both in respect of all the regular transactions and does the organisation have a system to determine the place of supply whenever a new type of transaction arises?

(ii) Does the contract with the Vendors/Customers mentions the Place of Supply of such transactions?

(iii) If yes, whether there is a proper control mechanism to determine whether the Place of supply determined in the Contract is correct?

(iv) Has any person been specifically entrusted with the responsibility of determination of the place of supply?

9. Value

(i) What is the mechanism to determine the value which is in accordance with the provisions of law to prevent allegations of undervaluation/overvaluation?

(ii) While determining incentives to dealers/distributors, warranty period, pre-supply discounts and post supply discounts, is there a system of ensuring that such offers are made prior to the date of supply?

(iii) Has the organisation analysed the optional valuation mechanisms available under the GST law?

10. Free supply

(i) Does the organisation ensure that free supplies received, provided as warranty or replacement and also supplied by third parties to customers as bought out components receive the treatment regarding their inclusion/exclusion of their value in the product in accordance with law?

11. Advance

(i) Does the organisation have a system of collecting advances linked to the specific supply of goods or services or both and tax-related thereto? When such advances are adjusted, is there a system to examine the GST liability to ensure that there is no double payment or failure to pay the tax?

(ii) Has the feasibility of changing the system of advance payment whether in the case of supplies received or made into a deposit not specifically linked to a supply to reduce cash flow been examined?

(iii) Has the management considered requirement of payment against specific activity relating to mobilisation as a supply in itself so that the recipient can take credit of the tax paid without waiting for completion of the contract?

12. Penalty or interest charged for late payment

(i) Whenever there is a collection of payment or interest or late fee, has the management got a system to ensure that as soon as such interest, penalty or late fee in terms of the contract is collected, tax due on such amount is paid even if the tax is not collected from the customer?

(ii) Has the management considered feasibility of incorporating a clause requiring payment of GST at the time of payment of interest, late fee or penalty and also introducing a system of raising debit note/ supplementary invoice for collection of interest, late fee or penalty with GST so that the recipient can take credit of such payment made?

13. Escalation Clause

(i) How does the organisation ensure that when amounts are collected in terms of escalation clause, GST is collected and paid?

(ii) Does the organisation ensure that where there is an escalation clause in the contract, GST liability is specifically mentioned in the contract?

14. Related person

(i) If there are any transactions involving the supply of goods/services to related person as defined in section 15 of CGST, has the management adopted the price in accordance with the valuation rules?

(ii) Does the management have a system to ensure that whenever transactions with a person take place for the first time, a check is made to ensure that the person with whom the transaction is going to be made is not a related person?

(iii) Does the management provide supplies without any consideration to related parties?

(iv) If yes, whether GST has been levied and discharged for such supplies?

15. Input tax credit management

General issues:

(i) Is the organization withholding any retention amount (typically seen in case of works contract where retention money is disbursed to vendor after a long period of time) and has analysed the impact on ITC?

(ii) Does the organisation have a system of verification of correctness of credits taken periodically and who verifies?

(iii) Is such verification on a random basis or hundred percent of all the documents being done? Does the organisation have a system of seeking clarification where there are doubts about the admissibility of credit and who takes a decision as to whether credit should be taken in such cases and if taken how the same should be treated?

(iv) Is there a system to ensure that such credits taken are treated as temporary and a final decision is taken after the issue is resolved?

(v) Does the organisation have a system of proper decision-making at the time of payment of tax about utilisation of credit available and determination of how much credit is available, how much is usable?

(vi) Has the organisation fixed responsibility on an officer or more than one officer to ensure credit matching takes place and when matching does not happen, the matter is pursued to its logical end and credit admissible is fully taken and utilised?

(vii) Is it ensured that original documents are available for all credits?

(viii) Whether the manner of determination of receipt of inputs/services for taking credit is proper? (When goods are received in lots, is the credit availed after receipt of the last lot wherever applicable? Method to be determined that input services have been received)

(ix) Does the record maintained ensure receipt of input/services is before taking credit?

(x) Does the organisation have the control system to ensure that the payment to Suppliers/Vendors is made within 180 days or subsequent credit reversal? Does the control system ensure that where the condition of payment is not be fulfilled, they are identified as such in advance?

(xi) Whether the input tax credit pertaining to an invoice has been claimed within September of the following financial year to which the invoice relates or within the due date of filing the annual return for the financial year to which the invoice relates whichever is earlier?

(xii) Does the internal control system differentiate between credit taken on the basis of bill of entry and other documents since the non availability of credit mentioned above is applicable to invoice or debit notes only?

(xiii) Has the organisation fixed control to restrict the input tax credit on goods and services which are explicitly blocked?

(xiv) Does the organisation have a proper control system to apportion the common credit and reverse the credit relating to exempt supplies?

(xv) Has control of utilisation of input tax credit is proper in the organisation?

(xvi) Has the management considered and examined the feasibility of making purchases from registered tax payers to ensure that input tax credit in respect of all eligible purchasers?

(xvii) Has the organisation devised a procedure whereby GST paid on travelling expenses of employees is available to the organisation as credit to the extent possible?

The credit of tax paid on capital goods:

(i) When capital goods are received or capital expenses are incurred, is there a system check whether credit of tax paid can be taken or not? (Does the management take into account the fact that if input tax credit is not available, the disadvantage is only to the extent of delay in availment of benefit because the depreciation is spread over many years whereas input tax credit is available immediately?)

(ii) Does the management have a system of cost-benefit analysis where the availability of credit is doubtful or where there is a possibility of dispute about eligibility before taking the credit?

(iii) When a decision to write off the capital goods or sell them is taken, is there a system of verification of legal provisions and recording the logic behind the decision which will help audit checks as well as decision making in future transactions?

(iv) Does the organisation have a proper control system to apportion the credit of the capital goods used to provide exempt supplies?

(v) In the case of works contract service received/to be received is there a system to consider the manner in which contracts have to be entered to ensure that the benefit of input tax credit can be availed to the full extent and also examination before decision to capitalise an expense is taken?

Has the organisation maintained books and accounts in such a manner that the information required for filing annual return with segregated data of credits availed under broad headings indicated in the annual return and to conduct reconciliation exercise?

(Refer – Annual return – Form 9 – Pt III –6 to 8)

(Refer – Reconciliation Statement – Part A – Pt IV – 14)

16. Input Service Distribution in GST

(i) Are the vendors supplying services, which are common input services for the organization, raising invoices on the ISD registration number?

(ii) Is there a mechanism to track the specific invoices which have not been declared by vendors in their GSTR-1 (because for ISD, the credit flows from vendor's GSTR-1 to GSTR-6A)?

(iii) Has registration as input service distributor been taken?

(iv) If yes, has the ratio of distribution of input tax credit for each service received and distributed to each the unit been determined in accordance with law?

(v) If the answer is yes, is there a write up explaining the basis so that legality and correctness can be examined?

(vi) Have you got the distribution method evaluated by an expert on GST? Are the recipient units aware of the process of arriving at the quantum of credit distributed, the basis for arriving at the amount and whether they have been given the write up relating to the input service distribution for their unit?

(vii) Has the organisation ensured that the credit received is distributed in the same month?

(ix) Has the management ensured that the units who are receiving the credit are aware of the fact they can take and utilise the credit only if they are eligible for the same even if the invoice is issued by their own head office or another office?

(x) Have the receivers of credit from ISD been made aware that according to the law, if credit taken is found to be wrong, action would be initiated against the unit which is taking the credit?

17. Cash ledger management

(i) Has the company introduced a system of proper management of cash ledger maintained by the GST network?

(ii) Is there clarity regarding the payments to be made to be credited into cash ledger and subsequent debits in the cash ledger?

(iii) Does the management ensure that the balance in the cash credit ledger of GST is kept at the minimum?

(iv) Have proper guidelines been issued for management of cash ledger and the input credit ledger so that the input credit is optimally utilised to improve cash flow? (While making payments for crediting in the cash ledger, what is the system to ensure that amounts are credited to CGST, SGST and IGST accounts correctly so that no surplus is left because of mistakes in making payments under the proper heads?)

(v) Does the organisation have a system of regular verification of liability register, verification of the figures given therein for their correctness and a decision at the appropriate level to make payments and settle or to keep the liability pending based on a cost-benefit and legal analysis?

(vi) Has the management ensured that amounts of interest, fee, penalty and other charges debited while filing monthly returns and showed in the annual return tallies with the books of accounts maintained each GSTIN wise? Is there a mechanism in place to ensure this?

(vii) Does the internal control system ensure that interest income, interest on corporate loans given, insurance claims etc which may be categorised as exempt income are appropriately accounted for and taken into account for the purpose of calculation of input tax credit to be reversed?

(viii) Is there a system in place to identify all deemed supplies (schedule III) like high seas sales/ global business/ trade to ensure that such incomes are not considered for reversal of ITC?

(Refer - Annual Return Form 9)

18. Job work done for the management

(i) Is there any supply to the job workers without payment of GST?

(ii) Does the management ensure that input tax credit has been taken in respect of all the inputs supplied to the job worker? (even if received directly by the JW)

(iii) Has credit been taken on such inputs? If credit has been taken and if the job worker has not returned the processed goods within one year, is there a system to ensure that credit is reversed as required by the law and proper reminders are sent to the job worker to ensure that he returns the processed goods within one year without fail?

(iv) Is there any supply of jigs, moulds, fixtures et cetera and if yes, has the management ensured that the credit has been taken on such items supplied?

(v) Is there any supply of other capital goods to the job worker and if yes, has it been ensured that capital goods are returned by the job worker within the specified time limit of three years?

(vi) Does the agreement with the job worker provide for the return of inputs and capital goods within the specified time limit after processing or after the completion of work and remedial action to be taken in case of failure?

(vii) Is the job worker undertaking manufacture on his own account and is able to utilise the credits of tax paid on inputs and capital goods purchased by him and used for job work? If the job worker is not engaged in manufacture of providing service on his own account, has the management taken care to ensure that all inputs required by the job worker are supplied and credit is taken in such cases, so that the manufacturing/provision of service cost does not increase because of the cascading effect of the taxation?

(viii) Does the job work generate any waste or scrap and if so, is the same returned by the job worker to the principal promptly and does the agreement with the job worker specify the quantum of waste/scrap that may arise and how it should be handled? (If waste and scrap that is generated are being sold by the job worker on his own account, does the agreement provide that applicable taxes should be paid by the job worker and it would be his responsibility to ensure that appropriate tax is paid and accounted for properly?)

(ix) Do the persons engaged in the accounting of job work process ensure that accounting system and management of issue of delivery challans is proper?

(x) Where the job worker does not return the entire quantity of inputs back after processing, is there a system to ensure that the job worker gives reference to the relevant delivery challan and indicates the balance quantity of inputs left with him to be processed in every delivery challan sent by him till the entire quantity of inputs is covered by the delivery challans sent by him?

(xi) Is the procedure adopted for supplies from the job worker's premises adequate?

(Refer – Annual return – Form 9 – Pt - VI –16 -B).

19. Job work management in case of job work done

(i) Does the management undertake job work for other service providers/manufacturers?

(ii) Is the management engaged only in job work or also undertakes the provision of service/manufacture?

(iii) Is the management discharging GST on waste and scrap that arises during job work? (If not, is the waste and scrap being returned to the principal? Does the management ensure that all materials supplied for job work are processed within the specified time limit and processed goods are returned to the principal?)

(iv) Have any capital goods or moulds, jigs or fixtures been supplied by the principal and if yes, have they been returned within the time limit specified? Is the management aware that such goods have to be returned within the specified time limit and has adequate system controls to ensure that the same is done in accordance with law?

(v) If the management is undertaking job work as well as the provision of service and manufacture, is the management availing credit of input tax paid on materials purchased and utilised for job work as well as the provision of service and manufacture on own account?

(Refer – Annual return – Form 9 – Pt - VI –16 -B).

20. Stock transfer/agent management

(i) Has the management established depots in different parts of the country? Is the management aware that the depot is considered as a distinct person for the purpose of levy of GST?

(ii) Alternatively, does the management have GST registered agents in different parts of the country who undertake sales/delivery of the products?

(iii) If yes, can the agent/depot take credit of tax paid on the materials supplied to them? If they are not entitled to credit, how the value of the materials supplied to them has been arrived at? (Has the management adopted open market value? If not, has the management adopted the value of goods of like kind and quality?)

(iv) If the depot or the agent can take credit of input tax, has the management taken care to ensure that the value adopted for transfer of goods to the depot or the agent is such that accumulation of input tax credit in the account is avoided?

(v) Is the management aware of the provisions relating to supplies to an agent in the valuation rules and has it ensured that the value adopted is in accordance with the valuation rules?

(vi) Does the nature of transactions and relationship with the agents, makes agents the related persons? If yes, has the management taken steps to ensure that value is determined considering agent as a related person?

(vii) Are there instances of the suppliers of goods or services or both acting as pure agents in respect of a portion of such supplies or in respect of all supplies? If yes, what is the system to ensure that in all such transactions there is a proper contract and the provisions relating to pure agent are followed?

(viii) Is the organisation acting as a pure agent to any receiver? If so, are the transactions backed by a proper agreement and is there a system to ensure that all the provisions relating to pure agent are followed?

21. Sales/outward supplies including continuous supply and e-commerce

(i) Has the management ensured that payments received in advance have been received without GST payable to the government?

(ii) In the case of continuous supply contracts, has it been ensured that the customer pays GST along with each milestone as specified?

(iii) In the case of government contracts has it been ensured that the terms of supply clearly state that taxes applicable at the time of supply would be payable separately? (If not, has the management taken care to ensure that the costing of supply has been made in such a manner that in spite of revision of rate of tax, the management would be able to supply and bear the taxation liability on own account?)

(iv) While working out the cost of supplies, has the management taken care of the fact that there may be tax deduction at source if the value of supply or contract is more than 2.5 lakhs?

(v) If not, has the management taken into account the fact that TDS would be deducted and even after deduction, the supply would not end up in a loss to the management?

(vi) In the case of e-commerce sales, has the management ensured that the input tax paid by the e-commerce operator for the purchases made from him is taken into account and taken as credit at the time of payment of GST?

(vii) In the case of a direct sale to a customer through e-commerce operator, has the management taken care to ensure that credit of input tax paid on the commission/remuneration paid to the e-commerce operator has been taken?

(ix) Has the management ensured that the accounts and records maintained in such a way that supplies in Schedule III to the Act are also accounted for to facilitate smooth reconciliation?

(x) There is no need to pay tax to the extent of the TCS deductions and duplicate the payment. Does the internal control mechanism take care of this?

(Refer – Annual return – Form 9 – Pt II –4 -F)

(Form 9C – Part II – Sl.No.5B)

21. Warranty provisions

(i) Does the management provide a warranty on the supplies made? (If so, when supplies of parts/components are made or warranty services are provided, has it been ensured that GST is not paid on such parts/components?)

(ii) Has the same principle been followed where an extended warranty is provided on payment of the extra amount on which GST has been collected?

(iii) In the case of warranty services provided on behalf of someone else, has it been ensured that GST on the cost of services levied/has been collected from the customer and paid to the government? Where warranty services are provided but the purchase of materials required is made, has the credit of input tax paid on such materials been taken or not?

22. Non-receipt and short receipt of consideration

(i) The law makes it obligatory for a receiver of supply to reverse the credit of the tax taken, if the payment is not made within 180 days. Since management has found that the payment would not come and has written off, it has to ensure that the receiver reports nonpayment and reverses the credit and supplier has to monitor and get at least the duty element back. Where the management is forced to write off the amount receivable for a supply already made whether in full or in part, has a system been introduced whereby steps are taken to claim the GST paid on such amounts back where eligible?

(ii) Does the contract provide that where such non-payment/short payment occurs and it happens because the payment is not received before September of the next year where the supplier is forced not to claim the GST paid back into their account; the receiver has to compensate the management for the loss?

(iii) Is there a system of proper follow-up of cases where there is delay in settlement by the receiver and such delay is concluded either way before the time-limit prescribed for claiming the GST back?

23. Sales returns

In the case of returns of the supplies made by the recipients, does the agreement provide that credit of input tax credit taken is reversed and necessary details are given by the recipient to facilitate GST refund claim? (Alternatively, does the agreement provide that the recipient should return the goods under invoice on payment of GST so that tax paid on such returns is taken as input tax credit?)

24. Accounting of cash

(i) Where payments or receipts are in cash, does the management have a system to ensure that the same are properly accounted for and there is an audit trail to show how the amount has been accounted for and whether it has been credited into the bank and if yes, is there a proper linkage with the bank account wherein the amount was credited?

(ii) Does the management have a system of ensuring that for every payment/receipt in cash, a voucher is prepared either manually or on the computer?

25. Receipts in convertible currency

(i) If there are receipts from customers/others in the form of convertible foreign currency for supplies made within the country attracting GST/IGST or in respect of export/imports of services, how is it ensured that GST is paid on the amount in Indian rupees in accordance with valuation rules relating to receipts in convertible currency?

(ii) Does the management have a system of maintenance of accounts to show the difference between exchange rate adopted for the purpose of imports/exports and actual amounts paid/realized which can be used for the purpose of reconciliation?

(Refer – Reconciliation Statement Form 9C)

26. Supplies to and from SEZ

(i) Is the organization obtaining the invoices duly endorsed by the Specified Officer of SEZ?

(ii) Has LUT been filed for the financial year?

(iii) Does the organization have a process to ensure that the GSTIN of the SEZ customer is appropriately tagged in the GSTN database as an SEZ?

(iv) Are the supplies made for authorized operations?

(v) If there are supplies to SEZ, how it is ensured that input tax credit in respect of all supplies made has been taken?

(vi) Is it ensured that refund has been claimed where credit is surplus and cannot be utilised? (Examine how it is ensured that proper documentation has been made to show that the recipient is an SEZ unit, the management ensure that a copy of the approval of SEZ unit and authorisation issued by the proper officer authorising the SEZ unit to receive the supplies of goods or services is obtained and kept on record)

(vii) Has the organisation made any supplies to SEZ units/developers on payment of taxes, if yes, have the same been declared in the returns? Has the refund of such amounts been claimed? Does the organisation have a system of categorization of inputs/input services under broad headings to facilitate reconciliation of details in Reconciliation statement –Part A – pt. iv -14 – items from B to Q with the books of account/Annual Financial Statement?

(Refer to Reconciliation Statement – Form 9C)

27. Exports

(i) Is it ensured that where the export is made on own account, shipping bills and other documents relating to such exports reflect the correct registration number of the exporter? (In case of the exports made through merchant exporter, if the waiver of export benefits in favour of merchant exporter has not been given, it is to be ensured that manufacturer's name also figures in the documents like shipping will, invoice et cetera.)

(ii) Has the management examined whether export on payment of GST is beneficial vis-à-vis export under bond without payment of GST? (The availability of drawback on the exports made vis a vis the customs duty paid on the inputs) If short claimed, has the management considered claiming special brand rate for drawback?

(iii) If without payment of IGST, whether LUT/Bond has been filed for the financial year?

(iv) If it is on payment of IGST, whether two types of invoices are issued i.e. Commercial invoice and Tax Invoice and if so, whether Tax Invoice is submitted for filing Bill of Export/Shipping bill?

(v) Does the organisation have a system of ensuring that correct drawback rates are applied and have a system to check whether their products are affected when drawback rates are changed by the government?

(vi) Has the organisation ensured that it need not have to opt for the special brand rate of drawback?

(vii) Has the management analysed the availability of export benefits under FTP like MEIS, SEIS, status holder benefits etc.?

(viii) Is there a system whereby whenever exports or deemed exports are made, there is a detailed consideration of the procedure to be followed so that benefits that are available for such exports/deemed exports are availed/claimed?

(ix) Whether there is proper control to ensure that goods meant for export are moved out of India within 3 months from the date of issuance of Invoice?

(x) Has the management intimated the Bank to link and issue the BRC for the Export Invoices?

(xi) Does the management have proper control to comply with the provisions of FEMA, FTP and Customs?

(xii) In case of exports through merchant exporters, does the management have a clear cut policy as to who will claim the export benefits. Further how it would be ensured that procedural requirements are fulfilled and the precautions to be taken by the personnel while entering into export contracts through merchant exporters?

28. Refund

(i) Does the assessee have consultants to look into refund claims made to see the correctness of such claims and advise?

(ii) Is there a system to look and consider whether any refund claims could/should have been filed?

(iii) Is there a proper control system in the organisation to apply for a refund within 2 years from the date of export?

29. Employee expenses

(i) Whenever supplies of services/goods are made to employees, is there any system to check whether GST is liable to be paid on such supplies?

(ii) If GST is liable to be paid on supplies made by employer to employee, is it ensured that the Open market value of such supply is considered for valuation purposes and not the value actually being recovered? Whether all the payment made to employees for the service provided by them is covered under an employment contract?

(iii) Whether there is proper control check that GST has been discharged on the gifts given to employees exceeding fifty thousand rupees in a financial year? Whenever any amount is recovered from employees, is there a system to check whether GST is to be paid on the basis of reverse charge mechanism?

30. Reverse Charge Mechanism

(i) Whether the organisation has a proper control system to verify the supplies received which are notified under the Reverse Charge Mechanism?

(ii) Has the organisation created a control check for the purpose of documentation to be made pertaining to supplies taxable under Reverse charge mechanism?

(iii) Does the organisation have proper control of claiming the credit of tax paid under reverse charge mechanism unless otherwise blocked?

(iv) Has the organisation undertaken an exercise to ensure that supplies are received from registered persons who pay non-composition tax?

(v) Has any exercise been undertaken to educate unregistered persons to take registration and supply on payment of tax so that input tax credit is taken by them and cascading effect of tax is reduced?

31. Records Management

(i) Does the management have a policy for management of records?

(ii) The period of storage of records in accordance with GST statute has to be 8 years. Has it been ensured that this would be done? (In case the entire Records Management is computerised, does the management have a system of proper storage of backup records and the availability of such records for the statutory period?)

(iii) Is the system ensuring that records which are relating to disputes with the department remain intact till the dispute is finally settled?

32. Investments

(i) Is there any liability of GST discharged, in the case of investments made? If the answer is yes, has the credit of GST paid in relation to services for such investments has been taken or not? Has the management examined the availability of such credit and taken the same promptly and correctly?

33. Assessment of GST

(i) Is there a system of ensuring that every time a new transaction, a new supply of goods or services or both is started, before the transaction is completed or immediately after it is completed, the assessment of the transaction and determination of tax liability is made?

(ii) Does the person who determines the tax liability after assessment, prepares a short note so that in case of a dispute at a later stage, the management is aware of the basis of the decision which can be very important?

(iii) Does the internal control system clearly lay down what is to be done (escalation, intimation expert opinion etc) where the personnel find it difficult to take a final decision in respect of any of the aspects of assessment such as classification, valuation, eligibility for exemption etc.

34. The issue of invoice, bill of supply etc.

(i) Are the formats adopted for invoice and bill of supply, in accordance with the legal provisions relating to invoice to be issued by a taxable person under section 31 read with the relevant rule? (Has the management introduced a system to verify any invoice or bill of supply received in respect of supply of goods or services or both to ensure that the invoice or bill of supply contains all the relevant information as per the rule and nothing is omitted before uploading?)

35. Registration-related accounting issues

(i) Does the Management ensure that at the time of supply of goods or services or purchase of goods or services, proper verification is made to check whether the supplier/recipient is a registered person?

36. Audit trail

(i) Does the software in use have a proper audit trail to ensure that entries in the software, corrections and administrative decisions made can be linked to the persons who are authorised to do so and in case more than one person is involved, the sequence of decision-making has been followed or not?

(ii) Is there a system of checking the audit trail by a person who is not involved and who is authorised to check the trail and suggest appropriate action?

(iii) Is the Information system and network encrypted and protected from unauthorised individuals?

(iv) Whether the management has a proper system of backing up of data and has a proper BCP?

37. Compliance in Return Filing

(i) Does the organisation have a system to ensure filing of the returns on or before the due date?

(ii) Is there a mechanism to undertake periodical reconciliation between ITC claimed by company and the corresponding entries appearing in GSTR-2A?

(iii) Is there a system of verifying the filing form GSTR-3B of the vendors where compliance is suspect?

(iv) Are the accounts maintained, whether computerised or not, in such a manner that all the information required in the annual return other than the ones already submitted as part of monthly returns can be made available easily (detailed below – annual return) so that the annual return filing can be done without errors and considerable investment of effort and time?

Zero rated supply (Export) on payment of tax (except supplies to SEZs)	
Supply to SEZs on payment of tax	
Deemed Exports	
Advances on which tax has been paid but invoice has not been issued (not covered under (A) to (E) above)	
Supplies/tax declared through Amendments (+)	
Supplies/tax reduced through Amendments (-)	
Zero rated supply (Export) without payment of tax	
Supply to SEZs without payment of tax	

Supplies declared through Amendments (+)	
Supplies reduced through Amendments (-)	
Inward supplies (other than imports and inward supplies liable to reverse charge but includes services received from SEZs)	Inputs
	Capital Goods
	Input Services
Inward supplies received from unregistered persons liable to reverse charge (other than B above) on which tax is paid & ITC availed	Inputs
	Capital Goods
	Input Services
Inward supplies received from registered persons liable to reverse charge (other than B above) on which tax is paid and ITC availed	Inputs
	Capital Goods
	Input Services
Import of goods (including supplies from SEZs)	Inputs
	Capital Goods
Import of services (excluding inward supplies from SEZs)	
Import of services (excluding inward supplies from SEZs)	
Amount of ITC reclaimed (other than B above) under the provisions of the Act	
Details of ITC reversed and ineligible ITC as declared in returns filed during the financial year as per Rule 37	
Details of ITC reversed and ineligible ITC as declared in returns filed during the financial year as per Rule 39	
Details of ITC reversed and ineligible ITC as declared in returns filed during the financial year as per Rule 42	
Details of ITC reversed and ineligible ITC as declared in returns filed during the financial year as per Rule 43	
Details of ITC reversed and ineligible ITC as declared in returns filed during the financial year as per section 17(5)	
Details of ITC reversed and ineligible ITC as declared in returns filed during the financial year as reversal of TRAN-I credit	
Details of ITC reversed and ineligible ITC as declared in returns filed during the financial year as reversal of TRAN-II credit Other reversals (pl. specify)	
ITC on inward supplies (other than imports and inward supplies liable to reverse	

charge but includes services received from SEZs) received during 2017-18 but availed during April to September, 2018
Supplies/tax declared through Amendments (+) (net of debit notes)
Supplies/tax reduced through Amendments (-) (net of credit notes)
Reversal of ITC availed during previous financial year
ITC availed for the previous financial year
Total Refund claimed
Total Refund Sanctioned
Total Refund Rejected
Total Refund pending
Total Demand of Taxes
Total taxes paid in respect of E above
Total demand pending out of E above
Supplies received from Composition taxpayers
Deemed supply under Section 143
Goods sent on approval basis but not returned

(Refer to annual return Form 9)

(v) Whether there is a control mechanism for reconciling the GSTR-1 and GSTR-3B?

(vi) Are the accounts maintained, whether computerised or not, in such a manner that the information required in the Reconciliation Statement Part – A - Pt. IV -12 and 14 can be made available easily?

(Refer to Reconciliation statement – Form 9C)

38. Audit reports of GST department, C & AG

Does the internal control system have a specific requirement on the action to be taken on audit reports received from the department, time for replies and the levels at which action has to be taken?

39. Previous Report Compliance where the organisation gets periodical GST reviews done.

(i) Whether the organisation responds to and rectifies the observations/ discrepancies mentioned in the report?

(ii) Whether there are pending issues as reported in the previous reports?

(iii) If yes, what is the stand of the management on it? Whether any steps have been initiated to resolve those issues?

40. Customs related internal control questionnaire.

The internal control questionnaire above covers several issues relating to customs also. Related person concept and valuation in such transactions, classification principles and examination of applicability of exemption, ITC in respect of imported goods and services and tax liability, processes relating to exports, refunds are some of the examples.

41. Customs Broker

Does the internal control system lay down any process for selection of the customs broker, to monitor his performance in the areas of statutory compliance, resolving disputes with the department, promptness in documentation and is there a system of cost benefit analysis relating to contribution of the broker?

42. Assessment

Has the internal control system ensured that the changes in rate of duty, exemptions and conditions for exemption are regularly monitored and necessary changes in documentation are ensured in view of the fact that in respect of imports also, it is self assessment regime now?

Does the internal control system ensure that in case the Customs department proposes re-assessment, the personnel dealing with the subject ensure that provisions of section 17 of *the Customs Act* requiring communication for re-assessment, written consent or speaking order are followed?

Has the internal control system devised a process whereby in cases of dispute the option for provisional assessment/payment under protest or acceptance of department proposal are made taking all factors into account for the benefit of the tax payer?

43. Valuation

(i) Does the internal control system ensure that the contracts entered into for implementation of JV projects, imports from holding company/JV partner abroad who may be considered as related persons or otherwise are examined from the point of view of Customs duty also?

(ii) Does the internal control system require import agreements, royalty agreements and dealership of imported goods etc are drafted and entered into taking into account the provisions of *the Customs Act, 1962* so that the value is declared correctly at the time of import itself and future disputes are avoided?

44. Warehousing

In cases where taxpayer has customs bonded warehouse, does the internal control system ensure that there is proper monitoring of the period of expiry of warehousing and application for extension where needed and ensure that warehoused goods do not become obsolete or deteriorate?

45. General

Has the internal control system been designed in such a manner that the decisions relating to investment, merger, demerger, take overs, joint ventures, agreements with partners, remunerations, accounting systems (changes/new introduction), director related decisions and outsourcing decisions are covered?

Chapter 15

Outward Supply

15.1 INTRODUCTION

The audit has to ensure that all aspects relating to GST are considered by the auditors, examined and reported. It is necessary that the relevant documents are scrutinised thoroughly by the auditors. The internal control questionnaire would be provided to the auditee in advance so that answers are provided earlier. Each of the answers in negative in the ICQ, would be examined by the auditors to see the legal correctness and also whether any alternative is available which may be beneficial to the assessee. If the management is unable to provide documents subject -wise or area -wise to cover many aspects then the documents would have to be selected at random as well as from larger value transactions. These would be verified in detail. This would indicate the existence, level and effectiveness of internal control mechanism.

It is quite possible that a single document would have several aspects to be examined. For example, if an invoice is taken up for outward supply, it would require examination of classification of goods and/or service, valuation, eligibility for exemption claimed, if any, nature of transaction etc. Therefore auditors cannot restrict themselves to a particular area while scrutinising the document but as far as possible ensure that as many areas as possible are covered.

15.2 VERIFICATION OF FINANCIAL STATEMENTS

Introduction

The financial accounts and records maintained by an assessee are reflected in the financial statements which are certified by the statutory auditors. The reconciliation of accounts and records with the returns filed under GST would indicate the discrepancies. These differences would have to be analysed further to examine whether there is any liability on account of GST.

The auditors would verify the reconciliation prepared by the management for the audits done on behalf of the management as well as the statutory audit under section 35 of the CGST Act.

The auditors would look into the following aspects and data in the financial accounts keeping in mind the provisions in the GST law and consider whether the financial statements and the data contained therein are compliant with GST law.

15.2.1 General

(1) Auditor would take the ratio of input tax credit to output tax paid in a financial year and compare it with the previous years and look for any significant variation. In case of variation, necessary verification would be conducted to see whether there are valid reasons for the difference that is found.

(2) Similar examinations would be conducted in respect of ratios of output tax paid to total turnover, input tax credit utilised to total turnover, tax paid on imports of goods and services to total turnover et cetera.

(3) Auditors invariably should comment on the significant accounting policies to be considered from the point of view of GST.

(4) The components of miscellaneous income/income and components of expenses are required to be seen, considered from the point of view of GST.

(5) The auditor's observations about transactions with directors may be considered. Auditors would have to bear in mind that the reconciliation statement contemplated requires information to be provided in Part A – Pt. – M. In case of transactions with related parties actual transaction value could be less than the taxable value and therefore it may have an impact on the overall turnover if adjustments are not made.

(Refer to GSTR – 9C Reconciliation Statement: Part A- Pt. II – M.)

(6) The expenses incurred on director fees is also indicated in the financial accounts and it is necessary to see whether such expenses include GST or whether GST has been accounted for separately by the company on such expenses.

(Refer to GSTR – 9C Reconciliation Statement: Part A- Pt. IV – N or P or Q .)

(7) In the case of partnership firms, services provided by partners or provided to the partners are to be looked into.

Part A – Pt.II – N of Reconciliation Statement also requires adjustment details to be given in the turnover for reasons other than A to M. Whether there are such adjustments and consequences thereof would have to be looked into.

(Refer to Reconciliation Statement: Part A- Pt.II – A to N).

15.2.2 Levy of GST

Determination of nature of supply and taxability

The determination of nature of supply of goods and/or services is a step that has to be taken before classification is attempted.

There are statutory provisions defining classification, composite supply and mixed supply. There are rules for classification and the method as to how to determine the rate of tax in case of supplies in the CGST act. If the supply taken up for verification is for supply of multiple goods and/or services, the first step would be to see whether supply has to be treated as composite supply or mixed supply.

Examination has to be done for as many goods or services or both provided by the assessee or received by the assessee by creating a table for each supply. The principle of materiality maybe kept in mind so that no major products or services supplied are left out.

Name of Goods or Services under consideration:

Nature of supply-Goods/ services/composite/mixed	Rationale for conclusion in column 1 according to assessee	Comments of the auditor

Some of the reasons for determining nature of supply by the assessee can be:

1. It is a composite supply because the four conditions required to be fulfilled have been fulfilled, viz. the supplies are naturally bundled; they are supplied in conjunction with each other in the ordinary course of business; one of the supplies is a principal supply and all the supplies are taxable supplies.
2. When the supply does not satisfy the test for composite supply and price for each supply is separately available, each supply has to be treated as a separate supply.
3. When a supply consists of many supplies but cannot be treated as a composite supply, it has to be treated as a mixed supply if it has failed the test of composite supply and there are no separate prices available for each supply.
4. There can be other reasons such as similar supplies have been classified by others as composite or mixed supply or goods or services.
5. Advice given by the department in writing.
6. Advice given by consultant in writing.
7. Advance Ruling to classify the supply as composite, non-composite or mixed supply obtained if useful for Customer to be convinced.

Inter branch transactions

It is necessary to ensure that in the case of inter branch transactions especially where goods and services or both are supplied from one branch to the other or from head office to the branch and vice versa, tax is paid even though there may be no consideration. The valuation would have to be done on open market value.

The exception is where the recipient branch is able to avail full ITC and does not have any exempt supplies. In such case the valuation can be based on invoice value as declared by the supplying branch / HO.

While doing so it is also necessary to check whether any of the transactions can be considered as supply of service by the Department even though the assessee feels otherwise.

It is also necessary to verify whether there are central support functions being undertaken from the head office to support the branches. In such a case, GST invoicing from the head office to the branch office may be required. Advance Ruling Authority in the case of Columbia Asia Hospitals (Advance Ruling No. KAR ADRG 15/2018, dt. 27 July 2018) has taken a view that this is necessary[1].

15.2.3 Classification

Introduction

After categorising the supply as composite, non-composite or mixed supply, verification of correctness of classification adopted in respect of supplies made or received by the assessee has to be taken up.

Even though, many categories of taxable persons are not required to mention the subheading of the classification, it would always be appropriate to check the classification up to eight-digit level in the HSN at least in the case of large organisations. Quite often exemptions are given only on the basis of headings in the tariff and in such cases, if the classification has not been correctly made, it can lead to a demand.

This table has to be filled up for as many supplies of the assessee as required/ possible and for supplies received from unregistered persons also.

The description of the goods and/or services in the invoice should always be given as it is known in the trade and not in the tariff by every person who has something to do with GST be it a trader, a manufacturer or a service provider. The classification has to be correctly made by considering the description of the goods/services or both adopted in the invoices or in the trade and checking with the description in the tariff and not the other way round.

Sl. No	Trade Name	Name in Schedule	Class Assessee	Rationale	Comments – auditor
1	2	3	4	5	6

1 The authors have some reservations with this view of the AAR which would be challenged. In a High court decision CCE Vs Nissin Brake Industries PO Ltd - 2019- TIOL- 151 (SC) ST in 2019, this was differed.

15.2.4 Rate of tax, claims for exemption and tax paid.

The auditors would also check whether the organisation has a system to verify the correctness of the rate of tax payable to outward supplies. (This would be important especially in cases where rate of tax has changed over a period of time)) The verification of inward supplies (RCM) by checking the classification, relevant notification ensuring that changes made are taken note of and given effect to.

Claim for exemption and the denial of such exemption by the Department account for substantial portion of the disputes that arise relating to levy of tax on goods and services. Wherever exemption has been claimed in the invoice, it is necessary to check whether exemption is admissible. If it is prima facie admissible, it has to be checked as to whether the conditions are fulfilled or not. Quite often exemptions are given subject to fulfilment of conditions relating to input tax credit availability or end use criteria. Fulfilments of such conditions are also required to be considered.

It is necessary that every claim for exemption is examined carefully with reference to the classification, description of the goods and/or services, conditions required to be fulfilled by the taxable person and existence of the notification. Quite often withdrawal of exemption is not noticed and assessees continue to avail the exemption. It is also possible that exemption introduced in the interim are missed.

Auditors also have to see abatements claimed/admissible for determination of tax payable; retrospective effect of the notification if given, clarifications issued by the Board etc. relating to exemptions.

Where exemption has been given but not taken note of and availed by the assessee, refund claim can be filed after issuing credit note to the customers subject to tax burden not being passed on. (Unjust enrichment)

Since reconciliation statement in form 9C requires details of non-taxable items also, in this statement it would be appropriate to include non-taxable supplies also so that reconciliation exercise becomes easier and simpler.

Sl. No	Desc.	Rate	Period	Notification No. Date	Rationale	Comments - Auditor
1	2	3	4	5	6	7

Sl. No	Desc.	Rate	Period	Notification No. Date	Taxable Value	Central Tax	State/UT Tax	Integrated tax	Cess
1	2	3	4	5	6	7	8	9	10

Note: If there was any change of rate of tax during the year of audit, the periods covered by each notification during the year would be filled. For each notification benefit availed there would be an entry in the table. The second table would help in providing information for Reconciliation and also verification of the correctness of the tax paid.

(Refer to Reconciliation Statement: 9C - Part A- Pt.III – A to K. and Form 9C– Part A - Part II – Sl.No.5B)

This table has to be used in respect of supplies from unregistered suppliers also if and when reverse charge is introduced.

15.2.5 Invoice/bill of supply

Sl. No	Particulars	Remarks Assessee	Remarks Auditor
1	Does the format of the invoice in use contain all the information required as per rule 46 of CGST Rules?		
2	Are the invoices being signed by the authorised representative digitally?		
3	Are the addresses of unregistered persons given in the invoices tallying with the addresses in the record maintained by the assessee?		

15.2.6 Time of Supply (TOS) of goods

Sl No	Particulars	Remarks Assessee	Remarks Auditor
1.	Whether the invoice is issued at the time of removal where it involved movement?		
2.	Whether the invoice is issued at the time of delivery or making the goods available to the recipient where it does not involve movement?		
3.	Whether TOS is correct in the case of vouchers issued?		
4.	Whether TOS is correct in the case of debit note raised for interest/ late fee/penalty?		
5.	Whether the TOS is correct of goods sent earlier on 'sale on approval basis' exceeding the time limit of 6 months?		

Sl No	Particulars	Remarks Assessee	Remarks Auditor
6.	In case the supply under the invoice/delivery challan is a part supply in continuous supply contract, does the tax liability arise in accordance with the terms of the contract and the document issued is the correct one?		

Time of supply of services

Sl No	Particulars	Remarks Assessee	Remarks Auditor
1.	Whether TOS is correct where invoice was issued within the time period prescribed under section 31(2) of the CGST Act?		
2.	Whether TOS is correct where invoice was not issued within the time period prescribed under section 31(2) of the CGST Act?		
3.	Whether TOS is correct in case of service received under reverse charge? (even when date of payment or date of issue of invoice are not ascertainable)		
4.	Whether TOS is correct for service from an associated enterprise?		
5.	Whether TOS is correct where the supply ceased prior to completion?		

Note: In most audits only part of the checklist would be relevant.

15.2.7 Valuation: Invoice Verification

Sl No	Particulars	Remarks Assessee	Remarks Auditor
1.	Whether advance amount received towards supply in the invoice is considered for tax payment?(Currently relevant only for advance received against services)		
2.	Whether the value of any bought out components, designs etc. supplied have been considered?		
3.	Whether the entire consideration has been considered for discharge of tax?		

Sl No	Particulars	Remarks Assessee	Remarks Auditor
4.	Whether the correct value is considered where the supply is a transfer to the branch?		
5.	Whether the value as part of barter/exchange arrangement is correct?		
6.	Whether value adopted for disposal of business assets on which input tax credit has been taken is correct?		
7.	Whether value adopted for disposal of business assets on which input tax credit has NOT been taken is correct?		
8.	Whether value adopted in cases of diversion of assets for private use is correct?		
9.	Whether the discount, cash discount or quantity discount passed on in the invoice is in order?		
10.	Whether prompt supply discounts are given later?		
11.	Whether rate of exchange of currency is correct? (u/r 34)		
12.	Whether the conditions are fulfilled where supplied as a pure agent?		

Note: In most invoices only part of the checklist would be relevant.

Valuation: Other than invoice verification

Sl No	Particulars	Remarks Assessee	Remarks Auditor
1	Whether there are any cases of reimbursement of expenses received from the customers in respect of supplies made which have not been considered in value of supply?		
2	Whether any supply has been subsidised by a private party?		
3	Whether the value adopted for stock transfer between distinct persons is correct?		
4	Whether the process adopted to arrive at the cost when the basis of value is cost of provision of supply or service is correct? (CAS4 etc.).		

Sl No	Particulars	Remarks Assessee	Remarks Auditor
5	Whether the procedure adopted to arrive at the value on the basis of value of similar/like kind of goods is correct?		
6	Whether the value adopted for supply to an agent is correct?		
7	Whether there are transactions where supplies have been made treating the recipients as unrelated persons but in GST law, they are related persons?		
8	Whether the value adopted for transactions with related persons and distinct persons is correct?		
9	Have the marketing schemes such as buy one get one free, buy two get two free etc. correctly reflected the value to be adopted?		
10	Whether the value of supply where the consideration is partly in money and partly in kind is correct?		
11	Whether the value in case of special transactions like lottery, betting, gambling and horse racing, is correct?		
12	Whether the value in respect of certain supplies according to rule 32 such as purchase or sale of foreign currency and money changing, travel agent, life insurance business, second-hand goods, valuation of token/ vouchers, notified services, is correct?		
13	Whether the value of supply made by the employer to employee is correct?		
14	Correctness of the treatment of advance received and treated as deposit not linked to any particular supply?		
15	Whether tax treatment of subsidised food provided by the employer to employee, if any, is correct?		
16	Whether tax treatment of subsidised transport/free transport provided by the employer to employee, if any is correct?		
17	Whether there are any supplies made at prices lower than the cost of production? (to capture the market and GST implications in such a case.)		

Sl No	Particulars	Remarks Assessee	Remarks Auditor
18	Whether the value adopted in shipping bills and related documents is correct?		
19	Whether the exchange rate adopted for the purpose of arriving at assessable value in the shipping bill is correct?		
20	Whether the lease charges offered to tax are as per the agreement between the parties?		
21	In case of mobilisation advance collected, has the tax liability been discharged?		

Value addition: In the case of large works contracts which may take years to complete, it may be better not to examine whether the advance paid is actually a mobilisation advance. Instead it may be collected for specific purposes and billed as and when the amount is spent for the purpose. This will facilitate availment of credit by the recipient.

Note: In most audits only part of the checklist would be relevant.

(Refer – Annual return – Form 9 – Pt II –4 - F).

15.2.8 Place of supply

Introduction

Every taxable person is required to indicate the place of supply in all the documents relating to outward supply. GST is a destination-based consumption tax and therefore the location where consumption takes place and where the goods or services have moved has to be determined. When the supplier determines the place of supply, he is actually determining the type of tax he is required to pay and to whom he is paying. If the supply happens to be interstate, IGST liability arises and if the supply happens to be intra-state, CGST and SGST would have to be paid. Another difficulty that arises is that merely because the delivery of the goods or services takes place to a place in the state would not necessarily mean that that is the place of supply. In the case of "Bill to, ship to" cases, the place of supply is determined based on the person who has placed the order and has requested the supplier to supply to a third party in a different place.

Place of supply (POS): System and records verification for conduct of audit.

Sl No	Particulars	Remarks Assessee	Remarks Auditor
1	Whether there is a proper process adopted by the organisation to determine the POS whenever a new type of transaction arises?		

Sl No	Particulars	Remarks Assessee	Remarks Auditor
2	Whether the fact that in the case of high sea sale transaction, there is no supply has been followed?		
3	Whether in determination of POS of services where either the supplier or recipient is located outside India in respect of services that are in respect of goods is correct?		
4	Has the Place of services been determined correctly where either the supplier or recipient is located outside India? Has the place of supply been determined correctly where services are supplied at multiple locations, including a location in the taxable territory?		
5	Whether the POS of services where either the supplier or recipient is located outside India (a) in respect of services of admission to an event that is organised may be cultural, artistic, sporting, scientific, education or entertainment or an amusement park including ancillary services. (b) where above services are supplied at multiple locations, including a location in the taxable territory. (c) where above services are supplied at multiple locations, including locations in different states in taxable territory.		

Note: In most audits only part of the checklist would be relevant.

Verification of POS during Invoice Verification

Sl No	Particulars	Remarks Assessee	Remarks Auditor
1	Whether the nature of supply as interstate supply/intrastate supply is done?		
2	Whether the address of delivery mentioned in the invoice tallies with the address of the recipient maintained in the records or not?		
3	Whether the determination of POS where 'supply involves movement' of goods is correct?		
4	Whether the POS of 'bill to ship to' is correctly done?		

Sl No	Particulars	Remarks Assessee	Remarks Auditor
5	Whether POS where goods are assembled or installed at site is correct?		
6	Whether POS, where the supply does not involve movement of goods is correct?		
7	Whether POS where goods are supplied on-board a conveyance, for supply by the operator of the conveyance during its journey to the passenger is correct?		
8	Whether POS in the case of export of goods is correct?		
9	Whether POS, in the case of supplies to SEZ/units in EHTP/EPZ/ESTP etc. is correct?		
10	Whether the POS in the case of supply to a person from customs bonded warehouse without filing a bill of entry is correct?		
11	Whether the POS in case of supply of services to a registered person in India is correct?		
12	Whether the POS in case of supply of services to an unregistered person in India is correct?		
13	Whether the POS in case of supply of services by an unregistered person in India is correct?		
14	Whether the POS in case of supply of services directly in relation to immovable property is correct?		
15	Whether the POS in case of supply of services of restaurant and catering, personal grooming, fitness, beauty treatment, health service including cosmetic and plastic surgery is correct?		
16	Whether the POS in case of supply of services of training and performance appraisal supplied to a registered/unregistered person is correct?		
17	Whether the POS in case of supply of services of admission to a venue/ event which could be cultural, artistic, sporting, scientific, education or entertainment or an amusement park including ancillary services is correct?		

Sl No	Particulars	Remarks Assessee	Remarks Auditor
18	Whether the POS in case of supply of services of organizing an event including ancillary services supplied to a registered/unregistered person is correct?		
19	Whether the POS in case of supply of services of transportation of goods supplied to a registered/ unregistered person is correct?		
20	Whether the POS in case of supply of services of transportation of passenger when supplied to a registered/ unregistered person is correct?		
21	Whether the POS in case of supply of services supplied on-board a conveyance is correct?		
22	Whether the POS in case of services of banking and financial services including stock broking services where address on record of the recipient is available and correct?		
23	Whether the POS in case of services of banking and financial services including stock broking services where address on record of the recipient is not available is correct?		
24	Whether the POS in case of Insurance services supplied to a registered or unregistered person is correct?		
25	Whether the POS of services where either the supplier or recipient is located outside India when the location of the recipient is known is correct?		
26	Whether the POS of services where either the supplier or recipient is located outside India that are supplied by remotely accessing the goods is correct?		
27	Whether the POS of services where the supplier or recipient is located outside India and the service provided is directly in relation to immovable correct?		
28	Whether the POS of services where either the supplier or recipient is located outside India in the case of services of transportation of goods is correct?		
29	Whether the POS of services where either the supplier or recipient is located outside India in the case of transportation of passengers is correct?		

Sl No	Particulars	Remarks Assessee	Remarks Auditor
30	Whether the POS of services where either the supplier or recipient is located outside India supplied on-board a conveyance is correct?		
31	Whether the POS of services where either the supplier or recipient is located outside India of online information and database access or retrieval is correct?		
32	Whether the POS of services where either the supplier or recipient is located outside India is correct for the following: (a) Services of a banking company or a financial institution or NBFC. (b) Intermediary services (c) Hiring of transport for a period up to one month.		
33	Whether place of supply determined in the case of reverse charge supplies is correct?		
34	Whether place of supply in the case of import of goods is correct?		

Note: In most invoices only part of the checklist would be relevant.

15.2.9 Exports and deemed exports

Auditors have to examine the answers given by the organisation and see whether the organisation is following the process and the procedures correctly so that the benefits of refund of taxes is availed to the full extent. Auditors would have to check whether any benefit has been availed wrongly which would invite penal consequences to the organisation. Claims for drawback, export scheme benefits, etc. have to be examined for their correctness. The answers to the questions would bring out the awareness of the management and the mechanism introduced by the management to ensure that export processes and procedures are followed correctly and all the benefits which are available are availed of.

Supplies to SEZ and SEZ developers are considered to be deemed exports (zero rated) if they fulfil the conditions. The supplier need not reverse the credit taken. Even though there is no specific provision in the law providing for refund claim by the unit in special economic zone, yet any tax which is not payable but has been paid can be claimed as refund either by the supplier or by the receiver in accordance with law. As regards the unit in the special economic zone, the supplies made to the domestic tariff area by such a unit is considered as an import by the domestic tariff area unit and import duties and IGST have to be paid in accordance with law.

Sl No	Particulars	Remarks Assessee	Remarks Auditor
1.	Whether the correct registration number of the assessee is mentioned in shipping bills and related documents?		
2.	Whether the description of the goods declared in the shipping bills is the correct description and the classification has been correctly done?		
3.	Whether the drawback claimed in shipping bills and related documents is correct? (Including special brand rate)		
4.	Whether the rebate claimed in shipping bills and related documents is correct and maintenance facilitates generation of information required for annual return? *(Refer – Annual return – Form 9 – Pt.IV – 4 A&B).*		
5.	Has the taxpayer opted for the benefits of any export scheme? If yes, has the export obligation been fulfilled?		
6.	Whether there are exports not taking place after clearance of the goods for export within 90 days? Further whether payment of tax has been made with interest where applicable?		
5.	Whether the description of the goods in the shipping bill and the drawback schedule match with each other and claim for drawback is correct?		
6.	Whether the claim for export benefits if the assessee has exported goods through merchant exporter is correct?		
7.	Whether supplies to special economic zone units are made for authorised operations? Does maintenance facilitates generation of information required for annual return? *(Refer – Annual return – Form 9 – Pt.IV – C).*		

Sl No	Particulars	Remarks Assessee	Remarks Auditor
8.	Whether in supplies on payment of tax to SEZ any claim for refund has been made by the assessee or by the SEZ? Does maintenance facilitates generation of information required for annual return? *(Refer – Annual return – Form 9 – Pt.IV – D).*		
9.	Whether supplies to SEZ have been treated as zero rated supplies and in the case of goods and services supplied to EOUs, the same are as per the approved list of supplies for which benefits can be availed? Does maintenance facilitates generation of information required for annual return in respect of all deemed exports? *(Refer – Annual return – Form 9 – Pt.IV – E).*		
10.	Whether in claim of refund of input tax credit accumulated because of exports, deemed exports et cetera is correct?		
11.	Whether the claim for rebate of tax paid on inputs used in the manufacture of goods for export is correct?		
12.	Whether in transaction involving reimport of exported goods by the assessee and claim for drawback is correct?		
13.	Whether in supplies to United Nations bodies and other similar agencies in respect of which domestic taxes are not levied and exemption is provided by way of refund the assessee has followed the procedure correctly?		
14.	Whether in supplies to distinct persons abroad made by the assessee have been dealt directly?		
15.	Whether the treatment of exports of goods or services made to Nepal/Bhutan is correct?		
16.	Whether the transaction in respect of exports to Nepal/ Bhutan when the consideration is received in Indian currency or in Convertible foreign exchange in respect of goods is correct?		
17.	Whether the taxpayer has claimed the benefit of MEIS and SEIS?		

Sl No	Particulars	Remarks Assessee	Remarks Auditor
18.	Whether the procedure followed for supplies to SEZ has been followed and documentation required for supplies to SEZ is complete?		
19.	Whether invoice issued to SEZ have been endorsed by the SO?		
20.	Whether LUT has been filed?		
21.	Whether consideration has been received within one year (interpretation issue)?		

(Refer – Annual return – Form 9 – Pt II –14 - D).

15.2.10 Credit Note

In view of the explanation to section 12 of the CGST act, the supply is deemed to have been made to the extent of consideration received. Therefore when a credit note is issued, the consideration to the extent of the amount for which credit note has been issued comes down and the CGST Law itself provides that it can be taken that the supply of goods or services was made to the extent of consideration received only.

As a result the tax paid on the goods or services or both supplied comes down and the assessee is entitled to claim refund subject to unjust enrichment. Therefore where the recipient has not availed any tax credit, if a credit note is issued because of reduction for the reasons specified in section 34 of CGST act, the benefit of refund would be available.

Sl No	Particulars	Remarks Assessee	Remarks Auditor
	Whether the credit note is issued with GST? If GST not considered then no implication as recipient would have availed the credit. If GST credit given further questions below:		
1.	Whether the credit notes issued by the assessee fulfil all the conditions?		
2.	Whether the assessee has declared the details of credit notes in the return filed?		
3.	Whether the claims for refund are filed where the recipient has taken input tax credit?		

Sl No	Particulars	Remarks Assessee	Remarks Auditor
4.	Whether the credit note is correctly linked to the original invoice?		
5.	Is the linkage of credit note with original invoice real or artificial? (in industries like FMCG etc., distributors undertake many functions including marketing for the manufacturer towards which the consideration is passed on by way of credit notes linked to a sale invoice. Such amounts should instead be recovered by distributors by issuing a GST invoice).		

(Refer – Annual return – Form 9 – Pt II –4 – I and 5 - H).

15.2.11 Debit Note

The Act contemplates issue of debit/credit note by a supplier when the taxable value shown in the invoice is less than the taxable value of the supply or the tax charged in the invoice is less than the tax payable on the supply.

Sl No	Particulars	Remarks Assessee	Remarks Auditor
1.	Whether the details of all debit notes is included in the return filed?		
2.	Whether the debit note shows the tax amount in addition to the taxable value? (If not it has to be seen whether the amount in the debit note has been treated as cum tax amount.)		

(Refer – Annual return – Form 9 – Pt II –4 – J and 5 - I).

15.2.12 Royalties

The documents in relation to royalty would be few and far between and sometimes may not even be in existence if the amount has been paid by book adjustments without any documentation between related parties. Therefore auditors have to check the financial accounts or make specific enquiry as to whether any royalty payments have been made or whether any royalty payments have been received and verify the same.

It would also be necessary to see what is the purpose of royalty and what is the impact of such royalty paid on valuation in the case of imports.

In the case of imports when royalty is linked to the value of imports, it may have to be added to the value of imported goods. Therefore it is necessary that royalty paid is reported to SVB when referred to even if the importer is convinced that it is not includible.

Sl No	Particulars	Remarks Assessee	Remarks Auditor
1.	Whether the assessee has collected any royalty during the audit period and whether tax has been paid on the same?		
2.	Is the tax treatment of any royalty been collected from recipients of services abroad correct?		
3.	Whether the tax treatment of any royalty paid to any person abroad is correct?		

15.2.13 Sale of waste/scrap

Selling of waste/scrap other than specific dealers is only incidental business activity. Waste and scrap disposed of for consideration is liable to tax.

The generation of scrap could be at the factory or job workers premises where the goods are processed. The proper accounting of the quantities would be important.

Sl No	Particulars	Remarks Assessee	Remarks Auditor
1.	Whether the waste and scrap disposed of during the audit period has been documented and tax paid where applicable?		
2.	Whether the disposal of waste/scrap by a job worker or unregistered person has been accounted for and tax paid correctly?		

15.2.14 Sale of capital goods

"Capital goods" means goods, the value of which is capitalised in the books of account of the person claiming the input tax credit and which are used or intended to be used in the course or furtherance of business;

In case of supply of capital goods or plant and machinery on which input tax credit has been taken or not taken, the registered person would have to pay tax. The process for the determination of amount of tax payable varies.

Capital goods lying at the job-workers premises would also be considered as 'capital goods' in the hands of the purchaser as long as the said capital goods are capitalized in his books of account. Therefore, disposal of such capital goods also are considered supplies.

Sl No	Particulars	Remarks Assessee	Remarks Auditor
1	Whether the input tax credit taken in respect of capital goods where capitalised considers, claim for depreciation, installation and erection and also the section 17 as regards credits blocked in respect of capital goods?		
2.	Whether the credit taken or not taken in the case of turnkey contracts is correct?		
3.	Whether on the cost of installation, erection etc. of capital goods capitalised, depreciation not claimed to the extent of input tax credit?		
4.	Whether ITC on capital goods sent for job work is correct and time for return fulfilled?		
5.	Whether the restriction on capital goods credit u/s 17(5) has been complied?		
6.	Whether treatment of capital goods transferred between branches is in line with the law?		
7.	Whether the conditions for transfer of capital goods in case of sale, merger, amalgamation is correct?		
8.	Whether the ITC on capital goods is reversed when written off fully?		
9.	Whether the ITC of CG in case when the assessee is engaged in the supply of exempted as well as taxable supplies is correct?		
10.	Whether the ITC of capital goods exclusively used in the supply of exempted supplies is not taken?		

15.2.15 Employee expenses

Any services provided by an employee to employer in the course of employment is neither a supply of goods or services.

The supply of goods and/or services by an employer to employee is considered a supply and both are considered related persons.

Therefore it becomes necessary that necessary internal control mechanism is in place when supply of services or goods are made to employees.

All recoveries made from the employees also have to be examined in the light of the definition of service and tax if payable paid.

Audit checks:

Sl No	Particulars	Remarks Assessee	Remarks Auditor
1	Whether transactions between the employer and the employee which attract the GST (such as gifts, subsidies and other benefits in cash or in-kind) if any payable is paid correctly?		
2.	Whether the notice period recovery made has been subjected to tax?		
3.	Whether tax is paid on appropriate value in transactions with the employee wherein the assets of the company are provided to the employee for his personal benefit either free of cost are at a nominal cost?		
4	Whether information required in the reconciliation statement can be generated? *(Refer – Reconciliation Statement – Part A – Pt.IV – 14 – H)*		

15.2.16 Works Contract and continuous supply contracts

Works contract as understood in the trade cannot be applied in the GST regime for the purpose of implementation of GST. Since works contract can also be a continuous contract, both types of contracts are being discussed together.

The expression 'works contract' is limited to contracts relating to immoveable property in the GST regime and covers not only construction but also repairs, renovation etc. A contract would amount to a 'works contract' only where there is a transfer of property in goods, while such a transfer may result in goods or anything else (i.e., immoveable property). A contract in relation to movable property, however, would be treated as a 'composite supply' of goods or services depending on the principal supply. Works contract as defined above would be treated as a supply of service.

Credit of GST paid on works contract services would be allowed only if the output is also works contract services. However in relation to installation of plant and machinery, credit is allowed. The activity which is not capitalised may also be examined for its admissibility.

Continuous supply of goods means recurrent supply of goods over a period of time under a contract. Such supply can be through a wire, pipeline or other conduit. In the case of services, period of three months has been fixed for provision of services to treat as continuous supply of services.

Sl No	Particulars	Remarks Assessee	Remarks Auditor
1	Whether in continuous supply contract which has provision for periodical/ milestone payments the time of issue of invoice and tax payment is correct?		
2.	Whether the assessee has kept separate account for each works contract correctly?		
3.	Whether the tax treatment in case of continuous contracts which were not completed as on 1 July 2017 and completed subsequently is correct?		
4.	Whether TDS has been taken as input tax credit or not?*		

15.2.17 Electronic commerce

This part includes both e commerce operator and the sellers who sell through him and purchase from the operator.

In the GST law, e commerce operator term includes aggregators (those who provide a platform for others to supply through them).

The Government is empowered to notify categories of services wherein the person responsible for payment of taxes would nether be the supplier nor the recipient of supply, but the e-commerce operator through whom the supply is affected.

If the e-commerce operator does not have physical presence in the country, he has to necessarily appoint a representative.

Sl No	Particulars	Remarks Assessee	Remarks Auditor
1	Whether the e-commerce operator has collected taxes and paid on goods (TCS)?		
2.	Whether the tax paid by the e-commerce operator is taken as credit at the time of payment of GST by supplier?		

15.2.18 Composition scheme

The composition levy is an alternative method of levy of tax designed for small taxpayers. At present the aggregate turnover limit for availing composition scheme is Rs. 1 crore. The threshold limit for opting into composition scheme recommended is to increase to Rs. 1.5 crores but is yet to be notified.

Verification of the records of the assessee who has opted for composition levy

Sl No	Particulars	Remarks Assessee	Remarks Auditor
1	Whether the taxable person is not engaged in supply of services other than restaurant services?		
2.	Whether the computation of aggregate turnover for eligibility is correct? (all businesses under the same pan number)		
3.	Is there any interstate supply of goods?		
4.	Whether no supply of goods through an electronic commerce operator is there?		
5.	Whether the phrase "composition taxable person, not eligible to collect tax on supplies" is provided or not in bill?		

(Refer – Annual Return – Pt.VI – 16 –A)

15.2.19 Actionable Claims

'Actionable claim' means a claim to any debt, other than a debt secured by mortgage of immovable property or by hypothecation or pledge of movable property or to any beneficial interest in movable property not in the possession, either actual or constructive, of the claimant, which the Civil Courts recognize as affording grounds for relief, whether such debt or beneficial interest be existent, accruing, conditional or contingent.

The definition of goods includes actionable claims. However Schedule III to CGST Act treats actionable claims other than betting, gambling and lottery as neither goods nor services.

The law relating to actionable claim is yet to settle in the case of service tax itself and in future also this area is expected to create disputes.

15.2.20 Supplies to/through an agent

"Agent" is a person, including a factor, broker, commission agent, *arhatia*, *del credere* agent, an auctioneer or any other mercantile agent, by whatever name called, who carries on the business of supply or receipt of goods or services or both on behalf of another;

Supply of goods by a principal to his **agent** where the **agent** undertakes to supply such goods on behalf of the principal and vice versa are considered as supplies.

Receipt of goods by the agent of the person is considered as the receipt by the principal.

Sl No	Particulars	Remarks Assessee	Remarks Auditor
1	Whether the taxable person has taken credit of tax paid on inputs or capital goods received by his agent?		
2.	Whether the taxable person has paid the tax amount to the person in respect of the supplies received by his agent within 180 days?		

15.2.21 Receipts in convertible currency

The rate of exchange in respect of goods has to be determined based on the time of supply and the rate of exchange applicable is as per the notification issued by Central Board of Excise and Customs and section 14 of customs act 1962. As regards services, the rule 34 of CGST Rules provides that the rate of exchange has to be determined in accordance with generally accepted accounting principles.

Sl No	Particulars	Remarks Assessee	Remarks Auditor
1	Whether the tax paid in respect of receipts in convertible foreign currency for supplies is correct?		
2.	If there is a difference between actual amount received/paid and as per the documents relating to export/import, does the account maintained show it so that it can be used for reconciliation? *(Refer – Reconciliation Statement – Part A – Pt. – 5 –N)*		

15.2.22 Financial Management

There may be some areas where there is a need to examine the GST liability even though the transaction could be considered as part of treasury management or financial management of the company. Even though the transactions in relation to money are exempt, there are implications in terms of requirement of reversal of input tax credit attributable to such receipts and also determination of credits which are to be considered as common credits. Therefore it becomes necessary to see whether there are any receipts or expenses in relation to money which may have financial implications under the GST regime in terms of input tax credit or liability to GST.

Implications in terms of output tax liability or exempted supply leading to requirement of reversal of input tax credit taken attributable to transactions and determination of common credit.

Sl No	Particulars	Remarks Assessee	Remarks Auditor
1	Check whether any bankruptcy dividend has been received as income.		
2	Check whether any loans have been extended or deposits have been made resulting in interest earnings by the assessee and examine whether the ITC requirements have been fulfilled.		
3	Check whether any insurance claims have been received and if so, examine whether there are any implications in respect of input tax credit on the item on which the insurance claim arises.		
4	Examine whether any bad debts have been written off and implications thereof in terms of GST liability.		
5	Examine whether credit of GST paid on interest liabilities of trade creditors, bills payable et cetera has been taken as credit.		
6	Examine GST liability in respect of loans, mortgages et cetera		
7	Examine the GST liability in respect of transactions with a subsidiary company, if any.		
8	Examine whether credit of GST paid on interest liabilities of trade creditors, bills payable etc., has been taken as credit.		

15.2.23 MERGERS/ACQUISITIONS/AMALGAMATIONS:

Sl No	Particulars	Remarks Assessee	Remarks Auditor
1	Review of process of merger/acquisition/ amalgamation in the light of GST provisions.		

15.2.24 BANK STATEMENT/RECONCILIATION:

Sl No	Particulars	Remarks Assessee	Remarks Auditor
1	Examine the bank statement to see whether there is any unexplained income which can be found by the departmental audit and result in demand for GST on such income. Examine the liability of such unexplained income to GST.		
2	Examine the bank reconciliation statement prepared and if any discrepancy has been found, consider the GST implications.		

Chapter 16

Inward Supply

16.1 INTRODUCTION

The proper verification of supplies of goods or services or both received in the GST regime can be beneficial to a taxpayer. It can identify credits missed out, duplicated, short/ excess availed and wrongly taken. This would enable remedial action and can serve as a guide for the management in making modifications in the purchase policy/ system. Answers given to the internal control questions and the documentation and record maintenance relating to input tax credit availment and their verification would help in proper input tax credit management. Legal provisions relating to reversal of credits in case of non-payment of consideration, reverse charge of GST, procedure relating to payment of taxes in respect of purchase from unregistered persons etc. have increased the onerous responsibilities of an assessee as regards compliance and compliance risks.

In view of the fact that GST regime aims at seamless credit flow the beginning of the trade cycle of a product or a service to the end consumer, the quantum of credit available is substantial and availment of all admissible credit would enhance the competitiveness of the business and increase profitability and proper compliance with the law would reduce risks involved. Therefore audit of records and documents connected with all inward receipts of goods or services or both by way of an internal thorough scrutiny and verification and consequent implementation would add value to every business.

16.2 INPUT TAX CREDIT

The auditors would look into the following aspects and data in the financial accounts keeping in mind the provisions in the GST law and consider whether the financial statements and the data contained therein are compliant with GST law.

Sl No	Particulars	Remarks Assessee	Remarks Auditor
1	Whether the original documents based on which credit is taken contain all particulars?		
2.	Whether the supply is received?		
3.	Whether the credit is eligible and not restricted? (With reference to section 17 of CGST Act)		

Sl No	Particulars	Remarks Assessee	Remarks Auditor
4.	Whether the payments in respect of all the supplies is made within 180 days?		
5.	Whether amounts reversed have been taken to a suspense account and credit availed on payment?		
6.	Whether the input tax credit pertaining to an invoice has been claimed within September of the following financial year to which the invoice relates or within the due date of filing annual return for the financial year to which the invoice relate whichever is earlier?		
7.	Whether apportionment of common input tax credit and reversal of inadmissible credit in such cases has been done correctly?		
8.	Whether the credit has been taken at the time of receipt of last instalment when the supply is made in instalments?		
9.	Whether in the case of 'bill to ship to' transactions, where the assessee is not the person who is billed, another invoice has been raised by the person who ordered and is available with the auditee?		
10.	Whether credit is NOT taken in respect of certain goods lost, stolen, destroyed, written of or disposed of by way of gift or free samples?		
11.	Whether credit in respect of construction of immovable property (other than plant and machinery) has NOT been taken?		
12.	Whether credit of tax paid to a composition scheme supplier has NOT been taken?		
13.	Whether credit has NOT been taken on goods or services are both used for personal consumption?		
14.	Where vendor has issued a credit note with GST, whether such amount of GST has been reversed and deducted from ITC availed?		

Sl No	Particulars	Remarks Assessee	Remarks Auditor
15.	Whether credit of tax paid as a result of order made under section 74 invoking extended period on the ground of miss declaration, suppression of facts etcetera, has NOT been taken?		
16.	Whether credit of tax paid has NOT been taken in respect of goods which were seized in transit and released?		
17.	Whether in case of cross change from branches/ HO credit is availed correctly?		
18.	Whether the assessee had issued invoices for the inputs or capital goods sent to job worker which are not received back or supplied further within in the time limit prescribed? *(Refer – Annual return – Form 9 – Pt - VI –16 -B).*		
19.	Whether self-invoice issued in respect of goods or services or both received from unregistered person is for the correct quantity of goods or the service received by the taxpayer?*		
20.	Whether the availment of credit in respect of inputs and capital goods sent for job work is correct?		
21.	Whether the contract for job work with the job worker specifically provides for the processed losses during the processing of inputs?		
22.	Whether in case of the assessee becoming liable to pay tax in the middle of the financial year, the declaration of goods contained in semi-finished or finished goods held in stock or the capital goods have been calculated correctly and if required a certificate obtained from Chartered/ Cost Accountant?		

(Refer – Annual return – Form 9 – Pt III –6).

(Refer – Reconciliation Statement – Part A – Pt. IV – 14)

16.3 ITC - CAPITAL GOODS

There is only one question given below in respect of capital goods. However it has to be noted that the verification of ITC on capital goods would be similar to input supplies of goods or services or both. The only difference that arises is in computation of eligible credit. The availment of ITC on capital goods requires thorough knowledge of methods of calculation of turnover, common credit, monthly eligible credit, principles relating to capitalisation and eligibility criteria. The one question given below comprises all these aspects and requires detailed study.

Sl No	Particulars	Remarks Assessee	Remarks Auditor
1	Whether the credit of tax paid on capital goods received and captialised is correct?		

(Refer – Annual return – Part III – 6)

The information required in the annual return has to be compiled from the books of account and filed. The total of credit taken in respect of inputs and capital goods in respect of each item should tally with the total credit availed. There is a need to maintain books of account, if not maintained, in such a manner that information can be easily taken out for annual return.

(Refer – Reconciliation Statement – Form 9C- Part A – Pt. IV – 14)

16.4 INPUT SERVICE DISTRIBUTION

The term 'input service distributor' means an office of the supplier of goods or services or both which receives tax invoices issued under section 31 of the CGST Act towards the receipt of input services and issues a prescribed document for the purpose of distributing the credit of tax paid having the same permanent account number as that of the said office. This facilitates use of tax credits when billing is done to a different or central office of the same tax payer other than to who the supply is made. The common expenses invoices may also be received at such office.

Sl No	Particulars	Remarks Assessee	Remarks Auditor
1	Whether the ratio of distribution of input tax credit for each service received and distributed is correct?		
2.	Whether the credit received is distributed in the same month?		

From 1986 onwards till the introduction of GST, maximum number of disputes have arisen in matters related to CENVAT credit. The provisions relating to input tax credit in the GST law does not give any hope this would undergo change. Therefore auditor needs to understand the eligibility and examine that no future exposure is there.

(Refer – Annual return – Form 9 – Pt II –6 -G).

16.5 REVERSE CHARGE MECHANISM

RCM would include notified goods or services or both even if the supplier is registered and other supplies made by unregistered supplier to a registered recipient.

In the case of notified goods or services or both, Persons required to pay tax under reverse charge are required to obtain registration whether or not they make any outward supplies. Threshold limits for registration do not apply. Composition tax rates are not applicable and therefore normal tax rates would apply. Registered persons availing composition tax rates also have to pay tax on supplies taxable on reverse charge basis at normal rates only. All provisions of the law would apply to the recipient of such goods and/or services, as if the recipient is the supplier of such goods and/or services.

Reverse charge levy from unregistered suppliers has been kept in abeyance at present.

Sl No	Particulars	Remarks Assessee	Remarks Auditor
1	Whether the assessee has paid the tax in respect of goods or services or both received from unregistered person as notified?		
2.	In all such cases whether the taxability, nature of tax, classification, rate of tax, value, eligibility for input tax credit/capital goods credit, time of supply, place of supply etc. is correct?		
3	Review of treatment of directors' sitting fees as regards discharge of GST liability and availment of credit of the input tax credit.		
4	Review of treatment of gifts/freebies provided to directors, if any and the treatment of expenses reimbursed to the directors as regards GST liability and ITC.		
5	Review of expenses incurred by the company on the directors in respect of which invoices are in the name of the company and availment of ITC.		

(Refer – Annual return – Form 9 – Pt III –6 – B, C and D).

16.6 IMPORTS

The import of goods has been defined in the IGST Act, 2017 as bringing goods into India from a place outside India. All imports shall be deemed as inter-State supplies and accordingly IGST would be levied in addition to the applicable

Custom duties. IGST is levied on value plus specified customs duties. In addition, GST compensation cess also would be leviable wherever applicable and would be collected on the value taken for levying integrated tax. The place of supply of goods in case of imports would be the location of the importer.

It has been clarified that IGST on high sea sale(s) transactions of imported goods, whether one or multiple, shall be levied and collected only at the time of importation i.e. when the import declarations are filed before the Customs authorities for the customs clearance purposes for the first time.

Most of the aspects to be covered have been covered in relevant places. An attempt has been made to cover some aspects which may not be relevant in the point of view of GST but would be useful to the assessee.

Sl No	Particulars	Remarks Assessee	Remarks Auditor
1	Whether in case the taxpayer has been extended the benefit of authorised economic operator and whether the accounts and records which are required to be maintained as per the requirements of customs have been maintained?		
2.	Whether the taxpayer has claimed the benefit of MEIS and SEIS scrips for payment of customs duty?		
3	Whether the drawback claimed on exports is correct?		
4	Whether the classification and rate of duty adopted for the purpose of import of goods by the taxpayer is correct?		
5	Whether the assessee has paid the interest and customs duties for delays?		
6	Whether the disputes with the customs Department (show cause notice/order) have been dealt with correctly?		

Furthermore, in view of the provisions contained in Schedule I of the CGST Act, 2017, the import of services by a taxable person from a related person or from a distinct person as defined in Section 25 of the CGST Act, 2017, in the course or furtherance of business shall be treated as supply even if it is made without any consideration.

(Refer – Reconciliation Statement – Part A – Pt. IV – 14 – D)

(Refer – Annual return – Form 9 – Pt III –6 – E and F).

16.7 SALES RETURNS

Auditors have to check whether there are any (supply) sales returns and how they have been dealt with to verify whether necessary internal control checks have been established and if established have actually been working.

The sales returns are at times made to a warehouse/branch other than the originating State. In such cases the stock transfer for goods returned to the GSTIN who received such goods is to be made from originating State. The branch/ warehouse may issue the credit note to the customer for the return.

16.8 VALUATION OF SUPPLIES RECEIVED

Sl. No.	Particulars	Remarks Assessee	Remarks Auditor
1.	Whether includability of expenses incurred on items like tools jigs, fixtures, engineering, design etc. paid separately for supply to the exporter of the goods or to any other person in the case of import of goods is correct?		
2.	Whether the correctness of the details furnished to the customs department and the legality of valuation adopted for transfer of goods from the supplier in the case of imports from related party is correct?		
3.	Whether the documents relating to special valuation branch investigation, adjudication and finalisation of provisional assessments and sanction of refunds etc. are correct?		
4.	Whether the value adopted in the case of free supplies from abroad, supplies of replacements for defective goods or parts supplied, supply of prototype, samples and their valuation is correct?		
5.	Whether the value of free supplies made for the purpose of charity under claim for exemption, if any is correct?		
6.	Whether taxability and value of services received from abroad is correct?		
7.	Whether the value adopted in the case of goods and services received from unregistered person if the registered person liable to pay tax is correct?		
8.	Whether reversal is done where payment is not made within 180 days for the goods or supplies received?		

Sl. No.	Particulars	Remarks Assessee	Remarks Auditor
9.	Whether the obligation of liability to pay tax in in respect of which reverse charge mechanism is applicable is correct?		
10.	Verify whether the value adopted for importation in the case of purchases made on high seas is correct?		

16.9 ASSETS/GOODS/SERVICES PROVIDED TO THE COMPANY BY SOMEONE ELSE

Sl No	Particulars	Remarks Assessee	Remarks Auditor
1	Check whether input tax credit admissible has been availed on assets/inputs/input services for which payment for made by others but the inputs or input services have been received and used in furtherance of business.		
2	In the case of imports also, check whether admissible ITC has been availed even when the supplier has borne the liability of IGST paid on imports.		

16.10 EMPLOYEE EXPENSES

Sl No	Particulars	Remarks Assessee	Remarks Auditor
1	Check whether travelling expenses have been reimbursed by the company to the employees and bills or invoices are in the name of the employees. Check whether inadmissible ITC has been taken in such cases.		
2	Check whether admissible ITC has been availed of the tax paid on travelling expenses for the employees have been borne by the auditee and bills or invoices are in the name of the auditee.		

16.11 PRELIMINARY EXPENSES OF BUSINESS

Any business before commencement has to incur preliminary expenses and while doing so would receive inputs or input services. In the GST regime, no credit is admissible unless the person is registered. Therefore as soon as a business is proposed to be set up, it would be advisable to take registration so that GST liability incurred in respect of inputs and input services received during the course of setting up the business can be taken and utilised.

Sl No	Particulars	Remarks Assessee	Remarks Auditor
1	Check whether the taxpayer has taken the credit of GST paid on inputs/input services at the time of setting up of business.		
2	if answer to 1 above is nil, check whether credit of GST paid on inputs and input services within one year prior to registration has been taken or not		

16.12 RESEARCH AND DEVELOPMENT

Sl No	Particulars	Remarks Assessee	Remarks Auditor
1	Check whether the activity of research and development undertaken by the auditee is liable to GST because the same is undertaken on the goods of the recipient who is abroad		
2	Check whether the credit has been taken on the inputs and input services used in research and development activities provided the output of research and development activity has not been supplied free of cost to anyone.		
3	If the research and development activity has been outsourced, check whether the credit of input tax paid on services received has been taken.		

16.13 FINANCIAL MANAGEMENT

There may be some areas where there is a need to examine the GST liability even though the transaction could be considered as part of treasury management or financial management of the company. Even though the transactions in relation to money are exempt, there are implications in terms of requirement of reversal of input tax credit attributable to such receipts and also determination of credits which are to be considered as common credits. Therefore it becomes necessary to see whether there are any receipts or expenses in relation to money which may have financial implications under the GST regime in terms of input tax credit or liability to GST.

Implications in terms of input tax credit leading to requirement of reversal of input tax credit taken attributable to transactions and determination of common credit.

Sl No	Particulars	Remarks Assessee	Remarks Auditor
1	Examine whether the credit of input tax paid on bill discounting fee has been availed.		
2	Examine whether credit of GST paid on interest liabilities of trade creditors, bills payable et cetera has been taken as credit.		
3	Examine GST liability in respect of loans, mortgages et cetera		
4	Examine the GST liability in respect of transactions with a subsidiary company, if any.		

16.14 MERGERS/ACQUISITIONS/AMALGAMATIONS:

Sl No	Particulars	Remarks Assessee	Remarks Auditor
1	Review of process of merger/acquisition/ amalgamation in the light of GST provisions.		

16.15 BANK STATEMENT/RECONCILIATION:

Sl No	Particulars	Remarks Assessee	Remarks Auditor
1	Examine the bank statement to see whether there is any unexplained income which can be found by the departmental audit and result in demand for GST on such income. Examine the liability of such unexplained income to GST.		
2	Examine the bank reconciliation statement prepared and if any discrepancy has been found, consider the GST implications.		

Note: In most audits only part of the checklist would be relevant. For specific industries there maybe a need to have additional check points.

Chapter 17

Procedural Aspects

17.1 REGISTRATION UNDER GST

17.1.1 Introduction

Procedure for registration and all issues related to registration have been discussed in the Chapter 1 & 2 [Basic Concepts and Procedures]. The auditors should consult the relevant portions in the overview to ensure that all issues are covered relating to registration during the audit.

The audit verification would involve verification of validity of the registration, correspondence with the department relating to registration, documents submitted for the purpose of registration and their correctness, omissions and commissions in taking registration from the department, registration of branches within the State undertaking business under different verticals etc. Verification is needed to see whether a separate registration should have been taken in respect of establishments elsewhere which are not registered but required to be registered et cetera.

17.1.2 Compliance Checkpoints

Various compliance checkpoints and procedural aspects that need to be reviewed in the registration process under GST are as under:

Sl No	Description	Remarks Assessee	Remarks Auditor
1	Whether auditee was registered under any of the following earlier laws viz., Service Tax/Central Excise/VAT/CST and ensures complete migration under GST. If not, ascertain the reasons?		
2	Whether the auditee falls under the category of persons who are not liable to be registered?		
3	If not, whether the aggregate turnover of auditee in financial year exceeded the prescribed limit Rs.10 lakhs or 20 lakhs as the case may be? (Rs. 40 lakh for supply of goods w.e.f 1st April 2019 in most of the States)		

Sl No	Description	Remarks Assessee	Remarks Auditor
4	Whether the auditee is compulsory liable to be registered u/s 24?		
5	Make a list of all the premises from where the supplies are made by the auditee to ensure that GST registration is obtained for all the premises in each State?		
6	Whether the auditee has obtained registration within the prescribed time period (i.e. 30 days from the date auditee is liable to be registered)?		
7	Where the auditee has multiple premises/business verticals has the review of options of separate registration been done?		
8	Where the auditee is falling under any of the prescribed persons for whom obtaining Unique Identity Number is mandatory- has it been applied?		
9	Whether the registration is obtained as an Input Service Distributor (ISD) in order to distribute the credits if done?		
10	Whether SEZ has obtained separate registration apart from the normal registration?		
11	Where the auditee is a casual taxable person or Non-resident taxable person- has registration been done?		
12	If yes, whether they have applied for registration at least five days in advance before making any supply? Also, whether they have deposited estimated tax liability and registration is granted only after they make advance deposit of the estimated tax liability?		
13	Whether in case of amendments in registration certificate the same is intimated to the department within 15 days of such amendments in GST Reg-14 (legal name of the business, or the State of place of business or additional place of business)?		
14	Whether the change in the constitution of any business that results in the change of the Permanent Account Number of a registered person, a fresh registration in Form GST REG-01 has been applied for?		

Sl No	Description	Remarks Assessee	Remarks Auditor
15	Whether any registrations were cancelled under GST to ensure that all the prescribed documents have been submitted as per Rule 20 for such cancellation and that the account is timely suspended?		
16	Whether all required returns are filed and tax dues are paid by the auditee at the time of cancellation of registration?		
17	Whether there is any transfer of business on account of amalgamation, de-merger, sale, change in constitution etc. and whether new GST registration has been taken by the transferee?		
18	Whether auditee has displayed certificate of registration and GSTIN at his place of business and on the name board respectively?		
19	Whether the authorised signatory satisfies all the norms specified in the rules?		
20	Where goods are stored at any transporter's warehouse, whether the premise is added as an additional place of business in RC? `		

17.2 RETURNS UNDER GST

17.2.1 Introduction

Returns are the means of communication between the tax payers and administrators. The auditor is required to check the compliance and disclosure requirements of the computations of the liability of the tax determined and paid along with the details as submitted in the various returns filed under GST. The auditor is to verify the timeliness, completeness and correctness of the filing of the returns and the information as submitted therein. Various areas of verification in the returns filed are as under.

Sl. No.	Description	Remarks Assessee	Remarks Auditor
1	Whether monthly returns have been filed within due date GSTR 1/GSTR 3B?		
2	Whether all the details w.r.t outward supplies such as in GSTR-1/3B are provided by auditee?		

Sl. No.	Description	Remarks Assessee	Remarks Auditor
3	Whether the auditee is maintaining the reconciliation b/w the total turnover as per GSTR-1 vs. Total Direct & Indirect incomes in P&L?		
4	Whether all the details w.r.t inward supplies including are properly disclosed in GSTR-3B by auditee?		
5	Whether the auditee is maintaining the reconciliation b/w the total expenses as per GSTR-3B vs. Total Direct & Indirect expenses in P&L? Whether Purchase register (books) has all required fields?		
6	Whether ITC as per 2A and 3B is reconciled? If any ITC is not availed the same has to be availed on or before September of the following year. If not, the ITC would lapse, unless extended		
8	Whether optimum ITC utilization considered based on the changes in the law on utilisation?		
7	Whether the auditee is required to file quarterly return? [Applicable in case of assessee who opted Composition scheme]		
8	If yes, whether the auditee has filed the quarterly (GSTR-4) return within the due date?		
9	Whether that auditee has furnished all the details in the return properly? Whether auditee has paid full tax dues as furnished in return?		
10	Whether monthly (GSTR-7) return for tax deducted, if applicable, has been filed within due date?		
11	If yes, whether the auditee (Non-Resident Foreign Taxpayer) has filed monthly (GSTR-5) return within the due date (before 20th of next month or within 7 days after 90th day of registration whichever is earlier)?		
12	Whether auditee is registered as Input Service Distributor?		
13	If yes, whether the auditee has filed monthly (GSTR-6) return within the due date?		
14	Whether auditee is registered as an E-Commerce operator required to collect TCS post 1st October 2018?		

Sl. No.	Description	Remarks Assessee	Remarks Auditor
15	If yes, whether the auditee has filed monthly (GSTR-8) return within the due date?		
16	Whether credits disclosed in the GST return are reconciled with electronic credit ledger?		
17	Whether returns for every month are filed whether or not any supplies have been made during the month - **Nil Returns?**		
18	Whether all the **mis-matches** are properly addressed and the reasons for the same are being documented?		
19	Whether auditee has declared the quantum of ineligible ITC which are for used for non-taxable supplies or other than business purposes in Form GSTR-3B?		
20	Whether any inward supplies which are ineligible, either fully or partially are specified in Form GSTR-3B by the auditee?		
21	Whether the auditee has filed Annual (GSTR-9) return. If yes, check whether the same has been filed within due date? [Not applicable in some cases]		
22	Whether the return has been filed within due date and the details furnished are accurate and proper?		
23	Whether auditee has **discontinued operations** from any of his branches, change in the constitution of business, not liable to be registered for other than persons in 25(3)? If yes, whether auditee has filed an application for cancellation of registration?		
24	Whether the auditee has filed **Final return** within due date?		
25	Whether auditee has made any **delay in filing of** any of the periodical returns? If yes whether late filing fees and interest if any has been paid?		
26	Whether auditee has received any **notice from the Dept.** requiring filing the returns?		
27	Whether the auditee has **reverted** within the stipulated time period?		

Sl. No.	Description	Remarks Assessee	Remarks Auditor
28	Whether the auditee is sending inputs and capital goods to **job worker** for further processing? If yes, whether details of inputs and capital goods sent to job worker and received back are furnished quarterly in Form **GST ITC-04?**		
29	Confirm that all the above points as relevant are compiled for all other registrations?		

17.2.2 Returns for Regular taxpayers other than casual taxable person

Form No.	Frequency	Due Date	Details to be Furnished
Form GSTR-1	Monthly	11th of succeeding month	Invoice level details of outward supplies.
Form GSTR-2A	Monthly	Auto populates (No due date/last date)	Inward supply details shall be auto populated on the basis GSTR-1 of the suppliers.
Form GSTR-2	Monthly	11th to 15th of succeeding month (The date for GSTR-2 deferred indefinitely).	Invoice level details of outward supplies. Shall be prepared on the basis of actions (Accept, reject, Modify, add, pending) of the recipient on the data auto-populated in GSTR-2A.
From GSTR-1A	Monthly	Accept or reject by 17th of next month *(Presently, ineffective)*	Any modifications/rejections made by the recipients, for the data submitted in GSTR-1 of supplier shall be auto-populated in GSTR-1A. Based on actions of supplier, his GSTR-1 gets updated.
Form GSTR-3	Monthly	20th of succeeding month (The date for GSTR-3 deferred indefinitely.)	Monthly return on the basis of finalization of details of GSTR-1 and GSTR-2, along with the payment of amount of tax, interest, fees… etc.
Form GSTR-3B	Monthly	20th of succeeding month	As simple statement type of return, introduced as an interim return for submission of gross amounts and payment of tax. This was introduced as

Form No.	Frequency	Due Date	Details to be Furnished
			the trade and GSTTN are not ready for complete structure of GSTR-1, 2 and 3. This is applicable up to March'19.
Form GSTR-9	Annually	By 31st Dec of the following financial year. Extended to 30th June 2019 for July 2017 – March 2018.	Annual Return – furnish the details of ITC availed and GST paid which includes local, interstate and import/exports.
Form GSTR-9C	Annually	By 31st Dec of the following financial year. Extended to 30th June 2019 for July 2017 – March 2018.	Reconciliation statement reconciling the outward supplies, inward supplies, ITC refund details etc between annual return in form GSTR-9 and financial statements.

17.2.3 Returns for Composite Tax Payers

Form Type	Frequency	Due Date	Details to be Furnished
Form GSTR-4A	Quarterly	Auto populated	Invoice wise details of inward supplies form registered persons gets auto-populated on the basis of GSTR-1 of the suppliers.
Form GSTR-4	Quarterly	18th of the month following the end of the quarter*	All outward and inward supply details to be furnished. This includes invoice level details of Inward supplies prepared on the basis of auto-populated details from Form GSTR-4A.
Form GSTR-9A	Annual	31st Dec of next financial year	Furnish the consolidated details of quarterly returns filed along with tax payment details.

***** ***For assessees opting for composition scheme based on notification 2/2019, G.S.R. 189(E) -Central Tax (Rate) dated 7th March 2019 – Payments have to be made by 18th of the month following the end of the quarter, although GSTR-4 can be filed on annual basis by 30th April following the end of such financial year.***

17.2.4 Returns for Non- Resident Taxpayers

Form Type	Frequency	Due Date	Details to be Furnished
Form GSTR-5	Monthly	20th of succeeding month or within 7 days after the expiry of registration	Details of imports, outward supplies, ITC availed, tax paid and closing stock

17.2.5 Returns for Online information and database access and retrieval services

Form Type	Frequency	Due Date	Details to be Furnished
Form GSTR-5A	Monthly	20th of succeeding month	Details of Service provided from a place outside India to a person in India other than a registered person.

17.2.6 Returns for Input Service Distributor

Form Type	Frequency	Due Date	Details to be Furnished
FORM GSTR-6A	Monthly	Auto populated	All the inward supply details shall get auto populated, on the basis of GSTR-1 filed by the suppliers.
Form GSTR-6	Monthly	13th of succeeding month	The details of eligible and ineligible credits and the details of distribution of credit to be provided.

17.2.7 Returns for Tax Deductor

Form Type	Frequency	Due Date	Details to be Furnished
Form GSTR-7	Monthly	10th of succeeding month	GSTIN wise details of the gross amounts paid and tax deducted from the payments made.

17.2.8 Returns for E-Commerce

Form Type	Frequency	Due Date	Details to be furnished
Form GSTR-8	Monthly	10th of succeeding month	Details of supplies effected through e-commerce operator and the amount of tax collected on supplies
Form GSTR-9B	Annually	31st Dec of next fiscal	Details of outward supplies of goods or services or both effected/returned through it and the amount of tax collected.

17.2.9 Final Return

Every taxable person whose registration has been surrendered or cancelled has to furnish this return.

Return Type	Frequency	Due Date	Details to be furnished
Form GSTR-10	One time return	Within 3 months of cancellation of registration	Furnish details of reversal of credit held in inputs, semi-finished, final goods and capital goods, tax payable and paid.

17.2.10 Returns for Government Departments and United Nation Bodies

Return Type	Frequency	Due Date	Details to be furnished
Form GSTR-11	Monthly	Not specified	Details of inward supplies to be furnished by a person having UIN.

In additions to the above specified returns, there are multiple special purpose returns under GST and all such returns should be filed online only.

17.2.11 Additional measures and Late Fee

(i) The time lines for filing GSTR-1 have been extended for the period July 2017 to September 2018 to 31st October 2018. The dates for GSTR-2 & GSTR-3 are deferred indefinitely.

(ii) Further, for filing of details in FORM GSTR-1 till March 2018, taxpayers had been divided into two categories as followed:

Taxpayers with annual aggregate turnover up to Rs. 1.5 crore need to file GSTR-1 on quarterly basis. The due dates from October 2018 to March

2019 till end of the month of the following quarter. The due date from July 2018 to September 2018 extended till 31st December 2018 (Persons obtained registration under Notification No. 31/2018 CT.

(iii) Taxpayers with annual aggregate turnover more than Rs. 1.5 crore need to file GSTR-1 on monthly basis. The due dates from October 2018 to March 2019 till the 11th day of succeeding month. The due date from July 2018 to November 2018 extended till 31st December 2018 (Persons obtained registration under Notification No. 31/2018 CT. (iv) The late fee is waived for the following months:

- Filed GSTR 3B for the period Jul'17-Sep'17.
- Filed GSTR 3B for the period Oct' 17 to April' 2018 those who have submitted but not filed Tran – 1 on or before 27.12.2017 and
- Filed GSTR 3B on or before 31.05.2018, Tran – 1 is to be filed on or before 10.05.2018.

(v) For GSTR-3B Oct'17 onwards and for GSTR-1, late fee payable by a taxpayer whose tax liability for that month was 'NIL' will be Rs. 20/- per day per return (Rs. 10/- per day each under CGST & SGST Acts) and for others it is Rs. 50/- (Rs. 25/- per day each under CGST & SGST Acts) per day per return instead of Rs. 200/- per day (Rs. 100/- per day each under CGST & SGST Acts).

(vi) For GSTR-4 the late fee payable by a taxpayer whose tax liability for that month was 'NIL' will be Rs. 10/- per day per return (Rs. 10/- per day each under CGST & SGST Acts) and for others it is Rs. 50/- (Rs. 25/- per day each under CGST & SGST Acts) per day per return.

(vii) For GSTR-5 the late fee payable by a taxpayer whose tax liability for that month was 'NIL' will be Rs. 10/- per day per return (Rs. 10/- per day each under CGST & SGST Acts) and for others it is Rs. 50/- (Rs. 25/- per day each under CGST & SGST Acts) per day per return.

(viii) For GSTR-6 the late fee payable by a taxpayer whose tax liability for that month was 'NIL' will be Rs. 10/- per day per return (Rs. 10/- per day each under CGST & SGST Acts) and for others it is Rs. 50/- (Rs. 25/- per day each under CGST & SGST Acts) per day per return.

(ix) Late fees against GSTR 1, GSTR 3B & GSTR 4 for the period July 2017 to September 2018 has been waived for persons who have not filed within due date but filed between 22nd December 2018 to 31st March 2019. Refer notification 75/76/77-2018, GSR No. 1252(E)/1253(E)/1254(E), dated 31st December 2018.

Note: Late fees against GSTR-1 is not auto-populating in the GST portal presently.

17.3 RECORDS UNDER GST

17.3.1 Introduction

Assessment in GST is mainly focused on self - assessment by the taxpayers themselves. The compliance verification is done by the department through scrutiny of returns, audit and/or investigation. Thus the auditor is required to check the compliance through documentary checks rather than physical controls. This requires certain obligations to be cast on the taxpayer for keeping and maintaining accounts and records.

Sl. No.	Description	Remarks Assessee	Remarks Auditor
1	Whether all the mandatory records are maintained at the place of business as mentioned in registration certificate? (a) production or manufacture of goods (b) inward and outward supplies Compare with details of supplies made to unregistered persons and registered persons (B2C and B2B) generated from monthly returns filed. *(Refer – Annual return – Form 9 – Part A – Pt. IV – 4 A&B).* (c) stock of goods (d) output tax payable and paid		
2	Whether records are maintained at such respective place of businesses in case of more than one place of business as per registration certificate		
3	Whether the records mentioned below are maintained? (a) Record of Goods, services imported, exported (b) Supplies liable under RCM (c) Invoices, Bill of Supply, Delivery Challan, Debit Note, Credit Note, payment, receipt and refund vouchers (d) Stock records (e) Advances paid/received (f) Tax paid, collected, details of ITC (g) E-way bills (h) Names and complete addresses of suppliers from whom goods/services chargeable to tax are received (i) Names and complete addresses of the persons to whom goods/services supplied where required under these rules		

Sl. No.	Description	Remarks Assessee	Remarks Auditor
	(j) The complete addresses of the premises where the goods are stored including goods stored during transit along with the particulars of the stock stored therein. (k) Monthly production accounts showing the quantitative details of raw materials or services used in the manufacture and quantitative details of the goods so manufactured including the waste and by products thereof. (l) Accounts showing the quantitative details of goods used in the provision of services, details of input services utilized and the services supplied.		
4	Whether the above records maintained by the auditee reflect the true and correct details. Also ensure that the said records are authenticated by authorised signatory?		
5	Whether records such as records of consignor, consignee and other relevant details of goods have been maintained by owner or operator of warehouse and transporter whether registered or not?		
6	Whether a registered person engaged in works contract services has maintained accounts showing the following? (a) The names and addresses of the persons on whose behalf the works contract is executed; (b) Description, value and quantity (wherever applicable) of goods or services received for the execution of works contract; (c) Description, value and quantity (wherever applicable) of goods or services utilized in the execution of works contract; (d) The details of payment received in respect of each works contract; and (e) The names and addresses of suppliers from whom he received goods or services.		
7	Whether agent of the registered person has maintained accounts depicting the following? (a) particulars of authorization received by him from each principal to receive or supply goods or services on behalf of such principal separately; (b) particulars including description, value and quantity (wherever applicable) of goods or services received on behalf of every principal;		

Sl. No.	Description	Remarks Assessee	Remarks Auditor
	(c) Particulars including description, value and quantity (wherever applicable) of goods or services supplied on behalf of every principal; (d) Details of accounts furnished to every principal; and (e) Tax paid on receipts or on supply of goods or services effected on behalf of every principal		
8	Whether the possibility of maintaining the records in electronic form in the case of auditee has been examined?		
9	If yes, whether they are properly preserved i.e. backup has been timely created, credentials are proper, access of same is restricted etc.?		
10	Whether the turnover during a financial year (12m) exceeds the prescribed limit (i.e. 2 crores)?		
11	If yes to the above then verify whether accounts are audited by a chartered accountant or a cost accountant?		
12	Whether the audited annual accounts and reconciliation statement are as per sec 44(2) of CGST Act, 2017		
13	Whether all the records as per sec 35(1) are maintained for last seventy two months before the annual return for the year preceding to the year for which audit is conducted?		
14	Whether the records/books pertaining to any appeal/revision/proceeding are maintained for a minimum specified period?		
15	Whether records are maintained regarding advances received and paid and also adjustment of such advances against invoices?		
16	Whether list of all indirect tax related reports are generated through software?		

17.3.2 Proforma for different types of records

(i) Inward supply (purchase register)

Sl. No.	Invoice/BOE details		Supplier details				Input receipt/service completion date
	Number	Date	Name	Type	GSTN	State	
				Foreign supplier			
				Unregistered			
				SEZ			
				Registered			

Details of Goods/Service			Value	Rate of Tax			
Description	HSN/SAC	Qty.		CGST	SGST	IGST	Cess

Place of Supply	Nature of Supply	Nature of credit	Liable under RCM (Y/N)	Payment date	Tax payment date (RCM)
	Inputs	Taxable			
	Capital goods	Common			
	Input services	Exempt			
	composition supplies	Non-business			

Type of purchase	Amount of tax				Date of ITC availment	Other Documents Received
	CGST	SGST	IGST	Cess		
Inter- State						
Intra-State						
Import						

(Refer – Reconciliation Statement – Part A – Pt. IV – 14 – B to Q)

(Refer – Annual return – Form 9 – Pt III –6 – A to O).

(ii) Outward Supply

Sl.No	Date of Invoice	Invoice No.	Recipient Details			Details of Goods/Services			Value
			Name	GSTN	State	Description	HSN/SAC	Qty.	

Rate of Tax				Amount of Tax			
CGST	SGST	IGST	Cess	CGST	SGST	IGST	Cess

Tax Payment date	RCM applicable(y/n)	Nature of Supply	Type of sale	Other Documents Issued
		Goods	Export	Supplementary Invoice
		Services	Inter-State	Debit note
			Intra-State	Credit

(Refer – Reconciliation Statement – Part A – Pt.III – 9 –A to O)
(Refer – Annual return – Form 9 – Pt III –5 – A to I).

(iii) Statement of advances received and adjusted:

Receipt of Advances for supply to be made						
Receipt Voucher Date	Receipt Voucher No.	Recipient Details			P.O. No.	Amount of Advance Received
		Name	GSTN	State		

Advance Adjustment												
Invoice No.	Details of Goods/Service			Value	Rate of Tax				Amount of Tax			
	Description	HSN/SAC	Qty		CGST	SGST	IGST	Cess	CGST	SGST	IGST	Cess

Advance Refunded	

(Refer – Reconciliation Statement – Part A – Pt. – 4 –F)

17.4 DOCUMENTATION UNDER GST

17.4.1 Introduction

Documents are keys to determine the trail of any transaction. It also plays an important role in all the audits under GST law and in general. It acts as evidence at the time of dispute and proper documentation also safeguards the taxpayers against frivolous demand notices. Following are the various checkpoints in respect of the documentation under GST.

Sl. No.	Description	Remarks Assessee	Remarks Auditor
	Tax Invoice		
1	Whether invoices are issued as per Rule 46?		
2	Whether registered person supplying taxable goods is issuing a tax invoice before or at the time of: (i) Removal of goods for supply to the recipient, where supply involves movement of goods? (ii) Delivery of goods or making available thereof to the recipient in other cases?		
3	Whether registered person supplying taxable services is issuing a tax invoice before or after the provision of service but within 30 days from such completion? Note: Where the transaction involves banks or financial institutions, the invoice should be issued within 45 days.		

Sl. No.	Description	Remarks Assessee	Remarks Auditor
4	Whether the Invoice is issued before or at the time each such statement is issued in case of continuous supply of goods, where successive statements of accounts are involved? Where successive payments are not involved, whether invoice is issued before or at the time each such payment is received?		
5	In case of Continuous Supply of services, where (1) The Due date of payment is ascertainable from the contract, whether invoice is issued on or before the due date of payment? (2) The Due date of payment is not ascertainable from the contract, whether invoice is issued before or at the time when the supplier of service receives the payment? (3) Payment is linked to the completion of an event, whether invoice is issued on or before the date of completion of that event?		
6	Whether the invoice is issued, in case of sale on approval basis; (i) before or at the time of supply or (ii) 6 months from the date of removal, whichever is earlier?		
7	Whether a *single invoice-cum-bill of supply* is issued for all such supplies where a registered person is supplying taxable as well as exempted goods or services or both to an unregistered person?		
8	Whether the invoice is issued in triplicate in case of goods? ORIGINAL FOR RECIPIENT DUPLICATE FOR TRANSPORTER TRIPLICATE FOR SUPPLIER		
9	Whether the invoice is issued in duplicate, in case of service? ORIGINAL FOR RECIPIENT DUPLICATE FOR SUPPLIER?		
10	Whether serial number of invoices issued during a tax period is furnished electronically through the common portal in FORM GSTR-1?		
11	Whether the self-invoice is issued for unregistered procurements liable under RCM?		

Sl. No.	Description	Remarks Assessee	Remarks Auditor
12	Whether the invoice contains an endorsement in case of export of goods or services that it is for "EXPORT/SUPPLY TO SEZ UNIT OR SEZ DEVELOPER, ON PAYMENT OF INTEGRATED TAX" or "UNDER BOND OR LETTER OF UNDERTAKING WITHOUT PAYMENT OF INTEGRATED TAX"?		
	Bill Of Supply		
13	Where the auditee has opted for Composition Scheme, Whether the auditee is issuing bill of supply (Bill of supply = invoice without tax)?		
14	Whether the bill of supply contains all the required details as per Rule 49?		
	Receipt Voucher		
15	Whether the auditee is in practice of issuing receipt voucher in case of receipt of any advances?		
16	Whether the receipt voucher contains all the required details as per Rule 50?		
	Other Documents		
17	Whether the auditee is in practice of issuing refund voucher for refund of advances received for which receipt voucher was issued earlier?		
18	If yes, whether the refund voucher contains all the required details as per Rule 51?		
19	Whether payment voucher is issued for payments made to the vendors covered under RCM under Sec 9(3) and is as per Rule 52?		
20	Whether Revised tax invoice and credit or debit notes issued is as per rule 53?		
21	Whether auditee has issued revised invoice for period from the date of effective registration to the date of grant of registration certificate as under? (a) Recipient wise consolidated invoices - registered/unregistered having supplies interstate supplies of more than 2.5 lakhs (b) State wise consolidated revised invoices - Unregistered + Interstate + <2.5L (c) Consolidated revised invoices - Unregistered persons		

Sl. No.	Description	Remarks Assessee	Remarks Auditor
22	Whether credit note is issued by auditee only in the following cases? (i) Where the taxable value or tax charged in the invoice exceeds the taxable value or tax payable in respect of such supply, or (ii) Where the goods are returned by the recipient, or (iii) Where goods or services or both supplied are found to be deficient.		
23	Whether debit note issued by auditee only when the taxable value or tax charged in the invoice is found to be less than the taxable value or tax payable in respect of such supply?		
24	Whether the invoices issued in accordance with sec 74/129/130 contains the words "INPUT TAX CREDIT NOT ADMISSIBLE"? E.g.: After the audit by the department, Search and Seizure, Confiscation.		
25	Whether the ISD invoices issued, if any, are as per rule 54 of CGST rules?		
	Delivery Challan		
26	Whether only delivery challan and not an invoice is issued for the following? (a) supply of liquid gas where the quantity at the time of removal from the place of business of the supplier is not known, (b) transportation of goods for job work, (c) transportation of goods for reasons other than by way of supply? *E.g.:* Intra state branch transfers; Sale on approval; Inter-state movement for repairs, Removal of warranty spares... etc.		
27	Whether delivery challan issued is as per rule 55 of CGST Rules?		
28	Whether Delivery challan is issued in triplicate? ORIGINAL FOR CONSIGNEE DUPLICATE FOR TRANSPORTER TRIPLICATE FOR CONSIGNER		
29	Whether invoices are issued after delivery of goods, in cases where the removal of goods for supply was made without invoice?		

Sl. No.	Description	Remarks Assessee	Remarks Auditor
30	Where goods are transported in a semi knocked down or completely knocked down, whether the condition complied as under? (a) The supplier issued complete invoice before dispatch of the first consignment, (b) The supplier issued DC for each of the subsequent consignments, giving reference of the invoice, (c) Each consignment is accompanied by copies of the corresponding delivery challan along with a duly certified copy of the invoice and (d) The original copy of Invoice is issued along with the last consignment?		
31	Whether any exemption from issuance of tax invoice is available to auditee? (i) The value of gods supplied is less than Rs.200/-, (ii) The recipient is not a registered person and (iii) The recipient does not require such invoice/bill of supply		
32	If yes, whether a consolidated invoice is issued for each day on such supplies?		

17.4.2 Contents of the invoices

Particulars	Tax Invoice	Bill of Supply	Credit note	Debit note	Delivery challan	Receipt voucher	Refund voucher	Payment voucher
Name, address and GSTIN of the supplier	✔	✔	✔	✔	✔	✔	✔	✔
Consecutive serial number	✔	✔	✔	✔	✔	✔	✔	✔
Date of its issue	✔	✔	✔	✔	✔	✔	✔	✔
Name, address and GSTIN of the recipient	✔	✔	✔	✔	✔	✔	✔	✔
HSN of Goods/ Services	✔	✔			✔			
Description of Goods / Services	✔	✔			✔	✔	✔	✔
Qty incase of goods	✔				✔			✔
Total value of supply	✔	✔	✔	✔	✔			
Taxable value of the supply after discount & Abatement	✔	✔						
Rate of tax	✔		✔	✔	✔	✔	✔	✔
Amt. of tax	✔		✔	✔	✔	✔	✔	✔
POS incase of Interstate Supply	✔				✔	✔		✔
Signature of authorised signatory	✔	✔	✔	✔	✔	✔	✔	✔
Whether tax payable on Reverse Charge	✔						✔	
Serial number and date of the corresponding tax invoice			✔	✔				

Note: Mandatory content requirements for credit availment are: Invoice no, name and address of supplier and recipient, GSTIN of both, description of Supply, value, tax amount, & place of supply.

17.5 PAYMENT UNDER GST

17.5.1 Introduction

Discharging the tax obligation is the ultimate objective of any tax compliance mechanism. The discharge of taxes is by way of payment of taxes either in cash or by way of utilization of the input tax credits. Further, under GST, returns cannot be filed without discharging the applicable liability.

For understanding the payment under GST, it is required to understand various ledgers of the assessee maintained by the GSTN. Following are the three ledgers maintained by for each registered person, which can be verified by logging into GST portal:

(i) Electronic Cash Ledger

(ii) Electronic Credit Ledger

(iii) Electronic Tax liability ledger

Sl. No.	Description	Remarks Assessee	Remarks Auditor
1	Whether tax payable is paid within the prescribed time as per the GST provision and rules made there under?		
2	Whether tax is being collected beyond tax payable? If yes, whether Sec. 76 is complied?		
3	Whether the tax payer charged wrongly IGST in place of CGST/SGST or vice versa?		
4	Whether refund has been claimed in accordance with sec 54 w.r.t excess credits in credit ledger at the end of the tax period?		
5	Whether interest is paid @18% in case of delayed payment of taxes?		
6	Whether the interest is calculated from the day succeeding the day on which such was due to be paid?		

Sl. No.	Description	Remarks Assessee	Remarks Auditor
7	Confirm that, in case of excess or undue claim of credit/undue or excess reduction in the output tax liability auditee shall pay interest on such undue or excess claim or on such undue or excess reduction as the case may be at rate of 24%?		

(Refer – Reconciliation Statement – Part A – Pt.III – 9 –L to O)

17.6 PAYMENT UNDER PROTEST IN GST REGIME

In the erstwhile indirect tax regime comprising of Central Excise, Service tax and Customs there was a provision for payment under protest in the following circumstances:

- when an assessee/tax payer did not agree with the stand taken by the department or
- advice by the department or
- where an assessee entertained doubts about the correctness of his own views about classification/valuation.

Initially there was a rule prescribing procedure for payment under protest. Subsequently the rule was omitted and intimation by the assessee that he is paying the tax under protest was sufficient. In this case as per the instructions, the proper officer was to pass a speaking order on the protest (which was not followed many a times in practice). If the speaking order was not passed, one could request for the same. Courts also took the view that once an appeal is filed against a decision or order, payments made in accordance with the appealed decision has to be considered as payment under protest.

There was another major advantage in making payments of taxes under protest. Once payment under protest was made, there was no time limit for filing the refund claim for amounts paid in excess.

In case Revenue disputes, provisions contained in sections 73 and 74 provide for issue of show cause notice. While show cause notice has to be issued with 6 years 9 months in case of liability arising because of fraud, mis-declaration, miss-statement etc. even in the case of normal cases of mistakes either on the part of Revenue or on the part of assessee, show cause notice for demanding tax/input tax/refund due, is 3 years and 9 months.

Even in cases where an assessee has a bona fide belief that what he is doing is legally right, if he disputes and does not pay the amount before issue of an order, interest would accrue and penalty of 10% of the tax determined or Rs.10,000 whichever is higher (mandatory) can be imposed on him. These options available to the government are disadvantageous to the taxpayers and lead to litigation which is costly not only in terms of delay but also in terms of cost.

However at times the assessees would definitely entertain doubts about the correctness of the approach adopted by them with regard to classification/ valuation for variety of reasons including advice by the departmental officers/auditing officers/investigating officers. Earlier the payments under protest or provisional assessment were the options available. In the GST regime, there is no specific provision for payment under protest at all.

Another option to get clarity is approaching Advance Ruling Authority. The spate of orders passed by such Advance Ruling Benches has failed to inspire confidence about the impartiality and fairness of the decisions. This is due to different views being taken by different benches on the same issue and many deeper aspects of law not being discussed while pronouncing orders. It is expected that this would result in further litigation. Moreover the decision of the Authority is binding on the taxpayer and this can result in higher payment of taxes till the issue is finally sorted out.

The second option available is to seek provisional assessment. In case of B2C transactions, this option would be useful since tax need not be passed on. The law provides for time bound finalisation of provisional assessment of six months and this would result in faster resolution of the dispute. In this process, option of payment of tax at higher rate without passing it on to the customer and claim of refund as and when the finalisation takes place also would be available. In case of bona fide belief on the part of the assessee with regard to value or classification of the goods and or services or both, this option would ensure that even when the assessee takes a contra view, penalty of 10% would not be levied and chances of issue getting settled within a reasonable time are higher. In any case total litigation period would come down.

In the case of B2B transactions also provisional assessment can be requested for in case of doubt and tax can be paid at higher rate if the customer can take credit and has no objection to pay higher rate of duty. In this case assessee has the option of choosing either payment at lower rate or at higher rate. If the credit has been taken, if tax has been paid at higher rate, refund cannot be claimed. Many tax payers from the earlier regime have doubts on the time limits prescribed being adhered to in GST as the officers are the same.

Another option in the case of B2C transaction is to pay tax at higher rate, intimate the department that it is being paid under protest but file a refund claim after 3 months, setting the process of litigation in motion. In such a case proper officer would be compelled to decide classification/valuation issue for deciding admissibility of refund. In this process the advantage is that the amount claimed as refund would earn 6% interest in case of delay in settlement and by filing periodical refund claim, assessee can safeguard its interest and urgency to settle the issue would be there for the department also. No penal action would arise.

In the case of input tax credit, an assessee can take the credit even where there is doubt about its admissibility and reverse it immediately and inform the department. Since the reversed credit has no time limit for re-availment, as and when the issue gets finalised, credit can be taken. This procedure would involve challenges like preservation of the documents, reference to details of credit taken and reversed, proof of correspondence with the department, regular monitoring of the issue so that when it becomes clear, credit can be taken. Maybe amounts on regular basis can be parked in a contingent asset account which would be reversed in the year end and in the new year the amount reversed re credited to this suspense account.

Note: Unlike the past when payments could be made directly under challan by giving the details of the nature of payments, in the GST regime payments have to be made by debits in the electronic cash ledger or electronic credit ledger only. The amount available in the electronic cash ledger may be used for making any payment towards tax, interest, penalty, fees or any other amount payable.

Chapter 18

Reconciliations

In any accounting system there is a need to see that all transactions are accounted completely, accurately and in a timely manner. Under GST, the need to capture the transactions which constitute a "supply" and exclude those which are not supplies, is an added requirement. A few reconciliations needed to file form- 9 & 9c are discussed hereunder.

18.1 RECONCILIATION OF SUPPLY (AFTER CONSIDERING THE RETURNS) ON WHICH OUTPUT TAX IS PAYABLE

Sl. No	Particulars	Total
	Data as per audited accounts for entity as whole:-	
Add	Revenue from operations	XXX
Less	Other Income	XX
	Amount as per financials	**XXX**
	Amount for period 1st April 2017 to 30th June 2017	(XX)
	Comparable Financials for July – March 18	**XXX**
Less	Revenue/Other Income pertaining to other registered/distinct persons: All different State/ business vertical turnover as per audited accounts	**(XX)**
Less	(a) Revenue items on which output GST is not payable (b) Zero rated supply without payment of tax: Export and supplies to SEZ (Confirm proper procedure followed like valid LUT, Receipt in CFE etc. This would not be applicable for Export under rebate where IGST paid by utilising the credit.) **Note-** Deemed exports: GST needs to be paid and refund claimed by either the recipient or supplier.	(XX)

Sl. No	Particulars	Total
	(c) Liable to tax under reverse charge mechanism u/s 9(3): Goods and services specified[1] 1. [A separate reconciliation for this may be prepared] (d) Amount of wholly Exempt Supplies not disclosed in returns. If disclosed no adjustment required, the return figure can be adopted. (e) Partly Exempt Supplies (exempt portion amount): If exempt portion disclosed no adjustment required, the return figure can be adopted. (f) Non-GST supplies: The specified 5 petroleum products and liquor for human consumption unless part of composite supply of taxable goods or services.[2] (g) Not a supply as per the definition of supply: Supplies not in course of business other than in import of services. It may be noted that the supplies set out in Schedule I are deemed supplies.[3] (h) Not a supply of goods or services as per Schedule III: [4] (i) Unbilled revenue (Considering the provisions of Section 13(2) of the CGST Act, 2017) if being accounted (j) Revenue by way of supplies made through agents where tax paid in previous year upon initial dispatch (k) Revenue (tax on advances) against which Time of Supply has occurred in the previous year[5] (l) Any other (please specify)	
	Adjusted Amount as per financials (in the State)[sub-total]	XXX

1 Goods- Cashew, Bidi wrapper leaves; tobacco leaves raw cotton by agriculturist to registered person, silk yarn manufacturer to registered person, lottery by Government to distributor or used vehicles by Government to registered person. Services by GTA opting for reverse charge to specified persons, advocate or firm or arbitral tribunal to business entity, sponsorship to body corporate to partnership firm, Govt supplies (except renting and specified services) by Government to business entity, renting by government to registered person, director to company, insurance agent to insurance companies, author, artist .. to publishers etc., Member of overseeing committee to RBI and priority lending certificate (we.f.28.5.18).

2 New Year Special in restaurant with food and liquor- Rs. 3000 per couple. GST payable on the composite offer.

3 Permanent transfer or disposal of business assets where ITC has been availed, Supplies between distinct persons (other States or business vertical) other than gifts not exceeding Rs.50,000/-, supply by principal to agent where agent supplies further or by agent to principal where agent receives goods on behalf of principal and import of services from related person in course of business.

4 Sale of land or building after completion, services of funeral, burial, crematorium or mortuary including transportation of dead, actionable claims other than lottery, betting and gambling. Notified w.e.f 28.6.17 activity in relation to a function entrusted to panchayat under Article 243G of Constitution of India.

5 The time of supply on services for which advance was received would have suffered service tax. Different treatment provided in transitional provisions.

Sl. No	Particulars	Total
Add	(a) Sale of capital assets (b) Opening balance of unbilled revenues if being accounted. (1st July 17) (c) Advances received in current period (d) Section 15 – Valuation Adjustments • taxes, duties, cess etc. levied under other laws charged by supplier • Amount incurred by recipient but liable to be paid by supplier • interest late fee or penalty for delayed payment of consideration • Incidental expenses charged by the supplier (e) Activities listed in Schedule I • Write off and disposal of business assets without consideration, if GST credit was availed • Supply of goods/services to related persons/distinct persons • To employees (excluding gifts per employee up to Rs.50,000 • Goods dispatched by to agents to the extent sale is not made/recognized (f) Revenue duplicated in returns. (g) Goods rejection for which credit notes not eligible for tax: Discounts not known at time of supply (h) Any other (please specify)	XXX
Add/ Less	(a) Exchange difference/ variation accounted in books separately (b) Profit/ loss on sale of(assets)	XXX
	Adjusted financials (in a State) Amount as per Annual Return (in a State)	XXX XXX
	Difference • Revenue omitted to be declared in the Annual Return • Reasons for difference	

In this outwards supply (simple) reconciliation the interpretation of few aspects required for arriving at the due taxes have not been considered. Some of them are enumerated hereunder

- Incorrect exemption or incorrect classification leading to no GST payment.
- Incorrect rate adopted leading to short/excess payment of taxes.
- Application of concept of composite, non-composite or mixed supply

- Whether the IGST or CGST and SGST should have been charged?
- The need to apply the proper valuation under section 15.

18.1.1 ITC Audit - GST

The industry and trade needs to carry out an input tax credit review before the last date of filing of September 2019 return [October 20th 2019] for the year 2018-19. GST being a new law there could be several challenges in availing the credit as under:

- Tax payers working under VAT or Excise or service tax would find some similarities and some variations. Some unlearning is needed. Most will continue to have their old views.
- There could be a number of errors of understanding the concepts which is not possible without a deeper reading of the related provisions.
- Old well set systems need to be changed, more emphasis on using automation. Mistakes cannot be corrected by manual filing.
- In configuration, integration, extraction of data there would be challenges as the person who knowns IT does not know GST and vice versa. System errors would repeat till rectified.
- Law even today is not clear to more than 5% of the tax payers, professionals and tax officers. Therefore there are bound to be many transactional mistakes in the year 2018-19.
- There are no well tested reconciliations utilities in place from the Government.
- The registered person has to ensure that total reconciliation and proper availment is carried out before this time limit expires. Those who miss this window may have to face disputes and litigation if they were to avail the ITC after this date.

The advantages of an ITC audit could be as under:

(1) It will ensure that all eligible credit of tax paid on inputs, capital goods and input services are availed in accordance with law and fulfilment of procedures for receipt, documentation, vendor compliance etc.

(2) It will ensure that the proper order of utilisation of credit for each IGST, SGST/ UTGST and CGST is adopted.

(3) It will ensure that rebate is claimed only after debit of IGST on export.

(4) It will ensure that the procurement/ purchase planning could negotiate better when they understand the ITC of vendor.

(5) The marketing could understand the impact of ITC on the customer to be able to negotiate the best price.

(6) The more eligible ITC is taken, it adds directly to the bottom line of the company.

(7) This review would avoid the future litigation at the time of audit or investigation.

The possible coverage of ITC review could be in 4 segments:

(i) A step wise ITC review sample list with comments;

(ii) Some of the expected common errors in this transition period;

(iii) Expenses reconciliation and

(iv) The ITC reconciliation itself.

18.1.2 Steps in ITC Review

(i) Understand the business: The general background of industry, company, challenges in indirect taxes faced by them, type of vendors and type of customers has to be understood. This would help in conduct of the review.

(ii) Confirm the existence of adequacy of systems and controls: Internal control in indirect taxes has not been put in most organisations and change to GST may have further delayed it. Reliance on the normal audit checks may not be adequate due to various reasons. The transactions which may not be reflected in the books of account like stock transfers to different states, Agent/ principal supply, supplies with related parties which are without consideration, reverse charge, etc., are normally not accounted in the financial system in the form of usual inward-outward supplies. These aspects may need confirmation of proper systems to comply and reconcile the liabilities as well as the credits.

(iii) Review of procurement policy of the organization including imports: The importance of the tax clause to ensure optimisation of the credits and ensuring vendor has paid taxes owed on the supply cannot be overemphasised. Further the knowledge of availability or otherwise of input tax credits to the procurement team may be limited.

(iv) Invoice Validity: The evidence of payment of taxes is the indication in the invoice along with specified particulars. Also, confirm that all invoices where credit has been taken are available for verification and preserved properly.

(v) Review the nature of services and goods: The nature of expenses incurred is required to ascertain GST impact and to assess GST credits. Any goods and services used in furtherance of business are eligible for credit other than those blocked. All the major inputs, capital goods and services need to be identified.

(vi) Review of Sources: The question of procurements made only through registered dealer/ manufacturer/service provider needs to be confirmed. In case of procurement from unregistered dealer, the possibility of credit chain being broken and consequent increase in costs to be confirmed.

(vii) Review the system of claiming credit: The time of supply would be important for availing credit in respect of Inputs, Capital goods and RCM expenses. Verify if the goods and services are actually received and in a verifiable manner.

(viii) Review the major agreements/ orders: This can be done by review of sample invoices based on which credits claimed to study impact under GST with respect to taxations and credits.

(ix) Review of expenses liable for GST under RCM: Most of the RCM payments could also be eligible for credits. If so, whether paid and availed to avoid payment of irrecoverable interest.

(x) Studying the nature of books of accounts maintained: The books to capture and identify that ITC has been availed. Review of financial ledgers to ensure that ITC are taken on all eligible heads. There may be a need to have bifurcation of accounts to enable the capture of such information.

(xi) Review of treatment of purchase returns to study the possible impact under GST: The tax paid on purchases returns on GST invoice is equal to credit on inputs.

(xii) Review the foreign currency payments: To ascertain RCM liability and availment of ITC.

(xiii) Review if goods/services at Branches/ Business verticals: Confirm if invoices are addressed properly for goods/services received at locations. Ensure that credit capture system and reconciliation is available in all branches within and outside the State. If expenses incurred at other than branches registered in the State, confirm that an input service distributor registration exists.

(xiv) Review terms of purchase orders vis a vis purchase invoices: Defective invoices can lead to disputes at a later date. They can however be rectified once identified.

(xv) Review of rate of taxes: This would be more important for goods or services supplied. It may also be value additive for the vendors if the customer confirms the taxes. This should not be the responsibility of the customer but as on date, it could be.

(xvi) Review of method of capitalising the work in progress: This is to examine whether ineligible credits exist or eligible credits are not availed. This should be as per Accounting Standards and GST law.

(xvii) Review of credit availment mechanism and conditions to be fulfilled for credit: The need for having received the goods or services; the issue of a valid invoice, goods and/or services used in furtherance business. There may be a need to suggest improvement to automatically record the credit which can later be confirmed. This would be important in bringing down the cost of procurement of goods or services.

(xviii) Review if payments are made within stipulated time for taking credit: There is a time limit for payment to vendors within 180- days. If it exceeds, ITC needs to be reversed without interest. On payment to the vendor is made, the credit can be claimed back. System to capture such reversals in recoverable accounts and their periodic nullifying may be suggested.

(xix) Review discounts agreed and valuation adopted by vendors: Ensure that they are in line with law and do not lead to loss of credits or double taxation

(xx) Review of debit notes and credit notes on sampling basis: This is to ascertain the impact on ITC: To confirm that the credit be availed only if receiver/ customer had reversed the credit.

(xxi) Review of credit register: Look for patterns and confirm evidence captured/ filed in order to satisfy the scrutiny by internal/external auditors.

(xxii) Review of import documents, job work inward invoices, stock transfer inward invoices, etc. Some of these may not be accounted in the system as they are not financial entries but have an impact on ITC.

(xxiii) Review if there are transactions of personal nature: In such cases credit is not available.

(xxiv) Review of goods issued free of cost or as samples: At times the value of such FOC supplies may have to be included in the final supply at which time if the credit of such FOC is lost it may not be competitive as credit in between has been lost.

(xxv) Review of credit apportionment in case of supply of taxable and exempted supplies: The capture of credit specific to each and only the common credits being allocated is a preferred way forward.

(xxvi) Review of credit availment in case of assets put partially for non-business/ non-taxable use: The reversal for personal use needs to be confirmed.

(xxvii) Review of various returns filed under GST such as GSTR 1 and GSTR 3B and identification of differences in ITC if any, between GSTR 3B and GSTR 2A. [Reconciliation to be provided by Auditee]

(xxviii) Review of TRAN-1, TRAN-2 filed: This is to be confirmed with what was eligible and if any excess availed to be reversed. If short availed disclosure could be made as last date is over. Courts have provided facility to those who have evidence of having technical issues in uploading and those as directed by GST Council (till 31st January 2019). The general facility to correct trans- 1 for all has however not been directed by Courts till date. This may also be expected in time.

(xxix) Review of disputable credits: These credits could be availed and reversed with intimation to revenue avoid time limitation and facility of availing in case of favorable court judgements in future.

(xxx) Review of credit accumulations: Reason to be ascertained and option if any exercised for encashment of such credits through refund or rebate.

(xxxi) Review of important ratios: The credit availed and utilised to total GST, ITC/ Total purchases and expenses among others.

(xxxii) Common Errors: Identifying and correcting the errors observed in the above review and also confirming with a list of common errors (provided further)

18.1.3 Common Errors in ITC

The errors in GST compliance are expected to be mainly centered around understanding of the ITC concept, interpreting the complex provisions, vendor compliances impacting ITC, doubtful credits, missed or short credits, excess or duplicate credits, debit/ credit note adjustments, capital goods credit vis a vis capitalization, reversal for exempt supplies, reverse charge credit, reversal requirements and more. Professionals can categorise them into conceptual errors, system errors or material transaction errors. We examine some of them in more detail hereunder:

1. **Considering ITC balance to payoff liability under reverse charge**
   - Recipient cannot utilize ITC for discharging RCM liabilities. GST portal also does not allow such adjustment while filing returns.
   - ITC can be claimed in the same month where taxes are paid by the recipient under RCM in end of previous month.

2. **Discharging GST under reverse charge on services u/s 9(3).**
   - Auditor needs to understand place of supply especially for export or import of services.

- The old service tax law and the GST Act differ and there are some transactions which no longer attract GST. If paid then refund can be sought as it is within limitation. Illustration: Rent a cab or manpower services which were liable for RCM under earlier tax regime but not notified services under GST regime.

3. ITC could be claimed on the taxes paid under RCM on the GTA services:

- ITC is only restricted for provider of GTA service who pays at 5%. The customer who pays taxes under RCM could avail ITC if eligible.

4. Treating export of goods/services as exempted goods/services and not availing eligible credits related to same

- Refund of taxes paid on the goods or services could be availed by the person making the exports even when output GST is not paid on exported goods/exported services.

5. Non-reversal of ITC in cases where payment is not made to supplier within 180 days from the date of invoice

- Reversal of ITC with interest is required. (Recently the amendment for no interest has been made- but retrospective applicability not made clear.)
- The care to enable re credit on future payment can be suggested.

6. Inter-State purchases made from unregistered persons

- Procure goods only from a registered vendor & avail eligible ITC.
- ITC availed on the basis of invoice of registered dealer provided by the unregistered person would not be available. Further availing ITC on the basis of photocopies may be disputed.
- No restriction for availing 100% of ITC on the purchase of capital goods. [50% credit was there in earlier central excise regime].

7. Availing ITC on supplies specifically blocked u/s 17.

- Not allowed and if availed - has to be reversed with interest if utilised.

8. Availing credit when the same is restricted by rate notification

- Where ITC was availed when the conditional of notification restricts. Credit to be reversed with interest if utilised.

9. Availing ITC merely on receipt of invoice without actual receipt of goods/services

- ITC could be availed only on receipt of invoice and goods (constructive receipts on instruction of purchaser included).

10. Non-reversal of proportionate ITC in respect of exempted supplies, non-business purpose use

- Non-business, non-taxable or exempt supplies not eligible for credit. It would amount to non-compliance of Rule 42 and 43 of the CGST Rules, 2017.

11. Non-availment of ITC on bank charges

- ITC could be availed as there is no specific restriction U/S 17(5)

12. Non-reversal of ITC in respect of goods lost, stolen, destroyed, written off or distributed as gifts/free samples

- Where ITC is availed and then the goods lost, stolen, destroyed, written off or distributed as gifts/free samples, ITC has to be reversed with interest.
- Written off could mean fully written off and therefore provision may not impact this.
- Inputs destroyed before putting into the production process would be covered.
- Inputs sent as samples are covered in this section. Inputs contained in final products would not be impacted.

13. Delay in availing ITC

- Avail the ITC on monthly basis and utilize for payment of output liability.
- The absence of proper mechanism/checklist to determine the eligibility of ITC of various purchase /procurement transactions.

14. Paying GST on exempted goods or services

- In GST tax payer cannot opt for payment when goods or services are exempted unconditionally. In service tax due to the law not having attained clarity one could pay the tax when in doubt.
- This means that the ITC would be denied where on pay tax on exempt transactions.

15. Not following procedure for export of goods or services

- The place of supply whether in India or outside in case of goods and services is provided in IGST Act. It would be more relevant in case of services as logic would not work.

- GST like earlier excise is a procedural law and one requires to follow proper prescribed procedures to get the ITC benefits encashed.
- Not following procedures could lead to payment of GST on exports or denial of rebate or refund.

16. Many dozens more...[6]

18.2 RECONCILIATION OF EXPENSES (NET INWARDS AFTER CONSIDERING THE RETURN OF SUPPLIES TO THE VENDORS) ON WHICH ITC IS AVAILABLE

(This is from the audited accounts to the GST Return summary for the year)

Reconciliation of Total Expenses (Net inward supplies) on which ITC Availed		
Sl. No.	**Particulars**	**Total**
	Operational Expenses	xx
	Other Expenses	xx
Less:		
A.	Expenses pertaining to other registered persons/distinct persons	
B.	Expenses on which input tax credit is not available due to the following:	
i.	Not a supply as per Schedule III or the definition of supply	
ii.	Inward supplies received from composition suppliers	
iii.	Exempt inward supplies	
iv.	Wholly Exempt Inward Supplies	
v.	Partly Exempt Inward Supplies (exempt portion)	
vi.	Non-GST Inward supplies	
vii.	Goods/services are not used in the course or furtherance of business	
viii.	Credit ineligible as the goods/services received are used wholly for effecting exempt supplies (excluding exports)	
ix.	Credit ineligible u/s 17(5)(a) : On motor vehicles and other conveyances	

6 Good analytical articles on various subjects of GST would be a source of addition to these checklists. idtc@icai.in has many publications/articles on GST including on ITC.

Reconciliation of Total Expenses (Net inward supplies) on which ITC Availed		
Sl. No.	**Particulars**	**Total**
x.	Credit ineligible u/s 17(5)(b)(i) : On food and beverages, outdoor catering, beauty treatment, health services, cosmetic and plastic surgery	
xi.	Credit ineligible u/s 17(5)(b)(ii) : On membership of a club, health and fitness centre	
xii.	Credit ineligible u/s 17(5)(b)(iii) : On rent-a-cab, life insurance and health insurance	
xiii.	Credit ineligible u/s 17(5)(b)(iv) : On travel benefits extended to employees on vacation	
xiv.	Credit ineligible u/s 17(5)(c) : On works contract services when supplied for construction of an immovable property	
xv.	Credit ineligible u/s 17(5)(d) : On goods/services received for construction of an immovable property on own account	
xvi.	Credit ineligible u/s 17(5)(g) : On goods or services or both used for personal consumption;	
xvii.	Credit ineligible u/s 17(5)(h) : On goods lost, stolen, destroyed;	
xviii.	Credit ineligible u/s 17(5)(h) : On goods fully written off;	
xix.	Credit ineligible u/s 17(5)(h) : On goods disposed of by way of gift;	
xx.	Credit ineligible u/s 17(5)(h) : On goods disposed of by way of free samples;	
xxi.	Credit ineligible u/s 17(5)(i) : In respect of tax paid in accordance with the provisions of sections 74, 129 and 130;	
xxii.	Credit not taken as the recipient's GSTIN was not mentioned/mentioned incorrectly	
xxiii.	Credit reversed u/s 17 (4) for a banking company/financial institution/non-banking financial company	
xxiv.	Credit not taken as the place of supply is outside the State	
C.	Expenses for Credit reversed u/s 16(2) (d) due to non-payment in 180 days	
D.	Prepaid expenses of previous year	
E.	Expenses omitted to be declared in the Annual Return	

Reconciliation of Total Expenses (Net inward supplies) on which ITC Availed		
Sl. No.	**Particulars**	**Total**
F.	Expenses on which input tax credit will be taken in the subsequent year	
G.	Any other (please specify)	
	Adjusted Expenses Amount as per financials (in the State)[sub-total]	xx
Add:		
A.	Expenses for Credit u/s 140- 143 – Transitional Credits: Not be applicable from 18-19 onwards.	
B.	Expenses for Credit available u/s 18 on registration opting out of composition etc.	
C.	Expenses for Credit missed in earlier returns: Including of previous year on which input tax credit has been taken this year: Not applicable for the 1st year	
D.	Expenses for Credit reversed due to 180 days now availed.	
E.	Purchase of capital assets	
F.	Prepaid expenses of this year	
G.	**Adjustments in Valuation Section 15**	
i.	Taxes, duties, cess etc. levied under other laws charged by supplier	
ii.	Amount incurred by recipient but liable to be paid by supplier	
iii.	Interest, late fee or penalty for delayed payment of consideration	
iv.	Incidental expenses charged by the supplier	
v.	Any other (please specify)	
	Final Adjusted Expenses as per financials	xx
	Expense Amount as per Annual Return (in a State)	xx
	Difference to be Analysed	xx

Notes:

18.3 RECONCILIATION OF ITC

(This would provide credits as per financials and the returns: It should ideally be credit available under law)

Sample Reconciliation Format - ITC for year		
Sl. No.	**Particulars**	**Total**
	Input Tax Credit as per Books	xx
Less:		
A.	Credit relating to other registered persons/distinct persons	
B.	Credit on which input tax credit is not available due to the following:	
i.	ITC used for transaction which are not a supply as per Schedule III or the definition of supply	
ii.	ITC on Inward supplies received from composition suppliers	
iii.	ITC on Goods/services are not used in the course or furtherance of business u/s 17(1)	
iv.	Credit ineligible as the goods/services received are used wholly for effecting exempt supplies (excluding exports)	
v.	Credit ineligible u/s 17(5)(a) : On motor vehicles and other conveyances	
vi.	Credit ineligible u/s 17(5)(b)(i) : On food and beverages, outdoor catering, beauty treatment, health services, cosmetic and plastic surgery	
vii.	Credit ineligible u/s 17(5)(b)(ii) : On membership of a club, health and fitness centre	
viii.	Credit ineligible u/s 17(5)(b)(iii) : On rent-a-cab, life insurance and health insurance	
ix.	Credit ineligible u/s 17(5)(b)(iv) : On travel benefits extended to employees on vacation	
x.	Credit ineligible u/s 17(5)(c) : On works contract services when supplied for construction of an immovable property	
xi.	Credit ineligible u/s 17(5)(d) : On goods/services received for construction of an immovable property on own account	
xii.	Credit ineligible u/s 17(5)(g) : On goods or services or both used for personal consumption;	

Sample Reconciliation Format - ITC for year		
Sl. No.	**Particulars**	**Total**
xiii.	Credit ineligible u/s 17(5)(h) : On goods lost, stolen, destroyed;	
xiv.	Credit ineligible u/s 17(5)(h) : On goods fully written off;	
xv.	Credit ineligible u/s 17(5)(h) : On goods disposed of by way of gift;	
xvi.	Credit ineligible u/s 17(5)(h) : On goods disposed of by way of free samples;	
xvii.	Credit ineligible u/s 17(5)(i) : In respect of tax paid in accordance with the provisions of sections 74, 129 and 130;	
xviii.	Credit not taken as the recipient's GSTIN was not mentioned/mentioned incorrectly	
xix.	Credit reversed u/s 17 (4) for a banking company/financial institution/non-banking financial company	
xx.	Credit not taken as the place of supply is outside the State	
C.	Proportionate reversal of Credit u/s 17(2): Reversal for exempt supplies.	
D.	Credit reversed u/s 16(2) (d) due to non-payment in 180 days	
E.	Credits which will be taken in the subsequent year	
F.	Credits reversed under protest: This may be due to doubt or direction of revenue	
G.	Any other (please specify)	
	Adjusted ITC Amount as per financials (in the State)[sub-total]	XX
Add:		
A.	Credit u/s 140-143- Transitional	
B.	Credit available u/s 18 on registration opting out of composition etc.	
C.	Credit reversed due to 180 days now availed.	
D.	Credit on purchase of capital assets	
E.	Credit on prepaid expenses of this year if missed	
F.	**Missed credit from 1st July 2017 till 31st March 2018**	

Sample Reconciliation Format - ITC for year		
Sl. No.	**Particulars**	**Total**
G.	Adjustments in Valuation Section 15	
H.	Any other (please specify)	
	Final Adjusted as per financials	xx
	Amount of ITC as per Annual Return (in a State)	xx
	Difference if any to be analysed	xx

The reconciliation would need a good understanding of the provisions applicable to ITC. It would also raise many issues which would be the reason for the differences. This statement could also be customised as many aspects may not be applicable to all tax payers.

18.4 IDENTIFICATION AND REVERSE CHARGE RECONCILIATION

The provision of reverse charge was existing in the VAT regime as purchase tax and in Service Tax for the purposes of providing a level playing field to the tax compliant and encouraging the unregistered entities to register. The unfair advantage to the entities outside India was also sought to be equalized through the additional duty of customs- CVD (now IGST) and reverse charge under service tax for import of services. The expansion of the list in GST to some specific goods and services similar to earlier regime was to safeguard the revenue where the trade is mainly carried out by unorganised and uneducated entrepreneurs.

In these cases the recipient pays the GST and the supplier cannot avail the input tax credit as he does not pay. The registered recipient however can avail the eligible credit after payment of the GST under reverse charge. The need to pay the RCM is cash and not by adjustment of the accumulated credit impacts the exporters of goods and services for whom no exemption is available as on date except for SEZ. They would have to necessarily go for a refund.

The reconciliation statement for arriving at RCM liability is as under:

Identification and Reconciliation of Reverse Charge Liability			
Sl. No.	**Particulars**	**Total Amount**	**GST Amount**
i.	Total Expenses in Foreign Exchange		
ii.	Value of imported services from related parties not recorded in books		
	Sub Total A		

Identification and Reconciliation of Reverse Charge Liability			
Sl. No.	**Particulars**	**Total Amount**	**GST Amount**
Less:			
i.	Goods on which Customs duty is paid		
ii.	Goods and Services provided and received outside India- Global trade		
	Sub Total B – (Any service supplied by any person who is located in a non-taxable territory to any person located in taxable territory other than non-taxable online recipient (Import of Services)[7]		
Add:			
I.	Specified Receipt of Goods under Section 9 (3)[8]:		
a.	Cashew nuts (0801), not shelled or peeled- Supplied by an Agriculturist to Registered person		
b.	Bidi wrapper leaves (914049010)[tendu]- Supplied by an Agriculturist to Registered person		
c.	Tobacco Leaves (2401)- Supplied by an Agriculturist to Registered person		
d.	Raw Cotton (5201)- Supplied by an Agriculturist to Registered person		
e.	Silk Yarn (5004- 06) - Supplied by any person who manufactured from raw silk or silk worm cocoons to Registered Person.		
f.	Lottery – Supplied by State/ Union territory Govt or local authority to Distributor or selling agent		
g.	Used Vehicles (seized, confiscated, old/used/ scrap) – Supplied by State/ Union territory Govt or local authority to Registered Person		

7 Under section 7 imports of services for a consideration whether or not in the course or furtherance of business is to be included. However non-taxable online recipient has been expressly excluded. Further import from related parties would be liable even if there is no consideration (Schedule I)

8 The rate of RCM for goods would be as applicable to the goods

Identification and Reconciliation of Reverse Charge Liability			
Sl. No.	**Particulars**	**Total Amount**	**GST Amount**
h.	Priority Sector Lending Certificate – Supplied by any registered person to any registered person.[9]		
	Sub Total – C		
II.	Specified receipt of service under section 9(3)[10]		
a.	Goods transport agency not paid GST on forward charge to Specified person[11]		
b.	Legal services by individual advocate (including senior advocate) or firm of advocates to any business entity in taxable territory.		
c.	Arbitral Tribunal to any business entity in taxable territory.		
d.	Sponsorship services to anybody corporate or partnership firm.		
e.	Any services by Central/ State/ Union Territory Government other than 1.		
f.	Renting of immovable property, by department of posts- speed post, express parcel, life insurance and agency to any business entity in taxable territory		
g.	Renting of immovable property by Central/ State/ Union Territory Government to any registered person.		
h.	Directorship services by director of body corporate or Company to that company/ body corporate.		
i.	Insurance agency service to person carrying on insurance business in taxable territory		

9 We.f. 13.102017

10 The rate of RCM would be as 5% for GTA and for others as applicable to specified services

11 (a) Any factory registered or governed by Factories Act; (b) any society registered under Societies Registration Act; (c) any co-operative society; (d) registered person; any body corporate; (e) any partnership firm; (f) any casual taxable person.

Identification and Reconciliation of Reverse Charge Liability			
Sl. No.	**Particulars**	**Total Amount**	**GST Amount**
j.	Services by Author, music composer, photographer, and artist by way of transfer or enjoyment of copyright relating to original literary work to publisher, music company, producer or the like located in the taxable territory.		
k.	Services by member of overseeing Committee to Reserve Bank of India		
l.	Services supplied by a recovery agent to a banking company or a financial institution or a nonbanking financial company		
m.	Services supplied by a person located in non-taxable territory by way of transportation of goods by a vessel from a place outside India up to the customs station of clearance in India to an importer.		
n.	Services supplied by individual Direct Selling Agents (DSAs) other than a body corporate, partnership or limited liability partnership firm to bank or non-banking financial company (NBFCs)		
	Sub Total – D		
	Total Reverse charge – B + C + D		Xx
	Total RCM Paid in Returns		Xx
	Difference to be Analysed		Xx

18.5 JOB WORK RECONCILIATION

Industry after introduction in VAT in 2003/5 had started to send raw material and components within the State on payment of excise duty and VAT. This would avoid some paper work. However a large part was sending out these inputs without payment of duty/ taxes. In GST also supplying on payment of tax and receipt back with tax on gross amount is possible.

However a registered person is allowed to send any inputs or capital goods for job work without payment of GST to a job worker in terms of Section 143 of CGST Act 2017. However, there are certain conditions such as intimation, receipt of goods after job work within the stipulated time period, filing ITC-04 form etc. The registered person is allowed to claim the input tax credit on goods which are directly sent to job worker subject to receipt back of goods.

The inputs sent for job work should be received back within a period of 1 year and capital goods sent should be received in 3 years. In case goods are not received within the time specified, the same would be treated as supply as on the date of challan through which goods were sent for job work. Applicable GST to be paid on such goods including interest, which could prove to be very expensive. Unlike earlier indirect tax laws, there is no provision in GST law to avail credit of such tax paid even after receipt of goods processed. Therefore, it would be very crucial for the registered person to keep track of goods sent and received back after job work.

Reconciliation could be undertaken in following manner:

(1) Compare the description, HSN, amount and quantity of goods sent and received as per stores job work register and security register. Where there is quantity sent in weight and received back in numbers, the comparative pieces to be accounted and displayed in the documents and records.

(2) Identify the differences and ascertain the reasons for the differences. While normal conversion losses are acceptable, the abnormal consumption may need debit to the job worker along with GST for excess usage.

(3) Ascertain if the inputs and capital goods sent for job work received back within 1 year and 3 years. Such restriction would not apply to tools, dies, moulds and fixtures.

(4) In case of transactions wherein the goods are not received within the normal cycle time as per stores job work register, ascertain if receipt entries are found in inward security register. Job work register could be updated based on entries found.

(5) Ascertain the differences between goods sent for job work register and outward security register. Reasons for differences to be ascertained. Instances like goods sent directly from vendor's site to job worker site should be considered for which there may not be any entry in security register.

(6) Year-end stock reconciliation to be undertaken as per job workers records and job work register. Reasons for differences to be ascertained.

(7) Details of scrap generated and sold, if any as per job worker to be matched with entries in job work register. Documentation of payment of tax kept by both principal and job worker.

(8) Identify the instances wherein goods actually not received to determine the tax amount and interest to be paid with disclosure in GST returns.

(9) Compare the details of goods sent/ received and ensure that taxes paid for non-receipts are appropriately disclosed in quarterly GST return in form ITC-04.

18.6 E-WAY BILL RECONCILIATION

E-way bill has been introduced for all interstate movement of goods with effect from 1st April 2018 and all State governments have implemented it by the end of June 2018. Non -issue of E-way bill could attract penal consequences in terms of Section 129 of CGST Act 2017.

This section makes it obligatory for the owner of the goods to pay the tax and 100% of the tax as penalty even to get the goods and the vehicle released. If the owner does not come forward, the transporter has to pay tax and 50% of tax towards penalty. In the case of exempted goods also penalty as a percentage of value has to be paid. Till such payment is made the goods and the vehicle remain detained.

Therefore, it is essential to ensure that all goods movement is accompanied by E-way bill and a proper invoice (Complete in all respects) wherever required. It is also to be noted that tax paid under section 129 is not available as credit to the receiver. Where for any reason, tax and penalty are paid and the goods got released, the tax need not be paid again while making payment with monthly returns.

Similarly, supply of goods without issue of tax invoice or issue of invoice without supply of goods would attract penalty in terms of Section 122 of CGST Act 2017. Department is also contemplating taking up reconciliation between the E-way bills generated with details of outward supplies in GSTR-1. It is essential to prepare a reconciliation statement on periodical basis to avoid any non-compliances.

The following table could be helpful in reconciliation of E-way bills generated between GSTR-1 and E-way bill report which could be generated on E-way bill portal:

Table A

Sl No	Particulars	Total Amount (Rs)
1	Total amount of E-way bill generated as per E-way bill report in E-way bill portal for the period………	XXX
2	Total amount of outward supplies as per GSTR-1 for the period ………. *	XXX
	Difference (if any) - reasons to be ascertained	XX

***Note:** The outward supplies as per GSTR 1 should not consider the debit notes, credit notes, invoice amendments, advance receipt and adjustments effected in GSTR 1.

Table B

SL No	Particulars	Total Amount (Rs)	Remarks
1	Total amount of supplies for which E-way bill generated as per E-way bill report for the period……….	**XXX**	**Remarks**
	To be reduced		
2	Total amount of goods sent for job work without GST payment		
3	Total amount of goods sent under delivery challan under warranty claim		
4	Total amount of goods sent as FOC supplies, samples under delivery challan		
5	Total amount of way bill issued towards unregistered procurements		
6	Total amount of way bill issued towards import consignment		
7	Total amount of way bill issued but not cancelled due to non-supply of goods. (Or) E-way bill issued but failed to cancel due to non-supply of goods		
8	Total Credit notes issued which is effected in GSTR-1 for the period		
	To be added		
10	Total amount of taxable supplies for which Way bills issued by the transporter		
11	Total amount of taxable supplies for which Way bills not issued where the consignment value is less than Rs.50,000/-*[12]		

12 This limit could vary in few states where limit is more than Rs.50,000/- for intra-state movement of goods.

SL No	Particulars	Total Amount (Rs)	Remarks
12	Total amount of taxable supplies for which Way bills not issued for the products exempted from e-way bill (i.e. Jewellery, precious stones, LPG etc.)		
	Total outward supplies amount as per GSTR-1 for the period		

18.7 RECONCILIATION BETWEEN GSTR-2A AND BOOKS OF ACCOUNT

The GSTR-2A is an auto-populated report which contains the details of invoices which are raised and uploaded by the supplier in his GSTR-1 returns. Initially this report was provided to help the taxpayer to file GSTR-2 returns. As the due dates for GSTR-2 were extended on regular basis and finally kept under abeyance, this auto-populated report was not of much significance.

However, the revenue department started comparing the ITC availed by the taxpayers in GSTR-3B with the auto-populated report of GSTR-2A and started issuing the ASMT-10 notices highlighting the differences between GSTR-3B & GSTR-2A. Such comparison is difficult for various reasons such as non-submission of GSTR-1 by the suppliers, errors in information submitted by the vendors, delay in claim in credit etc. The fact that this issue is not being pursued by revenue indicates that it may not stand scrutiny of the courts. The new returns also foster the view that compliance is the supplier's job and receiver cannot be penalised for no fault of his.

The tax payer is advised to undertake such comparison to identify the reasons for such differences as it could also result in detecting eligible but missed out credits including reconciliation with books of account. It would also avoid the need for answering the enquiry from the revenue which is inevitable. The following table could be helpful in identifying the differences and reconciling the ITC with books of accounts:

Table A

(Amount in rupees)

Sl No	Particulars	SGST	CGST	IGST	Cess	Total
1	ITC claimed in GSTR-3B as per books of accounts	XXX	XXX	XXX	XXX	XXX
2	ITC available as per GSTR-2A	XXX	XXX	XXX	XXX	XXX
	Difference (if any) - reasons to be ascertained – refer Table B	XX	XX	XX	XX	XX

Table B

(Amount in rupees)

SL No.	Particulars	CGST	SGST	IGST
1	ITC available as per GSTR-2A in rupees for the tax period ………….. (A)	XXX	XXX	XXX
	To be added:			
2	ITC availed, but invoices are not been uploaded by the supplier for a. Not filed the return b. Filed returns - but uploaded as B2C instead of B2B	XX	XX	XX
3	ITC availed on import of goods			XX
4	ITC availed on import of services			XX
5	ITC availed on self-invoice - Section 9(3) & 9(4) if supplier has not uploaded w.r.t 9(3)	XX	XX	XX
6	ITC availed as CGST & SGST, whereas uploaded by the supplier as IGST	-	-	XX
7	ITC availed on debit notes, but not been uploaded by the supplier	XX	XX	XX
	Sub-total (B)			
	To be deducted/reduced:			
8	ITC availed on the invoices of previous tax period	XX	XX	XX
9	Ineligible ITC not availed by the taxpayer	XX	XX	XX
10	Restricted under section 17(5) of CGST Act, 2017	XX	XX	XX
11	ITC availed as CGST & SGST, whereas uploaded by the supplier as IGST	XX	XX	-

SL No.	Particulars	CGST	SGST	IGST
12	ITC availed as per invoice, error in taxable value uploaded by the supplier. Ex: ITC claimed as per invoice Rs.1500/- ITC uploaded by the supplier is Rs.1200/- (error in uploading taxable value)	-	-	XX
13	Invoices uploaded by the supplier, but ITC is not availed by the taxpayer - to be availed within time limit prescribed in Section 39(9) of CGST Act, 2017	XX	XX	XX
	Sub-total (C)			
	ITC as per Books of accounts [(A)+(B)-(C)]			

18.8 RECONCILIATION BETWEEN GSTR-1 TO GSTR-3B

Initially the returns prescribed to be filed by the normal taxpayers were GSTR-1, 2 and 3 with the help of auto-populated reports which are GSTR-1A & 2A. Due to lot of technical problems faced at the stage of implementation of said returns, the due dates for filing GSTR-1, 2 and 3 were extended and later on GSTR-2 & 3 was kept under abeyance. As the due dates for GSTR-1, 2 & 3 were extended, rule 61(5) & 61(6) of CGST Rules, 2017 were substituted vide notification no. 17/2017-CT dated 27.07.2017 wherein a new monthly return was prescribed in form GSTR-3B summary return. The due date prescribed is 20th of subsequent month.

It is important to note that this reconciliation is essential to be done before the filing of the annual return in Form 9. Due to the extension provided it is expected that 90% of the assessees other than those under composition would comply for the year 2017-18 and more for the year 2018-19.

Though the due date of GSTR-3B is 20th of subsequent month which is 10 days after the due date of GSTR-1, due to extension of timeline for GSTR-1 filing could have resulted in differences in disclosure between GSTR-1 and GSTR-3B. Therefore, there is a need for the taxpayers to reconcile the differences for turnover disclosed between GSTR-1 and GSTR-3B to ascertain if there is any excess or short payment of CGST/SGST/IGST. In case of excess payment, the same may be adjusted towards subsequent period liability or refund needs to be claimed by the taxpayer. Any short payment is to be made good by payment along with interest payment. The following table could be helpful in reconciliation of turnover between GSTR-1 and GSTR-3B return:

Table A

Sl No	Particulars	Total Amount in Rs	GST Amount in Rs
1	Total outward turnover disclosed in Table 3.1 (a), (b), (c), (e) of GSTR-3B for the tax period	XXX	XXX
2	Total outward turnover disclosed in GSTR-1 for the tax period	XXX	XXX
	Difference (if any) - reasons to be ascertained	XX	XX

Table B

Sl No	Particulars	Total Amount in Rs	GST Amount in Rs	Remarks
	Total Turnover as disclosed in GSTR-3B Table 3.1 (a), (b), (c), (e) - **(A)***[13]	**XXX**	**XXX**	**Remarks**
	To be Added:			
3	The invoices which were raised during the tax period not considered while filing GSTR-3B	XX	XX	Creates additional liability
4	The debit notes which were raised during the tax period not considered while filing GSTR-3B	XX	XX	Creates additional liability
5	The credit notes raised during the tax period but not considered in GSTR-1	XX	XX	No additional liability, only disclosure error. Should be disclosed in GSTR-1 within time prescribed under Section 39(9).

13 Do not include the inward supplies turnover on which GST is paid under reverse charge mechanism.

Sl No	Particulars	Total Amount in Rs	GST Amount in Rs	Remarks
6	Short payment of tax due to error in computation of tax while filing GSTR-3B	-	XX	Creates additional liability
7	Payment of IGST instead of CGST and SGST	-	XX	Creates additional liability + file refund for payment made under wrong head
8	Payment of CGST and SGST instead of IGST	-	XX	Creates additional liability + file refund for payment made under wrong head
9	Advance received not considered in GSTR-1		XX	No additional liability, only disclosure error. Should be disclosed in GSTR-1 within time prescribed under Section 39(9)
	Sub-Total (B)		XXX	
	To be deducted:			
10	The invoices which were not considered in GSTR-1	XX	XX	No additional liability, only disclosure error. Should be disclosed in GSTR-1 within time prescribed under Section 39(9).
11	The debit notes raised but not considered while filing GSTR-1	XX	XX	No additional liability, only disclosure error. Should be disclosed in GSTR-1 within time prescribed under Section 39(9).
12	The credit notes raised during the tax period but not considered in GSTR-3B	XX	XX	Excess payment of tax, need to rectified within time prescribed under section 39(9)

Sl No	Particulars	Total Amount in Rs	GST Amount in Rs	Remarks
13	Excess payment of tax due to error in computation of tax while filing GSTR-3B	-	XX	Excess payment of tax, need to rectified within time prescribed under section 39(9)
	Sub-Total (C')		XXX	
	Total turnover as per GSTR-1 (A)+(B)-(C')		XXX	

18.9 IDENTIFICATION OF DISCLOSURE ERRORS BETWEEN GSTR-3B AND GSTR -1 FOR NORMAL REGISTERED PERSON (OTHER THAN PERSON REGISTERED AS SEZ)

		Compare with (table reference)	
Sl	**Particulars**	**GSTR-3B**	**GSTR-1**
1	Other taxable supplies (including deemed exports and sale from bonded warehouse)	3.1 (a)	Table 4, 5, 6C, 7, 9, 10 & 11
2	Zero rated supplies (SEZ)	3.1 (b)	Table 6B, 9 & 11
3	Zero rated supplies (Exports)	3.1 (b)	Table 6A, 9 & 11
4	Non-GST supplies	3.1 (e)	Table 8
5	Exempted Supplies	3.1 (c)	Table 8
6	Nil rates supplies	3.1 (c)	Table 8

18.10 EXPORTS RECONCILIATION

Exports of goods or services or both under GST is treated as Zero Rated supplies and accordingly in terms of provisions of section 16 of the IGST Act, 2017 supplier can either opt for exporting of goods or services without payment of taxes wherein refund can be for the input tax credit used in supplying such goods/ services. Alternatively, supplier can opt for exporting goods/ services with payment of taxes wherein the amount of output tax paid (in cash and by utilisation of credit) can be claimed as refund. Various reconciliations required in the context of export of goods/ services are as follows:

18.10.1 Reconciliation with Table 6A of GSTR 1

Export sales as shown under zero rated supplies should match with the amount of export sales shown in table 6A of GSTR-1. As per table 3.1(b) of the GSTR 3B tax payer needs to show the zero rated supplies which includes the supplies made to the SEZ also. However, tax payer would show only exports in the table 6A of GSTR 1 provided that supplies which are shown in the GSTR 1 should not exceed the supplies which are shown in the GSTR 3B. Hence it required to reconcile and match exports as per GSTR 3B is matching with the table 6A of GSTR 1.

18.10.2 Reconciliation with Shipping Bill

Shipping bill is a mandatory requirement to be filed with the custom authority for any exports of goods from India to a place outside India wherein he mentions the details of the export such as invoice number, date and value of goods exported etc. Hence tax payers can cross verify the exports as per books with the shipping bill. This is traditional way of reconciliation of the books with the shipping bill documents.

18.10.3 Reconciliation of Export Invoices and BRCs/FIRCs

Another traditional way of the reconciliation of the exports is with the reconciliation certification received from the banks. Bank issues these certificates shipping bill wise, hence it helps the assessees for the reconciliation of the exports with the realisation certificates received from the bank. Further, FIRC's are issued for every remittance received in the convertible foreign exchange. Since, one of the conditions for a transaction to be called as an export is that the monies must be received in the convertible foreign exchange therefore this reconciliation also helps in establishing remittance in foreign exchange and thereby claiming a refund of taxes paid.

18.10.4 Reconciliation with Export General Manifest (EGM) data at ICE GATE

Export General Manifest is a legal document mandatory to be filed by carrier of goods with customs department. This document is used by government authorities as proof of export. Assessee can match the exports made during the particular period with the details at the ICE GATE.

18.10.5 Reconciliation with the E Way bills generated

This is the new source for reconciliation in GST era. E way bill is one of the tools which is used for the monitor the movement of goods to check the tax evasion in GST. E way bill needs to be generated even for the export of goods which are required to be transported up to port (Airport/sea port) from where goods are being exported. While generation the E-way bill assessees are required to give the invoice wise details. Hence now assessees are required to reconcile the details of the as per E way bill portal with the books.

18.11 RECONCILIATION WITH SCRIP'S OBTAINED UNDER FOREIGN TRADE POLICY

One of the incentive schemes of exports is MEIS/ SEIS wherein incentive is granted by the DGFT as a percentage of the exports of such goods/ services. In order to ensure full benefit as available under the DGFT is availed and received, it becomes imperative to reconcile the value of goods/ services exported with that for which the benefits under FTP has been applied for and received.

18.12 REFUNDS RECONCILIATION

The provisions relating to claiming of refund in case of exports are contained in Section 54 of the CGST Act, 2017 read with Rules 89 to 97A of the CGST Rules and Circular Nos. 17/2017 dated 15/11/2017, 18/2017 dated 16/11/2017 and 24/2017 dated 21/12/2017 issued by the CBIC from time to time. Refund in relation to exports can be claimed by exercising any of or both the following two options:

- Refund of IGST in case of exports on payment of IGST (Rule 96);
- Refund of accumulated ITC in case of exports without payment of taxes under Bond/LUT (Rule 96A).
- Refund of accumulated ITC in case of inverted rate structuring;

As far as the refund is concerned, a complete and proper reconciliation and the account of the refunds applied for, sanctioned, pending and rejected must be kept. This would also enable focus on this area which at times is ignored due to the difficulty in getting the refund in the past. The same must also be matched with the entries passed in the books of accounts. Apart from the above, following reconciliations should be made by the assesse before application of the refund should made reconciliations of the following:

18.13 RECONCILIATION OF INPUT/ OUTPUT INVOICES WITH BOOKS OF ACCOUNTS

Assessee should reconcile the books with the dockets. This is one of correct and concrete way that the input tax credit reconciliation. This reconciliation helps assessee in timely correction of the inconsistencies. Various differences include instances such as credit claimed in the incorrect GST account, incorrect place of supply, improper type of credit availed viz., CGST & SGST instead of IGST or vice-versa. Based on the extent of internal controls, the number of invoices to be reconciled has to be determined and must be carried out.

This reconciliation can also be performed in respect of the claim of refunds viz., claim on output refund or input refund or interest refund for delayed refunds. It is pertinent to note that the claim of refund be rejected if the credit is availed on the expenses which are not eligible to be availed or is availed without any proper document as prescribed under rule 46 of the GST rules.

18.14 RECONCILIATION WITH ELECTRONIC CREDIT/ LIABILITY LEDGER

Assessee must continuously match the details of taxes as appearing in the electronic liability ledger and electronic credit ledger with the details of taxes as disclosed in the Duties & Taxes ledger in the financial statements such that the same is matching. Further, any differences therein must be reconciled in a timely manner and the adjustment to be given effect.

It is also important to match the amount of taxes paid in cash effecting the Cash in Hand / Bank ledger in the books of accounts with the monies as deposited in the electronic cash ledger and the mis-matches if any must be scrutinised. This can also assist assessee in timely claiming the refund of excess cash deposited in the electronic cash ledger.

Further, before applying of the refund, assessee needs to reconcile the amount of the input tax credit as per input tax register should match the input tax credit as per electronic ledger of the assessee. Every month while filing GSTR 3B assessee provides the details of the input tax credit in the return. Therefore before applying assessee should match the books with the portal (i.e. credit ledger of portal) and at the time of applying the refund, the value for which the refund claim is applied needs to be debited in the electronic credit ledger and the proof of such debit needs to be submitted along with the application for refund.

18.15 RECONCILIATION WITH THE SHIPPING BILL DATA

The IGST refund module has been designed in line with the above rule and has an in built mechanism to automatically grant refund after validating the Shipping Bill data with available in ICES against the GST Returns data transmitted by GSTN. The matching between the two data sources is done at Invoice level and any miss-match of the laid down parameters returns following error/response codes:

(i) **SB001:** Invalid Shipping Bill Number This may occur due to a mismatch between the SB No. furnished in GSTR-1/6A and the SB No. with customs. The possible reason for such mismatch could be a clerical error made by the exporter at the time of filling of GSTR-1/6A, which can be rectified by making amendments in GSTR-1 by using Form 9A. Form 9A has been made available by GSTN w.e.f. 15.12.2017 in exporter's login at the GST Common Portal.

(ii) **SB002:** EGM not filed Exporter may approach the Shipping Lines to file the EGM immediately.

(iii) **SB003:** GSTIN mismatch, this error occurs when GSTIN declared in the SB does not match with the GSTIN used to fill the corresponding GST Returns. In this case too, the Exporter may be asked to make necessary adjustments in GSTR-1 by use of amendment Form 9A. However, it is to be noted that there is no provision of amendment in the Shipping Bill once the EGM is filed.

(iv) **SB004:** Record already received, this error code occurs due to duplicate/repeat transmission of SB-Invoice record from GSTN. The previous transmission would have already been validated for IGST refund by ICES.

(v) **SB005:** Invalid Invoice Number This is the most common error faced by the exporters, which occurs due to mismatch of invoice number as declared in the Invoice Table in the SB and that declared in the GSTR 1 for the same supply. This can happen due to:

(a) Typographical mistake while entering data in GSTR 1 or the SB;

(b) The exporter uses two sets of invoices, one invoice for GST and another invoice for exports resulting in mismatch of invoice numbers.

(vi) **SB006:** Gateway EGM not available In case of ICDs, if the Gateway EGM is not filed electronically or is stuck in some error, response code SB006 shall appear. It is noticed that Gateway EGM in case of many ICD's Shipping Bills have been manually filed, which shall not suffice and the EGM shall have to be filed in ICES at the gateway port. Gateway EGM pendency and error reports can be viewed in New MIS role. In case of pending Gateway EGMs, Shipping Lines may be approached at gateway ports to file supplementary EGMs expeditiously.

18.16 OTHER RECONCILIATIONS

The focus of the revenue on tax evasion and leakage in the coming months would be very high due the following practices:

a. Tax payers not filing GSTR 3B returns after payment of taxes due and only filing GSTR1.

b. Registered tax payer not filing either 1 or 3B.

c. Unregistered tax payers using e way bill with their PAN number with value being depressed. At times using one e-way bill for movement of multiple supplies.

d. Not accounting for the supplies in their books.

e. Procuring invoices without any supply.

f. Under invoicing quantities / values to unregistered buyers and over invoicing to registered buyer.

g. Year-end entries to boost the turnover with or without payment of GST.

The auditor may need to examine for those registered the stock register against the dispatches and guard against fraud in these areas. This may require various reconciliations including stock to delivery challans/ invoices.

Chapter 19

Genesis of Dispute- Avoidance and mitigation

19.1 INTRODUCTION

In this chapter an attempt is made to identify the common errors in general that may be made by tax payers and the revenue department and what steps a taxpayer can take to ensure that the number of disputes are reduced. Further when the disputes arise how to tackle them better. The awareness of the errors of the Department that may be committed would help the taxpayer to be ready to deal with them.

The specific errors in different industries depending on the way business is done have not been covered in this book for which readers may refer to the sectoral books.

The statutory dispute resolution mechanism has been dealt with in the chapter 'Overview' which shows that the statutory dispute resolution mechanism is costly for a taxpayer in terms of time as well as cost.

19.2 REASONS FOR DISPUTES

(a) Lack of awareness of the GST law of revenue officers (especially the State GST Officers of services) at this point of time. Further officers in adjudication, appeals and advance ruling positions need to have advanced knowledge duly certified after having passed an examination.

(b) Long and complex legal provisions due to "consensus" based approach and haste without considering trade realities.

(c) Poor drafting of act, rules and frequent amending notifications and circulars leading to further confusion.

(d) Confusing clarifications press releases, FAQs and oral guidance provided by the revenue departments/ officers.

(e) GST law has major differences when compared with the erstwhile service tax or Local VAT law as regards levy classification, credits etc.

(f) Provisions relating to input tax credit are very complex and complicated. At times they are restrictive and defy logic.

(g) The persons in the parallel economy actively seeking to continue their off the record transactions using the loop holes available.

(h) Tendency on the part of the revenue officers to interpret legal provisions with a revenue bias and to hoist frivolous demands.

(i) Corruption in tax administration which has come down substantially in GST regime. However due to the problems in the portal and non implementation of matching, e-way bill implementation, the interaction with officers is continuing. It is expected that lakhs of notices on non reconciliation would be issued in the period post July 2019.

(j) Audit objections by the audit parties deputed by AG and the internal audit wing of the GST department without understanding the latest changes and settled law. This results in routine generation of disputes by issue of show cause notice which are in majority of adjudications as well as 1st appeal confirmed. Tax payers may get relief at Tribunal level after efflux of years.

(k) Lack of proper guidance by the officers to the tax payers.

(l) Lack of discipline in following judicial precedents and even departmental circulars.

(m) Advance rulings taking opposite views on the same issue relied on even though it is known that it is applicable only to the person who has applied.

(n) Total lack of trust in the tax payers on the part of officers. The presumption is tax payer is evading which is not fair.

(o) Lack of knowledge of latest legal position.

(p) Attitude of arrogance and superiority from earlier regimes carried forward to some extent.

(q) Discretionary powers available to the officers in some aspects though it has been reduced in GST.

(r) Inordinate delay in dispute resolution.

(s) Lack of proper training with evaluation for adjudicators, audit and appellate officers.

(t) Lack of attention to the law as it existed at the time of dispute.

(u) Fear of Audit, Vigilance machinery and CBI on the part of the Central tax officers leading to playing safe.

(v) Multiple agencies of the department looking to detect tax evasion/ tax avoidance by the tax payers and difference in their perception about the law.

(w) Provision in the law providing for penalty of 10% in the event of a tax payer not paying the tax demanded with interest within 30 days of issue of show cause notice (SCN) has to be kept in mind. Therefore as far as possible when a show cause notice is expected, tax payer should request for provisional assessment.

(wi) Provision of pre deposit at 1st and 2nd appellate stages. Especially unfair if the SCN is frivolous and ultimately tax payer would win.

(wii) State GST officers having inadequate knowledge of well settled concepts while dealing with the supply of services leading to re-inventing settled law under service tax.

19.3 COMMON ERRORS BY TAX PAYERS - RESOLUTION

(a) Ignorance of law and latest amendments – Attend the update programs conducted by trade/ industry association/ professionals. Keep professionals in house or external who are updated on the latest notification, circulars and decisions.

(b) Errors in filing returns and payment of tax - Filing of the returns in time after due verification after payment of tax in time. In case of any difficulty taking a snap shot of the error message and retaining that and also intimating the department about the difficulty promptly.

(c) Mistakes in arriving at aggregate turnover leading to errors in computation of threshold or composition limits – Ensure that internal controls are established to identify, prevent and correct errors in terms of law.

(d) Delayed registration after GST is due leading to denial of credit prior to registration and limiting the benefit of credit to customers as well – Staff engaged in the work should be asked to undergo training and their knowledge levels checked by the management.

(e) Incompetent and untrained officers maintaining records and returns and filing of the same - Staff engaged in the work should be asked to undergo training and their knowledge levels evaluated.

(f) Non-cooperation with audit /investigation – Management should pay attention to ensure that full co-operation is extended and document the submission of documents and discussions.

(g) Non-preservation of past correspondence with the Department – Management has to ensure proper preservation of records and filing systems.

(h) Statement given by a person of the company or the tax payer leading to the wrong conclusion/information for the Department - Management has to ensure that person who interacts with the department has sufficient legal knowledge, knowledge of business and policies of the company.

(i) Not taking qualified professional legal assistance at the appropriate time – The legal assistance should always be taken at the earliest time i.e. when there is a hint of a dispute arising.

(j) Tax related transactions, procedures and systems not vetted by an independent tax professional at reasonable intervals – GST review audit is one of the best preventive steps (explained later in this chapter).

(k) Lack of inter action with the department – Even though often departmental officers take revenue biased views, there is no harm in seeking clarifications from the department. It helps in establishing bona fides of the tax payer. If not satisfied at lower levels, meeting up with senior officers.

(l) Avoid disputes: Where the issue does not create recurring liability and cost benefit analysis shows it is not worthwhile pursuing litigation, better to pay tax and interest and even penalty.

(m) Lack of knowledge on the part of staff: Keeping some good commentaries specific to industry is available for reference. Staff should be deputed for seminars /training programs /workshops.

(n) Wrong claims for refunds/delayed claims for refunds: Tax payers should be aware of provisions relating to refunds and claim for refunds and prompt attention to this area can be very beneficial and the GST audit by independent professional could come handy in this regard.

(o) Lack of proper documentation: Documentation and details to be given in statutory documents have to be carefully taken note of and implemented so that no loss is caused to self or the customers.

(p) Procrastination (postponement) in making decision about the approach when investigation/ inquiry/audit queries are received or panic reaction of paying up dues which was no legal needs in such a situation.

19.4 SOME POSSIBLE SOLUTIONS TO REVENUE TO AVOID DISPUTES

(a) The 100s of good suggestions to make the GST law simple, fair and transparent, erring in favour of the honest assessee to be put in place within March of 2020 by Government. All issues before the GST Council should be cleared in time bound manner before March 2020.

(b) A serious and complete exercise in training of industry, trade and professionals on a war footing by trade and professional institutes.

(c) The lack of knowledge of officers across the Board with lower level of understanding in State ranks and Officers in charge of Advance Ruling has been observed. The trade is frustrated with the present lack of guidance with interest and penalties being imposed on hapless tax payers who do not understand the law. All officers have to go through a rigorous training with system of evaluation with the ones in charge of adjudication needing to have an expert level of knowledge certified.

(d) Methodology of good coordination between the assessees and CBIC as well as GSTN with time bound clarification with no demand recourse for incorrect advice from authorities up to March of 2020.

(e) All the clarifications/ FAQs etc. being collated and one consolidated document issued for compliance support as early as possible.

(f) The quick resolution of refunds and making it totally online without human intervention. Technology used to verify those that appear to be erroneous.

(g) In the case of any inspection, search, seizure, it is necessary to see whether the order passed under section 129 is appropriate and can be challenged and has been examined properly by the assessee. Similarly in the case of action under section 130 resulting in confiscation of goods and vehicle, steps taken by the assessee have to be seen to examine the correctness.

(h) If any investigation has been initiated, the replies given to the Department during the correspondence or statements given to the Departmental officers by the officers of the firm/company have to be examined and seen for the appropriateness of the responses. Quite often such investigations lead to show cause notice and result in losses because of delayed response.

(i) If the assessee has paid the entire amount of dues with interest, it is necessary to verify whether any remedial steps have to be taken since quite often even after payment of all the taxes, proceedings are initiated within the time available to the Department for collection of penalty which as mentioned earlier can be very high.

(j) The auditor has to verify whether the payments were made in accordance with the provisions in the GST law so that the interest of the assessee is safeguarded. He may seek expert opinion.

(k) If Department audit has been conducted, the audit queries raised, replies given and action taken with regard to the queries have to be examined.

(l) It is to be seen whether the system of correspondence maintained ensures that the show cause notices received, adjudication orders received and orders in appeal/revision passed by statutory authorities are kept intact and properly maintained and pursued till the logical end.

Tax payer may also get a review of the compliance till date done by knowledgeable professionals. If any issue identified by the assessee or internal auditor or statutory auditors or department, it has to be resolved by the assessee voluntarily and immediately. This would avoid additional interest as well as penalty.

Chapter 20

Common errors to be avoided in GST

20.1 INTRODUCTION

Prevention is better than cure. A professional as an auditor can prevent the impact of serious errors or mistakes of a client which otherwise could lead to increased demand of tax, penalty and interest having impact on continuity of business as well. In addition to this, clients could end up facing harassment from tax department for non-compliance. All these can be prevented by an auditor, if he understands the common errors of clients. Most of the errors could be industry specific. However, there are number of errors which are common and could be avoided by clients if an auditor proactively brings them to client's notice. Many a times, revenue (department) tries to deny credits or demand tax on frivolous grounds. This could be avoided with a few preventive actions. A few avoidable common errors to ensure better GST compliance are listed in this chapter. It may be noted that the list is only indicative in nature and could vary depending on the type of business and level of internal control and compliance existing. The list could be considered by the professionals for incorporating the check points in the audit program / audit checklist as well.

The possibility of these common errors along with impact could be discussed with the audit team as well so that major non-compliance issues get covered in the audit.

20.2 CONCEPTUAL ERRORS

Conceptual errors are those errors which occur as a result of wrong understanding of law. Such errors could bring the tax payers into serious problem in the long run unless corrective actions are taken to correct as impact would be repetitive in nature. Few of them are listed below:

(1) Incorrect classification of goods or services which could lead to incorrect GST rate/wrong exemption claim. Demand on multiple persons in supply chain possible without credit.

This could further result in incorrect input credit availment. Example could be classifying the service as 'Rent a cab service' instead of 'Lease of a car'.

(2) Deduction claimed for expenses incurred as pure agent without satisfying all the conditions prescribed in law for 'pure agent' deduction. Claiming of tax amount from customers later on also may not be easy in such situations. Especially if the time limit for claiming credit by customers has lapsed.

(3) Discharging GST under reverse charge mechanism without ascertaining place of supply for the transaction especially in case of services procured from overseas vendors. This could be expensive if the person is not eligible for claiming credit due to supply of exempted goods or services.

(4) Wrong type of tax paid on interstate supply of goods or services under reverse charge mechanism without ascertaining the place of supply.

(5) Though goods/service absolutely exempted, opting to pay GST with input tax credit benefit. In such cases, credit could be denied as there was absolute exemption from payment of GST.

(6) Claiming exemption or payment of GST at concessional rate without fulfilling the conditions attached to it. For example, claiming ITC when opting to pay 5% GST on renting of motor vehicle.

(7) Not remitting GST to government after collecting from customers. This could invoke demand under Section 74 resulting in denial of credit to customers as well. Business may take a big hit in such situations as customers may not like to do business with such vendors.

(8) Unregistered persons and composition dealers are prohibited from collecting any tax from customers. Non-compliance could lead to imprisonment if quantum of amount involved exceeds Rs. 1 Crore.

(9) Incorrect determination of place of supply which could lead to incorrect charging of type of tax or even taxing a non-taxable transaction or vice versa.

(10) Registration not taken by person making interstate taxable supplies. It is to be noted that registration is mandatory for person making interstate supplies of goods. The benefit of threshold exemption limit of Rs.40 lakh is only for goods and not available to services.

(11) Considering all payments received in foreign currency as exports/zero rated supplies as per GST without satisfying other prescribed conditions in the law to treat supplies as exports.

(12) Considering input tax credit balance to payoff liability under reverse charge. However, GST portal does not allow such adjustment while filing returns.

(13) Delay in availment of input tax credit in case of reverse charge transactions. Such credit can be availed in the same month of liability subject to payment. This could have impact on cash flow.

(14) Discharging GST under reverse charge on services which are no longer under list of notified services u/s 9(3). For example, paying GST on courier services equating them with GTA services.

(15) Non availment of ITC on GTA services when option of 5% GST payment opted under reverse charge mechanism. The credit restriction is only for GTAs and not on recipient paying under reverse charge. Paying GST under reverse charge even when GTAs are charging GST at full rate of 12% presently.

(16) Treating export of goods/services as exempted goods/services and not availing related eligible ITC.

(17) Non-reversal of input tax credit along with interest in cases where payment is not made to supplier within 180 days from invoice date.

(18) Not availing the credit reversed earlier due to non-payment after making payment to vendor.

(19) Non-payment of GST on advance money received towards taxable supply of services.

(20) GST deduction claimed on post sale discounts which are agreed post sale which is against the conditions prescribed in Section 15 for valuation.

(21) Non-payment of GST on transactions covered in Schedule I of CGST Act. For instance, GST not paid on taxable goods or services supplied to branch in other State without any consideration.

(22) As exporter of goods/services not claiming the refund of duties and input tax credit which he is entitled to.

(23) Mixed supply could be classified as composite supply and vice versa leading to excess/short payment of GST.

(24) Credits reversed on oral instructions of departmental officers/audit parties without ascertaining the legal requirement.

(25) Tax not discharged on exemptions discontinued under GST which were present in earlier tax regime.

(26) Availing credit on basis of photocopy of invoices/debit note/BOE without having the original invoices/debit note/BOE.

(27) Availing input tax credit on supplies which are blocked for credit under Section 17(5) of CGST Act.

(28) Not availing credit on goods or services covered in Section 17 due to wrong interpretation. Example: Motor vehicles are covered in the list

of ineligible credits with exceptions. However, credit could be eligible when such vehicles are used for transportation of goods or providing transport services.

(29) Claiming benefit of zero rated supplies to SEZ (raising invoice to SEZ without tax) without executing letter of undertaking or bond.

(30) Availing input tax credit merely on receipt of invoice without actual receipt of goods/services.

(31) Non-reversal of proportionate common input tax credit in respect of exempted supplies and non-business use.

(32) Advances classified as deposits in books of accounts which could lead to non-payment of tax on advance amounts.

(33) Non-availment of input tax credit on bank charges, vehicle insurance, asset insurance and telephone bills.

(34) Non-reversal of credit in respect of goods lost, stolen, destroyed, written off or distributed as gifts/free samples.

(35) Reversal of credit on warranty replacements made as a part of finished goods sent.

(36) Not considering time of supply for payment of GST which results in early/delayed payment of GST.

(37) Non-payment of GST on goods sent for job work not received after processing within due date.

(38) Non-payment of GST on waste or scrap generated during job work.

(39) Failure to distribute the common credits to other locations under ISD.

(40) Not considering non-monetary consideration for arriving at the value for paying GST.

(41) Interest/penalty collected for delayed payments from customers not considered for payment of GST.

(42) Taxable amounts recovered from employees such as notice period pay, canteen recoveries, transportation charges not considered for payment of GST.

(43) Considering wrong rate of interest for delayed payment of GST (18%) or wrong claim of input tax credits (24%).

(44) Treating tax paid on employee recoveries as RCM and taking back the amount of tax paid as credit. Output taxes cannot be availed as input credit.

(45) Reversing ITC on common inputs and capital goods using the same formula though different provisions exist in CGST provisions resulting in short or excess reversal of credits.

(46) Not computing the actual ITC reversal amount after the end of the financial year.

(47) Not registering / nor discharging GST under reverse charge mechanism by business entities on services procured from related /associated enterprises abroad by the non-taxable persons in accordance with Schedule I. Ex: Education institution claiming GST exemption not paying GST on taxable services imported from related entity outside India.

(48) Payment of tax at different rates in case of composite supplies instead of considering the rate as applicable for principal supply.

(49) Payment of tax at single rate in case of mixed supplies instead of considering the rates as applicable for each supplied goods /service at relevant rates.

(50) Time of supply considered as date of invoice instead of date of receipt of consideration in case of late payment penalty, fee or interest collected from customers.

(51) Payment of GST on ad-hoc value in case of related party transactions even though the recipient is not eligible for full credit.

(52) Claiming ITC on expenses such as food & beverages, hiring of vehicles which are restricted under GST law without ascertaining if they are obligatory for employer under any of the laws.

(53) Claim of ITC pertaining to other registered locations fully without opting for ISD option to distribute the credits.

(54) Wrongly treating turnover from high sea sale transactions, sale from customs warehouse before clearance for home consumption and merchanting sale transactions as exempt supply for the purpose of ITC reversals.

(55) Not paying GST in respect of capital goods or plant and machinery, on which input tax credit has been taken when such goods are disposed of or sold. Ex: Sale of old vehicles.

(56) Wrongly paying GST on tools, jigs, dies, fixtures and moulds for non- receipt within 1 year or 3 years from job workers.

(57) Not obtaining ‘casual taxable person’ registration when occasionally any transaction is undertaken in any State where there is no fixed place of business. Careful analysis required considering option of charging IGST in such cases.

(58) Non-issue of tax invoice where goods sent or taken for supply on approval basis when goods are supplied or on /before six 6 months from date of removal whichever is earlier.

(59) Not indicating the amount of GST being collected on the documents such as tax invoice from the customers.

(60) Claim of deduction towards GST paid to the extent credit note issued without ascertaining if the recipient reverses the ITC claimed earlier. Deduction is eligible only when ITC reversed by recipient.

(61) Not complying with maintenance of documentation as required under Section 35 of the CGST Act 2017 read with Rule 56 of the CGST Rules 2017.

(62) Claim of refund of GST paid on capital goods in case of exports though restricted for refund.

(63) Despatch of goods without supporting documents such as tax invoice / bill of supply/ delivery challan or e-way bill inviting penalty demand.

(64) Exporting goods or services but failing to satisfy all conditions of export.

(65) Not maintaining the books of account / GST related records at principal place of business leading to demand of penalties

(66) Electronic records not digitally signed as specified in Rule 56

20.3 SYSTEM ERRORS

System errors are those errors which occur due to lack of good internal control system in the organization. Unless preventive and corrective action taken, system error could lead to cash flow issues and increased demand as well. Few of them are listed below:

(1) Not having a proper system of authorisation based on monetary limits for GST transactions.

(2) Making accounting entries on gross basis and passing entries for eligible credit or tax payable at end of the month. Failure to have a system of reconciliation of procurements or outward supplies to ensure complete credit availment or tax paid.

(3) Impact of GST not considered while quoting for an order or planning of a large expansion/investment or drafting an agreement or repetitive transaction.

(4) Credit availment in books in case of reverse charge cases before making payment of tax.

(5) Absence of system of recording entry in job work control register when inputs/capital goods are being sent for job work to ensure receipt within due dates.

(6) Having improper system of internal communication with the accounting, purchase and indirect tax department in the organization.

(7) No proper system to determine place of supply, type of tax for various sales transactions.

(8) Absence of proper mechanism/checklist to determine eligibility of input tax credit for procurements.

(9) Not providing GST registration numbers to vendors leading to receipt of invoices without GST which could result in denial of credit.

(10) No standard operating procedures laid down in medium and large enterprises for better tax compliance.

(11) ERP or other accounting package system of an enterprise not linked with the figures used for paying GST resulting in complications during return filing, lack of control. The absence of proper reconciliation system between financial records and tax records.

(12) Input tax credit missed out due to errors (incorrect GSTIN, non-indication of tax amount in the invoice) of supplier. In such cases, follow up should be made with supplier to correct.

(13) Delay in availing input tax credit which could result in excess payment of tax in cash.

(14) Not having a system to ensure that vendors are filing their return and paying GST in time. [At least till new system of returns put in place where supplier responsible]

(15) Issue of invoice instead of bill of supply for GST exempted supplies.

(16) Not keeping track of correspondences with tax department especially ensuring replies to proper authority.

(17) Not keeping a separate file for export proof such as shipping bills.

(18) Not accounting the inward invoices on regular basis.

(19) Credit notes not issued within time limit (financial year end) specified in case of excess amount/GST rate charge, purchase returns due to no system of tracking such instances.

(20) System of identification of inputs/input services/capital goods used exclusively for taxable, non-taxable activities not present.

(21) Not having standard operating procedures for ensuring all compliances in GST.

(22) Not having system of reconciliation of inward supplies and outward supplies including credit and liability details.

(22) Not having the system of paying to vendors within 180 days to avoid need of reversal of credits and avoid paying interest.

(23) Absence of system of MIS (management information system) to management on ratio of tax liability against tax credits, total credits to total purchases which can highlight important aspects to management and take action, if needed.

(24) Absence of systems audit to ensure adequate controls on data, information stored in computer systems including access restriction to control unauthorised access.

(25) Not having the system of getting periodical GST compliance review done from professionals.

(26) Not verifying the GST rates charged by the vendors on periodical basis, especially when there are changes in rate of GST.

(27) Not exploring the option of refund claim in case of deemed exports considering the cost benefit analysis.

(28) Not exploring the export benefits in case of export transactions including FTP benefits.

(29) Not factoring the additional benefits while bargaining/ negotiating price with the vendors. Ex: MEIS scrip benefit of 3% on FOB value of exports not considered while negotiating price for export of goods.

(30) Purchase of goods from composition scheme dealers where cost of purchase is high for such dealers due to ineligibility of credits.

(31) Not considering the option of registration of additional business places in other States which could result in loss of credits on procurements meant for such additional places.

(32) No system of proper planning before going for major CAPEX spending considering the factors such as GST rate, ITC etc.

(33) Not educating/ training the travelling staff on GST credit impact on procurements made. Obtaining bills in individuals name could result in loss of credit. Obtaining invoices with local address could impact the place of supply and in turn impact credit eligibility.

(34) Not having proper system of filing for input invoices, department correspondences.

(35) Not replying to departmental letters within due date.

(36) Not having proper terms/ arrangement for customisation of ERP to meet the needs of changes in the law on regular basis.

(37) Too much dependency on manual systems leading to delay in compliances.

(38) Not updating customers masters with correct address, GSTIN in case of changes which could lead to cancellation of invoices with need of claim of refund of GST paid.

(39) Not using the tools provided by GSTIN such as bulk generation of way bills, creating masters to avoid duplication of entries.

(40) Not considering the GST aspects in purchase orders/ contracts/ agreements. Cut paste drafting in vogue.

(41) Not taking entries in security registers from department officials on their visits.

(42) Not keeping track of litigation issues pending with status including refund claims.

(43) Absence of system of providing regular training to those involved in GST compliance and other divisions such as marketing, stores etc. to understand the GST impact.

(44) GRNs not reconciled with input tax credit register to ensure completeness of credits.

20.4 COMPLIANCE ERRORS

Compliance errors are errors associated with compliance requirement in GST such as return filing, payment of taxes and filing replies etc. Ignoring such errors could have impact on GST compliance ratings as well. Few of them are listed below:

(1) Not paying GST or not filing GST returns within due date leading to interest and penalty.

(2) Depositing GST in wrong type of tax. Example could be depositing GST in IGST instead of CGST & SGST. Cash ledger is segregated into different heads wherein inter head adjustment is not permitted in GSTN portal. Payment in correct head and refund in the other would be the solution.

(3) Wrong data filled in offline excel utility. Example could be incorrect GSTIN of recipient, incorrect format of date or invoice number.

(4) Charging separate rate of tax or not charging tax at all for services ancillary to supply of goods such as packing charges, transportation charges. Generally, these services would form of composite supply and rate applicable on goods supplied to be charged on such services also.

(5) Non-disclosure of job worker premises as additional place of business where goods are supplied from unregistered job worker premises to customer.

(6) Not amending the additional places of business in registration certificate.

(7) Failure to obtain ISD registration to distribute the credits.

(8) Not filing ISD returns.

(9) Not issuing E-way bills for stock transfers under the assumption that E-way bills required only for sale transactions.

(10) Not displaying the registration number and registration certificate at prominent place of business

(11) Not maintaining the accounts/ records for GST at each place of business

(12) Not filing intimation for goods sent to job work in for ITC-04

(13) Not raising self-invoice, issue of payment vouchers, receipt vouchers, refund vouchers as required under the GST law.

(14) Wrong disclosures in the returns being filed

(15) Not maintaining all records as prescribed under Rule 56 of CGST Rules which could get qualified in audit certification in form GSTR-9C.

(10) Claim of ITC on defective invoices.

(11) Not adding additional place of business in the registration certificate.

(12) Not updating the details of authorised signatory in the registration details.

(13) Not making appropriate declaration in case of exports, SEZ supplies on invoices.

(14) Not considering payment of GST on inclusive method (treating total amount as inclusive of GST) in case GST is not collected separately.

(15) Providing wrong details in e-way bills with respect to amounts, HSN, rate of tax etc.

(16) Not filing returns after filing application for cancellation of registration till actual cancellation of registration.

(17) Not issuing bill of supply in case of exempt supplies.

(18) Not issuing receipt voucher for advances received, not issuing payment vouchers for procurements from vendors where the liability under RCM exists.

(19) Errors in filing returns with respect to registration status of customers. Not mentioning GSTIN of customers enabling them to take credit.

(20) Not having a system of ascertaining if the vendors have been paying GST. Non-payment of GST could result in loss of credit.

(21) Not intimating or following conditions in case of supplies to be treated as deemed export.

(22) Not filing extension application in case of casual taxable person registration and continuing even after expiry of validity.

(23) Not updating the changes in the registration certificate.

Chapter 21

Annual Return under GST

21.1 INTRODUCTION

Filing of the annual return is not an entirely new phenomenon for tax payers who were required to file annual return and submit reconciliation certificate by the specified persons including Chartered Accountant under the State VAT laws. Under central excise law also certain annual information was specified for some larger enterprises which however did not require any certification.

The challenges and requirements under the GST regime are different and unlike VAT regimes, scrutiny and assessments would be limited as indicated. In the present GST regime, the Government network (GSTN) is in possession of vast data (details furnished in the monthly returns) which can be analysed and mined. The detection of common mistakes and even frauds (circular trading or bill with GST to X and supply to Y in cash) would be easier for the GST Network. The revenue department has a minimum period of three year, (could extend to 3 years 9 months) after a bona fide mistake/error is detected, to take recovery action. If charge of suppression, misstatement, fraud etc exist, then the period would be minimum 5 years (could extend to 5 years 9 months), to make demands. If longer period is invoked, credit of differential tax paid would not be available to the customer. This can have devastating effect like closure of business etc. Since amounts are on gross basis, for large defaults on bona fide nature where tax collected are not paid, may be due to severe financial crunch, imprisonment is possible if tax is not paid. Demands in GST would be on percentage of gross and not on how much margin is there.

Therefore, annual return is to be taken very seriously and has to be considered as an opportunity to file the returns regularly, validate the tax and ITC, and have a relook at what has been done in the previous year, without any prejudice or bias. The ideal sequence for tax compliant is: file GSTR 3B, file the GSTR-1 and reconcile to GSTR-3B. Then rectify all mistakes before September return filing is due date by revising the GSTR1 and GSTR 3B. File the annual return and then conduct the audit under section 35(5) if required.

The monthly return filed for the month of September of subsequent year could be the last opportunity to make rectifications of omissions and commissions in the previous financial year.[1] Even though annual return is required to be filed only by 31st December of subsequent year for a financial year, it is better to prepare it as soon as possible and be ready to submit it early. There is no provision for rectification of annual return and late fee has to be paid for delayed filing which has to be kept in mind. Where the tax payer does not have the man power with expert knowledge of the law, it is better to get expert help at least for the first 2-3 years, even though there are challenges this year considering the number of knowledgeable professionals available. The verification by expert even after submission of the annual return would be useful to ensure that the tax payer can be confident that he is complied with the law or he has taken steps to rectify mistakes if any. There would be no surprises and demands in coming years.

In terms of section 44 of the CGST Act 2017, every registered person needs to furnish an annual return for every financial year electronically in such form and manner as may be prescribed on or before the 31st day of December following the end of such financial year. However, following categories of persons are not required to file annual return:

(i) Casual taxable person

(ii) Input service distributors

(iii) Non-resident taxable persons

(iv) Persons paying TDS/TCS under section 51 or 52 of the Act.

(v) Every electronic commerce operator who is required to collect tax at source (TCS) in terms of section 52 and required to file annual return in form 9B.

(vi) Department of the Central Government or a State Government or a local authority, whose books of account are subject to audit by the Comptroller and Auditor-General of India or an auditor appointed for auditing the accounts of local authorities under any law for the time being in force.[2]

Further, section 44(2) provides that every person who is required to get his accounts audited in accordance with the provision of section 35 (5) is required to furnish the annual return along with the copy of audited annual accounts and a reconciliation statement reconciling the value of supplies declared in the return

1 There is view that 3B is not a return under 3 therefore, the credit should be available beyond September of the year upto December 2018 or later. Court decision may have to be awaited for relying on this this interpretation.

2 Notification no.03/2019-C.T dated 01st February 2019. Further the persons covered under this limb are not required to file annual return and also not required to conduct GST Audit and file the reconciliation statement as per section 44(2). Refer CGST Amendment Act, 2018 w.e.f 01st February 2019.

furnished for the financial year with the audited annual financial statement, and such other particulars as may be prescribed.

Rule 80 of the CGST Rules lays down the manner in which annual return is required to be filed by the registered persons. Sub rule 1 provides that every registered person who is required to file annual return under section 44 needs to file it electronically in Form GSTR-9 through the common portal. In case of person paying tax under composition scheme under section 10, the annual return has to be filed in Form GSTR-9A. E commerce operator who are required to collect the tax under section 52 needs to file annual return in the form GSTR-9B. However, since the TCS provisions were made applicable w.e.f. 01st October 2018 (i.e. F.Y 2018-19) vide notification no.51/2018-central tax dated 13th September 2018, there is no requirement of form GSTR-9B for the financial year 2017-18. E commerce operator would have to file form GSTR-9 for the F.Y 2017-18.The last date for filing of the annual return for all categories of taxable persons is the 31st December following the end of financial year, unless extended. For each registration, a separate annual return to be furnished by the registered taxable person. The Government has released the format of annual return vide notification no. 39/2018-Central tax dated 4th September 2018 which has been further amended vide notification no.74/2018-central tax dated 31st December 2018.

It may so happen that a registered person registered under regular scheme could have opted for composition scheme or vice versa during the financial year. In such a case, there could be requirement of filing both GSTR-9 and GSTR-9A. The annual return in form GSTR-9A does not require following information which is required in GSTR-9:

(i) Bifurcation of supplies made for B2B, B2C, SEZ, deemed exports

(ii) Advance receipt details

(iii) Details of imports as composition scheme does not allow these.

(iv) Bifurcation of supplies between nil rate, exempt, no GST supplies.

(v) Details of ITC availed, reversed details not required.

21.2 IMPACT OF ANNUAL RETURN ON AUDIT REPORT

Annual return is a return to be filed every year by each registered person irrespective of the turnover. However, GST audit report under section 35(5) is required to be conducted for the registered persons having aggregate turnover exceeding Rs.2 crores[3] in the financial year. Annual return submission is the responsibility of the registered person. Audit report is also the responsibility of the registered person which requires to be certified by a qualified chartered or cost accountant. Verification of the details furnished in the annual return with the

3 Refer Rule 80(3) of CGST Rules 2017.

information furnished in the monthly returns (in cases where annual return tables are not auto populated) and the accounts and records of the tax payer could be the basis for GST Audit/certification. Therefore, due care needs to be taken while furnishing the annual return wherein the details of inward and outward supplies as per returns filed are to be furnished.

It is important to note that the present annual return provide opportunity of any rectification of details in relation to liabilities already furnished and information as per books of account. However, ITC unclaimed, pertaining to the financial year, is not allowed to be claimed through the annual return. Ideally, for F.Y 2017-18, registered person would file/disclose his liability in form GSTR-9 as per the books of account and if the assessee utilises this opportunity properly, then there may not be any additional recommended liability arising from Auditor apart from advanced issues like interpretational differences, classification issues etc.. Therefore, proper filing of form GSTR-9 after rectifying the GSTR-1 and GSTR-3B would be important to ensure that audit certification in form GSTR-9C is done smoothly and appropriately. This would ensure that the GST auditor need not have to provide for qualifications and disclaimers, which attract special audits and also investigation by Director General of Central Revenue Intelligence to raid/visit the tax payer.

21.3 ROLE OF PROFESSIONALS IN ANNUAL RETURN

GST law being new, the tax payers would be very keen to engage the professionals to comply with the annual return. The professionals who are engaged for this need to have good knowledge of the disclosure requirement in the periodical returns as well as the annual return. Some of the benefits which could be brought to the tax payers are as under:

(1) **Appropriate disclosure in the return:** Most of the information in the annual return would be taken from the periodical returns filed on monthly/quarterly basis. However, there are certain extra information which needs to be filled in the annual return such as break up between credits on inputs, input services and capital goods. Similarly, details of demands or refund status etc. Professional could assist the tax payer in appropriate disclosure of such information. Moreover, the registered person can disclose the unidentified/ non-disclosed/non-discharged liabilities, if any, for the financial year and discharge them through this annual return. In later years the configuration of accounts itself can be changed to take care of this compliance.

(2) **Adjustment of details in the return** – The due date for availment of input tax credit for the previous financial year invoices or debit notes would be the due date of filing the return for the month of September of the year. Similarly, the due date for issue of credit note would be

end of September. Any adjustment for the details furnished in the returns for the previous financial year should be done by September of this year. The annual return would require details of such adjustment details.

(3) **Giving effect to adjustments needed as per statutory audit -** There could be instances wherein need for certain adjustments arises as an outcome of statutory audit. The professional could go through such adjustments required in the periodical returns to be filed before filing of annual return.

(4) **Avoid litigation due to non-disclosure of information:** There is a risk of non-disclosure of information which could be considered as suppression under section 74 to make tax demand with penalties for larger period. Professionals could guide the tax payers to avoid such situation.

(5) **Compliance before September month**: The basis for audit certification under section 35(5) is the annual return. Any discrepancies in the annual return would have direct impact requiring the auditor to report on discrepancies while certification. A thorough compliance review before filing the annual return could avoid such situation if tax payer complies with all requirements highlighted by the professionals.

21.4 BASIC STEPS BEFORE FILING ANNUAL RETURN

The basic steps which could be considered for proper filing of GSTR-9 are as follows:

Step 1: Prepare a reconciliation statement between workings of GSTR-1 and GSTR-3B filed during the financial year.

Step 2: Download the summary GSTR-3B and GSTR-1 available in the GST portal and compare the same with workings. With this, taxable person could ascertain if data reflecting in the portal and the workings are matching or not. Differences, if any could be reconciled. The auto-populated columns in GSTR-9 would be reflected based on the data available in the portal based periodical returns filed.

Step 3: Categorise the data based on GSTR-3B as follows:

i. **Category A**: Data disclosed in GSTR-3B for the period April to March of financial year; (for FY 2017-18, it is July 17 to March 2018)

ii. **Category B**: Data disclosed in GSTR-3B for the period April to September of subsequent financial year;

iii. **Category C**: Data not disclosed in GSTR-3B for the period April to September of subsequent financial year.

This would help in identifying the data which needs disclosures in different parts of annual return.

Step 4: Sub-classify the **Category A** data in to B2B, B2Cs, B2Cl, exports/supply to SEZ with payment of duty or without payment of duty, exempt supply. These classifications can be taken from GSTR-1, limited to the disclosure made in GSTR-3B. For example, liability discharged as per GSTR-3B is 1.5 crores and liability disclosed as per GSTR-1 is 2 crores, the sub-classification as mentioned as above has to be limited to 1.5 crores.

Step 5: Based on the sub-classification made as per the previous step, bifurcate the transactions into outward supplies on which tax is payable and outward supplies on which tax is not payable.

Step 6: Bifurcate ITC availed in GSTR-3B filed for the financial year into ITC of inputs, input services and capital goods with HSN details.

Step 7: Maintain workings of reversal of ITC in terms of Rule 37 and bifurcate the same in to two categories as below:

i. ITC availed, reversed and reclaimed in same financial year;

ii. ITC availed, reverse and re-claimed in different financial year.

Step 8: Maintain the workings of reversal of ITC made u/r 39, 42/43, through ITC-03 etc.

Step 9: Prepare the reconciliation between GSTR-2A with books of account to compare ITC claimed in books as against the data available in GSTR-2A. Vendors should be instructed to update all the supply details before this.

Step 10: Summarise and maintain the details of GST refund applied, sanctioned, rejected, pending and details of demand of taxes i.e. as per the order passed by adjudicating authority and details of taxes paid and pending status against such demand.

Step 11: Maintain the details of inward supplies from composition tax payers, goods sent for job work but not received within time limit u/s 143, goods sent for supply on approval basis but not yet received within time u/s 31(7) of CGST Act.

Step 12: Summarise the HSN summary for outward supplies HSN wise and rate wise. If the same HSN had different tax rates during the financial year, it has to be reported separately.

Step 13: Identify the major inward supplies which comprises of 10% or more of the total inward supplies with HSN details.

Step 14: Fill the GSTR-9 form or edit the auto populated form with the relevant information which has been obtained at various stages in previous steps for filing.

21.5 DETAILS REQUIRED IN THE ANNUAL RETURN

Most of the details such as outward supplies made to registered persons, unregistered persons, ITC amount as per GSTR-3B return, ITC as per GSTR-2A etc., are auto populated in the GSTR-9 available on the portal after login. The registered person should thoroughly go through the form to fill the information as there are chances of mistakes due to technical issues. As most of information to be filled in the annual return has to be taken from either GSTR-3B/GSTR-1, it is important for the tax payer to match both GSTR-3B and GSTR-1 before filing annual return.

With the amendment made in format of GSTR-9 in December 2018, Government has clarified the following:-

i. GSTR-9 should be filled on the basis of GSTR-3B and detailed data could be extracted from GSTR-1;

ii. Additional disclosure and discharge of liabilities pertaining to the financial year can be made through GSTR-9;

iii. Unclaimed credits of the financial year could not be claimed through GSTR-9.

The details to be furnished in the annual return are discussed in detail in below paragraphs:

21.5.1 Part I – Basic information

Table 1	Financial Year	• The details could get auto populated • Reporting of GST registration number and name of the registered person. • Persons with multiple registrations would be required to submit annual return for each registration separately.
Table 2	GSTIN	
Table 3A	Legal Name	
Table 3B	Trade Name (if any)	

21.5.2 Part II – Outward supplies

Table 4

Table 4 provides for reporting of all supplies (i.e. outward supplies and RCM transactions) which includes details of advances, inward and outward supplies made during the financial year on which tax is payable. This table could include the transactions classified under **Category A and Category C** as mentioned in para 21.4

	Description	Reference to fill information	Instruction provided in form
A	Supplies	• Sum of supplies to all	Aggregate value of supplies

	Description	Reference to fill information	Instruction provided in form
	made to un-registered persons (B2C)	unregistered persons, consumers or registered persons who have not provided GSTIN • Amounts to be furnished should be net of debit/credit notes and amendments • Refer GSTR-1 Table 5,7,9 & 10 which covers taxable outward supplies to unregistered persons with invoice value more than Rs.2.5 lakh, taxable supplies with less than Rs.2.5 lakh, supplies through E-commerce operators, amendments made to supply details furnished in earlier tax periods. • Details with tax break up to be provided • This could also cover supply of services to customers outside India which do not qualify as export of services • Any omission made in GSTR-3B for the financial year may be added here unless already considered in GSTR-3B filed for April to September of subsequent year.	made to consumers and unregistered persons on which tax has been paid shall be declared here. These would include details of supplies made through E-Commerce operators and are to be declared as net of credit notes or debit notes issued in this regard. Table 5, Table 7 along with respective amendments in Table 9 and Table 10 of FORM GSTR-1 may be used for filling up these details.
B	Supplies made to registered persons (B2B)	• Sum of all B2B supplies (tax invoices issued) other than zero rated and deemed exports to be provided • Refer GSTR-1 Table 4A & 4C • Details with tax break up to be provided	Aggregate value of supplies made to registered persons (including supplies made to UINs) on which tax has been paid shall be declared here. These would include supplies made through E-Commerce operators but shall not include supplies on which tax is to be

	Description	Reference to fill information	Instruction provided in form
		• Details of supplies wherein recipient is liable not to be included • Any omission made in GSTR-3B for the financial year may be added here unless already considered in GSTR-3B filed for April to September of subsequent year	paid by the recipient on reverse charge basis. Details of debit and credit notes are to be mentioned separately. Table 4A and Table 4C of Form GSTR-1 may be used for filling up these details.
C	Zero rated supply (Export) on payment of tax (except supplies to SEZs)	• Sum of all Exports (Goods & Services) made against payment of tax excluding SEZ supplies to be provided • Exports made without payment of tax under LUT or bond should not be reported here • Refer GSTR-1 Table 6A • Details with tax break up to be provided • Any omission made in GSTR-3B for the financial year may be added here unless already considered in GSTR-3B filed for April to September of subsequent year.	Aggregate value of exports (except supplies to SEZs) on which tax has been paid shall be declared here. Table 6A of FORM GSTR-1 may be used for filling up these details.
D	Supply to SEZs on payment of tax	• Sum of all SEZ supplies made against payment of tax to be provided • Refer GSTR-1 Table 6B • Details with tax break up to be provided • Any omission made in GSTR-3B for the financial year may be added here unless already considered in GSTR-3B filed for April to September of subsequent year.	Aggregate value of supplies to SEZs on which tax has been paid shall be declared here. Table 6B of GSTR-1 may be used for filling up these details.

	Description	Reference to fill information	Instruction provided in form
E	Deemed Exports	• Sum of all deemed exports to be provided • Refer Table 6C of GSTR-1 • Details with tax break up to be provided • This includes supplies to EOUs, supplies against advance authorisation scheme, EPCG license and supply of gold by bank/PSU specified in notification no.50/2017-customs. • Any omission made in GSTR-3B for the financial year may be added here unless already considered in GSTR-3B filed for April to September of subsequent year.	Aggregate value of supplies in the nature of deemed exports on which tax has been paid shall be declared here. Table 6C of FORM GSTR-1 may be used for filling up these details.
F	Advances on which tax has been paid but invoice has not been issued (not covered under (A) to (E) above)	• Sum of all advances which remain unadjusted (i.e. tax invoice not raised) as on the last day of the previous financial year on which tax has been paid to be provided • Refer GSTR-1 Table 11A + 11B + Separate Workings to arrive at these details • Ex: Total advance received for FY 2017-18 is Rs.50 lakh. Invoices issued for Rs.40 lakh in the year. In this column, the balance amount of Rs.10 lakh which was subject to GST to be disclosed • At present advance for supply of services are subject to GST. Till 10.11.2017, advance for supply of goods were also	Details of all unadjusted advances i.e. advance has been received and tax has been paid but invoice has not been issued in the current year shall be declared here. Table 11A of FORM GSTR-1 may be used for filling up these details.

	Description	Reference to fill information	Instruction provided in form
		subject to GST. • Any omission made in GSTR-3B for the financial year may be added here unless already considered in GSTR-3B filed for April to September of subsequent year.	
G	Inward supplies on which tax is to be paid on reverse charge basis	• Sum of all supplies on which tax has been paid under reverse charge mechanism to be provided • Refer GSTR-3B Table 3.1(d) • This includes procurements under section 9(3) and 9(4) of the CGST Act 2017 including section 5(3) and 5(4) of IGST Act 2017 covering procurements from unregistered persons. • Only the net taxable amount to be disclosed in this. For ex: Total invoice value is Rs.10,000/- whereas taxable value is Rs.8,000/-. Then, only Rs.8,000/- to be disclosed here. • Procurement of goods and supplies from unregistered persons were subject to GST only till 13.10.2017 • Undisclosed liability can be disclosed in this column to discharge the tax provided the same has not been disclosed and discharged in GSTR-3B during the period April to September of subsequent financial year.	Aggregate value of all inward supplies (including advances and net of credit and debit notes) on which tax is to be paid by the recipient (i.e.by the person filing the annual return) on reverse charge basis. This shall include supplies received from registered persons, unregistered persons on which tax is levied on reverse charge basis. This shall also include aggregate value of all import of services. Table 3.1(d) of FORM GSTR-3B may be used for filling up these details.

	Description	Reference to fill information	Instruction provided in form
H	Sub-total (A to G above)	*Auto-Populated*	
I	Credit Notes issued in respect of transactions specified in (B) to (E) above (-)	• Sum of all credit notes issued against B2B supplies with payment of tax, including zero rated supplies & deemed exports to be reported which are issued in the financial year to be provided. • Any undisclosed credit notes issued for the financial year in GSTR-3B but disclosed in GSTR-1 of April to September of subsequent financial year can be considered here. Ex: Credit note dated 20.03.2018 not disclosed or given effect in GSTR-3B till September 2018 but shown GSTR-1. Such credit note details can be provided here. • Refer GSTR-1 Table 9B • Credit notes issued and disclosed in GSTR-3B by end of March month or un disclosed credit note could only be considered here. • Credit notes should have been issued in accordance with Section 34 of CGST Act 2017 which could be due to excess taxable value or tax amount or return of goods by customer or supplied goods/ services found to be deficient. Date of document important. Worksheet needed.	Aggregate value of credit notes issued in respect of B to B supplies (4B), exports (4C), supplies to SEZs (4D) and deemed exports (4E) shall be declared here. Table 9B of FORM GSTR-1 may be used for filling up these details.
J	Debit Notes issued in	• Sum of all debit notes issued against B2B	Aggregate value of debit notes issued in respect of B to B

	Description	Reference to fill information	Instruction provided in form
	respect of transactions specified in (B) to (E) above (+)	supplies with payment of tax, including zero rated supplies & deemed exports • Refer GSTR-1 Table 9B to be provided • Debit notes issued and disclosed in GSTR-1 should only be considered here • Debit notes issued till the end of March and disclosed after September of subsequent year could be disclosed here. If they are disclosed between April to September of subsequent year, then the same to be shown in part V of this form. • Debit notes should have been issued in accordance with Section 34 of CGST Act 2017 which could be issued when taxable value or tax amount charged found to be less than actuals.	supplies (4B), exports (4C), supplies to SEZs (4D) and deemed exports (4E) shall be declared here. Table 9B of FORM GSTR-1 may be used for filling up these details.
K	Supplies/tax declared through Amendments (+)	• Sum of amendments made to all supplies with payment of tax including B to B supplies, deemed exports on payment of tax, SEZ supplies on payment of tax, direct exports on payment of tax, credit and debit notes (except B2C supplies), which has resulted in addition in value of supplies/tax being reported • Refer GSTR-1 Table 9A & 9C • Amendments made within	Details of amendments made to B to B supplies (4B), exports (4C), supplies to SEZs (4D) and deemed exports (4E), credit notes (4I), debit notes (4J) and refund vouchers shall be declared here. Table 9A and Table 9C of FORM GSTR-1 may be used for filling up these details.

	Description	Reference to fill information	Instruction provided in form
		financial year (before end of March) should only be considered here.	
L	Supplies/tax reduced through Amendments (-)	• Sum of amendments made to all supplies with payment of tax including B to B supplies, deemed exports on payment of tax, SEZ supplies on payment of tax, direct exports on payment of tax, credit and debit notes (except B2C supplies), which has resulted in reduction in value of supplies/tax being reported • Refer GSTR-1 Table 9A & 9C • Amendments made within financial year (before end of March) should only be considered here.	Details of amendments made to B to B supplies (4B), exports (4C), supplies to SEZs (4D) and deemed exports (4E), credit notes (4I), debit notes (4J) and refund vouchers shall be declared here. Table 9A and Table 9C of FORM GSTR-1 may be used for filling up these details.
M	Sub-total (I to L above)	*Auto-Populated*	
N	Supplies and advances on which tax is to be paid (H + M) above	*Auto-Populated*	

Table 5

Table 5 provides for reporting of all other supplies (i.e. supplies without payment of tax and exempt) made by the registered person during the financial year

This table would include the transactions classified under **Category A and Category C** as mentioned in para 21.4

	Description	Reference to fill information	Instruction provided in form
A	Zero rated	• Sum of all direct exports	Aggregate value of exports

	Description	Reference to fill information	Instruction provided in form
	supply (Export) without payment of tax	(Goods & Services) made without payment of tax other than SEZ supplies to be declared ● Presumably Under Letter of Undertaking/ Bond Refer GSTR-1 Table 6A	(except supplies to SEZs) on which tax has not been paid shall be declared here. Table 6A of FORM GSTR-1 may be used for filling up these details.
B	Supply to SEZs without payment of tax	● Sum of all SEZ supplies made without payment of tax ● Refer GSTR-1 Table 6B	Aggregate value of supplies to SEZs on which tax has not been paid shall be declared here. Table 6B of GSTR-1 may be used for filling up these details.
C	Supplies on which tax is to be paid by the recipient on reverse charge basis	● Sum of supplies made by the registered persons, where the liability to pay tax is on the recipient under reverse charge ● Refer GSTR-1 Table 4B ● This could include sponsorship services, legal services provided, director services, GTA etc.	Aggregate value of supplies made to registered persons on which tax is payable by the recipient on reverse charge basis. Details of debit and credit notes are to be mentioned separately. Table 4B of Form GSTR-1 may be used for filling up these details.
D	Exempted	● Sum of all exempt supplies (i.e. taxable supplies which have been exempted under a specific Notification) ● Refer GSTR-1 Table 8 ● 'No supply' could be those activities which are covered in Schedule III to CGST Act 2017 such as supply of land or supply of building after completion certificate, high seas sale, reimbursement as pure	Aggregate value of exempted, Nil Rated and Non-GST supplies shall be declared here. Table 8 of Form GSTR-1 may be used for filling up these details. The value of "no supply" shall also be declared here.

	Description	Reference to fill information	Instruction provided in form
		agent.	
E	Nil Rated	• Sum of all supplies wherein the rate of GST is Nil/Zero • Refer GSTR-1 Table 8 • CGST Noti.no.12/2017 (Rate) covers list of services which are subject to 'Nil' rate.	Aggregate value of exempted, Nil Rated and Non-GST supplies shall be declared here. Table 8 of FORM GSTR-1 may be used for filling up these details. The value of "no supply" shall also be declared here.
F	Non-GST Supply	• Sum of all supplies which are outside the levy of GST such as supply of petrol, diesel, petroleum crude, natural gas, ATF and alcohol. • Refer GSTR-1 Table 8- - Worksheet for D, E and F items would be necessary which could help the auditor.	Aggregate value of exempted, Nil Rated and Non-GST supplies shall be declared here. Table 8 of FORM GSTR-1 may be used for filling up these details. The value of "no supply" shall also be declared here.
G	Sub-total (A to F above)	*Auto-Populated*	
H	Credit Notes issued in respect of transactions specified in A to F above (-)	• Sum of all credit notes reported with respect to above transactions • Refer GSTR-1 Table 9B • This covers even credit notes issued in respect of non-taxable/exempt supplies.	Aggregate value of credit notes issued in respect of supplies declared in 5A,5B,5C, 5D, 5E and 5F shall be declared here. Table 9B of FORM GSTR-1 may be used for filling up these details.
I	Debit Notes issued in respect of transactions specified in A to F above (+)	• Sum of all debit notes reported with respect to above transactions • Refer GSTR-1 Table 9B	Aggregate value of debit notes issued in respect of supplies declared in 5A,5B,5C, 5D, 5E and 5F shall be declared here. Table 9B of FORM GSTR-1 may be used for filling up these details.
J	Supplies declared through	• Sum of amendments made to all supplies	Details of amendments made to exports (except supplies to

	Description	Reference to fill information	Instruction provided in form
	Amendments (+)	without payment of tax, which has resulted in addition in value of supplies being reported • Refer GSTR-1 Table 9A & 9C	SEZs) and supplies to SEZs on which tax has not been paid shall be declared here. Table 9A and Table 9C of FORM GSTR-1 may be used for filling up these details.
K	Supplies reduced through Amendments (-)	• Sum of amendments made to all supplies without payment of tax, which has resulted in reduction in value of supplies being reported • Refer GSTR-1 Table 9A & 9C	Details of amendments made to exports (except supplies to SEZs) and supplies to SEZs on which tax has not been paid shall be declared here. Table 9A and Table 9C of FORM GSTR-1 may be used for filling up these details.
L	Sub-Total (H to K above)	*Auto-Populated*	
M	Turnover on which tax is not to be paid (G + L above)	*Auto-Populated*	
N	Total Turnover (including advances) (4N + 5M - 4G above	*Auto-Populated*	Total turnover including the sum of all the supplies (with additional supplies and amendments) on which tax is payable and tax is not payable shall be declared here. This shall also include amount of advances on which tax is paid but invoices have not been issued in the current year. However, this shall not include the aggregate value of inward supplies on which tax is paid by the recipient(i.e. by the person filing the annual return) on reverse charge basis.

21.5.3 Part III – Input tax credit

Table 6

Table 6 provides for reporting of gross input tax credit (ITC) availed by the registered person during the financial year

This table has to filled based on the ITC availed in GSTR-3B filed for the financial year.

	Description	Reference to fill information	Instruction provided in form
A	Total amount of input tax credit availed through Form GSTR-3B (sum total of Table 4A of Form GSTR-3B)	*Auto-Populated from Form GSTR-3B*	Total input tax credit availed in Table 4A of Form GSTR-3B for the taxpayer would be auto-populated here.
B	Inward supplies (other than imports and inward supplies liable to reverse charge but includes services received from SEZs)	• Sum of ITC availed on all intra-state and inter-state (within India) procurements, where the tax has been charged by the supplier. • Bifurcation of credits availed on inputs, input service and capital goods shall be provided. • It is interesting to note that such bifurcation is not being provided in present GSTR-3B return format. This adds extra burden to return filers.	Aggregate value of input tax credit availed on all inward supplies except those on which tax is payable on reverse charge basis but includes supply of services received from SEZs shall be declared here. It may be noted that the total ITC availed is to be classified as ITC on inputs, capital goods and input services. Table 4(A)(5) of Form GSTR-3B may be used for filling up these details. This shall not include ITC which was availed, reversed and then reclaimed in the ITC ledger. This is to be declared separately under 6(H) below.
C	Inward supplies received from unregistered persons liable to reverse charge (other than B above) on which	• Sum of ITC availed on tax paid under reverse charge for supplies received from unregistered persons which was liable till 13.10.2017 to be	Aggregate value of input tax credit availed on all inward supplies received from unregistered persons (other than import of services) on which tax is payable on reverse charge basis shall be declared

	Description	Reference to fill information	Instruction provided in form
	tax is paid & ITC availed	reported. • Refer GSTR-3B Table 4A(3) • Bifurcation to be made between inputs, input services and capital goods which could be challenging as such information is presently not being captured in GSTR-3B return. • Self invoice issued in respect of supplies received from unregistered persons could be referred to make this bifurcation. This could cover liability discharged under Section 9(3) and Section 9(4).	here. It may be noted that the total ITC availed is to be classified as ITC on inputs, capital goods and input services. Table 4(A)(3) of Form GSTR-3B may be used for filling up these details.
D	Inward supplies received from registered persons liable to reverse charge (other than B above) on which tax is paid and ITC availed	• Sum of ITC availed on tax paid under reverse charge for supplies received from registered persons • Refer GSTR-3B Table 4A(3) • Bifurcation to be made between inputs, input services and capital goods which could be challenging as such information is presently not being captured in GSTR-3B return.	Aggregate value of input tax credit availed on all inward supplies received from registered persons on which tax is payable on reverse charge basis shall be declared here. It may be noted that the total ITC availed is to be classified as ITC on inputs, capital goods and input services. Table 4(A)(3) of Form GSTR-3B may be used for filling up these details.
E	Import of goods (including supplies from SEZs)	• Sum of IGST credit availed on import of goods and procurements from SEZ on which IGST paid • Bifurcation to be made	Details of input tax credit availed on import of goods including supply of goods received from SEZs shall be declared here. It may be noted that the total ITC availed is to

	Description	Reference to fill information	Instruction provided in form
		between inputs and capital goods Refer GSTR-3B Table 4A(1) + ITC on SEZ	be classified as ITC on inputs and capital goods. Table 4(A)(1) of Form GSTR-3B may be used for filling up these details.
F	Import of services (excluding inward supplies from SEZs)	• Sum of IGST paid credit availed on import of services • Refer GSTR-3B Table 4A(2)	Details of input tax credit availed on import of services (excluding inward supplies from SEZs) shall be declared here. Table 4(A)(2) of Form GSTR-3B may be used for filling up these details.
G	Input Tax credit received from ISD	• Sum of credit availed based on ISD Invoice (credit distribution) • Refer GSTR-3B Table 4A(4)	Aggregate value of input tax credit received from input service distributor shall be declared here. Table 4(A)(4) of Form GSTR-3B may be used for filling up these details
H	Amount of ITC reclaimed (other than B above) under the provisions of the Act	• Sum of ITC reclaimed (which was availed and subsequently reversed) • Section B of this table requires reporting of ITC availed originally • Credits which are reversed and subsequently reclaimed within the same financial year, shall be reported under this section Ex: ITC availed on invoice dated 02nd July 2017, since payment has not been made the ITC been reversed with interest in the GST return for the period January 2018 and	Aggregate value of input tax credit availed, reversed and reclaimed under the provisions of the Act shall be declared here.

	Description	Reference to fill information	Instruction provided in form
		payment made to vendor on 12th March 2018 and reclaimed the credit in March 2018 GSTR-3B.	
I	Sub-Total (B to H above)	*Auto-Populated*	
J	Difference (I - A above)	*Auto-Populated* Ideally there should not be difference considering the fact that the total of 'I' above is break up of credits as per column 'A' which is auto populated from GSTR form 3B	The difference between the total amount of input tax credit availed through Form GSTR-3B and input tax credit declared in row B to H shall be declared here. Ideally, this amount should be zero.
K	Transition Credit through TRAN-I (including revisions if any)	• Transitional credits received in Electronic Credit Ledger from Form GST TRAN-I • Refer Electronic Credit Ledger	Details of transition credit received in the electronic credit ledger on filing of Form GST TRAN-I including revision of TRAN-I (whether upwards or downwards), if any shall be declared here.
L	Transition Credit through TRAN-II	• Transitional credits received in Electronic Credit Ledger from Form GST TRAN-II • Refer Electronic Credit Ledger • The transitional credit claimed till March 18 should only be considered in this.	Details of transition credit received in the electronic credit ledger after filing of Form GST TRAN-II shall be declared here.
M	Any other ITC availed but not specified above	Details of ITC availed through Form ITC-01 (conversion from composition to regular) and Form ITC-02 (Transfer of credit due to sale, merger, amalgamation, transfer of asset etc.)	Details of ITC availed but not covered in any of heads specified under 6B to 6L above shall be declared here. Details of ITC availed through Form ITC-01 and Form ITC-02 in the financial year shall be declared here.

	Description	Reference to fill information	Instruction provided in form
N	Sub-total (K to M above)	*Auto-Populated*	
O	Total ITC availed (I + N above)	*Auto-Populated*	

Table 7

Table 7 provides for reporting of ITC reversed by the registered person and Ineligible credits for financial year

	Description	Reference to fill information	Instruction provided in form
A	As per Rule 37	• Sum of ITC reversed on account of non-payment to vendor within 180 days in terms of Section 16(2) read with Rule 37 of CGST Rules to be reported. • This restriction would not be applicable for transactions of Schedule I and no reporting needed. • Refer GSTR-3B Table 4(B)(2) + Workings	Details of input tax credit reversed due to ineligibility or reversals required under rule 37, 39,42 and 43 of the CGST Rules, 2017 shall be declared here. This column should also contain details of any input tax credit reversed under section 17(5) of the CGST Act, 2017 and details of ineligible transition credit claimed under Form GST TRAN-I or Form GST TRAN-II and then subsequently reversed. Table 4(B) of Form GSTR-3B may be used for filling up these details. Any ITC reversed through Form ITC -03 shall be declared in 7H.
B	As per Rule 39	• Sum of ITC reversed on account of ISD Credit Notes. • Refer GSTR-3B Table 4(B)(2) + Workings	
C	As per Rule 42	• Sum of ITC reversed on common input and input services (used for	

	Description	Reference to fill information	Instruction provided in form
		exempt supplies) • Does not include the final annual reversal made in the subsequent financial year. This needs to be shown in separate table in subsequent part. • Refer GSTR-3B Table 4(B)(1) + Workings	
D	As per Rule 43	• Sum of ITC reversed on capital goods (used partially for exempt supplies) • Refer GSTR-3B Table 4(B)(1) + Workings	
E	As per section 17(5)	• Sum of ineligible credits under section 17(5) which have been reversed • The said amount shall be disclosed only when credit has been availed and reversed in Form GSTR-3B. • Mere reporting of values in GSTR-3B Table 4(D)(1) shall not be reported in this section, as it would be adjusted against total ITC availed as reported in Table 6 • Credits which are availed and subsequently identified as restricted under Section 17(5) should also be added here.	
F	Reversal of TRAN-I credit	• Reversal of TRAN-I credits	-

	Description	Reference to fill information	Instruction provided in form
		• Refer Electronic Credit Ledger • This could include E.Cess, SHE Cess, KKC credit which could have been reversed by the registered persons by the end of March. • Any reversals made from April month of subsequent year; the details could be disclosed in GSTR-9 of such subsequent financial year.	
G	Reversal of TRAN-II credit	• Reversal of TRAN-II credits • Refer Electronic Credit Ledger	-
H	Other reversals (pl. specify)	Any other reversals –ITC reversed on account of ITC-03 (regular scheme to composition scheme). This includes credit reversed as per Rule 44 in case of special circumstances such as conversion to exempted supply.	-
I	Total ITC Reversed (A to H above	*Auto-Populated*	-
J	Net ITC Available for Utilization (6O-7I)	*Auto-Populated*	-

Table 8

Table 8 provides for a summary of ITC available as per GSTR-2A & IGST paid on import of goods and a comparison with ITC availed

	Description	Reference to fill information	Instruction provided in form
A	ITC as per GSTR-2A (Table 3 & 5 thereof)	*Auto-Populated from GSTR-2A.* Registered person should follow up with the vendors to file GSTR-1 pending if any before end of September of subsequent financial year. Any amendment for entries of GSTR-1 of particular financial year can be made by end of September of subsequent financial year. *The due date for filing GSTR-1 for FY 2017-18 was extended till the due date of filing GSTR-1 for the month of April 2019.	The total credit available for inwards supplies (other than imports and inwards supplies liable to reverse charge but includes services received from SEZs) received during 2017-18 and reflected in FORM GSTR-2A (table 3 & 5 only) shall be auto-populated in this table. This would be the aggregate of all the input tax credit that has been declared by the corresponding suppliers in their FORM GSTR-I.
B	ITC as per sum total of 6(B) and 6(H) above	*Auto-Populated from Table 6* ITC as per GSTR-3B would be auto populated here.	The input tax credit as declared in Table 6B and 6H shall be auto-populated here.
C	ITC on inward supplies (other than imports and inward supplies liable to reverse charge but includes services received from SEZs) received during 2017-18 but availed during April to September,	• Sum of ITC availed during the period April 2018 to September 2018, w.r.t. invoices issued by the vendor for supplies received up to 31st March 2018. • This section is provided to capture credits availed by the registered period in the subsequent financial year, which pertain to FY 2017-18 • Refer ITC ledger/ GSTR-3B workings for	Aggregate value of input tax credit availed on all inward supplies (except those on which tax is payable on reverse charge basis but includes supply of services received from SEZs) received during July 2017 to March 2018 but credit on which was availed between April to September 2018 shall be declared here. Table 4(A)(5) of FORM GSTR-3B may be used for filling up these details.

	Description	Reference to fill information	Instruction provided in form
	2018	the period April to September 2018.	
D	Difference [A-(B+C)]	*Auto-Populated* • If values arrived is negative, it would mean that the total availment of credit is more than the credit reported by the vendor.	Aggregate value of the input tax credit which was available in FORM GSTR2A (table 3 & 5 only) but not availed in FORM GSTR-3B returns shall be computed based on values of 8A, 8B and 8C. However, there may be circumstances where the credit availed in FORM GSTR-3B was greater than the credit available in FORM GSTR-2A. In such cases, the value in row 8D shall be negative
E	ITC available but not availed (out of D)	• ITC reflected in Form GSTR-2A for FY 2017-18 which is eligible but not availed. • ITC not reflected in Form GSTR-2A but not availed, would not be reported in this section	The credit which was available and not availed in FORM GSTR-3B and the credit was not availed in FORM GSTR-3B as the same was ineligible shall be declared here. Ideally, if 8D is positive, the sum of 8E and 8F shall be equal to 8D.
F	ITC available but ineligible (out of D)	• Transactions reflected in Form GSTR-2A for FY 2017-18 which is available but not eligible • Transactions not reflected in Form GSTR-2A, would not be reported in this section	
G	IGST paid on import of goods (including supplies from SEZ)	• Actual IGST paid on import of goods and procurements from SEZ shall be reported • Refer Bill of entries filed and duty payment challans	Aggregate value of IGST paid at the time of imports (including imports from SEZs) during the financial year shall be declared here.
H	IGST credit	*Auto-Populated*	The input tax credit as

	Description	Reference to fill information	Instruction provided in form
	availed on import of goods (as per 6(E) above)	• Represents actual ITC availed on import of goods and procurements from SEZ from G above	declared in Table 6E shall be auto-populated here.
I	Difference (G-H)	*Auto-Populated*	
J	ITC available but not availed on import of goods (Equal to I)	*Auto-Populated* • The form does not provide the option of reporting ITC availed on import of goods in 2018-19, on which IGST was paid in 2017-18. • Due to this, any eligible amount of ITC could get disclosed as lapse credit in column K below. Therefore, until and unless it is corrected, the amount of credit available as ITC on import of goods for declaration in this column be restricted to amount of credit availed as per column H above.	
K	Total ITC to be lapsed in current financial year (E + F + J)	*Auto-Populated*	The total input tax credit which shall lapse for the current financial year shall be computed in this row.

21.5.4 Part IV – Details of tax paid

Table 9

Table 9 provides for reporting of tax paid by the registered person during the financial year

	Integrated Tax	Details to be reported under the following heads • Tax payable - While reporting the details, one
	Central Tax	

	State Tax/UT Tax	shall also ensure that the details reported in Table 4 is in line with the total tax payable • Paid through cash – Ensure that the amount of tax paid in cash reported in the Table 9 is matched with the actual cash payments • Paid through ITC - Ensure that the amount of tax paid in cash reported in the Table 9 is matched with the actual credit utilisation as per the returns **Also refer Table 6.1 of Form GSTR-3B filed** **Instruction** - Part IV is the actual tax paid during the financial year. Payment of tax under Table 6.1 of Form GSTR-3B may be used for filling up these details
	Cess	
	Interest	
	Late Fee	
	Penalty	
	Other	

21.5.5 Part V – Transactions of previous FY disclosed in present FY April to September

Table 10 – 13

Table 10-13 provides for reporting of transactions pertaining to previous financial year which are reported by the registered person during the period April to September of present financial year or up to date of filing annual return whichever is earlier

	Description	Reference to fill information	Instruction provided in form
10	Supplies/tax declared through Amendments (+) (net of debit notes)	• Outward supplies of previous FY reported in current FY – Additional invoice reported in GSTR-1 of current FY pertaining to previous FY. • Details of debit notes reported in current FY between April to September against supplies reported in previous FY to be provided here. • Amendments made in the value of supplies/tax paid against invoices	Details of additions or amendments to any of the supplies already declared in the returns of the previous financial year but such amendments were furnished in Table 9A, Table 9B and Table 9C of Form GSTR-1 of April to September of the current financial year or date of filing of Annual Return for the previous financial year, whichever is earlier shall be declared here.

	Description	Reference to fill information	Instruction provided in form
		reported in previous FY – Refer GSTR-3B Table 9 and Table 10.	
11	Supplies/tax reduced through Amendments (-) (net of credit notes)	• Details of credit notes reported in current FY between April to September against supplies reported in previous FY to be provided here. • Amendments made in the value of supplies/tax paid against invoices reported in previous FY – Refer GSTR-3B Table 9 and Table 10.	Details of additions or amendments to any of the supplies already declared in the returns of the previous financial year but such amendments were furnished in Table 9A, Table 9B and Table 9C of Form GSTR-1 of April to September of the current financial year or date of filing of Annual Return for the previous financial year, whichever is earlier shall be declared here.
12	Reversal of ITC availed during previous financial year	• ITC availed in the PFY which has been reversed in the current FY (example: Ineligible credit availed in previous FY, reversed in current FY) • This could also cover the amount of credits reversed under Rule 42 for the previous FY after ascertaining the actual taxable and exempted turnover.	Aggregate value of reversal of ITC which was availed in the previous financial year but reversed in returns filed for the months of April to September of the current financial year or date of filing of Annual Return for previous financial year, whichever is earlier shall be declared here. Table 4(B) of Form GSTR-3B may be used for filling up these details.
13	ITC availed for the previous financial year	• ITC availed in the current FY pertaining to supplies received in the previous FY	Details of ITC for goods or services received in the previous financial year but ITC

	Description	Reference to fill information	Instruction provided in form
		• Reference should also be made to Table 8 of the Annual Return – Reporting of ITC availed in current FY till September month for supplies received in previous FY	for the same was availed in returns filed for the months of April to September of the current financial year or date of filing of Annual Return for the previous financial year whichever is earlier shall be declared here. Table 4(A) of FORM GSTR-3B may be used for filling up these details. However, any ITC which was reversed in the FY 2017-18 as per second proviso to sub-section (2) of section 16 but was reclaimed in FY 2018-19, the details of such ITC reclaimed shall be furnished in the annual return for FY 2018-19.

Table 14

Table 14 provides for disclosing details of differential tax paid on account of declaration in table 10 & 11 above

	Description	Reference to fill information	Instruction provided in form
14	Details of IGST, CGST, SGST/UTGST, Cess or Interest payable and paid	Details of differential taxes paid on account of disclosure of transactions in present FY which are pertaining to previous FY for which annual return is being filed to be provided in this table.	-

21.5.6 Part VI – Other information

Table 15 – 18

Table 15 provides for reporting of Demands and Refunds claims by the registered person during the PFY

	Description	Reference to fill information	Instruction provided in form
15	A. Total Refund claimed B. Total Refund Sanctioned C. Total Refund Rejected D. Total Refund pending E. Total Demand of Taxes F. Total taxes paid in respect of E above G. Total demand pending out of E above	• Details as at end of the previous FY could be provided in this table. • Sum of all refunds claimed, sanctioned, rejected and pending for processing. • Refund claims filed in the financial year and would include refunds which have been sanctioned, rejected or are pending for processing. • Refund pending would be the aggregate amount in all refund application for which acknowledgement has been received and would exclude provisional refunds received. • Sum of all demands of taxes for which an order confirming	• Aggregate value of refunds claimed, sanctioned, rejected and pending for processing shall be declared here. Refund claimed would be the aggregate value of all the refund claims filed in the financial year and would include refunds which have been sanctioned, rejected or are pending for processing. Refund sanctioned means the aggregate value of all refund sanction orders. Refund pending would be the aggregate amount in all refund application for which acknowledgement has been received and would exclude provisional refunds received. These would not include details of non-GST refund claims. • Aggregate value of demands of taxes for which an order confirming the demand has been issued by the adjudicating authority shall be declared here. Aggregate value of taxes paid out of the total

	Description	Reference to fill information	Instruction provided in form
		the demand has been issued by the adjudicating authority, along with details of taxes paid and unpaid demands.	value of confirmed demand as declared in 15E above shall be declared here. Aggregate value of demands pending recovery out of 15E above shall be declared here.

Table 16 provides for Information on supplies received from composition taxpayers, deemed supply under section 143 and goods sent on approval basis

	Description	Reference to fill information	Instruction provided in form
16	A. Supplies received from Composition taxpayers B. Deemed supply under section 143 C. Goods sent on approval basis but not returned	• Sum of all supplies received from composition taxpayers. Refer Form GSTR-3B Table 5. Many would not have filled this information in GSTR-3B form. • Sum of all deemed supplies from the principal to the job-worker in terms of sub-section (3) and sub-section (4) of section 143 of the CGST Act. For FY 2017-18 this would not be applicable as the time limit specified for inputs is 1 year which completes only on 1st July 2018. • Sum of deemed supplies for goods which were sent on	• Aggregate value of supplies received from composition taxpayers shall be declared here. Table 5 of Form GSTR-3B may be used for filling up these details. • Aggregate value of all deemed supplies from the principal to the job-worker in terms of sub-section (3) and sub-section (4) of section 143 of the CGST Act shall be declared here. • Aggregate value of all deemed supplies for goods which were sent on approval basis but were not returned to the principal supplier within one eighty days of such supply shall be declared here.

	Description	Reference to fill information	Instruction provided in form
		approval basis but were not returned to the principal supplier within one eighty days of such supply. ● Information on procurement of goods or services from unregistered persons, composite scheme suppliers are expected to be provided in the income tax form no.3CD as well with effect from March 2018. Therefore, tax payers could start maintaining the details completely.	

Table 17 and 18 provides reporting of HSN wise summary of Outward and Inward Supplies reported in the previous FY

	Description	Reference to fill information	Instruction provided in form
17	Outward Supplies	● HSN wise summary of outward supplies reported during the PFY including details of quantity, taxable value and taxes to be provided in this column ● Refer Form GSTR-1 Table 12 ● The data has to be entered HSN wise and rate wise.	Summary of supplies effected and received against a particular HSN code to be reported only in this table. It will be optional for taxpayers having annual turnover up to ₹ 1.50 Cr. It will be mandatory to report HSN code at two digits level for taxpayers having annual turnover in the preceding year above ₹ 1.50 Cr but up to ₹ 5.00 Cr and at four digits' level for

	Description	Reference to fill information	Instruction provided in form
			taxpayers having annual turnover above ₹ 5.00 Cr. UQC details to be furnished only for supply of goods. Quantity is to be reported net of returns. Table 12 of FORM GSTR1 may be used for filling up details in Table 17. It may be noted that this summary details are required to be declared only for those inward supplies which in value independently account for 10 % or more of the total value of inward supplies.
18	Inward Supplies	• HSN wise summary of inward supplies reported during the PFY including details of quantity, taxable value and taxes to be provided in this column • Present Form 3B does not require reporting of HSN wise supplies. This could be a challenge. Some relaxation could be expected from this disclosure. • The system of maintaining the purchase/expense register with complete details including HSN would help in filling this information. • This would include	Summary of supplies effected and received against a particular HSN code to be reported only in this table. It will be optional for taxpayers having annual turnover upto ₹ 1.50 Cr. It will be mandatory to report HSN code at two digits level for taxpayers having annual turnover in the preceding year above ₹ 1.50 Cr but upto ₹ 5.00 Cr and at four digits' level for taxpayers having annual turnover above ₹ 5.00 Cr. UQC details to be furnished only for supply of goods. Quantity is to be reported net of returns. Table 12 of FORM GSTR1 may be used for filling up details in Table 17. It may be noted that this summary details are required to be declared only for those inward

	Description	Reference to fill information	Instruction provided in form
		disclosure of only those supplies which account for 10% or more of total value of inward supplies.	supplies which in value independently account for 10 % or more of the total value of inward supplies.

Table 19 provides reporting of Late Fees

	Description	Reference to fill information	Instruction provided in form
19	Late fees payable and paid	Late fee payable details to be provided here. This would be applicable only if annual return delayed beyond the due date.	Late fee would be payable if annual return is filed after the due date.

The last part is verification wherein the authorized person for the tax payer needs to affirm and declare that the information given is true and correct to best of his knowledge and nothing has been concealed. Interestingly, he should also confirm that in case of any reduction in output tax liability, the benefit has been passed on the recipient of supply. It is not clear if such declaration is required only when there is a reduction due to reduction in rate of tax.

Few tax payers would have ignored the aspect of anti-profiteering. It is also possible that tax payers file the annual return accepting the above declaration. It may be advisable where such liability is possible to take a certificate from a Chartered Accountant on the absence of anti-profiteering. If such declaration is found to be false, then there could only be general penalty under Section 125 of CGST Act 2017 as there are separate specific provisions for non-compliance with anti-profiteering provisions in addition to the general penalties applicable.

DISCHARGE OF ADDITIONAL LIABILITY

Towards the end of the return, taxpayers are being given an option to pay any additional liability declared in this form, through Form DRC-03. Taxpayers need to select 'Annual Return' in the drop down provided in Form DRC-03. It may be noted that such liability can be paid through electronic cash ledger only as per the instruction provided to GSTR-9.

It is relevant to note that section 41(2) of CGST Act, 2017 allows utilisation of credit for payment of self-assessed output tax as per return. According to section 2(97) of CGST Act 2017, 'return' means any return prescribed or otherwise required to be furnished by or under this Act or the rules made thereunder. Even annual return is a return which is prescribed under the GST provisions and therefore, utilisation of credit should be allowed.

21.6 DETAILS NOT REQUIRED TO BE FURNISHED IN THE ANNUAL RETURN

It is important to know that the annual return does not warrant submission of some information as per understanding today, which are provided below:

(1) Details of goods sent and received back within time limit/ after job work.

(2) Details of supplies made without consideration.

(3) Details of free issues, gifts, free samples etc.

(4) Details of transactions covered in schedule III to CGST Act such as sale of land, building after obtaining completion certificate etc.

(5) Details of deductions claimed as pure agent towards the taxable supplies made.

(6) Details of goods received free of cost from customers.

21.7 CONSEQUENCES OF NON-COMPLIANCE

Non-filing of annual return could have the following consequences:

(1) Notice under section 46 could be issued to file the return within 15 days.

(2) Late fee for delayed filing of annual return could be demanded under section 47(2) of the Act which would be lower of Rs.100 per day during which such failure continues or quarter percent of turnover in the state or union territory. Equal late fee would be applicable in SGST law as well.

(3) General penalty as per section 125 of the Act could also be applicable which may extend up to Rs.25000/- with equal penalty under SGST law as well.

21.8 REVISION OF ANNUAL RETURN

There is no option provided in the law to revise the annual return filed. The return is meant to disclose the details as per books of accounts based on returns filed in form GSTR-3B and GSTR-1 forms with few additional details such as refund claims made and rejected, reconciliation of credit amounts as per GSTR-2A. Therefore, due care needs to be taken while filing the return. This would be more important when the tax payers are subject to mandatory audit as the comparison would be made between the annual return and financial statements. Wrong information in annual return could lead to demands in later periods.

Since there is no facility for revised return to avoid penalties and longer period demands, corrections needed maybe indicated by way of a communication by way of speed post or RPAD mentioning the date of rectification in the subsequent GSTR-1 and 3B.

21.9 IMPORTANT FORMATS

Following are few formats which could be used while preparation of annual return. The formats are provided for the information which are not readily available from either GSTR-3B or GSTR-1 return:

F-1: Details of ITC availed on Inward supplies (other than imports and inward supplies liable to reverse charge but includes services received from SEZs) *[Refer Part III]*

Month	Particulars	HSN	(Input/CG/Input Services)	Value of goods/services	Tax [CGST]	Tax (SGST)	Tax [IGST]	Cess

F-2: Details of ITC availed on Inward supplies received from unregistered persons liable to reverse charge (other than B above) on which tax is paid - *[Refer Part III]*

Month	Particulars	HSN	(Input/CG/Input Services)	Value of goods/services	Tax [CGST]	Tax (SGST)	Tax [IGST]	Cess

F-3: Details of ITC availed on Inward supplies received from registered persons liable to reverse charge (other than B above) on which tax is paid - *[Refer Part III]*

Month	Particulars	HSN	(Input/CG/Input Services)	Value of goods/services	Tax [CGST]	Tax (SGST)	Tax [IGST]	Cess

F-4: Details of ITC availed on Import of goods (including supplies from SEZs) - *[Refer Part III]*

Month	Particulars	HSN	(Input/Capital goods)	Value of goods/services	IGST

F- 5: Details of ITC availed on Import of services (excluding inward supplies from SEZs) - *[Refer Part III]*

Month	Particulars	HSN	Value of goods/services	IGST

F- 6: Details of ITC reclaimed (other than B above) under the provisions of the Act - *[Refer Part III]*

Month	Particulars	HSN	(Input/CG/Input Services)	Value of goods/services	Tax [CGST]	Tax (SGST)	Tax [IGST]	Cess

F-7: Details of amount of ITC reversal u/s 16(2) r/w Rule 37 for not making payment in 180 days - *[Refer Part III]*

Invoice reference	Party	Particulars/HSN	Value of goods/services	Tax [CGST]	Tax [SGST]	Tax [IGST]	Interest (if any)

F-8: Details of Amount of ITC Reversal u/s 16(2) r/w Rule 42 in respect of inputs/input services - *[Refer Part III]*

Month	Tax [CGST]	Tax [SGST]	Tax [IGST]	Interest (if any)

F-9: Details of Amount of ITC Reversal u/s 16(2) r/w Rule 43 in respect of capital goods - *[Refer Part III]*

Month	Tax [CGST]	Tax [SGST]	Tax [IGST]	Interest (if any)

Month	Tax [CGST]	Tax [SGST]	Tax [IGST]	Interest (if any)

F-10: Details of amount of ineligible ITC u/s 17(5) - *[Refer Part III]*

Month	Particulars/HSN	Nature of restriction	Value of goods/services	Tax [CGST]	Tax [SGST]	Tax [IGST]

F-11: Details of ITC on inward supplies (other than imports and inward supplies liable to reverse charge but includes services received from SEZs) received during 2017-18 but availed during April to September, 2018 - *[Refer Part III]*

Month	Particulars	HSN	(Input/CG/Input Services)	Value of goods/services	Tax [CGST]	Tax (SGST)	Tax [IGST]	Cess

F-12: Total IGST paid on import of goods (including supplies from SEZ) - *[Refer Part III]*

Month	Particulars	HSN	Value of goods	Tax [IGST]	Cess

F-13: Details of ITC availed in July 17 to Mar 18 but reversed in Apr 18 to Sep 18 *[Refer Part V]*

Invoice reference	Particulars	HSN	Value of goods/services	Tax [CGST+SGST]	Tax [IGST]	Cess

F-14: Details of ITC availed in July 17 to Mar 18 but reversed in Apr 18 to Sep 18 *[Refer Part V]*

Invoice reference	Particulars	HSN	Value of goods/services	Tax [CGST+SGST]	Tax [IGST]	Cess

F-15: Details of additions made to supplies made in July 17 to Mar 18 but details furnished in GSTR-1 of Apr 18 to Sep 18 *[Refer Part V]*

Invoice reference	Particulars	HSN	Value of goods/services	Tax [CGST+SGST]	Tax [IGST]	Cess

F-16: Details of deductions made to supplies made in July 17 to Mar 18 but details furnished in GSTR-1 of Apr 18 to Sep 18 *[Refer Part V]*

Invoice reference	Particulars	HSN	Value of goods/services	Tax [CGST+SGST]	Tax [IGST]	Cess

F-17: Details of supplies received from composition tax payers for July 17 to Mar 18 *[Refer Part VI]*

Month	Particulars	Value of supplies
Jul 17		
Aug 17		
Sep 17		
Oct 17		
Nov 17		
Dec 17		
Jan 18		
Feb 18		
Mar 18		

F-18: Details of goods supplied for job work but treated as deemed supply due to non- receipt as per section 143 *[Refer part VI]*

JW challan reference	Particulars	HSN	Value of goods	Tax [CGST+SGST]	IGST	Cess

F-19: Details of goods sent on approval but not returned in 180 days *[Refer Part VI]*

DC reference	Particulars	HSN	Value of goods	Tax [CGST+SGST/IGST]	Cess

21.10 BRIEF CHECKLIST FOR USE OF PROFESSIONALS

It is important that the professionals use a checklist for preparation of the annual return to ensure that the important aspects are not missed out while assisting the tax payers in filing their annual return. There is no revision option provided for the annual return and therefore, due care needs to be taken while filing the return in form GSTR-9. Following is the checklist which could be useful for the professionals.

Sl. No.	Description	Remarks
	GSTR-1	
1	Check whether all the outward supplies for the period July 2017 to March 2018 has been disclosed in GSTR-1	
2	Check whether the outward turnover is disclosed separately in GSTR-1 • B2B • B2C • Export • SEZ • Deemed supply • Exempted/nil rated/non-GST supply • HSN Summary	
3	Check whether the turnover of outward supplies disclosed in GSTR- 1 is reconciled with the books of accounts	
4	Check whether all the debit notes/credit notes raised during the	

Sl. No.	Description	Remarks
	period July 2017 to March 2018 is disclosed in the GSTR-1	
5	Check whether advances received towards goods (up to 13.10.2017) and services are disclosed in GSTR-1	
6	Check whether invoices are raised against such advances received and disclosed in GSTR-1 and adjusted against the liability payable in GSTR-3B	
7	Check whether the balance advances received on which invoices is not yet raised during the financial year is identified and reconciled	
8	Check any changes of outward supplies of 17-18 is made during April 18 to Sept 18. If yes, reconciliation of the same is to be checked.	
9	Check whether any amendments have been done with respect to July 17 to Mar 18 outward supply and adjustment to that extent is done. Further, also see whether the client has maintained details of changes/amendments during April 18 to Sept 18	
10	Check whether any turnover of July 17 to Mar 18 is not disclosed in the GSTR-1 return	
	GSTR-3B	
11	Check whether the turnover disclosed in the GSTR-3B for the period July 17 to Mar 18 is matching with the corresponding GSTR-1 return	
12	Check whether the client has maintained reconciliation for the difference if any between GSTR-1 and GSTR-3B	
13	Check whether the client has maintained reconciliation for the information of July 17 to Mar 18 in April 18 to Sept 18	
14	Check whether the credit note/debit note for the supplies made during period July 17 to Mar 18 by Sept 18 and also disclosed in GSTR-1 & GSTR-3B	
15	Check whether the client has paid the GST on inward supplies attracting GST under reverse charge [Sec 9(3) and 9(4)]	
16	Check whether the client has reversed ITC wherever the payment to supplier is not made within 180 days. Also check, if the payment is made to the supplier after reversal, the ITC is reclaimed back.	
17	Check whether the reclaimed credit is identified and kept separately	
18	Check whether the reversal of ITC under Rule 42 & 43 is	

Sl. No.	Description	Remarks
	done month on month basis (if applicable)	
19	Check whether the reversal of ITC under Rule 42 is recomputed, • If recomputed ITC towards exempted supplies is more than the actual reversal – check whether the differential ITC has been reversed by Sept 18 along with interest. • If recomputed ITC towards exempted supplies is less than the actual reversal – check whether the excess ITC reversal has been availed back by Sept 18, if not ITC would get lapsed	
20	Check whether the reconciliation between GSTR-2A and ITC as per GSTR-3B is reconciled. If not, ask the client to do it and avail any missed out ITC by the due date for filing the return for the period March 2019.	
21	Check whether the payment made in GSTR-3B is off set with the corresponding liability.	
22	Check whether the interest is paid on delay payment made in GSTR-3B	
23	Check whether the Non-GST inward supply, exempt inward supply and composition and NIL rated inward supplies are disclosed in GSTR-3B separately	
	Books of Accounts	
24	Check whether the turnover disclosed in the GSTR-1 & GSTR-3B is matching with books of accounts.	
25	Check whether the ITC availed in the books of accounts is matching with table 4 of GSTR-3B	
26	Check whether any reconciliation between books to GSTR-1 & books to GSTR-3B is done. If any difference identified, check whether the same is rectified in Sept 18 return. If the same is not rectified, ensure that additional liability if any has been disclosed and discharged through GSTR-9.	
27	The credit balance of profit and loss account is required to be reconciled with the GSTR-1 & 3B and any difference, reconciliation statement need to be prepared.	
28	Check whether the advance at the end of the year is identified and matched with the books of accounts	
29	Check whether registered person has complied with Schedule I transactions, made any adjustments like netting off expenses etc.	

Sl. No.	Description	Remarks
	GSTR-9	
30	Check whether the transactions of F.Y 2017-18 have been categorised by registered person as mentioned in Para 21.4	
29	Check whether the details of the turnover which has tax implication has been separately identified.	
30	Check whether the details of the turnover (tax implication + no tax implication) is bifurcated as follows: • B2C • B2B • Exports with payment of tax • SEZ with payment of tax • Deemed exports • Advances at the end of the year on which invoice is not raised • Inward supplies on which tax to be paid under RCM	
31	Check whether the turnover on which recipient is made liable to pay the GST is identified separately	
32	Check whether the details of credit notes/debit notes raised during the July 17 to Mar 18 details is available.	
33	Check whether the amendments made with respect to the outward supplies during July 17 to Mar 18 are identified and summarised.	
34	Check whether the ITC register is maintained by the client and wherein ITC is classified as inputs, input services or capital goods.	
35	Check whether the ITC availed in GSTR-3B is matched with books of accounts as well as GSTR-2A. If any ITC not availed by due date of filing the return of March 2019, would get lapsed.	
36	Check wherever the GST is made under reverse charge on import of goods/services, the ITC on the same is availed and disclosed in the GST returns.	
37	Check whether the ITC on ISD invoices is availed and shown in the GSTR-3B	
38	Check whether the client has filed TRAN-1 & II properly and ITC is auto-populated in Electronic Credit Ledger	
39	Check whether the client has reversed the ITC (if any) under Rule 37, 39, 42, 43 & section 17(5)	
40	Check whether the client is opted out/opted in to composition	

Sl. No.	Description	Remarks
	scheme, if yes see whether the corresponding availment/reversal of ITC is done	
41	Check whether the ITC as per GSTR-2A and GSTR-3B is reconciled. If any ITC is not availed, inform client to avail it in Sept 18. If not, ITC would lapse	
42	Check whether any ineligible ITC is availed, if yes inform the client to reverse the same at the earliest.	
43	Compare the output tax payable as per the reconciled turnover with tax paid as per GSTR-3B. if any liability arises the same is required to be made with interest and disclosed in the returns	
44	Check whether the client has maintained the details of refund claimed and status as on Mar 18 is prepared	
45	Check whether any demand notices are received by the client, if yes details of the same is required to be provided	
46	Check whether the client has maintained HSN wise outward supplies/inward supplies along with quantity details.	

Note: *There could be a much more exhaustive checklist prepared for complex multi locational tax payers and also with the problems faced in compliance which experience would be available by end of the year. Further depending on the nature of trade/industry or service, the above checklist could be customised.*

The professionals/industry could also refer to the Technical Guide on Annual Return and GST Audit published in October 2018 by The Institute of Chartered Accountants of India for guidance.

There have been some grey areas in filling of this annual return and the Government is expected to come out with clarification/s. It may be noted that the format of GSTR-9, 9A cannot go beyond the rules or the GST Act.

Chapter 22

Reconciliation & Certification under Section 35(5)

22.1 INTRODUCTION

GST functions on the concept of self-assessment wherein assessee is expected to assess the taxes on goods and services supplied and pay the taxes after adjusting eligible ITC within the due date. The transactions undertaken over a period are required to be disclosed by way of filing of the periodic tax returns. In a self-assessment environment, there would be a less intervention of the tax officers in the day to day business transactions and the onus of routine checking of completeness, correctness of the assessment, disclosure of taxes is on the assessees themselves. Annual return only ensures that the returns are filed by all registered entities and is intended for small assessees. Audit which is for larger entities beyond the limit of Rs. 2 crores turnover involves the following addition activities:

- The judgement of the correctness/completeness of classification/ exemption claimed, place of supply, valuation, time of supply in the tax paid, tax credit claimed, turnover declared, refund claimed and compliance of GST overall which has any implication on tax.
- Audited Financials need to be uploaded.
- Reconciliation and audit report certified by the Chartered or Cost Accountant which is to be conducted after filling the annual return. However practically to be filed along with the annual return and financials.

Therefore, in order to have proper checks and balances in the system and to ensure that there is a compliance of the law and timely detection of non-compliance (if any), various mechanisms are required to be inbuilt. One of the mechanisms of keeping vigilance is to get the accounts of the assessee audited under any other law like- Companies Act, Income Tax Act etc. GST law has envisaged audits of the following nature:

(i) Compulsory audit by Chartered Accountant or Cost Accountant, of the registered person having aggregate turnover exceeding Rs. 2 Crore under section 35 (5)

(ii) Audit by Commissioner or any officer authorised by him under section 65 of the Act

(iii) Special audit by a Chartered Accountant or Cost Accountant in exceptional circumstances as nominated by the Commissioner – section 66 of the Act

The present discussion is on the mandatory audit to be conducted by the professionals i.e. CA's/CMA's as per the requirement of section 35(5) of the Act.

22.2 NEED FOR RECONCILIATION & CERTIFICATION

The reconciliation statement is required to be furnished in Form GSTR-9C as notified vide Notification No. 49/2018-Central Tax. The need for reconciliation statement arises as the annual return is prepared by the assessees based on the transactions reported in the books of accounts, Form GSTR 1 and GSTR 3B in various periodical returns wherein the supplies of all nature are required to be reported. The books of account are maintained based on different principles i.e. the Generally Accepted Accounting Principles (GAAPs). There can be a possibility that the annual returns which is prepared on the basis of self-assessment by the taxpayer themselves, would miss out on reporting of various transactions in the annual returns but are reflected in the books of accounts and *vice versa.* The objective of reconciliation statement is to reconcile the details furnished in the audited financial statement *vis-a-vis* the details in the annual return. In case of any difference, the reasons need to be explained. In case of errors, rectifications need to be done.

Further, similar to the tax audit as required under the Income Tax Act, the GST audit is also in the nature of an independent verification/check carried out by professionals to safeguard the interest of the GST revenue. Further, the audit by professionals also helps assessees in identification of any process or transactional non-compliances so that the corrective action can be taken on timely basis. The burden of high costs of interests and penalties can be reduced on the old proverb – "*a stitch in time saves nine*". It also helps in reducing the unnecessary and avoidable litigation and disputes between the department and the taxpayers.

This reconciliation statement has to be certified by a Chartered Accountant or a Cost Accountant as required under section 35(5) in the Part B of the form GSTR-9C. This may be applicable in any of the following manners:

- Certification in case where reconciliation statement (GTR-9C) is drawn by the person who had conducted the audit;
- Certification in case where reconciliation statement (GTR-9C) is drawn by the person other than the person who had conducted the audit.

Different certification formats have been prescribed for the above.

22.3 LEGAL PROVISIONS OF THE AUDIT BY CA/CMA

22.3.1 Requirement of audit under section 35(5) read with section 44(2) and rule 80(3)

Section 35(5) of the Goods and Service Tax Act, 2017 read with section 44(2) and rule 80(3) of the GST rules provides that every registered person whose turnover during a financial year exceeds Rs. 2 crores shall get his accounts ***audited*** by a Chartered Accountant or a Cost Accountant and submit a copy of the audited annual accounts, the reconciliation statement under sub-section (2) of section 44 and such other documents in such form and manner as may be prescribed. This should be filed in **FORM GSTR-9C,** electronically through the common portal either directly or through a Facilitation Centre notified by the Commissioner.

Further, section 44(2) of Goods and Service Tax, 2017 states that every registered person who is required to get his accounts audited in accordance with the provisions of sub-section (5) of section 35 shall furnish, electronically the following:

(i) Annual Return under section 44(1) CGST Act, 2017;

(ii) Audited Annual Accounts;

(iii) Reconciliation Statement;

(iv) Such other particulars as may be prescribed.

The term **"Audit"** is defined under section 2(13) of the CGST Act, 2017 as:

"examination of the records, returns and other documents maintained or furnished by the registered person under this Act or the rules made thereunder or under any other law for the time being in force to verify the correctness of turnover declared, taxes paid, refund claimed and input tax credit availed, and to assess his compliance with the provisions of this Act or the rules made thereunder".

Thus, the definition of the term 'audit' entails following essential characteristics:

(i) Audit involves examination of
   - (a) Records;
   - (b) Returns; and
   - (c) Other documents maintained or furnished.

(ii) By the registered person.

(iii) Either under the Act (CGST/SGST/IGST Act) or rules made thereunder or *under any other law for the time being in force.*

(iv) To verify the correctness of
   - (a) turnover declared,
   - (b) taxes paid,
   - (c) refund claimed and
   - (d) input tax credit availed.

(v) To assess the compliance under the Act or rules made thereunder.

22.3.2 Analysis/Issues

22.3.2.1 Coverage of the term 'Audit'

The coverage and scope of the term 'Audit' has been given a very wide meaning as provided above u/s 2(13) of the GST Act. The same can be broken into three limbs as under:

(i) Examination of the records/documents maintained;

(ii) Verifying the correctness of the turnover declared, taxes paid, refund claimed and input tax credit claimed; and

(iii) Assessing the compliance under the Act or rules made thereunder.

We would now understand each of the above limbs of the audit in detail and the duty casted upon the auditor in this regard.

(I) Examination of the various records/documents maintained

The first limb of the definition of the term audit requires an examination of the records, returns and other documents maintained or furnished by the registered person either under the GST act or rules made thereunder or under any other law for the time being in force.

Further, it is important to note that auditors i.e. CA's/CMA's while certifying the reconciliation statement are required to comment as to whether the registered person has/has not maintained the books of accounts/records/documents as required under the GST Act, rules and notifications made/issued thereunder.

Therefore, an auditor needs to know the various records, documents, accounts that are required to be maintained by the assessees. He is required to verify the completeness and correctness of the same in accordance with the various provisions of the GST law.

Accounts & Records to be maintained: In terms of section 35(1) of the GST Act, every registered person shall keep and maintain, at his principal place of business, a true and correct account of:

(a) Production or manufacture of goods: Every registered person manufacturing goods shall maintain monthly production accounts showing quantitative details of raw materials or services used in the manufacture and quantitative details of the goods so manufactured including the waste and by products thereof.

(b) Inward and outward supply of goods or services or both;

(c) Stock of goods: Further, every registered person, other than a person covered under composition scheme, shall maintain the accounts of stock in respect of goods received and supplied by him, and such accounts shall contain particulars of the opening balance, receipt, supply, goods lost, stolen, destroyed, written off or disposed of by way of gift or free sample and the balance of stock including raw materials, finished goods, scrap and wastage thereof.

(d) Input tax credit availed.

(e) Output tax payable and paid and a separate account of advances received, paid and adjustments made thereto.

(f) Such other particulars as prescribed in Rule 56 of CGST Rules as provided below:

Goods at additional places: It is critical to note here that if any taxable goods are found to be stored at any place(s) other than those declared as above without the cover of any valid document, the proper officer can determine the amount of tax payable on such goods as if such goods have been supplied by the registered person.

Goods at godown or warehouse: The owner or the operator of the godown shall store the goods in such manner that they can be identified item-wise and owner-wise and would facilitate any physical verification or inspection by the proper officer on demand.

Every registered person shall keep the particulars of -

(a) Names and complete addresses of suppliers from whom he has received the goods or services chargeable to tax under the Act;

(b) Names and complete addresses of the persons to whom he has supplied goods or services.

(c) The complete address of the premises where goods are stored by him, including goods stored during transit along with the particulars of the stock stored therein.

Section 35 (*2*) provides that every owner or operator of warehouse or godown or any other place used for storage of goods and every transporter, irrespective of whether he is a registered person or not, shall maintain records of the consigner, consignee and other relevant details of the goods in such manner as may be prescribed.

Persons executing works contracts: Every registered person executing works contract would keep separate accounts for works contract showing -

(a) The names and addresses of the persons on whose behalf the works contract is executed;

(b) Description, value and quantity (wherever applicable) of goods or services received for the execution of works contract;

(c) Description, value and quantity (wherever applicable) of goods or services utilized in the execution of works contract;

(d) The details of payment received in respect of each works contract; and

(e) The names and addresses of suppliers from whom he received goods or services.

Persons acting as an agent: Every agent shall maintain accounts depicting the-

(a) Particulars of authorisation received by him from each principal to receive or supply goods or services on behalf of such principal separately;

(b) Particulars including description, value and quantity (wherever applicable) of goods or services received on behalf of every principal;

(c) Particulars including description, value and quantity (wherever applicable) of goods or services supplied on behalf of every principal;

(d) Details of accounts furnished to every principal; and

(e) Tax paid on receipts or on supply of goods or services effected on behalf of every principal.

Further, any person having custody over the goods in the capacity of a carrier or a clearing and forwarding agent for delivery or dispatch thereof to a recipient on behalf of any registered person would maintain true and correct records in respect of such goods handled by him on behalf of such registered person and would produce the details thereof as and when required by the proper officer.

Documents to be maintained: Apart from the above records, assessee is also required to maintain various documents as required under GST Act and rules as under:

(a) **Tax Invoice** in case of supply of goods or services or both as per the requirement laid down in rule 46 to 48 of GST Rules

(b) **Bill of supply** in case of supply of exempted goods or services or supplies by the persons covered under the composition scheme as per the requirement laid down in rule 49 of GST Rules

(c) **Receipt voucher** for receipt of advance payment as per the requirement laid down in rule 50 of GST Rules

(d) **Refund voucher** in case no supply or no Tax invoice is issued against the receipt voucher as per the requirement laid down in rule 51 of GST Rules

(e) **Self invoice** in case of receipt of goods/services which are liable for tax under reverse charge u/s 9(3) or 9(4) of the GST Act from the supplier who is not registered under the GST Act

(f) **Payment voucher** in case of making payment to the supplier towards the supply of goods or services covered under reverse charge as per the requirement laid down in rule 52 of GST Rules

(g) **Debit/Credit Notes** as required under the provisions of section 34 of the GST Act

(h) **Delivery challan** in case of movement of goods without invoice i.e. stock transfers, job work etc. as per the requirement laid down in rule 55 of the GST rules.

(i) **E-Way Bill** as required to be generated in terms of rule 138 of the GST rules.

Accounts, records, documents in electronic form: Rule 57 of the GST rules, provides that proper electronic back-up of records shall be maintained and preserved in such manner that, in the event of destruction of such records due to accidents or natural causes, the information can be restored within a reasonable period of time.

The registered person maintaining electronic records shall produce, on demand, the relevant records or documents, duly authenticated by him, in hard copy or in any electronically readable format.

Where the accounts and records are stored electronically by any registered person, he shall, on demand, provide the details of such files, passwords of such files and explanation for codes used, where necessary, for access and any other information which is required for such access along with a sample copy in print form of the information stored in such files.

The provisions allow maintenance of records in electronic form subject to the condition that such records are authenticated by digital signature. Many tax payers would have maintained records like ITC register, stock register which needs to be authenticated with digital signature which otherwise could attract general penalty extending upto Rs.50,000/-.

One must also know the provisions of section 4 of the Information Technology Act, 2000, which gives the legal recognition to the maintenance of the records in the electronic form stating that where any law provides that information or any other matter would be in writing or in the typewritten or printed form, then, notwithstanding anything contained in such law, such requirement would be deemed to have been satisfied if such information or matter is

(a) Rendered or made available in an electronic form; and

(b) Accessible so as to be usable for a subsequent reference.

The above provision in the Information Technology Act has a binding effect notwithstanding anything contained in any other law for the time being in force, therefore the documents, records that are required to be maintained in the GST law would be deemed to have been maintained if the same is rendered or made available in the electronic form and the same is accessible therefrom.

Question 1: *Registered person has maintained records/documents at each State/branch level, what is the auditor's responsibility while certifying GSTR-9C?*

Ans: If the records pertaining to additional place of business are maintained in electronic form which can be retrieved separately from principal place of business, it could be considered a sufficient compliance of the law and auditor may not be required to comment upon separately on it. However, if the records are maintained in the physical form and separate records have not been maintained at such additional place of business, the auditor may have to make appropriate observations in the certification in part B of GSTR-9C.

Places at which records are to be maintained: Every registered person would keep the books of account at the principal place of business and books of account relating to additional place of business mentioned in his certificate of registration and such books of account would include any electronic form of data stored on any electronic device.

Where such accounts and documents are maintained manually, be kept at every related place of business mentioned in the certificate of registration and would be accessible at every related place of business where such accounts and documents are maintained digitally. Further, in case where more than one place of business is specified in the certificate of registration, the accounts relating to each place of business shall be kept at such places of business.

Retention of the Accounts and records: Accounts maintained by the registered person together with all the invoices, bills of supply, credit and debit notes, and delivery challans relating to stocks, deliveries, inward supply and outward supply would be preserved until the expiry of seventy two months from the due date of furnishing of annual return for the year pertaining to such accounts and record for the period as provided.

Auditor's responsibility is to examine the completeness and correctness with which the above accounts, records and documents are maintained by the assessee and in case of any non-compliance therein, the same needs to be reported by way of a qualification in part B of the certification.

(II) Correctness of turnover declared, taxes paid, refund claimed and input tax credit availed

There is a specific requirement laid out here wherein an auditor is expected to verify the correctness of the turnover declared, taxes paid, refund claimed and the input tax credit availed. In fact, if one closely goes through the structure in which form GSTR 9C is designed, it can be well appreciated that the form is designed in a manner to cover the verification of all the above aspects as under:

- Correctness of Turnover Declared (Sl. No. 5, 6, 7 & 8 in Part II of the form GSTR 9C)
- Correctness of the Taxes paid (Sl. No. 9 & 10 in Part III of the form GSTR 9C)
- Correctness of the refund claimed (Part V of the form GSTR 9C)

- Correctness of the Input Tax credit availed (Sl. No.12, 13, 14 & 15 of Part IV of the GSTR 9C)
- Recommendation on erroneous refund to be paid back (Part V of GSTR 9C)

Details of various aspects that needs to be verified by the auditor in respect of the above is covered in Chapter 15 to 17 of this Book. Further, we would also understand the verification requirement for each of the above heads in step by step discussion of the form GSTR 9C in detail later in this chapter.

(III) Assessing compliance with the provisions of this Act or the rules made thereunder

The third limb of the definition of the term 'Audit' is generic in nature and calls for assessing of the compliance with the provisions of the act or the rules made thereunder. Therefore, one has to note that apart from the above specific compliance requirement, there are various other key statutory provisions in the GST law whose compliance needs to be verified by the auditor as under:

- Classification & rate of tax adopted by the assessee for the goods/services supplied.
- Composite & mixed supply principles are being followed for the goods/services supplied.
- Time of supply, Place of supply and valuation principles as laid out in the act and rules thereunder.

The readers are advised to understand the concepts of each of the above. The details of various aspects need to be verified by the auditor are covered in Chapter 15 to 17 of this Book.

22.3.2.2 Turnover v/s Aggregate Turnover for audit Threshold limit

The requirement to get the accounts audited under section 35 arises when the turnover exceeds Rs. 2 crore. Here, one could encounter confusion as to whether turnover has to be considered at all India level for a particular PAN or the turnover in the State has to be considered. The section only refers to the term 'turnover' whereas Rule 80 refers to the term 'aggregate turnover'. The law has not defined the term 'turnover'. Only definition given under the Act is either 'aggregate turnover' or 'turnover in the State'. In the absence of any definition of the term 'turnover' in the Act and specific reference of the term 'aggregate turnover' in the Rule 80 could give an indication that the turnover to be considered has to be aggregate turnover at all India level. It is important to note that if the coverage of audit is based on the 'aggregate turnover' at all India level, then audit would be required for all the States of an entity GSTIN wise, whether or not the turnover for that particular registration crosses the limit. There could be dissent from the businesses on this as even a small branch office in other State having turnover of a meagre say Rs.10 lakhs in a year would also need to get the accounts audited and submit the reconciliation statement and the certification. To comply with this that GSTIN may need to have a separate trial balance! However, one must note that the audit remains incomplete and full mapping with the financial statements is not possible unless all the registrations of an entity are subjected to the audit. In order to avoid the interpretation issues, it is expected that a suitable clarification would be issued by the Government in this regard to avoid any confusion or the alternative interpretation in this regard.

22.3.2.3 Applicability of turnover limit for the period 01.07.2017 to 31.03.2018

GST has been implemented with effect from 01.07.2017. As a consequence, during the financial year 2017-18, GST is in force only for a period of nine months from 01.07.2017 to 31.03.2018. Now, the question which arises here is whether the above-mentioned annual turnover limit of Rs. 2 Crore for audit purposes would apply proportionately in the given case for a period of nine months or whether the foregoing limit would apply to twelve months.

It is important to understand the meaning of the term 'aggregate turnover' which not only includes taxable supplies but also covers exempt supplies and export of goods/services. One must now reckon the meaning of the term 'exempt supplies' which as per section 2(47) of the GST Act would also cover supply of any goods or services which attract nil rate of tax or which may be wholly exempt from tax and also includes non-taxable supply. The term 'non-taxable supplies' as per section 2(78) of the GST Act means a supply of goods or services or both which is not leviable to tax under CGST, SGST or IGST Act.

The taxes levied in the financial year 17-18 under erstwhile laws viz., VAT/CST Service Tax etc. would get covered within the meaning of the term "non-taxable supplies" as these were the supplies levied to tax under any other laws. Further section 35(5) uses the expression 'financial year' and therefore, although for the year 2017-18, the GST period comprises of 9 months, it is reasonable to include the first quarter of the financial year 2017-18. A clarification from the Government(s) in this regard can help avoid unnecessary dispute.

22.3.2.4 Calculation of threshold of two crore for audit

Section 2(6) of the GST Act, 2017 provides the value of the aggregate turnover to be, *"the aggregate value of all taxable supplies (excluding the value of inward supplies on which tax is payable by a person on reverse charge basis), exempt supplies, exports of goods or services or both and inter-State supplies of persons having the same Permanent Account Number, to be computed on all India basis but excludes central tax, State tax, Union territory tax, integrated tax and cess."*

A careful reading of above definitions reveal that first of all it is an exhaustive definition because the expression "means" [and not includes] has been used.

Further, while computing the value of "Aggregate Turnover", following inclusions would be made:

(a) Value of all Taxable Supplies: The term "Taxable Supply" means a supply of goods or services or both which is leviable to tax under the GST Act.

(b) Value of all Exempt Supplies: The term "Exempt Supply" means supply of any goods or services or both which attracts nil rate of tax or which may be wholly exempt from tax under section 11 of the CGST Act/SGST Act. It is also worth highlighting here that the term "exempt supply" includes non-taxable supply also. The term "Non-taxable Supply" means a supply of goods or services or both which is not leviable to tax under the CGST Act/SGST Act or under the IGST Act. For ex: Non-taxable supply are Alcoholic Liquor for Human Consumption and five specified Petroleum Products i.e. Petroleum Crude, Motor Spirit (Petrol), High Speed Diesel [HSD], Natural Gas and Aviation Turbine Fuel [ATF]

(c) Value of the supplies which in the nature of export of goods or services or both.

However, following must not be included while computing the value of the aggregate turnover:

(a) Value of Inward supplies on which tax is payable by a person on reverse charge basis. For Ex: Sponsorship services, legal services by advocate, Services supplied by a Director of a Company to the said company.

(b) Central Tax, State Tax, Union territory Tax, Integrated Tax and Cess.

This is an essential requirement in the audit as the auditor must be clear as to which are the entities that would get covered within the meaning of the term 'Audit'. Following practical illustrations would help the readers:

Question 2: *XYZ limited is fully into the business of export of services and it supplies the services under LUT without any payment of any taxes. Whether XYZ limited needs to get the audit done as per section 35(5) of the GST Act?*

Ans: Meaning of the term 'Aggregate Turnover as defined u/s 2(6) of the GST Act also covered exports of goods and services. Therefore, in the given case if the total value of export supplies made by XYZ limited exceeds Rs.2 Crores then it needs to get audit done under the GST Act.

Question 3: *As per the Audited financial statements for the FY 2017-18, the total turnover of ABC limited is Rs.1.8 Crores, Does that mean that ABC limited would not be required to subject itself to GST Audit?*

Ans: The fact that the turnover as per the audited financial statements is less than Rs. 2 Crores (i.e. Rs.1.8 Crores in the given case) cannot be the decisive factor for the purpose of determining the mandatory requirement of the audit. It is important to note that the meaning of the term 'aggregate turnover' as discussed above is having a wider import and would cover the 3 months turnover between April 2017 to June 2017 and all the taxable supplies under the GST act. For instance, cross charge between the branches, stock transfers, taxes on advances etc. may not be covered within the meaning of the term 'Turnover' in the financial statements as the same are prepared as per Generally Accepted Accounting Principles (i.e. GAAPs). These need to be included while calculating the threshold limit of Rs. 2 Crores in the aggregate turnover and therefore in the given case one has to take the cognizance of the various taxable, exempt, non-taxable and export supplies made by ABC limited as are reported in the returns filed and accordingly a conclusion as to applicability of the GST Audit needs to be arrived at.

Question 4: *Surya Transporters is a Goods Transport Agency having a turnover of Rs.10 Crores which is fully covered under reverse charge and the tax is paid by the recipient of the transportation services. It has obtained registration under the GST Act due to specific requirement from the customer. Whether it needs to get audited under the GST Act?*

Ans: The supplies covered under reverse charge would also tantamount to 'taxable supplies' in so much so that the levy of tax on such supplies is also attracted u/s 9(2) of the CGST Act. The only exception being carved out in section 9(3) and 9(4) that the liability to pay tax on such supplies is shifted onto the recipient of the supplies or any other category of the person(s) as specified in this regard. Further, since the turnover of inward supplies which is liable under reverse charge is excluded from the definition of the 'aggregate turnover' and the 'exempt supplies', therefore taking analogy from the same, it can be said that the said turnover needs to be considered in the taxable supplies of the person who is supplying such outward supplies for the purpose of determining the threshold limit for audit under GST and in the given case Surya Transporters would require to get their accounts audited under the GST act. However, since the strict interpretation of the legal provisions of the GST act leads to a situation where in the persons who are not liable to pay any taxes under the GST act are also being mandated to get the accounts audited under the GST act. Further, the liability in respect of the transactions covered under reverse charge are indirectly getting audited twice one at the supplier's end by its auditors and secondly by the auditors of the recipient. It must be noted that the taxes are not paid twice on the same truncation both by the supplier and the recipient and when in doubt, the auditor of the supplier/recipient as the case may be must make an adequate communication with the other auditors to avoid the clanger of double taxation.

Question 5: *Ashok Petroleum limited is a company into the business of sale of petroleum products i.e. HSD and Petrol having turnover of Rs.50 Crores in a Financial year. Whether it is covered by the audit under GST?*

Ans: Section 35(5) states that the requirement for audit is in respect of registered persons. Since, in the given case, Ashok Petroleum limited is not required to obtain registration under GST as per section 22 of the GST Act. Therefore, even if the turnover of non-taxable supplies of Ashok Petroleum limited exceeds Rs. 2 Crores in the financial year, it is not required to get itself audited under GST.

Question 6: *In the above case, if Ashok Petroleum Limited registers under the GST Act in order to pay taxes under reverse charge, then whether it needs to undertake the mandatory audit?*

Ans: In case Ashok Petroleum limited registers under GST for paying taxes under reverse charge then it would be covered by the mandatory requirement of audit as the threshold limit calculation of 'aggregate turnover' also includes 'non-taxable supplies' and since supply of petroleum is a non-taxable supply therefore the turnover of sale of petrol/diesel needs to be counted for the purpose of calculation of the threshold limit of Rs. 2 Crores and hence audit under GST needs to be carried out.

Question 7: *Hero Holding Limited has an Interest income of Rs. 1.90 Crores and a Rental Income of Rs. 30 Lakhs, whether it needs to undertake the GST Audit u/s 35(5)?*

Ans: Assuming that the interest received is on account of deposits, loans, advances etc. the same would amount to be an exempt supply since interest is specifically exempted from the clutches of GST vide entry 27 of Notification No.12/2017-Central Tax (Rate). Since, one needs to consider the 'Aggregate Turnover' for the purpose of deriving the threshold of Rs. 2 Crore for audit and since the said aggregate turnover also includes exempt supplies, in the given case Hero Holding limited needs to consider the total taxable as well as exempt turnover and since the same exceeds the threshold limit of Rs. 2 Crore, the GST audit is required to be undertaken.

Question 8: *HR Holding Limited has an Interest income of Rs. 1.90 Crores and a Dividend income of Rs. 3 Crores, whether it needs to undertake the GST Audit u/s 35(5)?*

Ans: Assuming that the interest received is on account of deposits, loans, advances etc. the same would amount to be an exempt supply since interest is specifically exempted from the clutches of GST vide entry 27 of Notification No.12/2017-Central Tax (Rate). Since, one needs to consider the 'Aggregate Turnover' for the purpose of deriving the threshold of Rs. 2 Crore for audit and since the said aggregate turnover also includes exempt supplies, therefore in the given case HR Holding limited needs to consider the interest income. However, it is important to note that the dividends received are not on account of any supply of goods or services and therefore the same is not a transaction of supply at all and therefore the same needs to be excluded from the threshold of the aggregate turnover limit of Rs. 2 Crore. Since, the aggregate turnover is less than Rs. 2 Crores, there is no requirement for GST audit.

Question 9: *Unity Constructions Limited has an income from Sale of land worth Rs. 2 Crores and a Rental Income of Rs. 50 lakhs, whether it needs to undertake the GST Audit u/s 35(5)?*

Ans: Sale of land is not liable to tax under GST as the same is covered under schedule III of the GST Act being a transaction neither amounting to be a supply of goods nor as a supply of service. Since, one needs to consider the 'Aggregate Turnover' for the purpose of deriving the threshold of Rs. 2 Crore for audit and the said aggregate turnover includes taxable supplies, exempt supplies and export supplies. Therefore in the given case the transaction covered under schedule III being the nature of neither a supply or goods nor services would not fall within the meaning of either 'taxable supplies' or 'exempt supplies' or 'export supplies' and therefore the same needs to be excluded from the aggregate turnover limit of Rs. 2 Crore. Since, the aggregate turnover in the given case is less than Rs. 2 Crores, there is no requirement for GST audit.

Question 10: *Diversity Constructions Limited has an income from Sale of land worth Rs. 2 Crores and Sale of flats Post occupancy certificate of Rs. 10 Crores, whether it needs to undertake the GST Audit u/s 35(5)?*

Ans: Sale of land and sale of flats post receipt of the occupancy certificate are not liable to tax under GST as the same are covered under schedule III of the GST Act being a transaction neither amounting to a supply of goods nor as a supply of service. Since, one needs to consider the 'Aggregate Turnover' for the purpose of deriving the threshold of Rs. 2 Crore for audit and since the said aggregate turnover includes taxable supplies, exempt supplies and export supplies in the given case the transaction covered under schedule III being in the nature of neither a supply or goods nor services would not fall within the meaning of either 'taxable supplies' or 'exempt supplies' or 'export supplies' and therefore the same needs to be excluded from the threshold of the aggregate turnover limit of Rs. 2 Crore. Since, the aggregate turnover in the given case is less than Rs. 2 Crores, therefore there is no requirement for GST audit.

Question 11: *Shyam Lal Gupta is into a proprietorship business with a trade name Srinath collections. Its total aggregate turnover out of its trading business is Rs. 1.8 Crore. However, in FY 2017-18, Mr. Gupta also earns a rental income in his personal capacity of Rs. 30 Lakhs, whether Srinath collections would require to undertake the GST Audit u/s 35(5)?*

Ans: Definition of the term 'Aggregate Turnover' covers all the taxable, exempt supplies under the same Permanent Account Number (PAN) to be computed on all India basis and therefore in the given case assuming that Mr. Shyam Lal Gupta holds a single PAN for its trade and individual incomes, supplies from its trading business and also the rental income needs to be added for the purpose of determining liability to audit under GST. In the given case, since the same exceeds the threshold limit of Rs. 2 Crores, audit would be required.

Question 12: *Supreme limited has turnover exceeding Rs. 2 Crores and it has 10 GST registrations in various states, one of the registrations is in the state of New Delhi which is the ISD registration. Whether audit needs to be carried out for the State of New Delhi having the ISD registration?*

Ans: It is pertinent to note that the ISD registration in itself cannot undertake or report the activities of any supplies of goods or services or both, the said registration is taken merely to distribute the credits. Further, the reconciliation needs to be performed between the financial statements and the annual returns. In the given case, since as per section 44(1) of the GST Act, no annual return is required to be filed by ISD, the question of GST audit does not arise.

Question 13: *MRP Private limited has obtained registration under the GST Act in the month of Nov 2017, whereas its turnover for the period Jul 17 to Oct 17 was Rs. 20 Lakhs and turnover for the period Nov 17 to Mar 18 is Rs. 1.9 Crores, whether MRP Private Limited would require to undertake the GST Audit u/s 35(5)?*

Ans: The term 'aggregate turnover' not only includes taxable supplies but also covers exempt supplies and export of goods/services. One must now reckon the meaning of the term 'exempt supplies' which as per section 2(47) of the GST Act would also cover supply of any goods or services which attract nil rate of tax or which may be wholly exempt from tax and also includes non-taxable supply.

Although for the period Apr 17 to Oct 17, the assessee was not registered, it is reasonable to understand that in order to reckon the turnover limit prescribed for audit i.e., Rs. 2 crores one has to consider the turnover for the whole of the financial year (12 Months) which would also include the turnover in respect of supplies made prior to the registration and therefore since the aggregate turnover in the entire financial year exceeds Rs. 2 Crore, audit under GST would be required in this case. However, a suitable and immediate clarification from the Government(s) in this regard can help avoid unnecessary dispute on the issue.

Question 14: *XYZ Private limited is having a taxable turnover of Rs. 30 Crores, however it has not obtained any registration under GST and has also not complied with any of the provisions of the GST Act. Whether XYZ Private Limited would be required to get itself audited under the GST Act?*

Ans: Audit u/s 35(5) of the CGST Act to be conducted by CA or CWA is applicable only to a Registered Person. Unregistered Person who is liable to take registration under Section 25 of the CGST Act is a taxable person but the said unregistered Person is not a Registered Person defined under Section 2(94) of the CGST Act 2017. Hence in terms of Section 35(5) of the Act, it is not required to get the audit done.

However, under Section 63 of the CGST Act, where a taxable person (i.e. a person liable to take registration) fails to obtain registration, the proper officer may decide to assess the tax liability of the said taxable person to his best judgment for the relevant tax periods and issue an assessment order within a period of five years from the due date for filing of the annual return for the year to which the tax not paid relates to.

Question 15: *M/s ABC & Co. was registered under GST in the FY 17-18. However the business was closed in the FY 18-19 and it has surrendered its GST registration. Whether ABC & Co. would require to be subjected to GST Audit u/s 35(5) for the FY 17-18?*

Ans: Section 35(5) which prescribes the requirement for audit under GST states that 'Every Registered Person' having turnover above a prescribed limit would require to get the accounts audited under GST. In the given case, since ABC & Co. was a registered person in FY 17-18 and assuming that the turnover in the said financial year exceeded the prescribed limit and it would require to get the accounts audited under the GST Act.

Question 16: *M/s. Ramchand Jewellers obtains registration as a Casual Taxable person in the state of Delhi for the purpose of Business exhibition held in the state in the month of March 2018. Total value of sales made in the exhibition in the month of March 2018 amounts to Rs. 5 Crores. Whether Ramchand Jewellers would require to undertake the GST Audit u/s 35(5) for the FY 17-18?*

Ans: It is pertinent to note that the reconciliation needs to be performed between the financial statements and the annual returns. In the given case, since as per section 44(1) of the GST Act, no annual return is required to be filed by the assessee registered as a Casual Dealer under the GST Act, the question of GST audit does not arise for the state of Delhi. However, it is to be noted that M/s. Ramchand Jewellers would need to get the accounts audited under the GST Act for its registrations in other States and also the turnover of the supplies made through the casual dealer registration needs to be included for the purpose of determining the turnover threshold limit of Rs. 2 Crores for the audit.

22.3.2.5 Whether accounts to be separately audited under GST Act?

Section 35(5) provides that the registered person is required to furnish the audited annual accounts along with the reconciliation statement. Again, the point of discussion arises as to what is meant by the term 'audited annual accounts'. This question gains more significance from the point of view that the assessee may have already got his accounts audited under other laws i.e. Companies Act, Income Tax Act or any other law governing the audit of the accounts. When the audit has already been done, whether the books of account audited under those Acts are contemplated to be submitted or there has to be separate audit under GST Act. There is no specific mention about this under the Act or Rules made thereunder.

However, authors are of the view that when the audit has been done under any other laws for the time being in force, then the audited accounts under those Acts should be permitted to be submitted. This also finds support from part 1 of the

GSTR-9C which requires the auditor to mention as to whether accounts have been audited under any Act. Also, part B of the GSTR-9C has reference of the examination of balance sheet, profit and loss account and cash flow statement. As there is no requirement to prepare these statements/records under the GST Act, it cannot be said that these are required to be audited under the GST Law. However, the language of certification format in part B of the GSTR-9C indicates that there has to be separate GSTIN wise audit but it may be practically very difficult considering that the balance sheet, P&L and cash flow may not be prepared GSTIN wise.

Combined reading of the section 35(5), 44(2) along with forms notified, give rise to two situations, first being a case where entities are not required to be audited under any other statute. In such a situation, audit has to be carried out in terms of Section 35(5) and reconciliation statement has to be drawn under Section 44(2) duly certified. However, in case where the entity is already required to be audited under any other statutes like Companies Act, Income-tax Act, Co-operative Societies Act, etc., then the reconciliation statement can be drawn up by the same auditor who has audited the annual accounts. Alternatively, the reconciliation statement can be drawn up and certified by another Chartered Accountant or Cost Accountant. However, in case where the accounts are not audited under any other act, then the interpretation that the audit of annual accounts is to be carried under the GST Act must be suitably clarified by the Government to avoid the confusion.

22.3.2.6 Key Points to be noted in appointment of Chartered Accountant/Cost Accountant

Section 35(5) requires the accounts to be audited by a Chartered Accountant or a Cost Accountant. Therefore, assessees while appointing the professionals for the purpose of undertaking the mandatory audit under the GST Act must take cognizance of the important aspects which are discussed in subsequent paras.

Section 2(13) of the GST Act, defines the term "Chartered Accountant" means a chartered accountant as defined in clause (*b*) of sub-section (*1*) of section 2 of the Chartered Accountants Act, 1949.

Cost Accountant has not been defined under the GST Act. Meaning could be understood from CWA Act 1959 which is defined as member of institute of cost accountants of India.

In terms of Section 2(1)(b) of The Chartered Accountants Act (No. 38 of 1949) [as amended by The Chartered Accountants (Amendment) Act, 2006 (No. 9 of 2006) "Chartered Accountant" means a person who is a member of the Institute of Chartered Accountants of India.

Further, in terms of section 6 of The Chartered Accountants Act, no member of the Institute shall be entitled to practice whether in India or elsewhere unless he has obtained from the Council a certificate of practice. Therefore, only a chartered accountant holding certificate of practice can audit accounts.

Similarly, section 2(2) of The Chartered Accountants Act. provide that a member of the Institute is also deemed to be in practice when he provides services in partnership with chartered accountant(s). In view of this provision, the audit can also be conducted by a Firm of chartered accountants. In such a case, it would be necessary to state the name of the partner who has signed an audit report on behalf of the Firm.

Question 17: *Whether a Chartered Accountant is required to be registered as a GST practitioner for the purpose of certifying Form GSTR 9C?*

Ans: Reference must be given to section 48 of the CGST/SGST Act read with Rule 83(8) of the CGST/SGST Rules which authorizes a GST practitioner to undertake the following activities:

(a) furnish the details of outward and inward supplies;

(b) furnish monthly, quarterly, annual or final return;

(c) make deposit for credit into the electronic cash ledger;

(d) file a claim for refund; and

(e) file an application for amendment or cancellation of registration:

The GST Act/Rules do not vest a GST practitioner with the power to audit u/s 35(5). The power to audit is granted only to a Chartered Accountant or Cost Accountant. Therefore, a Chartered Accountant is not required to be registered as a GST practitioner for the purpose of certifying Form GSTR 9C.

Internal Auditor cannot be appointed as a Tax Auditor: The council of the Institute of Chartered Accountants of India, in its 378th meeting held on 28th September 2018 made an announcement clarifying that "an Internal Auditor of an entity cannot undertake GST Audit of the same entity". The announcement is made based on similar view taken in the context of audit under Income-tax Act or VAT audit being audits under statutes.

Preface to the standards on Internal Audit issued by ICAI in the scope of the standards on internal audit provides that ***'Internal audit'*** *is an independent management function, which involves a continuous and critical appraisal of the functioning of an entity with a view to suggest improvements thereto and add value to and strengthen the* ***overall governance mechanism*** *of the entity, including the entity's strategic risk management and internal control system. Internal audit, therefore, provides assurance that there is transparency in reporting, as a part of good governance.*

Term 'Internal auditor' must be understood accordingly based on the meaning and scope of the 'Internal Audit' function.

The doubt whether part of the internal audit function if carried out would also disentitle an auditor to conduct a GST audit may be clarified in due course of time by the Ethical Standards Board of both Bodies.

Procedure of appointment: There are no specific provisions either under the GST Act or rules made there under. However, as a matter of general principle, based on the request made by the assessee, auditor must send a proposal/offer letter clearly giving the scope and coverage of the audit, roles and responsibility of the auditors and the management and the proposed Fees.

Later, the registered person appointing the auditor must issue a letter of appointment appointing him/them as the GST Auditor. The said letter of appointment must be signed by a person competent to appoint such GST Auditor. In case of non-corporate entities, a letter from the authorized person may be obtained.

The letter of appointment must be in terms of "SA 210 – Terms of Audit Engagement" indicating the terms of the engagement, the scope and the extent of the coverage. The letter of appointment may stipulate the fee/remuneration. Normally, the said letter of appointment must be duly acknowledged by the GST auditor and accordingly a letter of acceptance of audit should be issued to the registered person *[Refer to Appendix 8 for suggested format of Engagement Letter]*.

Question 18: *Whether audit under the GST Act needs to be performed only by the statutory auditor's appointed under the Companies Act or other similar statutes who have signed the accounts of the company? Can it be done by any other Chartered Accountant in Practice?*

Ans: The GST audit can be conducted by the statutory auditor or by any other chartered accountant who is in full time practice or by a Firm of chartered accountants.

Question 19: *Can a member in part time practice be appointed as a statutory auditor under the GST Act?*

Ans: the ICAI Council had passed a Resolution, effective from 1st April 2005, that any member in part time practice (holding certificate of practice and also engaging himself in other business or occupation) is not entitled to perform attest function. Therefore, any member in part time practice cannot perform an audit under the GST Act even if a partner of Firm of chartered accountants.

Question 20: *In GST, a single assessee would be required to get the accounts audited for each of the registrations obtained. Therefore does an assessee need to appoint only single Chartered Accountant/Firm of Chartered Accountants as a GST Auditor or it can appoint various CA's/Firms of CA's as auditors for its different registrations?*

Ans: There is no specific provision or restriction in the GST Act or the rules. Therefore, an entity can appoint two or more chartered accountants for the purpose of audit under the GST Laws.

Question 21: *Whether audit is required in case where the assessee has cancelled the GST registration for the State or has surrendered the GST registration?*

Ans: Every registered person who had a valid registration during any part of the year is required to file the annual return. However, if the person has applied for surrender of the registration in the year which has been accepted by the department, such supplier may not have the access to the GST portal & accordingly may not be able to file annual return. Due to this practical difficulty clarification from government for manual submission/alternative procedure would be required.

Question 22: *A partnership firm is having an income of Rs. 5 crore from other sources and thereby it is not required to be audited under any other law including Income Tax Act. Whether there is requirement of audit under this Act?*

Ans: In the given case since the turnover exceeds Rs. 2 crore and though audit has not been conducted under any other law since the same is not required under any other law, it would be compulsory to get the accounts audited under the GST Act. The audited financial statements would be required to be given in Part B of GSTR-9C along with comment/ qualification of additional liability on unreconciled differences as per Part A of the GSTR-9C.

22.4 RELATIONSHIP BETWEEN PERIODICAL RETURNS (GSTR-1 & GSTR-3B), ANNUAL RETURNS (GSTR-9 & 9B) AND RECONCILIATION STATEMENT (GSTR-9C)

There are different reporting/compliance requirements under GST which could be either periodical compliance or annual compliance. Each person liable to be registered under GST is required to undertake such compliances. This also necessitates understanding of the nature of all the returns and interrelationship between them as explained below:

22.4.1 Form GSTR-1 – Declaration of details of outward supplies

This is a periodical submission of outward supplies made by registered taxable person. In this, the information is segregated between the B2B supplies, B2C large and small supplies, export, deemed exports, supplies to SEZ, non-taxable supplies, advances received and advances adjusted. Further, there are also tables giving details of debit notes and credit notes issued in respect of the supplies made including amendments made in the original invoices/debit notes/credit notes/advances, if any. The turnover/outward supply under different categories declared in GSTR-1 should match with the supplies as per books of account. There is no provision for the revision of GSTR-1 returns. Any errors or omissions therein have to be reported in the subsequent period. Proviso to section 37 (3) provides that the details of all such invoices may be disclosed latest by the due date of filing of the return for the month of the September of the succeeding financial year or annual return whichever is earlier.[1]

There could be many instances where there are errors or omissions in the financial year. All such corrections have to be made in the GSTR-1 of the period between April to September of succeeding FY. (For FY 2017-18, the corrections/additions/modifications have to be made in the period April 2018 to September 2018 GSTR-1 Returns). Later for FY 2017-18, the same was extended upto March 2019. Presuming corrections have been made in this interval, the total outward supply of the registered person for the FY 2017-18 would be determined by considering the GSTR-1 filed during period July 2017 to March 2019 (period of 21 months).[2]

22.4.2 Form GSTR-3B – Summary of outward supplies, input tax credit & payment of taxes

This is a return filed by the registered person giving summarized information of the outward supplies made, input tax credits availed, taxes and other sums payable and paid to the Government. Unlike GSTR-1, the information has to be given in summary form. It is needless to mention that the details of outward supply as submitted in the GSTR-1 should match with the details furnished in the GSTR-3B and any difference/deficiency in the one has to be corrected by submitting the details in the subsequent period returns but not later than the due date of filing of the Return for the month of September of the succeeding financial year. Similar to discussion made above in case of GSTR-1, the details of all transactions made in the last FY may be gauged from the GSTR-3B filed for the period July 2017 to September, 2018.

Importance of basic returns:

- The importance of the return whether GSTR 3B or 1 cannot be undermined. If incorrect information is filed, then additional liability has to be disclosed either by way of annual return or audit and taxes needs to be paid along with the applicable interest.
- If only GSTR 3B is filed which is providing no break up, it would also not serve the purpose. If only GSTR-1 is filed, then it means that payment have not been done but only invoices disclosed.
- If there are mistakes in the return and they have not been rectified by the due date of filing of the return for the month of September, then the same needs to be corrected in the annual return or in audit.

---

1 This restriction for the year 2017-18 is unfair with the changing law as on date not being understood by the tax authorities. Maybe challenged in the High Courts.

2 It is estimated that more than 25% have not been able to file the returns upto September 2018.

- If GSTR-3B and GSTR-1 are not reconciled, then this would come up and be reported in GSTR 9.
- Tax compliant assessees would be advised for the year 2018-19 to ensure that these mis-match or rectification of mistakes is carried out in the subsequent months return.

22.4.3 Form GSTR-9 – Annual return providing details submitted in GSTR 1 & GSTR 3B and books

The GSTR 1 & GSTR 3B have the limitation of not allowing revision. This makes it difficult for the business and government to ascertain the consolidated details of all transactions undertaken in the concerned period or financial year. Annual Return overcomes the limitation by consolidating all the returns filed in respect of transactions pertaining to the last year in single return and assesse can also carry out various adjustments, correct the errors and report the liability in accordance with the books of accounts and make the payment for the additional liability.

Similarly, in the Annual Return one can disclose the transactions which have been omitted to be disclosed in the periodical returns. It is not merely a consolidation of details submitted to the Government over a period of time through periodical returns. Hence as stated earlier the errors or omissions, if any, have to be carried out/adjusted in the periodical returns (i.e. GSTR-1 and GSTR-3B) and in case any adjustments still remain, then the same can be carried out by the assesse in the annual returns.

22.4.4 GSTR-9C – Audit/Reconciliation statement reconciling the differences between books of accounts and the annual returns and certifying the same

Filing of Annual Return does not mean that all the transactions have been reported therein. There is a possibility of many transactions which are shown in the audited financial statements but not in the Annual Return. These could arise due to different principles under GST Law *vis-a-vis* the principles adopted for preparation and presentation of books of account and financial statements or it could be due to under reporting of transactions in annual return. GSTR 9C is intended to provide the details of all such transactions which constitute difference between the books of account and the Annual Return.

Some of the transactions may be of temporary difference as under:

- Income accrued as per books of account but time of supply not occurred in the current FY),
- Foreign exchange transaction- due to difference in rates,
- Income accounted on cash basis but GST would be on accrual basis- Professionals like CA's have the option to do so etc.

Some others may be permanent difference as under:

- Non-monetary consideration which may not be considered for the purpose of preparation of books of account but considered for the purpose of valuation under GST).
- Stock transfer
- Cross charge for services across States
- Employee recoveries towards canteen facilities, transportation facilities etc.

The GSTR-9C is intended to reconcile all such differences and certification thereafter. In case of multi-locational assessees, the reconciliation and certification thereof become more challenging.

22.5 STRUCTURE OF RECONCILIATION STATEMENT IN FORM GSTR-9C

The reconciliation statement is required to be prepared in two parts. Part A is the reconciliation statement whereas Part B is the certification by the chartered accountant or the cost accountant who has drawn the Part A. The summarized discussion on both the parts is as under:

Part A: This part is further sub divided in 5 parts as discussed below:

Part I	Basic Details	
1	Financial Year	
2	GSTIN	
3	Legal Name	
4	Trade Name (if any)	
5	Liable to audit under any Act?	

Part II: This part requires the reconciliation of turnover declared in audited financial statement with the turnover declared in Annual return (GSTR 9). It has following Tables:

Sr. No	Particulars	Description
Table 5	Reconciliation of Gross Turnover	It requires making addition and subtraction of various specified categories of items from the gross turnover of the audited annual financial statement to arrive at the gross turnover as per the GSTR-9. The difference between two is reported as un-reconciled turnover.

Sr. No	Particulars	Description
Table 6	Reasons for Un-Reconciled difference in Annual Gross Turnover	The auditor is required to explain the reasons of the un-reconciled differences in the annual gross turnover.
Table 7	Reconciliation of Taxable Turnover	This table requires reconciliation of taxable turnover as declared in the audited annual financial statement with the GSTR-9 taxable turnover. The difference between Table 5 and Table 7 is that in case of Table 5, the reconciliation is between gross turnover (which includes taxable as well as non-taxable turnover) whereas Table 7 provides for reconciliation between taxable turnover.
Table 8	Reasons for Un-Reconciled difference in Taxable Turnover	Explanation of reason of difference between taxable turnover is required to be given in this Table.

Part III: This part deals with reconciliation of taxes paid. It has following tables:

Sr. No	Particulars	Description
Table 9	Reconciliation of rate wise liability and amount payable thereon	This table requires reconciliation of GST rate wise liability and amount payable thereon. The turnover in the audited annual financial statement may be liable to tax at different rates. There is need to provide details of taxable value and tax payable for goods or services supplied at various rates. This amount is required to be compared with the total turnover and tax liability declared in the Annual Return.
Table 10	Reasons for un-reconciled payment of amount	This table requires auditor to explain the reasons for un-reconciled payment of amount
Table 11	Additional amount payable but not paid (due to reasons specified under Tables 6,8 and 10 above)	This table is summary of additional amount payable by virtue of differences which have arisen in the Table 6, 8 and 10 above. The tax declared under this table has to be paid in cash.

Part IV: This part deals with reconciliation of Input Tax Credits as per books of account and ITC as declared in the Annual Return. Following are tables required to be reported/reconciled with respect to the ITC:

Sr. No	Particulars	Description
Table 12	Reconciliation of Net Input Tax Credit (ITC)	Reconciliation of net input tax credits as per audited annual financial statements for the GSTIN vis-a-vis Input Tax Credit availed in the GSTR-9 suitably adjusted for the credits pertaining to the one financial year availed in different financial year. The difference between the two is un-reconciled ITC.
Table 13	Reasons for un-reconciled difference in ITC	Reasons for un-reconciled ITC have to be declared in the Table 13.
Table 14	Reconciliation of ITC declared in Annual Return (GSTR-9) with ITC availed on expenses as per audited Financial Statement of books of account	This table requires submission of details as to the credits availed on various categories of expenses as per audited annual financial statement or books of account. This detail has to be reconciled with the credits availed in the GSTR-9
Table 15	Reason for un-reconciled difference in ITC	The reason of difference in credits as per books of account and GSTR-9 as arrived under Table 14 has to be reported under this table.
Table 16	Tax payable on un -reconciled difference in ITC (due to reasons specified in 13 and 15 above)	This part requires the auditor to comment upon the tax payable on un-reconciled differences in ITC which has arisen in table 13 and Table 15.

Part V: This part requires auditor to recommend additional liability arising due to non-reconciliation. The additional liability has to be mentioned separately under various categories of rates of tax, input tax credits, interest, late fees, penalty, any other amount not included in the GSTR-9, erroneous refund to be paid back, outstanding demands to be settled and others if any.

Part B: This part provides the format of certification by the auditor. Format I is applicable when the certification is done either by chartered accountant/cost accountant who had conducted the audit of the accounts whereas format II is applicable where the reconciliation statement (FORM GSTR-9C) is drawn up by a person other than the person who had conducted the audit of the accounts.

22.6 STEP BY STEP UNDERSTANDING OF FORM GSTR 9C

Since, various information has to be filled into the Form GSTR 9C, therefore this section provides the step by step understanding of form GSTR 9C along with analysis of the specific issues and challenges and its resolutions as explained below.

22.6.1 Part I – Basic details

Pt I	Basic Details	
1	Financial Year	
2	GSTIN	
3A	Legal Name	<Auto>
3B	Trade Name (if any)	<Auto>
4	Are you liable for audit under any Act? << Please Specify>>	

Serial No.	Instructions in the Form
1	*It is mandatory to file all your FORM GSTR-1, FORM GSTR-3B and FORM GSTR -9 for the FY 2017-18 before filing this return. The details for the period between July 2017 to March 2018 are to be provided in this statement for the financial year 2017-18. The reconciliation statement is to be filed for every GSTIN separately.*
2	*The reference to current financial year in this statement is the financial year for which the reconciliation statement is being filed for.*

Introduction

This part requires the submission of the basic information of the assessee i.e. the financial year, GST No., Trade Name, Legal Name, liability to audit under any act. The same is as explained below.

Financial Year: The financial year for which the Reconciliation statement is being submitted must be filled here.

GSTIN: GSTIN means the "Goods and Services tax Identification Number" of the tax payer or the Registered Person. Each tax payer, on his successful registration would be assigned a State-wise PAN based 15-digit GSTIN. The first 2 digits of the said GSTIN would represent the State code as per the Indian Census 2011. The next 10 digits would be the PAN of the tax payer. The 13th digit would be based on the number of registrations within a State, while the 14th digit would be assigned based on the nature of the business of the Registered person. The 15th

digit is a check code which can be a "numeral" or an "alphabet". Since, the reconciliation statement cannot be filed at an entity level and the same needs to be separately filed by each registered person, such registered person is required to submit the GSTIN in this field. Auditor can cross verify the GST No. based on the registration certificate issued in Form REG 06.

Legal Name: Once the GSTIN is filled in by the registered person, the legal name would auto-populate based on the details as submitted in the GST common portal. Assessee needs to re-validate the details so auto-populated.

Trade Name: Once the GSTIN is filled in by the registered person, the trade name would auto-populate based on the details as submitted in the GST common portal. Assessee needs to re-validate the details so auto-populated.

Are you liable to audit under any Act: If the registered person is liable to audit under any Act (other than GST Act), he has to mention the same in this part of the format. The audit under any other Act may include the Companies Act, Income Tax Act etc. Therefore, in case assessee has got the Books of accounts audited as per the requirement of the any act, then details of the same must be appropriately mentioned in this field.

Analysis

Legal Name v/s Trade Name: A business name is the official name of the person or entity which is used on the Government forms and applications. It is also determined by how you set up your business i.e. if the business is operated as a sole proprietorship, the legal name can be a full name of the proprietor or by any other name kept as a legal name. In case of the partnership concerns, the business name is written in the partnership agreement. Further, in case of companies, the name may end with Private Limited, Limited, LLP etc. The legal name is a part of the memorandum and articles of the association of the companies.

Sometimes, business owner wants to operate under a name other than the company's legal name which is known as a 'Trade Name'. It is different from a business's legal name. Business owners can use a trade name for advertising and sales purposes. The trade name is the name the public sees, like on signboards and the internet. The business name and trading name can be different. A trade name does not need to include Limited, Pvt Ltd, LLP etc. For example, McD is a trade name. The company's legal business name is McD Inc. Bottom line is that if an entity wants to operate under a different name which it wants to be recognised as in public, than the business name, then it needs register the trade name.

Different periodicity of the financial statement: Generally, the financial year would commence from April of the year to March of the subsequent year. However, in case any assessee wishes to adopt different financial year other than April to March, then the same can also be opted for in case of companies by making an application to the Companies law Board and in case of other constitutions such as Partnership firms, societies, AOP etc. as per the need of the assessee. In the given case, since reconciliation has to be performed on the audited financial statements, it would be difficult for such companies to prepare reconciliation statement based on the audited financial year other than April to March. Therefore, such entities would have to prepare an interim financial statement duly audited for the period April to March and accordingly the reconciliation statement must be prepared or another option would be to file the certification on belated basis once the financial statements are fully audited for entire financial year being reviewed.

The assessee has the option of adopting different financial year in the Companies Act 2013 based on the practice of foreign holding company. He could adopt the financial year which can be even January to December. However for the purpose of income tax audit compliance, the audit has to be conducted for April to March period under the Income tax provisions. Therefore, in most cases, the GST auditor may find the audited financial statements for the period April to March either in Companies Act 2013 or in Income tax Act 1961 or both which could be relied on for GST audit certification.

Reconciliation statement to be separately provided GSTIN wise: It is important to note here that the reconciliation statement needs to be separately submitted for each GSTIN of the entity. For ex: If a company has multiple registrations within the state, even then it has to submit the reconciliation statement for each registration even though covered within the same state.

Mandate of audit of the Books of accounts for GST Audit: The provisions in section 35(5) read with section 44(2) provides for the requirement of the auditing of the accounts and submission of the same with the reconciliation statement. In other words, the GST auditor cannot reconcile the Annual returns with the unaudited financial statements. Therefore, whenever the audit has not been done under any other Act, then it would not be possible for the GST auditor to perform the audit under the GST Act as the reconciliation under the GST Act can be certified only by keeping audited financial statements as the base. In the event that there is no need to get the audit done under any law in force the reasons for the same may be recorded.

The GST auditor needs to suggest to the assessee to prepare the audited financial statements and get the books of accounts audited. He would then based on that, commence the GST Audit. This is also evident from the requirement as laid out in Part B of the certification in Form 9C which requires the GST Auditor to comment upon the qualification, observations etc. on the audit of accounts and also submit the audited financial statement, cash flow statement etc.

The audit under others laws may have been conducted by another professional. In such a case the auditor must conduct a due diligence and conclude that the earlier audit was done properly. After that he can rely on such audited statements and disclose such fact in his report.

22.6.2 Part II – Reconciliation of turnover declared in the audited annual financial statement with turnover declared in Annual Return (GSTR 9)

Pt II	Reconciliation of turnover declared in the Audited Annual Financial Statement with turnover declared in Annual Return (GSTR 9)

Serial No.	Instructions in the Form
Part II	*Part II consists of reconciliation of the annual turnover declared in the audited Annual Financial Statement with the turnover as declared in the Annual Return furnished in FORM GSTR-9 for this GSTIN.*

Introduction

This part requires the reconciliation of turnover as declared in the books of accounts/financial statement with the turnover as declared in the Annual Return. Here, the reconciliation of turnover starts from the financial statements and arrives at the annual returns. For multi locational units, this turnover has to be taken from the audited financial statement of that particular GSTIN (management can derive this) and then the adjustments must be carried out to the turnover to arrive at the turnover as disclosed in the annual returns.

Analysis

It is pertinent to note that turnover as per the financial statement may have followed the accounting principles based on the Generally Accepted Accounting Policies (GAAP's) adopted by the organization on a consistent basis as discussed in 22.4 above. The basic tenets of disclosure as per accounting and GST are different.

Sl. No. 5 – Reconciliation of Gross Turnover

5	Reconciliation of Gross Turnover

Introduction

This field requires reconciliation of the turnover on gross basis i.e. without considering any exemptions or non-taxable or zero rated supplies. The idea behind this reconciliation is to identify the difference on account of any values of supplies (Taxable or exempted) on gross basis which has been missed for consideration in the annual returns.

This reconciliation is only on the outward supplies and the values pertaining to reverse charge need not be considered here. Since, this is only first part of the reconciliation exercise all the reconciliation differences noted here may not straight away lead to additional tax liability. Since the reconciliation here is on gross turnover basis, it is possible that the turnover is exempted or the same is export supply etc. Further, it is also possible that there is a reconciliation difference at gross turnover level but actually the tax element on such tax base has been rightly paid by the assessee. Therefore, auditor must be vigilant while computing the reconciliation and more so updating the reasons for the differences. A holistic and a 360 degree view of the reconciliation differences must be taken into account by the auditor before giving the reasons for differences and recommending the additional tax liability.

The reconciliation difference can be on account of various reasons, auditor needs to identify the differences, its reasons, quantify the same and fill such details in the respective bucket of the specific differences as specified in column 5A to 5N of Form GSTR 9C. In case, auditor is of the view that the quantified difference is not falling in any of the specific columns, then the same needs to be updated in column 5O (residuary column) of the reconciliation statement. Further, in case the difference is leading to any additional tax liability, then instead of adjusting the same in column 5O, the auditor needs to keep the difference open and reasons for the same must be given in Column 6 of the form.

Sl. No. 5A – Turnover (Including exports) as per audited financial statements for the state/UT (for multi-GSTIN units under same pan the turnover shall be derived from the Audited Financial Statement)

5A	Turnover (Including exports) as per audited financial statements for the state/UT (for multi-GSTIN units under same pan the turnover shall be derived from the Audited Financial Statement)	

Serial No.	Instructions in the Form
5A	*The turnover as per the audited Annual Financial Statement shall be declared here. There may be cases where multiple GSTINs (State-wise) registrations exist on the same PAN. This is common for persons/entities with presence over multiple States. Such persons/entities, will have to internally derive their GSTIN wise turnover and declare the same here. This shall include export turnover (if any). It may be noted that reference to audited Annual Financial Statement includes reference to books of accounts in case of persons/entities having presence over multiple States.*

Introduction

In this field auditor is required to declare the turnover as per the audited financial statements for the respective State/UT or the GSTIN under the same PAN.

Analysis

Meaning of the term 'Turnover' is not defined in the GST act or the rules made thereunder. 'Turnover in the State' is defined in section 2(112) of the CGST Act.

However, in this field Turnover as per audited financial statements is required to be disclosed. We would understand the general meaning of the term 'turnover' in order to understand the requirement of disclosure in this field.

As per Collins Dictionary, the term 'Turnover' is defined as *"The turnover of a company is the value of the goods or services sold during a particular period of time."*

As per Business Dictionary, the term 'Turnover' is defined as *"The annual sales volume net of all discounts and sales taxes. (2) The number of times an asset (such as cash, inventory, raw materials) is replaced or revolves during an accounting period."*

In the "Guidance Note on Terms Used in Financial Statements" published by the Institute, the expression "Sales Turnover" (Item 15.01) has been defined as under:- *"The aggregate amount for which sales are effected or services rendered by an enterprise. The term `gross turnover' and `net turnover' (or gross sales and net sales) are sometimes used to distinguish the sales aggregate before and after deduction of returns and trade discounts.*

The Guide to Company Audit issued by the Institute in the year 1980, while discussing "sales", stated as follows: *"Total turnover, that is, the aggregate amount for which sales are effected by the company, giving the amount of sales in respect of each class of goods dealt with by the company and indicating the quantities of such sales for each class separately. Note (i) The term 'turnover' would mean the total sales after deducting therefrom goods returned, price adjustments, trade discount and cancellation of bills for the period of audit, if any. Adjustments which do not relate to turnover should not be made e.g. writing off bad debts, royalty etc. Where excise duty is included in turnover, the corresponding amount should be distinctly shown as a debit item in the profit and loss account."*

Details of incomes to be disclosed: Income is defined in the framework for preparation and presentation of financial statements (issued by ICAI) as increase in economic benefits during the accounting period in the form of inflows or enhancements of assets or decrease of liabilities that result in increase in equity, other than those relating to contributions from equity participants.

Income encompasses revenue and gains. Since the details of turnover as per financial statements is required to be filled in here, auditor needs to ascertain whether the income is disclosed as per Ind AS 11 on Recognition, measurement, presentation & disclosure of revenues & Ind AS 11 for recognition, measurement etc. for Construction contracts. In general terms, the meaning of the term 'turnover' would cover the direct revenues from operations i.e. Sale of products, services and other operating revenues.

However, apart from the turnover of revenues from the operations, an entity may have sources of income from non-operational areas as well. An illustrative list of various incomes that an organisation would have from other sources are as follows"

- Interest & Dividends income;
- Royalties;
- Income from sale of investments;
- Other Direct & Indirect Incomes;
- Other miscellaneous incomes.

As per the meaning of the turnover as explained above, it is mainly the turnover of sales i.e. the income from operations would need to be disclosed here in Sl. No. 5A of the reconciliation statement. The revenues from other sources can be disclosed in the various other relevant fields as explained below. If the same does not fit in any specific field then the same needs to be disclosed in the residuary field i.e. Sl. No. 5O of the reconciliation statement. However, for the ease of computation of the reconciliation statement one may also do a summation of all the incomes (operational and others) as reported in the income statement of the audited financial statements and be disclosed in full here whether or not such incomes are taxable or exempted or exported etc.

The possible omissions which need to be included could be notice pay recoveries, credits journal entries in the debtors/income accounts, debit journal entries in creditors/income accounts, all schedule I items, interest and no supply items in schedule III among others.

Gross Turnover to be disclosed: It is to be noted that the details of the turnover must be disclosed on Gross basis i.e. before deduction on account of discounts. Any trade discounts given are to be later adjusted in the subsequent fields.

Turnover to be considered for FY 2017-18: It is important to note that since the reconciliation is w.r.t the supplies made in the GST regime, the turnover for the period between Apr'17 to Mar'18 must be considered here and later the turnover pertaining to the Pre-GST regime (i.e. Apr' 17 to Jun' 17) would be excluded vide Sl. No. 5G below. In case of assessees who have not migrated from the existing tax regime and have obtained for new registration under GST at a later point in time after 1st July 2017 due to various reasons (i.e. exempted, below threshold limit etc.) then such assessees also may disclose the turnover recognized in the financial statements from the beginning of the financial year i.e. 17-18 even though they have registered under GST at a later date and any difference arising thereby in the turnover as disclosed in the Annual returns can either be disclosed in any other specific field or in the residuary field viz., 5O or it would need to be explained in Column 6 based on the turnover of the entire financial year.

Turnover to be considered in case of multiple GSTIN's: Audited financial statements are prepared at an entity level for each PAN and the same are not audited separately at each GSTIN level. However, the reconciliation in the GST law is separately required for each registration number. Therefore in order to reconcile the differences one has to bifurcate the audited financial statements for each GSTIN so that the exercise of reconciliation can be smoothly conducted. Here, it is very important to note that auditor is entrusted to draw the reconciliation statement at each GSTIN level and since the annual returns are also prepared at each GSTIN level, therefore in order to perform the comparison and the reconciliation thereof with the turnover declared in the annual returns, auditor needs to bifurcate the turnover as per the audited financial statements at each GSTIN level. Since the financial statements are audited at the entity level and the turnover reflected therein is also at an entity level, therefore the question that arises is how can the auditor identify and bifurcate the turnover at each GSTIN level. Various methods that an auditor can adopt in this regard are as under:

(1) **Splitting of the Financial Statements:** Auditor must demand the financial statements i.e. Profit & loss account and Balance sheet at each GSTIN level from the assessee. Once this is received, auditor needs to compare such financials being the true and correct representative with the audited set of the financial statements. Upon achieving an absolute assurance over such split financial statements, auditor can then pick the details of turnover from such financial statements and update the same in this column.

(2) **Splitting of the Trial Balance:** Auditor must demand the trial balance at each GSTIN level. Once the trial balance is obtained at each GSTIN level, auditor needs to map all the trial balances and match the same with the audited financial statements which gives auditor an absolute assurance over the trial balance being a true and correct representative of the audited financial statements. Once this is achieved, auditor can then pick the details of various revenues/incomes from the trial balance and update the same in this column.

(3) **Splitting of GL's in the Chart of Accounts:** Since, this being a first year of implementation of GST, it may be possible that accounting modules/software of the assessee have not been configured in a manner to allow extraction of the trial balance for each GSTIN, this is more so in cases where there is no cost category bifurcation done at the preliminary stage of passing the accounting entry itself or in case where the bifurcation can at most be done at a state level but the multiple GST registrations have been obtained by the auditee in the same state. In such a situation, auditor needs to verify the working papers and various schedules annexed to the audited financial statements and accordingly must identify the various GL accounts that having impact on the turnovers declared in the audited financial statements. Once the list of GL accounts are identified, auditor needs to then obtain the breakup of such GL accounts with various additions and subtractions at each GSTIN level. Once auditor gets an absolute assurance over the GL's pertaining to the turnover being a true and correct representative of the audited financial statements auditor can then pick the details from such GL's and update the same in this column.

(4) **Splitting at Invoicing level:** Many assessees keep different sequencing of the invoice numbers issued at various states for ex: Invoicing series for Maharashtra is MH/17-18/001 whereas the series maintained for one at Gujarat is GJ/17-18/001, similarly the bifurcation can also be based on any other criteria. Auditor needs to identify the category of bifurcation and based on the listing of the various sales invoices issued, the turnovers for each such cost category reflecting a separate GST number can be bifurcated. Auditor can place reliance on the working papers of the audited financial statements to avoid discrepancies and ensure completeness of this exercise. Further, the impact of supplementary invoices, debit notes and credit notes must also be given effect to while achieving the turnover. This exercise can be more cumbersome for the auditor and therefore must be applied only in case where the above methods are not adaptable.

(5) **Segment Reporting of the Audited Financial Statements:** Accounting Standard 17 on "Segment Reporting" or Ind-AS 108 on "Operating Segments" as the case maybe, require companies to disclose various segment wise reporting of the information. Since, the legal requirement of obtaining separate registrations under GST is also linked to the business verticals as per the above standards, therefore auditor must review this information provided by the companies statutory auditors and the relevant working papers therein which may provide the GST auditor with an adequate information to bifurcate the turnovers at the GSTIN level.

Note: It must be noted that providing of the proper details of the turnover at each GSTIN level should be the responsibility of the management and auditor needs to agree the same with management in the engagement letter entered into for this purpose and can also be a part of management representation letter to be obtained from the assessee. Auditor needs to perform various substantive audit procedures to ensure correctness of the information so provided and accordingly place reliance on the same.

The auditor should get the following information from the management:

(i) GSTIN wise gross trial balance, where available or certificate of all GSTIN wise turnover matched to the audited statements.

(ii) Major contracts for implication of cross charge.

(iii) Cost centre wise accounts or MIS.

(iv) Transactions between the foreign branch and the entities in India.

(v) Sharing of intangibles, shared expenses (AMC rentals, insurance etc.) across the entities.

Where above information is not available ensure it is part of the management representation.

He may further communicate with the other GSTIN auditors if different firms appointed.

Multiple GST Auditors for the single entity: It is important to note that the above activity becomes more challenging when an entity appoints different auditors for performing audit for its various GST numbers. In such a situation auditor needs to communicate with the other joint auditors and accordingly the above comparison must be made so that the error of reporting of turnovers twice in various GSTIN's and also the chances of turnovers getting missed to be reported in all the GSTIN's is effectively avoided. Auditor needs to take cognizance of SA 299 issued by ICAI on *"Responsibility of Joint Auditors"* and SA 600 on *"Using the work of another auditor." [Refer Chapter 11 of this book for more details on the same]*

Effective usage of Technology: Since, this exercise of segregating the details at each GSTIN level can involve high time & efforts and would be less reliable when performed manually. Therefore, auditor should aid the usage of technology in this exercise such as effective usage of various MS excel tools including Pivot tables, Vlookup, Macros etc. Auditor can tag the respective category wise bifurcation of various profit centres at each entry and transaction level which forms as basis for segregation of the financial statements. Auditor can also look at generation of various reports from the accounting system of the assessee and apply the same on various external tools and software which can use various logics simultaneously and throw the desired results. The more advanced usage of the technology can be integration of these software within the assessee's accounting system itself such that the accounting system and the software perform the above logics on live basis and the reports can be accessed directly from the systems software on need basis as and when required.

Precautions to be noted in usage of Technology: Although, usage of technology can ease the function of the auditor but is important to note that the same comes with many inherent risks and limitations. One must note that any technological tool or software works on the principle of "Garbage In Garbage Out", therefore if the data entry itself passed in the assessee's accounting system or the report being uploaded onto the software is itself wrong, then no software can help ease in the performance of the work, in fact it can lead to substantial discrepancies in the audit. Even if the correct and proper reports or data is been picked up by the software, auditor must take note that various bugs in the software and improper testing of the same can lead to incorrect output information being thrown by such software. Therefore, auditor needs to perform a thorough testing of the input data and the output information provided by the software. Auditor can use the system generated reports only when he gets the substantially absolute level of assurance on the same.

Cash system of Accounting: In case of cash system of accounting, auditor may disclose the turnover as followed by the assessee on receipt basis. However, since the payment of taxes and declaration of the details thereon by the assessee is as per the principles of Time of supply under the GST Act, it may lead to higher reconciliation differences.

Turnover of the Foreign Branch/Operations: Although, the turnover pertaining to the foreign branch or operations of the assessee may not be leviable to GST, in order to complete the entire reconciliation cycle with the financial statements and to map the same fully, it is suggested to include the said turnover details here and the same can be excluded again in Sl. No. 5O of this form. The turnover could be considered in the report of branch/office which is directly concerned with such foreign branch/operations.

Question 23: *What is the meaning of turnover as per audited annual financial statement? Does it includes the recovery made which are netted from the expenses and accordingly do not appear in the credit side of P&L Account?*

Ans: The term 'Turnover is not defined under the GST Act or rules made thereunder. The Guide to Company Audit issued by the Institute in the year 1980, while discussing "sales", stated as follows: "Total turnover, that is, the aggregate amount for which sales are effected by the company, giving the amount of sales in respect of each class of goods dealt with by the company and indicating the quantities of such sales for each class separately. Note (i) The term 'turnover' would mean the total sales after deducting therefrom goods returned, price adjustments, trade discount and cancellation of bills for the period of audit, if any. Adjustments which do not relate to turnover should not be made e.g. writing off bad debts, royalty etc. Where excise duty is included in turnover, the corresponding amount should be distinctly shown as a debit item in the profit and loss account." Taking clue form the above, it can be stated that Turnover would not include the recovery made which are netted off from the expenses.

Question 24: ABC Ltd has a branch office outside India. Whether auditor is required to report and comment upon the liability on transactions with the branch office?

Ans: In this case the branch office located outside India falls outside the taxable territory, and accordingly the transactions of such branch office are not liable for GST, therefore there would not be requirement for any audit/ certification as per the law. However, the transactions pertaining to the branch office outside India would be included in the financial statements of the head office in India. If the turnover pertaining to the branch is included in the head office turnover, the reconciliation statement would be prepared after excluding the turnover of branch from the head office turnover in the Table 5A. However, alternatively if it is not excluded, the adjustment should be made for the turnover of the branch in the Table 5O. As far as the transaction with the branch offices are concerned, it tantamount to be a distinct person and there would be a liability to pay tax under the schedule I of the GST Act, even if there is no consideration. Such transactions have to be reported under table 5C of GSTR-9C.

Sl. No. 5B – Unbilled revenue at the beginning of the Financial Year – [to be added]

5B	Unbilled Revenue at the beginning of Financial Year	(+)	

Serial No.	Instructions in the Form
5B	*Unbilled revenue which was recorded in the books of accounts on the basis of accrual system of accounting in the last financial year and was carried forward to the current financial year shall be declared here. In other words, when GST is payable during the financial year on such revenue (which was recognized earlier), the value of such revenue shall be declared here.* *(For example, if rupees Ten Crores of unbilled revenue existed for the financial year 2016-17, and during the current financial year, GST was paid on rupees Four Crores of such revenue, then value of rupees Four Crores rupees shall be declared here)*

Introduction

The recognition of revenue in financial statements is as per the standards prescribed in this regard wherein once it is probable that any future economic benefits associated with the item of revenue would flow to the entity and the amount of revenue can be measured with reliability, then having regard to the GAAP of the organization, the revenue can be recognized.

There may be possibility that the revenue recognition criteria are met under the relevant accounting standard and hence revenue is recognised in the books of account but invoice has not been raised to the recipient as the milestone of raising of invoice as per contractual terms has not arisen. To the contrary, as far as GST law is concerned, the provisions of time of supply state that the liability in respect of supply of goods/service would arise upon issuance of invoice. Further, explanation (1) to section 12(2) of the GST Act states that "supply" would be deemed to have been made to the extent it is covered by the invoice or, as the case may be, the payment.

Therefore, invoice in respect of unbilled revenue items would be raised in the current financial year (for ex: FY 17-18) whereas revenue on the same item must have already been recognized in the books of accounts in the previous financial year (for ex: FY 16-17), Since GST liability would be created for and paid on this transaction only when the tax invoice is raised (assuming no advances received), the details of the same would also be disclosed in the Annual Returns of FY 17-18. Therefore, such items of revenues must be added in field 5B of Form 9C in order to reconcile them with the annual returns.

The possibility of unbilled revenues could be in the following illustrated activities:

- Long term software development,
- BPO Companies who bill at the start of the next month,
- Yearly, quarterly, monthly Rentals/Lease premiums,
- Insurance contracts,
- Continuous construction contracts
- Supply of RMC/oil through pipelines,
- AMCs or service contracts etc.

However, following the prudent principle of accounting the revenue needs to be recognized in the same financial year to the extent of the work completed in that year (July 17 to March 18). The value of the unbilled revenue which is measured with reliability and such details is available and considered in the financials needs to be declared in this column as GST would be only paid on invoicing.

Analysis

Tax invoices raised between April 17 to June 17: It is possible that in respect of some supply transactions the revenue is recognized in the previous financial year i.e. FY 16-17 and it remains to be an opening unbilled revenue. In this situation, such items even though being unbilled revenues at the beginning of the financial year must not be disclosed here as the tax invoice in its respect is issued prior to the implementation of the GST.

Tax invoice not raised even in the subsequent financial year: It may be possible that an item is recognized as revenue in the books of accounts based on the principles of revenue recognition in the previous financial year. This remains as opening unbilled revenue at the beginning of the financial year. However in case the invoice is not raised on such opening item even in the subsequent financial year, then such items also does not warrant disclosure in this field. Instructions issued in this regard clearly state the disclosure is required for those revenue items which are considered for GST in the current financial year.

Segregation of unbilled revenue in case of audit of multiple GSTINs: The details of unbilled revenue as reflecting in the previous year's financial statements and in the Notes to accounts for entity a whole needs to bifurcate the unbilled revenue at each GSTIN level. Auditor may use various methodology of bifurcation as explained above for this purpose. Further, if an entity may appoints different auditors for performing an audit for its various GST numbers, in such a situation auditor needs to communicate with the other joint auditors. Auditor needs to take cognizance of SA 299 issued by ICAI on "Responsibility of Joint Auditors" and SA 600 on "Using the work of another auditor." *[Refer Chapter 11 of this book for more details on the same]*

The disclosure that one is relying on another auditor may be made.

Reference in financials/returns

The details of the unbilled revenue can be obtained from the Notes to Accounts of the financial statements or from the balance Sheet Schedule. Unbilled revenue would appear in the profit and loss account of the previous year. In order to get information of unbilled revenue at the beginning of Financial Year, reference may be had to previous year's audited financial statements.

Sl. No. 5C - Unadjusted Advances at the end of the Financial year - [to be added]

5C	Unadjusted Advances at the end of the Financial Year	(+)	

Serial No.	Instructions in the Form
5C	*Value of all advances for which GST has been paid but the same has not been recognized as revenue in the audited Annual Financial Statement shall be declared here.*

Introduction

The liability to pay GST arises in accordance with the principles of time of supply as given under section 12 and 13 of the GST Act. The liability arises on the earlier of receipt of money or raising of invoice. However, presently the tax on advances is payable only in case of supply of services and the same is suspended in case of supply of goods w.e.f. 13th October 2018 vide Notification 40/2017-CT Dated 13.10.2017. This was for assessees engaged in supply of goods having aggregate turnover of less than Rs.1.5 Crores and later the same was extended to all the assesees in the category of supply of goods vide Notification 66/2017-CT Dated 15.11.2017. Therefore, in case of any supplies on which GST is paid on advances and the invoice for such supply is also issued in the same financial year, then there is no implication of reconciliation. However, in all cases where GST is paid on the advances and no tax invoice is issued or tax invoice is partially issued up to the end of the financial year, then details of such advances need to be reflected here.

Relevant Statutory Provisions

For Supply of Goods:

Sec 12(2): The time of supply of goods shall be the earlier of the following dates, namely:

(a) *the date of issue of invoice by the supplier or the last date on which he is required, under sub-section (1) of section 31, to issue the invoice with respect to the supply; or*

(b) *the date on which the supplier receives the payment with respect to the supply:*

The Government issued NN 40/2017-CT dated 13th October 2017 in terms of section 148 of CGST Act to relax Registered Persons having aggregate turnover less than Rs. 1.5 crores from paying tax on such advances. This facility was extended to all Registered Persons without threshold limit vide NN 66/2017-Central tax, dated 15th Nov 2017 but only in case of supply of goods.

For Supply of services:

Sec 13(2): The time of supply of services shall be the earliest of the following dates, namely: —

(a) the date of issue of invoice by the supplier, if the invoice is issued within the period prescribed under section 31 or the date of receipt of payment, whichever is earlier; or

(b) the date of provision of service, if the invoice is not issued within the period prescribed under section 31 or the date of receipt of payment, whichever is earlier; or

(c) the date on which the recipient shows the receipt of services in his books of account, in a case where the provisions of clause (a) or clause (b) do not apply:

Explanation—For the purposes of clauses (a) and (b)—

(i) the supply shall be deemed to have been made to the extent it is covered by the invoice or, as the case may be, the payment;

(ii) *"the date of receipt of payment" shall be the date on which the payment is entered in the books of account of the supplier or the date on which the payment is credited to his bank account, whichever is earlier.* Analysis Advance received and invoice issued in the same FY: In case where the advance on which tax is paid gets adjusted in the same financial year by way of issuance of invoice against such advance, then no disclosure is warranted here as the details of the invoice issued would have already been recognised as a revenue and disclosed in Sl. No. 5A above. It is to be noted that advances received can be for various purposes. Therefore, the advances on which GST is liable to be paid should only be considered for the adjustment. The various types of advances and whether or not to be included / excluded are as follows:

(a) Advance received in respect of services for which the supply has not been made as on 31st March 2018. Since, in case of these advances, revenue is not recognized in the books of accounts, but it is offered to tax for GST – To be included for the purpose of adjustment.

(b) Advance received for Goods before 15th Nov 2017 and the supply of goods is not completed as on 31st March 2018. Since, in case of these advances, revenue is not recognized in the books of accounts, but it is offered to tax for GST – to be included for the purpose of adjustment.

(c) Advance received for exempted services as on 31st March 2018. Since GST is not applicable on these transactions, it does not tantamount any adjustment.

(d) Advance received for goods after 15th Nov 2017. Since GST is not applicable on these advances as being specifically deferred to the date of issue of invoice, it does not tantamount any adjustment.

(e) Financial advances (loans) received which are not adjustable against any services. Since these are capital transactions and not being received against any supply of goods or services, it does not tantamount any adjustment.

Question 25: *Advance of Rs.1,00,000/- is received for goods in October'17 and invoice for the same is issued in March'18 for Rs.1,00,000/-. Whether the details of such advance needs to be disclosed here?*

Ans: This field does not warrant disclosure of all the advances and instead only those advances on which tax was earlier paid and which remain unadjusted even at the end of the financial year. In the given case, since invoice has been issued for GST paid on advance received already, therefore as already adjusted, does not warrant any disclosure here.

Advance received in FY and invoice issued in the subsequent FY: The essential reason for disclosure in this field is for a situation where the GST has been paid on the advances and the same is not invoiced/remain unadjusted upto end of the financial year. Various situations in which advances even though unadjusted do not warrant disclosure here are as under:

(1) Advances received in respect of goods but not liable to GST in terms of provision of time of supply.

(2) Advances only partially adjusted from the invoice and the balance part remains unadjusted.

(3) Advance received in respect of zero rated supply of goods/services.

(4) Advance received in respect of supplies that are exempted from GST or advances received in respect of non-taxable supplies.

Question 26: *Advance of Rs.50,000/- was received for goods in 25th October'17 but invoice issued in May'18 for Rs.50,000/-. Whether the details of such unadjusted needs to be disclosed here?*

Ans: The GST on advances was suspended in case of supply of goods w.e.f. 13th October 2018 for assessees engaged in supply of goods having aggregate turnover of less than Rs.1.5 Crores and later the same was extended to all the assesees in the category of supply of goods vide Notification 66/2017-CT Dated 15.11.2017. Therefore, in the given case auditor must first identify the effective date of exemption from advances for the class of assessee getting audited and in case where there is no implication of GST on advances then the same would not warrant disclosure here. However, in all other cases where GST is paid/payable on the advances and no tax invoice is issued, disclosure necessary.

Question 27: *Advance of Rs.1,00,000/- is received for goods in September'17 but invoice issued in February'18 for Rs.60,000/- and balance Rs.40,000/- invoice was raised in May'18. Whether the details of any unadjusted needs to be disclosed here?*

Ans: In this case, GST would have been paid on full advance i.e. Rs.1,00,000/- but no invoice would have been raised for Rs.40,000/- and it would be treated as unadjusted advance for the Financial year 2017-18. Therefore, unadjusted advance to the tune of Rs.40,000/- only must be disclosed here.

Question 28*: Advance of Rs.1,00,000/- is received for Goods in Dec'17 but invoice issued in April'18 for Rs.1,00,000/-. Whether the details of any unadjusted needs to be disclosed here?*

Ans: In this case, GST would not have been paid on full advance i.e. Rs.1,00,000/- as advance received after November, the liability to pay GST on advances in respect of goods is removed. Therefore, no disclosure required.

Question 29: *Advance of Rs.1,00,000/- is received for services (exempted supply) in July'17 and invoice on the same is issued in May'18. Whether the details of any advances need to be disclosed here?*

Ans: In this case, GST is not payable on this transaction of supply as it is exempted. Therefore even though the advance remains unadjusted it does not warrant any disclosure here.

Question 30: *Advance of Rs.1,00,000/- is received for export of services in July'17 and invoice for the same is issued in May' 18. Whether the details of any unadjusted needs to be disclosed here?*

Ans: In this case, if the export of services is done without LUT upon payment of GST, then the details of such unadjusted advance of Rs.1,00,000/- would form a part of unadjusted advance for the Financial year 2017-18 needs to be disclosed here. However if export of services is done under LUT without payment of GST not require to be disclosed here.

Spill over transactions between Pre-GST Regime and the GST regime: While the transactions prior to the GST regime needs to be segregated even though it is in the nature of unadjusted advances as there is no liability for payment of GST on the same. Various possible scenarios that may arise in this regard are as under:

(1) Advances liable for taxes under the erstwhile tax laws and adjusted in the GST regime.

(2) Advances liable for taxes under the erstwhile tax laws and again liable for taxes in the GST regime upon adjustment of the same as per sec 142(11)(c).

(3) Advances not liable for taxes under the erstwhile tax laws and adjusted in the GST regime.

In order to understand the implication of the unadjusted advances that are being carried forward from the Pre-GST regime, one has to understand the statutory provisions governing such transactions. Reference must be made to section 142(10) & 142(11) for the same as under:

Relevant Statutory Provisions

Sec 142 (10): Save as otherwise provided in this Chapter, the goods or services or both supplied on or after the appointed day in pursuance of a contract entered into prior to the appointed day shall be liable to tax under the provisions of this Act.

Sec 142(11)(a): notwithstanding anything contained in section 12, no tax shall be payable on goods under this Act to the extent the tax was leviable on the said goods under the Value Added Tax Act of the State;

Sec 142(11)(b): notwithstanding anything contained in section 13, no tax shall be payable on services under this Act to the extent the tax was leviable on the said services under Chapter V of the Finance Act, 1994;

Sec 142(11)(c): where tax was paid on any supply both under the Value Added Tax Act and under Chapter V of the Finance Act, 1994, tax shall be leviable under this Act and the taxable person shall be entitled to take credit of value added tax or service tax paid under the existing law to the extent of supplies made after the appointed day and such credit shall be calculated in such manner as may be prescribed.

From the above, it can be noted that if a transaction is leviable to only VAT or Service Tax, then no further taxes would be paid on the said transactions to the extent the same was leviable to under the said erstwhile acts. For instance, the levy of VAT was on sale of goods and therefore even if any advance received, the same was not liable for VAT. However, the service tax levy was on providing or agreeing to provide the service or on receipt of payment whichever is earlier based on Point of Taxation rules of Service tax. As a result, the levy also attracted upon receipt of advances for the provision of services. Following illustrations can help understanding the concept:

Question 31: *Advance of Rs.1,00,000/- is received for sale of goods in April'17 (Pre-GST Period) and VAT on the same has not been paid. Invoice for such advances was raised in July'18 (Post GST period). Whether the details of such unadjusted advances needs to be reflected here?*

Ans: In this case, VAT was not applicable as per the erstwhile VAT laws on the receipt of advances and since the sale did not take place in the pre-GST regime, the levy of tax is not attracted under the VAT laws. Since, the supply of goods has taken place in the GST regime, this transaction would be liable for GST. However, the details of the unadjusted advance need not be reflected on this transaction as no tax was paid on the advance element.

Question 32: *Advance of Rs.1,00,000/- is received for Services in April'17 (Pre GST Period) and service tax on the same has been paid. Invoice was raised in July'18 (post GST period). Whether the details of such unadjusted advances needs to be reflected here?*

Ans: In this case, as per section 140(11)(b) the transaction of receipt of advance was liable to service tax and since service tax is already paid on the same, the same would again not be liable for GST. Since, no GST is applicable on the advances and also at the invoicing stage, the advances although is remaining unadjusted, the same would not be disclosed here as Service tax was already paid earlier. Where no GST is payable such turnover would not form part of this column. This may still be an open reconciliation item which can be disclosed in the residuary field i.e. Column 5O of this form.

Segregation of unadjusted advances in case of audit of multiple GSTINs: Since, audited financial statements are prepared at an entity level for each PAN, the details of unadjusted advances as reflecting in the financial statements is for entity a whole. In such circumstances, auditor needs to bifurcate such unadjusted advances at each GSTIN level. Auditor may use various methods for bifurcation as explained above for this purpose. Further, if an entity appoints different auditors for performing an audit for its various GST numbers, the auditor needs to communicate with the other auditors and accordingly the above comparison must be made, so that the error of reporting of unadjusted advances multiple times in various GSTIN's is avoided. Auditor needs to take cognizance of SA 299 issued by ICAI on "Responsibility of Joint Auditors" and SA 600 on "Using the work of another auditor." *[Refer Chapter 11 of this book for more details on the same]*

Advances liable for GST but not paid: Information reported in GSTR 1 may not be required to be adopted at face value. An auditor has to cross check the data which is available in the Trial Balance. Preparation of GSTR 9 would involve summation of data from GSTR 3B filed for Jul 2017 to Mar 2018 and transactions recorded in books and not considered in the monthly/ quarterly returns whether reported during 2017-18 or 2018-19 (up to Oct 31, 2018 or Dec 31, 2018) as well as any advances which was omitted and not reflected in those returns. The auditor needs to ascertain all such advances that are liable for GST but not paid by the assessee and the quantification of the unadjusted advances must be reported here. These reversal entries for advances and adjustment of advances are prevalent throughout the year, are reversed usually at the end of every month. Thus, the only entry which is to be given effect for the reconciliation between Audited Financials and Annual Returns is the unadjusted entries that are lying at the end of the financial year.

Advances whether to be considered net of taxes?: In case an assessee has paid GST on advances on cum tax basis then for the purpose of disclosure here the details of advances must be disclosed on net of taxes basis i.e. the value of tax must be segregated and only the advance after taxes must be disclosed here. However, in case where the assessee has paid GST on ex-tax basis, then the actual value of the advance must be considered and the same need not be netted off.

Financial advances/deposits: It is pertinent to note that auditor must not consider all the unadjusted advances here and only those advances which are liable for GST. Therefore, advances received which are merely in the nature of transaction in money such as loans or deposits which are not part of the consideration for the purpose of levy of GST must be suitably excluded from these calculations.

Reference in Financials/Returns

Auditor can obtain this information from various sources i.e. the details of unadjusted advances can be taken from advances received from customer account or could be reflecting as a credit item in the Sundry Debtors account or separately disclosed under the Current Liabilities. In case the liability to pay GST is separately accounted for and adjusted in the books of accounts, then the details can be taken from the books of accounts. Further, details of tax paid on advances to the extent declared in the financial year and reflecting in GSTR 1 and the Annual returns in GSTR 9 can be taken from column 4F of the Annual Returns. Further, the details of tax on advances is separately disclosed in Column 11A(1) & (2) of GSTR 1 and the details of adjustment of advances is also disclosed in column 11B (1) & (2) of the GSTR 1 which can be helpful to the auditor in filling these details.

Sl. No. 5D - Deemed Supply under Schedule I - [to be added]

5D	Deemed Supply under Schedule I	(+)	

Serial No.	Instructions in the Form
5D	*Aggregate value of deemed supplies under Schedule I of the CGST Act, 2017 shall be declared here. Any deemed supply which is already part of the turnover in the audited Annual Financial Statement is not required to be included here.*

Introduction

Certain supplies are constituted as deemed supplies under schedule I of the GST Act which are liable for tax even if there is no consideration involved in such transactions. This clause comes with the exception that 'consideration' is not needed to treat the specified activities as 'supply'. It is worth noting that schedule I is applied only when the specified transactions are made without consideration. If the same are made with consideration same would fall under first clause i.e. (a) of Section 7(1) and not under this clause. These transactions may not be recognized as revenues in the financial statements but since they constitute deemed supply in GST, details of the same are disclosed in various returns filed under GST i.e. GSTR 3B, GSTR 1 and the Annual Return in Form GSTR 9.

Analysis

Various supplies that constitute deemed supply as per schedule I in GST are as under:

(1) Permanent transfer/disposal of business assets:

There are mainly three ingredients that should be present in this transaction to be constituted as a deemed supply i.e.

- There should be **permanent transfer or disposal** - Implies that goods should be transferred without any intention or requirement of having to receive the goods back by a person. Eg. Intentional destruction or disposal of assets, Assets donated, decommissioning of an entire plant, impairment of assets, assets taken over by a proprietor on completion of its useful life etc.
- Transfer/disposal should be of '**business assets**' - All type of assets current or non-current, tangible or intangible which are owned or controlled to produce value and that are held by an entity to produce positive economic value are assets.
- **ITC on such** 'business assets' should have been availed - ITC should have been availed on the same assets which are getting disposed or transferred. Therefore, if the assessee has not availed ITC, then the transaction may not come under the ambit. For eg: Free samples manufactured & distributed may not be deemed supply as ITC on such assets was not availed. However, there could be need for reversal of ITC availed on inputs used in such manufactured samples.

(2) Supplies between related/distinct persons:

Supply of goods or services to related/distinct persons or between related/distinct persons amount to supply whether or not there is any consideration involved in the transaction. For Eg: Stock transfer.

- Related Person: Any relationship as per explanation to section 15 of the Act are deemed to be related persons.

- Distinct person: GST Act treats each branch or establishment if separately registered as a distinct person.

As per AS 21 consolidated financial statements "Intragroup balances and intragroup transactions, including sales, expenses and dividends, are eliminated in full". Therefore, if the intra company sales i.e. deemed supplies are:

(i) eliminated in the annual financial statement or the consolidated financial statement considered at Column 5A only then the reconciliation difference would arise and the same needs to be considered for the disclosure in column 5D.

(ii) not eliminated and are part of the Annual financial statement at column 5A then the said turnover details even though in the nature of deemed supply would not require disclosure in this column i.e. 5D.

It is important to note that employer and employee are related persons and supplies between then are deemed supplies. The major implications of this can be seen in the cases of facilities like house, car, mobile phones, canteen, transport etc given to the employees. Such supplies including gifts could be liable to GST. However, a concession of up to Rs.50,000/- per employee in any financial year is provided in case of gifts where a transaction would not be treated as deemed supply. One must note that, if the facilities are part of employment contract without recovery of any amount, then it can be called as consideration for employment and not liable as "gift". Following elements are required to be satisfied: -

- It must be made without any contractual obligation. If it is made under a contractual obligation, it cannot be termed as a 'gift'.
- It must be made without any consideration in money or money's worth. Hence, anything made out of love and affection or such other non- legal considerations can only be termed as 'gifts'.

Reference must also be given to the press release issued by Central Board of Indirect Tax (CBIC) on 10th July, 2017 which clarifies as follows:

"The question arises as to what constitutes a gift. Gift has not been defined in the GST law. In common parlance, gift is made without consideration, is voluntary in nature and is made occasionally. It cannot be demanded as a matter of right by the employee and the employee cannot move a court of law for obtaining a gift. In business are gifts actually given or there is some quid pro quo is a moot question which would be decided by courts.

Another issue is the taxation of perquisites. It is pertinent to point out here that the services by an employee to the employer in the course of or in relation to his employment are outside the scope of GST (neither supply of goods nor supply of services). It follows therefrom that supply by the employer to the employee in terms of contractual agreement entered into between the employer and the employee, would not be subjected to GST. Further, the input tax credit (ITC) scheme under GST does not allow ITC of membership of a club, health and fitness centre [section 17(5)(b)(ii)]. It follows, therefore, that if such services are provided free of charge to all the employees by the employer then the same would not be subjected to GST, provided appropriate GST was paid when procured by the employer. The same would hold true for free housing to the employees, when the same is provided in terms of the contract between the employer and employee and is part and parcel of the cost-to-company (C2C)."

Further, it is important to note that the services by an employee to the employer are covered in Schedule III i.e. No supply and details of the same would not be required to be provided here. Auditor may face practical challenges in identifying these transactions as such transactions may not get recorded in the books as gifts. May be one could verify the staff welfare and similar accounts.

(3) Supply of goods between principal to his agent and vice-versa:

During pre-GST regime, there was no levy of VAT/sales tax on these kind of transactions as there was no sale between them. The compliance was ensured asking the taxpayers to produce the prescribed forms like 'Form F'

This entry covers the transactions involving supply of goods between the principal and agent. In order to tax the movement of goods between 'principal' and 'agent' which happens without any consideration, the same are specifically listed in the Schedule I. The main intent behind this clause is to levy GST at every stage of movement of goods and also to ensure seamless movement of goods through supply chain without need of exchange of various forms.

Section 2(5) of CGST Act, 2017 defines 'Principal' as *"a person on whose behalf an agent carries on the business of supply or receipt of goods or services or both"*

Section 2(5) of CGST Act, 2017 defines 'agent' as "*a person, including a factor, broker, commission agent, arhatia, del credere agent, an auctioneer or any other mercantile agent, by whatever name called, who carries on the business of supply or receipt of goods or services or both on behalf of another.*"

The combined reading of the above two definitions makes it clear that the 'agent' should make/receive supplies on behalf of the principal. As the movement of goods between the principal and agent are deemed as 'supply', there are specific provisions for valuing the supply for payment of GST, similarly the raising of invoice etc.

While determining the liability in respect of transactions between Principal and Agent, reference must be made to the Circular No. 57/31/2018-GST Dated the 4th September, 2018 read with Corrigendum issued dated 5th November, 2018. It may be kept in mind that circulars not in line with the law are *non est in law.*[3]

(4) Import of services from related person/establishment outside India:

Imports are made with consideration are liable to GST even if the same are not in the course or furtherance of business. This is in alignment of the principles of Customs. As per 2(11) of IGST Act 'import of services' means the supply of any service, where:

(i) the supplier of service is located outside India;

(ii) the recipient of service is located in India; and

(iii) the place of supply of service is in India.

For ex: Support services provided by branch/holding/subsidiary company outside India to a taxable person in India. Such service is an import of services which could be liable for GST under reverse charge. These transactions need not be considered in table 5D of GSTR-9C as it is not outward supply.

Reference in financial/Returns

(i) In case the cost center category wise entries are booked in the financial statements, then these details can be identified based on inter-branch accounts maintained. Further, in case a separate invoicing series maintained in the GST law, then it helps assessees to segregate these transactions from general revenue transactions.

(ii) **Same GSTIN:** GSTR 1 contains details of all B2B transactions with GSTIN of parties. A comparison of same GSTIN can help obtain the information. Example: Supplies between branches within the same state with same GSTIN could be a base. However, as the supply does not take place within same GSTIN, this is not required to be disclosed.

(iii) **Same PAN but different GSTIN:** GSTIN is PAN based and PAN for an entity would be same throughout India. GSTR 1 contains details of all B2B transactions with GSTIN of parties. A comparison of same PAN number with GSTIN from GSTR 1 would give details of deemed supplies between the same entities (common PAN) but separate GSTIN (could be Separate vertical, Different state)

---

3 Ratan Melting Wires- Constitutional bench Supreme Court.

(iv) **HR Policy/employee pay-sheets:** Details of recoveries from employee for food provided (canteen), Transportation provided (Cab services), Uniform and Shoe etc. Even valuation aspects to be verified for payment of GST.

(v) **E-way Bill/Delivery Challans:** Details in respect of various movement of goods which has not been treated as supply by the assessee can be obtained from the e-way bill database of the listing of various movement of goods caused by the assessee under the cover of a delivery challan.

(vi) **Multiple GSTIN's:** In case of audit of multi location entities would require examination (among others) of the following:

(a) Cost incurred commonly at or by the Head Office for other branches or by one branch for HO or other branches – E.g. Marketing and Brand Building Costs, software costs, common administration etc;

(b) Head Office providing support to Branches – E.g. Centralized Accounting Services; HR Services etc.,

(c) Branches without billings to any third parties but merely providing support to HO;

(d) Branches with billings to third parties and taking support from HO;

(e) Identification of Branches which have not been registered although supplying goods/ services from the other state;

(f) E-Way bill to track supplies which have been marked as stock transfers;

(g) Credit of 'State A' availed in 'State B' especially in cases of where the place of supply is State B (E.g. Accommodation Services of employee of 'State A' availed as credit in 'State B');

(h) Basis of bifurcation of credits into ISD;

Question 33: *Table 5D requires reporting of the deemed supply under Schedule I. Whether such reporting has to made as per the valuation provisions or the value at which supply has been declared by the registered persons?*

Ans: Part II of GSTR-9C is meant for reconciliation of the turnover as per books of account with the turnover as declared in the GSTR-9. Considering the same, the value to be shown in the Table 5D would be the value as per the schedule I in accordance with the provisions of section 15 read with valuation rules. If auditor finds that the valuation adopted by the client is not in accordance with the valuation provisions of the GST Act or rules made thereunder which could result in additional liability then the proper valuation as per auditor must be disclosed in this table and recommendation must be given as a disclosure in Part V i.e. auditors recommendation on additional liability.

Sl. No. 5E – Credit notes issued after the end of the Financial Year but reflected in the Annual Return - [to be deducted]

5E	Credit notes issued after the end of the Financial Year but reflected in the Annual Return	(-)	

Serial No.	Instructions in the Form
5E	*Aggregate value of credit notes which were issued after 31st of March for any supply accounted in the current financial year but such credit notes were reflected in the annual return (GSTR-9) shall be declared here.*

Introduction

This serial no. requires the disclosure in respect of the value of credit notes which were issued after Mar 31, 2018 in respect of any supply accounted in the current financial year (i.e. 2018-19) but such credit notes were reflected in the annual return (GSTR –9 for the financial year 2017-18).

Analysis

It is very uncommon from accounting perspective that a credit note dated after Apr 1, 2018 and is given effect to in the financial accounts in the year 18-19 on principles of revenue recognition standard. Normally the details of said credit note is disclosed in the annual returns of FY 17-18. One of the reasons for the difference can be the delay in accounting of such credit note or physically the credit note was issued later in FY 18-19 but accounted in the annual returns immediately.

This Sl. No. requires one to collate information recorded in the returns filed during the period April to September 2018 in respect of Credit Notes/Adjustments made for the transactions pertaining to the previous financial year. All such Adjustments made/Credit Notes issued and reflected in GSTR 1 for the above period should be considered for filling this information. Value of transactions collated as cited supra would be considered for adjustment of turnover reflected in the Audited Financial Statements to derive the turnover as per Annual Return in GSTR 9. By the above adjustment, the turnover derived from audited annual financial statements does not contain the 'effect' of these credit notes but GSTR 9 already may contain its 'effect' due to inclusion in GSTR 1 'for' 2017-18. In reconciling turnover in financial statements and GSTR 9, it is important to 'reduce' the turnover in financial statements (at 5A) to enable it to reconcile with turnover in GSTR 9.

Steps to be followed:

Step 1: Prepare a list credit notes dated after Apr 1, 2018.

Step 2: Prepare another list of credit note adjusted in Table 9A, 9B and 9C of GSTR 1 'for' 2017-18 file (on-time or belatedly).

Step 3: Map the list of credit notes identified in step 1 with those identified in step 2 and the common credit notes needs to be segregated.

Step 4: Common credit notes so identified needs to be validated that these credit notes have not been 'given effect to' in the financials for the FY 17-18 and therefore the same needs to be given effect to here.

Credit notes of FY 17-18 declared whether or not through amendments needs to be declared: It is pertinent to note that the disclosure of all the credit notes affecting the taxable supplies made in the previous year needs to be made here. However, it is pertinent to note that the Form GSTR 9C is to be prepared for transactions effected in the FY 17-18 and therefore certain credit notes may be issued afresh in the subsequent financial year and not as an amendment in the GSTR1. Since these credit notes relate to the subsequent events and the transactions that are reported in FY 18-19 and therefore would not warrant disclosure here. They need to be disclosed while filing of the GSTR 9C certification for FY 18-19.

Sl. No.5F – Trade Discounts Accounted for in the Audited Financial Statement but are not permissible under GST - [to be added]

5F	Trade Discounts Accounted for in the Audited Financial Statement but are not permissible under GST	(+)	

Serial No.	Instructions in the Form
5F	*Trade discounts which are accounted for in the audited Annual Financial Statement but on which GST was leviable (being not permissible) shall be declared here.*

Introduction

Details of trade discounts given in the normal course of business but which are not permissible for reduction from the value of supply must be added here. Since, assessee has already paid GST on the same and has considered this liability in the GSTR 1 and the same is disclosed in the annual returns, therefore the details of impermissible trade discounts needs to be added here.

Relevant statutory provisions

Tax Treatment of discounts in GST is governed by section 15 which states that *the value of the supply shall not include any discount which is given—*

(a) *before or at the time of the supply if such discount has been duly recorded in the invoice issued in respect of such supply; and*

(b) after the supply has been effected, if—

(i) such discount is established in terms of an agreement entered into at or before the time of such supply and specifically linked to relevant invoices; and

(ii) input tax credit as is attributable to the discount on the basis of document issued by the supplier has been reversed by the recipient of the supply.

Analysis

As per Business Dictionary, "Trade Discount" is an "*An amount or rate by which the catalogue, list, or retail price of an item is reduced when sold to a reseller. The trade discount reflects the reseller's profit margin and usually varies directly with the quantity of the item purchased.*"

It is pertinent to note that in a business scenario, discounts are of various types such as trade discounts, cash discounts, turnover discount, target discount, seasonal discount etc. From the above, it can be noted that trade discount is the one which varies directly with the quantity of the items sold. Generally, the trade discount is given in the invoice itself at the time of supply of goods. Therefore, it is important to note that only such discounts which are given directly on the invoice needs to be reported here. The other post supply discounts such as cash discounts, turnover discount, target discount, seasonal discount etc. are given by way of credit notes and the reporting in respect of the same would need to be done Sl. No. 5J below.

Trade discounts reduced from the Gross revenue in the financial statements: Trade discounts and volume rebates which are provided would be reduced for revenue recognition in annual financial statement. As per Accounting Standard 9 (AS 9) "*Trade discounts and volume rebates received are not encompassed within the definition of revenue, since they represent a reduction of cost. Trade discounts and volume rebates given should be deducted in determining revenue*". Therefore, the revenue recognized in the books of accounts would be net of the discounts.

Discount which are allowed before or at the time of supply and which are linked to such supply of goods or services are permissible deductions in GST from the transaction value and the same should have been reduced from the turnover in the financial statements. However, in case these trade discounts which do not fit into the compliance requirement in section 15(3) of the CGST Act then the said discount element would be taxable and needs to be reported here by way of the addition.

Example: Assessee has recorded revenue in the books of accounts of say Rs. 10 crores and a discount is given say for Rs. 10 lakhs, then as per the accounting standard as explained above, the net revenue would be disclosed in the financial statements of Rs. 9.90 crores. Assessee must have also taken the reduction of this discount in the annual returns filed and the taxable value as per Annual returns is also Rs. 9.9 crores. Now auditor during the course of the audit notices that this discount was not separately disclosed by the assessee on the Tax invoice and therefore as per section 15(3) the same should not be allowed as deduction. Hence, auditor would add back this discount element in this field thereby the value of taxable supply increases to Rs. 10 Crores and the taxable value as per Annual returns is still of Rs. 9.90 Crores and thereby leads to recommendation of the auditor for additional tax payable to the extent of deduction of discount claimed.

Trade discounts reported as expenses in the financial statements: Sometimes, it is possible that assessee reports the trade discounts as expenditure in the books of accounts as per his practice or in order to inflate the turnover even though that is not in line with the accounting standards. In such a situation the auditor must not perform any adjustment to the turnover and thereby in the above example full Rs. 10 crore as reported as the sale would be considered as the Gross turnover by the auditee and recommendation for payment of taxes would be made accordingly.

Sl. No. 5G - Turnover from April 2017 to June 2017 - [to be deducted]

5G	Turnover from April 2017 to June 2017	(-)	

Serial No.	Instructions in the Form
5G	*Turnover included in the audited Annual Financial Statement for April 2017 to June 2017 shall be declared here*

Introduction

Annual financial statements is the starting point of this table which is normally prepared for period ending 31st march of every year, thus would cover transaction from April 2017 to March 2018. However, GSTR 9 annual returns would be for the period between July 2017 to March 2018. Therefore, in order to bring both Annual financial statements and Annual returns on same level, the turnover for period Apr 2017 to June 2017 would be reduced from turnover in annual financial statements.

Analysis

One must note that the exclusion of turnover here cannot be merely based on the transactions accounted as revenue in the books of accounts between the period April 2017 to June 2017. The books are updated based on the principle of accounting in accordance with the revenue recognition as per AS 9 or Ind AS 115 whereas the levy of taxes are based on the taxable event i.e. Point of taxation in case of services, removal of goods from the factory gate in case of Central Excise and sale of goods in case of VAT/CST. Therefore, under this field one must remove only those transactions which are leviable to tax under the erstwhile tax laws irrespective of its accounting treatment. This aspect also gets strength from the law as provided in section 142(11)(a) and (b) of CGST/SGST Act, which states that transactions that are leviable to tax under VAT/service tax would not be liable to GST. Although there is no such saving clause mentioned for excise duty however reference must be given to Notification.No.12/2017 CE dated.30.06.2017 which grants exemption to goods manufactured prior to 30.06.2017 but cleared after 01.07.2017, provided appropriate GST is leviable on such goods. In services, in case an advance is received in the month of April 2017 and the service is provided in the month of August 2017, this transaction would be recorded as revenue in the books in the month of August 2017. However, as per the point of taxation rules, service tax was liable to be paid on receipt of advance and therefore it must be deducted here.

Transactions leviable to both Service Tax and VAT: In case of works contract service both VAT as well as service tax was liable to be paid, therefore where advance was received during the period April 2017 to June 2017, but supply is effected after June 2017, then the value of amount received during the period April 2017 to June 2017 needs to be deducted under this Sl. No. WCT being a service the advance was liable to tax on receipt basis as per service tax law but not under State level VAT laws. Further the same value needs to be added back in Sl. No. 5(O) again, since the aforesaid supplies would be again liable to tax under GST law in view of exception carved out in section 142(11)(c). Therefore, while auditing these kind of transactions auditor must give due regard to the transitional provisions as laid out in section 142(10) and 142(11) and the tax treatment as accorded by the assessee for the spillover transactions.

Continuous supply of services: In case of continuous supply of services, the liability to pay service tax once the relevant event occurs requires the recipient to make the tax payment. Auditor should verify the occurrence of the relevant taxable event under the erstwhile service tax law. In case such event has occurred prior to 01.07.2017, then notwithstanding the fact that consideration is received on or after 01.07.2017, such turnovers would be liable for service tax and must be reflected in this Sl. No. as turnover from April 2017 to July 2017.

Question 34: *Continuous supply of service in the nature of construction service is being provided. The construction started on 1.5.2017 and is yet to be completed as on 31.3.2018. As per agreement for sale, the customers are liable to be pay on completion method. As of 30.6.2017, the 'first floor slab' of construction work has been completed, at which point every customer is required to pay Rs.2,00,000/-. Only 50 customers have paid out of 200 customers. Revenue has been recognised only for 50 customers as on 30.6.2017. 110 customers have paid during the period 1.7.2017 to 31.3.2018, which has been recognised as revenue for the period ended March 2018. Please also state the effect to be given in respect of the balance 40 customers who have not paid any consideration?*

Ans: As per proviso to Rule 3(b) of Clause of Service tax Rules, 2011, in case of continuous supply of service, the point of taxation would be the point in time which requires the service recipient to make payment to service provider. In this case, the service recipient is liable to pay to the service provider as per the agreement on completion of construction related to 'first floor slab' completed on 30.6.2017. If invoices are raised on or before 30.7.2017, the date of raising the invoice would be the point of taxation. If invoices are not raised before 30.7.2017, the date of completion of service i.e. 30.6.2017 would be the point of taxation. Thus, service tax is liable to be paid on consideration of Rs.2,00,000/- relating to each of the 200 customers, irrespective of whether consideration is received or not from the 200 customers by the builder. Since consideration received from 160 customers have been received (50 + 110), the relevant turnovers (160 customers multiplied by Rs.2,00,000/-) has to be reduced from turnover under this Sl. No., though service tax would be payable on product of 200 customers into Rs.2,00,000/-.

Reference in financials/returns

- Central Excise/Service Tax/VAT Returns filed for the period April 2017 to June 2017.
- TRAN-1 form filed under GST for details of tax under Section 140(11) (c).
- Cut off procedures in the form of verification of Gate Passes on 30.06.2017 with corresponding invoices/delivery challans/e-way bills (under the erstwhile laws) etc. may be checked to validate the correctness of data for goods.
- There could be cases where books of accounts are closed quarterly, or financial statements are drawn up quarterly. In such cases, the quarterly turnovers can be adopted, and adjustments can be made relating to point of taxation under excise law, State level vat law and service tax law to arrive at taxable values as per the erstwhile laws.

Sl. No. 5H - Unbilled Revenue at the end of Financial Year - [to be deducted]

5H	Unbilled Revenue at the end of Financial Year	(-)	

Serial No.	Instructions in the Form
5H	*Unbilled revenue which was recorded in the books of accounts on the basis of accrual system of accounting during the current financial year but GST was not payable on such revenue in the same financial year shall be declared here.*

Introduction

The recognition of revenue in financial statements is as per the standards prescribed in this regard. Once it is probable that any future economic benefit associated with the item of revenue would flow to the entity and the amount of revenue can be measured with reliability, then having regard to the Generally accepted accounting principles of the organization, the revenue can be recognized.

It is possible that in case of some business transactions all the criteria required for recognition of revenue are satisfied in a transaction and accordingly the revenue is recognized in the books of accounts but no billing or invoicing is done in respect of such revenue item. To the contrary, as far as GST law is concerned, the provisions of time of supply states that the liability in respect of supply of goods/service would arise upon issuance of invoice. Further, explanation (1) to section 12(2) of the GST Act states that "supply" would be deemed to have been made to the extent it is covered by the invoice or, as the case may be, the payment. Therefore, invoice in respect of these items would be raised in the current financial year (for ex: FY 18-19) whereas revenue on the same item must have already been recognized in the books of accounts in the previous financial year (for ex: FY 17-18). The GST liability would arise only on issue of the tax invoice (assuming no advances received). This would be disclosed in the Annual Returns of FY 18-19. Therefore, such items of revenues must be reduced in this field in order to match the numbers with the annual returns. *[For more discussion, readers may refer to the discussion made in respect of the treatment for Un-billed revenue for Sl. No. 5B above]*

Reference in financials/returns

The details of the unbilled revenue can be obtained from the Notes to Accounts of the financial statements or from the Head of Debtors where all these items are separately grouped instead of tagging it to any customer. Detailed discussion has been made above with respect to balance of unbilled revenue at the beginning of the year. Similar logic would be equally applicable on the closing unbilled revenue at year end.

Sl. No.5I – Unadjusted Advances at the beginning of the Financial Year - [to be deducted]

5I	Unadjusted Advances at the beginning of the Financial Year	(-)	

Serial No.	Instructions in the Form
5I	*Value of all advances for which GST has not been paid but the same has been recognized as revenue in the audited Annual Financial Statement shall be declared here.*

Introduction

The liability to pay GST accrues once the event as specified in section 12 & section 13 of the GST Act providing for time of supply in case of goods/services arises. GST also needed to be paid upon receipt of advance for the supply upto 15th November 2017. However, presently the tax on advances is payable only in case of supply of services as it was suspended in case of supply of goods. [Notification 66/2017-CT dt. 15.11.2017.]

Therefore, in case of any supplies on which GST is paid on advances and the invoice for such supply is also issued in the same financial year, then there is no implication of reconciliation. In all cases where GST is paid on the advances in the previous year and the tax invoice is issued in the subsequent year, then details of such advances must be reflected here.

Analysis

Unadjusted advances as on 01.04.2017: This situation may not arise in the first year of implementation of GST as there would not be any unadjusted advances pertaining to the previous financial year as an opening in the beginning of the financial year. The implication for the subsequent financial years would be similar to that of discussion for advances as made for explanation of Column 5C. However, since the GST was implemented from the middle of the financial year and therefore if there exists any unadjusted advances at the time of implementation of GST, then one may disclose the same here. *[For more discussion, readers may refer to the discussion made in respect of the treatment for Unadjusted advances for Sl. No. 5C above]*

Example: In case of advances received in the pre-GST regime and the sum of Rs.1,00,000/- is received for Services in April'17 (Pre GST Period) and service tax on the same has been paid. Invoice was raised in July'17 (post GST period).

In this case, no GST was applicable as Service tax was already paid earlier on the advance received. Therefore one may disclose the details in the residuary field and not here as this field is exclusively for those unadjusted advances which are opening at the beginning of the FY.

Reference in Financials/Returns: Auditor can obtain this information from various sources i.e. in case the liability to pay GST is separately accounted for and adjusted in the books of accounts, then the details can be taken from the books of accounts. Further, details of tax paid on advances to the extent declared in the financial year and reflected in GSTR 1 and the Annual returns in GSTR 9 can be taken from column 4F of the Annual Returns. Further, the details of tax on advances is separately disclosed in Column 11A (1) & (2) of GSTR 1 and the details of adjustment of advances is also disclosed in column 11B (1) & (2) of the GSTR 1 which can be helpful to the auditor in filling these details.

Sl. No.5J – Credit Notes Accounted for in the Audited Annual Financial Statement but are not Permissible under GST - [to be Added]

5J	Credit Notes Accounted for in the Audited Annual Financial Statement but are not Permissible under GST	(+)	

Serial No.	Instructions in the Form
5J	*Aggregate value of credit notes which have been accounted for in the audited Annual Financial Statement but were not admissible under Section 34 of the CGST Act shall be declared here.*

Introduction

Credit notes are issued by taxable person where there is a short supply of goods or services or both or when improper tax is charged or in case of post supply discounts. When credit notes are raised there is a reduction in the said turnover as well as reduction in the output tax liability. Therefore, in case assessee raises any credit notes which has impact on the financial statements by way of reduction of the turnover but if such corresponding reduction is not permissible in the GST then the value of such credit note must be added here.

Relevant Statutory Provision

Section 34(1) of the GST provides for various situations in which credit note can be issued and adjusted against the outward taxable supply. It states as under:

> *"Where a tax invoice has been issued for supply of any goods or services or both and the taxable value or tax charged in that tax invoice is found to exceed the taxable value or tax payable in respect of such supply, or where the goods supplied are returned by the recipient, or where goods or services or both supplied are found to be deficient, the registered person, who has supplied such goods or services or both, may issue to the recipient a credit note containing such particulars as may be prescribed."*

Analysis

From the above statutory provision, it can be understood that credit note can be issued against a tax invoice. It is important to note that credit notes issued without GST could also be a valid financial transaction and does not lead to any impact on the GST payable. Treatment for that is discussed later. Various business transactions in which the credit note are issued with GST are as under:

- Sales returns of goods supplied against a tax invoice either partially or fully;
- Deficiency in supply of any service not in accordance with the agreement;
- Rate difference due to post supply reduction in prices;
- Post supply discounts issued to the customer as per the pre-agreed terms or otherwise;
- Adjustment of the incorrect taxable value or tax charged by the supplier.

Implication based on accounting treatment of credit notes: The impact of reporting in this field depends on how the credit notes have been accounted in the books of accounts of the assessee. Generally, credit notes directly impact the revenues and accordingly income would be recognised in the books of accounts as net of the credit notes. In this situation, the turnover is reduced to that extent and therefore as an auditor if such credit notes are permissible for deduction, then there is no further impact, however if such credit notes cannot be deducted as the same do not fall within the requirement of section 34 or is not a permissible discount, then the auditor should add back the value of such credit notes here.

To the contrary, sometimes, it is possible that assessee reports the credit notes as an expenditure in the books of accounts or gives the impact only in the trade receivables/ payables without reducing the actual turnover. If such credit note is not permissible, then auditor need not perform any adjustment here as the turnover is anyway on the higher side to that extent and the difference would lead to additional tax liability as a part of auditor's recommendation.

Impact of permissible credit notes: It is possible that the credit note is a valid permissible credit note under GST. However assessee has not recorded such credit note as a reduction in the turnover in the books of accounts. Instead the same is either recorded as an expenditure in the books of accounts or impact is given only in the trade receivables/payables without reducing the actual turnover. In such a situation, auditor must reduce the turnover to that extent in order to match with the taxable value as per the annual returns. However since this field is to increase the turnover due to impermissible credit notes, the impact of this situation of permissible credit note must be given in the residual field i.e. Sl. No. 5O as a reduction in the turnover.

Post-supply discounts given through credit notes: Various discounts such as cash discounts, volume discount, seasonal discount etc. are issued post supply of the goods/services. The impact of such credit notes given for the discounts must be declared in this field only. However, while adjusting any credit note for the discount, the auditor must take note of the applicability of discount in terms of section 15 of the GST act as referred above. In other words, if the terms of the discount are not pre-agreed and the same is not linked to any tax invoice issued earlier and where the customer has not reversed the corresponding tax credit, auditor must disallow the reduction and add back the value of credit note here.

Customer confirmations to be verified: It is important to note that as per section 15 of the GST act, the deduction on account of credit notes issued for discounts is available only when the corresponding input tax credit is reversed by the customer. Therefore, auditor must suggest to the assessee to obtain declarations from the customer in this regard and also verify the same on sample basis covering the material values of deduction involved.

Implication of Financial credit notes: In a business environment where multiple credit notes are issued against a single invoice or where the volume of credit notes is very high typically in the automobile industry, it is possible that the supplier issued the financial credit note without giving any effect of the same on the GST. In other words, the deduction on account of GST is not claimed on such credit notes. However, since the turnover is reduced by the assessee to that extent, auditor must add back the value of such financial credit notes here.

Credit note issued against the Pre-GST supply: It may be possible that the assessee issues a credit note against the supply made by him in the Pre- GST regime. In such a situation, if such credit note is issued for the downward revision of the price, then the same is valid and allowed as deduction as per section 142(2) of the GST Act, if the same is issued within 30 days of such price revision and the recipient has reduced the corresponding input tax credit. Therefore, auditor must have regard to the conditions as mentioned in section 142(2) and accordingly if the deduction on account of such credit notes is permissible then no adjustment must be carried out here. However, if such credit note issued is not permissible, then the value of such credit note must be added back.

Credit note with only tax impact: It is possible that the credit note is issued against a tax invoice on which the taxable value is proper but the tax element is wrongly excess charged. In such a situation the turnover would not be effected and therefore based on the treatment given in the annual returns, auditor must give implication of such transaction either in the residuary field i.e. 5O or in table 9 of this form as a tax impact.

Question 35: *M/s PQR & Co. supplies goods to the customer and later based on the prompt payment made by the customer, PQR & Co issues a credit note with a discount of 5%, without GST. Whether this credit note issued without GST needs to be added here?*

Ans: Yes, since this is a financial credit note and as the turnover is reduced to the extent of this credit note issued but the corresponding reduction to that extent is not made in the annual returns. PQR & Co has not reduced any GST on the basis of this credit note, this financial credit note must be added here.

Reference in Financials/Returns:

- Credit notes register/Discounts ledger;
- Terms of agreement with the customer.

Sl No. 5K – Adjustments on Account of Supply of Goods by SEZ Units to DTA Units - [to be deducted]

5K	Adjustments on Account of Supply of Goods by SEZ Units to DTA Units	(-)	

Serial No.	Instructions in the Form
5K	*Aggregate value of all goods supplied by SEZs to DTA units for which the DTA units have filed bill of entry shall be declared here.*

Introduction

It is pertinent to note that supplies by SEZ to DTA units is treated as import of goods as the premises of the authorised operations of SEZ is deemed to the outside the taxable territory as per the provisions of the SEZ Act. Since, outward supply of goods by SEZ would not be disclosed in the annual returns and also in the GSTR 1 and the same is recorded by the recipient of supply as an import of goods under the cover of the bill of entry, in order to match the turnover of the SEZ declared in its financial statements with the Annual return, the outward supply of goods made by SEZ needs to be deducted from here.

Analysis

SEZ unit supplies goods to a DTA unit and the relevant bill of entry is filed by the DTA unit. This transaction would be a sale transaction for the SEZ and would also be disclosed as revenue in the books of accounts. However, it would not be considered as supply for GST purposes and hence it is deducted from the turnover as per GSTR 9. This transaction would be treated as an import of goods in the hands of the DTA. However, it is possible that SEZ unit can itself file the bill of entry based on the authorization received from the DTA unit.

Supply of services by the SEZ unit: It is important to note that supply of services by the SEZ unit is treated on par with any other supplies and the said SEZ is required to charge applicable GST on the invoices issued for the outward supply and the details of the same are also declared in the annual returns filed. Therefore, the element of services would not create any open reconciliation and hence the details w.r.t. services supplied by SEZ would not warrant declaration here.

Reference in Financials/Returns

- Copy of the invoice endorsed by the specified officer of the concerned SEZ.
- List of authorised operations of the SEZ and the fact that the goods supplied from such authorised operations.
- GST common portal would also provide the details of the registered persons as to whether such registration under GST has been obtained as SEZ or otherwise.
- SEZ units are required to maintain records of the assets/goods admitted into the SEZ unit and the details of disposal of such goods. Such records can assist an Auditor in identifying the outward supply made by an SEZ unit. Additionally, disposal of capital goods would be disclosed as deletion in Fixed Asset Registers.

Sl. No. 5L – Turnover for the period under Composition Scheme - [to be deducted]

5L	Turnover for the period under Composition Scheme	(-)	

Serial No.	Instructions in the Form
5L	*There may be cases where registered persons might have opted out of the composition scheme during the current financial year. Their turnover as per the audited Annual Financial Statement would include turnover both as composition taxpayer as well as normal taxpayer. Therefore, the turnover for which GST was paid under the composition scheme shall be declared here.*

Introduction

Assessees covered under the composition scheme as eligible for under section 10 of the GST Act based on the turnover limit would require to transfer the GST registration to the normal scheme in case the turnover limit as prescribed under the act for coverage under the composition scheme is crossed. Such assessees are required to file the Annual returns in Form GSTR 9C to the extent covered under the composition scheme. Further, for the period the assessee is covered under normal scheme, the Annual return is required to be filed under Form GSTR 9. Since, in the given situation the turnover as disclosed in the financial statements is matched with the annual returns filed under Form GSTR 9, the turnover covered under the composition scheme should be reduced. Therefore, Sl. No. 5L of GSTR 9C should match with the turnover declared in Sl. No. 6C of GSTR 9A, which is the sum of Table 6 and 7 of GSTR-4 of relevant period.

Question 36: *Mr. X is a composition dealer who has opted out of the composition scheme during the current financial year. Whether he needs to declare the turnover separately when he was covered under composition scheme? If yes where it has to be disclosed?*

Ans: Since their turnover as per the audited Annual Financial Statement would include turnover both as composition taxpayer as well as normal taxpayer., Mr. X needs to calculate the turnover for the period during which he was covered under composition scheme separately and disclose the same under table 5L of part II of the form.

Sl. No. 5M – Adjustments in turnover under Section 15 and Rules thereunder - [to be added/deducted]

5M	Adjustments in turnover under Section 15 and Rules thereunder	(+)/ (-)	

Serial No.	Instructions in the Form
5M	*There may be cases where the taxable value and the invoice value differ due to valuation principles under section 15 of the CGST Act, 2017 and rules thereunder. Therefore, any difference between the turnover reported in the Annual Return (GSTR 9) and turnover reported in the audited Annual Financial Statement due to difference in valuation of supplies shall be declared here.*

Introduction

Section 15 of the CGST Act states that the supply of goods must be valued at the transaction value in all situations where price is the sole consideration for the supply and the supplier and receiver are not related to each other. However, in certain situations, it is provided that the supply has to be valued in accordance with the mechanism as provided in the rules for valuation on the basis of Open

Market value or based on the value of similar goods or on the basis of cost of provision of goods/services etc. as under:

- Transactions between related persons;
- Transactions between distinct persons;
- Supplies involving consideration in non-monetary form etc.

In these cases the value in the books of accounts would be "nil". This would not match with the one adopted for calculating GST, the differences on this account need to be appropriately reported here. Further examples: partial recovery of amounts from employees towards supply of food; barter/exchange arrangements; subsidies other than direct Government subsidies – solar, fertiliser, irrigation; corporation tax recovered from tenant; second hand car dealing, value of land etc.In terms of Rule 28, the value in case of related persons transaction would be open market value (OMV). If OMV is not available, then value of supply of goods or services of like kind and quality has to be adopted. If both are not available, cost + 10% or residual method has to be considered for GST payment. In such cases, value as per annual return would be more than the value accounted in financial statements. Similarly, free supply of goods by the customers could also have impact for which circular no.47/21/2018 dated 8th June 2018 could be referred.

Question 37: *How to reconcile in case the incomes which are in the nature of pure agent are reported in the financial statements as income?*

Ans: If the amount recovered as pure agent*[4] has been routed through Balance Sheet in the books of account, it does not form part of the turnover as per books. Also, the same has not been disclosed in the GSTR-9. In view of this, it does not become a reconciliation item and accordingly does not require disclosure in the GSTR- 9C. On the other hand, if the same is included in the turnover as per books of account, adjustment has to be made in the table 5O of the GSTR- 9C.

Sl. No. 5N – Adjustments in turnover due to Foreign Exchange Fluctuations - [to be added/deducted]

5N	Adjustments in turnover due to Foreign Exchange Fluctuations	(+)/ (-)	

Serial No.	Instructions in the Form
5N	*Any difference between the turnover reported in the Annual Return (GSTR9) and turnover reported in the audited Annual Financial Statement due to foreign exchange fluctuations shall be declared here.*

4 The deduction for pure agent under GST needs to be done only if the conditions are complied with.

Introduction

Taxable person might be involved in foreign exchange related transactions. This could include foreign operations and foreign currency transactions recorded in books at transaction date but at every balance sheet date requires items to be reported as per AS 11 and IND AS 21 "The Effects of Changes in Foreign Exchange Rates".

Monetary items such as cash, accounts receivable, notes receivable, and investments etc would be recorded at the exchange rates prevailing on the date of transaction. On the said exchange rate of the transaction, GST would be paid and disclosed in GSTR 1 and same disclosed in GSTR 9.

However as on the balance sheet date, changes are done based on accounting standards which affect the turnover that is to be shown in annual financial statements. The turnover may be increased or decreased, such adjustment in turnover due the foreign exchange fluctuations shall be declared in this entry.

Rule 34 maybe referred and value in books and as per GST for the foreign exchange transactions are different. That should be adjusted here. There is also another entry for the financials of gain or loss in respect of foreign exchange which is not to be considered here unless it is taken as turnover as per financials.

Sl. No. 5O – Adjustments in turnover due to reasons not listed above - [to be added/deducted]

5O	Adjustments in turnover due to reasons not listed above	(+)/ (-)	

Serial No.	Instructions in the Form
5O	*Any difference between the turnover reported in the Annual Return (GSTR9) and turnover reported in the audited Annual Financial Statement due to reasons not listed above shall be declared here.*

Introduction

Any other turnover differences as per annual financial statement and annual return which are not covered must be reported here. A separate worksheet maybe needed to compile all those transactions not taxable and reported here. Impact of section 142(11)(C), if any, maybe reported here.

The differential amounts to be categorized as items which needs addition and items which needs to be deducted. Income items such as interest on FD, dividend and duty drawback should be deducted if accounted in financial statements as revenue. Transactions which are treated as supply for GST such as deemed supply due to non-receipt of goods within 1 year after job work or goods sent on approval but not sold in 6 months which are held as deemed supply could be added.

Question 38: *XYZ is a construction company and its annual financial statements are prepared based on the percentage of completion method whereas GST liability is discharged treating the transactions as in the nature of continuous supply of services and accordingly based on the principles of time of supply. How to report the difference between two sets of records?*

Ans: Turnover as per audited annual financial statements (percentage completion method as per the relevant GAAP's) shall be declared in Part III table 5A, and it shall be adjusted according to 5B to 5N to get the turnover as declared in GSTR 9. Further, in case the differences does not fit into the various specific categories of reconciliation issues, then the reasons for the same needs to be given in 5O and must be reported accordingly.

Question 39: *Capital Goods have been sold on which earlier ITC was availed. Profit earned on sale of such capital goods have been reported in the financial statements. How to reconcile the same in the GSTR-9C?*

Ans: In line with the principles of the accounting, profit on sale of the fixed assets is shown in the credit side of P&L account which gets included in the turnover as per audited financial statement. However, the turnover as per GST law includes the sale value of fixed assets. Hence, the adjustment needs to be made by reducing the profit earned from the turnover as per audited financial and addition should be made for the sale value realized to arrive at the value as per GSTR-9. Both the adjustments must be carried out and reported in Table 5O.

Question 40: *Assessee is having various transactions reported as income in the financial statements as under, how to make adjustment of the following categories of income in the GSTR-9C?*

- Divided income
- Duty drawback received
- Excess creditors written back
- TDS appearing in form 26AS but invoice not issued
- Profit on sale of mutual fund units

Ans: These are in the nature of income for the business where no supply is involved. As these items must have already been included in the turnover as per books of account but not in the GSTR-9, it has to be reported in Table 5O as other adjustments.

Question 41: *Whether assessee is required to disclose details of Notice pay recovery from employees in GSTR-9C? If yes, where should it be reported?*

Ans: If the taxable person has considered the notice pay recovered from employees as a taxable supply but has not disclosed the same as an income in the

Profit and Loss account, it would be reported under SI.No.5O of GSTR-9C for the purpose of reconciliation. Data for such recoveries can be ascertained from credits in the Salary / Wages ledger maintained in the books of accounts.

Question 42: *Are there any transactions which appear under the expense head, but has an impact on the outward taxable supplies for the purpose of GST?*

Ans: Yes, there may be such transactions viz., incentives / rebate received from supplier which is considered as a supply under GST is one of such case. Incentives / rebate received from the supplier can be taxable supply under GST depending upon the nature of such incentives. In usual scenarios the taxable person reduces the incentive / rebate received from the cost of purchase in the books of accounts and the said amount will be added under SI. No. 5O, so as to reconcile with value declared in Form GSTR 9.

Question 43: *What is the implication in the reconciliation statement for Inputs and Capital Goods which is sent to a job worker but is not returned within the prescribed period?*

Ans: As per Section 143(3) and 143(4) of the CGST Act, where inputs or capital goods are sent to job worker and such goods are not received within the prescribed period of one year or three years respectively, it will be deemed as a supply on the date when such goods were sent to the job worker. However, such supply may not be treated as an income in the audited annual Financial Statements. In such a situation, the value on which GST is liable to be paid on the goods sent to the job worker is liable to be added under SI No 5O. Data for such transactions can be ascertained from the inventory records and Form ITC-04.

Question 44: *How to disclose the reconciliation differences in case of transactions supplied in the Pre-GST regime and effected as return in the post GST regime?*

Ans: As per the transition provisions [Section 142(1)], taxable person is required to consider return of pre-GST inward supplies as an outward supply and raise a tax invoice for the same. However, for the purpose of accounts, the same would be considered as a purchase return and reduced from the total purchase value instead of being disclosed as a revenue in the books of accounts. In such a situation, the aggregate value of the returns which has been considered as an outward supply under GST has to be adjusted in SI. No. 5O for the purpose of reconciliation.

SI. No. 5P – Annual turnover after adjustments as above – Auto

5P	Annual turnover after adjustments as above	

Introduction

These details would be auto-populated based on the various adjustments as done above.

Sl. No. 5Q – Turnover as declared in Annual Return (GSTR9)

5Q	Turnover as declared in Annual Return (GSTR9)	

Serial No.	Instructions in the Form
5Q	*Annual turnover as declared in the Annual Return (GSTR 9) shall be declared here. This turnover may be derived from Sr. No. 5N, 10 and 11 of Annual Return (GSTR 9).*

Introduction

These details would be auto-populated from Sr. No. 5N, 10 and 11 of Annual Return (GSTR 9).

Sl. No. 5R – Un-Reconciled Turnover (Q - P)-AT1

5E	Un-Reconciled turnover	

Introduction

These details of un-reconciled turnover would be reflected here and the reasons for the same be given by the auditor as explained below. A worksheet of all transaction which are taxable and not captured elsewhere maybe reported here

Sl. No. 6 – Reasons for Un-Reconciled difference in Annual Gross Turnover

6	Reasons for Un-Reconciled difference in Annual Gross Turnover	
A	Reason 1	<<Text>>
B	Reason 2	<<Text>>
C	Reason 3	<<Text>>

Serial No.	Instructions in the Form
6	*Reasons for non-reconciliation between the annual turnover declared in the audited Annual Financial Statement and turnover as declared in the Annual Return (GSTR 9) shall be specified here.*

Introduction

This is the difference between the above two fields is the open un-reconciled turnover. Further, the reasons for the above difference need to be manually entered into the form. The reasons may result in additional tax liability for the taxpayer if there is any short payment of tax due to turnover mismatch.

Sl. No. 7 – Reconciliation of Taxable Turnover

7	Reconciliation of Taxable Turnover

Serial No.	Instructions in the Form
7	*The table provides for reconciliation of taxable turnover from the audited annual turnover after adjustments with the taxable turnover declared in annual return (GSTR-9).*

Introduction

Once the reconciliation of turnover is done on gross basis which may also include certain exempt supplies or non-taxable supplies on which no tax is paid, in order to arrive at the reconciliation of the taxable turnover, this second level of reconciliation is required to be performed. The objective of this reconciliation is to remove the impact of the exempt supplies, non-taxable supplies, zero rated supplies etc. on which no tax is required to be paid by the assessee. In other words, auditor would not be able to achieve the quantification of the additional tax payable unless this reconciliation is carried out.

Sl. No. 7A – Annual Turnover after Adjustments (from 5P)

7A	Annual turnover after adjustments as above	

Serial No.	Instructions in the Form
7A	*Annual turnover as derived in Table 5P above would be auto-populated here.*

Introduction

This field would be auto populated with the amount calculated in Table 5P. Table 5(P) is directly considered as the base for calculating the taxable turnover. Since the total tax liability would be calculated based on the taxable turnover arrived, it is to be noted that all the inputs required to arrive at this field i.e. Table 5P would be accurately calculated and disclosed.

Sl. No. 7B – Value of exempted, nil rated, Non-GST Supplies, No-Supply Turnover

7B	Value of exempted, nil rated, Non-GST Supplies, No-Supply Turnover	

Serial No.	Instructions in the Form
7B	*Value of exempted, nil rated, non-GST and no-supply turnover shall be declared here. This shall be reported net of credit notes, debit notes and amendments if any.*

Introduction

Value of exempted, nil rated and Non-GST supplies have to be reported here. Brief explanation of all these types of transactions is as explained below:

(A) **Exempt Supplies**: Supplies which are leviable to GST but are exempted under section 11 or Section 6 of IGST act shall be reported here. Reference can be given to notification 2/2017-CTR for exempted goods list, 12/2017-CTR for exempted services.

(B) **Nil Rated Supply**: Supplies that are leviable to GST but at presently liable for tax at Nil rated under section 9 of GST Act. Reference can be given to notification 11/2017-CTR.

(C) **Non-GST Supply**: Supplies which excluded from of levy of GST shall be covered here. Example: alcoholic liquor for human consumption. Petrol, ATF and natural gas (presently not covered under the levy)

(D) **No-Supply**: This is a new term used but indicates the supplies which are covered by schedule III of the CGST Act. Example: Sale of land. It is proposed to amend the GST law to include even transactions such as High-sea sales, supply of warehoused goods before home consumption, etc in schedule III.

This column would be aggregate turnover of column 5D i.e. exempted, 5E i.e. Nil rated and 5F i.e. non GST supply, of Annual returns. All such turnovers which shall not form a part of taxable turnover would be reduced on net basis (i.e. after considering debit/credit notes of such supplies). Table 5(P) arrives at the Total GST turnover which is inclusive of all types of supplies under GST. Therefore, in order to arrive at the total **Taxable turnover**, a net off of all the exempt, nil rated, non-GST, and no-supply needs to be done.

Impact of incorrect claim of exemption: Auditor must cross verify the transactions on which any exemption, non-taxability etc. is claimed by the assessee. It must be noted that any exemption notification must be given a strict interpretation and therefore auditor must thoroughly verify the transaction and be satisfied on the correctness of such a claim by the assessee. In case the exemption claimed by the assessee is not proper, then auditor must report this revenue in Sl. No. 5O and not in this field. However, in case there is dis-agreement with the assessee on the claim of such exemption, then auditor can report the same as an observation in part II of the form instead of reporting the transaction as a recommendation in Sl. No. 5O and Part V disclosure.

Reference in financials/returns

- Credit side of the Profit & Loss Account.
- Relevant fields in GSTR 1, GSTR 3B & GSTR 9.
- Returns filed under Central Excise & State VAT/CST for goods liable to tax under the said act.

Sl. No. 7C – Zero Rated Supplies without Payment of Tax

7C	Zero Rated Supplies without Payment of Tax	

Serial No.	Instructions in the Form
7C	*Value of zero rated supplies (including supplies to SEZs) on which tax is not paid shall be declared here. This shall be reported net of credit notes, debit notes and amendments if any.*

Introduction

"Zero rated supply" means any of the following supplies of goods or services or namely:

(a) Export of goods or services or both; or

(b) Supply of goods or services or both to a special economic zone developer or a special economic zone unit.

Zero rated supplies can be with payment or without payment of Tax.

(1) Zero rated supplies made with payment of GST: Already a part of taxable turnover in annual return and thus shall not be declared here.

(2) Zero rated supply made without payment of GST: In order to arrive at the taxable turnover, zero rated supplies made without payment of tax needs to be reduced i.e. to be declared here.

Analysis

Bifurcation of the zero rated supplies: It may be possible that the assessee has supplied the goods/services with payment of tax in one month and has opted for supply of goods/services without payment of tax in the subsequent month. This is also possible for two transactions in the same month. Therefore the auditor must take suitable precautions before reporting the transactions here.

Disclosure of the Zero rated supplies in GSTR 1 & GSTR 3B returns: While reporting the transactions here auditor must note that there is a possibility of incorrect disclosure of the zero rated supplies wrongly as exempt supplies in the GSTR 3B or GSTR 1 return and therefore, auditor may err in the disclosure in case the same is made merely based on such returns without having regard to the verification of the documents or invoice concerning such transaction.

Non-submission of LUT: As explained above, the option to export or supply goods or services to SEZ without payment of tax is available but the responsibility to ensure that export takes place is of the assessee and if the export does not take place within the specified period, tax liability would arise. Therefore, auditor would have to see whether necessary controls exist and whether exports have taken place and where exports did not take place, tax was paid. In such a case there would be variation in the nature of turn over and there could be variation in the turnover itself if the value has changed because of conversion of export to domestic sale.

Reference in financials/returns

In case of exports of goods without payment of tax:

- Credit side of the Profit & loss account;
- Relevant fields in GSTR 1, GSTR 3B and GSTR 9;
- Shipping Bill/Bill of lading, Commercial invoice along with packing list issued for export of goods;
- Application seeking refund of input tax credit, if any along with the details/documents filed therewith;
- Verification of shipping bills from ICEGATE portal on sample basis;

In case of export of services without payment of tax:

- Credit side of the Profit & loss account;
- Relevant fields in GSTR 1, GSTR 3B and GSTR 9;
- Invoices issued for export of services;
- Application seeking refund of input tax credit, if any along with the details/documents filed therewith;
- Bank statement or the certificate issued by the bank for inward remittance of foreign exchange or the FIRC's;

In case supply of services to SEZ without payment of taxes:

- As a practice, the SEZ-recipient issues a copy of the invoice endorsed by the specified officer of the concerned SEZ. Copy of such invoice.
- Default list of authorised operations list of the SEZ recipient if available with the supplier may be verified.
- Declaration from the supplier that the goods/services supplied to SEZ are used only in the authorised operations of the SEZ.
- GST common portal would also provide the details of the registered persons as to whether such registration under GST has been obtained as SEZ or otherwise.

Sl. No. 7D – Supplies on which Tax is to be paid by the recipient on Reverse Charge Basis

7D	Supplies on which Tax is to be paid by the recipient on Reverse Charge Basis	

Serial No.	Instructions in the Form
7D	*Value of reverse charge supplies on which tax is to be paid by the recipient shall be declared here. This shall be reported net of credit notes, debit notes and amendments if any.*

Introduction

GST needs to be paid by recipient on reverse charge basis for certain transactions liable for tax under reverse charge as under:

(a) Section 9(3): Specified category of goods as notified from time to time eg: Raw cotton, cashew etc.

(b) Section 9(3): Specified category of services as notified from time to time eg: GTA, advocate services, importer of services etc.

(c) Section 9(4): procurement of goods or services from unregistered persons by a registered person. Further there is exemption from reverse charge in respect of supplies made by unregistered person not exceeding taxable supplies of Rs. 5,000 per day. This provision is presently deferred w.e.f 13th October 2017 and up to Sept 2019.

Since adjusted annual turnover at column 5P shall not differentiate between whether tax on the same is forward chare or reverse charge. Thus, to arrive at taxable turnover ie. taxed in the hands of the supplier, transactions on which the customer being recipient is liable to pay tax is reduced. The said column would have been declared at column 5C and 5H & I i.e. net of credit/debit notes.

Analysis

Expenses liable under reverse charge need not be disclosed: Expenses on which tax is paid by the assessee as recipient of service under reverse charge should not be disclosed here and the same must be disclosed in table 9. Since, table 7 is concerned with the transactions pertaining to the sales/outward supplies of the assessee, therefore only such transactions on which the supplier has not collected and paid the taxes since the same is paid by the recipient under reverse charge only must be disclosed here.

Customer confirmations not required: As long as the auditor verifies the transactions and satisfies that the transaction is covered within the ambit of reverse charge and the supplier is not liable to collect and pay any taxes on the same, the same is sufficient. It is not expected of the auditor to obtain confirmations from the recipient of supply as to whether or not they have paid tax on this transaction.

Further, even if the recipient has not paid the taxes on such supplies, the liability cannot fall on the supplier as there is no levy to that extent.

Reference in financials/returns

- Credit side of the Profit & loss account;
- Data entered Table 4B of GSTR 1 (Supplies attracting tax on reverse charge);
- Table 3.1(c) (Other outward supplies – Nil rated, exempted) of GSTR 3B

Sl. No. 7E – Taxable turnover as per adjustments above (a-b-c-d)

7E	Taxable turnover as per adjustments above	

Serial No.	Instructions in the Form
7E	*The taxable turnover is derived as the difference between the annual turnover after adjustments declared in Table 7A above and the sum of all supplies (exempted, non-GST, reverse charge etc.) declared in Table 7B, 7C and 7D above.*

Introduction

This column is auto populated with taxable turnover which shall form a base for tax liability to be computed. The value disclosed here represents the actual taxable value for the entire financial year on which tax is required to be paid by the assessee. In other words, any short taxable value considered by the assessee as compared to this value would lead to the additional tax liability.

Sl. No. 7F – Taxable Turnover as per liability declared in Annual Return (GSTR9)

7F	Taxable Turnover as per liability declared in Annual Return (GSTR 9)	

Serial No.	Instructions in the Form
7F	*Taxable turnover as declared in Table (4N – 4G) + (10-11) of the Annual Return (GSTR 9) shall be declared here.*

Taxable turnover at column 7E needs to be compared with the turnover (i.e. Supplies and advances on which tax is to be paid) disclosed in the annual return for differences as per Table (4N-4G) + (10-11) of GSTR 9 is to be replicated here.

Sl. No. 7G – Un-reconciled Taxable Turnover (F-E)

7G	Un-reconciled Taxable Turnover	

The difference between the column 7 F and 7 E would be auto populated in column 7G. The reasons for the same needs to be analyzed and the same needs to be reported in table 8 of the form. Some of the common reasons for such difference could be on account of the following:

(1) Un-reconciled turnover itself at Column 5R

(2) Incorrect disclosure in any of the column of table 5 of GSTR 9C which is considered as the base for further adjustments.

(3) Incorrect disclosure in the annual return with respect to any turnover.

Sl. No. 8 – Un-reconciled Taxable Turnover (F-E)

8	Reasons for Un-Reconciled difference in Taxable Turnover	
A	Reason 1	<<Text>>
B	Reason 2	<<Text>>
C	Reason 3	<<Text>>

Serial No.	Instructions in the Form
8	*Reasons for non-reconciliation between adjusted annual taxable turnover as derived from Table 7E above and the taxable turnover declared in Table 7F shall be specified here.*

Introduction

The reconciliation carried out in table 7 removes the impact of the exempt, non-taxable, zero rated supplies etc. on which tax is not payable and therefore the set of differences which would have impact on tax Liability would actually be part of Table 8 again. This part of GSTR 9C identifies the taxable turnover differences to be placed on record for explaining the differences between the GST Returns and the Audited Financials.

Values are based on which the taxes are computed and therefore any differences in the element of values gets captured in Part II. However, it is possible that the value is properly considered but the actual tax is not proper due to rates or otherwise. Such differences would get highlighted here. In Part III of the Form 9C, Auditor reconciles the rate wise liability of tax, total amount payable thereon with tax actually paid as declared in Annual Return. The additional tax payable due to non-reconciliation of taxable value for any other reason is recommended here. The relevant Part III of the Form 9C is bifurcated into 3 tables i.e. Table 9, 10 and 1122.7. Part III – Reconciliation of Tax Paid.

Question 45: *What can be the various instances of unreconciled differences to be reported in SI No.8 of Form GSTR-9C?*

Ans: Following illustrations can be considered for having the reconciliation differences to be reported in SI No.8 of Form GSTR-9C:

(a) Zero-rated supply made by the registered person during the previous year. However, conditions relevant for the supply has not been complied by the registered person, can be construed to be a regular supply.

(b) Transaction reported in a delivery challan during the financial year for supply on sale or approval basis beyond a period of six months shall be deemed to be a supply under GST. However, that may not be a sale for revenue recognition in the books of accounts for such transaction. Assuming GST returns carry the supply details and no revenue recognition has been done in the books of accounts, this shall call for the reconciliation.

(c) Exemption conditions not fulfilled by the registered person while exercising the option to supply either a Nil rated or Exemption, shall be reported as Regular Supply.

Pt. III	**Reconciliation of Tax Paid**					
9	**Reconciliation of Rate wise liability and amount payable thereon**					
			Tax Payable			
	Description	**Taxable Value**	**Central Tax**	**State Tax**	**Integrated Tax**	**Cess, if Applicable**
	1	2	3	4	5	6
A	5%					
B	5% (RC)					
C	12%					
D	12% (RC)					
E	18%					
F	18% (RC)					
G	28%					
H	28% (RC)					
I	3%					
J	0.25% (RC)					

Pt. III	Reconciliation of Tax Paid					
9	**Reconciliation of Rate wise liability and amount payable thereon**					
			Tax Payable			
	Description	**Taxable Value**	**Central Tax**	**State Tax**	**Integrated Tax**	**Cess, if Applicable**
	1	**2**	**3**	**4**	**5**	**6**
K	0.1%					
L	Interest					
M	Late Fee					
N	Penalty					
O	Others					
P	Total amount to be paid as per tables above		<Auto>	<Auto>	<Auto>	<Auto>
Q	Total amount paid as declared in Annual Return (GSTR 9)					
R	Un-reconciled payment of amount				PT1	

Serial No.	Instructions in the Form
9	*The table provides for reconciliation of tax paid as per reconciliation statement and amount of tax paid as declared in Annual Return (GSTR 9). Under the head labelled —"RC", supplies where tax was paid on reverse charge basis by the recipient (i.e. the person for whom reconciliation statement has been prepared) shall be declared.*
9P	*The total amount to be paid as per liability declared in Table 9A to 9O is auto populated here.*
9Q	*The amount payable as declared in Table 9 of the Annual Return (GSTR9) shall be declared here. It should also contain any differential tax paid on Table 10 or 11 of the Annual Return (GSTR9).*

Introduction

Table 9, 9P & 9Q of the reconciliation statement requires auditor to perform reconciliation of the tax paid with the details of actual tax paid as declared in Annual Returns (GSTR 9). The tax liability needs to be reported rate wise in Table 9. Further, the taxable value and liability of tax on which the assessee has paid tax under Reverse Charge Mechanism is also required to be reported rate-wise separately. The details of total tax payable for the Financial Year 2017-18 as declared in table 9 of the Annual Return is also required to be disclosed along with the differential tax paid vide table 10 & 11 of the Annual Return along with the Interest, Late Fees and Penalty Payable.

Analysis

Sl. No. 11 of form GSTR 9C requires an auditor to compute the additional amount of tax payable but not paid. It is important to note that in order to compute the tax, the values of taxes (i.e. tax base) that is liable for GST needs to be apportioned at an individual rate wise level. We would now briefly understand the information that needs to be disclosed in various columns of the table 9 as under:

Column	Particulars	Explanation
1	Description	This is merely the description of the rate wise bifurcation. It should be available as it is and nothing needs to be filled in by the auditor in this column.
2	Taxable Value	<<Discussed in detail below>>
3	Central Tax	Auditor need to manually calculate the tax payable based on the details of the value provided against the relevant description. For instance, if the taxable value of Rs.1,00,000/- is filled in against the description of 5%, then the tax amount in field must be manually calculated by the auditor i.e. Rs.2,500/- (CGST element) in this case. Whether the manual calculation errors would be auto-corrected and whether the details in this field would be editable or not would be known only once the forms are available on the common portal.
4	State/UT Tax	<Same as above> i.e. the relevant SGST portion needs to be updated here.
5	Integrated Tax	<Same as above> i.e. the relevant IGST portion needs be updated here.
6	Cess, If applicable	<Same as above> i.e. the relevant Cess portion needs be updated here. Since, cess has its own rates of taxes, auditor needs to compute the actual rate of cess and filled in here instead of the rates of taxes as mentioned in column 1 above. Since, compensation cesses is not charged unilaterally and the same is backed with CGST/SGST or IGST, the relevant field of the GST taxes paid on such taxable value would be kept as the base for filling in the details of the cess in the appropriate field.

Taxable values are to be reported in column 2 of the table 9 would be in respect of the following:

(A) Rate wise Taxable value of outward supplies;

(B) Rate wise Taxable value of inward supplies liable under reverse charge.

(A) Taxable value for outward supplies – Sl. No. 9A, C, E, G, I, J, K:

In order to compute the rate wise liability of the taxes payable, auditor needs to update the rate wise details of the taxable value of the outward supplies in column 3 of the Table in the relevant fields as mentioned above. It is important to note that there are total 8 rates of taxes viz., Nil, 0.10%, 0.25%, 3%, 5%, 12%, 18% & 28%.Note: The possibility of the incorrect rate having been used exists. In these cases, the differential tax could be additional to the rates set out. Once the return is finalised, the additional rows maybe be enabled in due course of time.

Mapping with Table 7E of the Reconciliation statement: While updating the details in table 9, auditor must take note of the taxable turnover after adjustments has already been reported by the auditor in table 7. Table 7E already takes into consideration all the adjustments in the turnover reported by the auditor and only the details of the taxable turnover as per the books of accounts is reported in table 7E. Since, the tax rate that is to be applied in this table is only on the taxable turnover as declared in the reconciliation statement, the values that are to be reported in Table 9 should be taxable value as reported under Table 7E of GSTR 9C i.e. Adjusted Total turnover for the FY 2017-18 under GST and amount of tax (rate wise) should be derived accordingly. Therefore, in order to better understand the mechanism of computation of the taxable values, auditor can follow one of the approaches i.e. the Top-Down approach or the Bottom-up approach. Top-Down approach is as under:

(I) Top-Down approach to determine the taxable values:

In this approach auditor ignores the actual taxable values considered by the assessee in its books of accounts and the GSTR 1 returns filed and arrives at the turnover as reported in the financial statements. He performs all the adjustments to the said turnover as given in Sl. No. 5B to 5O and 7B to 7D and then arrives at the taxable values. In other words, this approach is nothing but an extension of the workings already performed by the auditor in table 5B to 5O and 7B to 7D. He maps these workings on monthly basis at rate wise level so that the information available in the working papers is straight away available to be disclosed in table 9.

***Illustrative format of Working Papers in Top-Down Approach:**

S. No.	Particulars	Frequency	0%	0.10 %	0.25 %	3%	5%	12%	18%	28%
A	Turnover (including exports) as per audited financial statements for the State/UT (For multi-GSTIN units under same PAN the turnover shall be derived	Monthly	10	5	10	2	20	50	80	20

S. No.	Particulars		Frequency	0%	0.10 %	0.25 %	3%	5%	12%	18%	28%
	from the audited Annual Financial Statement)										
B	Unbilled revenue at the beginning of Financial Year	(+)	Yearly								
C	Unadjusted advances at the end of the Financial Year	(+)	Yearly								
D	Deemed Supply under Schedule I	(+)	Monthly		2	1	3	6	8	10	
E	Credit Notes issued after the end of the financial year but reflected in the annual return	(+)	Yearly								
F	Trade Discounts accounted for in the audited Annual Financial Statement but are not permissible under GST	(+)	Monthly								
G	Turnover from April 2017 to June 2017	(-)	Monthly								
H	Unbilled revenue at the end of Financial Year	(-)	Yearly								
I	Unadjusted Advances at the beginning of the Financial Year	(-)	Yearly								
J	Credit notes accounted for in the audited Annual Financial Statement but are not permissible under GST	(-)	Monthly								
K	Adjustments on account of supply of goods by SEZ units to DTA Units	(-)	Monthly								
L	Turnover for the period under composition scheme	(-)	Monthly								
M	Adjustments in turnover under section 15 and rules Thereunder	(+/-)	Monthly		5	8	10	2	1	6	6
N	Adjustments in turnover due to foreign exchange Fluctuations	(+/-)	Monthly								
O	Adjustments in turnover due to reasons not listed above	(+/-)	Monthly								
7B	Value of Exempted, Nil Rated, Non-GST supplies, No-Supply	(-)	Monthly		1	2	1	2	2	2	1
7C	Zero rated supplies without payment of tax	(-)	Monthly								
7D	Supplies on which tax is to be paid by the recipient on reverse	(-)	Monthly								
7E	Taxable turnover as per adjustments above (A-B-C-D)			10	11	21	16	30	61	98	27

(*Source: Technical Guide on Annual Return GST Audit issued by ICAI)

(II) Bottom-Up approach to determine the taxable values:

In this approach, auditor would consider the turnovers as disclosed in Annual returns i.e. GSTR 9 which in turn considers various GSTR 1 returns filed by the assessee as the base and later various additions/reductions and adjustments must be performed on such base to achieve the adjusted taxable turnover as reflected in table 7E of the Part II. Various step-wise adjustments that the assessee needs to perform in this approach are as under:

Step 1: Derive the value of turnover as declared in Annual returns (i.e. GSTR 9) from field 5Q of Part II which is to be taken from Sl. No. 5N, 10 & 11 of Form GSTR 9.

Step 2: Review the workings of the GSTR 9 and extract the details as reflected on monthly basis in Form GSTR 1 i.e. monthly returns pertaining to details disclosed in Sl. No. 5N, 10 & 11 of the annual return.

Step 3: Segregate the tax rate wise breakup of such supplies which would be readily available from the data of GSTR 1 in case of B2B supplies. In case of B2C supplies, these details are not be straight away be available from Form GSTR 1. Therefore the auditor can rely upon the books of accounts of the auditee or the working papers maintained in respect of the GSTR 1 to extrapolate this information.

Step 4: Once the rate wise and month wise break-up of the value disclosed in the field 5Q of part II of Form 9C is available, then auditor would add the additional taxable value arising out of the adjustments performed in table 5 from Sl. No. 5B to 5O of Part II and the reasons for such additional liability is disclosed in Table 6.

Step 5: After the above calculations, auditor must reduce the turnover pertaining to exempted supplies, nil rated supplies, non-taxable supplies, No supply, Zero rated supplies (with LUT) and outward reverse charge supplies as given in Sl. No. 7B to 7D of table 7 of this form.

Step 6: The resultant figure after the above adjustment would be the adjusted taxable turnover as reflected in 7E and the auditor possesses the month-wise and rate wise break-up of such taxable turnover which then needs to be disclosed in column 2 of table 9.

(B) Taxable value for inward supplies liable under reverse charge – Sl. No. 9B, D, F, H:

Similar to above, auditor needs to arrive at GST rate wise details of taxable value for inward supplies which are liable to tax under reverse charge. It is pertinent to note that inward supplies are liable to tax under RCM in the following two scenarios:

- Specified category of inward supplies received under Section 9(3) and 5(3) of the CGST Act 2017 and various SGST Acts 2017 and IGST Act 2017 respectively. To understand the specified category of services liable to tax under RCM, refer notification no.13/2017-CGST rate & notification no.10/2017-IGST rate in case of services. Notification no.4/17 CGST Rate and notification no. 4/17 IGST rate in case of goods as amended from time to time can be referred.
- Inward supplies received from an unregistered persons to a registered persons liable to tax as RCM under Section 9(4) and 5(4) of the CGST Act 2017 and various SGST Acts 2017 and IGST Act 2017 respectively. The said details should be taken for a period upto 12th October 2017 only.*[5]

In order to update the details of the taxable value in column 2 of the table 9, the value of inward supply liable for reverse charge needs to be taken from the books of accounts maintained by the assessee. The various steps that an auditor need to take to compute the taxable value is as under:

Step 1: Map the taxable value for reverse charge identified by the assessee and tax paid thereon based on the various tax ledgers created in the books of accounts. These ledgers need to be mapped with the GSTR 3B filed by the assessee.

Step2: Check completeness and correctness of the above in terms of classification, value, rate of tax etc.

Step 3: Check timelines of the above values derived in the books of accounts. Reference must be given to the provisions of time of supply in this regard. Auditor needs to verify that the liability of RCM has been booked in books of accounts accordingly. In case where the liability has not been booked in accordance with happening of aforesaid events, then in that case, reliance can be placed on proviso to Section 12(3) and 13(3) of the GST Acts 2017. The date on which the entry of the inward supplies is made in the books of accounts is made, can be assumed to be the date and thus value of taxable supply along with the rate wise tax liability needs to be decided.

Step 4: Various expense/ asset (capitalization aspect) ledgers needs to be scrutinized and any transaction that is liable for tax under reverse charge

---

5 Suspended from that date due to reason that RCM is not practicable (due in the level of compliance presently in place, ignoring the threshold exemption available to the supplier and fastening the liability of the supplier on the buyer – all being unfair). However care was not taken to do it retrospectively from 1st July 18 (to avoid confusion and make things simple), therefore need to be disclosed.

and not considered above needs to be identified. The debit entries in the income/credit ledgers may also be relevant.

Step 5: Once the taxable values of the transactions liable to reverse charge has been identified, then auditee need to make a segregation tax rate wise.

Step 6: The resultant figure needs to be updated in column 2 of table 9.

Question 46: *Auditor identifies the liability to pay tax under RCM at the time preparation of GSTR-9C. Whether tax on the same may be paid and availed as credits even after expiry of September?*

Ans: Yes, tax on the same can be paid under RCM through this form. However, as per section 16(4) of the CGST ACT, 2017 auditee cannot take input credit after the due date of furnishing return in Form GSTR 3B for the month of September or date of furnishing the relevant Annual return, whichever is earlier. Hence, the input tax credit on such expenses may not be claimed at the time of preparation of GSTR-9 /GSTR-9C which is prepared after end of due date of month of September.*[6]

Implication of Interest: Section 49 of CGST act provides explanation that "other dues" means interest, penalty, fee or any other amount payable under this Act or the rules made thereunder. Where the person liable to pay tax fails to pay the tax within the due date to pay, then interest at specified rate would be levied on the outstanding tax payable from succeeding day of due date till the date of actual payment. Auditor should deduce the above calculations of the taxable values and taxes on outward supplies and reverse charge on monthly basis. This can be compared with the actual tax paid as per GSTR 3B and the tax payment challans (DRC-03). The difference would be the total interest payable.

Late Filing Fee: Section 47 of CGST Act provides for Levy of late fee - Any registered person who fails to furnish the details of outward or inward supplies required under section 37 or section 38 or returns required under section 39 or section 45 by the due date shall pay a late fee. Presently, the late filing fee is as under:

(a) GSTR 1: Delay in filing- nil as due date for the same is extended till 31st October 2018.

(b) GSTR 3B: If tax liability exists- late fee of Rs.50/day. If Nil returns are filed then Rs.20/Day.

(c) GSTR 9: Delay in filing then late fee of Rs.100/Day with maximum fee capped.

---

6 ITC is an indefeasible right and the provision may need tob read down by Courts. Till then only ITC can be taken GSTR 3B and reversed under protest.

Penalty: Various penalties would be paid by the assessee during departmental audits, assessments etc. The auditee may have paid penalty under Section 129 of the GST Acts for non-compliance in respect of e-way bill requirement for movement of goods or without compliance of Rule 138 of the GST Rules. Auditor need to review the ledger of penalties, if any maintained by assessee or any other similar ledger maintained in the books of accounts to identify these transactions. It is important to note that late filing fee is not a penalty. Therefore, the details of the late filing fee only must be reported and penalty is not be reported here.

Note: It must be noted that in the present structure of form, the details of interest, late fee and penalty is demanded to be entered with a break up of CGST, SGST, IGST and cess, which would be very challenging for the auditor to compute. It is expected that a suitable amendment in the said fields would be made.

Challenges/Issues

Difference in the taxable values or tax paid as per GSTR 1 & GSTR 3B: It must be noted that in this approach auditor prepare the workings keeping the details as reflected in GSTR 1 as the base. There may be a difference between GSTR 3B and GSTR 1 data filed by the assessee. The nature and the reason of such differences can be numerous as this is the first year of implementation of GST. Therefore, auditor must firstly understand the nature of such difference, reason for such error etc. Further he is to assess what should be the correct disclosure and which record shows the correct figures. Then proper effect for each of such difference must be given based on facts of each case.

Rate wise bifurcation of the taxable values/taxes: The reporting in this table becomes easy if the taxable values and the taxes are kept with the rate wise bifurcation in the books of accounts. However, it must be noted that practically based on the system of accounting followed by the assessee, following permutations and combinations of reporting is possible:

(a) Taxable values and also tax ledgers are segregated and kept various rate-wise;

(b) Ledgers for taxable values is maintained rate wise but the tax ledgers is a single consolidated without any such bifurcation.

(c) Ledgers for taxes is maintained rate wise but the taxable values ledgers is a single consolidated without any such bifurcation.

(d) Neither the ledgers for taxable values nor the ones of tax is maintained with a bifurcation of rate-wise.

While the practice in (a) above eases the work of the auditor, the practice followed in (d) complicates the task of this reporting. Therefore, in order to break and segregate the taxable values rate wise, auditor may advise the tax payer to use various tools such as Micros in MS excel or special software tools to cull out this information. If no such tool available and the volume of the transactions is very high and different rates are applicable with no rate wise bifurcation of tax, it would be difficult to verify the accuracy of data. The auditor may consider making an observation that due to lack of availability of rate wise tax liability from the books of accounts, he is not in a position to furnish details in the given table.

Reporting on classification matters: One of the contentious issue that may arise is in respect of the reporting of the classification disputes in Table 9 under Part III of GSTR 9C. An issue may arise as to how an auditor should deal with classification and place of supply issues. This is explained with the following illustration:

Question 47: *X a Registered Person has classified EPC Contract of Solar Power Plants as Supply of Goods classifiable under Chapter 85 and has reflected it under 5% GST rate. The Works Contract Service rate is 18%. Auditor feels it is 18%. What should he do?*

Ans: Where client agrees with the contention of Auditor then it should be shown under 18% rate. Auditor to recommend for payment of additional tax.

In case client does not agree the Auditor qualify in the main certificate under the opinion paragraph stating that the proper classification is WCT and rate of GST should be 18%.

Question 48: *Due to the nature of business of a Registered Person, types of supply, complexities of transactions and size of operations, the Auditor is unable to identify or comment upon each and every classification of outward and inward supplies. How should Auditor approach to punch data in Table 9?*

Ans: The Auditor in such a case, may put in his comments in the main certificate under opinion paragraph (4 or 5, as the case may be). He can state that the classification aspect has been considered as noticed during audit and is subject to the information and declaration or management representation as provided by the Registered Person. It should be clearly specified that all aspects of classification have not been considered. Due to the lack of availability of rate wise tax liability from the books of accounts, the Auditor should state that he is not in a position to punch the details in the given table. Further, Auditor should get signed by management in Management Representation letter (MRL) that the above information was not available as required which may result into a limitation for an audit.

Limitations in the audit: In case the auditor is unable to identify or comment upon each and every classification of outward and inward supplies then in such case, auditor may put in his comment in the main certificate under opinion paragraph (4 or 5, as the case maybe) as under;

That all aspects of classification have not been considered.

That the issues that may arise on account of classification have not been dealt with in detail and only those as noticed during the course of audit have been duly considered and have been reported.

That the classification aspect has been considered as noticed during the course of audit. That it is subject to the information and declaration or management representation as received from the client.

Similarly, for identification of tax liability on RCM or the time of supply then it should be reported that it was not possible to identify.

Sl. No. 9P – Total amount to be paid as per tables above

The total tax liability along with late fee, interest, penalty and other amount paid and shown above would be auto populated here.

Sl. No 9Q- Total amount paid as declared in the annual return GSTR 9

Details of tax paid as declared in returns filed during the financial year along with differential tax paid (As at Column 14 of Annual return) on account of declaration of the transactions for the previous FY declared in returns of April to September of current FY or up to the date of filing of annual return of previous FY whichever is earlier would be declared here. Amount of Service tax or VAT paid/adjusted, then:

(1) Paid and adjusted before June 2017 then shall not form a part of disclosure here

(2) Paid before June, 17 but adjusted in March 18 shall not form a part of disclosure here as such reduction shall not be through GST credit note.

Sl. No. 9R – Un-Reconciled Payment of Amount

The difference between the column 9P and 9Q would be auto populated in column 9R. The reasons for the same needs to be analyzed and it needs to be reported in table 10 of the form. Some of the common reasons for such difference could be on account of the following:

(1) Unreconciled turnover itself at Column 5R

(2) Incorrect disclosure in any of the column of table 5 of GSTR 9C which is considered as the base for further adjustments.

(3) Difference of opinion on classification of goods/services and rate tax on that.

Sl. No. 10 – Reasons for Un-Reconciled Payment of Amount

10	Reasons for Un-Reconciled payment of tax	
A	Reason 1	<<Text>>
B	Reason 2	<<Text>>
C	Reason 3	<<Text>>

Serial No.	Instructions in the Form
10	*Reasons for non-reconciliation between payable/liability declared in Table 9P above and the amount payable in Table 9Q shall be specified here.*

Introduction

For each identified non-reconciliation, auditor would provide reasons and enter manually. The reasons may result in additional tax liability for the taxpayer if there is any short payment of tax due to non/short consideration of the taxable value by the assessee, incorrect rate of tax applied etc.

Analysis

Some of the reasons for non-reconciliation of the taxes paid with that of the taxes payable can be as under:

Mis-match with GSTR 3B: Non-disclosure or incorrect disclosure of the taxable values or tax amount in GSTR 3B. It may be possible that such incorrect disclosure is also carried out in the GSTR 1 and also the books of accounts of the assessee. However, it may also be possible that the incorrect disclosure is only made in GSTR 3B but the GSTR 1 or the books of accounts properly discloses the taxable values. In case, the values and taxes are properly reflecting in the GSTR 1 or books of accounts but the same is not considered in GSTR 3B, then such difference would get reflected here.

Mis-match with books of accounts: It is also possible that GSTR 1 and GSTR 3B inter se matches but the figure reported therein does not match with the books of accounts. In such a situation, the difference would get reflected in the reconciliations carried in Part II. The reasons for such reconciliation would already get reported in table 6 or 8 case the case may be. Here, auditor must be careful to not include the additional tax liability. Therefore, once the differences are arrived at in table 10, auditor must report the reasons for such differences based on the differences already covered earlier in table 6 and 8 and the additional differences noted here.

Mis-match with GSTR 1: It is also possible that the mis-match is only with the GSTR 1 whereas the books properly match with the GSTR 3B. In such a situation, the difference may not result in any additional tax liability as the same must have already been considered and paid in GSTR 3B. Therefore, the auditor must take note of this scenario and need not recommend for the payment of additional tax liability again.

Sl. No. 11 – Additional amount payable but not paid (due to reasons specified under tables 6, 8 and 10 above)

11	Additional amount payable but not paid (due to reasons specified under Tables 6,8 and 10 above)					
			To be paid through Cash			
	Description	Taxable Value	Central tax	State tax/UT tax	Integrated tax	Cess, if applicable
	1	2	3	4	5	6
	5%					
	12%					
	18%					
	28%					
	3%					
	0.25%					
	0.10%					
	Interest					
	Late Fee					
	Penalty					
	Others (please specify)					

Serial No.	Instructions in the Form
11	*Any amount which is payable due to reasons specified under Table 6, 8 and 10 above shall be declared here.*

Introduction

Additional liability to pay tax for non-reconciled items due to various reasons specified at table 6, 8 and 10 would be determined with different rate of taxes applicable with declaration at respective fields of table 11. These additional amounts are to be paid in cash only even though the taxable person may have sufficient credit in electronic credit ledger. Further these payments made in cash may not be available as input tax credit to any recipient (B2B) and may have to be borne by taxable person. It is also to be noted only the disclosure of the **additional amount** payable in cash must be disclosed here and not the whole tax liability which is already paid. Section 41(2) of CGST Act provides utilisation of ITC only for self-assessed tax. As the liability under this table 11 is determined by auditor, it appears that the table specifies for cash payment without utilising ITC.

Analysis

After all the workings carried out in respect of the outward supplies and reverse charge, the final values of the additional tax liability that needs to be paid must be reported here. At this juncture, it becomes important for an auditor to understand the relationship between the various reconciliations carried out above in table 5, 7 and 9 and the reasons reported therein in table 6, 8 and 10.

Relationship between various reconciliations in table 5, 7 and 9: Auditor must note that all the reconciliation differences cannot lead to additional tax liability, therefore explained below is the relationship between the various reconciliations:

(1) **Table 5 - Reconciliation of Gross Turnover:** The reconciliation carried out in table 5 is on the gross turnover and therefore the difference in turnover noted and the reasons mentioned therein in table 6 also includes the impact of exempt, non-taxable, zero rated supplies etc. which are not liable for tax. Further, in other types of non-reconciliations reported in Table 6, there can be an impact on the tax Liability to be paid. The instances for same would principally cover such cases where there is difference in taxable turnover in GST Returns and Adjusted Total turnover.

(2) **Table 7 - Reconciliation of Taxable Turnover:** The reconciliation carried out in table 7 removes the impact of the exempt, non-taxable, zero rated supplies etc. on which tax is not payable and therefore the set of differences which have an impact on tax Liability should actually be part of Table 8 again.

(3) **Table 9 – Reconciliation of the Tax Paid:** In both the above reconciliations carried out, the auditor is merely arriving at the taxable value. However, in order to arrive at the actual tax payable, one has to apply the tax rates on the taxable values determined in table 7. Further, the impact of reverse charge is also not seen in above tables and the impact of short payment of taxes on this count is also reported here.

In other words, it must be noted that all the above reconciliations carried out are not independent exercises and instead the reconciliation in table 5 supplements the reconciliation in table 7 and a first level of filtering takes place. From the taxable value computed in table 7, the second level of filtering takes place whereby the tax which is already paid on the taxable value through challans and reported in GSTR 3B would get reconciled and only the balance additional tax payable would remain as un-reconciled here.

Impact of excess tax paid by the assessee: It is very much possible that in the process of reconciliation auditor notes that there is an excess tax paid by the assessee. In such a case, no reporting should be done in Table 11 as there may not be provision of negative reporting in Table 11. Auditor cannot recommend the payment of taxes netting of with the excess tax paid otherwise. However, auditor can separately report to the management. Auditee would be required to pay additional tax as reported by the auditor in table 11 and claim refund of the excess tax paid at his option.

22.6.2.1 Part IV – Reconciliation of net Input Tax Credit (ITC) declared in audited annual financial statement with net ITC declared in annual return (GSTR 9)

Introduction

This part focuses on reconciliation in respect of the input tax credits availed by the assessee between the ITC declared as per audited financial statements and ITC as declared in the annual returns. The process of reconciliation as laid out in Form 9C is to start from the ITC as per financial statements and make necessary adjustments to reconcile with the credits disclosed in the annual returns.

In other words, assessees would have to derive the ITC as per the audited financial statements and then the adjustments must be carried out to the said ITC to arrive at the ITC as disclosed in the annual returns. Therefore, in the process of preparation of Form 9C, auditor must first plot the numbers as per the audited financial statements and then work backwards to match the same with the annual returns. Adjustments which have already been considered between GSTR-3B and Annual Return (GSTR-9) need not be considered here.

Sl. No. 12 – Reconciliation of Net Input Tax Credit (ITC)

This field requires reconciliation of ITC on net basis i.e. after considering reversals if any.

12	Reconciliation of Net Input Tax Credit (ITC)

I. No.12A - ITC availed as per audited annual financial statement for the State/UT (for multi-GSTIN units under same PAN this should be derived from books of accounts)

12A	ITC availed as per audited Annual Financial Statement for the State/UT (For multi-GSTIN units under same PAN this should be derived from books of accounts)	

Serial No.	Instructions in the Form
12A	*ITC availed (after reversals) as per the audited Annual Financial Statement shall be declared here. There may be cases where multiple GSTINs (State wise) registrations exist on the same PAN. This is common for persons/entities with presence over multiple States. Such persons/entities, will have to internally derive their ITC for each individual GSTIN and declare the same here. It may be noted that*

Serial No.	Instructions in the Form
	reference to audited Annual Financial Statement includes reference to books of accounts in case of persons/entities having presence over multiple States.

Introduction

In this field assessee has to enter ITC availed as per annual financial statement for the State/UT. It is pertinent to note here that, for entities having multiple presence across the country and having centralized accounting, SL.NO.12A requires ITC availed separately for each of the GSTIN i.e. for each registration the ITC as per books of accounts have to be segregated as the same needs to be entered here, even when centralized accounting is carried out for all the units across India.

Analysis

Net ITC to be disclosed: It is pertinent to note here that Net ITC as availed in the books of accounts has to be disclosed after considering the effect of the following:

- Reversals due to ineligible credits, lapse of the time limit, non-payment to vendor within 180 days or on account of both taxable and exempt supplies etc.;
- Debit notes issued by the supplier if any;
- Credit note issued by the supplier if any.

ITC availed from July 17 to Mar 18 to be considered for the FY 2017-18: As GST was rolled out from 1st July'17, GST have been levied and collected in the current financial year only for a period of 9 months. For the period April'17 to June'17, as there was no GST (taxes like service tax, excise duty, VAT were being levied), the ITC claimed under earlier laws would not to be considered under this column.

Aggregate of ITC claimed during the year needs to be disclosed: Aggregate of the ITC claimed on the following during the year has to be disclosed under SL.NO.12A:

- ITC on all eligible inputs, capital goods and input services;
- ITC on transactions on which tax has been paid on reverse charge basis.

This would be relevant for all transactions pertaining to FY 2017-18 in respect of which input tax credit has been taken in the period April 2018 to September 2018. Here, it is important to note that irrespective of when the credits have been claimed in the returns or whether or not such credits are eligible, auditor must fill the details of the credit if the accounting of same has been done in the financial statements for FY 17-18. In case, any credits eligible for in 17-18 but has been availed in the books in the FY 18-19, then such credits must not be disclosed here.

ITC availed in the ISD registration: In case where an ISD registration is taken by the assessee, the credits are first availed by the ISD unit and then said credit is distributed to its different units based on their turnover. These credits should be considered and disclosed under this serial no. by the units only when the said credit has been distributed by the ISD unit. When the credit is availed by the ISD unit and not distributed to various other GSTIN units of the said entity, it cannot be considered by these other units and no disclosure of the same is required under this head. Such undistributed credits could be ineligible as well as they are completely used at respective registered place of business.

Disclosure of Compensation Cess: Credit of compensation cess can be used only for payment of outward compensation cess. In case an entity is eligible to avail the credit of compensation cess, the same needs to be disclosed under this serial number. For Example: In case of luxury car dealer, his inputs are liable to cess and also he is liable for cess on his outward sales. Therefore, such dealer needs to disclose the ITC availed on cess under this head. However, it is important to note that where the entity is not eligible to avail credit of input cess, it will result as cost to the company and the disclosure is not required under this head.

Tax Ledgers maintained in the books of accounts: In case of separate ledgers maintained, the amounts could be directly related to the GSTIN for reporting. The information would be collated from net of debit and credits (other than payments) of such account codes/ledger names in the accounting software. However, in case assessee is maintaining single accounting ledger for all the states, then it would be a challenge for the auditor to bifurcate such credits. Although, auditor can take the segregated details from the returns filed for each of the GST number, yet it is recommended to the auditor as it would defeat the purpose of this exercise since the matching of returns to returns may not throw any reconciliation difference. Where the task becomes too cumbersome wherein auditor would have to verify each invoice to ascertain the GSTIN for which the credit relates, in such a situation, he may certify the amount of ITC availed and thus, suitable assurance in form of corroborative evidence should be taken by the Auditor.

ITC claimed as refund: It is pertinent to note that in case of zero rated supplies, inverted tax rate structure, assessee can claim refund of the input taxes credit availed. Therefore, even in case of a situation where the assessee is claiming a refund of the taxes paid, since the input tax credit was initially availed, the details of such credit must be reflected here.

Segregation of the transitional credits: Due care must be taken by the assessee to segregate and remove the transitional credits from the total credits availed. The details of the transitional credits must be disclosed in the subsequent tab i.e. in the Sl. No. 12B. For example, Total credit availed by the assessee in the FY 2017-18 in the books of accounts is Rs. 1 crore which also includes the credit availed through the Form TRAN 1 of Rs. 20 lakhs, then the ITC to be disclosed here would be only Rs. 80 lakhs and balance Rs. 20 lakh needs to be disclosed in sl.no.12B.

Reference from Financials/Returns

ITC as per books of accounts can be taken from the credit ledgers (like input CGST ledger, input SGST ledger, input IGST ledger, etc.) under the head current assets provided that they have been correctly accounted for during the year after considering the impact of ineligible credits and reversals if any.

Sl. No.12B - ITC booked in earlier financial years claimed in current financial year

12B	ITC booked in earlier Financial Years claimed in current Financial Year	(+)	

Serial No.	Instructions in the Form
12B	*Any ITC which was booked in the audited Annual Financial Statement of earlier financial year(s) but availed in the ITC ledger in the financial year for which the reconciliation statement is being filed for shall be declared here. This shall include transitional credit which was booked in earlier years but availed during the Financial Year 2017-18.*

Introduction

In this field assessee is required to fill in information regarding ITC which is accounted for in the books of accounts in the earlier year but the credit of which is being claimed in the returns filed during the current financial year. As GST has been rolled out in the year 2017 itself, there will be no credit of GST which must have been accounted for by the assessee in the year 2016 and claimed in the return during the year 2017. Therefore, practically this field will not be required to be entered for FY 17-18 in respect of GST credits. However, going forward from next FY 18-19 this field will be applicable.

Analysis

Transitional credits of closing balance to be disclosed here: One must note here that information regarding transitional credits, i.e. credit of erstwhile taxes like service tax, excise duty, VAT, etc. which have been accounted for in the FY 16-17, but the credit of which has been taken by the assessee during this FY 17-18 has to be entered in this filed. In simple words for the current FY 17-18, a taxpayer has to enter the amount of transitional credit claimed by him under Form TRAN-1. However, it must be noted that all the transitional credits do not warrant disclosure here as only those transitional credits on which credit was already taken in the earlier financial years must be disclosed here. The following table would assist auditor in determining the various credits to be claimed here:

Nature of credit	Disclosure Table	Remarks
Closing balance in service tax, excise, VAT returns transferred to GST u/s 140(1)	12A & 12B	Auditor must break the credits from the closing balance transferred in TRAN 1 and the ones availed in FY 16-17 and earlier needs to be reported in Sl. No. 12B. Further, the closing balance of the transitional credits which has been availed in Apr 17 to Jun 17 must be disclosed in Sl. No. 12A.
50% credit of capital goods availed by the assessee through Form TRAN 1	12A	These credits in respect of the capital goods were not availed by the assessee in the earlier financial year and the same is availed for the first time in this financial year. Therefore, the same needs to be disclosed in Sl. No. 12A.
Credit on stocks availed by the assessee in Form TRAN 1	12A	These credits in respect of the stocks were not availed by the assessee in the earlier financial year and the same is availed for the first time in this financial year in Form TRAN 1. Therefore, the same needs to be disclosed in Sl. No. 12A.
Credit on stocks availed by the assessee in Form TRAN 2	12A	These credits in respect of the stocks were not availed by the assessee in the earlier financial year and the same is availed for the first time in this financial year in Form TRAN 2. Therefore, the same needs to be disclosed in Sl. No. 12A.
Credit is availed by the assessee under section 142(11)(C) in Form TRAN 1 in case where both VAT and service tax is been paid on the transaction mainly in works contracts and construction service	12A	These credits were not availed by the assessee in the earlier financial year and the same is availed for the first time in this financial year in Form TRAN 2. Therefore the same needs to be disclosed in Sl. No. 12A.

Reference in Financials/Returns

The information to be filled in this column for the current year i.e. 17-18 can be taken from Form TRAN - 1 & TRAN - 2 i.e. the aggregate value of the credit transferred from earlier regime to GST regime.

Sl. No.12C - ITC booked in current financial year to be claimed in subsequent financial year

12C	ITC booked in current Financial Year to be claimed in subsequent Financial Years	(-)	

Serial No.	Instructions in the Form
12C	*Any ITC which has been booked in the audited Annual Financial Statement of the current financial year but the same has not been credited to the ITC ledger for the said financial year shall be declared here.*

Introduction

This serial number requires the value of ITC which is accounted for in the current financial year in the books of accounts, but the credit of which is going to be claimed in the next financial year in the GST returns. The auditor must verify the ITC which are appearing in the GST credit ledgers in the books of accounts but are not reflected in the ITC register reported in GSTR 3B of FY 2017-18. The difference of such unclaimed balance would be reported here.

Analysis

For Example: Invoice dated 30th March'18 received by the recipient on April '18. ITC on these purchases have been accounted for in the books of accounts for the year ended 31st March '18. In this case, ITC of tax paid would be availed in the GSTR 3B for the month of April'18 or thereafter.

Value of ITC on such transactions has to be entered under SL.NO.12C. A few of the reasons for booking the ITC in the current year and claiming it in the return in the next financial year can be as under:

- Year End purchases – cut off procedures, ITC not availed as goods/services not received;
- Credit missed to be considered while filing the return;
- Hard copy invoice not received;
- Credit note issued by the vendor.
- Credit on stock transfer of goods claimed by receiving branch before receipt of goods.

The objective behind reducing this value from the ITC as per audited financial statements is that when the assessee has not claimed the ITC in return in this year, the scrutiny of such ITC would result in duplication of work. Once when accounted in books and secondly when the same is claimed in the GST returns.

Once the ITC is claimed in returns, it affects the government revenue and it is only then, when its correctness and eligibility needs to be verified.

RCM credit availed in subsequent month: In cases where the entity avails credit on transactions covered under reverse charge basis in the following month in which tax has been paid, at the year ending (e.g. March'18) it may so happen that the transaction has been accounted for in the previous year (17-18) while credit availed in the returns in subsequent year (18-19). Hence, ITC over such transactions is required to be considered under this head.

Credit claimed under different GSTN: Many entities have presence over multiple States having separate GSTN numbers for each of its location. However, the accounting is carried out centrally. Therefore, it may so happen that credit is accounted for in the books of accounts under the head of a different location while in GSTR-3B the said ITC is claimed in some other location. **For Example:** In books of accounts credit on purchases accounted under Gujarat division, however the said credit is taken in GSTR 3B of Maharashtra division.

Credit claimed based on the GSTR 2A reflected in the portal: GSTR 2A is a return which is auto populated based on the suppliers' outward return (GSTR - 1). Many times it so happens that the recipient misses to avail credit on few of its purchases, however the same are reflected in GSTR 2A. The recipient may avail the credit by accepting the said entry in form GSTR 2A, however the same may not be accounted in books of accounts. However, it must be noted that un-reconciled transactions appearing in GSTR 2A should not be directly disclosed here. The amounts appearing in GSTR 2A could be for various reasons including vendor uploading transactions with wrong GSTIN – This credit cannot be availed by the recipient since the purchase does not belong to him though appearing in his GSTR 2A.

Sl. No.12D - ITC availed as per audited financial statements or books of account

12D	ITC availed as per audited financial statements or books of account	<Auto>

Serial No.	Instructions in the Form
12D	*ITC availed as per audited Annual Financial Statement or books of accounts as derived from values declared in Table 12A, 12B and 12C above will be auto-populated here.*

Based on the amount declared under SL.NO.12A, 12B and 12C, this field would be auto populated. After the aforesaid adjustments are done this field will reflect only that amount of ITC which has been claimed in the GST returns in the current financial year irrespective of the year in which it has been accounted for in the books of accounts. Assessee needs to re-validate the details so auto-populated.

Sl. No.12E – ITC claimed in the annual return (GSTR 9)

12E	ITC claimed in the annual return (GSTR 9)	

Serial No.	Instructions in the Form
12E	*Net ITC available for utilization as declared in Table 7J of Annual Return (GSTR9) shall be declared here.*

This field requires the disclosure of the amount of ITC that has been claimed by the assessee in form GSTR 9. i.e. the aggregate of ITC claimed by the assessee in GSTR-3B filed for the period July'17 to March'18. The required value in this field would be auto populated from the table 7J of Form GSTR 9.

Sl. No.12F – Un-reconciled ITC

12F	Un-reconciled ITC	ITC 1

The difference between ITC claimed as per audited financial statements and annual return (GSTR 9) will get auto populated here. This is the un-reconciled ITC of the assessee which may be disputed by the department and reasons for non-reconciliation will have to be figured out by the assessee. Assessee needs to re-validate the details so auto-populated.

Sl.No.13 – Reasons for Un-reconciled difference in ITC

13	Reasons for Un-Reconciled difference in ITC	
A	Reason 1	<<Text>>
B	Reason 2	<<Text>>
C	Reason 3	<<Text>>

Serial No.	Instructions in the Form
13	*Reasons for non-reconciliation of ITC as per audited Annual Financial Statement or books of account (Table 12D) and the net ITC (Table12E) availed in the Annual Return (GSTR9) shall be specified here.*

Introduction

Auditor needs to provide the reasons for the difference in ITC availed as per audited financial statements and as per Annual return derived in Sl.No.12F.

Analysis

In case the difference is positive, possible reasons for difference can be due to the following:

- The amount of ITC for the financial year claimed in the point 13 of Annual return form which is the amount of ITC claimed in returns of subsequent year for the financial year;
- The amount of ITC available but not availed either due to non-eligibility for ITC or simple non-availment in return or ITC which has lapsed as credit not availed.

In case the difference is negative, the matter is of concern as it is a clear indication of more than available ITC has been claimed. This could be on account of following reasons:

- ITC of another GSTIN claimed in returns of GSTIN under audit;
- Duplicate ITC availed;
- ITC of subsequent year where goods/services were received later but ITC availed based on the invoice received earlier.

Various reasons for differences noted here can be due to the following:

Credit of tax paid on Reverse Charge: As per section 9(3) and 9(4) of the CGST Act, on the notified goods and services and supplies from unregistered persons, tax is to be paid on reverse charge basis. In case of such transactions, as taxable invoice is not received from the supplier, it may so happen that the input tax credit is missed to be accounted for such transactions in the books of accounts at the time of invoice booking. However, while filing GSTR-3B, the tax and credit on the said transaction is rightly paid and credit is also availed. There is high probability of differences in ITC occurring due to this reason.

Year End Purchases: Invoice dated 30th March'18 received by the recipient in April '18. Hence, ITC on these purchases will be accounted for in the books of accounts for the year ended 31st March '18, However, credit of tax paid will be availed in the return for the month of April'18.

Timing of availing the credit: Similarly, one must note that conditions as prescribed in section 16 needs to be complied with, in order to avail the input tax credit. Therefore, credit is not available merely on receipt of the invoice and its accounting thereon. Auditor must check that the following conditions are also satisfied:

(a) He is in possession of a tax invoice or debit note issued by a supplier registered under this Act;

(b) He has received the goods or services or both.

(c) The tax charged in respect of such supply has been actually paid to the Government

(d) He has furnished the return under section 39

(e) He has made the payment within 180 days.

Transitional Credit: Many taxpayers have not been able to file their Tran 1 form and claim credit due to technical glitches in the GST portal. However, these credits have been accounted by the taxpayers in their books of accounts for the year 17-18.

Ineligible Credits Claimed: It may so happen that ineligible ITC may be availed in the books of accounts by the taxpayer, however the same is rightly reversed while filing of form GSTR 3B, resulting into difference between books and returns.

There may be several other reasons for differences in ITC as per Audited financial statements and as per Annual Return. One of the fundamental features of GST is the seamless flow of input credit across the chain (from the manufacture of goods, supplier of service till it is consumed) and across the country. ITC is equivalent to cash for a taxpayer. Therefore, excess availment or incorrect availment and utilization of credit has a direct nexus with reduction in revenue for the Government. Hence, in order to avoid the leakage of credits, assessee must reconcile the Input tax credit on timely basis.

Question 49: *An entity is required to reverse the credits after expiry of 180 days on account of non-payment to supplier did not have sufficient balance of credit. The reversal was made by discharging the tax liability in cash. How to adjust in the GSTR-9 or GSTR-9C?*

Ans: Any tax payments made in cash for discharging tax liability for the previous FY needs to be shown in part IV table 9 and for current FY in part V table 12 of GSTR 9. There is no disclosure requirement of the same in GSTR- 9C.

Question 50: *Certain eligible credits have been availed in the books of account but missed in the annual return. Whether same has to be reversed through the reconciliation statement?*

Ans: Last date of availment of credit for any FY is till due date of filing GST return for September of next FY or date of filing the Annual returns whichever is earlier. As the credits have not been taken in GSTR-3B till the due date of filing of return of month of September, it cannot be taken in GSTR-9. The difference between ITC as per books of account and GSTR-9 is required to be reported in Table 12F and reason of such difference to be explained in Table 13. However, this may not arise any additional liability as such credit has never been utilized for payment of liability under GST.

Question 51: *Many taxpayers have not been able to file their TRAN 1 credit due to technical portal issues. However, these credits have been accounted by the taxpayers in their books of accounts for the year 17-18. Does this affect the ITC reconciliation and is it required to be disclosed?*

Ans: Yes, the above issue will lead to difference in reconciliation under table 12F i.e. ITC between annual audited financial statement and Annual Return (Form GSTR 9). The difference on account of Tran 1 credit which has been booked in the audited financial statement of current year but the same has not been credited to the ITC ledger for the said financial year will result in one of the reconciliation item and required to be explained by auditor.

This maybe reversed under protest as the GST portal had several issues and tax payer cannot be an expert ion filing.

Sl.No.14 – Reconciliation of ITC declared in the annual return (GSTR 9) with ITC availed on expenses as per audited annual financial statement or books of account

14	Reconciliation of ITC declared in Annual Return (GSTR9) with ITC availed on expenses as per audited Annual Financial Statement or books of account			
	Description	**Value**	**Amount of Total ITC**	**Amount of eligible ITC availed**
	1	**2**	**3**	**4**
A	Purchases			
B	Freight/Carriage			
C	Power and Fuel			
D	Imported goods (Including received from SEZs)			
E	Rent and Insurance			
F	Goods lost, stolen, destroyed, written off or disposed of by way of gift or free samples			
G	Royalties			
H	Employees' Cost (Salaries, wages, Bonus etc.)			
I	Conveyance charges			
J	Bank Charges			
K	Entertainment charges			
L	Stationery Expenses (including postage etc.)			

14	**Reconciliation of ITC declared in Annual Return (GSTR9) with ITC availed on expenses as per audited Annual Financial Statement or books of account**			
	Description	**Value**	**Amount of Total ITC**	**Amount of eligible ITC availed**
	1	**2**	**3**	**4**
M	Repair and Maintenance			
N	Other Miscellaneous expenses			
O	Capital goods			
P	Any other expense 1			
Q	Any other expense 2			
R	Total amount of eligible ITC availed			<<Auto>>
S	ITC claimed in Annual Return (GSTR9)			
T	Un-reconciled ITC			ITC 2

Serial No.	**Instructions in the Form**
14	*This table is for reconciliation of ITC declared in the Annual Return (GSTR9) against the expenses booked in the audited Annual Financial Statement or books of account. The various sub-heads specified under this table are general expenses in the audited Annual Financial Statement or books of account on which ITC may or may not be available. Further, this is only an indicative list of heads under which expenses are generally booked. Taxpayers may add or delete any of these heads but all heads of expenses on which GST has been paid/was payable are to be declared here.*

Introduction

This table requires reconciliation of ITC availed on various expenses as per books of accounts and as per Annual Return. The assessee needs to disclose the ITC availed under each head of expense during the year and it needs to be reconciled with the figures in Annual Return. In case auditor notes that there is any ineligible input tax credit has been claimed, then he needs to highlight the same. This would lead to a reconciliation difference and eventual liability. The various expense heads which are given under table 14 are as above in the table.

Analysis

The list of expense head given in the form is indicative: It is very important to note here that the list of expenses as given under table 14 of form GSTR 9C is only an indicative list and not exhaustive. Entities may have various major heads of expenses based on their nature of business and may vary from the list as given above. Therefore, entities can edit the above given list of expense head by adding the expenses which are not given in the above list. Also, it is not mandatory to enter value in each of the expense head as given above. If any of the expenditures is not applicable for the entity the same may be left blank.

Disclosure of prepaid expenses: Prepaid expenses are not reflected in the profit & loss account of the entity. However, they are recorded in the balance sheet. It may so happen that all the expenses as reflected in the Profit & Loss account are considered for disclosure under this head and the expenses recorded in the balance sheet may get missed out. Prepaid expenses recorded in the balance sheet is to considered for disclosure under the relevant head.

Situation where ineligible ITC is booked to costs: As ITC of tax paid on a few expenses is blocked and is ineligible like ITC of tax paid on food and beverages, motor vehicles, etc. entities follow a policy of not considering these ineligible ITC's and directly account the ITC in respect of these items as their cost i.e. no bifurcation of taxes is done. Even in GSTR -3B though disclosure of the value of reversal of ineligible ITC is required, not many disclose this value under the required head. Therefore, for such entities it is important to note here that table 14 of this form requires bifurcation and disclosure of both total value of ITC (i.e. eligible + ineligible) and value of eligible ITC is required. Hence, these entities who book ineligible ITC as their cost need to start accounting for ineligible ITC's and subsequently show these as reversals. This would help the assessee also since all details of credits not availed would be available for audit review. It is common that auditor finds out cases where credit was available which has not been availed.

Disclosure of value of the expenditure and the value of ITC on it required: Table 14 requires the taxpayer to disclose the total amount of ITC available on each of the expense head under column (3). However, what is important is that the taxpayer also needs to disclose appropriately the eligible ITC availed i.e. the net ITC availed after reversals required due to ineligible credit under section 17(5) of the CGST Act or for any other reason.

Example: An insurance company raised an invoice of Rs. 30,000 on which ITC amounts to Rs. 5,400. The details of which are as follows:

Life Insurance – Rs 10,000 + GST Rs. 1,800

Fire Insurance – Rs 20,000 + GST Rs. 3,600

The disclosure of the above in table 14 will be as under:

Under column 2 'Value' – Rs. 30,000 to be entered

Under column 3 'Amount of ITC' – Rs. 5,400 to be entered

Under column 4 'Amount of eligible ITC availed" – Rs 3,600 to be entered as ITC on life insurance is blocked and ineligible credit under GST

Value of ITC claimed on capital goods also to be disclosed: Though the table 14 majorly covers general expense heads, it is very important to highlight that credit availed on capital goods also needs to be disclosed under this table. The details of ITC on capital goods need to be disclosed in SL.NO.14O of the form.

Value of expenses and the Total ITC only to be disclosed: It is important for the assessee to note that the value of expenditure under each head of expense (i.e. column 2) and the amount of total ITC (i.e. column 3) are to be filled only for the purpose of disclosure. The reconciliation of the basic value would not be required to be carried out. Reconciliation of the eligible ITC only (i.e. column 4) would be carried out with the ITC as per annual returns.

Question 52: *Some blocked credit availed by the assessee is noticed by the auditor at the time preparation of GSTR-9C. What is the course of action?*

Ans: If such instances are noticed in the course of reconciliation, he may be required to disclose it as recommended liability in part V of GSTR 9C.

Reference in Financials/Returns

The information required for this table can be majorly taken from the Profit & loss account under the indirect expenses head. All the expenses as stated under the indirect expenses needs to be disclosed in this table. Further, in case entity maintains separate GL for ineligible credits availed, then the same can be used for disclosure of details in ineligible ITC. Further, any addition to the capital assets also needs to be considered.

Question 53: *In table 14A to 14Q of Form 9C the auditor is required to show gross ITC with respect to each expense or net ITC i.e. Gross minus ITC reversed for that expense?*

Ans: The auditor is required to show net ITC with respect to each expense. It could be challenging for the auditor the determine the amount to be reversed for each expense individually as the assesse would have done reversal from credits (say under Rule 42) on aggregate basis.

Sl. No.15 – Reasons for Un-reconciled difference in ITC

15	Reasons for Un-Reconciled difference in ITC	
A	Reason 1	<<Text>>
B	Reason 2	<<Text>>
C	Reason 3	<<Text>>

Serial No.	Instructions in the Form
15	*Reasons for non-reconciliation between ITC availed on the various expenses declared in Table 14R and ITC declared in Table 14S shall be specified here.*

The assessee has to provide his comments or reasons for the difference in ITC availed on the various expenses as per books of account and as per Annual return derived in field 12F.

Sl. No.16 - Tax payable on Un-reconciled difference In ITC (due to reasons specified in 13 and 15 above)

16	Tax payable on Un-reconciled difference In ITC (due to reasons specified in 13 and 15 above)	
	Description	Amount Payable
	Central Tax	
	State/UT Tax	
	Integrated Tax	
	Cess	
	Interest	
	Penalty	

Serial No.	Instructions in the Form
16	*Any amount which is payable due to reasons specified in Table 13 and 15 above shall be declared here. Towards, the end of the reconciliation statement taxpayers shall be given an option to pay their taxes as recommended by the auditor.*

Introduction

This field requires the auditor to calculate the tax payable on the following non-reconciled amounts:

- Difference in Net ITC as per audited financial statements vis-à-vis ITC claimed in Annual Return (Calculated under SL.No.12F)
- Difference in ITC availed on expenses as per audited financial statement vis-à-vis ITC declared in Annual Return (Calculated under SL.No.14T)

The auditor is required to calculate the tax payable, interest and penalty, if any, in respect of the said differences and mention these details under this serial number.

Analysis

Option to make payment of additional liability may be provided: Any amount which is found to be payable in addition to the taxes already paid, towards the end of the reconciliation statement, taxpayers will be given an option to pay their taxes as recommended by the auditor. Instruction 8 to the form GSTR 9C states that facility of payment of tax would be provided to the taxpayer at the end of the reconciliation statement.

22.6.2.2 Part V - Auditor's recommendation on additional liability due to non-reconciliation

Part V	Auditor's recommendation on additional liability due to non-reconciliation					
	Description	**Value**	**Central Tax**	**State/UT Tax**	**Integrated Tax**	**Cess, if applicable**
	1	**2**	**3**	**4**	**5**	**6**
	5%					
	12%					
	18%					
	28%					
	3%					
	0.25%					
	0.10%					
	Input Tax Credit					
	Interest					
	Late Fee					
	Penalty					
	Any other amount paid for supplies not included in Annual Return (GSTR 9)					
	Erroneous refund to be paid back					
	Outstanding demands to be settled					
	Other (Pl. specify)					

Serial No.	Instructions in the Form
Part V	*Part V consists of the auditor's recommendation on the additional liability to be discharged by the taxpayer due to non-reconciliation of turnover or non-reconciliation of input tax credit. The auditor shall also recommend if there is any other amount to be paid for supplies not included in the Annual Return. Any refund which has been erroneously taken and shall be paid back to the Government shall also be declared in this table. Lastly, any other outstanding demands which is recommended to be settled by the auditor shall be declared in this Table.* *Towards the end of the return, taxpayers shall be given an option to pay any additional liability declared in this form, through FORM DRC-03. Taxpayers shall select "Reconciliation Statement" in the drop down provided in FORM DRC-03. It may be noted that such liability shall be paid through electronic cash ledger only.*

Introduction

Once the reconciliation statement is drawn up by the auditor and after noticing the non-reconciled differences in the turnover, ITC, etc. he needs to provide his recommendations on the differences observed and the tax payable in cash thereon has to be disclosed under this serial number. Further the auditor would also be required to provide his recommendation on the following:

- If there is any other amount to be paid for supplies not included in the annual return (GSTR – 9);
- If there is any refund which has been erroneously taken and is required to be paid back to the Government;
- Any other outstanding demands to be settled may be recommended by the auditor.

At the end of the form the auditor has to provide verification stating that the information given is true and correct to the best of his knowledge and belief and nothing has been concealed therefrom.

Analysis

Assessee possesses the option to pay: It is noteworthy here to note that, the words used are "possesses an option to pay". Therefore, even after the auditor has recommended the amount of tax that is payable by the assessee, it is at the discretion of the assessee whether to pay or not, as the assessee is being given an option to pay and it is not mandatory to pay. The assessee may choose to pay the liability due at a later date along with additional interest thereon or may await show cause notice and adjudication process. However, it is expected that an enquiry would start once this report is scrutinised by the revenue.

(2) Whether liability only upon reconciliation difference needs to be recommended:

The auditor is primarily required to report on the liability arising on the non-reconciled amounts under Form GSTR 9C. However, his scope is not restricted only to reporting of the un-reconciled amounts. On a perusal of the heading to Part V of GSTR 9C, it appears that the responsibility of the auditor is restricted to report only the additional liability which may arise on account of non-reconciliation matters only. An Auditor may take a view that he is not required to step into the shoes of an assessing officer, revisionary authority or an investigator to mine any undisclosed supplies which are neither reported in the annual return nor in the financial statements. The instruction provided to fill in the relevant GSTR 9C plays an important role. Para 7 of instructions provided to the relevant GSTR 9C makes it clear that apart from recommending any additional tax liability that may arise on account of reconciliations matters, an auditor is also required to recommend such of those cases relating to supplies not reported in the annual return, refunds erroneously taken, any outstanding demands that may be settled by the Registered Person, wrong availment of exemption etc.

Performing this reconciliation accurately and analysing the reasons for the differences falls within the responsibility of auditor's responsibility.

Liability to be payable through Cash only: If any amount is found to be payable by the assessee under table V, it has to be paid only in cash. No option to pay the liability by usage of ITC credit lying in the electronic credit ledger. This could be due to restriction on usage of ITC only for self-assessed tax in terms of section 41(2) of CGST Act 2017. Taxpayers shall be given an option to pay any additional liability declared in this form, through FORM DRC-03. Taxpayers shall select "Reconciliation Statement" in the drop down provided in FORM DRC-03. It may be noted that such liability shall be paid through electronic cash ledger only.

Question 54: *Whether auditor needs to identify the reasons for reconciliation difference at a gross level or the same needs to be further identified at the individual transaction/invoice level?*

Ans: Mere difference between turnover as per audited annual financial statement and GSTR- 9 does not mean there is liability on such un-reconciled amount. The auditor is required to further drill down to identify the reason of difference. If the transaction leading to such difference creates additional liability, same has to be reported as liability in the GSTR- 9C. At invoice level as auditor needs to recommends whether to pay CGST/SGST or IGST.

Question 55: *Is the determination of additional liability determined by the Auditor binding on the registered person?*

Ans: At the outset, it can be inferred from the heading to Part V of GSTR 9C that the auditor only has a recommendatory power while furnishing his report. Any recommendations given by the auditor may or may not be acceptable to the registered person. If it is acceptable, the payment of tax is to be made by the registered person. However, if it is not acceptable then the question arises as to how the auditor resolves the issue. At this juncture, the auditor needs to exercise his professional diligence, skill, legal knowledge and care in determination of any additional tax liability which in his opinion, may be payable by the registered person. The registered person has an option to accept, reject or partially accept the recommended additional tax liability. In line with such recommendations though not explicitly stated anywhere in the relevant Form or GST laws.

(i) the registered person can choose to make the payment of the additional tax liability in full or in part;

(ii) the registered person can even choose to reject the complete recommendations of the Auditor and not make the payment at all.

Before an auditor ventures into recommending any additional tax liability due care, caution and diligence must be exercised. For instance, in respect of commodity classification based on HSN if an auditor believes that there are two possibilities then he may choose to place reliance on an expert opinion obtained by the registered person. In such a situation a proper disclosure may suffice.

However, when looked at from the perspective of the Government, the recommendation shall form the foundation for an effective show cause notice and enquiry into the affairs of the registered person.

Verification:

I hereby solemnly affirm and declare that the information given herein above is true and correct to the best of my knowledge and belief and nothing has been concealed there from.

** (Signature and stamp/Seal of the Auditor)

Place: ....

Name of the signatory ....

Membership No.................

Date: ....

Full address ....**Verification of registered person:**

I hereby solemnly affirm and declare that I am uploading the reconciliation statement in FORM GSTR-9C prepared and duly signed by the Auditor and nothing has been tampered or altered by me in the statement. I am also uploading other statements, as applicable, including financial statement, profit and loss account and balance sheet etc.

Place: Signature

Date:

Name of Authorised

Signatory

Designation/ Status

Analysis

Understanding the verification declaration is important for an auditor. Auditor is required to confirm on the truth and correctness of information including confirmation on non-concealment. Concealment could be understood to be hiding or keeping secret of some information. Auditor needs to be make sure that none of the information is concealed with a *mala fide* intention.

Later, auditor needs to submit the signed form to the assesse who needs to counter sign and ultimately submit the form by uploading and filing the same online on the GST common portal.

22.7 PART B – CERTIFICATION

As per section 35(5) of the CGST Act read with rule 80(3) of the CGST rules, the auditor is not only required to conduct an audit of the annual accounts of the assessee, but also he is required to duly certify the reconciliation statement drawn under form GSTR 9C. This part of the form provides for a format in which due certification is to be provided by the auditor. Two formats have been prescribed by the government which are as follows:

- **Format I** – This format has to be adopted when the audit of the annual accounts and the reconciliation statement is drawn up by the same auditor;
- **Format II** – This format has to be adopted when two different persons have been appointed by the assessee, one for conducting the audit and the other for drawing the reconciliation statement.

22.7.1 Format I - Certification in cases where the Reconciliation Statement (Form GSTR 9C) is drawn up by the person who had conducted the audit

Under this format the same person is responsible to conduct the audit of the books of accounts of the assessee as required under section 35(5) and he is also responsible to draw the reconciliation statement as required under section 44(2).

Therefore, the auditor has to first examine the following annual accounts of the assessee:

- Balance sheet;
- Profit & Loss Account;
- Cash Flow statement for the year;
- Books of accounts as maintained by the assessee for the year.

Based on the examination of the above documents by the auditor, he is required to provide his comments and report the following aspects:

(1) Whether the books and the documents have been maintained by the assessee in conformity with the GST Acts and rules issued thereunder;

(2) Whether the balance sheet, P&L account, cash flow statement are in line with the books of accounts;

(3) Whether he was provided with all the information required for conducting the audit.

If answer to any of the questions stated above is in the negative, the auditor is required to provide the discrepancies observed along with his remarks/comments.

Further once the audit of the annual accounts has been conducted by the auditor, he is further required to provide his opinion on the reconciliation statement drawn in part A of the Form GSTR 9C. He is required to verify the reconciliation statement and then certify that the statement drawn in his opinion is true and correct. If on verification any inconsistency is observed the auditor is required to highlight the same along with his comments and qualify his audit report subject to these discrepancies.

Therefore, under the first format the auditor is placed with dual responsibility of conducting the audit of the books of accounts of the assessee as well as the responsibility of certifying the reconciliation statement.

22.7.2 Format II - Certification in cases where the Reconciliation Statement (Form GSTR 9c) is drawn up by the person other than the person who had conducted the audit of the accounts

This format has to be adopted when 2 distinct auditors have been appointed by the assessee

- **First Auditor** – To perform the audit of the books of accounts of the company;
- **Second Auditor** – To duly certify the reconciliation statement drawn under the Form GSTR - 9C.

This format of certification has to be adopted by the auditor who is appointed to duly certify the reconciliation statement of the assessee under GST.

As per **"SA 600 – Using the Work of another Auditor"** the auditor can place his reliance on the audit performed by the other auditor and based on these audited annual accounts can proceed to examine the particulars entered in the reconciliation statement.

However, the auditor is required to specifically mention in his certificate the name and address of the other auditor who has conducted the audit of the books of accounts of the assessee and attach along with his certificate the following audited documents:

- Balance sheet;
- Profit & Loss Account;
- Cash Flow statement;
- Any other documents which are required to be annexed thereto.

  Based on the verification the auditor has to ***report*** the following:

- Whether the books and the accounts have been maintained by the assessee in conformity with the GST Acts and rules issued thereunder.

If the said books of accounts have not been maintained, the same has to be reported by the auditor.

Further the auditor needs to ***certify*** whether the particulars entered into the Form GSTR 9C are true and correct in his opinion. If on verification any inconsistency is observed the auditor is required to highlight the same along with his comments and qualify his audit certificate subject to these discrepancies.

Analysis

Key difference in certification as given in sub-parts I & II: The key difference between the two formats given is as under:

- **Format I** – This format has to be adopted when the audit of the annual accounts and the reconciliation statement is drawn up by the same auditor;
- **Format II** – This format has to be adopted when two different persons have been appointed by the assessee, one for conducting the audit and the other for drawing the reconciliation statement.

This can be better understood by way of an example

Example: *M/s. ABC appoints two separate chartered accountants as follows:*

Mr. Z for conducting annual audit; and

Mr. Y for certifying the reconciliation statements as per GSTR 9C.

In this scenario where separate persons are appointed, Mr. Y will not be required to comment on appropriateness of the balance sheet, profit and loss account, cash flow statement and the books of accounts of M/s. ABC. Mr. Y's opinion would be restricted to certification of the reconciliation statements given under Form GSTR 9C. Mr. Y will be required to provide his opinion in format given under Roman II of Part B of Form GSTR 9C. However Y may confirm that the audit was done adequately before relying on Z.

Difference between True & Fair and True & Correct: The certification format as provided in the Form GSTR -9C requires the auditor to provide a certificate duly signed by the auditor stating that the particulars entered are true and correct.

There is a gap between usage of the words "true and fair" and "true and correct". The difference between the two phrases has been highlighted as below:

Sl. No	Particulars	True and Correct	True & Fair
1	Meaning	This phrase is used to indicate absolute level of assurance expected to be provided. Absolute assurance indicates that procedures have been performed as considered appropriate. This means though not 100% correct, the records are substantially correct	This phrase is used when absolute assurance cannot be given, however to a great extent reliance can be placed. Test Check of controls and also in depth of sample as needed done.
2	Risk involved	The person using this phrase is exposed to high risk comparatively, as he is stating that the contents are substantially correct.	The person using this phrase is exposed to a comparatively lower risk, as he is not giving an absolute assurance. There exits some level of ambiguity
3	Association of the Phrase	This phrase is generally associated when any certification work is carried out. When a certificate is being issued there cannot exist any ambiguity, substantial assurance has to be provided.	This phrase is generally associated when any report has to be issued. When a report is being issued reasonable assurance can suffice.
4	Examples	Under Income tax Act as under Form 3CB and 3CD the auditor is required to give a declaration as "true and correct" and not "true and fair".	In statutory audits like audit under Companies Act, the auditor enjoys the leniency by usage of the words "true and fair".

Commenting upon the accounts/documents/records not maintained: In the formats as given in the form GSTR – 9C the auditor is required to comment upon the accounts, documents or records as required by the Act which are not maintained by the assessee. The following is a list of few records/documents that are required to be maintained by the assessee as per section 35

(1) Every registered person is required to keep and maintain at his principal place of business a true and correct account of:

- Production or manufacture of goods;
- Inward and outward supply of goods or services or both;
- Stock of goods;
- Input tax credit availed;
- Output tax payable and paid; and

(2) In addition to above, there are other records prescribed in Rule 56 of CGST Rules 2007.

(3) Every owner or operator of warehouse or godown or any other place used for storage of goods and every transporter needs to maintain records of the consigner, consignee and other relevant details of the goods in such manner as may be prescribed.

If, on verification any of the documents are found missing or not being recorded by the assessee, the auditor is required to report the same in his certificate.

Submission of Form GSTR-9C: Having prepared all the forms at GSTIN level, they should be submitted on the common portal. It should be ensured that all submissions are made on or before 31st December*[7] to ensure that the compliance can be made timely and there is no late fee. When a person fails to get his accounts audited, then he would be liable with a penalty of Rs.25,000/-. (Sec 125 of CGST Act, 2017).

Question 56: *What are the consequences of the failure in submitting the annual return and not getting the accounts audited?*

Ans: The following are the consequences of the failure in submitting the annual return and not getting the accounts audited:

a) Section 44(2) of the CGST Act and State /Union Territory GST Act provides that every Registered Person shall file electronically an annual return in Form GSTR 9 along with a reconciliation statement in Form GSTR 9-C, reconciling the value of supplies declared in the

7 Representations from industry and professional organisations have requested for 31st March due to the fact that even in November neither form 9 or 9C can be uploaded. Also clarity to fill the forms has also not been provided.

return furnished for the financial year with the audited annual financial statement.

b) Section 47(2) of the CGST Act provides for levy of a late fee of Rs. 100/- per day for delay in furnishing annual return in GSTR 9, subject to a maximum amount of quarter percent (0.25%) of the turnover in the State or Union Territory. Similar provisions for levy of late fee exist under the State / Union Territory GST Act. Therefore it can be concluded that a late fee of Rs.200/- per day (Rs. 100 under CGST law +Rs. 100/- under State / Union Territory GST law) could be levied which would be capped to a maximum amount of half percent (0.25% under the CGST Law + 0.25% under the SGST / UTGST Law) of turnover in the state or Union territory.

c) In a situation where a registered person fails to furnish both GSTR 9 and GSTR 9C on the common portal, the provisions of late fee cited in clause "c" supra would equally apply.

Further, there is no separate penalty or late fee provided in the law for failure to get the accounts audited. Hence, in absence of any specific provision there may be general penalty of Rs. 25,000/- each under section 125 of the CGST Act/SGST Act.

'Observation' and 'Qualification': Auditor needs to provide various observations and qualifications subject to which the opinion is formed. Difference between the terms 'observation' and qualification' is as under:

Observation: The word 'observation' has not been defined under the CGST Act or under the Standards of Auditing issued by the ICAI. Therefore, dictionary meaning would have to be taken. As per the Law Lexcion, authored by P Ramanatha Iyer observation means 'view' or 'remark'.

Qualification: The word 'qualification' has not been defined under the CGST Act. As per SA 705 issued by the ICAI the Auditor shall express a qualified opinion when:

(a) The auditor, having obtained sufficient appropriate audit evidence, concludes that misstatements, individually or in the aggregate, are material, but not pervasive, to the financial statements; or

(b) The auditor is unable to obtain sufficient appropriate audit evidence on which to base the opinion, but the Auditor concludes that the possible effects on the financial statements of undetected misstatements, if any, could be material but not pervasive

Therefore, while certifying Form GSTR 9C the Chartered Accountant should take utmost care in reporting a matter as an 'observation' or as a 'qualification'.

Audit Certificate and Audit Report: Para 2.2 of the 'Guidance Note on Audit Report and certificates for Special Purpose' issued by the ICAI notes the difference between the term 'certificate' and 'report' as under;

"**A Certificate** is a written confirmation of the accuracy of facts stated there in and does not involve any estimate or the opinion."

"**A Report**, on the other hand, is a formal statement usually made after an enquiry, examination or review of specified matters under report and includes the reporting auditor's opinion thereon".

Thus, where a certificate is issued, the Chartered Accountant would be responsible for factual accuracy of what is stated therein. In case of a report, he is responsible for ensuring that the report is based on the factual data, true and fair (or in some cases true and correct) to the best of his belief, knowledge and information furnished to him.

The word 'certificate' as described in the laws and regulations or even in the contracts that an entity might have entered into can normally be associated with reasonable assurance. However, depending upon the circumstances and based upon the nature, timing and extent of the procedures which a practitioner can perform, the practitioner can conclude that a reasonable assurance cannot be expressed on the subject matter of the "certificate" and only limited assurance/conclusion can be given. The practitioner's procedures in case where reasonable assurance is to be expressed would be substantially different (and more extensive) from circumstances where limited assurance is to be expressed.

Comment on Accounts/records/documents that are required to be maintained by assessee: Auditor needs to comment upon the non-compliance in respect of various accounts/records/documents maintained. **[See** in introduction of this chapter].

Submission of Profit and loss/income and expenditure a/c and cash flow statement: Auditor's certification on examination of these statements has to be provided. Although it appears from the form that these statements would be required for each GSTIN i.e. each location wise, the intention could be only to provide the certification on examination of these statements on the entire entity level. Thus, assessee would not be required to prepare these statements again for each GSTIN location.

Additional certification for the auditor who has conducted the audit of accounts: Having conducted the audit of accounts, the said statutory auditors of the entity are required to additionally report in para 3 of part B (I) the observation/comment/discrepancies found during the audit of accounting of transactions. Therefore, the statutory auditors are required to comment upon the accounting also in addition to the comments, observations, qualifications that are to be reported in para 5 as per GSTR 9C i.e. GST audit.

Sample observations/qualifications in para 5: All the particulars required in GSTR 9C being reported as certified to be true and correct by the auditor, subject to certain observations/qualifications, few are as under:

(a) Basis of classification adopted could not be verified as the details were not available.

(b) Refund claim of IGST on services are made but the convertible foreign exchange on the same are not received within 1 year.

(c) Goods removed under DC to job work not received back within 1 year.

(d) Outdoor catering services procured by taxable person for serving food to employees which is mandatory under other statutes are blocked ITC but assessee has availed such credits.

(e) Krishi Kalyan Cess paid under Section 140(1) needs to be reversed in terms of the proposed amendment to Section 140(1) but assessee has not reversed the same.

(f) Fuel which is a non-GST supply are required to be declared in GSTR 3B and accordingly get effected in GSTR 9 but is not disclosed by assessee.

(g) RCM payments and ITC on the same requires self-invoicing and declaration of the same in GSTR 1 but the assesse has not maintained such self-invoicing process.

(h) Recovery from employee (canteen, cab and notice pay) requires employer to pay GST as these are covered under schedule 1 but assesse has not paid GST on the same.

(i) Assessee has paid GST under RCM on adhoc basis for all inward transportation but certain transporters are GTO which did not require assessee to pay GST under RCM.

(j) Carried forward credit balance of earlier return period is Rs.XXXX but ITC in TRAN 1 is Rs.XXXX and the difference is for the reasons…

(k) Assessee outward classifications details could not be verified and accordingly ITC reversal if any required also could not be verified.

Question 57: *There is difference of opinion between auditor and the client as to eligibility of exemption notification. How to treat the same at the time of reconciliation?*

Ans: The auditor's primary responsibility is to comment on the reason of differences between turnover, taxes paid and ITC claimed as per books of account viz a viz declared in the annual return. The exemption claimed by the client does not results in the difference of the turnover and hence the same may not require to be commented upon by the auditor in table 11. Also, part V which requires auditor to comment on additional liability also intends to cover the cases which has arisen due to non-reconciliation. Hence, it can be stated that, it may not be required in this column also. However, more clarity is expected from Government in such cases. The auditor may mention his comment on such difference in opinion as one of the observations in part B para 4 of the certification GSTR-9C.

Question 58: *There is service tax demand pending against the assessee. For similar issue, notice has been issued under GST also. What is the responsibility of auditor to report the same under GSTR-9C?*

Ans: Part V of the GSTR-9C provides for auditor recommendation on the outstanding demand which is recommended to be settled by the auditor. If, in view of the auditor, the demand under GST is sustainable, he may make his recommendation to pay the outstanding demand. However, it is not compulsory for the auditor to comment on the same. There is no need to report the demand under service tax in any part of GSTR-9C.

Question 59: *Can the Form GSTR 9C filed be revised?*

Ans: There is no provision enabling an assessee to file revised Form GSTR 9C. As such, some experts opine that, the Certificate once issued/filed cannot be revised in view of no such revision being permitted to audited reports by a Chartered Accountant. However, there is another view that since there are is no specific bar/restrictions under the GST law to file a revised audit report/certificate, a revised audit report/certificate can be issued/filed. Caution is advised in taking such a position unless Government issues any clarification in this regard. While one can appreciate that mistakes apparent which can creep in and therefore warrant a revision, it must be ensured that due professional care is exercised at the time of filing this reconciliation statement.

22.8 FILING OF GSTR 9C ON GST PORTAL

Introduction to GSTR 9C offline Utility: GSTR-9C Offline utility is an Excel-based tool to facilitate the creation of reconciliation statement required to be furnished by Normal taxpayer having turnover above Rs. 2 Crores duly verified and signed by Chartered Accountant/Cost Accountant, along with filing of his/her annual return in Form GSTR-9. Chartered Accountant/Cost Accountant will use the GSTR-9C Offline utility to fill up details. Once GSTR-9C return is prepared using offline tool, it is to be uploaded on the GST portal by the taxpayer along with a copy of Balance Sheet, Income and Expenditure Account/ Profit and Loss Account and any other related document.

The taxpayer should file Form GSTR-9C after filing his/her annual return in Form GSTR-9. In case assessee has not filed Form GSTR-9, GST Portal would not allow the taxpayer to file Form GSTR-9C. The excel based GSTR-9C offline utility is designed to help the taxpayer to prepare the GSTR-9C return offline. The utility can be downloaded from this link.

Steps to prepare reconciliation statement in form GSTR-9C: Various steps that needs to be taken by the taxpayers while filing GSTR 9C are as under:

- Download the GSTR-9C Offline Utility;
- Along with the GSTR-9C Offline Utility excel file, following files also would be made available as under:
    - Readme Notepad: Open it to read about Prerequisites before installation of the Offline Tool, Installation instructions and key functionalities.
    - 'wsweb' HTML File: HTML file name 'wsweb' and 'GSTR_9C_Offline_Utility' should be in same folder to generate the JSON."
- Open the GSTR-9C Offline Utility Excel Worksheet.
- Add table-wise details in the Worksheet.
- Generate Preview file to view Draft Form GSTR-9C.
- Generate JSON File to Upload on the GST Portal.
- Open Downloaded GSTR-9C JSON Files.
- Open Downloaded Error GSTR-9C JSON File(s), if any.
- Upload the generated JSON File on GST Portal.
- Download Processed GSTR-9C JSON File(s) from GST Portal.
- Download Error Report, if any, from the GST Portal and Correct the Errors.
- Download GSTR-9C Tables Derived from GSTR-9(PDF).
- Initiate Filing of Form GSTR-9C.
- View the Updated Tile of the Filed Form GSTR-9C on the "File Annual Returns" Page.

Question 60: *Will assessee be allowed to file Form GSTR-9C if he has not filed the annual return?*

Ans: No, Form GSTR-9C can be filed only after filing the annual return in Form GSTR-9. GSTR-9C tile shall be enabled only after successful filing of GSTR-9 for the financial year.

Question 61: *What are the pre-conditions for filing Form GSTR 9C?*

Ans: Various pre-conditions for filing Form GSTR 9C are as under:

- User should be registered and should have a valid GSTIN;
- User should have valid login credentials (i.e., User ID and password);

- User has filed GSTR-9 for the relevant financial year;
- The aggregate turnover of such registered person during the financial year exceeds two crore rupees;
- User should have got his accounts audited as specified.

Question 62: *When does the system enable filing of Form GSTR 9C?*

Ans: GSTR-9C tile shall be enabled only after successful filing of GSTR-9 for the financial year. Form GSTR-9C shall be made available to all taxpayers to whom GSTR-9 is applicable for the financial year. System would not validate whether the turnover of taxpayer exceeds 2 crore rupees or not.

Question 63: *How can the details in Form GSTR 9C be filled?*

Ans: The taxpayer, or the auditor can download GSTR-9C offline tool (.zip file) from GST Portal and unzip the downloaded file to open excel based offline tool. Details needs to be filled in the downloaded offline sheet and validate sheet.

Question 64: *From where can the GSTR-9C Offline Utility be downloaded and used in the system?*

Ans: To download and open the GSTR-9C Offline Utility in the system from the GST Portal, perform following steps:

- Access the GST Portal: www.gst.gov.in.
- Go to Downloads > Offline Tools > GSTR-9C Offline Tool option and click on it.
- Unzip the downloaded Zip file which contain GSTR_9c_Offline_Utility.xls excel sheet.
- Open the GSTR_9c_Offline_Utility.xls excel sheet by double clicking on it.
- Read the 'Read Me' instructions on excel sheet and then fill the worksheet accordingly.

Question 65: *Do assessee has to login to GST Portal to upload the generated JSON file using GSTR-9C Offline Utility?*

Ans: Yes, Taxpayer must login in to the GST Portal to upload the generated JSON file using GSTR-9C Offline Utility. Log in to GST portal-Annual return-Select Financial year and click on Search-Click on 'Prepare Offline' option in GSTR-9C tile-Go to 'upload' tab.

Question 66: *What are the basic system requirements/configurations required to use GSTR-9C Offline Tool?*

Ans: The offline functions work best on Windows 7 and above and MS EXCEL 2007 and above.

Questions 67: *Will there be any system computed fields and data auto-populated in Form GSTR 9C?*

Ans: Taxpayer can download the 'System generated summary based on GSTR-9' in PDF file from the portal by clicking on 'Download GSTR-9C tables derived from GSTR-9 (PDF)' button. Downloaded PDF can be handed over/passed on to auditor. Auditor can use the same to fill the GSTR-9 related fields in GSTR-9C. 'System generated summary based on GSTR-9' filed shall have the following fields:

- Turnover as declared in Annual return (GSTR-9)
- Taxable turnover as per liability declared in Annual Return (GSTR-9)
- Total amount of Tax paid as declared in Annual Return (GSTR- 9)
- ITC claimed in Annual Return (GSTR-9)
- ITC claimed in Annual Return (GSTR-9)

Questions 68: *How would Form GSTR 9C be verified and signed by Chartered Accountant/ Cost Accountant?*

Ans: Chartered Accountant/Cost Accountant shall use the offline tool to fill up the required details and the Certificate. He would generate a JSON file after validation and upload the file. After generating JSON the Auditor needs to affix his digital signature.

Question 69: *Who would upload the Form GSTR 9C?*

Ans: Chartered Accountant/ Cost Accountant after verification and signing shall pass on the signed JSON file to taxpayer for upload of Form GSTR 9C. It is to be uploaded on GST portal by the taxpayer, after verification, along with a copy of the following documents: Balance Sheet, Income and Expenditure Account/ Profit and Loss Account and any other document.

Question 70: *Can draft Form GSTR 9C be downloaded before filing?*

Ans: Yes, Draft GSTR-9C in PDF format can be downloaded after the upload of JSON file.

Question 71: *What is the format to be used for uploading of Form GSTR 9C?*

Ans: Upload format allowed for GSTR-9C is JSON only and upload format allowed for Balance Sheet, Profit and Loss Account/ Income and Expenditure Account and any other document is PDF only.

Question 72: *Is there any limit on the size of documents required to be uploaded?*

Ans: Limit of upload for following documents under each section shall be 2 files and each file size should not exceed 5 MB:

- Balance Sheet
- Profit and Loss Account/Income and Expenditure Account
- Other document 1, if any
- Other document 2, if any

Question 73: *Can any changes be made in the JSON file uploaded by the Auditor?*

Ans: No, one cannot make any changes in the JSON file uploaded by the Auditor. System shall validate that no changes have been made by taxpayer in JSON signed by auditor.

Question 74: *What can be done if Auditor has made recommendation on additional liability to be discharged by taxpayer?*

Ans: In such a situation, an option would be given to navigate to GST DRC 03 for making payment towards additional liability. After making payment through GST DRC 03, you will be navigated back to Form GSTR 9C.

Question 75: *What can be done in case of any error shown by system on uploading the Form GSTR 9C with necessary documents?*

Ans: Download the JSON error file and handover it to auditor. Auditor has to open it in offline tool by clicking on "Open downloaded error JSON file". He would correct errors as per details mentioned in "GST Validation errors" and sign it again after generating JSON. On upload of signed JSON; system shall validate that no changes have been made in signed JSON by taxpayer.

Question 76: *Can the status of Form GSTR 9C be tracked?*

Ans: Taxpayer can track the status of form GSTR-9C through 'Track return status' option in Services menu. Once return is filed successfully, then you can check the details in 'View e-filed returns' option under Services menu.

Question 77: *In case of uploading GSTR-9C JSON File again, after making changes. What will happen to details of the previous upload?*

Ans: If some details exist from previous upload, it will be updated with latest uploaded details. All new entries will be added as new entries.

Question 78: Does one need to click on 'save' button in 'upload relevant documents page' after every upload?

Ans: Yes, one need to click on 'Save' button after the status is 'Processed'. Save button shall be enabled only after successful upload of mandatory documents (Balance sheet and Profit & loss statement/Income & expenditure statement)

Question 79: *What will happen if one clicks on 'proceed to file' without clicking on 'save' button?*

Ans: Error message shall be displayed if you click on 'proceed to file' without clicking on 'Save' button.

Question 80: *When proceed to file button shall be enabled?*

Ans: 'Proceed to file' button shall be enabled only after successful upload of

- Signed JSON file
- Balance sheet in PDF/JPEG format
- Profit & Loss statement/ Income & Expenditure statement in PDF/JPEG format and save

Question 81: *When 'File GSTR-9C' button will be enabled?*

Ans: 'File GSTR-9C' button will be enabled only after Proceed to file and select the declaration/verification check box.

Question 82: *Can one add/delete the uploaded PDF/JPEG file after clicking on 'Proceed to file' or 'File GSTR-9C' button?*

Ans: Yes, one can add/delete PDF/JPEG file till successful filing of GSTR-9C. If you have deleted/added any documents, then you have to click on save and proceed file again.

Question 83: *Can the reconciliation statement be downloaded in excel format before/after filing of GSTR-9C?*

Ans: Yes. You can download the reconciliation statement details in excel format.

Question 84: *Can the uploaded PDF/JPEG (Balance sheet, profit & loss statement etc.) and JSON file be downloaded after successful filing?*

Ans: Yes, you can download the GSTR-9C JSON/PDF/Excel files by clicking on 'Download GSTR-9C' button in GSTR-9C tile on the and PDF/JPEG uploaded by taxpayer can be downloaded by clicking on 'View GSTR-9C' button in GSTR-9C tile.

Source: FAQ's and User Manual released by GST Network

22.9 CHECKLIST ON FORM GSTR 9C – RECONCILIATION STATEMENT

PROGRAMME FOR CONDUCTING GST AUDIT

Sl. No.	Particulars	Comments
1	Entities having multiple GSTIN have to derive their GSTIN wise turnover as per audited financial statements.	
2	Identify the transactions causing differences between turnover as per books of account/audited financial statement and the Annual Return i.e. GSTR-9	
3	Derive the taxable turnover from annual turnover after adjustments of: • Exempted/Non-GST/Nil rated/No-supply turnover • Zero rated supply without payment of tax • Supplies on which tax is to be paid by the recipient on reverse charge basis.	

Sl. No.	Particulars	Comments
4	Understand the reason of differences between two records to identify as to whether: • it is a reconciliation item between two sets of records requiring disclosure in GSTR-9C; or • error or omission which may result in addition liability	
5	Obtain the reason of differences from the client and report in the GSTR-9C	
6	Identify the taxable value and GST rate wise liability, obtain and understand the difference, if any, is there between above and amount paid as declared in GSTR 9 and report the reason in GSTR-9C	
7	Derive the additional amount payable (to be paid in cash) on account of differences obtained in table 5 & 6 above.	
8	Identify the credits availed in the books of account at aggregate level (for each GSTIN) as well as separately for each of the expenses	
9	Obtain the working papers of GSTR 3B and map the credits as per the entries passed in the Books of accounts with that of GSTR 3B.	
10	Reconcile the difference in credits as per GSTR-9 and books of account. Report the un-reconciled difference in ITC along with reasons.	
11	Derive the amount of tax payable if any on un-reconciled difference in ITC as per table 9.	
12	Identify any other transactions/observations where additional liability may arise which is to be reported as per recommendation of the auditor	
13	Prepare and submit the GSTIN level GSTR-9 and GSTR-9C on the common portal. Similar exercise to be done for all GSTR-9 and GSTR-9C at entity level.	

CHECKLIST FOR CONDUCTING GST AUDIT

Sl. No.	Particulars
A.	**UNDERSTANDING OF BUSINESS**
1	Peruse the website of entity and google other information available on industry as well as the business
2	Physical walk through in visit to principal place of business / head office/ factory and other premises to understand the business operations
3	Review of audited financial statements, cashflow and gross trial balance for last 2 financial years
4	Review of product / service including advertisement material and literature
5	Review the organisational structure including related parties
6	Ascertaining the associated inherent, control and detection risks in conduct of the audit
7	Preliminary discussion with HODs to get clarity - challenges in business
8	State wise Registration / Business Verticals/ Additional place of business - Understanding
C.	**UNDERSTANDING THE AUTOMATION / ERP**
9	Review of automation/ computerisation in the organisation covering hardware, software, physical, access controls
10	Review if the software/ ERP including link to GSTN has controls / options to take care all the updated legal provisions of GST.
11	Review if there are any adverse comments in Internal Audit, Earlier GST reports and in IS audit if nay conducted
12	Review if there is a system of updating the masters / ledgers with updated information of customers, vendors etc.
11	Review of books and records maintained to ascertain if there in accordance with GST law
D.	**REVENUE / SUPPLY - GOODS / SERVICES**
12	Review of Profit of Loss account to ascertain

Sl. No.	Particulars
13	a. Exemptions / Concessions / Composition scheme opted
	b. Supply in DTA / Exports
14	c. Transactions with related parties / distinct persons according to Schedule I
	d. Special transactions such as SEZ, EOU, UN etc.
15	Review of nature of supply and implication - Composite supply / Mixed supply
	Verification of system of advance receipts to study GST impact and treatment
16	Verification of adjustments made for advance receipts with sale invoices
	Verification of treatment of sales / service return and tax adjustments
17	Verification of conditions fulfilled for deductions claimed for sale / service return, defects
	Verification of discount policy in organization and impact under GST
18	Verification of conditions fulfilled for deductions against discounts allowed
	Verification of unbilled revenues, adjustments and GST impact
19	Verification of Inter unit supplies and GST impact on such supplies - Schedule I
	Verification of benefits adopted for exports and ful-fillment of conditions
20	Verification of terms of agreements entered with customers having impact on valuation
21	Verification of recoveries from employees and GST impact on such recoveries
22	Verification of rate of tax adopted for taxable supplies made
23	Verification of rates adopted in case of changes in rates in between different rates
24	Verification of sales to SEZ to ascertain if they are zero rated
25	Verification of exports made with tax payment or without tax payment
26	Verification of rebate/ refunds claimed against exports

Sl. No.	Particulars
27	Verification of sales made as deemed export
28	Verification of refund claims in respect of deemed exports
29	Verification of sale of fixed assets and impact under GST
30	Verification if any goods / services liable under RCM are being provided
31	Verification if billings for support services to own branches / units are done - Schedule I
32	Verification of sales made on approval basis to ascertain GST compliance
33	Verification of sales made from exhibitions to ascertain GST compliance
34	Verification of sales made as casual taxable person in any state to ascertain GST compliance
35	Verification different sale schemes and impact in GST
36	Reconciliation of details of supplies as per annual return and books of accounts
E.	**PROCUREMENT OF GOODS AND SERVICES**
37	Review of procurement policy and system of the organization including imports
38	Review the nature of services and goods procured to ascertain GST impact
39	Verification of procurements made through different class such as registered dealer/manufacturer/service provider / unregistered dealer
40	Verification of purchase and expense invoices on sampling basis to study impact under GST with respect to taxations and credits
41	Verification of expenses liable for GST under RCM, credits in them for reimbursements etc.
42	Verification of financial ledgers where ITC are taken /not taken
43	Verification of treatment of purchase returns to study the possible impact under GST
44	Verification the foreign currency payments to ascertain RCM liability
45	Verification if goods / services are sourced at respective branches to

Sl. No.	Particulars
	claim credit benefit- ISD registration
46	Review of classification of goods as inputs or capital goods based on accounting
47	Review system of claiming credit and timing involved for taking credit
48	Verification of payments made within stipulated time for taking credit and reversals made if any
49	Review if invoices are addressed to goods / services receiving location
50	Verification of reconciliation of all expenses on which ITC availed been prepared and verified along with annual return
F	**CLASSIFICATION AND VALUATION**
51	Review the system of recognising sales / services and system of invoicing customers
52	Verification of classification policy of goods/services
53	Review if schedule II to CGST considered for deemed service / goods
54	Review terms of agreement/ invoices to ensure description / classification is matching
55	Verification of the rate of tax adopted
56	Review present valuation mechanism adopted for regular sales to customers, supplies to related parties, supplies without monetary consideration
57	Review free supplies if any to study GST impact
58	Review of reimbursements claimed and impact on GST valuation
59	Review if there are advance receipts and its impact on valuation
60	Review valuation adopted for supplies to agents, own branches or godowns
61	Verification of valuation principles followed in case of different sale schemes
62	Verification of valuation adopted in case of recoveries from employees such cab, canteen, telephone
63	Verification of valuation of gifts issued to related parties or others

Sl. No.	Particulars
G	**FINANCIAL STATEMENTS REVIEW**
64	Review the shareholding pattern by investment by group companies / associated enterprises
65	Review of employee / director/ partner benefits provided which could be treated as supplies and have impact under GST
66	Studying the nature of accounts maintained by the organization
67	Review of GSTIN wise books of accounts maintained and accounts related to that for disclosure in GST-9c statement
68	Review of notes to accounts to understand the transactions with related parties, accounting principles etc.
69	Review of debit notes and credit notes which are in line with GST / not in line with GST
70	Verification of adjustments on account of foreign exchange fluctuations for disclosure in GSTR-9C
71	Verification of adjustments on account of advances from customers for disclosure in GSTR-9C
72	Verification of non-operating incomes, impact in GST and disclosure in GSTR-9C
73	Reconciliation of difference between annual return and financial statements for the differences after understanding reasons from management
74	Ascertaining the taxes payable and paid along with interest implication
75	Review the income and customer ledgers, gross trial balance for credits other than payments
H	**REVIEW OF DOCUMENTATION**
76	Verification of tax invoices issued for time of supply and place of supply on test check
77	Verification of tax invoices or bill of supply issued for disclosure compliance in GST
78	Verification of delivery challans issued for movement of goods for approval, job work etc.
79	Review of various returns filed under GST such as GSTR-1, GSTR-3B and annual return
80	Review of relevant reconciliation statements prepared

Sl. No.	Particulars
81	Review of litigations and related documents as necessary for audit certification
82	Review of various reports generated for compliance such as sales register, credit register, fixed asset register
83	Review of registration certificates and places added
84	Review of documentation at branches or additional places for compliance with GST law
85	Review of export and import documents for taxes paid, zero rate claim, credits claim
86	Review of registration certificate display compliance
87	Taking management representational letters where needed
I.	**REVIEW OF AGREEMENTS / CONTRACTS**
88	Review of agreements / contracts / orders to identify important clauses with customers or vendors which could have major impact under GST
89	Review of agreements to ascertain type of supplies being made
90	Review of agreements to understand the discount policy
91	Review of agreements to understand various sale schemes
92	Review of agreements to understand the time of supply
93	Review of agreements to understand payment terms
J.	**TAX CREDITS**
94	Review nature of expenses incurred to assess GST credits
95	Verification if there are transactions of personal nature where credits being disallowed
96	Verification of credit availment mechanism and suggest on improvement requirement
97	Verification of goods issued free of cost or as samples and GST credit impact
98	Verification of purchases for credit optimisation
99	Verification of credit apportionment in case of supply of taxable and exempted supplies

Sl. No.	Particulars
100	Verification of credit availment in case of assets put partially for non-business /non-taxable use
101	Verification of documents based on which credits claimed
102	Verification of credit register and contents
103	Verification of conditions fulfilled for credit claim
104	Verification the reconciliation of the ITC prepared and disclosures made in financials and annual return
K.	**REVIEW OF PERIODICAL RETURNS**
105	Verification of GSTR-3B and GSTR-1 filed along with Annual return filed
106	Ensuring that the disclosures are made in annual return for reconciliation in GSTR-9C
107	Verification of taxes paid at different rates and disclosure
108	Verification of type of taxes paid and disclosure
109	Verification of procurement details disclosed with classification
110	Verification of interest and penalties paid along with disclosure
L.	**CERTIFICATION IN FORM GSTR-9C**
111	Quantification of tax liabilities to be discharged based on information provided by management
112	Quantification of interest liabilities to be discharged based on information provided by management
113	Quantification of wrong / ineligible credits claimed based on information provided by management
114	Reconciliation of details of sales, procurements, expenses, tax, credits between financials and GST annual return
115	Certifying as required including reporting on non-compliances, providing observations, suggestions for improvement in book keeping
116	Obtaining the Management Representation as per ICAI Guidelines

Note: This checklist is only indicative and not comprehensive. For specific industries it may need Customisation

22.10 GOOD ACCOUNTING PRACTICES TO BE FOLLOWED FOR EASE IN RECONCILIATION

For accounting GST related transactions in books as per IGAAP, the first and foremost step is to create proper GL heads of accounts in the Chart of Accounts (COA). Besides proper financial accounting, the purpose of proper COA is also to serve/help the reconciliations/matching/validation of sales, purchases, ITC etc with the outward/inward supplies and the electronic cash/credit ledger balances as per the various returns filed and the data on the GST portal.

The Chart of Accounts should be made keeping various types of business transactions in mind. Few important transactions are:

(1) Outward supply
(2) Inward supply
(3) RCM transaction
(4) Import of goods & services
(5) Receipt of advances for goods or services
(6) Credit Note
(7) Debit Note
(8) Discounts

In all the above transactions, the General Ledger Accounts for GST Input Tax Credit (Current Asset grouping) and GST liability (Current Liability grouping) under CGST, SGST and IGST should be properly and separately created in the COA. Hitherto, there was no need to bifurcate the GL Accounts for inputs, input services and capital goods. However, in view of the requirements of mentioning the details of ITC separately for each of the above in the Annual Return – Form GSTR – 9, it is necessary that the GL Accounts are created catering to this need.

As an example, following GL Accounts should be part of the chart of accounts:

(A) The below accounts should be used for accounting ITC on inward supply of inputs, input services and capital goods as mentioned at serial no 2 above.

CGST ITC Receivable A/c –Inputs (Part of Current Assets)	For recording the CGST ITC receivable on input tax invoice/credit note
SGST ITC Receivable A/c –Inputs (Part of Current Assets)	For recording the SGST ITC receivable on input tax invoice/credit note
IGST ITC Receivable A/c –Inputs (Part of Current Assets)	For recording the IGST ITC receivable on input tax invoice/credit note
CGST ITC Receivable A/c –Inputs Services (Part of Current Assets)	For recording the CGST ITC receivable on input services tax invoice/credit note

SGST ITC Receivable A/c –Inputs Services (Part of Current Assets)	For recording the SGST ITC receivable on input services tax invoice/credit note
IGST ITC Receivable A/c –Inputs Services (Part of Current Assets)	For recording the IGST ITC receivable on input services tax invoice/credit note
CGST ITC Receivable A/c –Capital Goods (Part of Current Assets)	For recording the CGST ITC receivable on capital goods tax invoice/credit note
SGST ITC Receivable A/c –Capital Goods (Part of Current Assets)	For recording the SGST ITC receivable on capital goods tax invoice/credit note
IGST ITC Receivable A/c –Capital Goods (Part of Current Assets)	For recording the IGST ITC receivable on capital goods tax invoice/credit note

(B) For accounting GST on outward supply (Sr No 1 above), following GL accounts should be used:

Head of Account	Grouping	Nature of transaction
CGST Payable A/c- Outward Supply	Current Liability	For recording the CGST liability charged in the tax invoice/debit note
SGST Payable A/c - Outward Supply	Current Liability	For recording the SGST liability charged in the tax invoice/debit note
IGST Payable A/c - Outward Supply	Current Liability	For recording the IGST liability charged in the tax invoice/debit note

(C) For recording GST transactions related to RCM/Import of goods/Import of services (Sr. No 3 & 4 above), following chain of entries are recommended:

(1) For recording the GST liability under the above three cases:

CGST Receivable A/c – RCM/Imp of Goods/Imp of Services.....Dr

CGST Payable A/c – RCM/Imp of Goods/Imp of Service..........Cr

(2) For paying the GST liability in cash/bank:

Electronic Cash Ledger A/c ....Dr

Bank A/c...Cr

(3) For transferring the GST liability to the Electronic Liability Register

CGST Payable A/c – RCM/Imp of Goods/Imp of Services........Dr

Electronic Liability Register A/c....................................Cr

(4) For showing the payment of GST liability in Govt. books/ledgers

Electronic Liability Register A/c ....Dr

Electronic Cash Ledger A/c ....Cr

(5) For availing the GST credit in books matching to Govt. books/ledgers

Electronic Credit Ledger A/c ....Dr

CGST Receivable A/c – RCM/Imp of Goods/Imp of Services .....Cr

The above example is for CGST. Similar entries/GL Accounts should be made for SGST in case of RCM and IGST in case of import of goods/services.

(D) For recording GST transactions related to receipt of advance against goods & services (Sr. No 5 above)

(1) For recording the GST liability on receipt of advance

CGST Receivable on Advances A/c....................Dr

CGST Payable on Advances A/c.......................................Cr

(2) For adjusting the advance in the month of supply

CGST Payable A/c –Outward Supply.................................Dr

CGST Receivable on Advances A/c.................................Cr

(E) For recording Debit/Credit Note/Discounts transactions (Sl No 6,7 & 8 above)

These entries will be similar to outward supply/inward supply entries where GST is involved.

Reporting of the GST Transactions:

ERP/Accounting software should be configured to provide reports to cover following aspects to facilitate easy reconciliation of GST Returns with the books of accounts:

(1) Classification/HSN Code/SAC wise reports – GSTIN wise;

(2) Inward supply register to throw HSN wise/SAC wise, supplier wise, GSTIN wise, head of account wise, ITC wise data;

(3) Outward supply register to throw HSN wise/SAC wise, customer wise, GSTIN wise, head of account wise data;

(4) Expenses register to throw HSN wise/SAC wise, supplier wise, GSTIN wise, head of account wise, ITC wise data;

(5) Ultimately the amount disclosed in the current assets as the credit taken must match with the Electronic credit ledger;

(6) Tagging to the cost centres in order to extract the reports GSTIN wise;

(7) Mapping of ITC with the expenditure respective GL's.

22.11 ROLE OF PROFESSIONALS IN AUDIT ENGAGEMENT

As per section 35(5) of CGST act, 2017 read with rule 80 (3) of the CGST rules, 2017 every registered person whose turnover during a financial year exceeds Rs. 2 Crore shall get his accounts audited by a Chartered accountant or a Cost accountant.

Section 2(1)(b) of the CA Act, 1949 defines the term 'Chartered Accountant' to mean a person who is a member of the Institute.

Section 2(1)(c) of the Cost & works accountants act, 1959 defines the term 'Cost accountant, to mean a person who is the member of the Institute. Section 6 provides that a member cannot practice without obtaining Certificate of Practice Thus, only a member of ICWAI having a Certificate of Practice (COP), or a firm of Cost Accountants can take up the GST Audit.

The GST audit demands significant preparation from both the auditor and auditee. Auditor must possess the following in order to smoothly complete the assignment:

- understanding of the business of the auditee and the nature of the supplies undertaken.
- an expert knowledge/understanding of the GST laws and common issues faced in the client industry,
- IT infrastructure of the auditee, the method in which the GST portal operates,
- applicability of the various notifications, circulars, clarifications, classification of goods and/or services, the nature of supplies,
- the manner of availment of credits together with its allowability or otherwise,
- maintenance of various records and documents specified therein,
- the basic functioning of the e-governance model. The audit coverage of all these records and documents would need substantial amount of preparation and time,
- requirements of reporting and source of information.

To start with, the following (among others) are the various steps an auditor can take in connection with the GST audit assignments:

(a) Inform the concerned assessee about the applicability of GST audit;

(b) Confirm the eligibility to be the GST auditor under the related legislation and the guidelines issued by ICAI;

(c) Assess the conflict of interest, if any, and the independence required for the conduct of the audit;

(d) Upon acceptance of the assignment, formal engagement letter must be sent and signed off between both the parties;

(e) Understand the nature of business, the products or services, requirements of records to be maintained, and advice the auditee to maintain the accounts and records so required, beforehand;

(f) Prepare a questionnaire to understand the operations/activities of the auditee, and specifically develop questions on those issues on which the GST law would have a bearing;

(g) Preparation of the detailed audit program and list of records to be verified;

(h) Special attention must be paid to transactions not appearing in the Financial Accounts, but having GST implications;

(i) Prepare various Reconciliation Statements.

22.11.1 Audit Proposal

Audit proposal must include an overview of what information the audit will provide. It should also provide a time-line, an estimate of the costs and a strong connection to the mission and objective of company goals. It should include client's profile, few reasons detailing the importance of an audit for an organization, list of partners conducting the audit, their role, title and contact information, detailed scope and area of coverage along with the milestones of the deliverables, management responsibility, fees, deliverables and engagement team.

22.11.2 Acceptance/Conflict of Interest

An auditor needs to consider various aspects before acceptance of the engagement in terms of any possible impendence issue of conflict of interest etc. Some of the areas are listed below:

(a) Section 2(2) of CA act, 1949 provides that a member would be deemed to be in practice if he engages himself, for a consideration, in the specified activities, which includes inter alia audit. Section 6 inter alia provides that a member cannot practice without obtaining Certificate of Practice Thus, only a member of ICAI having a Certificate of Practice (COP), or a firm of Chartered Accountants can take up the GST Audit. Additionally, a Chartered Accountant must bear in mind the following:

(b) Member in part time practice (including an employee having a COP) is not entitled to perform attest function. (241st Council Meeting Resolution);

(c) Member having substantial interest in an assessee cannot take up its audit. (Clause 4 of Part I of the Second Schedule of the Chartered Accountants Act, 1949 ("the CA Act") read with Appendix 9 of CA Regulations 1988);

(d) Member not to accept the audit of a person to whom he is indebted for more than Rs. 10,000/- (Chapter X of ICAI Guidelines);

(e) Member not to charge professional fees based on a percentage of profit or which are contingent upon the finding or the result of the professional employment. (Clause 10 of part I of the First Schedule to the CA Act);

(f) Internal auditor of an assessee cannot be appointed as his tax auditor (281st Council Meeting Resolution).

(g) In case of joint audits, all the auditors would have to sign the audit report and should issue separate reports where they have different opinions. (Ref SA 299).

(h) The restrictions applicable for appointment of a statutory auditor where fee for other services are more than the statutory audit fee, in case of specified entities, are not applicable to GST auditors (Chapter IX of ICAI Guidelines).

(i) An assessee may have GST registrations in more than one State. In such cases, the assessee may appoint a single/multiple auditor(s) for the distinct registrations under the same PAN. It is possible that accounts and records that are kept in different States may be in the local language of that State. In such cases, it is suggested that the auditor should not accept the audit of accounts written in a language which he/his staff do not understand.

(The code of conduct under both the regulatory Acts is provided in the Appendices to the Book.)

22.11.3 Audit Engagement

Communication with the previous Auditor – Since the GST audit is applicable for the first time (for the financial year 2017-18), the requirement of communication with the previous auditor prior to accepting the engagement (based on the provisions of the CA Act) does not arise. However, as a healthy practice, the GST auditor may choose to communicate with the previous auditor (under the erstwhile provisions of State Level Laws) so as to get a better insight into the auditee's business practices. Such communication would, however, become mandatory in the subsequent years (where the retiring auditor is a Chartered Accountant).

Engagement letter - Engagement letter states the terms and conditions of the engagement, principally addressing the scope of the engagement and the terms of compensation for the firm. Audit engagement letter would include:

- Scope & objective
- Fees
- Time frame
- Confidentiality of information
- Limitation of liability
- Acknowledgement & acceptance
- Other matters if any.

[Format of engagement letter is provided in the appendices to this book]

22.11.4 Management Representation Letter

MRL is a letter written by the auditor which is subsequently signed by senior management of auditee. The letter could state that the information submitted for the purpose of certification is complete and accurate, the limitation of the audit, non-provision of information with disclosure of all material information which could have impact under GST. Auditor needs to identify all important areas which needs representation of the management which would also become important audit evidence to prove that he has taken due care and has not been negligent. Representation letter could cover following aspects for confirmation from management:

(i) Reporting of all outward supplies in books of account and returns filed under GST provisions such as GSTR-3B, GSTR-1 and GSTR-9.

(ii) Confirmation on not supplying goods or services from unregistered places.

(iii) Reporting of supplies to registered customers and unregistered customers under respective columns in GST returns filed.

(iv) Valuation of supplies to related/distinct persons in accordance with valuation provisions.

(v) Reporting of all inward supplies in books of account and returns filed under GST provisions such as GSTR-3B, GSTR-9.

(vi) Maintenance of all records and documents as specified under Section 35(5) of CGST Act 2017 read with Rule 56 of CGST Rules 2017. This could include production register, stock register, self invoices, payment vouchers, refund vouchers, receipt voucher for advances, details of suppliers, details of customers and ITC registers.

(vii) Maintenance of electronic register with DSC.

(viii) Issue of invoices and delivery challans according to GST provisions

(ix) Movement of goods based on invoice or delivery challan along with e-way bill as required under the law from time to time.

(x) Classification of goods or services in accordance with GST provisions in accounting of inward supplies.

(xi) Classification of outward supplies in accordance with GST provisions.

(xii) Claim of exemptions/deductions in accordance with GST provisions.

(xiii) Declaration of all place of business at the time of audit and inclusion in registration certificate including reasons for non-inclusion of any of the place, if any.

(xiv) Confirmation on accounting of goods received from job work including scrap generated.

(xv) Claim of transitional credits in accordance with transitional provisions in TRAN-1 and TRAN-2 form.

(xvi) Confirmation on reconciliation of details disclosed in books of account with returns and other records maintained in GST law.

(xvii) Confirmation on break-up of information for each GSTIN from the audited financial statements/books of accounts only with segregation of information for pre-GST (April 2017 to June 2017 and GST period.

(xviii) Confirmation on claim of credit on only inputs, capital goods and input received with tax invoices.

(xix) Payment to vendors within 180 days or else reversal in accordance with ITC provisions.

(xx) Claim and utilisation of different types of GST according to order of utilisation.

(xxi) Credits are not claimed on restricted inputs, capital goods or services which are specified in Section 17(5) of CGST Act 2017.

(xxii) Confirmation on identification and reversal of inputs or capital goods which are subsequently lost, destroyed, issued as gift or samples to reverse/pay back the amount equal to ITC.

(xxiii) Confirmation on issue of invoices according to time of supply provisions of GST.

(xxiv) Confirmation on issue of invoices with correct place of supply to discharge the correct type of GST.

(xxv) Computations made for proportionate credits only in accordance with Rule 42 and Rule 43 in case of inputs, input services and capital goods in case of supplies involving exempted supplies in addition to taxable supplies.

(xxvi) All transactions without consideration with related/distinct persons considered for discharging GST.

(xxvii) Confirmation on correctness and completeness of tax invoices, bill of supplies, debit notes, credit notes, delivery challans provided for the purpose of certification.

(xxviii) Any other aspect as may relevant and decided by the auditor during the course of audit.

Chapter 23

Customs Audit

23.1 INTRODUCTION

What started as offerings as gifts to the King for permission to sell his goods became a custom and then became tax levied on imports and exports which came to be known as 'customs duties. There is a reference to Customs duty in Kautilya's Arthashastra also which shows that customs duties have been levied and collected from time immemorial.

The British rule in India made customs statutory levy with the introduction of Sea Customs Act, 1878. The three enactments of the British rule in India viz. Sea Customs Act, 1878, Inland Bounded Warehousing Act, 1896 and the Land Customs Act, 1924 were consolidated into the Customs Act, 1962 as it stands now. The Indian Tariff Act, 1934 was replaced by Customs Tariff Act, 1975 which underwent drastic changes in the year 1985 to be in tune with technological and industrial development in the world.

The constitution empowers the Parliament to make laws and entry 83 of the union list of the seventh schedule empowers the Central Government to levy duties of Customs on imports and exports.

The levy is on taxable event which is import of goods into India and export of goods out of India. The assessment exercise is conducted to arrive at duties payable after determining the classification of the goods in the schedule, rate of duty in the schedule read with exemption notifications if any and other levies such as IGST, anti-dumping duty, compensation cess, safeguard duty etc. After the assessment, duties have to be paid and thereafter goods are released to the importer or allowed to be exported

23.1.1 Audit in Customs

Audit of records relating to imports and exports is a very recent phenomenon. In the case of taxation on domestic manufacture under central excise law, even though there was a requirement of assessment of the tax by the departmental officer till 1995, there was provision for audit of the records of the assessees in their premises by the departmental officers as well the officers of the C & AG. However, in customs, till 2011, the practice was to assess the bills of entry/shipping bill or other import/export documents and only after assessment and examination of the cargo (selectively) and payment of applicable duties, goods were released to the importer or allowed to be exported. In the Custom houses, there was a practice of concurrent audit with assessment and C&AG used to the audit the records submitted for import and export in the Custom house itself.

A proper system of risk management was introduced around 2005 and Accredited Client Programme (ACP) was also introduced in the same year. The accredited clients got several facilities once their application was accepted. After gaining experience for about 5-6 years, in 2011, self-assessment was introduced in Customs also and On-site Post Clearance Audit at the Premises of Importers and Exporters Premises, 2011 was also notified. This was the beginning of the post clearance statutory audit in Customs. In 2016, the government introduced Authorised Economic Operator programme. (AEO). AEO is a programme under the aegis of the World Customs Organization (WCO) SAFE Framework of Standards to secure and facilitate (SAFE) Global Trade. All these liberalisation steps had to be accompanied by some safeguards and verification system.

Audit regulations of 2011 provided only for audit of the records of importer and exporters. Customs Audit Regulations, 2018 provides for audit of the records of an importer or exporter or custodian approved under section 45 or licensee of a warehouse and any other person concerned directly or indirectly in clearing, forwarding, stocking, carrying, selling or purchasing of imported goods or export goods or dutiable goods. The regulations also provided for audit either in the office of the proper officer or in any other premises. Section 99A was also introduced in the Customs Act, 1962 this year to provide statutory support. Statutory provisions can be seen in Appendix.

23.1.2 Consequences of the changes

(i) Assessment is an option for the proper officer of customs. He has the support of risk management system which identifies where examination of goods/documents/assessment may be required.

(ii) Importer/exporter has no such luxury. He is responsible for correctness of whatever he has declared/submitted.

(iii) When goods have not been assessed by the proper officer, the chances of invocation of suppression/mis-declaration or fraud to demand the duty/differential duty are high and the importer/exporter runs the risk of payment of duty, interest and penalty equal to the duty payable.

(iv) Earlier Customs scrutiny was limited to documents called for during assessment or examination. Conclusions that can be reached were based on the documents.

(v) When an audit is taken up, the possibility of different interpretations coming up are high.

(vi) Verification of post import activities can quite often result in demands proposing revision of value.

(vii) The Customs brokers may not be capable of understanding complex technical details relating to the goods imported and quite often may like to follow the instructions of the officers.

(viii) Valuation is an area in which a large number of disputes arise in Customs and quite often expert advice/detailed knowledge of the law can be very useful.

(ix) In the case of exports, mistakes, if made, can result in loss of benefits.

(x) Lack of knowledge of the processes relating to imports and exports, can result in delays and delays in customs processes can be very costly and result in increase in transaction costs.

(xi) Because of the cost of storage, cost of waiting etc. in import is very high, decisions made either after long procrastination or in panic can result in huge losses.

(xii) It is not only the knowledge of the Customs Act which is required but also other enactments. The Customs department also enforces other acts along with the Customs Act.

(xiii) The risk management system also some-times would miss withdrawal of exemptions and later it can become a demand invoking suppression.

(xiv) It cannot be said that Customs brokers can be relied upon to monitor notifications, circulars etc. even though many of them do it.

23.1.3 Possible solutions for better compliance under customs law could be as follows:

(i) There is nothing better than knowledge of law and making decisions after considering all the pros and cons.

(ii) Proper maintenance of records and accounts is also equally important since non maintenance of proper records itself can lead to loss of credibility.

(iii) Regular monitoring of issue of notifications, circulars with regard to the products concerned and also changes in rates etc. is a must.

(iv) Periodical review of overall customs activities has to be undertaken.

(v) Foreign Trade Policy and the benefits available thereunder should be verified and availed.

(vi) Regular training of personnel concerned is a must.

(vii) If possible knowledgeable professionals can be asked to do a periodical audit of all customs activities (can be clubbed with GST if necessary). If periodical audit is not possible, an audit can be got done prior to departmental audit.

23.1.4 Importance of periodical internal customs review

IGST paid on import of goods would be eligible as credit in terms of Section 16 of CGST Act 2017. According to Rule 36 of CGST Rules 2017, ITC of GST would not be eligible as credit when such GST has been paid in pursuance of any order where any demand has been confirmed on account of fraud, wilful misstatement or suppression of facts. This could have been caused by factors such as undervaluation, wrong classification or wrong claim of exemption etc. Therefore, any IGST which was not paid correctly but paid subsequent to any demand, would become ineligible for credit. GST auditor needs to ascertain if any such IGST paid due to fraud, misstatement or suppression of facts has been claimed as ITC to report the same.

The basic customs duty paid on import of goods would not be eligible as input tax credit and therefore, adds to the cost of procurement for the tax payer. Any undervaluation of goods for payment of customs duty which is found later would result in additional customs duty payment including interest and penalty. The importer may not be in position to collect such additional costs from his customer as well.

In initial days of GST, there were doubts on levy/ non-levy of GST for first importer in case of high sea sale transaction which was put to rest later through clarification vide customs circular no.33/2017 subject to condition that the last buyer furnished entire set of documents such as original invoice, high sea sale contract, commission details etc. Failure to comply with any condition could invite trouble from the department.

23.2 CUSTOMS REVIEW PROGRAMME

A periodical review of customs provisions compliance could help the businessmen to avoid / mitigate big surprises from the department in form of big tax demands. A brief customs review programme which can cover important areas as suggestions for review of implications of imports, exports or related activities is given below which could be customised based on nature of business of the auditee. Few check points added to check on FTP benefits as well which could add value to clients during GST audit though impact is not much for certification.

India has fulfilled its obligations to the World Customs Organisation as regards implementation of Authorised Economic Operator programme which provides expedited clearance to AEOs and other benefits with regard to their imports and exports. Another important part the objective of which is to safeguard revenue interests i.e. post clearance audit in the premises of the importer has not yet been implemented.

As a precursor to introduction to post clearance audit, regulations have been notified in the year 2018 and legal provisions to empower customs officers have also been introduced (available in Appendix 19).

So far after completion of importation or exportation which used to happen after verification /non verification of documents, in very exceptional cases, investigation used to be taken up to detect commercial frauds. In future when the post clearance audit work starts records maintained relating to import/export and subsequent activities relating to import/export would be verified in detail. Therefore imports/ exporters and all other associated persons specified in the regulations have to be prepared for the post clearance audit.

It is felt that a review by knowledgeable professionals periodically would not only ensure that actions relating to import /export are legal but also certain benefits missed to be availed could be availed.

23.2.1 Importer/ Exporter

CUSTOMS REVIEW PROGRAMME	
Name of the concern	
Address	
Contact persons	
Phone numbers	
E-mail Id	
Nature of Business	
Audit team	
Date of commencement of review	
Date of conclusion of review	
Review period	

Sl. No.	Particulars	Reviewed by	Remarks, If Any
1.	**Review of various reports**		
A	Review of previous audit report if any, to ensure compliance of the issues raised/found.		
B	Review of statutory audit report to ascertain the position on statutory dues related to Customs and to ascertain the existence of related party transactions which could have impact on valuation of goods.		

Sl. No.	Particulars	Reviewed by	Remarks, If Any
C	Review of the annual stock reports/statements to ascertain whether differences exist between book stock and actual stock figures as the same could have customs duty implications.		
D	Review of internal audit reports to ascertain the issues pertaining to Customs noted by internal auditors and compliance of the same.		
E	Review of audit notes/reports issued by the tax authorities and compliance of the same.		
F	Reviewing of SOP established by the organization (if any) with respect to Customs procedures and comments thereon to management, if any deviation noticed.		
2.	**Registration under DGFT/ As Authorised Economic Operator (AEO) under Customs.**		
A	Review of Import Export Code certificate obtained (IEC) for importing or exporting activity including inclusion of all branches in the IEC.		
B	Review of registration certificate obtained under GST provisions for trading activity (as importer dealer).		
C.	Review of quality of accounts and records and also to see whether accounts are maintained as per Ind AS/IFRS (Indian accounting standards or International Financial Reporting system in case the auditee is an AEO and review of fulfillment of obligations cast on the AEO.		

Sl. No.	Particulars	Reviewed by	Remarks, If Any
3.	**Classification, Rate of tax, claims for exemption and tax paid**		
A.	Review of the classification of all the products imported/exported by the auditee		
B.	Review of rate of tax, claims for exemption and tax paid. Auditor has to check and see whether other exemptions, if any, are available for the goods imported or exported. Review of the stand taken by the importer in the case of denial of exemption by Customs. Check whether acceptance was given in writing as required under the law and whether it is justified and if not whether any remedial action is possible.		
4.	**Review of Valuation, Taxability of Goods**		
A	Review the valuation mechanism applied for the goods imported or exported to ensure that the same are in accordance with Customs Valuation provisions		
B	Review the correctness of valuation for payment of IGST		
C	Review value applied for payment of other duties like safeguard duty, anti-dumping duty, calamity cess, compensation cess etc.		
D	Review of various agreements entered with major customers/suppliers/parent company/subsidiary and study the implication thereof. Check whether there are any conditions relating to post import activities which can be considered as condition of sale of any imported goods.		

Sl. No.	Particulars	Reviewed by	Remarks, If Any
E	Review the SVB documents if there are transactions with related persons referred to SVB and check whether submissions reflect the correct facts and legal provisions have been applied correctly to facts.		
F.	Check whether IGST on ocean freight has been paid correctly and separately.		
G.	If there are imports by air, check whether freight has been calculated correctly.		
H.	If the imports have been made for charitable purpose, examine the valuation process adopted and its correctness. If the import for charitable purpose has been made under an ad-hoc exemption notification, see whether post import conditions imposed in the notifications have been fulfilled.		
I.	Check whether the importer has accepted the value enhanced by Customs. Check whether acceptance was given in writing as required under the law and whether it is justified and if not whether any remedial action is possible.		
J.	Check whether all the documents relating to imports have been maintained properly.		
5.	**Review of Exports and Deemed exports**		
A	Review if proper documents are maintained in case of export of goods outside India while clearing under LUT or under Bond without payment of duty		

Sl. No.	Particulars	Reviewed by	Remarks, If Any
B	Review if proper documents are maintained in case of deemed export of goods without payment of taxes. Review for existence of exemption certificate and other documentation		
C	Review of payment of export duty, if any, including impact on refund claimed under GST		
D	Review the process and the procedure followed for exports after the goods leave the premises to ensure that actual exports take place within the period prescribed.		
E.	Review the process and the procedure followed and their correctness in respect of exports through merchant exporter, if any.		
F	Review of various benefits availed for exports under FTP including suggestions on claiming benefits, if any, eligible.		
G	Review the process of exports and see whether refund of indigenous taxes has been claimed or not where relevant.		
H	Review dutiable exports to see whether there is any change in duty payable because of verification of sample, quantity exported or revision of value.		
I	Where assessment is on the basis of tariff value, check whether correct tariff value has been applied.		
J	Where imported goods have been re-exported, see whether the process and procedure followed are correct?		

Sl. No.	Particulars	Reviewed by	Remarks, If Any
K	In the case of re-export, check whether taxes paid at the time of import have been correctly claimed as drawback as admissible.		
L	In the case of import for job work under the relevant notification, examine the correctness of the procedure followed and method of accounting. See whether all the conditions have been fulfilled.		
M	In the case of job work see whether the benefit of MEIS/SEIS is admissible and has been taken.		
6.	**Review of Imports**		
A	Review if proper documents are maintained in case of import of goods.		
B	Review if proper documents are maintained in case entity has availed the benefit of Advance authorisation or EPCG authorisation and imported goods without payment of taxes.		
C	Review whether the conditions to be fulfilled in terms of advance authorisation or EPCG authorisation with regard to export obligations have been fulfilled correctly or not.		
D	Review whether completion of formalities such as obtaining EODC from DGFT and closure of bonds executed before customs have been completed properly.		
E	Review imports made under exemption notifications which requires the importer to follow the procedure under Customs (Import		

Sl. No.	Particulars	Reviewed by	Remarks, If Any
	of goods at concessional rate of duty for manufacture of excisable goods) Rules, 1996 to check whether post importation conditions have been fulfilled.		
F	Review payment of import duties, credits, exemptions claimed etc. Check whether alternate exemption notifications are available but missed.		
G	Review the customs correspondence file to evaluate issues that can arise or have arisen in the past.		
H	Review ongoing litigation files to understand the issues and make suggestions.		
I	If any machine or article has been sent for repair after importation, see whether the value adopted for payment of duty is in accordance with law. (The law requires tax to be paid on freight both ways and repair charges).		
J	Was there any case of short landing during importation? If yes, did the importer claim refund of duty paid?		
7.	**Samples**		
A.	If sample has been drawn in the case of any import, review the effect of report on the sample in respect of the transaction.		
B.	If the report is adverse, review action taken by the importer and whether it is appropriate.		

Sl. No.	Particulars	Reviewed by	Remarks, If Any
C	If the report is favourable, see whether the importer had paid duty at higher rate and if so, whether he has claimed refund of excess duty paid.		
D	If provisional assessment was resorted to and the test report is favourable, see whether the provisional assessment has been finalised and the importer has been able to get the bank guarantee /security released. This applies to all cases of provisional assessment.		
E	If duty at higher rate had been paid under protest and the report is favourable, check whether refund claim has been filed. This applies to cases where duty at higher rate had been paid under protest for other reasons also.		
F	If there are cases where duty has been paid under protest, check whether excess duty paid has been passed on to the buyers. If not check whether necessary entries in the books of accounts and the financial statements have been made so that refund claim does not get affected by the unjust enrichment clause.		
8.	**Assessment Process**		
A	Review and see whether any self assessment was not accepted and examine the correctness of the procedure and process.		
B	Check whether declarations in bills of entry/shipping bills have been made correctly.		

Sl. No.	Particulars	Reviewed by	Remarks, If Any
9.	**Payment of duties**		
A.	Review the import/export management as regards payment of duties. Is the auditee paying interest on duties which could have been avoided?		
B	Review if the auditee has a system of monitoring movement/processing bills of entry/shipping bills filed to ensure that queries are promptly answered and documents called for are submitted without delay and transaction costs are reduced?		
10	Compliance with requirements of other statutes enforced/implemented by the Customs.		
A. D	In addition to the implementation and enforcement of provisions of Customs Act, GST law, the customs department is responsible for enforcement of many other statutes. Further when an importer/exporter is undertaking international transaction, it is necessary that he knows his obligations under other statutes and the auditor has to see whether the auditee has fulfilled the obligations. A list (not exhaustive) of statutes is given below: 1. Explosives Act, 1884 and Explosive Rules, 1983. 2. Live Stock Importation Act, 1898. 3. Drugs and Cosmetics Act, 1940 and Drug and Cosmetics Rules, 1945. 4. Copyright Act, 1957 and Copyright Rules, 1958. 5. Arms Act, 1959.		

Sl. No.	Particulars	Reviewed by	Remarks, If Any
	6. Atomic Energy Act, 1962. 7. Insecticide Act, 1968. 8. Patents Act, 1970 and Patent Rules, 2003 9. Wild Life Protection Act, 1972. 10. Gas Cylinder Rules, 1981 and S & MPV (Unfired) Rules, 1981. 11. Environment (Protection) Act, 1986 and Rules, 1986. 12. The Bureau of Indian Standards Act, 1986 and Rules, 1987. 13. Motor Vehicles Act, 1988. 14. Plants, Fruits and Seeds (Regulation of Import into India) Order, 1989. 15. Trade Marks Act, 1999. 16. Hazardous Waste (Management and Handling) Rules, 2003. 17. Plant Quarantine (Regulation of Import Into India) Order, 2003. 18. Food Safety and Standards Act, 2006. 19. Legal Metrology Act, 2009 and Legal Metrology (Packaged Commodities) Rules, 2011.		
11.	**Review of financial statements**		
A	Review of Balance sheet to – • Identify the assets purchased and ascertain the eligibility of IGST refund • Identify investments made in associates/group companies if any. If any investments are made, then ascertain the impact of Customs valuation for imports or exports clearances made to such associates or group		

Sl. No.	Particulars	Reviewed by	Remarks, If Any
	companies. Examination of SVB (Special Valuation Branch) valuation requirement ● Identify the major customers/ clients to trace the realizations and the pattern of charging them to study the implications under Customs law.		
B	Review of Profit & Loss account – ● Ascertain the nature of revenue – Sales (Exporting goods) and other incomes. ● Review for existence of any export of goods and the satisfaction of conditions for availing such exemption of duty for exporting ● Review for impact of insurance claims made and received on damaged goods. ● Review the remission of duty on lost/destroyed abandoned goods ● Review the abatement of duty on damaged/deteriorated goods. ● Review the refund of export or import duty if any.		
C	Review the debit notes – ● Ascertain additional consideration/amounts debited to customers to study the impact under Customs law. ● Review for purchase returns to study impact under Customs law.		
D	Review the credit notes - ● Review for Sales returns to study impact under customs law. ● Review for discounts if any allowed and impact of the same on valuation of goods		

Sl. No.	Particulars	Reviewed by	Remarks, If Any
12.	**Review of Input tax credit and Input tax setoff**		
A	Review the import transactions to ensure that eligible import duties paid are availed as credit in accordance with the provisions of GST law		
B	Review the GRNs' to ensure that credits/set offs have been claimed in case of all eligible import purchases		
C	Review the raw materials ledger to find out if the goods on which input tax credit is claimed are issued towards exempted activities		
13.	**Benefits**		
A	Review if the entity is availing the benefit of Duty drawback and its correctness.		
B	Suggestion on choosing of rate of drawback i.e. All industry Rate or Brand Rate		
C	Review if the entity is availing any benefits under FTP (Foreign Trade Policy) such as MEIS, SEIS etc.		
14.	**Miscellaneous**		
A	Review of Baggage provisions, if applicable.		
B	Review of procedures relating to goods imported or exported through post/courier.		
C	Review of procedures for goods sent/received for repairs to/from outside India.		

Sl. No.	Particulars	Reviewed by	Remarks, If Any
D	Review the transactions to find out cases of any goods re-imported or re-exported goods and exemption if any claimed.		
E	Review the list of documents filed with the department, list of authorized signatories.		
F	Review for transactions wherein the goods are being imported or exported as samples and the customs implications on such transactions.		
G	Review of free of cost (FOC) exports as export promotion activity.		

23.2.2 Customs Broker

Sl No	Particulars	Reviewed	Remarks, If any
1.	General review		
A	Review whether KYC norms for customers has been followed by the broker by verifying correctness of Importer Exporter Code (IEC) number, Goods and Services Tax Identification Number (GSTIN), identity of his client and functioning of his client at the declared address by using reliable, independent, authentic documents, data or information.		
B.	Review the system of maintenance of accounts and records by the Broker.		
C.	Review the operations of the Broker to see whether broker is fulfilling his obligations under the licensing regulations.		
D	Review the steps taken by the Broker to ensure that his staff have the up to date knowledge and are capable of advising the clients		

Sl No	Particulars	Reviewed	Remarks, If any
E	Review some of the documents filed relating to import/export to see the correctness of classification, exemption claimed, valuation etc.		
F	Review the quality of advice given to the clients by the broker.		
G	See the correspondence files to check whether the department has found any activity of the broker wrong.		
H	Check whether licence is valid? Whether any change in the constitution of the firm has taken place and if so whether the broker has applied for a fresh licence as required.		
I	Study the billing procedure adopted by the Customs broker to check whether he has ensured that amounts collected for third party services are obtained as a pure agent so that his customers are not deprived of the credit of taxes paid.		
J	See whether broker has ensured that customs queries are promptly replied without any delay so that importer/exporter is not affected adversely.		
K	Has the broker maintained up to date records such as bill of entry, shipping bill, transshipment application, etc., all correspondence, other papers relating to his business as Customs Broker and accounts including financial transactions in an orderly and itemised manner as required in the regulations?		
L	Has the broker maintained all records and accounts that are required to be maintained under these regulations and preserved for at least five years as required under the regulations.		
M	As in the case of importer/exporter carry out **Review of financial statements** (Sl.No.11 above).		
N.	Since the broker would be liable to pay GST on services rendered by him, the checks suggested for GST audits would be applicable to the Customs broker also. The details therefore are not reproduced.		

23.2.3 Warehouse:

Notifications from 67/2016 to 72/2016 are regulations notified by CBIC on 14/5/2016 after the revision of warehousing provisions in the Customs Act, 1962. Even though regulations cover different categories of warehouses, the audit checks required do not differ greatly. In the private bonded warehouse, only the owner's goods can be stored. In the public bonded warehouse, anyone can store the goods in respect of which warehousing bill of entry has been filed. Special warehouses are for notified goods and they are subject to physical control of the bond officer and no storage, no removal can take place without the presence of the bond officer. A warehouse keeper would be paying GST also and would be taking credit of input taxes also. Therefore the detailed audit proposed for GST and the process would be applicable to the warehouses also. Therefore only a few checks which are necessary for audit relating to warehousing process are incorporated herein below.

Sl No	Particulars	Reviewed	Remarks, If any
A.	Check whether the auditee has (a) maintained detailed records of the receipt, handling, storing, and removal of any goods into or from the warehouse and they reflect the correct position and also provide a record of each activity, operation or action taken in relation to the warehoused goods. (b) maintained a record of drawal of samples from the warehoused goods. (c) kept copies of the bills of entry, transport documents, Forms for transfer of goods from a warehouse, shipping bills or bills of export or any other documents evidencing the receipt or removal of goods into or from the warehouse and copies of the bonds executed.		
B	Check whether the insurance cover taken, the amount for which bond has been executed are adequate.		
C	Examine whether warehouse keeper appointed fulfils the requirements of regulations in terms of qualification, experience etc.		
D	Check the account maintained for one time locks by the auditee vis-à-vis actual stock.		
E	Call for and check the audit reports/inspection notes of the department/AG/Internal auditor of the auditee and examine whether the auditee has missed any obligations to be fulfilled.		

Sl No	Particulars	Reviewed	Remarks, If any
F	Review of the correspondence file with the department.		
G	Is any manufacturing or other operations being done on the imported goods in the warehouse? If yes, examine whether the obligations to be fulfilled as per Manufacture & Other Operations in Warehouse Regulations, 1966.		

23.2.4 Container Freight Stations (CFS):

CFS were allowed to be set up to act as custodians when the global trade gradually shifted to containerization and also to reduce congestion in the ports. Unlike the port, the CFS can be set up anywhere near the port. All over India several CFS have been set up and they are appointed under section 45 of the Customs Act, 1962. CFSs have to work in accordance with the provisions of Handling of Cargo in Customs Areas Regulations, 2009. Being service providers and located in the taxable territory, they have to discharge **GST.** Therefore the auditing process and procedure provided for others would apply to them also.

Sl No	Particulars	Reviewed	Remarks, If any
A	Review of books of accounts maintained, processes and procedures followed to consider whether the obligations under the Handling of Cargo in Customs Areas Regulations, 2009, have been fulfilled.		
B	Review of steps taken to dispose of uncleared and unclaimed cargo by auction		
C	Review of correspondence file with the department		
D	Review of audit reports from department/internal audit/AG's audit etc.		
E	Review of action taken on the previous audit reports		

Chapter 24

Important Year End Action Points in GST

24.1 INTRODUCTION

At the end of the financial year, it is important for the tax payers in GST to undertake a few actions to ensure that the GST transactions are reported appropriately in financial statements and periodical GST returns. This would be important considering the fact that the disclosures made in periodical GST returns would need to be collated into the annual return under GSTR-9 and further compared with financial statements at the time of certification in form GSTR-9C by the auditor. Differences in disclosures made in periodical returns as compared to financial statements would increase the reconciliation items needing more explanation. This could also invite department's audit, DGGSTI attention. Due care needs to be taken to reconcile the differences and take corrective actions. The action points could vary depending on the nature of business. Some of them could be common for most tax payers which include the following:

24.2 CROSS CHARGE TO RELATED/DISTINCT PERSONS

Supply of goods or services to own branches/units/employees without consideration would be treated as supply liable for GST in terms of schedule I to CGST Act 2017. There could be many support services or other supplies undertaken by the tax payer which needs to be identified on periodical basis to cross charge with GST. Before finalization of annual accounts, it is important to identify the cost to be allocated to such other locations of the same entity. Tax invoice could be issued after adopting appropriate valuation mechanism to discharge GST. The details of such cross charge should be reflected in GST return with appropriate treatment in financial statements as well.

The difference between cross charge and Input Service Distributor (ISD) needs to be understood. Many tax payers use the concept interchangeably which is not legally correct and would lead to demands. ISD option could be used for distribution of credits on only input services which are commonly used for multiple locations or any dedicated units. Distribution should be done based on the ratio of turnover. Cross charge mechanism could be opted for services supplied to other distinct persons for which various expenses including inputs, input services or capital goods are incurred. In the first one, tax payer takes the total credit and distributes them to the locations. In the second one, he avails the credit if eligible and then charges the GST on supplies of goods or services made within the entity to the different GSTIN.

24.3 REVIEW OF ITC LEDGER AND VENDOR INVOICES

Considering the challenges in terms of availment of input tax credits (ITC) at State level as compared to a centralized level under service tax regime, there is a possibility that invoices may have been prepared incorrectly or disclosed incorrectly as B2C instead of B2B. Further certain credits could have been availed in the wrong State or wrong GSTIN within the same State. All conditions under section 16 are to be met for availing credit. Any wrong claim of credit could result in reversal at subsequent stage along with interest. As there is a time limit for taking the credit, there would be no option to take back the credit after lapse of time limit. Therefore, ITC ledgers could be thoroughly verified for correctness of type of credit claimed and correctness of registration in which it is claimed. There could also be defective invoices issued by the vendors which could result in dispute of input tax credits. Those invoices could be identified to instruct the vendors to take necessary actions before close of the financial statements.

24.4 E-WAY BILL COMPLIANCE AND RECONCILIATION

E-way bill compliance is made mandatory for most transactions involving movement of goods. E-way bills are important even for movement which may not be as a result of supply such as removal for job work, sale on approval etc. As a year end process, a reconciliation could be made to ascertain if tax invoice or bill of supply wherever necessary has been issued within the due time based on E-way bills issued.

24.5 ITC DISTRIBUTION UNDER ISD

In case of multiple registered units under GST, there could be common expenses with ITC availed at one unit including credits which relate to some other unit but payment made by the HO or branch. Such ITC needs to be distributed to other units specifically as well as for the common expenses based on the proportionate turnover on monthly basis under input service distributor concept. Tax payers could make it a point to check if all common expenses are identified including distribution of credits for the financial year. Considering the fact there is a time limit for taking ITC, importance to be given for such distribution. Any ITC which is found to be claimed in wrong unit after the time limit and not distributed, could lapse.

24.6 ITC REVERSAL AND YEAR-END ADJUSTMENTS

In case of taxpayers having taxable and exempt supplies, the ITC could be claimed on those inputs, capital goods and input services which are used for taxable supplies. Where they are common, the proportionate credit needs to be reversed/paid based on monthly turnovers. After the end of financial year, by end of September, the credit reversal needs to be re-computed based on actual turnover. Tax payers should ensure that such re-computation is made taking actual turnover which could result in excess claim or short claim of credit when there is a change in turnover considered for monthly computations made. Any short claim of credit could be re-claimed by end of September after end of financial year. Delay could result in loss of credit. Excess claimed credit, if any to be paid back along with interest.

24.7 RECONCILIATION

Taxpayers should reconcile the electronic cash ledgers, electronic credit ledgers and electronic liability ledgers with books of accounts. Further, the reconciliation of the GSTR 3B returns must also be performed with that of GSTR 1 and any discrepancies needs to be reported/rectified. The reconciliation could result in identifying excess or short claim of credit, excess or short payment of taxes including differences in turnover disclosed. Key reconciliations that needs be done would be between the monthly GSTR-3B and GSTR-1 statements. ITC reconciliation with books of account and GSTR-2A could be another important reconciliation. All these would ensure that there are minimum differences between returns leading to correct filing of annual returns which in turn reduces the reconciliation items in the GST audit certification in form GSTR-9C.

24.8 GST PAYMENT UNDER REVERSE CHARGE

In terms of Section 7 read with Schedule I to the CGST Act 2017, import of services by any person from related persons or establishments outside India would be deemed to be supply even if there is no consideration paid by importing person. Valuation should be undertaken in terms valuation principles in the CGST Rules 2017. In case of multinational entities, receiving support from related entities or establishment outside India could be common. Such services if missed need to be identified by the registered person at the end of the year to ensure that necessary compliance is taken care including discharge of GST when place of supply is in India.

24.9 ISSUE OF DEBIT/CREDIT NOTE

At the year end, the taxable person could assess the need of issue of debit note in case of purchase returns, short collection of taxable amount or GST amount. In case of sale return, excess collection of taxable amount or GST amount, there would be a need to issue credit note. If required, debit notes /credit notes to be issued at the earliest so that additional cost in form of loss of ITC, risk of non-payment by customers, interest, if any could be avoided.

24.10 RETURN FILING FOR THE MONTH OF SEPTEMBER

GST return for the month of September after the end of financial year would be key as it provides the last opportunity to the tax payers to rectify mistakes/make good the omissions in the returns filed in previous financial year. Therefore, tax payers have to do a review of all GST related accounts and the ledgers to ensure that they do not miss this last opportunity. The annual return to be filed in GSTR-9 for the previous financial year would also cover a few adjustments made in present financial year for the period April to September. This annual return becomes basis for GSTR-9c as well. Following are important points to be considered while filing the returns for September month:

- Ensure that the turnover as reported in the GSTR-3B for previous financial year matches with the turnover as reported in the GSTR-1. If there is any error in GSTR-1, same is required to be corrected. If there is any error in GSTR-3B, the correct details should be shown in GSTR-1. Liability arising could be discharged with interest by disclosing the details in GSTR-3B of September or earlier. Items such as taxable/non-taxable supplies, exempt supplies, non-GST supplies, RCM, Zero rate supplies could be considered for the reconciliation.
- Ensure that the turnover as reported in the audited financial statement for the concerned GSTIN matches with the turnover declared in the GSTR-1 and the difference, if any, is due to the difference between statutory provisions and not due to mistakes/omissions in maintenance of accounts and records.
- Any amendment in the invoices pertaining to the last year's transaction has to be done in the GSTR-1. The amendment may be in the GSTIN, value, nature of tax, place of supply etc. The need could arise on account of communication received from the customer where he may have noticed the error in the GSTR-2A due to which he may not be in position to avail the ITC or it may have been noticed in the course of internal verification. Any credit note for the previous financial year should be issued by end of September of present financial year. Otherwise, deduction of tax paid would not be possible.
- Any supplies in respect of which a mistake has been made in identification of place of supply, time of supply or in its classification or with regard to claim for exemption, rectification has to be made. It is necessary to check whether any supply which is export has been shown as domestic supply and vice versa and rectify.
- All the advances received in previous year where time of supply has arisen in the previous year have to be included in the GSTR-1 and ensure that the same matches with the details furnished in the books of

account. Attention is required to be paid to continuous supply contracts to ascertain if time of supply concept has been followed or not.

- Exports to distinct person is not considered as export. This may have to be kept in mind.
- Disposal of business assets for consideration/for no consideration to related persons have to be reflected in the returns.
- Payments to employees/from employees for waiver of notice periods, payments to employees for services rendered in non-employee category, if any, have to be examined in terms of GST liability
- Necessary corrections, if required, in the disclosures made between B2B supply and B2C supply has to be made.
- Ensure that where services provided are liable to RCM, same have been disclosed in the GSTR-1 with specific indication about the liability under RCM so that the same is auto populated in the GSTR-2A of recipient and he pays RCM thereon.
- The due date of filing the GST return for September month is also last date for claiming the credit pertaining to previous financial year. Tax payers need to find out missed out credits if any which could be based on reconciliation of credit registers with physical invoices, GSTR-2A generated based on GSTR-1 filed by the vendors. Appropriate disclosure to be made in GST return and accounting in the month of September which otherwise could result in loss of credit.

24.11 OTHER ASPECTS

Following are various other aspects which could be considered by the tax payers which are important to ensure better compliance:

- According to GST provisions, invoice numbers should be unique for a financial year. There is no need to start invoice series from first number every year. Previous year's series could be continued or fresh number series could be started at the option of tax payer.
- There are specified returns for compliance of ISD provisions, job work provisions, TDS/TCS provisions etc., which need to be filed on periodical basis. Status of such returns filed could be ascertained at the year end.
- If needed, the HSN classification including number of digits disclosed on the invoices/ delivery challans could be re-examined.

Chapter 25

Other Certifications under GST

25.1 INTRODUCTION

GST is a major tax reform in the Country and has been a game changer. There has been a paradigm shift in the indirect tax structure with the GST rollout with effect from 1st July 2017. As a professional, it is imperative to understand and assimilate the new taxation structure, associated compliances and the changes in business processes emanating therefrom.

GST audit has to be periodically conducted on entities registered under GST by practicing chartered accountants or GST officers to ensure that there is proper compliance. The requirement of audit and certification requirement on reconciliation by chartered accountants and cost accountants under section 35(5) have been discussed at length in the other chapters. Other than the GST audit under section 35(5) of the CGST Act, 2017, there are various other certifications under GST that would have to be provided by a practicing chartered accountant, cost accountant, chartered engineer, etc. from time to time. In this chapter, we are going to discuss the various other certifications required to be provided by professionals.

A brief summary of various other certifications required under GST are as follows:

1. **ITC Claim under special circumstances *(Section 18(1) read with rule 40)*** Chartered accountant (CA) or a cost accountant certificate is required in case of input tax credit claim under special circumstances on the inputs held in stock, in semi-finished or finished goods, or the credit claimed on capital goods.

2. **Transfer of credit on sale, merger, amalgamation, lease or transfer of a business (Rule 41(2))**

   A certificate issued by a CA or cost accountant is required for certifying that the sale, merger, de-merger, amalgamation, lease or transfer of business has been done with a specific provision for the transfer of liabilities.

3. **Manner of reversal of credit under special circumstances (Sec 18(4) read with Rule 44)**

   In case of situations where the taxpayer opts to pay tax under section 10, or goods or services become subsequently exempt, the manner of reversal of credit needs to be duly certified by a CA or Cost accountant.

Application for refund of tax, interest, penalty, fees or any other amount (Rule 89(2))

Any application for refund needs to be accompanied with a certificate issued by a CA or cost accountant that the incidence of tax or any other amount claimed as refund has not been passed on to any other person.

TDS Certificate

Section 51 of the CGST Act, 2017 prescribes the authority and procedure for 'Tax Deduction at Source'. The Government may order the following persons (the deductors) to deduct tax at source:

(a) a department or establishment of the Central Government or State Government; or

(b) local authority; or

(c) Governmental agencies; or

(d) such persons or category of persons as may be notified by the Government on the recommendations of the Council.

The tax would be deducted @1% of the payment made to the supplier (the deductee) of taxable goods or services or both. At present no notification has been issued specifying others. The provisions came into effect from 1st October 2018.

Claiming of reimbursement of tax paid under 'Seva Bhoj Yojana' (C.B.I. & C. Circular No. 75/49/2018-GST, dated 27-12-2018)

To claim reimbursement of the tax paid by the specified organizations, a CA certificate certifying a list of details needs to be furnished with the application.

To determine whether the supply is taxable under GST (Schedule II)

In respect of construction, where the entire consideration has been received after issuance of the completion certificate, where required, by the competent authority, the said amount will not be liable to tax under GST. Hence, certification from such competent authority like a chartered engineer, etc. would be required under this circumstance.

Reduced rate of GST on houses constructed under Credit Linked Subsidy Scheme (CLSS)

The builder may charge a reduced rate of GST on houses constructed/acquired under CLSS on the basis of the certificate issued by the Primary Lending Institutions.

Before we proceed with the discussion of the various above mentioned certifications in detail, it is imperative to analyze the authenticity, reliability, and validity of these certificates issued by the various professionals.

25.2 AUTHENTICITY AND RELIABILITY OF THE CERTIFICATES ISSUED BY THE PROFESSIONALS

Financial statements and other relevant documents of an enterprise depict the wholesome financial situation of the enterprise for a particular period/at a particular time. The information in these statements is of vital importance for a large section of the society, which deals with that enterprise. It may be suppliers of material, customers, investors, banks, financial institutions, insurers, government, tax authorities, employees, collaborators, and even their competitors.

Keeping in view the importance of these statements and the large section of the society who use these statements for taking many vital decisions, it is necessary that these statements are attested by some person who is an expert in the field so that the objectivity, integrity, reliability, and credibility of the information is assured to a large extent. This function of attestation is done by various professionals like chartered accountants, cost accountants, advocates, chartered engineers, etc.

It has been, however, observed that there have been a number of cases in banks and financial institutions wherein due to the erroneous/ambiguous advice tendered by the respective professionals, borrower accounts have had to face quick mortality resulting in a loss for the bank. Many a time this has also resulted in vigilance cases being initiated with the allegations of connivance/malafide/gross negligence being attributed to the concerned users. Such cases bring into question the reliability and authenticity of the various reports and certificates issued by the professionals.

It is a generally accepted principle of law that certificates, reports issued by competent professionals like a chartered accountant, cost accountant, advocate are acceptable in the court of law unless and until any contrary evidence is submitted or its reliability or genuineness is challenged before the court.

Reference can be made to the judgment of the Supreme Court in case of **Commissioner v Akay Cosmetics (P) Ltd., 2001 (129) E.L.T. A82 (S.C)** wherein it was held that, that a chartered accountant's certificate is an acceptable basis for allowing admissible deductions such as turn over tax, octroi, freight and insurance unless revenue leads any evidence contrary to that.

Further, reference can also be made to the decision of The Delhi High Court in **YU Televentures Pvt. Ltd. v Union of India, 2017 (358) E.L.T. 81 (Del.)** wherein it was held that the Chartered Accountant's certificate produced by the importer showing incidence of Countervailing Duty (CVD) not passed on to the customers, was sufficient to rebut the presumption of unjust enrichment for refund especially when such certificate had already been accepted in earlier proceedings.

However, even though in most of the cases such certifications by the professionals can be relied on, there are circumstances under which these certificates are inappropriate and their reliability can be questioned for various reasons.

Reference can be made to the case of **Apollo Exports v Collector, 1999 (105) E.L.T. A126 (S.C)** wherein it was held that a chartered accountant's certificate was not acceptable in view of various discrepancies therein as -

- They are not the regular CAs of the appellant Company.
- The chartered accountant has nowhere set out what records had been verified by him before the issue of the certificate of consumption of stamping foils in leather bags and Wallets manufactured by the appellants.
- Further, the quantity imported and utilized has been referred without any indication of the quantity of damage/wastage shown to be nil while the appellants themselves stated that 118 inches of stamping foils were left as lost on account of handling/calculation/ measurement.

It was noticed that financial documents/certificates were being attested/issued by third persons misrepresenting themselves as professional members of the ICAI misleading the Authorities and Stakeholders. To curb the malpractices, the Professional Development Committee of the ICAI has implemented the innovative concept of UDIN i.e. Unique Document Identification Number. All the practicing chartered accountants are required to get the UDIN for every certificate issued by them. It will secure the certificates attested/certified by practicing professionals. This will also enable the Regulators, banks, third parties to check the authenticity of the documents.

The professionals should exercise due diligence and prepare their certificate with utmost care.

We now proceed to discuss the above various certifications in further detail.

25.3 CERTIFICATION OF THE ITC CLAIMED UNDER SPECIAL CIRCUMSTANCES

Under GST, ITC is generally available to all registered persons. However, following are the special cases where credit on the inputs held in stock, inputs contained in semi-finished and finished goods held on the date immediately preceding the date from which the person becomes liable to pay tax will be made available to such person subject to the certification by a CA or a cost accountant of the ITC claimed:

- A supplier who applies for registration within 30 days of becoming liable for registration (as the threshold limit of Rs. 20/40 lakhs has been crossed) and obtains registration.

- Voluntary Registration under GST by a person.
- Where a person ceases to pay tax under composition scheme and is now liable to pay tax under regular scheme.
- Where an exempt supply of goods or services or both by a registered person becomes a taxable supply.

Analysis:

Few important checkpoints and aspects that need to be considered by a Chartered Accountant or a Cost Accountant before certifying are as follows:

a) This certificate is required to be issued only if the aggregate value of the claim on account of SGST/CGST/UTGST and IGST exceeds Rs. 2 lakhs.

b) The certificate to be issued should be in accordance with the Guidance note on Reports and Certificates for special purpose issued by the ICAI.

c) Credit on input services is not available under any circumstance.

d) Declaration in Form GST ITC-01 is filed by the assessee on GST portal for entitlement to claim such credits within 30 days of being entitled to do so.

e) To ensure that the applicant has applied for registration within 30 days from the date from when he is liable to obtain registration under the GST law.

f) The tax invoices on which ITC is being claimed should not be older than one year on the on the day immediately preceding the date on which the Applicant is liable to pay tax.

g) Books and records and other relevant documents and registers relating to inputs lying in stock on the date preceding the date of grant of registration needs to be checked for verifying quantity of goods held/lying in stock.

h) Eligibility of such credits also needs to be checked as per Section 16 and Section 17 of the Act.

i) The books of account and relevant documents/records of the assessee should be thoroughly verified to understand if it is actually entitled to benefit of credit under section 18(1).

j) Where credit is available on capital goods, it needs to be ensured that the input tax credit on capital goods has been reduced by five percentage points per quarter of a year or part thereof, from the date of invoice and depreciation has not been claimed on the GST portion of the cost of the capital goods.

k) Compliance with Rule 40(1) (e) needs to be ensured regarding verification of the credits claimed with the details furnished by the supplier in Form GSTR-1 or Form GSTR-4 or GSTR-2A, as applicable.

Examples:

(i) A person becomes liable to pay tax on 1st January 2019 and has obtained registration on 15th January 2019. Such person is eligible for input tax credit on inputs held in stock as on 31st December 2018.

(ii) Mr. XYZ, registered person was paying tax under composition scheme up to 30th July 2018. However, with effect from 31st July 2018. Mr. XYZ becomes liable to pay tax under regular scheme. Mr. XYZ is eligible for input tax credit on inputs held in stock as on closure of business hours on 30th July 2018.

25.4 CERTIFICATION ON TRANSFER OF CREDIT ON SALE, MERGER, AMALGAMATION, LEASE OR TRANSFER OF A BUSINESS (RULE 41(2))

In the event of sale, merger, de-merger, amalgamation, lease or transfer or change in the ownership of business for any reason, the details of such event have to be furnished by the registered person in FORM GST ITC-02 with a request for transfer of unutilized input tax credit lying in his electronic credit ledger to the transferee.

A certificate needs to be issued by a practicing CA or cost accountant certifying that the sale, merger, de-merger, amalgamation, lease or transfer of business has been done with a specific provision for the transfer of liabilities. The transferor is required to submit a copy of the above certificate along with the Form GST ITC-02.

The registered person is thus allowed to transfer the input tax credit remaining unutilized in the electronic credit ledger to such sold, merged, demerged, amalgamated, leased or transferred business.

Analysis:

Few important checkpoints and aspects that need to be considered by a CA or cost accountant before certifying are as follows:

a) This certificate is to be issued in respect of a person who has sold/merged/de-merged/amalgamated/leased/transferred its business with a specific provision for the transfer of liabilities.

b) The Amalgamation/Merger Order or relevant Business Transfer Agreements should be thoroughly perused to ensure that there is a specific provision for transfer of liabilities.

25.5 CERTIFICATION ON REVERSAL OF CREDIT UNDER SPECIAL CIRCUMSTANCES (SEC 18(4) READ WITH RULE 44)

As per section 18(4) and section 29(5) credit on the inputs held in stock, inputs contained in semi-finished and finished goods and on capital goods needs to be reversed in the following cases:

- Where any registered person who has availed of input tax credit opts to pay tax under section 10 i.e. under composition scheme; or
- Where the goods or services or both supplied by a registered person have become wholly exempt.
- Every registered person whose registration has been cancelled

It is pertinent to note that, where the tax invoices related to the inputs held in stock are not available, the registered person needs to estimate the amount of ITC based on the prevailing market price of the goods on the effective date of the occurrence of any of the events specified above.

These details i.e. the estimated amount of ITC to be reversed in absence of tax invoices related to the stock, by such registered person needs to be certified by a CA or a cost accountant.

Analysis:

Few important checkpoints and aspects that need to be considered by a CA or cost accountant before certifying are as follows:

a) This certificate is required to be issued only if the tax invoices related to the inputs held in stock, inputs contained in semi-finished or finished goods held in stock and on capital goods are not available. It may be noted that the the above said Rule 44(3) stipulates issuance of a Certificate only in cases of non-possession of invoices. The said Rule does not speak of issuance of Certificate if the registered person is in possession of the relevant tax invoices.

b) Declaration in Form GSTR-10 is filed by the taxpayer on GST portal declaring the above amounts in the respective columns.

c) In case there are stocks-in-transit as on the specified date of eligibility of credits, appropriate treatment to be considered.

(Note: Practical difficulty may arise to determine the credit amount and invoice-wise details of items consumed at WIP/semi-finished and finished goods stage. This may be computed by way of a fixed percentage and relevant assumptions/note may be included in the Certificate).

d) To ensure that a declaration is taken from the applicant with regard to non-availability of tax invoices and reasons for the same.

e) Certificate is to be issued in respect of a person whose registration has been cancelled, or converted to composition scheme, or whose goods/services have become exempt.

f) Reversal of credit in Electronic Credit Ledger and payment in Electronic Cash Ledger of the amount as specified in GSTR -10 is to be ensured.

g) Declaration in Form GST ITC-03 is filed by the tax payer on GST portal declaring the above amounts in the respective columns.

h) The date on which the applicant has opted to pay tax u/s 10 of the CGST Act should be thoroughly verified. The applicability of conditions under the GST laws for a tax payer opting to pay tax u/s 10 should be checked to confirm the above said date.

i) The details which have been filed in Form GST CMP-02 which is an intimation to opt to pay tax under Section 10 need to be verified and cross checked.

j) The books of accounts and relevant documents/records of the applicant should be thoroughly verified to identify the supplies that were earlier taxable and have now become exempted. The relevant notifications issued by the Government should be meticulously perused to identify the date on which such taxable supplies have become exempted supplies.

25.6 APPLICATION FOR REFUND OF TAX, INTEREST, PENALTY, FEES OR ANY OTHER AMOUNT (RULE 89(2))

A person can claim refund of taxes, interest, fees, etc. paid by him under certain circumstances. In respect of these refunds, a certificate in Annexure 2 of FORM GST RFD-01 is required to be issued by a chartered accountant or a cost accountant to the effect that the incidence of tax, interest or any other amount claimed as refund has not been passed on to any other person. However, such certification is not required in case of refund of the following:

- Refund of tax paid on zero-rated supply of goods or services or both.
- Refund of tax on inputs or input services used in making zero-rated supply.
- Refund of unutilized input tax credit accumulated on account of inverted duty structure.
- Refund of tax paid on a supply which is not provided, either wholly or partially, and for which invoice has not been issued or where a refund voucher has been issued.
- Refund of tax in pursuance of section 77 which means a registered person who has paid CGST and SGST/UTGST on a transaction

considered by him as INTRASTATE supply but held to be INTER-STATE supply and vice versa.

Analysis:

Few important checkpoints and aspects that need to be considered by a CA or cost accountant before certifying are as follows:

a) This certificate is required to be issued only if the aggregate value of the refund claim exceeds Rs. 2 lakhs.

b) Invoices and agreements, if any, have to verified to see whether duty liability has been passed on.

c) Comparison of the GST rate of inputs vis-à-vis the GST rate of outputs should be done.

d) A declaration from the supplier have to be obtained to the effect that they have not claimed refund or drawback in respect of central tax on the supplies made i.e. this proviso forming part of 54(3) to ensure that there is no double refund/revenue loss to Government.

e) Documentary evidence to be obtained from the applicant for ensuring that there is no unjust enrichment of the refund amount claimed.

f) Ensure compliance with provisions of Section 54(10) with respect to default in furnishing any returns, non-payment of tax, interest or penalty etc.

25.7 TAX DEDUCTION AT SOURCE UNDER SECTION 51

Section 51 requires a department or establishment of the central government or state government; or local authority; or governmental agencies to deduct tax at source @ 1% of the value of the contract exceeding Rs.2.5 lakhs while making payment. The amount of tax deducted at source should be deposited to the Government account by the deductor by 10th of the succeeding month. The certificate is required to be issued in Form GST 7A after making payment made to the government within 5 days to the supplier. The supplier can take credit of the tax deducted at source only on the basis of this certificate.

It is to be noted that when both the supplier as well as place of supply are different from that of the recipient, no tax deduction at source would be made.

Analysis:

a) The CA or the cost accountant has to verify and ensure that the TDS certificate is in proper form and has been issued after payment of the tax by the issuer.

b) In the absence of definition of the word 'contract' used in the section, the definition of contract in the Indian Contract Act, 1872 can be adopted. Contract means "an agreement enforceable by law".

c) Tax is to be deducted in respect of all payments released on or after 1st Oct 2018.

d) Value for the purpose of tax deduction is the value excluding central tax, State tax, Union territory tax, integrated tax and cess indicated in the invoice.

e) Tax is to be deducted in case of any supply received from registered person having value exceeding Rs.2,50,000/-.

f) Rate of TDS: 1% CGST + 1% SGST/UTGST or 2% IGST (in case of Interstate supply).

g) TDS has to be made in all cases of supplies by registered persons.

h) The value of contract is to be considered individually and not consolidated when there are multiple contracts with a single supplier.

i) TDS is applicable on advance payment made for supply of goods or services.

j) In case of Reverse charge no tax is required to be deducted.

25.8 CERTIFICATION FOR CLAIMING OF REIMBURSEMENT OF TAX PAID UNDER 'SEVA BHOJ YOJANA' (C.B.I. & C. CIRCULAR NO. 75/49/2018-GST, DATED 27-12-2018)

The Ministry of Culture has introduced a Central Sector Scheme with effect from 1st August 2018 called the "Seva Bhoj Yojana" for the reimbursement of central tax and the Central Government's share of integrated tax paid on the purchase of certain raw food items as follows:

- ghee,
- edible oil,
- sugar/burra/jaggery,
- rice,
- atta/maida/rava/flour and pulses ;

which are used for distributing free food to general public/by charitable/religious institutions like Gurudwaras, temples, Dharmik Ashrams, Mosques, Dargahs, Churches, Math, Monasteries, etc.

All applications for reimbursement of the said taxes need to be submitted to the nodal officer of the State/Union territory in whose jurisdiction the claimant undertakes the specified activity, on a quarterly basis in FORM SBY-03, before the expiry of six months from the last day of the quarter in which the purchases of the specified items have been made.

This application needs to be signed by authorised signatory of the claimant along with a Chartered Accountant's Certificate. The CA certificate is required to certify the following aspects:

- Quantity, price and amount of central tax, State tax/Union territory tax or integrated tax paid on the purchase of the specified items during the quarter for which the claim is filed;
- The claimant is involved in charitable/religious activities;
- The reimbursement claimed in the current quarter/year is not more than the purchases in the previous corresponding quarter/year plus a maximum of 2.5%/10% for the current quarter/year, as the case may be;
- The claimant is using the specified items for only distributing free food to the public/devotees etc. during the claim period;
- The claimant fully satisfies the prescribed conditions.

Hence, the certificate from a CA certifying the above details is of extreme importance for claiming the reimbursement of tax paid on the specified items used for the specified activity.

Analysis:

Few important checkpoints and aspects that need to be considered by a Chartered Accountant or a cost accountant before certifying are as follows:

a) To ensure that the claimant has a Unique 10 digit Identity Number called as the Seva Bhoj Yojana - Unique Identity Number (hereinafter called as the "SBY-UIN"),issued by the Ministry of Culture.

b) Separate SBY-UIN for each State or Union territory in which the specified activity is undertaken has been obtained.

c) Goods on which reimbursement is being claimed are procured after the claimant has obtained the SBY-UIN.

d) Application for reimbursement of taxes has been filed by the claimant under Form SBY-03.

e) The terms and conditions for reimbursement of taxes related to the specified goods purchased its usage and distribution whether satisfied.

f) Ensure that the claimant has applied for reimbursement within the specified time limit and any reimbursement of tax which has been time barred are not being claimed.

g) The books and records and other relevant documents and registers relating to inputs need to be thoroughly verified.

h) The tax invoice must be the one containing the prescribed particulars (Section 16(2) of read along with Rule 46).

i) Computation of input tax credit from tax invoices/bills of entry or other relevant documents needs to be ensured.

j) Ensure that the debit notes/credit notes, if any, are recorded/accounted against the vendor invoice.

k) Ensure that the certificate issued is in accordance with the Guidance note on Reports and Certificates for special purpose issued by the ICAI.

l) Ensure that a letter of representation is taken from the management for the details and information provided by them.

25.9 CERTIFICATIONS RELATED TO REAL ESTATE INDUSTRY (SCHEDULE II & OTHER AMENDMENTS)

Certifications by professionals play an important role in case of the construction sector. Based on these certificates the nature of supply, whether to be treated as goods or service is determined.

Schedule II of the Act specifies the transactions which have to be treated as supply of goods and which are to be treated as supply of services. In respect of construction, where the entire consideration has been received after issuance of the completion certificate, where required, by the competent authority, the said amount will not be liable to tax under GST.

Therefore, if a completion certificate has been issued by the competent authority, any consideration received after obtaining this certificate will not be liable to tax under GST.

Competent Authority means the Government or any authority authorized to issue completion certificate under any law for the time being in force and in case of non-requirement of such certificate from such authority, from any of the following, namely:

- An architect registered with the Council of Architecture constituted under the Architects Act, 1972; or
- A chartered engineer registered with the Institution of Engineers (India); or

- A licensed surveyor of the respective local body of the city or town or village or development or planning authority;

Further, the 34th GST Council meeting has brought some series of changes for the Real Estate industry. The GST Council approved a transition plan for the implementation of a new tax structure for the real estate sector is applicable from April 1, 2019. The new tax structure which has been made applicable also requires a couple of certifications from the professionals. We proceed to discuss this newly required certification for the real estate industry.

For a smooth transition from the old scheme to the new scheme, the Government has provided an option for the promoters in respect of the ongoing projects, to either opt for a new scheme or continue with the old scheme. Hence, at this stage, it becomes imperative to understand the meaning of the term 'ongoing projects'.

It is a project which meets all the following conditions, namely-

- Commencement certificate issued - on/before 31.03.2019
- Construction has started – on/before 31.03.2019
- Completion certificate not issued on/before 31.03.2019
- Booking - on/before 31.03.2019

The commencement certificate in respect of the project, where required to be issued by the competent authority, has been issued on or before 31st March 2019, and it is certified by any of the following, that construction of the project has started on or before 31st March 2019:

- An architect registered with the Council of Architecture constituted under the Architects Act, 1972 (20 of 1972); or
- A chartered engineer registered with the Institution of Engineers (India); or
- A licensed surveyor of the respective local body of the city or town or village or development or planning authority.

Thereby there are two conditions i.e. commencement certificate should be there plus the certificate as to the start of actual construction.

Hence, both the certificates i.e. commencement, as well as certificate as to start of actual construction, are of huge importance for the builders/developers to prove whether their project is covered within the ambit of the term 'ongoing project' and thereby avail the benefit of the old or new scheme.

However, this certification has been brought for the limited purpose of certifying the ongoing projects for the smooth transition of the real estate industry. Hence, once the transition period is over these certifications will not be required going forward.

25.10 CERTIFICATION TO OBTAIN THE CONCESSIONAL RATE OF GST ON HOUSES CONSTRUCTED UNDER CREDIT LINKED SUBSIDY SCHEME (CLSS)

Credit Linked Subsidy Scheme is provided for a civil structure or any other original works pertaining to the houses constructed for:

- Economically Weaker Section (EWS)
- Lower Income Group (LIG)
- Middle Income Group-1 (MIG- 1)
- Middle Income Group-2 (MIG-2)

under the Housing for All (Urban) Mission/Pradhan Mantri Awas Yojana (Urban) and attracts concessional GST of 8% provided value of land is included in the price of the house.

Credit Linked Subsidy Scheme (CLSS) is one of the components of Housing for All (Urban) Mission/Pradhan Mantri Awas Yojana (PMAY) (Urban). Under this component, the subsidy would be provided on home loans taken by eligible urban poor (EWS/LIG/MIG-I/MIG-II) for acquisition and construction of the house. Credit-linked subsidy would also be available for housing loans availed for new construction and for the addition of rooms, kitchen, toilet, etc., to existing dwellings as incremental housing.

The benefit of Credit Linked Subsidy Scheme may be taken by the Economically Weaker sections or Low/Middle Income Groups for purchase of houses under any project. The maximum annual income for eligibility of beneficiaries under the scheme can be up to Rs.18 lakhs. It covers a very large section of the population which aspires to own a home.

Initially, houses acquired under CLSS attracted GST rate of 18% (effective GST rate of 12% after deducting the value of land). But later, the buyers were entitled to interest subsidy under the Scheme as well to a lower concessional rate of GST of 8% (effective rate after deducting the value of land).

To avail the CLSS benefit, the interest subsidy will be credited to the loan account of beneficiaries through Primary Lending Institutions (PLIs), resulting in reduced effective housing loan and Equated Monthly Installments (EMI).

The PLIs such as banks, housing finance corporations, NBFCs, etc. are required to register with Central Nodal Agencies (CNAs). The CNAs are required to release subsidy under the scheme to the PLIs in respect of loans sanctioned by them to borrower/beneficiaries resulting in reduced effective housing loan and Equated Monthly Installments (EMI).

The PLIs are required to provide the utilization/end use certificate and a certificate in relation to the physical progress of the construction of the housing unit financed under the scheme to the CNAs on a quarterly basis.

Certificate by PLIs on the basis of which the builder may charge a reduced rate of GST on houses constructed/acquired under CLSS. The certificate may be addressed to the beneficiary with a copy to the builder, certifying that the borrower is a beneficiary of the CLSS.

Therefore, the certificate issued by the PLIs is of utmost importance to the buyer to obtain a reduced rate of GST on its purchase.

However, it is imperative to note that the 34th GST Council meeting has brought a series of changes for the Real Estate industry. The GST Council approved a transition plan for the implementation of a new tax structure for the real estate sector being applicable from April 1st, 2019. The rate of GST on real estate has undergone significant change. Therefore, the above certification by the PLIs will be required for the limited purpose of certifying the ongoing projects. Hence, once the transition period is over these certifications will be required to be adopted as per the requirement of the new scheme under the real estate.

Appendices

Appendix 1: Abstract of provisions of audit under Goods and Service Tax Act, 2017

Appendix 1: Abstract of provisions of audit under Goods and Service Tax Act, 2017

SECTION 2(13) DEFINITION OF 'AUDIT'

(13) "audit" means the examination of records, returns and other documents maintained or furnished by the registered person under this Act or the rules made thereunder or under any other law for the time being in force to verify the correctness of turnover declared, taxes paid, refund claimed and input tax credit availed, and to assess his compliance with the provisions of this Act or the rules made thereunder;

SECTION 35(5) ACCOUNTS AND OTHER RECORDS

(5) Every registered person whose turnover during a financial year exceeds the prescribed limit shall get his accounts audited by a chartered accountant or a cost accountant and shall submit a copy of the audited annual accounts, the reconciliation statement under sub-section (*2*) of section 44 and such other documents in such form and manner as may be prescribed.

Provided that nothing contained in this sub-section shall apply to any department of the Central Government or a State Government or a local authority, whose books of account are subject to audit by the Comptroller and Auditor-General of India or an auditor appointed for auditing the accounts of local authorities under any law for the time being in force.

SECTION 65 AUDIT BY TAX AUTHORITIES

(1) The Commissioner or any officer authorised by him, by way of a general or a specific order, may undertake audit of any registered person for such period, at such frequency and in such manner as may be prescribed.

(2) The officers referred to in sub-section (*1*) may conduct audit at the place of business of the registered person or in their office.

(3) The registered person shall be informed by way of a notice not less than fifteen working days prior to the conduct of audit in such manner as may be prescribed.

(4) The audit under sub-section (1) shall be completed within a period of three months from the date of commencement of the audit:

Provided that where the Commissioner is satisfied that audit in respect of such registered person cannot be completed within three months, he may, for the reasons to be recorded in writing, extend the period by a further period not exceeding six months.

Explanation.—For the purposes of this sub-section, the expression "commencement of audit" shall mean the date on which the records and other documents, called for by the tax authorities, are made available by the registered person or the actual institution of audit at the place of business, whichever is later.

(5) During the course of audit, the authorised officer may require the registered person,—

(*i*) to afford him the necessary facility to verify the books of account or other documents as he may require;

(*ii*) to furnish such information as he may require and render assistance for timely completion of the audit.

(6) On conclusion of audit, the proper officer shall, within thirty days, inform the registered person, whose records are audited, about the findings, his rights and obligations and the reasons for such findings.

(7) Where the audit conducted under sub-section (*1*) results in detection of tax not paid or short paid or erroneously refunded, or input tax credit wrongly availed or utilised, the proper officer may initiate action under section 73 or section 74.

SECTION 66 SPECIAL AUDIT IN CERTAIN CASES

(1) If at any stage of scrutiny, inquiry, investigation or any other proceedings before him, any officer not below the rank of Assistant Commissioner, having regard to the nature and complexity of the case and the interest of revenue, is of the opinion that the value has not been correctly declared or the credit availed is not within the normal limits, he may, with the prior approval of the Commissioner, direct such registered person by a communication in writing to get his records including books of account examined and audited by a chartered accountant or a cost accountant as may be nominated by the Commissioner.

(2) The chartered accountant or cost accountant so nominated shall, within the period of ninety days, submit a report of such audit duly signed and certified by him to the said Assistant Commissioner mentioning therein such other particulars as may be specified:

Provided that the Assistant Commissioner may, on an application made to him in this behalf by the registered person or the chartered accountant or cost accountant or for any material and sufficient reason, extend the said period by a further period of ninety days.

(3) The provisions of sub-section (1) shall have effect notwithstanding that the accounts of the registered person have been audited under any other provisions of this Act or any other law for the time being in force.

(4) The registered person shall be given an opportunity of being heard in respect of any material gathered on the basis of special audit under sub-section (1) which is proposed to be used in any proceedings against him under this Act or the rules made thereunder.

(5) The expenses of the examination and audit of records under sub-section (1), including the remuneration of such chartered accountant or cost accountant, shall be determined and paid by the Commissioner and such determination shall be final.

(6) Where the special audit conducted under sub-section (1) results in detection of tax not paid or short paid or erroneously refunded, or input tax credit wrongly availed or utilized, the proper officer may initiate action under section 73 or section 74.

Appendix 2: Procedure of Audit in GST Rules, 2017

RULE 80(3) OF CGST RULES, 2017 – ANNUAL RETURN

(3) Every registered person other than those referred to in the proviso to sub-section (5) of section 35 whose aggregate turnover during a financial year exceeds two crore rupees shall get his accounts audited as specified under sub-section (5) of section 35 and he shall furnish a copy of audited annual accounts and a reconciliation statement, duly certified, in FORM GSTR-9C, electronically through the common portal either directly or through a Facilitation Centre notified by the Commissioner.

RULE 101 OF CGST RULES, 2017 – AUDIT

(1) The period of audit to be conducted under sub-section (1) of section 65 shall be a financial year or part thereof or multiples thereof.

(2) where it is decided to undertake the audit of a registered person in accordance with the provisions of section 65, the proper officer shall issue a notice in FORM GST ADT-01 in accordance with the provisions of sub-section (3) of the said section.

(3) The proper officer authorised to conduct audit of the records and the books of account of the registered person shall, with the assistance of the team of officers and officials accompanying him, verify the documents on the basis of which the books of account are maintained and the returns and statements furnished under the provisions of the Act and the rules made there under, the correctness of the turnover, exemptions and deductions claimed, the rate of tax applied in respect of the supply of goods or services or both, the input tax credit availed and utilised, refund claimed, and other relevant issues and record the observations in his audit notes.

(4) The proper officer may inform the registered person of the discrepancies noticed, if any, as observed in the audit and the said person may file his reply and the proper officer shall finalise the findings of the audit after due consideration of the reply furnished.

(5) On conclusion of the audit, the proper officer shall inform the findings of audit to the registered person in accordance with the provisions of sub-section (6) of section 65 in **FORM GST ADT-02.**

RULE 102 OF THE CGST RULES, 2017 – SPECIAL AUDIT

(1) Where special audit is required to be conducted in accordance with the provisions of section 66, the officer referred to in the said section shall issue a direction in **FORM GST ADT-03** to the registered person to get his records audited by a chartered accountant or a cost accountant specified in the said direction.

(2) On conclusion of the special audit, the registered person shall be informed of the findings of the special audit in **FORM GST ADT-04.**

Appendix 3: E-flier on GST special audit issued by CBIC

The CBIC has released an E-flier which explains about the types of audit (normal/ special) and procedure thereof under GST

GST is a trust based taxation regime wherein the assessee is required to self-assess his returns and determine tax liability without any intervention by the tax official. Therefore a tax regime that relies on self-assessment has to put in place a robust audit mechanism to measure and ensure compliance of the provisions of law by the taxable person.

"Audit" has been defined in section 2(13) of the CGST Act, 2017 and it means the examination of records, returns and other documents maintained or furnished by the registered person under the GST Acts or the rules made there under or under any other law for the time being in force to verify the correctness of turnover declared, taxes paid, refund claimed and input tax credit availed, and to assess his compliance with the provisions of the GST Acts or the rules made thereunder.

TYPES OF AUDIT

GST envisages three types of Audit.

(a) The first audit is by a chartered accountant or a cost accountant. Every registered person whose aggregate turnover during a financial year exceeds two crore rupees has to get his accounts audited by a chartered accountant or a cost accountant and furnish a copy of audited annual accounts and a reconciliation statement, duly certified, in FORM GSTR-9C.

(b) In the second type which is the normal audit, the Commissioner or any officer authorised by him, can undertake audit of any registered person for such period, at such frequency and in such manner as may be prescribed.

(c) The third type of audit is called the Special Audit. In Special Audit the registered person can be directed to get his records including books of account examined and audited by a chartered accountant or a cost accountant during any stage of scrutiny, inquiry, investigation or any other proceedings; depending upon the complexity of the case.

PROCEDURE

1. During the scrutiny, inquiry, investigation or any other proceedings of a registered person, the Assistant Commissioner or any officer senior to him, having regard to the nature and complexity of the case and the interest of revenue, might be of the opinion that the value has not been correctly declared or the credit availed is not within the normal limits.

2. In such cases, with the prior approval of the Commissioner, the Assistant Commissioner or any officer senior to him can direct the registered person in FORM GST ADT-03 to get his records including books of account examined and audited by a specified chartered accountant or a cost accountant. The chartered accountant or a cost accountant will be nominated by the Commissioner
3. The chartered accountant or cost accountant so nominated has to submit a report of such audit within the period of ninety days, duly signed and certified by him to the Assistant Commissioner.
4. On an application made by the registered person or the chartered accountant or cost accountant or for any material and sufficient reason, the Assistant Commissioner can extend the said period by a further period of ninety days.
5. The provisions of special audit shall have effect even if the accounts of the registered person have been audited under any other provisions of the GST Act or any other law for the time being in force.
6. The registered person shall be given an opportunity of being heard in respect of any material gathered on the basis of special audit and which is proposed to be used in any proceedings against him under this Act or the rules made thereunder.
7. The expenses of the examination and audit of records, including the remuneration of such chartered accountant or cost accountant, shall be determined and paid by the Commissioner.
8. On conclusion of the special audit, the registered person shall be informed of the findings of the special audit in FORM GST ADT-04.
9. Where the special audit results in detection of tax not paid or short paid or erroneously refunded, or input tax credit wrongly availed or utilised, the process of demand and recovery will be initiated against the registered person.

CONCLUSION

Special audit provides a lawful and legal way for the GST officers to take the assistance of a chartered accountant or cost accountant to determine tax liabilities in complex cases. The professional expertise of a chartered accountant or cost accountant will be of great significance in ensuring that the interest of revenue is safeguarded at all times.

Appendix 4: Relevant extracts about "audit" in the concept paper on 'Goods and Service Tax (GST) concept & status' issued by CBIC dated 01.05.2019

CBIC has issued GST – Concept & Status (Updated as on 1st May 2019)

"10.17 Self-assessment of the taxes payable by the registered person shall be the norm. Audit of registered persons shall be conducted on selective basis. Limitation period for raising demand is three (3) years from the due date of filing of annual return or from the date of erroneous refund for raising demand for short-payment or non-payment of tax or erroneous refund and its adjudication in normal cases. Limitation period for raising demand is five (5) years from the due date of filing of annual return or from the date of erroneous refund for raising demand for short-payment or non-payment of tax or erroneous refund and its adjudication in case of fraud, suppression or willful mis-statement."

"13.3 The design of GST systems is based on role based access. The taxpayer can access his own data through identified applications like registration, return, view ledger etc. The tax official having jurisdiction, as per GST law, can access the data. Data can be accessed by audit authorities as per law. No other entity can have any access to data available with GSTN."

Appendix 5: FAQ's Issued by CBIC dated 01.01.2018 – Abstract related to Audit

CBIC has issued FAQ's on GST as on 1.1.2018 and extract of audit related FAQ's are provided

1. What recourse may be taken by the officer in case proper explanation is not furnished for the discrepancy detected in the return filed, while conducting scrutiny under section 61 of CGST ACT?

If the taxable person does not provide a satisfactory explanation within 30 days of being informed (extendable by the officer concerned) or after accepting discrepancies, fails to take corrective action in the return for the month in which the discrepancy is accepted, the Proper Officer may take recourse to any of the following provisions:

(a) Proceed to conduct audit under Section 6 5 of the Act;

(b) Direct the conduct of a special audit under Section 66 which is to be conducted by a Chartered Accountant or a Cost Accountant nominated for this purpose by the Commissioner; or

(c) Undertake procedures of inspection, search and seizure under Section 67 of the Act; or

(d) Initiate proceeding for determination of tax and other dues under Section 73 or 74 of the Act.

2. Who can conduct audit of taxpayers?

There are three types of audit prescribed in the GST Act(s) as explained below:

(a) Audit by Chartered Accountant or a Cost Accountant: Every registered person whose turnover exceeds Rs. Two crore, shall get his accounts audited by a chartered accountant or a cost accountant. (Section 35(5) of the CGST/SGST Act).

(b) Audit by Department: The Commissioner or any officer of CGST or SGST or UTGST authorized by him by a general or specific order, may conduct audit of any registered person. The frequency and manner of audit will be prescribed in due course. (Section 65 of the CGST/SGST Act)

(c) Special Audit: If at any stage of scrutiny, inquiry, investigations or any other proceedings, if department is of the opinion that the value has not been correctly declared or credit availed is not within the normal limits, department may order special audit by chartered accountant or cost accountant, nominated by department. (Section 66 of the CGST/SGST Act)

3. Whether any prior intimation is required before conducting the audit?

Yes, prior intimation is required and the taxable person should be informed at least 15 working days prior to conduct of audit

4. What is the period within which the audit is to be completed?

The audit is required to be completed within 3 months from the date of commencement of audit. The period is extendable for a further period of a maximum of 6 months by the Commissioner.

5. What is meant by commencement of audit?

The term 'commencement of audit' is important because audit has to be completed within a given time frame in reference to this date of commencement. Commencement of audit means the later of the following:

(a) the date on which the records/accounts called for by the audit authorities are made available to them, or

(b) the actual institution of audit at the place of business of the taxpayer.

6. What are the obligations of the taxable person when he receives the notice of audit?

The taxable person is required to:

(a) facilitate the verification of accounts/records available or requisitioned by the authorities,

(b) provide such information as the authorities may require for the conduct of the audit, and

(c) render assistance for timely completion of the audit.

7. What would be the action by the proper officer upon conclusion of the audit?

The proper officer shall, on conclusion of audit, within 30 days inform the taxable person about his findings, reasons for findings and the taxable person's rights and obligations in respect of such findings.

8. Under what circumstances can a special audit be instituted

A special audit can be instituted in limited circumstances where during scrutiny, investigation, etc. it comes to the notice that a case is complex or the revenue stake is high. This power is given in section 66 of CGST /SGST Act.

9. Who can serve the notice of communication for special audit?

The Assistant/Deputy Commissioner is to serve the communication for special audit only after prior approval of the Commissioner.

10. Who will do the special audit?

A Chartered Accountant or a Cost Accountant so nominated by the Commissioner may undertake the audit.

11. What is the time limit to submit the audit report?

The auditor will have to submit the report within 90 days or within the further extended period of 90 days.

12. Who will bear the cost of special audit?

The expenses for examination and audit including the remuneration payable to the auditor will be determined and borne by the Commissioner.

13. What action the tax authorities may take after the special audit?

Based on the findings/observations of the special audit, action can be initiated under Section 73 or Section 74 of the CGST/SGST Act.

14. Can a CGST/SGST officer access business premises under any other circumstances?

Yes. Access can also be obtained in terms of Section 65 of CGST/SGST Act. This provision of law is meant to allow an audit party of CGST/SGST or C&AG or a cost accountant or chartered accountant nominated under section 66 of CGST/SGST Act, access to any business premises without issuance of a search warrant for the purposes of carrying out any audit, scrutiny, verification and checks as may be necessary to safeguard the interest of revenue.

However, a written authorization is to be issued by an officer of the rank of Commissioner of CGST or SGST. This provision facilitates access to a business premise which is not registered by a taxable person as a principal or additional place of business but has books of accounts, documents, computers etc. which are required for audit or verification of accounts of a taxable person.

Appendix 6: Forms on Audit issued under GST as provided in CGST Rules, 2017

FORM GST ADT-01 [SEE RULE 101(2)]

To ------------------------------

GSTIN ....

Name ....

Address ....

Period - F.Y.(s) - ....

Notice for conducting audit whereas it has been decided to undertake audit of your books of account and records for the financial year(s) .... to .... in accordance with the provisions of section 65. I propose to conduct the said audit at my office/at your place of business on .... And whereas you are required to :

(i) afford the undersigned the necessary facility to verify the books of account and records or other documents as may be required in this context, and

(ii) furnish such information as may be required and render assistance for timely completion of the audit.

You are hereby directed to attend in person or through an authorised representative on .... (date) at .... (place) before the undersigned and to produce your books of account and records for the aforesaid financial year(s) as required for audit. In case of failure to comply with this notice, it would be presumed that you are not in possession of such books of account and proceedings as deemed fit may be initiated as per the provisions of the Act and the rules made thereunder against you without making any further correspondence in this regard.

Signature ....

Name ....

Designation ....

FORM GST ADT-02 [SEE RULE 101(5)]

GSTIN ....

Name ....

Address ....

Audit Report No. .... Dated ....

Audit Report under section 65(6) Your books of account and records for the F.Y. ....has been examined and this Audit Report is prepared on the basis of information available/documents furnished by you and the findings are as under :

[Upload pdf file containing audit observation]

You are directed to discharge your statutory liabilities in this regard as per the provisions of the Act and the rules made thereunder, failing which proceedings as deemed fit may be initiated against you under the provisions of the Act.

Signature ....

Name ....

Designation ....

FORM GST ADT-03 [SEE RULE 102(1)]

To,

GSTIN ....

Name ....

Address ....

Tax period - F.Y.(s) - .... Communication to the registered person for conduct of special audit under section 66 Whereas the proceedings of scrutiny of return/enquiry/investigation/..................are going on; And whereas it is felt necessary to get your books of account and records examined and audited by .... (name), chartered accountant/cost accountant nominated by the Commissioner; You are hereby directed to get your books of account and records audited by the said chartered accountant/cost accountant.

Signature ....

Name ....

Designation ....

FORM GST ADT-04 [SEE RULE 102(2)]

To,

GSTIN ....

Name ....

Address ....

Information of findings upon Special Audit. Your books of account and records for the F.Y............ has been examined by .... (chartered accountant/cost accountant) and this Audit Report is prepared on the basis of information available/documents furnished by you and the findings/discrepancies are as under:

[Upload pdf file containing audit observation]

You are directed to discharge your statutory liabilities in this regard as per the provisions of the Act and the rules made thereunder, failing which proceedings as deemed fit may be initiated against you under the provisions of the Act.

Signature ....

Name ....

Designation ....

Appendix 7: Accounting entries of GST

Outward supply	SGST payable A/c CGST payable A/c IGST payable A/c (Separate account for each registration and separate account for services distributed as Input Service Distributor)
Inward supply	SGST receivable A/c CGST receivable A/c IGST receivable A/c (Separate account for each registration and separate account for services distributed as Input Service Distributor)
Reverse Charge	SGST receivable RCM A/c CGST receivable RCM A/c IGST receivable RCM A/c (Separate account for each registration and separate account for services distributed as Input Service Distributor)
Others	**Additional ledgers should be created for:** Taxes payable for Un registered dealer purchases Keeping track of advance payments/receipts and taxes paid for the same etc. Keeping track of balances in electronic cash ledger/credit ledger of GSTIN.

Ref No.	Accounting	Entries
1	Sales	I. In case of Local (intra state) supply Customer name A/c To SGST payable A/c To CGST payable A/c To Sales II. In case of inter-state supply Customer name A/c To IGST payable To Sales
2	Sales return(When treated as separate supply) (From auditee point of view)	I. In case of Local (intra state) supply Purchases A/c SGST receivable A/c CGST receivable A/c To Customer Name A/c II. In case of inter-state supply Purchases A/c IGST receivable A/c To Customer A/c
3	Sales return(When Credit note is issued) (From auditee point of view)	I. In case of Local (intra state) supply Sales returns A/c SGST receivable A/c CGST receivable A/c

Ref No.	Accounting	Entries
		To Customer name A/c II. In case of inter-state supply Sales returns A/c IGST receivable A/c To Customer name A/c
4	Sale of approval basis (On the expiry of 6 months)	I. In case of Local (intra state) supply Customer A/c To SGST payable A/c To CGST payable A/c II. In case of inter-state supply Customer A/c To IGST payable A/c
5	EOU Sales	refer point 12 for entry if the same are considered as deemed sales under GST/ However if the EOU sales are considered as Normal sales refer point 1 for entry
6	Sales in Transit (From Vendor To Auditee)	I. In case of Intra-state purchase Expenditure A/c/Capital Good A/c CGST receivable A/c SGST receivable A/c To Vendor A/c II. In case of inter-state purchase where POS is receiver state Expenditure A/c IGST receivable A/c To Vendor A/c
7	Sales in Transit (From Auditee To Customer)	I. In case of Local (intra state) supply Customer name A/c To SGST payable A/c To CGST payable A/c To Sales II. In case of inter-state supply Customer name A/c To IGST payable To Sales
8	Depot sales/Dealer sales (There is no concept of dealer or depot sales under GST, hence the same would be treated as normal sales)	I. In case of Local (intra state) supply Customer name A/c To SGST payable A/c To CGST payable A/c To Sales II. In case of inter-state supply Customer name A/c To IGST payable To Sales
9	Purchases	I.In case of Intra-state purchase Expenditure A/c/Capital Good A/c

Ref No.	Accounting	Entries
		CGST receivable A/c SGST receivable A/c To Vendor A/c II. In case of inter-state purchase Expenditure A/c IGST receivable A/c To Vendor A/c III. In case of inter/intra-state purchase (Credit of GST is not available) Expenditure A/c (incl. CGST/SGST/IGST of that state) To Vendor A/c
10	Stock transfer(When same set of books are maintained)	I. In case of Local (intra state) supply(With Two separate GSTN registration No's with common books) CGST Receivable(Branch-1) A/c SGST Receivable(Branch-1) A/c To SGST payable (Branch-2)A/c To CGST payable (Branch-2)A/c II. In case of inter-state supply (With Two separate GSTN registration No's with common books) IGST receivable(Branch-1) A/c To IGST payable(Branch-2) A/c
11	Stock transfer(When separate set of books are maintained)	I. In case of intra state supply (With two separate GSTN registration No's) Branch A/c To SGST payable A/c To CGST payable A/c To Sales II. In case of inter-state supply Branch A/c To IGST payable To Sales
12	Exports/Deemed Exports/SEZ Sales-Without Payment of Duty	I. In case of Local (intra state) supply Customer name A/c To Sales II. In case of inter-state supply Customer name A/c To Sales
13	Exports/Deemed Exports/SEZ Sales-Refund route	I. On Export sale Customer name A/c GST Refund receivable A/c To IGST payable To Sales II. On Payment of GST IGST Payable A/c

Ref No.	Accounting	Entries
		To IGST receivable A/c To Bank III. On receipt of Refund Bank A/c To IGST Refund receivable A/c
14	Free samples	I. In case of Local (intra state) supply P & L A/c To SGST Payable A/c To CGST Payable A/c II. In case of inter-state supply P & L A/c To IGST Payable A/c
15	Disposals	I. In case of Local (intra state) supply P & L A/c To SGST Payable A/c To CGST Payable A/c II. In case of inter-state supply P & L A/c To IGST Payable A/c
16	Captive consumption	No concept of captive consumption
17	Job work (job work - received within the specified time)	Shall not be treated as Supply under GST.(For inter-state clarity is awaited)
18	Job work (job work - Not received within the specified time - Treated as supply)	Treated as normal supply, refer 1 for entry
19	Job work (job work - Goods sent for job work, treated as supply on expiry of 1 year, received now)	I. In case of Local (intra state) supply Purchases A/c SGST receivable A/c CGST receivable A/c To Job worker A/c II. In case of inter-state supply Purchases A/c IGST receivable A/c To Job worker A/c
20	Interest charged/Late Fee for late payment	I. In case of Local (intra state) supply Bank A/c To SGST payable A/c To CGST payable A/c To Interest/ Late fee income A/c II. In case of inter-state supply Bank A/c To IGST payable A/c To Interest/ Late fee income A/c

Ref No.	Accounting	Entries
21	Advances received - For supply of goods or services	I. In case of Local (intra state) supply Bank A/c To SGST payable A/c To CGST payable A/c To Customer Advance Account II. In case of inter-state supply Bank A/c To IGST payable To Customer Advance Account
22	Composite & Mixed Supply	I. In case of Local (intra state) supply Customer A/c To SGST payable A/c To CGST payable A/c To Sales (goods/services/Both) II. In case of inter-state supply Customer A/c To IGST payable To Sales (goods/services/Both)
23	reverse charge (Specified Services or unregistered Dealer Purchases)	I. In case of Local (intra state) supply Purchases/Services A/c SGST receivable RCM A/c CGST receivable RCM A/c To SGST payable RCM A/c To CGST payable RCM A/c To Vendor A/c II. In case of inter-state supply Purchases/Services A/c IGST receivable RCM A/c To IGST payable RCM A/c To Vendor A/c
24	Imports (Deemed as Interstate Supplies)	Purchases A/c (Incl. BCD) IGST Receivable A/c To Vendor
25	Deposits received (refundable or not) - Applied Towards consideration of supply of goods or services	I. In case of Local (intra state) supply Refundable deposit A/c To SGST payable A/c To CGST payable A/c To Customer A/c II. In case of inter-state supply Refundable Deposit A/c To IGST payable To Customer A/c
26	For payment of IGST	IGST Payable A/c To IGST Receivable A/c To Bank A/c

Ref No.	Accounting	Entries
27	For payment of CGST	CGST Payable A/c To CGST Receivable A/c To IGST Receivable A/c To Bank A/c
28	For payment of SGST	SGST Payable A/c To SGST Receivable A/c To IGST Receivable A/c To Bank A/c
29	Related parties (Value arrived on the basis of ALP/ Standard Cost/ Cost plus margin)	I. In case of Local (intra state) supply Customer A/c P & L A/c (Differential amount * tax rate) To SGST payable A/c To CGST payable A/c To Sales II. In case of inter-state supply Customer A/c P & L A/c (Differential amount * tax rate) To IGST payable To Sales

Appendix 8: Audit Report under the Companies (Auditor's Report) Order, 2016 in relation to Indirect Taxes

Form of Audit Report

The MCA has issued the Companies (Auditor's Report) Order, 2016 (CARO 2016), on 29th March 2016. This order has been issued in supersession of the Companies (Auditor's Report) Order, 2015, and is applicable for reporting on financial statements of companies whose financial year commences on or after 1st April 2015. CARO 2015 was issued by MCA in supersession of CARO 2003 which was issued earlier in pursuance with the provision of Section 227 (4A) of Companies Act 1956.

Now, the MCA has relaxed the applicability of CARO 2016 to private companies by increasing applicability thresholds. CARO 2016 will not apply to the auditor's report on consolidated financial statements. The total number of clauses in the new CARO is 16. CARO 2016 has enhanced the auditor's reporting requirements in certain areas, such as related party transaction and managerial remuneration. The provisions of the CARO 2016 are furnished below:

CARO 2016 is applicable from FY 2015-16 and the matters specified therein shall be included in each report made by the auditor under Section 143 of the Companies Act, 2013 on the account of every company to which CARO 2016 applies.

Section 143 (11) of the Act stipulates that the Central Government may order for the inclusion of statement on specified matter in the auditor's report for specified class or description of companies. Accordingly, CARO 2016 is issued in pursuance of Section 143 (11) of Companies Act 2013 for inclusion of the matters specified therein in auditors' report. Hence, CARO 2016 should be complied by the statutory auditor of every company on which it applies.

CARO 2016 applicable to every company including a foreign company as defined in clause (42) of Section 2 of the Companies Act 2013.

The following classes of companies are outside the purview of the CARO 2016.

(a) Banking company as defined under Section 5 (c) of the Banking Regulation Act, 1949.

(b) Insurance company as defined under the Insurance Act 1938.

(c) Company licensed to operate under Section 8 of the Companies Act 2013 (companies registered with charitable object).

(d) A one person company (OPC) as defined under clause (62) of Section 2 of Companies Act 2013 (OPC means a company which has only one person as a member)

(e) A small company under Section 2 (85) of the Companies Act, 2013.

  (1) As per sec 2(85) of Companies Act 2013 small company means a company, other than a public company:

(a) Paid up share capital of which does not exceed ` 50 lacs or such higher amount as may be prescribed which shall not be more than ` 5 crore, and

(b) Turnover of which as per its last profit and loss account does not exceed ` 2 crore or such higher amount as may be prescribed which shall not be more than ` 20 crore.

(2) The following company shall not qualify as a small company:

(a) A holding company or a subsidiary company.

(b) A company registered under Section 8 of the Act.

(c) A company or body corporate governed by any special act

(f) The auditor of following type of Private Companies are not required to comment on the matter prescribed under CARO 2016:

(1) A private company which is not holding or subsidiary company of a public company, and

(2) A private company having a paid up capital and reserve and surplus not more than Rs. 1 crore as on the balance sheet date, and

(3) A private company which does not have total borrowing exceeding Rs. 1 crore from any bank and financial institution at any point of time during the financial year, and

(4) A private company which does not have total revenue exceeding Rs. 10 crore during the financial year.

MATTERS INCLUDED IN CARO 2016 IN RELATION TO INDIRECT TAX ARE DISCUSSED BELOW

Statutory Dues [Clause 3 (vii)]

(a) Whether the company is regular in depositing undisputed statutory dues with the appropriate authorities including Provident fund, Employees State Insurance fund, income tax, sales tax, service tax, duty of custom, duty of excise, value added tax, cess or any other statutory dues. If the company is not regular in depositing such statutory dues, the extent of arrears of outstanding statutory dues as at the last day of the financial year concerned for a period of more than six months from the date they become payable, shall be indicated by the auditor.

(b) In case dues of income tax and sales tax or service tax or duty of custom or duty of excise or value added tax have not been deposited on account of any dispute, then the amount involved and the forum where dispute is pending shall be disclosed.

Related Party Transaction [Clause 3 (xiii)]

Whether all transaction with the related party is in compliance with Section 177 and 188 of the Companies Act, 2013 where applicable and the details have been disclosed in the financial statement etc., as required by the applicable accounting standard.

Non Cash Transaction [Clause 3 (xv)]

Whether the company has entered into any non-cash transaction with the director or person concerned with his and if so, whether the provision of Section 192 of Companies Act, 2013 has been complied with.

Appendix 9: Statements on Standard Auditing Practices of ICAI

Preface to Standards on Quality Control, Auditing, Review, Other Assurance and Related Services

Auditing and Assurance Standard Board
Quality Control and Engagement Standards

S. No.	No. of Standard	Title of the Standard
1	SQC 1	Quality Control for Firms that Perform Audits and Reviews of Historical Financial Information, and Other Assurance and Related Services Engagements
2	SA 200	Overall Objectives of the Independent Auditor and the Conduct of an Audit in Accordance with Standards on Auditing
3	SA 210	Agreeing the Terms of Audit Engagements
4	SA 220	Quality Control for an Audit of Financial Statements
5	SA 230	Audit Documentation
6	SA 240	The Auditor's responsibilities Relating to Fraud in an Audit of Financial Statements
7	SA 250	Consideration of Laws and Regulations in an Audit of Financial Statements
8	SA 260	Communication with Those Charged with Governance
9	SA 265	Communicating Deficiencies in Internal Control to Those Charged with Governance and Management
10	SA 299	Responsibility of Joint Auditors
11	SA 300	Planning an Audit of Financial Statements
12	SA 315	Identifying and Assessing the Risks of Material Misstatement through Understanding the Entity and its Environment
13	SA 320	Materiality in Planning and Performing an Audit
14	SA 330	The Auditor's Responses to Assessed Risks
15	SA 402	Audit Considerations Relating to an Entity Using a Service Organization
16	SA 450	Evaluation of Misstatements Identified during the Audits
17	SA 500	Audit Evidence
18	SA 501	Audit Evidence - Specific Considerations for Selected Items
19	SA 505	External Confirmations
20	SA 510	Initial Audit Engagements-Opening Balances
21	SA 520	Analytical Procedures

S. No.	No. of Standard	Title of the Standard
22	SA 530	Audit Sampling
23	SA 540	Auditing Accounting Estimates, Including Fair Value Accounting Estimates, and Related Disclosures
24	SA 550	Related Parties
25	SA 560	Subsequent Events
26	SA 570	Going Concern
27	SA 580	Written Representations
28	SA 600	Using the Work of Another Auditor
29	SA 610	Using the Work of Internal Auditors
30	SA 620	Using the Work of an Auditor's Expert
31	SA 700	Forming an Opinion and Reporting on Financial Statements
32	SA 701	Communicating Key Audit Matters in the Independent Auditor's Report
33	SA 705	Modifications to the Opinion in the Independent Auditor's Report
34	SA 706	Emphasis of Matter Paragraphs and Other Matter Paragraphs in
		the Independent Auditor's Report
35	SA 710	Comparative Information – Corresponding Figures and Comparative Financial Statements
36	SA 720	The Auditor's Responsibility in Relation to Other Information in Documents Containing Audited Financial Statements
37	SA 800	Special Considerations-Audits of Financial Statements Prepared in Accordance with Special Purpose Framework
38	SA 805	Special Considerations-Audits of Single Purpose Financial Statements and Specific Elements, Accounts or Items of a Financial Statement
39	SA 810	Engagements to Report on Summary Financial Statements
40	SRE 2400	Engagements to Review Historical Financial Statements

STANDARD ON QUALITY CONTROL (SQC) 1: QUALITY CONTROL FOR FIRMS THAT PERFORM AUDITS AND REVIEWS OF HISTORICAL FINANCIAL INFORMATION, AND OTHER ASSURANCE AND RELATED SERVICES ENGAGEMENTS

Introduction

1. The purpose of this Standard on Quality Control (SQC) is to establish standards and provide guidance regarding a firm's responsibilities for its system of

quality control for audits and reviews of historical financial information, and for other assurance and related services engagements. This SQC is to be read in conjunction with the requirements of the Chartered Accountants Act, 1949, the Code of Ethics and other relevant pronouncements of the Institute1 (hereinafter referred to as "the Code").

2. Additional standards and guidance on the responsibilities of firm personnel regarding quality control procedures for specific types of engagements are set out in other pronouncements of the Auditing and Assurance Standards Board (AASB) issued under the authority of the Council. For example, standard on Auditing (SA) 220, "Quality Control for an Audit of Financial Statements", establishes standards and provides guidance on quality control procedures for audits of historical financial information.

3. The firm should establish a system of quality control designed to provide it with reasonable assurance that the firm and its personnel comply with professional standards and regulatory and legal requirements, and that reports issued by the firm or engagement partner(s) are appropriate in the circumstances.

4. A system of quality control consists of policies designed to achieve the objectives set out in paragraph 3 and the procedures necessary to implement and monitor compliance with those policies.

5. This SQC applies to all firms. The nature of the policies and procedures developed by individual firms to comply with this SQC will depend on various factors such as the size and operating characteristics of the firm, and whether it is part of a network.

Definitions

6. In this SQC, the following terms have the meanings attributed below:

(a) *Engagement documentation* – the record of work performed, results obtained, and conclusions the practitioner reached (terms such as "working papers" or "work papers" are also sometimes used). The documentation for a specific engagement is assembled in an engagement file;

(b) *Engagement partner* – the partner or other person in the firm who is a member of the Institute of Chartered Accountants of India and is in full time practice and is responsible for the engagement and its performance, and for the report that is issued on behalf of the firm, and who, where required, has the appropriate authority from a professional, legal or regulatory body.

(c) *Engagement quality control review* – a process designed to provide an objective evaluation, before the report is issued, of the significant judgments the engagement team made and the conclusions they reached in formulating the report.

(d) *Engagement quality control reviewer* – a partner, other person3 in the firm, suitably qualified external person, or a team made up of such individuals, with sufficient and appropriate experience and authority to objectively evaluate, before the report is issued, the significant judgments the engagement team made and the conclusions they reached in formulating the report. However, in case the review is done by a team of individuals, such team should be headed by a member of the Institute.

(e) *Engagement team* – all personnel performing an engagement, including any experts contracted by the firm in connection with that engagement.

(f) *Firm* – a sole practitioner/proprietor, partnership, or any such entity of professional accountants, as may be permitted by law.

(g) *Inspection* – in relation to completed engagements, procedures designed to provide evidence of compliance by engagement teams with the firm's quality control policies and procedures.

(h) *Listed entity* – an entity whose shares, stock or debt are quoted or listed on a recognized stock exchange, or are traded under the regulations of a recognized stock exchange or other equivalent body.

(i) *Monitoring* – a process comprising an ongoing consideration and evaluation of the firm's system of quality control, including a periodic inspection of a selection of completed engagements, designed to enable the firm to obtain reasonable assurance that its system of quality control is operating effectively.

(j) *Network firm*– A firm or entity that belongs to a network.

(k) Network – A larger structure:

   (i) That is aimed at co operation, and

   (ii) That is clearly aimed at profit or cost-sharing or shares common ownership, control or management, common quality control policies and procedures, common business strategy, the use of a common brand name, or a significant part of professional resources.

(l) *Partner* – any individual with authority to bind the firm with respect to the performance of a professional services engagement.

(m) *Personnel* – partners and staff.

(n) *Professional standards* – engagement standards, as defined in the AASB's "Preface to the Standards on Quality Control, Auditing, Review, Other Assurance and Related Services," and relevant ethical requirements as contained in the Code.

(o) *Reasonable assurance*–in the context of this SQC, a high, but not absolute, level of assurance.

(p) *Staff* – professionals, other than partners, including any experts which the firm employs.

(q) *Suitably qualified external person* – an individual outside the firm with the capabilities and competence to act as an engagement partner, for example a partner or an employee (with appropriate experience) of another firm.

Elements of a System of Quality Control

7. The firm's system of quality control should include policies and procedures addressing each of the following elements
   (a) Leadership responsibilities for quality within the firm.
   (b) Ethical requirements.
   (c) Acceptance and continuance of client relationships and specific engagements.
   (d) Human resources.
   (e) Engagement performance.
   (f) Monitoring.
8. The quality control policies and procedures should be documented and communicated to the firm's personnel. Such communication describes the quality control policies and procedures and the objectives they are designed to achieve, and includes the message that each individual has a personal responsibility for quality and is expected to comply with these policies and procedures. In addition, the firm recognizes the importance of obtaining feedback on its quality control system from its personnel. Therefore, thefirmencouragesitspersonneltocommunicatetheirviewsorconcernsonqualityco ntrolmatters

Leadership Responsibilities for Quality within the Firm

9. The firm should establish policies and procedures designed to promote an internal culture based on the recognition that quality is essential in performing engagements. Such policies and procedures should require the firm's chief executive officer (or equivalent) or, if appropriate, the firm's managing partners (or equivalent), to assume ultimate responsibility for the firm's system of quality control.
10. The firm's leadership and the examples it sets significantly influence the internal culture of the firm. The promotion of a quality-oriented internal culture depends on clear, consistent and frequent actions and messages from all levels of the firm's management emphasizing the firm's quality control policies and procedures, and the requirement to:
    (a) Perform work that complies with professional standards and regulatory and legal requirements; and
    (b) Issue reports that are appropriate in the circumstances.

    Such actions and messages encourage a culture that recognizes and rewards high quality work. They may be communicated by training seminars, meetings, formal or informal dialogue, mission statements, newsletters, or briefing memoranda. They are incorporated in the firm's internal documentation and training materials, and in partner and staff appraisal procedures such that they will support and reinforce the firm's view on the importance of quality and how, practically, it is to be achieved.

11. Of particular importance is the need for the firm's leadership to recognize that the firm's business strategy is subject to the overriding requirement for the firm to achieve quality in all the engagements that the firm performs. Accordingly:
    (a) The firm assigns its management responsibilities so that commercial considerations do not override the quality of work performed;
    (b) The firm's policies and procedures addressing performance evaluation, compensation, and promotion (including incentive systems) with regard to its personnel, are designed to demonstrate the firm's overriding commitment to quality; and

    The firm devotes sufficient resources for the development, documentation and support of its quality control policies and procedures.
12. Any person or persons assigned operational responsibility for the firm's quality control system by the firm's chief executive officer or managing board of partners should have sufficient and appropriate experience and ability, and the necessary authority, to assume that responsibility.
13. Sufficient and appropriate experience and ability enables the responsible person or persons to identify and understand quality control issues and to develop appropriate policies and procedures. Necessary authority enables the person or persons to implement those policies and procedures.

Ethical Requirements

14. The firm should establish policies and procedures designed to provide it with reasonable assurance that the firm and its personnel comply with relevant ethical requirements.
15. Ethical requirements relating to audits and reviews of historical financial information, and other assurance and related services engagements are contained in the Code. The Code establishes the fundamental principles of professional ethics, which include:
    (a) Integrity;
    (b) Objectivity;
    (c) Professional competence and due care;
    (d) Confidentiality; and
    (e) Professional behavior.
16. The Code includes a conceptual approach to independence for assurance engagements, including aspects such as threats to independence, accepted safeguards and the public interest.
17. The firm's policies and procedures should emphasize the fundamental principles, which are reinforced in particular by (a) the leadership of the firm, (b) education and training, (c) monitoring, and (d) a process for dealing with non-compliance. Independence for assurance engagements is so significant that it is addressed separately in paragraphs 18-27 below. These paragraphs need to be read in conjunction with the Code.

Independence

18. The firm should establish policies and procedures designed to provide it with reasonable assurance that the firm, its personnel and, where applicable, others subject to independence requirements (including experts contracted by the firm and network firm personnel), maintain independence where required by the Code. Such policies and procedures should enable the firm to:
    - (a) Communicate its independence requirements to its personnel and, where applicable, to others subject to them; and
    - (b) Identify and evaluate circumstances and relationships that create threats to independence, and to take appropriate action to eliminate those threats or reduce them to an acceptable level by applying safeguards, or, if considered appropriate, to withdraw from the engagement.

19. Such policies and procedures should require:
    - (a) Engagement partners to provide the firm with relevant information about client engagements, including the scope of services, to enable the firm to evaluate the overall impact, if any, on independence requirements;
    - (b) Personnel to promptly notify the firm of circumstances and relationships that create a threat to independence so that appropriate action can be taken; and
    - (c) The accumulation and communication of relevant information to appropriate personnel so that:
        - (i) The firm and its personnel can readily determine whether they satisfy independence requirements;
        - (ii) The firm can maintain and update its records relating to independence; and
        - (iii) The firm can take appropriate action regarding identified threats to independence.

20. The firm should establish policies and procedures designed to provide it with reasonable assurance that it is notified of breaches of independence requirements, and to enable it to take appropriate actions to resolve such situations. The policies and procedures should include requirements for:
    - (a) All who are subject to independence requirements to promptly notify the firm of independence breaches of which they become aware;
    - (b) The firm to promptly communicate identified breaches of these policies and procedures to:
        - (i) The engagement partner who, with the firm, needs to address the breach; and
        - (ii) Other relevant personnel in the firm and those subject to the independence requirements who need to take appropriate action; and
    - (c) Prompt communication to the firm, if necessary, by the engagement partner and the other individuals referred to in subparagraph (b) (ii) of

the actions taken to resolve the matter, so that the firm can determine whether it should take further action.

21. Comprehensive guidance on threats to independence and safeguards, including application to specific situations are contained in the Code.

22. A firm receiving notice of a breach of independence policies and procedures promptly communicates relevant information to engagement partners, others in the firm, as appropriate and, where applicable, experts contracted by the firm and network firm personnel, for appropriate action. Appropriate action by the firm and the relevant engagement partner includes applying appropriate safeguards to eliminate the threats to independence or to reduce them to an acceptable level, or withdrawing from the engagement. In addition, the firm provides independence education to personnel who are required to be independent.

23. ***At least annually, the firm should obtain written confirmation of compliance with its policies and procedures on independence from all firm personnel required to be independent in terms of the requirements of the Code.***

24. Written confirmation may be in paper or electronic form. By obtaining confirmation and taking appropriate action on information indicating non-compliance, the firm demonstrates the importance that it attaches to independence and makes the issue current for, and visible to, its personnel.

25. The Code discusses the familiarity threat that may be created by using the same senior personnel on an assurance engagement over a long period of time and the safeguards that might be appropriate to address such a threat. Accordingly, the firm should establish policies and procedures:

    (a) Setting out criteria for determining the need for safeguards to reduce the familiarity threat to an acceptable level when using the same senior personnel on an assurance engagement over a long period of time; and

    (b) For all audits of financial statements of listed entities, requiring the rotation of the engagement partner after a specified period in compliance with the Code.

26. Using the same senior personnel on assurance engagements over a prolonged period may create a familiarity threat or otherwise impair the quality of performance of the engagement. Therefore, the firm should establish criteria for determining the need for safeguards to address this threat. In determining appropriate criteria, the firm considers such matters as (a) the nature of the engagement, including the extent to which it involves a matter of public interest, and (b) the length of service of the senior personnel on the engagement. Examples of safeguards include rotating the senior personnel or requiring an engagement quality control review.

27. The familiarity threat is particularly relevant in the context of financial statement audits of listed entities. For these audits, the engagement partner should be rotated after a pre-defined period, normally not more than seven

years Acceptance and Continuance of Client Relationships and Specific Engagements

28. The firm should establish policies and procedures for the acceptance and continuance of client relationships and specific engagements, designed to provide it with reasonable assurance that it will undertake or continue relationships and engagements only where it:

(a) Has considered the integrity of the client and does not have information that would lead it to conclude that the client lacks integrity;

(b) Is competent to perform the engagement and has the capabilities, time and resources to do so; and

(c) Can comply with the ethical requirements.

The firm should obtain such information as it considers necessary in the circumstances before accepting an engagement with a new client, when deciding whether to continue an existing engagement, and when considering acceptance of a new engagement with an existing client. Where issues have been identified, and the firm decides to accept or continue the client relationship or a specific engagement, it should document how the issues were resolved.

29. With regard to the integrity of a client, matters that the firm considers include, for example:

- The identity and business reputation of the client's principal owners, key management, related parties and those charged with its governance.
- The nature of the client's operations, including its business practices.
- Information concerning the attitude of the client's principal owners, key management and those charged with its governance towards such matters as aggressive interpretation of accounting standards and the internal control environment.
- Whether the client is aggressively concerned with maintaining the firm's fees as low as possible.
- Indications of an inappropriate limitation in the scope of work.
- Indications that the client might be involved in money laundering or other criminal activities.
- There a sons for the proposed appointment of the firm and non-reappointment of the previous firm.

The extent of knowledge a firm will have regarding the integrity of a client will generally grow within the context of an ongoing relationship with that client.

30. Information on such matters that the firm obtains may come from, for example:

- Communications with existing or previous providers of professional accountancy services to the client in accordance with the Code, and discussions with other third parties.
- Inquiry of other firm personnel or third parties such as bankers, legal counsel and industry peers.
- Background searches of relevant databases.

31. In considering whether the firm has the capabilities, competence, time and resources to undertake a new engagement from a new or an existing client, the firm reviews the specific requirements of the engagement and existing partner and staff profiles at all relevant levels. Matters the firm considers include whether:

- Firm personnel have knowledge of relevant industries or subject matters;
- Firm personnel have experience with relevant regulatory or reporting requirements, or the ability to gain the necessary skills and knowledge effectively;
- The firm has sufficient personnel with the necessary capabilities and competence;
- Experts are available, if needed;
- Individuals meeting the criteria and eligibility requirements to perform engagement quality control review are available, where applicable; and
- The firm would be able to complete the engagement within the reporting deadline.

32. The firm also considers whether accepting an engagement from a new or an existing client may give rise to an actual or perceived conflict of interest6. Where a potential conflict is identified, the firm considers whether it is appropriate to accept the engagement.

33. Deciding whether to continue a client relationship includes consideration of significant matters that have arisen during the current or previous engagements, and their implications for continuing the relationship. For example, a client may have started to expand its business operations into an area where the firm does not possess the necessary knowledge or expertise.

34. Where the firm obtains information that would have caused it to decline an engagement if that information had been available earlier, policies and procedures on the continuance of the engagement and the client relationship should include consideration of:

(a) The professional and legal responsibilities that apply to the circumstances, including whether there is a requirement for the firm to report to the person or persons who made the appointment or, in some cases, to regulatory authorities; and

(b) The possibility of withdrawing from the engagement or from both the engagement and the client relationship.

35. Policies and procedures on withdrawal from an engagement or from both the engagement and the client relationship address issues that include the following:

- Discussing with the appropriate level of the client's management and those charged with its governance regarding the appropriate action that the firm might take based on the relevant facts and circumstances.
- If the firm determines that it is appropriate to withdraw, discussing with the appropriate level of the client's management and those charged with

its governance withdrawal from the engagement or from both the engagement and the client relationship, and the reasons for the withdrawal.

- Considering whether there is a professional, regulatory or legal requirement for the firm to remain in place, or for the firm to report the withdrawal from the engagement, or from both the engagement and the client relationship, together with the reasons for the withdrawal, to regulatory authorities.
- Documenting significant issues, consultations, conclusions and the basis for the conclusions.

Human Resources

36. The firm should establish policies and procedures designed to provide it with reasonable assurance that it has sufficient personnel with the capabilities, competence, and commitment to ethical principles necessary to perform its engagements in accordance with professional standards and regulatory and legal requirements and to enable the firm or engagement partners to issue reports that are appropriate in the circumstances.

37. Such policies and procedures address the following personnel issues:
    (a) Recruitment;
    (b) Performance evaluation;
    (c) Capabilities;
    (d) Competence;
    (e) Career development;
    (f) Promotion;
    (g) Compensation; and
    (h) Estimation of personnel needs.

    Addressing these issues enables the firm to ascertain the number and characteristics of the individuals required for the firm's engagements. The firm's recruitment processes include procedures that help the firm select individuals of integrity as well as the capacity to develop the capabilities and competence necessary to perform the firm's work.

38. Capabilities and competence are developed through a variety of methods, including the following:
    - Professional education.
    - Continuing professional development, including training.
    - Work experience.
    - Coaching by more experienced staff, for example, other members of the engagement team.

39. The continuing competence of the firm's personnel depends to a significant extent on an appropriate level of continuing professional development so that personnel maintain and also enhance their knowledge and capabilities. The firm therefore emphasizes in its policies and procedures, the need for continuing

training for all levels of firm personnel, and provides the necessary training resources and assistance to enable personnel to develop and maintain the required capabilities and competence. Where internal technical and training resources are unavailable, or for any other reason, the firm may use a suitably qualified external person for that purpose.

40. The firm's performance evaluation, compensation and promotion procedures give due recognition and reward to the development and maintenance of competence and commitment to ethical principles. In particular, the firm:

(a) Makes personnel aware of the firm's expectations regarding performance and ethical principles;

(b) Provides personnel with evaluation of, and counseling on, performance, progress and career development; and

Helps personnel understand that advancement to positions of greater responsibility depends, among other things, upon performance quality and adherence to ethical principles, and that failure to comply with the firm's policies and procedures may result in disciplinary action.

41. The size and circumstances of the firm will influence the structure of the firm's performance evaluation process. Smaller firms, in particular, may employ less formal methods of evaluating the performance of their personnel.

Assignment of Engagement Teams

42. The firm should assign responsibility for each engagement to an engagement partner. The firm should establish policies and procedures requiring that:

(a) The identity and role of the engagement partner are communicated to key members of the client's management and those charged with governance;

(b) The engagement partner has the appropriate capabilities, competence, authority and time to perform the role; and

(c) The responsibilities of the engagement partner are clearly defined and communicated to that partner.

43. Policies and procedures include systems to monitor the workload and availability of engagement partners so as to enable these individuals to have sufficient time to adequately discharge their responsibilities.

44. The firm should also assign appropriate staff with the necessary capabilities, competence and time to perform engagements in accordance with professional standards and regulatory and legal requirements, and to enable the firm or engagement partners to issue reports that are appropriate in the circumstances.

45. The firm establishes procedures to assess its staff's capabilities and competence. The capabilities and competence considered when assigning engagement teams, and in determining the level of supervision required, include the following:

- An understanding of, and practical experience with, engagements of a similar nature and complexity through appropriate training and participation.

- An understanding of professional standards and regulatory and legal requirements.
- Appropriate technical knowledge, including knowledge of relevant information technology.
- Knowledge of the relevant industries in which the clients operate.
- Ability to apply professional judgment.

An understanding of the firm's quality control policies and procedures.

Engagement Performance

46. The firm should establish policies and procedures designed to provide it with reasonable assurance that engagements are performed in accordance with professional standards and regulatory and legal requirements, and that the firm or the engagement partner issues reports that are appropriate in the circumstances.

47. Through its policies and procedures, the firm seeks to establish consistency in the quality of engagement performance. This is often accomplished through written or electronic manuals, software tools or other forms of standardized documentation, and industry or subject matter-specific guidance materials. Matters addressed include the following:

- How engagement teams are briefed on the engagement to obtain an understanding of the objectives of their work.

Processes for complying with applicable engagement standards

- Processes of engagement supervision, staff training and coaching.
- Methods of reviewing the work performed, the significant judgments made and the form of report being issued.
- Appropriate documentation of the work performed and of the timing and extent of there view.
- Processes to keep all policies and procedures current.

48. It is important that all members of the engagement team understand the objectives of the work they are to perform. Appropriate team-working and training are necessary to assist less experienced members of the engagement team to clearly understand the objectives of the assigned work.

49. Supervision includes the following:

- Tracking the progress of the engagement.
- Considering the capabilities and competence of individual members of the engagement team, whether they have sufficient time to carry out their work, whether they understand their instructions and whether the work is being carried out in accordance with the planned approach to the engagement.
- Addressing significant issues arising during the engagement, considering their significance and appropriately modifying the planned approach appropriately.

- Identifying matters for consultation or consideration by more experienced engagement team members during the engagement.

50. Review responsibilities are determined on the basis that more experienced engagement team members, including the engagement partner, review work performed by less experienced team members. Reviewers consider whether:
    (a) The work has been performed in accordance with professional standards and regulatory and legal requirements;
    (b) Significant matters have been raised for further consideration;
    (c) Appropriate consultations have taken place and the resulting conclusions have been documented and implemented;
    (d) There is a need to revise the nature, timing and extent of work performed;
    (e) The work performed supports the conclusions reached and is appropriately documented;
    (f) The evidence obtained is sufficient and appropriate to support the report; and

    The objectives of the engagement procedures have been achieved.

Consultation

51. The firm should establish policies and procedures designed to provide it with reasonable assurance that:
    (a) Appropriate consultation takes place on difficult or contentious matters;
    (b) Sufficient resources are available to enable appropriate consultation to take place;
    (c) The nature and scope of such consultations are documented; and
    (d) Conclusions resulting from consultations are documented and implemented.

52. Consultation includes discussion, at the appropriate professional level, with individuals within or outside the firm who have specialized expertise, to resolve a difficult or contentious matter.

53. Consultation uses appropriate research resources as well as the collective experience and technical expertise of the firm. Consultation helps to promote quality and improves the application of professional judgment. The firm seeks to establish a culture in which consultation is recognized as strength and encourages personnel to consult on difficult or contentious matters.

54. Effective consultation with other professionals requires that those consulted be given all the relevant facts that will enable them to provide informed advice on technical, ethical or other matters. Consultation procedures require consultation with those having appropriate knowledge, seniority and experience within the firm (or, where applicable, outside the firm) on significant technical, ethical and other matters, and appropriate documentation and implementation of conclusions resulting from consultations.

55. A firm needing to consult externally, for example, a firm without appropriate internal resources may take advantage of advisory services provided by (a) other firms, or (b) professional and regulatory bodies. Before contracting for such services, the firm considers whether the external provider is suitably qualified for that purpose.

56. The documentation of consultations with other professionals that involve difficult or contentious matters is agreed by both the individual seeking consultation and the individual consulted. The documentation is sufficiently complete and detailed to enable an understanding of:

    (a) The issue on which consultation was sought; and

    (b) The results of the consultation, including any decisions taken, the basis for those decisions and how they were implemented.

Differences of Opinion

57. The firm should establish policies and procedures for dealing with and resolving differences of opinion within the engagement team, with those consulted and, where applicable, between the engagement partner and the engagement quality control reviewer. Conclusions reached should be documented and implemented.

58. Such procedures encourage identification of differences of opinion at an early stage, provide clear guidelines as to the successive steps to be taken thereafter, and require documentation regarding the resolution of the differences and the implementation of the conclusions reached. The report should not be issued until the matter is resolved.

59. A firm using a suitably qualified external person(s) to conduct an engagement quality control review recognizes that differences of opinion can occur and establishes procedures to resolve such differences, for example, by consulting with another practitioner or firm, or a professional or regulatory body.

Engagement Quality Control Review

60. The firm should establish policies and procedures requiring, for appropriate engagements, an engagement quality control review that provides an objective evaluation of the significant judgments made by the engagement team and the conclusions reached in formulating the report. Such policies and procedures should:

    (a) Require an engagement quality control review for all audits of financial statements of listed entities;

    (b) Set out criteria against which all other audits and reviews of historical financial information, and other assurance and related services engagements should be evaluated to determine whether an engagement quality control review should be performed; and

    (c) Require an engagement quality control review for all engagements meeting the criteria established in compliance with sub-paragraph (b).

61. The firm's policies and procedures should require the completion of the engagement quality control review before the report is issued.

62. Criteria that a firm considers when determining which engagements other than audits of financial statements of listed entities are to be subject to an engagement quality control review include the following:

- The nature of the engagement, including the extent to which it involves a matter of public interest.
- The identification of unusual circumstances or risks in an engagement or class of engagements.
- Whether laws or regulations require an engagement quality control review.

63. The firm should establish policies and procedures setting out:

(a) The nature, timing and extent of an engagement quality control review;

(b) Criteria for the eligibility of engagement quality control reviewers; and

(c) Documentation requirements for an engagement quality control review.

Nature, Timing and Extent of the Engagement Quality Control Review

64. An engagement quality control review ordinarily involves discussion with the engagement partner, a review of the financial statements or other subject matter information and the report, and, in particular, consideration of whether the report is appropriate. It also involves a review of selected working papers relating to the significant judgments that the engagement team made and the conclusions they reached. The extent of the review depends on the complexity of the engagement and the risk that the report might not be appropriate in the circumstances. The review does not reduce the responsibilities of the engagement partner

65. An engagement quality control review for audits of financial statements of listed entities includes considering the following:

- The engagement team's evaluation of the firm's independence in relation to the specific engagement.
- Significant risks identified during the engagement and the responses to those risks.
- Judgments made, particularly with respect to materiality and significant risks.
- Whether appropriate consultation has taken place on matters involving differences of opinion or other difficult or contentious matters, and the conclusions arising from those consultations.
- The significance and disposition of corrected and uncorrected misstatements identified during the engagement.
- The matters to be communicated to management and those charged with governance and, where applicable, other parties such as regulatory bodies.

- Whether working papers selected for review reflect the work performed in relation to the significant judgments and support the conclusions reached.
- The appropriateness of the report to be issued.

Engagement quality control reviews for engagements other than audits of financial statements of listed entities may, depending on the circumstances, include some or all of these considerations.

66. The engagement quality control reviewer conducts the review in a timely manner at appropriate stages during the engagement so that significant matters may be promptly resolved to the reviewer's satisfaction before the report is issued.

67. Where the engagement quality control reviewer makes recommendations that the engagement partner does not accept and the matter is not resolved to the reviewer's satisfaction, the report is not issued until the matter is resolved by following the firm's procedures for dealing with differences of opinion.

Criteria for the Eligibility of Engagement Quality Control Reviewers

68. The firm's policies and procedures should address the appointment of engagement quality control reviewers and establish their eligibility through:
    (a) The technical qualifications required to perform the role, including the necessary experience and authority; and
    (b) The degree to which an engagement quality control reviewer can be consulted on the engagement without compromising the reviewer's objectivity.

69. The firm's policies and procedures on the technical qualifications of engagement quality control reviewers address the technical expertise, experience and authority necessary to perform the role. What constitutes sufficient and appropriate technical expertise, experience and authority depends on the circumstances of the engagement. In addition, the engagement quality control reviewer for an audit of the financial statements of a listed entity is an individual with sufficient and appropriate experience and authority to act as an audit engagement partner on audits of financial statements of listed entities.

70. The firm's policies and procedures are designed to maintain the objectivity of the engagement quality control reviewer. For example, the engagement quality control reviewer:
    (a) Is not selected by the engagement partner;
    (b) Does not otherwise participate in the engagement during the period of review;
    (c) Does not make decisions for the engagement team; and
    (d) Is not subject to other considerations that would threaten the reviewer's objectivity.

71. The engagement partner may consult the engagement quality control reviewer during the engagement. Such consultation need not compromise the

engagement quality control reviewer's eligibility to perform the role. Where the nature and extent of the consultations become significant, however, care is taken by both the engagement team and the reviewer to maintain the reviewer's objectivity. Where this is not possible, another individual within the firm or a suitably qualified external person is appointed to take on the role of either the engagement quality control reviewer or the person to be consulted on the engagement. The firm's policies provide for the replacement of the engagement quality control reviewer where the ability to perform an objective review may be impaired.

72. Suitably qualified external persons may be contracted where sole practitioners or small firms identify engagements requiring engagement quality control reviews. Alternatively, some sole practitioners or small firms may wish to use other firms to facilitate engagement quality control reviews. Where the firm contracts suitably qualified external persons, the firm follows the requirements and guidance in paragraphs 69-72.

Documentation of the Engagement Quality Control Review

73. Policies and procedures on documentation of the engagement quality control review should require documentation that:
    (a) The procedures required by the firm's policies on engagement quality control review have been performed;
    (b) The engagement quality control review has been completed before the report is issued; and
    (c) The reviewer is not aware of any unresolved matters that would cause the reviewer to believe that the significant judgments the engagement team made and the conclusions they reached were not appropriate.

Engagement Documentation

Completion of the Assembly of Final Engagement Files

74. The firm should establish policies and procedures for engagement teams to complete the assembly of final engagement files on a timely basis after the engagement reports have been finalized.

75. Law or regulation may prescribe the time limits by which the assembly of final engagement files for specific types of engagement should be completed. Where no such time limits are prescribed in law or regulation, the firm establishes time limits appropriate to the nature of the engagements that reflect the need to complete the assembly of final engagement files on a timely basis. In the case of an audit, for example, such a time limit is ordinarily not more than 60 days after the date of the auditor's report.

76. Where two or more different reports are issued in respect of the same subject matter information of an entity, the firm's policies and procedures relating to time limits for the assembly of final engagement files address each report as if it were for a separate engagement. This may, for example, be the case when the firm issues an auditor's report on a component's financial information for

group consolidation purposes and, at a subsequent date, an auditor's report on the same financial information for statutory purposes.

Confidentiality, Safe Custody, Integrity, Accessibility and Retrievability of Engagement Documentation

77. The firm should establish policies and procedures designed to maintain the confidentiality, safe custody, integrity, accessibility and retrievability of engagement documentation.

78. Relevant ethical requirements establish an obligation for the firm's personnel to observe at all times the confidentiality of information contained in engagement documentation, unless specific client authority has been given to disclose information, or there is a legal or professional duty to do so. Specific laws or regulations may impose additional obligations on the firm's personnel to maintain client confidentiality, particularly where data of a personal nature are concerned.

79. Whether engagement documentation is in paper, electronic or other media, the integrity, accessibility or irretrievability of the underlying data may be compromised if the documentation could be altered, added to or deleted without the firm's knowledge, or if it could be permanently lost or damaged. Accordingly, the firm designs and implements appropriate controls for engagement documentation to:

    (a) Enable the determination of when and by whom engagement documentation was created, changed or reviewed;

    (b) Protect the integrity of the information at all stages of the engagement, especially when the information is shared within the engagement team or transmitted to other parties via the Internet;

    (c) Prevent unauthorized changes to the engagement documentation; and

    (d) Allow access to the engagement documentation by the engagement team and other authorized parties as necessary to properly discharge their responsibilities.

80. Controls that the firm may design and implement to maintain the confidentiality, safe custody, integrity, accessibility and retrievability of engagement documentation include, for example:

    - The use of a password among engagement team members to restrict access to electronic engagement documentation to authorized users.
    - Appropriate back-up routines for electronic engagement documentation at appropriate stages during the engagement.
    - Procedures for properly distributing engagement documentation to the team members at the start of Engagement, processing it during engagement, and collating it at the end of engagement.
    - Procedures for restricting access to, and enabling proper distribution and confidential storage of, hardcopy engagement documentation.

81. For practical reasons, original paper documentation may be electronically scanned for inclusion in engagement files. In that case, the firm implements appropriate procedures requiring engagement teams to:

(a) Generate scanned copies that reflect the entire content of the original paper documentation, including manual signatures, cross-references and annotations;

(b) Integrate the scanned copies into the engagement files, including indexing and signing off on the scanned copies as necessary; and

(c) Enable the scanned copies to be retrieved and printed as necessary.

The firm considers whether to retain original paper documentation that has been scanned for legal, regulatory or other reasons.

Retention of Engagement Documentation

82. The firm should establish policies and procedures for the retention of engagement documentation for a period sufficient to meet the needs of the firm or as required by law or regulation.

83. The needs of the firm for retention of engagement documentation, and the period of such retention, will vary with the nature of the engagement and the firm's circumstances, for example, whether the engagement documentation is needed to provide a record of matters of continuing significance to future engagements. The retention period may also depend on other factors, such as whether local law or regulation prescribes specific retention periods for certain types of engagements, or whether there are generally accepted retention periods in the jurisdiction in the absence of specific legal or regulatory requirements. In the specific case of audit engagements, the retention period ordinarily is no shorter than seven years7 from the date of the auditor's report, or, if later, the date of the group auditor's report.

84. Procedures that the firm adopts for retention of engagement documentation include those that:

- Enable the retrieval of, and access to, the engagement documentation during the retention period, particularly in the case of electronic documentation since the underlying technology may be upgraded or changed overtime.
- Provide, where necessary, a record of changes made to engagement documentation after the engagement files have been completed.
- Enable authorized external parties to access and review specific engagement documentation for quality control or other purposes.

Ownership of Engagement Documentation

85. Unless otherwise specified by law or regulation, engagement documentation is the property of the firm The firm may, at its discretion, make portions of, or extracts from, engagement documentation available to clients, provided such disclosure does not undermine the validity of the work performed, or, in the case of assurance engagements, the independence of the firm or its personnel.

Monitoring

86. The firm should establish policies and procedures designed to provide it with reasonable assurance that the policies and procedures relating to the system of quality control are relevant, adequate, operating effectively and complied with in practice. Such policies and procedures should include an ongoing consideration and evaluation of the firm's system of quality control, including a periodic inspection of a selection of completed engagements.

87. The purpose of monitoring compliance with quality control policies and procedures is to provide an evaluation of:

    (a) Adherence to professional standards and regulatory and legal requirements;

    (b) Whether the quality control system has been appropriately designed and effectively implemented; and

    (c) Whether the firm's quality control policies and procedures have been appropriately applied, so that reports that are issued by the firm or engagement partners are appropriate in the circumstances.

88. The firm entrusts responsibility for the monitoring process to a partner or partners or other persons with sufficient and appropriate experience and authority in the firm to assume that responsibility. Monitoring of the firm's system of quality control is performed by competent individuals and covers both the appropriateness of the design and the effectiveness of the operation of the system of quality control.

89. Ongoing consideration and evaluation of the system of quality control includes matters such as the following:

    - Analysis of:

        (a) New developments in professional standards and regulatory and legal requirements, and how they are reflected in the firm's policies and procedures where appropriate;

        (b) Written confirmation of compliance with policies and procedures on independence;

        (c) Continuing professional development, including training; and

        (d) Decisions related to acceptance and continuance of client relationships and specific engagements.

            - Determination of corrective actions to be taken and improvements to be made in the system, including the provision of feedback into the firm's policies and procedures relating to education and training.
            - Communication to appropriate firm personnel of weaknesses identified in the system, in the level of understanding of the system, or compliance with it.
            - Follow-up by appropriate firm personnel so that necessary modifications are promptly made to the quality control policies and procedures.

90. The inspection of a selection of completed engagements is ordinarily performed on a cyclical basis. Engagements selected for inspection include at least one engagement for each engagement partner over an inspection cycle, which ordinarily spans no more than three years. The manner in which the inspection cycle is organized, including the timing of selection of individual engagements, depends on many factors, including the following:

- The size of the firm.
- The number and geographical location of offices.
- The results of previous monitoring procedures.
- The degree of authority both personnel and offices have (for example, whether individual offices are authorized to conduct their own inspections or whether only the head office may conduct them).
- The nature and complexity of the firm's practice and organization.
- The risks associated with the firm's clients and specific engagements.

91. The inspection process includes the selection of individual engagements, some of which may be selected without prior notification to the engagement team. Those inspecting the engagements are not involved in performing the engagement or the engagement quality control review. In determining the scope of the inspections, the firm may take into account the scope or conclusions of an independent external inspection program. However, an independent external inspection program does not act as a substitute for the firm's own internal monitoring program.

92. Small firms and sole practitioners may wish to use a suitably qualified external person or another firm to carry out engagement inspections and other monitoring procedures. Alternatively, they may wish to establish arrangements to share resources with other appropriate organizations to facilitate monitoring activities.

93. The firm should evaluate the effect of deficiencies noted as a result of the monitoring process and should determine whether they are either:

(a) Instances that do not necessarily indicate that the firm's system of quality control is insufficient to provide it with reasonable assurance that it complies with professional standards and regulatory and legal requirements, and that the reports issued by the firm or engagement partners are appropriate in the circumstances; or

(b) Systemic, repetitive or other significant deficiencies that require prompt corrective action.

94. The firm should communicate to relevant engagement partners and other appropriate personnel deficiencies noted as a result of the monitoring process and recommendations for appropriate remedial action.

95. The firm's evaluation of each type of deficiency should result in recommendations for one or more of the following:

(a) Taking appropriate remedial action in relation to an individual engagement or member of personnel;

(b) The communication of the findings to those responsible for training and professional development;

(c) Changes to the quality control policies and procedures; and

(d) Disciplinary action against those who fail to comply with the policies and procedures of the firm, especially those who do so repeatedly.

96. Where the results of the monitoring procedures indicate that a report may be inappropriate or that procedures were omitted during the performance of the engagement, the firm should determine what further action is appropriate to comply with relevant professional standards and regulatory and legal requirements. It should also consider obtaining legal advice.

97. At least annually, the firm should communicate the results of the monitoring of its quality control system to engagement partners and other appropriate individuals within the firm, including the firm's chief executive officer or, if appropriate, its managing partner(s). Such communication should enable the firm and these individuals to take prompt and appropriate action where necessary in accordance with their defined roles and responsibilities. Information communicated should include the following:

(a) A description of the monitoring procedures performed.

(b) The conclusions drawn from the monitoring procedures.

(c) Where relevant, a description of systemic, repetitive or other significant deficiencies and of the actions taken to resolve or amend those deficiencies.

98. The reporting of identified deficiencies to individuals other than the relevant engagement partners ordinarily does not include an identification of the specific engagements concerned, unless such identification is necessary for the proper discharge of the responsibilities of the individuals other than the engagement partners.

99. Some firms operate as part of a network and, for consistency, may implement some or all of their monitoring procedures on a network basis. Where firms within a network operate under common monitoring policies and procedures designed to comply with this SQC, and these firms place reliance on such a monitoring system:

(a) At least annually, the network communicates the overall scope, extent and results of the monitoring process to appropriate individuals within the network firms;

(b) The network communicates promptly any identified deficiencies in the quality control system to appropriate individuals within the relevant network firm or firms so that the necessary action can be taken; and

(c) Engagement partners in the network firms are entitled to rely on the results of the monitoring process implemented within the network, unless the firms or the network advises otherwise.

100. Appropriate documentation relating to monitoring:

(r) Sets out monitoring procedures, including the procedure for selecting completed engagements to be inspected;

(s) Records the evaluation of:

  (i) Adherence to professional standards and regulatory and legal requirements;

  (ii) Whether the quality control system has been appropriately designed and effectively implemented; and

  (iii) Whether the firm's quality control policies and procedures have been appropriately applied, so that reports that are issued by the firm or engagement partners are appropriate in the circumstances; and

(t) Identifies the deficiencies noted, evaluates their effect, and sets out the basis for determining whether and what further action is necessary.

Effective Date

This Standard on Quality Control is recommendatory for all engagements relating to accounting periods beginning on or after April 1, 2008 and is mandatory for all engagements relating to accounting periods beginning on or after April 1, 2009

STANDARD ON AUDITING 200: OVERALL OBJECTIVES OF THE INDEPENDENT AUDITOR AND THE CONDUCT OF AN AUDIT IN ACCORDANCE WITH STANDARDS ON AUDITING

Introduction

Scope of this SA

1. This Standard on Auditing (SA) establishes the independent auditor's overall responsibilities when conducting an audit of financial statements in accordance with SAs. Specifically, it sets out the overall objectives of the independent auditor, and explains the nature and scope of an audit designed to enable the independent auditor to meet those objectives. It also explains the scope, authority and structure of the SAs, and includes requirements establishing the general responsibilities of the independent auditor applicable in all audits, including the obligation to comply with the SAs. The independent auditor is referred to as "the auditor "hereafter.
2. SAs are written in the context of an audit of financial statements by an auditor. They are to be adapted as necessary in the circumstances when applied to audits of other historical financial information

An Audit of Financial Statements

3. The purpose of an audit is to enhance the degree of confidence of intended users in the financial statements. This is achieved by the expression of an opinion by the auditor on whether the financial statements are prepared, in all material respects, in accordance with an applicable financial reporting

framework. In the case of most general purpose frameworks, that opinion is on whether the financial statements are presented fairly, in all material respects, or give a true and fair view in accordance with the framework. An audit conducted in accordance with SAs and relevant ethical requirements enables the auditor to form that opinion. (Ref: Para.A1)

4. The financial statements subject to audit are those of the entity, prepared and presented by management of the entity with oversight from those charged with governance. SAs do not impose responsibilities on management or those charged with governance and do not override laws and regulations that govern their responsibilities. However, an audit in accordance with SAs is conducted on the premise that management and, where appropriate, those charged with governance have responsibilities that are fundamental to the conduct of the audit. The audit of the financial statements does not relieve management or those charged with governance of those responsibilities. (Ref: Para.A2-A11)

   As the basis for the auditor's opinion, SAs require the auditor to obtain reasonable assurance about whether the financial statements as a whole are free from material misstatement, whether due to fraud or error. Reasonable assurance is a high level of assurance. It is obtained when the auditor has obtained sufficient appropriate audit evidence to reduce audit risk (i.e., the risk that the auditor expresses an inappropriate opinion when the financial statements are materially misstated) to an acceptably low level. However, reasonable assurance is not an absolute level of assurance, because there are inherent limitations of an audit which result in most of the audit evidence on which the auditor draws conclusions and bases the auditor's opinion being persuasive rather than conclusive. (Ref: Para. A28-A52)

5. The concept of materiality is applied by the auditor both in planning and performing the audit, and in evaluating the effect of identified misstatements on the audit and of uncorrected misstatements, if any, on the financial statements1. In general, misstatements, including omissions, are considered to be material if, individually or in the aggregate, they could reasonably be expected to influence the economic decisions of users taken on the basis of the financial statements. Judgments about materiality are made in the light of surrounding circumstances, and are affected by the auditor's perception of the financial information needs of users of the financial statements, and by the size or nature of a misstatement, or a combination of both. The auditor's opinion deals with the financial statements as a whole and therefore the auditor is not responsible for the detection of misstatements that are not material to the financial statements as a whole.

6. The SAs contain objectives, requirements and application and other explanatory material that are designed to support the auditor in obtaining reasonable assurance. The SAs require that the auditor exercise professional judgment and maintain professional skepticism throughout the planning and performance of the audit and, among other things:

- Identify and assess risks of material misstatement, whether due to fraud or error, based on an understanding of the entity and its environment, including the entity's internal control.
- Obtain sufficient appropriate audit evidence about whether material misstatements exist, through designing and implementing appropriate responses to the assessed risks.
- Form an opinion on the financial statements based on conclusions drawn from the audit evidence obtained.

7. The form of opinion expressed by the auditor will depend upon the applicable financial reporting framework and any applicable laws or regulations. (Ref: Para.A12-A13)

8. The auditor may also have certain other communication and reporting responsibilities to users, management, those charged with governance, or parties outside the entity, in relation to matters arising from the audit. These may be established by the SAs or by applicable laws or regulations.

Overall Objectives of the Auditor

9. In conducting an audit of financial statements, the overall objectives of the auditor are:

   (a) To obtain reasonable assurance about whether the financial statements as a whole are free from material misstatement, whether due to fraud or error, thereby enabling the auditor to express an opinion on whether the financial statements are prepared, in all material respects, in accordance with an applicable financial reporting framework; and

   (b) To report on the financial statements, and communicate as required by the SAs, in accordance with the auditor's findings.

10. In all cases when reasonable assurance cannot be obtained and a qualified opinion in the auditor's report is insufficient in the circumstances for purposes of reporting to the intended users of the financial statements, the SAs require that the auditor disclaim an opinion or withdraw from the engagement, where withdrawal is legally permitted.

Definitions

11. For purposes of the SAs, the following terms have the meanings attributed below:

   (a) Applicable financial reporting framework – The financial reporting framework adopted by management and, where appropriate, those charged with governance in the preparation and presentation of the financial statements that is acceptable in view of the nature of the entity and the objective of the financial statements, or that is required by law or regulation.

   The term "fair presentation framework" is used to refer to a financial reporting framework that requires compliance with the requirements of the framework and:

I. Acknowledges explicitly or implicitly that, to achieve fair presentation of the financial statements, it may be necessary for management to provide disclosures beyond those specifically required by the framework; or

II. Acknowledges explicitly that it may be necessary for management to depart from a requirement of the framework to achieve fair presentation of the financial statements. Such departures are expected to be necessary only in extremely rare circumstances.

The term "compliance framework" is used to refer to a financial reporting framework that requires compliance with the requirements of the framework, but does not contain the acknowledgements in (i) or (ii) above.

(b) Audit evidence – Information used by the auditor in arriving at the conclusions on which the auditor's opinion is based. Audit evidence includes both information contained in the accounting records underlying the financial statements and other information. For purposes of the SAs:

Sufficiency of audit evidence is the measure of the quantity of audit evidence. The quantity of the audit evidence needed is affected by the auditor's assessment of the risks of material misstatement and also by the quality of such audit evidence.

Appropriateness of audit evidence is the measure of the quality of audit evidence; that is, its relevance and its reliability in providing support for the conclusions on which the auditor's opinion is based.

(c) Audit risk – The risk that the auditor expresses an inappropriate audit opinion when the financial statements are materially misstated. Audit risk is a function of the risks of material misstatement and detection risk.

(d) Auditor – "Auditor" is used to refer to the person or persons conducting the audit, usually the engagement partner or other members of the engagement team, or, as applicable, the firm. Where an SA expressly intends that a requirement or responsibility be fulfilled by the engagement partner, the term "engagement partner" rather than "auditor" is used. "Engagement partner" and "firm" are to be read as referring to their public sector equivalents where relevant.

(e) Detection risk – The risk that the procedures performed by the auditor to reduce audit risk to an acceptably low level will not detect a misstatement that exists and that could be material, either individually or when aggregated with other misstatements.

(f) Financial statements – A structured representation of historical financial information, including related notes, intended to communicate an entity's economic resources or obligations at a point in time or the changes therein for a period of time in accordance with a financial reporting framework. The related notes ordinarily comprise a summary of significant accounting policies and other explanatory information. The term "financial statements" ordinarily refers to a complete set of financial statements as determined by the requirements of the applicable financial reporting framework, but can also refer to a single financial statement.

(g) Historical financial information – Information expressed in financial terms in relation to a particular entity, derived primarily from that entity's accounting system, about economic events occurring in past time periods or about economic conditions or circumstances at points in time in the past.

(h) Management – The person(s) with executive responsibility for the conduct of the entity's operations. For some entities in some jurisdictions, management includes some or all of those charged with governance, for example, executive members of a governance board, or an owner-manager.

(i) Misstatement – A difference between the amount, classification, presentation, or disclosure of a reported financial statement item and the amount, classification, presentation, or disclosure that is required for the item to be in accordance with the applicable financial reporting framework. Misstatements can arise from error or fraud.

When the auditor expresses an opinion on whether the financial statements are presented fairly, in all material respects, or give a true and fair view, misstatements also include those adjustments of amounts, classifications, presentation, or disclosures that, in the auditor's judgment, are necessary for the financial statements to be presented fairly, in all material respects, or to give a true and fair view.

(j) Premise, relating to the responsibilities of management and, where appropriate, those charged with governance, on which an audit is conducted – That management and, where appropriate, those charged with governance have the following responsibilities that are fundamental to the conduct of an audit in accordance with SAs. That is, responsibility:

(i) For the preparation and presentation of the financial statements in accordance with the applicable financial reporting framework; this includes the design, implementation and maintenance of internal control relevant to the preparation and presentation of financial statements that are free from material misstatement, whether due to fraud or error; and

(ii) To provide the auditor with:

(a) All information, such as records and documentation, and other matters that are relevant to the preparation and presentation of the financial statements;

(b) Any additional information that the auditor may request from management and, where appropriate, those charged with governance; and

(c) Unrestricted access to those within the entity from whom the auditor determines it necessary to obtain audit evidence.

In the case of a fair presentation framework, the responsibility is for the preparation and *fair* presentation of the financial statements in accordance with the financial reporting framework; or the preparation of financial statements *that give a true and fair view* in accordance with the financial reporting framework. This applies to all references to "preparation and presentation of the financial statements" in the SAs.

The "premise, relating to the responsibilities of management and, where appropriate, those charged with governance, on which an audit is conducted" may also be referred to as the "premise".

(k) Professional judgment–The application of relevant training, knowledge and experience, within the context provided by auditing, accounting and ethical standards, in making informed decisions about the courses of action that are appropriate in the circumstances of the audit engagement.

(l) Professional skepticism – An attitude that includes a questioning mind, being alert to conditions which may indicate possible misstatement due to error or fraud, and a critical assessment of audit evidence.

(m) Reasonable assurance – In the context of an audit of financial statements, a high, but not absolute, level of assurance.

(n) Risk of material misstatement – The risk that the financial statements are materially misstated prior to audit. This consists of two components, described as follows at the assertion level:

(iii) Inherent risk – The susceptibility of an assertion about a class of transaction, account balance or disclosure to a misstatement that could be material, either individually or when aggregated with other misstatements, before consideration of any related controls.

(iv) Control risk – The risk that a misstatement that could occur in an assertion about a class of transaction, account balance or disclosure and that could be material, either individually or when aggregated with other misstatements, will not be prevented, or detected and corrected, on a timely basis by the entity's internal control.

(o) Those charged with governance – The person(s) or organization(s) (e.g., a corporate trustee) with responsibility for overseeing the strategic direction of the entity and obligations related to the accountability of the entity. This includes overseeing the financial reporting process. For some entities in some jurisdictions, those charged with governance may include management personnel, for example, executive members of a governance board of a private or public sector entity, or an owner-manager.

Requirements

Ethical Requirements Relating to an Audit of Financial Statements

12. The auditor shall comply with relevant ethical requirements, including those pertaining to independence, relating to financial statement audit engagements. (Ref: Para.A14-A17)

Professional Skepticism

13. The auditor shall plan and perform an audit with professional skepticism recognizing that circumstances may exist that cause the financial statements to be materially misstated.(Ref:Para.A18-A22)

Professional Judgment

14. The auditor shall exercise professional judgment in planning and performing an audit of financial statements. (Ref: Para.A23-A27)

Sufficient Appropriate Audit Evidence and Audit Risk

15. To obtain reasonable assurance, the auditor shall obtain sufficient appropriate audit evidence to reduce audit risk to an acceptably low level and thereby enable the auditor to draw reasonable conclusions on which to base the auditor's opinion. (Ref: Para.A28-A52)

Conduct of an Audit in Accordance with SAs

Complying with SAs Relevant to the Audit

16. The auditor shall comply with all SAs relevant to the audit. An SA is relevant to the audit when the SA is in effect and the circumstances addressed by the SA exist. (Ref: Para.A53-A56)
17. The auditor shall have an understanding of the entire text of an SA, including its application and other explanatory material, to understand its objectives and to apply its requirements properly. (Ref: Para.A57-A65)
18. The auditor shall not represent compliance with SAs in the auditor's report unless the auditor has complied with the requirements of this SA and all other SAs relevant to the audit.

Objectives Stated in Individual SAs

19. To achieve the overall objectives of the auditor, the auditor shall use the objectives stated in relevant SAs in planning and performing the audit, having regard to the interrelationships among the SAs, to: (Ref: Para.A66-A68)
    (a) Determine whether any audit procedures in addition to those required by the SAs are necessary in pursuance of the objectives stated in the SAs; and (Ref: Para.A69)

(b) Evaluate whether sufficient appropriate audit evidence has been obtained. (Ref: Para.A70)

Complying with Relevant Requirements

20. Subject to paragraph 23, the auditor shall comply with each requirement of an SA unless, in the circumstances of the audit:
    (a) The entire SA is not relevant; or
    (b) The requirement is not relevant because it is conditional and the condition does not exist. (Ref: Para. A71-A72)

21. In exceptional circumstances, the auditor may judge it necessary to depart from a relevant requirement in an SA. In such circumstances, the auditor shall perform alternative audit procedures to achieve the aim of that requirement. The need for the auditor to depart from a relevant requirement is expected to arise only where the requirement is for a specific procedure to be performed and, in the specific circumstances of the audit, that procedure would be ineffective in achieving the aim of the requirement. (Ref: Para.A73)

Failure to Achieve an Objective

22. If an objective in a relevant SA cannot be achieved, the auditor shall evaluate whether this prevents the auditor from achieving the overall objectives of the auditor and thereby requires the auditor, in accordance with the SAs, to modify the auditor's opinion or withdraw from the engagement. Failure to achieve an objective represents a significant matter requiring documentation in accordance with SA 230 3. (Ref: Para. A74-A75)

Effective Date

23. This SA is effective for audits of financial statements for periods beginning on or after April 1, 2010

STANDARDS ON AUDITING (SA) 210: AGREEING THE TERMS OF AUDIT ENGAGEMENTS

Introduction

Scope of this SA

1. This Standard on Auditing (SA) deals with the auditor's responsibilities in agreeing the terms of the audit engagement with management and, where appropriate, those charged with governance. This includes establishing that certain preconditions for an audit, responsibility for which rests with management and, where appropriate, those charged with governance, are present. SA 2201 deals with those aspects of engagement acceptance that are within the control of the auditor. (Ref: Para.A1)

Objective

2. The objective of the auditor is to accept or continue an audit engagement only when the basis upon which it is to be performed has been agreed, through:
   (a) Establishing whether the preconditions for an audit are present; and
   (b) Confirming that there is a common understanding between the auditor and management and, where appropriate, those charged with governance of the terms of the audit engagement.

Definitions

3. For purposes of the SAs, the following term has the meaning attributed below:
   Preconditions for an audit – The use by management of an acceptable financial reporting framework2 in the preparation of the financial statements and the agreement of management and, where appropriate, those charged with governance to the premise3 on which an audit is conducted.
4. For the purposes of this SA, references to "management" should be read hereafter as "management and, where appropriate, those charged with governance".

Requirements Preconditions for an Audit

5. In order to establish whether the preconditions for an audit are present, the auditor shall:
   (a) Determine whether the financial reporting framework to be applied in the preparation of the financial statements is acceptable; and (Ref: Para.A2-A9)
   (b) Obtain the agreement of management that it acknowledges and understands its responsibility: (Ref: Para A10-A13, A19)
      - For the preparation of the financial statements in accordance with the applicable financial reporting framework, including where relevant their fair presentation; (Ref: Para.A14)
      - For such internal control as management determines is necessary to enable the preparation of financial statements that are free from material misstatement, whether due to fraud or error; and (Ref: Para.A15-A18)
      - To provide the auditor with:
        (i) Access to all information of which management is aware that is relevant to the preparation of the financial statements such as records, documentation and other matters;
        (ii) Additional information that the auditor may request from management for the purpose of the audit; and
        (iii) Unrestricted access to persons within the entity from whom the auditor determines it necessary to obtain audit evidence

Limitation on Scope Prior to Audit Engagement Acceptance

6. If management or those charged with governance impose a limitation on the scope of the auditor's work in the terms of a proposed audit engagement such that the auditor believes the limitation will result in the auditor disclaiming an opinion on the financial statements, the auditor shall not accept such a limited engagement as an audit engagement, unless required by law or regulation to do so.

Other Factors Affecting Audit Engagement Acceptance

7. If the preconditions for an audit are not present, the auditor shall discuss the matter with management. Unless required by law or regulation to do so, the auditor shall not accept the proposed audit engagement:
   (a) If the auditor has determined that the financial reporting framework to be applied in the preparation of the financial statements is unacceptable, except as provided in paragraph 19;or
   (b) If the agreement referred to in paragraph 6(b) has not been obtained

Agreement on Audit Engagement Terms

8. The auditor shall agree the terms of the audit engagement with management or those charged with governance, as appropriate. (Ref: Para.A20)
9. Subject to paragraph 11, the agreed terms of the audit engagement shall be recorded in an audit engagement letter or other suitable form of written agreement and shall include: (Ref: Para.A21-A24)
   (a) The objective and scope of the audit of the financial statements;
   (b) The responsibilities of the auditor;
   (c) The responsibilities of management;
   (d) Identification of the applicable financial reporting framework for the preparation of the financial statements; and
   (e) Reference to the expected form and content of any reports to be issued by the auditor and a statement that there may be circumstances in which a report may differ from its expected form and content.
10. If law or regulation prescribes in sufficient detail the terms of the audit engagement referred to in paragraph 10, the auditor need not record them in a written agreement, except for the fact that such law or regulation applies and that management acknowledges and understands its responsibilities as set out in paragraph 6(b). (Ref: Para. A21, A25-A26)
11. If law or regulation prescribes responsibilities of management similar to those described in paragraph 6(b), the auditor may determine that the law or regulation includes responsibilities that, in the auditor's judgment, are equivalent in effect to those set out in that paragraph. For such responsibilities that are equivalent, the auditor may use the wording of the law or regulation to describe them in the written agreement. For those responsibilities that are not prescribed by law or regulation such that their effect is equivalent, the written agreement shall use the description in paragraph 6(b). (Ref: Para.A25)

Recurring Audits

12. On recurring audits, the auditor shall assess whether circumstances require the terms of the audit engagement to be revised and whether there is a need to remind the entity of the existing terms of the audit engagement. (Ref: Para.A27)

Acceptance of a Change in the Terms of the Audit Engagement

13. The auditor shall not agree to a change in the terms of the audit engagement where there is no reasonable justification for doing so. (Ref: Para.A28-A30)

14. If, prior to completing the audit engagement, the auditor is requested to change the audit engagement to an engagement that conveys a lower level of assurance, the auditor shall determine whether there is reasonable justification for doing so. (Ref: Para.A31-A32)

15. If the terms of the audit engagement are changed, the auditor and management shall agree on and record the new terms of the engagement in an engagement letter or other suitable form of written agreement.

16. If the auditor is unable to agree to a change of the terms of the audit engagement and is not permitted by management to continue the original audit engagement, the auditor shall:

    (a) Withdraw from the audit engagement where possible under applicable law or regulation; and

    (b) Determine whether there is any obligation, either contractual or otherwise, to report the circumstances to other parties, such as those charged with governance, owners or regulators.

Effective Date

17. This SA is effective for audits of financial statements for periods beginning on or after April 1, 2010

STANDARDS ON AUDITING (SA) 220: QUALITY CONTROL FOR AN AUDIT OF FINANCIAL STATEMENTS

Introduction

Scope of this SA

1. This Standard on Auditing (SA) deals with the specific responsibilities of the auditor regarding quality control procedures for an audit of financial statements. It also addresses, where applicable, the responsibilities of the engagement quality control reviewer. This SA is to be read in conjunction with relevant ethical requirements.

System of Quality Control and Role of Engagement Teams

2. Quality control systems, policies and procedures are the responsibility of the audit firm. Under SQC 1, the firm has an obligation to establish and maintain a system of quality control to provide it with reasonable assurance that:

   (a) The firm and its personnel comply with professional standards and regulatory and legal requirements; and

   (b) The reports issued by the firm or engagement partners are appropriate in the circumstances1.

   This SA is premised on the basis that the firm is subject to SQC 1. (Ref: Para. A1)

3. Within the context of the firm's system of quality control, engagement teams have a responsibility to implement quality control procedures that are applicable to the audit engagement and provide the firm with relevant information to enable the functioning of that part of the firm's system of quality control relating to independence.

4. Engagement teams are entitled to rely on the firm's system of quality control, unless information provided by the firm or other parties suggests otherwise. (Ref: Para.A2)

Objective

The objective of the auditor is to implement quality control procedures at the engagement level that provide the auditor with reasonable assurance that:

(a) The audit complies with professional standards and regulatory and legal requirements; and

(b) The auditor's report issued is appropriate in the circumstances

Leadership Responsibilities for Quality on Audits

5. The engagement partner shall take responsibility for the overall quality on each audit engagement to which that partner is assigned. (Ref: Para.A3)

Relevant Ethical Requirements

6. Throughout the audit engagement, the engagement partner shall remain alert, through observation and making inquiries as necessary, for evidence of non-compliance with relevant ethical requirements by members of the engagement team. (Ref: Para.A4-A5)

7. If matters come to the engagement partner's attention through the firm's system of quality control or otherwise that indicate that members of the engagement team have not complied with relevant ethical requirements, the engagement partner, in consultation with others in the firm, shall determine the appropriate action. (Ref: Para.A5)

Independence

8. The engagement partner shall form a conclusion on compliance with independence requirements that apply to the audit engagement. In doing so, the engagement partner shall:
   (a) Obtain relevant information from the firm and, where applicable, network firms, to identify and evaluate circumstances and relationships that create threats to independence;
   (b) Evaluate information on identified breaches, if any, of the firm's independence policies and procedures to determine whether they create a threat to independence for the audit engagement; and
   (c) Take appropriate action to eliminate such threats or reduce them to an acceptable level by applying safeguards, or, if considered appropriate, to withdraw from the audit engagement, where withdrawal is permitted by law or regulation. The engagement partner shall promptly report to the firm any inability to resolve the matter for appropriate action. (Ref: Para.A5-A7)

Acceptance and Continuance of Client Relationships and Audit Engagements

9. The engagement partner shall be satisfied that appropriate procedures regarding the acceptance and continuance of client relationships and audit engagements have been followed, and shall determine that conclusions reached in this regard are appropriate. (Ref: Para.A8-A9)

10. If the engagement partner obtains information that would have caused the firm to decline the audit engagement had that information been available earlier, the engagement partner shall communicate that information promptly to the firm, so that the firm and the engagement partner can take the necessary action. (Ref: Para.A9)

Assignment of Engagement Teams

11. The engagement partner shall be satisfied that the engagement team, and any auditor's experts who are not part of the engagement team, collectively have the appropriate competence and capabilities to:
    (a) Perform the audit engagement in accordance with professional standards and regulatory and legal requirements; and
    (b) Enable an auditor's report that is appropriate in the circumstances to be issued. (Ref: Para.A10-A12)

Engagement Performance

Direction, Supervision and Performance

12. The engagement partner shall take responsibility for:

(a) The direction, supervision and performance of the audit engagement in compliance with professional standards and regulatory and legal requirements; and (Ref: Para. A13-A15, A20)

(b) The auditor's report being appropriate in the circumstances.

Reviews

13. The engagement partner shall take responsibility for reviews being performed in accordance with the firm's review policies and procedures. (Ref: Para. A16-A17, A20)

14. On or before the date of the auditor's report, the engagement partner shall, through a review of the audit documentation and discussion with the engagement team, be satisfied that sufficient appropriate audit evidence has been obtained to support the conclusions reached and for the auditor's report to be issued. (Ref: Para.A18-A20)

Consultation

15. The engagement partner shall:

(a) Take responsibility for the engagement team undertaking appropriate consultation on difficult or contentious matters;

(b) Be satisfied that members of the engagement team have undertaken appropriate consultation during the course of the engagement, both within the engagement team and between the engagement team and others at the appropriate level within or outside the firm;

(c) Be satisfied that the nature and scope of, and conclusions resulting from, such consultations are agreed with the party consulted; and

(d) Determine that conclusions resulting from such consultations have been implemented. (Ref: Para. A21-A22)

Engagement Quality Control Review

16. For audits of financial statements of listed entities, and those other audit engagements, if any, for which the firm has determined that an engagement quality control review is required, the engagement partner shall:

(a) Determine that an engagement quality control reviewer has been appointed;

(b) Discuss significant matters arising during the audit engagement, including those identified during the engagement quality control review, with the engagement quality control reviewer; and

(c) Not date the auditor's report until the completion of the engagement quality control review. (Ref: Para. A23-A25)

17. The engagement quality control reviewer shall perform an objective evaluation of the significant judgments made by the engagement team, and the conclusions reached in formulating the auditor'sreport

This evaluation shall involve:

(a) Discussion of significant matters with the engagement partner;

(b) Review of the financial statements and the proposed auditor's report;

(c) Review of selected audit documentation relating to the significant judgments the engagement team made and the conclusions it reached; and

(d) Evaluation of the conclusions reached in formulating the auditor's report and consideration of whether the proposed auditor's report is appropriate. (Ref: Para. A26-A27, A29-A31)

18. For audits of financial statements of listed entities, the engagement quality control reviewer, on performing an engagement quality control review, shall also consider the following:

(a) The engagement team's evaluation of the firm's independence in relation to the audit engagement;

(b) Whether appropriate consultation has taken place on matters involving differences of opinion or other difficult or contentious matters, and the conclusions arising from those consultations; and

(c) Whether audit documentation selected for review reflects the work performed in relation to the significant judgments made and supports the conclusions reached. (Ref: Para.A28-A31)

Differences of Opinion

19. If differences of opinion arise within the engagement team, with those consulted or, where applicable, between the engagement partner and the engagement quality control reviewer, the engagement team shall follow the firm's policies and procedures for dealing with and resolving differences of opinion.

Monitoring

20. An effective system of quality control includes a monitoring process designed to provide the firm with reasonable assurance that its policies and procedures relating to the system of quality control are relevant, adequate, and operating effectively. The engagement partner shall consider the results of the firm's monitoring process as evidenced in the latest information circulated by the firm and, if applicable, other network firms and whether deficiencies noted in that information may affect the audit engagement. (Ref: Para A32-A34)

Documentation

21. The auditor shall document:

(a) Issues identified with respect to compliance with relevant ethical requirements and how they were resolved.

(b) Conclusions on compliance with independence requirements that apply to the audit engagement, and any relevant discussions with the firm that support these conclusions.

(c) Conclusions reached regarding the acceptance and continuance of client relationships and audit engagements.

(d) The nature and scope of, and conclusions resulting from, consultations undertaken during the course of the audit engagement. (Ref: Para.A35)

22. The engagement quality control reviewer shall document, for the audit engagement reviewed, that:

(a) The procedures required by the firm's policies on engagement quality control review have been performed;

(b) The engagement quality control review has been completed on or before the date of the auditor's report; and

(c) The reviewer is not aware of any unresolved matters that would cause the reviewer to believe that the significant judgments the engagement team made and the conclusions they reached were not appropriate.

STANDARDS ON AUDITING (SA) 230: AUDIT DOCUMENTATION

Introduction

Scope of this SA

1. This Standard on Auditing (SA) deals with the auditor's responsibility to prepare audit documentation for an audit of financial statements. It is to be adapted as necessary in the circumstances when applied to audits of other historical financial information. The specific documentation requirements of other SAs do not limit the application of this SA. Laws or regulations may establish additional documentation requirements.

Nature and Purposes of Audit Documentation

2. Audit documentation that meets the requirements of this SA and the specific documentation requirements of other relevant SAs provides:

(a) Evidence of the auditor's basis for a conclusion about the achievement of the overall objectives of the auditor; and

(b) Evidence that the audit was planned and performed in accordance with SAs and applicable legal and regulatory requirements.

3. Audit documentation serves a number of additional purposes, including the following:

- Assisting the engagement team to plan and perform the audit.
- Assisting members of the engagement team responsible for supervision to direct and supervise the audit work, and to discharge their review responsibilities in accordance with SA 220[1].
- Enabling the engagement team to be accountable for its work.
- Retaining a record of matters of continuing significance to future audits.
- Enabling the conduct of quality control reviews and inspections in accordance with SQC1[2].

- Enabling the conduct of external inspections in accordance with applicable legal, regulatory or other requirements.

Effective Date

4. This SA is effective for audits of financial statements for periods beginning on or after April 1, 2009.

Objective

5. The objective of the auditor is to prepare documentation that provides:
   (a) A sufficient and appropriate record of the basis for the auditor's report; and
   (b) Evidence that the audit was planned and performed in accordance with SAs and applicable legal and regulatory requirements.

Definitions

6. For purposes of the SAs, the following terms have the meanings attributed below:
   (a) *Audit documentation*–The record of audit procedures performed, relevant audit evidence obtained, and conclusions the auditor reached (terms such as "working papers" or "work papers" are also sometimes used).
   (b) *Audit file*– One or more folders or other storage media, in physical or electronic form, containing the records that comprise the audit documentation for a specific engagement.
   (c) *Experienced auditor*– An individual (whether internal or external to the firm) who has practical audit experience, and a reasonable understanding of:
      (i) Audit processes;
      (ii) SAs and applicable legal and regulatory requirements;
      (iii) The business environment in which the entity operates; and
      (iv) Auditing and financial reporting issues relevant to the entity's industry.

Requirements Timely Preparation of Audit Documentation

7. The auditor shall prepare audit documentation on a timely basis. *(Ref: Para.A1)*

Documentation of the Audit Procedures Performed and Audit Evidence Obtained Form, Content and Extent of Audit Documentation

8. The auditor shall prepare audit documentation that is sufficient to enable an experienced auditor, having no previous connection with the audit, to understand: *(Ref: Para. A2-A5, A16-A17)*

(a) The nature, timing, and extent of the audit procedures performed to comply with the SAs and applicable legal and regulatory requirements; *(Ref: Para.A6-A7)*

(b) The results of the audit procedures performed, and the audit evidence obtained; and

(c) Significant matters arising during the audit, the conclusions reached thereon, and significant professional judgments made in reaching those conclusions. *(Ref: Para. A8-A11)*

9. In documenting the nature, timing and extent of audit procedures performed, the auditor shall record:

   (a) The identifying characteristics of the specific items or matters tested; *(Ref: Para.A12)*

   (b) Who performed the audit work and the date such work was completed; and

   (c) Who reviewed the audit work performed and the date and extent of such review? *(Ref: Para.A13)*

10. The auditor shall document discussions of significant matters with management, those charged with governance, and others, including the nature of the significant matters discussed and when and with whom the discussions took place. *(Ref: Para.A14)*

11. If the auditor identified information that is inconsistent with the auditor's final conclusion regarding a significant matter, the auditor shall document how the auditor addressed the inconsistency. *(Ref:Para.A15)*

Departure from a Relevant Requirement

12. If, in exceptional circumstances, the auditor judges it necessary to depart from a relevant requirement in a SA, the auditor shall document how the alternative audit procedures performed achieve the aim of that requirement, and the reasons for the departure. *(Ref: Para. A18-A19)*

Matters arising after the Date of the Auditor's Report

13. If, in exceptional circumstances, the auditor performs new or additional audit procedures or draws new conclusions after the date of the auditor's report, the auditor shall document: *(Ref: Para.A20)*

   (a) The circumstances encountered;

   (b) The new or additional audit procedures performed, audit evidence obtained, and conclusions reached, and their effect on the auditor's report; and

   (c) When and by whom the resulting changes to audit documentation were made and reviewed.

Assembly of the Final Audit File

14. The auditor shall assemble the audit documentation in an audit file and complete the administrative process of assembling the final audit file on a timely basis after the date of the auditor's report. *(Ref: Para. A21-A22)*

15. After the assembly of the final audit file has been completed, the auditor shall not delete or discard audit documentation of any nature before the end of its retention period. *(Ref: Para.A23)*

16. In circumstances other than those envisaged in paragraph 13 where the auditor finds it necessary to modify existing audit documentation or add new audit documentation after the assembly of the final audit file has been completed, the auditor shall, regardless of the nature of the modifications or additions, document: *(Ref: Para. A24-A25)*

    (a) The specific reasons for making them; and

    (b) When and by whom they were made and reviewed.

STANDARDS ON AUDITING (SA) 240: THE AUDITOR'S RESPONSIBILITIES RELATING TO FRAUD IN AN AUDIT OF FINANCIAL STATEMENTS

Introduction

Scope of this SA

1. This Standard on Auditing (SA) deals with the auditor's responsibilities relating to fraud in an audit of financial statements. Specifically, it expands on how SA 315, "Identifying and Assessing the Risks of Material Misstatement Through Understanding the Entity and Its Environment," and SA 330, "The Auditor's Responses to Assessed Risks," are to be applied in relation to risks of material misstatement due to fraud.

Characteristics of Fraud

2. Misstatements in the financial statements can arise from either fraud or error. The distinguishing factor between fraud and error is whether the underlying action that results in the misstatement of the financial statements is intentional or unintentional.

3. Although fraud is a broad legal concept, for the purposes of the SAs, the auditor is concerned with fraud that causes a material misstatement in the financial statements. Two types of intentional misstatements are relevant to the auditor–misstatements resulting from fraudulent financial reporting and misstatements resulting from misappropriation of assets. Although the auditor may suspector, in rare cases, identify the occurrence of fraud, the auditor does not make legal determinations of whether fraud has actually occurred. (Ref: Para. A1- A6)

Responsibility for the Prevention and Detection of Fraud

4. The primary responsibility for the prevention and detection of fraud rests with both those charged with governance of the entity and management. It is important that management, with the oversight of those charged with governance, place a strong emphasis on fraud prevention, which may reduce opportunities for fraud to take place, and fraud deterrence, which could persuade individuals not to commit fraud because of the likelihood of detection and punishment. This involves a commitment to creating a culture of honesty and ethical behavior which can be reinforced by an active oversight by those charged with governance. In exercising oversight responsibility, those charged with governance consider the potential for override of controls or other inappropriate influence over the financial reporting process, such as efforts by management to manage earnings in order to influence the perception so analysts as to the entity's performance and profitability.

Responsibilities of the Auditor

5. An auditor conducting an audit in accordance with SAs is responsible for obtaining reasonable assurance that the financial statements taken as a whole are free from material misstatement, whether caused by fraud or error. Owing to the inherent limitations of an audit, there is an unavoidable risk that some material misstatements of the financial statements may not be detected, even though the audit is properly planned and performed in accordance with the SAs.

6. As described in SA 2002, the potential effects of inherent limitations are particularly significant in the case of misstatement resulting from fraud. The risk of not detecting a material misstatement resulting from fraud is higher than the risk of not detecting one resulting from error. This is because fraud may involve sophisticated and carefully organized schemes designed to conceal it, such as forgery, deliberate failure to record transactions, or intentional misrepresentations being made to the auditor. Such attempts at concealment may be even more difficult to detect when accompanied by collusion. Collusion may cause the auditor to believe that audit evidence is persuasive when it is, in fact, false. The auditor's ability to detect a fraud depends on factors such as the skillfulness of the perpetrator, the frequency and extent of manipulation, the degree of collusion involved, the relative size of individual amounts manipulated, and the seniority of those individuals involved. While the auditor may be able to identify potential opportunities for fraud to be perpetrated, it is difficult for the auditor to determine whether misstatements in judgment areas such as accounting estimates are caused by fraud or error.

7. Furthermore, the risk of the auditor not detecting a material misstatement resulting from management fraud is greater than for employee fraud, because management is frequently in a position to directly or indirectly manipulate accounting records, present fraudulent financial information or override control procedures designed to prevent similar frauds by other employees.

8. When obtaining reasonable assurance, the auditor is responsible for maintaining professional skepticism throughout the audit, considering the

potential for management override of controls and recognizing the fact that audit procedures that are effective for detecting error may not be effective in detecting fraud. The requirements in this SA are designed to assist the auditor in identifying and assessing the risks of material misstatement due to fraud and in designing procedures to detect such misstatement.

Effective Date

9. This SA is effective for audits of financial statements for periods beginning on or after 1st April, 2009.

Objectives

10. The objectives of the auditor are:
    (a) To identify and assess the risks of material misstatement in the financial statements due to fraud;
    (b) To obtain sufficient appropriate audit evidence about the assessed risks of material misstatement due to fraud, through designing and implementing appropriate responses; and
    (c) To respond appropriately to identified or suspected fraud

Definitions

11. For purposes of the SAs, the following terms have the meanings attributed below:
    (a) *Fraud* - An intentional act by one or more individuals among management, those charged with governance, employees, or third parties, involving the use of deception to obtain an unjust or illegal advantage.
    (b) *Fraud risk factors* - Events or conditions that indicate an incentive or pressure to commit fraud or provide an opportunity to commit fraud.

Requirements

Professional Skepticism

12. In accordance with SA 2003, the auditor shall maintain professional skepticism throughout the audit, recognizing the possibility that a material misstatement due to fraud could exist, notwithstanding the auditor's past experience of the honesty and integrity of the entity's management and those charged with governance. (Ref: Para. A7- A8)
13. Unless the auditor has reason to believe the contrary, the auditor may accept records and documents as genuine. If conditions identified during the audit because the auditor to believe that a document may not be authentic or that terms in a document have been modified but not disclosed to the auditor, the auditor shall investigate further. (Ref: Para.A9)
14. Where responses to inquiries of management or those charged with governance are inconsistent, the auditor shall investigate the inconsistencies.

Discussion among the Engagement Team

15. SA 315 requires a discussion among the engagement team members and a determination by the engagement partner of matters which are to be communicated to those team members not involved in the discussion4. This discussion shall place particular emphasis on how and where the entity's financial statements may be susceptible to material misstatement due to fraud, including how fraud might occur. The discussion shall occur notwithstanding the engagement team members' beliefs that management and those charged with governance are honest and have integrity. (Ref: Para.A10-A11)

Risk Assessment Procedures and Related Activities

16. When performing risk assessment procedures and related activities to obtain an understanding of the entity and its environment, including the entity's internal control, required by SA 3155, the auditor shall perform the procedures in paragraphs 17-24 to obtain information for use in identifying the risks of material misstatement due to fraud.

Management and Others within the Entity

17. The auditor shall make inquiries of management regarding:
    (a) Management's assessment of the risk that the financial statements may be materially misstated due to fraud, including the nature, extent and frequency of such assessments; (Ref: Para.A12-A13)
    (b) Management's process for identifying and responding to the risks of fraud in the entity, including any specific risks of fraud that management has identified or that have been brought to its attention, or classes of transactions, account balances, or disclosures for which a risk of fraud is likely to exist; (Ref: Para.A14)
    (c) Management's communication, if any, to those charged with governance regarding its processes for identifying and responding to the risks of fraud in the entity; and
    (d) Management's communication, if any, to employees regarding its views on business practices and ethical behavior.
18. The auditor shall make inquiries of management, and others within the entity as appropriate, to determine whether they have knowledge of any actual, suspected or alleged fraud affecting the entity. (Ref: Para.A15-A17)
19. For those entities that have an internal audit function, the auditor shall make inquiries of internal audit to determine whether it has knowledge of any actual, suspected or alleged fraud affecting the entity, and to obtain its views about the risks of fraud. (Ref: Para.A18)

Those Charged with Governance

20. Unless all of those charged with governance are involved in managing the entity6, the auditor shall obtain an understanding of how those charged with governance exercise oversight of management's processes for identifying and

responding to the risks of fraud in the entity and the internal control that management has established to mitigate these risks. (Ref: Para.A19-A21)

21. The auditor shall make inquiries of those charged with governance to determine whether they have knowledge of any actual, suspected or alleged fraud affecting the entity. These inquiries are made in part to corroborate the responses to the inquiries of management.

Unusual or Unexpected Relationships Identified

22. The auditor shall evaluate whether unusual or unexpected relationships that have been identified in performing analytical procedures, including those related to revenue accounts, may indicate risks of material misstatement due to fraud.

Other Information

23. The auditor shall consider whether other information obtained by the auditor indicates risks of material misstatement due to fraud. (Ref: Para.A22)

Evaluation of Fraud Risk Factors

24. The auditor shall evaluate whether the information obtained from the other risk assessment procedures and related activities performed indicates that one or more fraud risk factors are present. While fraud risk factors may not necessarily indicate the existence of fraud, they have often been present in circumstances where frauds have occurred and therefore may indicate risks of material misstatement due to fraud. (Ref: Para.A23-A27)

Identification and Assessment of the Risks of Material Misstatement Due to Fraud

25. In accordance with SA 315, the auditor shall identify and assess the risks of material misstatement due to fraud at the financial statement level, and at the assertion level for classes of transactions, account balances and disclosures7.

26. When identifying and assessing the risks of material misstatement due to fraud, the auditor shall, based on a presumption that there are risks of fraud in revenue recognition, evaluate which types of revenue, revenue transactions or assertions give rise to such risks. Paragraph 47 specifies the documentation required when the auditor concludes that the presumption is not applicable in the circumstances of the engagement and, accordingly, has not identified revenue recognition as a risk of material misstatement due to fraud.(Ref: Para. A28-A30)

27. The auditor shall treat those assessed risks of material misstatement due to fraud as significant risks and accordingly, to the extent not already done so, the auditor shall obtain an understanding of the entity's related controls, including control activities, relevant to such risks. (Ref: Para.A31-A32)

Responses to the Assessed Risks of Material Misstatement Due to Fraud

Overall Responses

28. In accordance with SA 330, the auditor shall determine overall responses to address the assessed risks of material misstatement due to fraud at the financial statement level.8 (Ref: Para.A33)

29. In determining overall responses to address the assessed risks of material misstatement due to fraud at the financial statement level, the auditor shall:

 (a) Assign and supervise personnel taking account of the knowledge, skill and ability of the individuals to be given significant engagement responsibilities and the auditor's assessment of the risks of material misstatement due to fraud for the engagement; (Ref: Para.A34-A35)

 (b) Evaluate whether the selection and application of accounting policies by the entity, particularly those related to subjective measurements and complex transactions, may be indicative of fraudulent financial reporting resulting from management's effort to manage earnings; and

 (c) Incorporate an element of unpredictability in the selection of the nature, timing and extent of audit procedures. (Ref: Para.A36)

Audit Procedures Responsive to Assessed Risks of Material Misstatement Due to Fraud at the Assertion Level

30. In accordance with SA 330, the auditor shall design and perform further audit procedures whose nature, timing and extent are responsive to the assessed risks of material misstatement due to fraud at the assertion level.9 (Ref: Para.A37-A40)

Audit Procedures Responsive to Risks Related to Management Override of Controls

31. Management is in a unique position to perpetrate fraud because of management's ability to manipulate accounting records and prepare fraudulent financial statements by overriding controls that otherwise appear to be operating effectively. Although the level of risk of management override of controls will vary from entity to entity, the risk is nevertheless present in all entities. Due to the unpredictable way in which such override could occur, it is a risk of material misstatement due to fraud and thus a significant risk.

32. Irrespective of the auditor's assessment of the risks of management override of controls, the auditor shall design and perform audit procedures to:

 (a) Test the appropriateness of journal entries recorded in the general ledger and other adjustments made in the preparation of the financial statements. In designing and performing audit procedures for such tests, the auditor shall:

(i) Make inquiries of individuals involved in the financial reporting process about inappropriate or unusual activity relating to the processing of journal entries and other adjustments;

(ii) Select journal entries and other adjustments made at the end of a reporting period; and

(iii) Consider the need to test journal entries and other adjustments throughout the period. (Ref: Para.A41-A44)

(b) Review accounting estimates10 for biases and evaluate whether the circumstances producing the bias, if any, represent a risk of material misstatement due to fraud. In performing this review, the auditor shall:

(i) Evaluate whether the judgments and decisions made by management in making the accounting estimates included in the financial statements, even if they are individually reasonable, indicate a possible bias on the part of the entity's management that may represent a risk of material misstatement due to fraud. If so, the auditor shall re-evaluate the accounting estimates taken as a whole; and

(ii) Perform a retrospective review of management judgments and assumptions related to significant accounting estimates reflected in the financial statements of the prior year11. (Ref: Para. A45-A46)

(c) For significant transactions that are outside the normal course of business for the entity, or that otherwise appear to be unusual given the auditor's understanding of the entity and its environment and other information obtained during the audit, the auditor shall evaluate whether the business rationale (or the lack thereof) of the transactions suggests that they may have been entered into to engage in fraudulent financial reporting or to conceal misappropriation of assets. (Ref: Para.A47)

33. The auditor shall determine whether, in order to respond to the identified risks of management override of controls, the auditor needs to perform other audit procedures in addition to those specifically referred to above (i.e., when there are specific additional risks of management override that are not covered as part of the procedures performed to address the requirements in paragraph 32).

Evaluation of Audit Evidence (Ref: Para. A48)

34. The auditor shall evaluate whether analytical procedures12 that are performed when forming an overall conclusion as to whether the financial statements as a whole are consistent with the auditor's understanding of the entity and its environment indicate a previously unrecognized risk of material misstatement due to fraud. (Ref: Para.A49)

35. When the auditor identifies a misstatement, the auditor shall evaluate whether such a misstatement is indicative of fraud. If there is such an indication, the auditor shall evaluate the implications of the misstatement in relation to other aspects of the audit, particularly the reliability of management representations,

recognizing that an instance of fraud is unlikely to be an isolated occurrence. (Ref: Para. A50)

36. If the auditor identifies a misstatement, whether material or not, and the auditor has reason to believe that it is or may be the result of fraud and that management (in particular, senior management) is involved, the auditor shall re-evaluate the assessment of the risks of material misstatement due to fraud and its resulting impact on the nature, timing and extent of audit procedures to respond to the assessed risks. The auditor shall also consider whether circumstances or conditions indicate possible collusion involving employees, management or third parties when reconsidering the reliability of evidence previously obtained. (Ref: Para.A51)

When the auditor confirms that, or is unable to conclude whether, the financial statements are materially misstated as a result of fraud the auditor shall evaluate the implications for the audit. (Ref: Para. A52)

Auditor Unable to Continue the Engagement

37. If, as a result of a misstatement resulting from fraud or suspected fraud, the auditor encounters exceptional circumstances that bring into question the auditor's ability to continue performing the audit, the auditor shall:

(a) Determine the professional and legal responsibilities applicable in the circumstances, including whether there is a requirement for the auditor to report to the person or persons who made the audit appointment or, in some cases, to regulatory authorities;

(b) Consider whether it is appropriate to withdraw from the engagement, where withdrawal from the engagement is legally permitted; and

(c) If the auditor withdraws:

(i) Discuss with the appropriate level of management and those charged with governance, the auditor's withdrawal from the engagement and the reasons for the withdrawal; and

(ii) Determine whether there is a professional or legal requirement to report to the person or persons who made the audit appointment or, in some cases, to regulatory authorities, the auditor's withdrawal from the engagement and the reasons for the withdrawal. (Ref: Para.A53-A56)

Management Representations

38. The auditor shall obtain written representations from management and, where applicable, those charged with governance that:

(a) They acknowledge their responsibility for the design, implementation and maintenance of internal control to prevent and detect fraud;

(b) They have disclosed to the auditor the results of management's assessment of the risk that the financial statements may be materially misstated as a result of fraud;

(c) They have disclosed to the auditor their knowledge of fraud or suspected fraud affecting the entity involving:

   (i) Management;

   (ii) Employees who have significant roles in internal control; or

   (iii) Others where the fraud could have a material effect on the financial statements; and

(d) They have disclosed to the auditor their knowledge of any allegations of fraud, or suspected fraud, affecting the entity's financial statements communicated by employees, former employees, analysts, regulators or others. (Ref: Para.A57-A58)

Communications to Management and with Those Charged with Governance

39. If the auditor has identified a fraud or has obtained information that indicates that a fraud may exist, the auditor shall communicate these matters on a timely basis to the appropriate level of management in order to inform those with primary responsibility for the prevention and detection of fraud of matters relevant to their responsibilities. (Ref: Para.A59)

40. Unless all of those charged with governance are involved in managing the entity, if the auditor has identified or suspects fraud involving:

   (a) Management;

   (b) Employees who have significant roles in internal control; or

   Others where the fraud results in a material misstatement in the financial statements.

   The auditor shall communicate these matters to those charged with governance on a timely basis. If the auditor suspects fraud involving management, the auditor shall communicate these suspicions to those charged with governance and discuss with them the nature, timing and extent of audit procedures necessary to complete the audit. (Ref: Para. A60-A62)

41. In accordance with SA 260, Communication with Those Charged with Governance13, the auditor shall communicate with those charged with governance any other matters related to fraud that are, in the auditor's judgment, relevant to their responsibilities. (Ref: Para.A63)

Communications to Regulatory and Enforcement Authorities

42. If the auditor has identified or suspects a fraud, the auditor shall determine whether there is a responsibility to report the occurrence or suspicion to a party outside the entity. Although the auditor's professional duty to maintain the confidentiality of client information may preclude such reporting, the auditor's legal responsibilities may override the duty of confidentiality in some circumstances. (Ref: Para. A64-A66)

Documentation

43. The auditor's documentation of the understanding of the entity and its environment and the assessment of the risks of material misstatement required by SA 315[14] shall include:
    (a) The significant decisions reached during the discussion among the engagement team regarding the susceptibility of the entity's financial statements to material misstatement due to fraud; and
    (b) The identified and assessed risks of material misstatement due to fraud at the financial statement level and at the assertion level.
44. The auditor's documentation of the responses to the assessed risks of material misstatement required by SA 330[15] shall include:
    (a) The overall responses to the assessed risks of material misstatement due to fraud at the financial statement level and the nature, timing and extent of audit procedures, and the linkage of those procedures with the assessed risks of material misstatement due to fraud at the assertion level; and
    (b) The results of the audit procedures, including those designed to address the risk of management override of controls.
45. The auditor shall document communications about fraud made to management, those charged with governance, regulators and others.

    When the auditor has concluded that the presumption that there is a risk of material misstatement due to fraud related to revenue recognition is not applicable in the circumstances of the engagement, the auditor shall document the reasons for that conclusion.

STANDARDS ON AUDITING (SA) 250: CONSIDERATION OF LAWS AND REGULATIONS IN AN AUDIT OF FINANCIAL STATEMENTS

Introduction

Scope of this SA

1. This Standard on Auditing (SA) deals with the auditor's responsibility to consider laws and regulations when performing an audit of financial statements. This SA does not apply to other assurance engagements in which the auditor is specifically engaged to test and report separately on compliance with specific laws or regulations.

Effect of Laws and Regulations

2. The effect on the financial statements of laws and regulations varies considerably. Those laws and regulations to which an entity is subject constitute the legal and regulatory framework. The provisions of some laws or regulations have a direct effect on the financial statements in that they determine the reported amounts and disclosures in an entity's financial

statements. Other laws or regulations are to be complied with by management or set the provisions under which the entity is allowed to conduct its business but do not have a direct effect on an entity's financial statements. Some entities operate in heavily regulated industries (such as banks and chemical companies). Others are subject only to the many laws and regulations that relate generally to the operating aspects of the business (such as those related to occupational safety and health). Non-compliance with laws and regulations may result in fines, litigation or other consequences for the entity that may have a material effect on the financial statements.

Responsibility of Management for Compliance with Laws and Regulations

3. It is the responsibility of management, with the oversight of those charged with governance, to ensure that the entity's operations are conducted in accordance with the provisions of laws and regulations, including compliance with the provisions of laws and regulations that determine the reported amounts and disclosures in an entity's financial statements. *(Ref: Para.A1-A2)*

Responsibility of the Auditor (Ref: Para. A3-A6)

4. The requirements in this SA are designed to assist the auditor in identifying material misstatement of the financial statements due to non-compliance with laws and regulations. However, the auditor is not responsible for preventing non-compliance and cannot be expected to detect non-compliance with all laws and regulations.

5. The auditor is responsible for obtaining reasonable assurance that the financial statements, taken as a whole, are free from material misstatement, whether caused by fraud or error. In conducting an audit of financial statements, the auditor takes into account the applicable legal and regulatory framework. Owing to the inherent limitations of an audit, there is an unavoidable risk that some material misstatements in the financial statements may not be detected, even though the audit is properly planned and performed in accordance with the SAs.3 In the context of laws and regulations, the potential effects of inherent limitations on the auditor's ability to detect material misstatements are greater for such reasons as the following:

   - There are many laws and regulations, relating principally to the operating aspects of an entity that typically do not affect the financial statements and are not captured by the entity's information systems relevant to financial reporting.
   - Non-compliance may involve conduct designed to conceal it, such as collusion, forgery, deliberate failure to record transactions, management override of controls or intentional misrepresentations being made to the auditor.
   - Whether an act constitutes non-compliance is ultimately a matter for legal determination by a court of law.

Ordinarily, the further removed non-compliance is from the events and transactions reflected in the financial statements, the less likely the auditor is to become aware of it or to recognize the non-compliance.

6. This SA distinguishes the auditor's responsibilities in relation to compliance with two different categories of laws and regulations as follows:

   (a) The provisions of those laws and regulations generally recognized to have a direct effect on the determination of material amounts and disclosures in the financial statements such as tax and labour laws. (see paragraph 13);and

   (b) Other laws and regulations that do not have a direct effect on the determination of the amounts and disclosures in the financial statements, but compliance with which may be fundamental to the operating aspects of the business, to an entity's ability to continue its business, or to avoid material penalties (for example, compliance with the terms of an operating license, compliance with regulatory solvency requirements, or compliance with environmental regulations); non-compliance with such laws and regulations may therefore have a material effect on the financial statements (see paragraph14).

7. In this SA, differing requirements are specified for each of the above categories of laws and regulations. For the category referred to in paragraph 6(a), the auditor's responsibility is to obtain sufficient appropriate audit evidence about compliance with the provisions of those laws and regulations. For the category referred to in paragraph 6(b), the auditor's responsibility is limited to undertaking specified audit procedures to help identify non-compliance with those laws and regulations that may have a material effect on the financial statements.

8. The auditor is required by this SA to remain alert to the possibility that other audit procedures applied for the purpose of forming an opinion on financial statements may bring instances of identified or suspected non-compliance to the auditor's attention. Maintaining professional skepticism throughout the audit, as required by SA 200, 4 is important in this context, given the extent of laws and regulations that affect the entity.

Effective Date

9. This SA is effective for audits of financial statements for periods beginning on or after April 1, 2009.

Objectives

10. The objectives of the auditor are:

    (a) To obtain sufficient appropriate audit evidence regarding compliance with the provisions of those laws and regulations generally recognized to have a direct effect on the determination of material amounts and disclosures in the financial statements;

(b) To perform specified audit procedures to help identify instances of non-compliance with other laws and regulations that may have a material effect on the financial statements; and

(c) To respond appropriately to non-compliance or suspected non-compliance with laws and regulations identified during the audit.

Definition

11. For the purposes of this SA, the following term has the meaning attributed below:

Non-compliance – Acts of omission or commission by the entity, either intentional or unintentional, which are contrary to the prevailing laws or regulations. Such acts include transactions entered into by, or in the name of, the entity, or on its behalf, by those charged with governance, management or employees. Non-compliance does not include personal misconduct (unrelated to the business activities of the entity) by those charged with governance, management or employees of the entity.

Requirements

The Auditor's Consideration of Compliance with Laws and Regulations

12. As part of obtaining an understanding of the entity and its environment in accordance with SA 315, the auditor shall obtain a general understanding of:

(a) The legal and regulatory framework applicable to the entity and the industry or sector in which the entity operates; and

(b) How the entity is complying with that framework. *(Ref: Para.A7)*

13. The auditor shall obtain sufficient appropriate audit evidence regarding compliance with the provisions of those laws and regulations generally recognized to have a direct effect on the determination of material amounts and disclosures in the financial statements. *(Ref: Para.A8)*

14. The auditor shall perform the following audit procedures to help identify instances of non-compliance with other laws and regulations that may have a material effect on the financial statements:

(a) Inquiring of management and, where appropriate, those charged with governance, as to whether the entity is in compliance with such laws and regulations; and

(b) Inspecting correspondence, if any, with the relevant licensing or regulatory authorities. *(Ref:Para.A9-A10)*

15. During the audit, the auditor shall remain alert to the possibility that other audit procedures applied may bring instances of non-compliance or suspected non-compliance with laws and regulations to the auditor's attention. *(Ref: Para.A11)*

16. The auditor shall request management and, where appropriate, those charged with governance to provide written representations that all known instances of non-compliance or suspected non-compliance with laws and regulations whose

effects should be considered when preparing financial statements have been disclosed to the auditor. *(Ref: Para.A12)*

17. In the absence of identified or suspected non-compliance, the auditor is not required to perform audit procedures regarding the entity's compliance with laws and regulations, other than those set out in paragraphs 12-16

Audit Procedures When Non-Compliance is Identified or Suspected

18. If the auditor becomes aware of information concerning an instance of non-compliance or suspected non-compliance with laws and regulations, the auditor shall obtain: *(Ref: Para.A13)*
    (a) An understanding of the nature of the act and the circumstances in which it has occurred; and
    (b) Further information to evaluate the possible effect on the financial statements. *(Ref: Para.A14)*

19. If the auditor suspects there may be non-compliance, the auditor shall discuss the matter with management and, where appropriate, those charged with governance. If management or, as appropriate, those charged with governance do not provide sufficient information that supports that the entity is in compliance with laws and regulations and, in the auditor's judgment, the effect of the suspected non- compliance may be material to the financial statements, the auditor shall consider the need to obtain legal advice. *(Ref: Para.A15-A16)*

20. If sufficient information about suspected non-compliance cannot be obtained, the auditor shall evaluate the effect of the lack of sufficient appropriate audit evidence on the auditor's opinion.

21. The auditor shall evaluate the implications of non-compliance in relation to other aspects of the audit, including the auditor's risk assessment and the reliability of written representations, and take appropriate action. *(Ref: Para.A17-A18)*

Reporting of Identified or Suspected Non-Compliance

Reporting Non-Compliance to Those Charged with Governance

22. Unless all of those charged with governance are involved in management of the entity, and therefore are aware of matters involving identified or suspected non-compliance already communicated by the auditor, the auditor shall communicate with those charged with governance matters involving non-compliance with laws and regulations that come to the auditor's attention during the course of the audit, other than when the matters are clearly inconsequential.

23. If, in the auditor's judgment, the non-compliance referred to in paragraph 22 is believed to be intentional and material, the auditor shall communicate the matter to those charged with governance as soon as practicable.

24. If the auditor suspects that management or those charged with governance are involved in non- compliance, the auditor shall communicate the matter to the

next higher level of authority at the entity, if it exists, such as an audit committee or supervisory board. Where no higher authority exists, or if the auditor believes that the communication may not be acted upon or is unsure as to the person to whom to report, the auditor shall consider the need to obtain legal advice.

Reporting Non-Compliance in the Auditor's Report on the Financial Statements

25. If the auditor concludes that the non-compliance has a material effect on the financial statements, and has not been adequately reflected in the financial statements, the auditor shall, in accordance with SA 705, express a qualified or adverse opinion on the financial statements.

26. If the auditor is precluded by management or those charged with governance from obtaining sufficient appropriate audit evidence to evaluate whether non-compliance that may be material to the financial statements has, or is likely to have, occurred, the auditor shall express a qualified opinion or disclaim an opinion on the financial statements on the basis of a limitation on the scope of the audit in accordance with SA705

27. If the auditor is unable to determine whether non-compliance has occurred because of limitations imposed by the circumstances rather than by management or those charged with governance, the auditor shall evaluate the effect on the auditor's opinion in accordance with SA705

Reporting Non-Compliance to Regulatory and Enforcement Authorities

28. If the auditor has identified or suspects non-compliance with laws and regulations, the auditor shall determine whether the auditor has a responsibility to report the identified or suspected non-compliance to parties outside the entity. *(Ref: Para. A19-A20)*

Documentation

29. The auditor shall document identified or suspected non-compliance with laws and regulations and the results of discussion with management and, where applicable, those charged with governance and other parties outside the entity.8 *(Ref: Para.A21)*

STANDARD ON AUDITING (SA) 260 (REVISED): COMMUNICATION WITH THOSE CHARGED WITH GOVERNANCE

Introduction

Scope of this SA

1. This Standard on Auditing (SA) deals with the auditor's responsibility to communicate with those charged with governance in an audit of financial statements. Although this SA applies irrespective of an entity's governance

structure or size, particular considerations apply where all of those charged with governance are involved in managing an entity, and for listed entities. This SA does not establish requirements regarding the auditor's communication with an entity's management or owners unless they are also charged with a governance role.

2. This SA is written in the context of an audit of financial statements, but may also be applicable, adapted as necessary in the circumstances, to audits of other historical financial information when those charged with governance have a responsibility to oversee the preparation of the other historical financial information.

3. Recognizing the importance of effective two-way communication in an audit of financial statements, this SA provides an overarching framework for the auditor's communication with those charged with governance, and identifies some specific matters to be communicated with them. Additional matters to be communicated, which complement the requirements of this SA, are identified in other SAs (see Appendix 1). In addition, SA 2651 establishes specific requirements regarding the communication of significant deficiencies in internal control the auditor has identified during the audit to those charged with governance. Further matters, not required by this or other SAs, may be required to be communicated by law or regulation, by agreement with the entity, or by additional requirements applicable to the engagement, for example, the standards of a national professional accountancy body. Nothing in this SA precludes the auditor from communicating any other matters to those charged with governance. (Ref: Para.A33–A36)

The Role of Communication

4. This SA focuses primarily on communications from the auditor to those charged with governance. Nevertheless, effective two-way communication is important in assisting:
   (a) The auditor and those charged with governance in understanding matters related to the audit in context, and in developing a constructive working relationship. This relationship is developed while maintaining the auditor's independence and objectivity;
   (b) The auditor in obtaining from those charged with governance information relevant to the audit. For example, those charged with governance may assist the auditor in understanding the entity and its environment, in identifying appropriate sources of audit evidence, and in providing information about specific transactions or events; and
   (c) Those charged with governance in fulfilling their responsibility to oversee the financial reporting process, thereby reducing the risks of material misstatement of the financial statements.

5. Although the auditor is responsible for communicating matters required by this SA, management also has a responsibility to communicate matters of governance interest to those charged with governance. Communication by the auditor does not relieve management of this responsibility.

Similarly, communication by management with those charged with governance of matters that the auditor is required to communicate does not relieve the auditor of the responsibility to also communicate them. Communication of these matters by management may, however, affect the form or timing of the auditor's communication with those charged with governance.

6. Clear communication of specific matters required to be communicated by SAs is an integral part of every audit. SAs do not, however, require the auditor to perform procedures specifically to identify any other matters to communicate with those charged with governance.

7. Law or regulation may restrict the auditor's communication of certain matters with those charged with governance. For example, laws or regulations may specifically prohibit a communication, or other action, that might prejudice an investigation by an appropriate authority into an actual, or suspected, illegal act. In some circumstances, potential conflicts between the auditor's obligations of confidentiality and obligations to communicate may be complex. In such cases, the auditor may consider obtaining legal advice.

Effective Date

8. This SA is effective for audits of financial statements for periods beginning on or after April 1, 2017.

Objectives

9. The objectives of the auditor are:
   (a) To communicate clearly with those charged with governance the responsibilities of the auditor in relation to the financial statement audit, and an overview of the planned scope and timing of the audit;
   (b) To obtain from those charged with governance information relevant to the audit;
   (c) To provide those charged with governance with timely observations arising from the audit that are significant and relevant to their responsibility to oversee the financial reporting process; and
   (d) To promote effective two-way communication between the auditor and those charged with governance.

Definitions

10. For purposes of the SAs, the following terms have the meanings attributed below:
   (a) Those charged with governance– The person(s) or organization(s) (e.g., a corporate trustee) with responsibility for overseeing the strategic direction of the entity and obligations related to the accountability of the entity. This includes overseeing the financial reporting process. For some entities, those charged with governance may include management personnel, for example, executive members of a governance board of a

private or public sector entity, or an owner-manager. For discussion of the diversity of governance structures, see paragraphs A1–A8.

(b) Management– The person(s) with executive responsibility for the conduct of the entity's operations. For some entities, management includes some or all of those charged with governance, for example, executive members of a governance board, or an owner-manager.

Requirements

Those Charged with Governance

11. The auditor shall determine the appropriate person(s) within the entity's governance structure with whom to communicate. (Ref: Para. A1–A4)

Communication with a Subgroup of Those Charged with Governance

12. If the auditor communicates with a subgroup of those charged with governance, for example, an audit committee, or an individual, the auditor shall determine whether the auditor also needs to communicate with the governing body. (*Ref: Para.A5–A7*)

When All of Those Charged with Governance Are Involved in Managing the Entity

13. In some cases, all of those charged with governance are involved in managing the entity, for example, a small business where a single owner manages the entity and no one else has a governance role. In these cases, if matters required by this SA are communicated with person(s) with management responsibilities, and those person(s) also have governance responsibilities, the matters need not be communicated again with those same person(s) in their governance role. These matters are noted in paragraph 16(c). The auditor shall nonetheless be satisfied that communication with person(s) with management responsibilities adequately informs all of those with whom the auditor would otherwise communicate in their governance capacity. (Ref: Para.A8)

Matters to Be Communicated

The Auditor's Responsibilities in Relation to the Financial Statement Audit

14. The auditor shall communicate with those charged with governance the responsibilities of the auditor in relation to the financial statement audit, including that:

(a) The auditor is responsible for forming and expressing an opinion on the financial statements that have been prepared by management with the oversight of those charged with governance; and

(b) The audit of the financial statements does not relieve management or those charged with governance of their responsibilities. (Ref: Para. A9–A10)

Planned Scope and Timing of the Audit

15. The auditor shall communicate with those charged with governance an overview of the planned scope and timing of the audit, which includes communicating about the significant risks identified by the auditor. (Ref: Para.A11–A16)

Significant Findings from the Audit

16. The auditor shall communicate with those charged with governance: (Ref: Para.A17–A18)
    (a) The auditor's views about significant qualitative aspects of the entity's accounting practices, including accounting policies, accounting estimates and financial statement disclosures. When applicable, the auditor shall explain to those charged with governance why the auditor considers a significant accounting practice, that is acceptable under the applicable financial reporting framework, not to be most appropriate to the particular circumstances of the entity; (Ref: Para.A19–A20)
    (b) Significant difficulties, if any, encountered during the audit; (Ref: Para.A21)
    (c) Unless all of those charged with governance are involved in managing the entity:
        (i) Significant matters arising during the audit that were discussed, or subject to correspondence, with management; and (Ref: Para.A22)
        (ii) Written representations the auditor is requesting;
    (d) Circumstances that affect the form and content of the auditor's report, if any; and (Ref: Para.A23–A25)

    Any other significant matters arising during the audit that, in the auditor's professional judgment, are relevant to the oversight of the financial reporting process. (Ref: Para. A26–A28)

Auditor Independence

17. In the case of listed entities, the auditor shall communicate with those charged with governance:
    (a) A statement that the engagement team and others in the firm as appropriate, the firm and, when applicable, network firms have complied with relevant ethical requirements regarding independence; and
        (i) All relationships and other matters between the firm, network firms, and the entity that, in the auditor's professional judgment, may reasonably be thought to bear on independence. This shall include total fees charged during the period covered by the financial statements for audit and non-audit services provided by the firm and network firms to the entity and components controlled by the entity. These fees shall be allocated to

categories that are appropriate to assist those charged with governance in assessing the effect of services on the independence of the auditor; and

(ii) The related safeguards that have been applied to eliminate identified threats to independence or reduce them to an acceptable level. (Ref: Para.A29–A32)

The Communication Process

Establishing the Communication Process

18. The auditor shall communicate with those charged with governance the form, timing and expected general content of communications. (Ref: Para.A37–A45)

Forms of Communication

19. The auditor shall communicate in writing with those charged with governance regarding significant findings from the audit if, in the auditor's professional judgment, oral communication would not be adequate. Written communications need not include all matters that arose during the course of the audit. (Ref: Para. A46–A48)

20. The auditor shall communicate in writing with those charged with governance regarding auditor independence when required by paragraph17.

Timing of Communications

21. The auditor shall communicate with those charged with governance on a timely basis. (Ref: Para. A49–A50)

Adequacy of the Communication Process

22. The auditor shall evaluate whether the two-way communication between the auditor and those charged with governance has been adequate for the purpose of the audit. If it has not, the auditor shall evaluate the effect, if any, on the auditor's assessment of the risks of material misstatement and ability to obtain sufficient appropriate audit evidence, and shall take appropriate action. (Ref: Para.A51–A53)

Documentation

23. Where matters required by this SA to be communicated are communicated orally, the auditor shall include them in the audit documentation, and when and to whom they were communicated. Where matters have been communicated in writing, the auditor shall retain a copy of the communication as part of the audit documentation. (*Ref: Para.A54*)

STANDARD ON AUDITING (SA) 265: COMMUNICATING DEFICIENCIES IN INTERNAL CONTROL TO THOSE CHARGED WITH GOVERNANCE AND MANAGEMENT

Introduction

Scope of this SA

1. This Standard on Auditing (SA) deals with the auditor's responsibility to communicate appropriately to those charged with governance and management deficiencies in internal control24 that the auditor has identified in an audit of financial statements. This SA does not impose additional responsibilities on the auditor regarding obtaining an understanding of internal control and designing and performing tests of controls over and above the requirements of SA 315 and SA 330. SA 260 establishes further requirements and provides guidance regarding the auditor's responsibility to communicate with those charged with governance in relation to the audit.
2. The auditor is required to obtain an understanding of internal control relevant to the audit when identifying and assessing the risks of material misstatement27. In making those risk assessments, the auditor considers internal control in order to design audit procedures that are appropriate in the circumstances, but not for the purpose of expressing an opinion on the effectiveness of internal control. The auditor may identify deficiencies in internal control not only during this risk assessment process but also at any other stage of the audit. This SA specifies which identified deficiencies the auditor is required to communicate to those charged with governance and management.
3. Nothing in this SA precludes the auditor from communicating to those charged with governance and management other internal control matters that the auditor has identified during the audit.

Effective Date

4. This SA is effective for audits of financial statements for periods beginning on or after April 1, 2010.

Objective

The objective of the auditor is to communicate appropriately to those charged with governance and management deficiencies in internal control that the auditor has identified during the audit and that, in the auditor's professional judgment, are of sufficient importance to merit their respective attentions.

Definitions

5. For purposes of the SAs, the following terms have the meanings attributed below:

    (a) Deficiency in internal control – This exists when:

(i) A control is designed, implemented or operated in such a way that it is unable to prevent, or detect and correct, misstatements in the financial statements on a timely basis; or

(ii) A control necessary to prevent, or detect and correct, misstatements in the financial statements on a timely basis is missing.

(b) Significant deficiency in internal control – A deficiency or combination of deficiencies in internal control that, in the auditor's professional judgment, is of sufficient importance to merit the attention of those charged with governance. (*Ref: Para.A5*)

Requirements

6. The auditor shall determine whether, on the basis of the audit work performed, the auditor has identified one or more deficiencies in internal control. (*Ref: Para.A1-A4*)

7. If the auditor has identified one or more deficiencies in internal control, the auditor shall determine, on the basis of the audit work performed, whether, individually or in combination, they constitute significant deficiencies. (*Ref: Para.A5-A11)*

8. The auditor shall communicate in writing significant deficiencies in internal control identified during the audit to those charged with governance on a timely basis. (*Ref: Para. A12- A18, A27*)

9. The auditor shall also communicate to management at an appropriate level of responsibility on a timely basis: (*Ref: Para. A19, A27*)

   (a) In writing, significant deficiencies in internal control that the auditor has communicated or intends to communicate to those charged with governance, unless it would be inappropriate to communicate directly to management in the circumstances; and (*Ref: Para. A14, A20-A21*)

   (b) Other deficiencies in internal control identified during the audit that have not been communicated to management by other parties and that, in the auditor's professional judgment, are of sufficient importance to merit management's attention. (*Ref: Para. A22-A26*)

10. The auditor shall include in the written communication of significant deficiencies in internal control:

   (a) A description of the deficiencies and an explanation of their potential effects; and (*Ref: Para.A28*)

   (b) Sufficient information to enable those charged with governance and management to understand the context of the communication. In particular, the auditor shall explain that: (*Ref: Para.A29-A30*)

      (i) The purpose of the audit was for the auditor to express an opinion on the financial statements;

      (ii) The audit included consideration of internal control relevant to the preparation of the financial statements in order to design audit procedures that are appropriate in the circumstances, but not for the purpose of expressing an opinion on the effectiveness of internal control; and

The matters being reported are limited to those deficiencies that the auditor has identified during the audit and that the auditor has concluded are of sufficient importance to merit being reported to those charged with governance.

STANDARD ON AUDITING (SA) 299: RESPONSIBILITY OF JOINT AUDITORS

Introduction

1. The practice of appointing more than one auditor to conduct the audit of large entities is in vogue these days. Such auditors, known as joint auditors, conduct the audit jointly and report on the financial statements of the entity. This Standard deals with the professional responsibilities which the auditors undertake in accepting such appointments as joint auditors. The Standard does not deal with the relationship between a principal auditor who is appointed to report on the financial statements of an entity and another auditor who is appointed to report on the financial statements of one or more divisions or branches included in the financial statements of the entity, e.g., the relationship between a company auditor appointed under section 224 of the Companies Act, 1956 and a branch auditor appointed under section 228 of the said Act.

Division of Work

2. Where joint auditors are appointed, they should, by mutual discussion, divide the audit work among themselves. The division of work would usually be in terms of audit of identifiable units or specified areas. In some cases, due to the nature of the business of the entity under audit, such a division of work may not be possible. In such situations, the division of work may be with reference to items of assets or liabilities or income or expenditure or with reference to periods of time. Certain areas of work, owing to their importance or owing to the nature of the work involved, would often not be divided and would be covered by all the joint auditors.
3. The division of work among joint auditors as well as the areas of work to be covered by all of them should be adequately documented and preferably communicated to the entity.

Coordination

4. Where, in the course of his work, a joint auditor comes across matters which are relevant to the areas of responsibility of other joint auditors and which deserve their attention, or which require disclosure or require discussion with, or application of judgment by, other joint auditors, he should communicate the same to all the other joint auditors in writing. This should be done by the submission of a report or note prior to the finalization of the audit.

Relationship among Joint Auditors

5. In respect of audit work divided among the joint auditors, each joint auditor is responsible only for the work allocated to him, whether or not he has prepared a separate report on the work performed by him. On the other hand, all the joint auditors are jointly and severally responsible–
   (a) in respect of the audit work which is not divided among the joint auditors and is carried out by all of them;
   (b) in respect of decisions taken by all the joint auditors concerning the nature, timing or extent of the audit procedures to be performed by any of the joint auditors. It may, however, be clarified that all the joint auditors are responsible only in respect of the appropriateness of the decisions concerning the nature, timing or extent of the audit procedures agreed upon among them; proper execution of these audit procedures is the separate and specific responsibility of the joint auditor concerned;
   (c) in respect of matters which are brought to the notice of the joint auditors by any one of them and on which there is an agreement among the joint auditors;
   (d) for examining that the financial statements of the entity comply with the disclosure requirements of the relevant statute; and
   (e) For ensuring that the audit report complies with the requirements of the relevant statute.
6. If any matters of the nature referred to in paragraph 4 above are brought to the attention of the entity or other joint auditors by an auditor after the audit report has been submitted, the other joint auditors would not be responsible for those matters.
7. Subject to paragraph 5(b) above, it is the responsibility of each joint auditor to determine the nature, timing and extent of audit procedures to be applied in relation to the area of work allocated to him. The issues such as appropriateness of using test checks or sampling should be decided by each joint auditor in relation to his own area of work. This responsibility is not shared by the other joint auditors. Thus, it is the separate and specific responsibility of each joint auditor to study and evaluate the prevailing system of internal control relating to the work allocated to him. Similarly, the nature, timing and extent of the enquiries to be made in the course of audit as well as the other audit procedures to be applied are solely the responsibility of each joint auditor.
8. In the case of audit of a large entity with several branches, including those required to be audited by branch auditors, the branch audit reports/returns may be required to be scrutinized by different joint auditors in accordance with the allocation of work. In such cases, it is the specific and separate responsibility of each joint auditor to review the audit reports/returns of the divisions/branches allocated to him and to ensure that they are properly incorporated into the accounts of the entity. In respect of the branches which do not fall within any divisions or zones which are separately assigned to the various joint auditors, they may agree among themselves as regards the division of work relating to

the review of such branch returns. It is also the separate and specific responsibility of each joint auditor to exercise his judgment with regard to the necessity of visiting such divisions/branches in respect of which the work is allocated to him.

9. A significant part of the audit work involves obtaining and evaluating information and explanations from the management. This responsibility is shared by all the joint auditors unless they agree upon a specific pattern of distribution of this responsibility. In cases where specific divisions, zones or units are allocated to different joint auditors, it is the separate and specific responsibility of each joint auditor to obtain appropriate information and explanations from the management in respect of such divisions/zones/units and to evaluate the information and explanations so obtained by him.

10. Each joint auditor is entitled to assume that the other joint auditors have carried out their part of the audit work in accordance with the generally accepted audit procedures.2 It is not necessary for a joint auditor to review the work performed by other joint auditors or perform any tests in order to ascertain whether the work has actually been performed in such a manner. Each joint auditor is entitled to rely upon the other joint auditors for bringing to his notice any departure from generally accepted accounting principles or any material error noticed in the course of the audit.

11. Where separate financial statements of a division/branch are audited by one of the joint auditors, the other joint auditors are entitled to proceed on the basis that such financial statements comply with all the legal and professional requirements regarding the disclosures to be made and present a true and fair view of the state of affairs and of the working results of the division/branch concerned, subject to such observations as may be communicated by the joint auditor concerned.

Reporting Responsibilities

12. Normally, the joint auditors are able to arrive at an agreed report. However, where the joint auditors are in disagreement with regard to any matters to be covered by the report, each one of them should express his own opinion through a separate report. A joint auditor is not bound by the views of the majority of the joint auditors regarding matters to be covered in the report and should express his opinion in a separate report in case of a disagreement.

Effective Date

13. This Standard on Auditing becomes operative in respect of all audits relating to accounting periods beginning on or after April 1, 1996

STANDARD ON AUDITING (SA) 300: PLANNING AN AUDIT OF FINANCIAL STATEMENTS

Introduction

Scope of this SA

1. This Standard on Auditing (SA) deals with the auditor's responsibility to plan an audit of financial statements. This SA is framed in the context of recurring audits. Additional considerations in initial audit engagements are separately identified. (Ref: Para.A1-A4)

Effective Date

2. This SA is effective for audits of financial statements for periods beginning on or after 1st April l2008.

Objective

3. The objective of the auditors to plan the audit so that it will be performed in an effective manner.

Requirements

Involvement of Key Engagement Team Members

4. The engagement partner and other key members of the engagement team shall be involved in planning the audit, including planning and participating in the discussion among engagement team members. (Ref: Para.A5)

Preliminary Engagement Activities

5. The auditor shall under take the following activities at the beginning of the current audit engagement:
   (a) Performing procedures required by SA 2201, "Quality Control for an Audit of Financial Statements" regarding the continuance of the client relationship and the specific audit engagement;
   (b) Evaluating compliance with ethical requirements, including independence, as required by SA2202; and
   (c) Establishing an understanding of the terms of the engagement, as required by SA 2103. (Ref: Para. A6- A8)

Planning Activities

6. *The auditor shall establish an overall audit strategy that sets the scope, timing and direction of the audit, and that guides the development of the audit plan.*
7. *In establishing the overall audit strategy, the auditor shall:*
   (a) Identify the characteristics of the engagement that define its scope; Ascertain the reporting objectives of the engagement to plan the timing of the audit and the nature of the communications required;
   (b) Consider the factors that, in the auditor's professional judgment, are significant in directing the engagement team's efforts;

(c) *Consider the results of preliminary engagement activities and, where applicable, whether knowledge gained on other engagements performed by the engagement partner for the entity is relevant; and*

(d) *Ascertain the nature, timing and extent of resources necessary to perform the engagement. (Ref: Para. A9-A12)*

8. *The auditor shall develop an audit plan that shall include a description of:*

   (a) *The nature, timing and extent of planned risk assessment procedures, as determined under SA 315 "Identifying and Assessing the Risks of Material Misstatement through Understanding the Entity and Its Environment".*

   (b) *The nature, timing and extent of planned further audit procedures at the assertion level, as determined under SA 330 "The Auditor's Responses to Assessed Risks".*

   (c) *Other planned audit procedures that are required to be carried out so that the engagement complies with SAs. (Ref: Para.A13)*

9. *The auditor shall update and change the overall audit strategy and the audit plan as necessary during the course of the audit. (Ref: Para.A14)*

10. *The auditor shall plan the nature, timing and extent of direction and supervision of engagement team members and the review of their work. (Ref: Para.A15-A16)*

Documentation

11. The auditor shall document:

    (a) *The overall audit strategy;*

    (b) *The audit plan; and*

    (c) *Any significant changes made during the audit engagement to the overall audit strategy or the audit plan, and the reasons for such changes. (Ref: Para.A17-A20)*

Additional Considerations in Initial Audit Engagements

12. *The auditor shall undertake the following activities prior to starting an initial audit:*

    (a) *Performing procedures required by SA 220 regarding the acceptance of the client relationship and the specific audit engagement4;and*

    (b) Communicating with the predecessor auditor, where there has been a change of auditors, in compliance with relevant ethical requirements. (Ref: Para.A21)

STANDARD ON AUDITING (SA) 315: IDENTIFYING AND ASSESSING THE RISK OF MATERIAL MISSTATEMENT THROUGH UNDERSTANDING THE ENTITY AND ITS ENVIRONMENT

Introduction

Scope of this SA

1. This Standard on Auditing (SA) deals with the auditor's responsibility to identify and assess the risks of material misstatement in the financial statements, through understanding the entity and its environment, including the entity's internal control.

Effective Date

2. This SA is effective for audits of financial statements for periods beginning on or after April1, 2008.

Objective

3. The objective of the auditor is to identify and assess the risks of material misstatement, whether due to fraud or error, at the financial statement and assertion levels, through understanding the entity and its environment, including the entity's internal control, thereby providing a basis for designing and implementing responses to the assessed risks of material misstatement. This will help the auditor to reduce the risk of material misstatement to an acceptably low level.

Definitions

4. For purposes of the SAs, the following terms have the meanings attributed below:

   (a) Assertions – Representations by management, explicit or otherwise, that are embodied in the financial statements, as used by the auditor to consider the different types of potential misstatements that may occur.

   (b) Business risk – A risk resulting from significant conditions, events, circumstances, actions or inactions that could adversely affect an entity's ability to achieve its objectives and execute its strategies, or from the setting of inappropriate objectives and strategies.

   (c) Internal control – The process designed, implemented and maintained by those charged with governance, management and other personnel to provide reasonable assurance about the achievement of an entity's objectives with regard to reliability of financial reporting, effectiveness and efficiency of operations, safeguarding of assets, and compliance with applicable laws and regulations. The term "controls" refers to any aspects of one or more of the components of internal control.

   (d) Risk assessment procedures – The audit procedures performed to obtain an understanding of the entity and its environment, including the entity's internal control, to identify and assess the risks of material misstatement, whether due to fraud or error, at the financial statement and assertion levels.

(e) Significant risk – An identified and assessed risk of material misstatement that, in the auditor's judgment, requires special audit consideration.

Requirements

Risk Assessment Procedures and Related Activities

5. The auditor shall perform risk assessment procedures to provide a basis for the identification and assessment of risks of material misstatement at the financial statement and assertion levels. Risk assessment procedures by themselves, however, do not provide sufficient appropriate audit evidence on which to base the audit opinion. (Ref: Para.A1-A5)

6. The risk assessment procedures shall include the following:

   (a) Inquiries of management and of others within the entity who in the auditor's judgment may have information that is likely to assist in identifying risks of material misstatement due to fraud or error. (Ref: Para.A6)

   (b) Analytical procedures. (Ref: Para.A7-A10)

   (c) Observation and inspection. (Ref: Para.A11)

7. The auditor shall consider whether information obtained from the auditor's client acceptance or continuance process is relevant to identifying risks of material misstatement.

8. Where the engagement partner has performed other engagements for the entity, the engagement partner shall consider whether information obtained is relevant to identifying risks of material misstatement.

9. When the auditor intends to use information obtained from the auditor's previous experience with the entity and from audit procedures performed in previous audits, the auditor shall determine whether changes have occurred since the previous audit that may affect its relevance to the current audit. (Ref: Para. A12- A13)

10. The engagement partner and other key engagement team members shall discuss the susceptibility of the entity's financial statements to material misstatement, and the application of the applicable financial reporting framework to the entity's facts and circumstances. The engagement partner shall determine which matters are to be communicated to engagement team members not involved in the discussion. (Ref: Para. A14-A16)

The Required Understanding of the Entity and Its Environment, Including the Entity's Internal Control

The Entity and Its Environment

11. The auditor shall obtain an understanding of the following:
    (a) Relevant industry, regulatory, and other external factors including the applicable financial reporting framework. (Ref: Para.A17-A22)
    (b) The nature of the entity, including:
        (i) its operations;
        (ii) its ownership and governance structures;
        (iii) the types of investments that the entity is making and plans to make, including investments in special-purpose entities; and
        (iv) The way that the entity is structured and how it is financed; to enable the auditor to understand the classes of transactions, account balances, and disclosures to be expected in the financial statements. (Ref: Para.A23-A27)
    (c) The entity's selection and application of accounting policies, including the reasons for changes thereto. The auditor shall evaluate whether the entity's accounting policies are appropriate for its business and consistent with the applicable financial reporting framework and accounting policies used in the relevant industry. (Ref: Para.A28)
    (d) The entity's objectives and strategies, and those related business risks that may result in risks of material misstatement. (Ref: Para.A29-A35)
    (e) The measurement and review of the entity's financial performance. (Ref: Para.A36-A41)

The Entity's Internal Control

12. The auditor shall obtain an understanding of internal control relevant to the audit. Although most controls relevant to the audit are likely to relate to financial reporting, not all controls that relate to financial reporting are relevant to the audit. It is a matter of the auditor's professional judgment whether a control, individually or in combination with others, is relevant to the audit. (Ref: Para.A42-A65)

Nature and Extent of the Understanding of Relevant Controls

13. When obtaining an understanding of controls that are relevant to the audit, the auditor shall evaluate the design of those controls and determine whether they have been implemented, by performing procedures in addition to inquiry of the entity's personnel. (Ref: Para.A66-A68)

Components of Internal Control

Control environment

14. The auditor shall obtain an understanding of the control environment. As part of obtaining this understanding, the auditor shall evaluate whether:
    (a) Management, with the oversight of those charged with governance, has created and maintained a culture of honesty and ethical behavior; and
    (b) The strengths in the control environment elements collectively provide an appropriate foundation for the other components of internal control, and whether those other components are not undermined by deficiencies in the control environment. (Ref: Para.A69-A78)

The entity's risk assessment process

15. The auditor shall obtain an understanding of whether the entity has a processor:
    (a) Identifying business risks relevant to financial reporting objectives;
    (b) Estimating the significance of the risks;
    (c) Assessing the likelihood of their occurrence; and
    (d) Deciding about actions to address those risks. (Ref: Para.A79)
16. If the entity has established such a process (referred to hereafter as the 'entity's risk assessment process'), the auditor shall obtain an understanding of it, and the results thereof. Where the auditor identifies risks of material misstatement that management failed to identify, the auditor shall evaluate whether there was an underlying risk of a kind that the auditor expects would have been identified by the entity's risk assessment process. If there is such a risk, the auditor shall obtain an understanding of why that process failed to identify it, and evaluate whether the process is appropriate to its circumstances or determine if there is a significant deficiency in internal control with regard to the entity's risk assessment process.
17. If the entity has not established such a process or has an ad hoc process, the auditor shall discuss with management whether business risks relevant to financial reporting objectives have been identified and how they have been addressed. The auditor shall evaluate whether the absence of a documented risk assessment process is appropriate in the circumstances, or determine whether it represents a significant deficiency in internal control. (Ref: Para. A80)

    The information system, including the related business processes, relevant to financial reporting, and communication.

18. The auditor shall obtain an understanding of the information system, including the related business processes, relevant to financial reporting, including the following areas:
    (a) The classes of transactions in the entity's operations that are significant to the financial statements;
    (b) The procedures, within both information technology (IT) and manual systems, by which those transactions are initiated, recorded, processed,

corrected as necessary, transferred to the general ledger and reported in the financial statements;

(c) The related accounting records, supporting information and specific accounts in the financial statements that are used to initiate, record, process and report transactions; this includes the correction of incorrect information and how information is transferred to the general ledger. The records may be in either manual or electronic form;

(d) How the information system captures events and conditions, other than transactions, that are significant to the financial statements;

(e) The financial reporting process used to prepare the entity's financial statements, including significant accounting estimates and disclosures;

(f) Controls surrounding journal entries, including non-standard journal entries used to record non- recurring, unusual transactions or adjustments. (Ref: Para.A81-A85)

19. The auditor shall obtain an understanding of how the entity communicates financial reporting roles and responsibilities and significant matters relating to financial reporting, including:

(a) Communications between management and those charged with governance; and

(b) External communications, such as those with regulatory authorities. (Ref: Para. A86-A87) Control activities relevant to the audit

20. The auditor shall obtain an understanding of control activities relevant to the audit, being those the auditor judges it necessary to understand in order to assess the risks of material misstatement at the assertion level and design further audit procedures responsive to assessed risks. An audit requires an understanding of only those control activities related to significant class of transactions, account balance, and disclosure in the financial statements and the assertions which the auditor finds relevant in his risk assessment process. (Ref: Para.A88-A94)

21. In understanding the entity's control activities, the auditor shall obtain an understanding of how the entity has responded to risks arising from IT. (Ref: Para.A95-A97)

Monitoring of controls

22. The auditor shall obtain an understanding of the major activities that the entity uses to monitor internal control over financial reporting, including those related to those control activities relevant to the audit, and how the entity initiates remedial actions to deficiencies in its controls. (Ref: Para.A98-A100)

23. If the entity has an internal audit function, the auditor shall obtain an understanding of the following in order to determine whether the internal audit function is likely to be relevant to the audit:

(a) The nature of the internal audit function's responsibilities and how the internal audit function fits in the entity's organizational structure; and

(b) The activities performed, or to be performed, by the internal audit function. (Ref: Para.A101-A103)

24. The auditor shall obtain an understanding of the sources of the information used in the entity's monitoring activities, and the basis upon which management considers the information to be sufficiently reliable for the purpose. (Ref: Para.A104)

Identifying and Assessing the Risks of Material Misstatement

25. The auditor shall identify and assess the risks of material misstatement at:

    (a) the financial statement level; and (Ref: Para.A105-A108)

    (b) The assertion level for classes of transactions, account balances, and disclosures; (Ref: Para. A109- A113)

    To provide a basis for designing and performing further audit procedures.

26. For this purpose, the auditor shall:

    (a) Identify risks throughout the process of obtaining an understanding of the entity and its environment, including relevant controls that relate to the risks, and by considering the classes of transactions, account balances, and disclosures in the financial statements; (Ref: Para.A114-A115)

    (b) Assess the identified risks, and evaluate whether they relate more pervasively to the financial statements as a whole and potentially affect many assertions;

    (c) Relate the identified risks to what can go wrong at the assertion level, taking account of relevant controls that the auditor intends to test; and (Ref: Para.A116-A118)

    (d) Consider the likelihood of misstatement, including the possibility of multiple misstatements, and whether the potential misstatement is of a magnitude that could result in a material misstatement.

Risks that Require Special Audit Consideration

27. As part of the risk assessment as described in paragraph 25, the auditor shall determine whether any of the risks identified are, in the auditor's judgment, a significant risk. In exercising this judgment, the auditor shall exclude the effects of identified controls related to the risk.

28. In exercising judgment as to which risks are significant risks, the auditor shall consider at least the following:

    (a) Whether the risk is a risk of fraud;

    (b) Whether the risk is related to recent significant economic, accounting, or other developments like changes in regulatory environment, etc., and, therefore, requires specific attention;

    (c) The complexity of transactions;

    (d) Whether the risk involves significant transactions with related parties;

(e) The degree of subjectivity in the measurement of financial information related to the risk, especially those measurements involving a wide range of measurement uncertainty; and

(f) Whether the risk involves significant transactions that are outside the normal course of business for the entity, or that otherwise appear to be unusual. (Ref: Para.A119-A123)

29. When the auditor has determined that a significant risk exists, the auditor shall obtain an understanding of the entity's controls, including control activities, relevant to that risk. (Ref: Para.A124-A126)

Risks for Which Substantive Procedures Alone Do Not Provide Sufficient Appropriate Audit Evidence

30. In respect of some risks, the auditor may judge that it is not possible or practicable to obtain sufficient appropriate audit evidence only from substantive procedures. Such risks may relate to the inaccurate or incomplete recording of routine and significant classes of transactions or account balances, the characteristics of which often permit highly automated processing with little or no manual intervention. In such cases, the entity's controls over such risks are relevant to the audit and the auditor shall obtain an understanding of them. (Ref: Para.A127-A129)

Revision of Risk Assessment

31. The auditor's assessment of the risks of material misstatement at the assertion level may change during the course of the audit as additional audit evidence is obtained. In circumstances where the auditor obtains audit evidence from performing further audit procedures, or if new information is obtained, either of which is inconsistent with the audit evidence on which the auditor originally based the assessment, the auditor shall revise the assessment and modify the further planned audit procedures accordingly. (Ref: Para. A130)

Documentation

32. The auditor shall document:

(a) The discussion among the engagement team where required by paragraph 10, and the significant decisions reached;

(b) Key elements of the understanding obtained regarding each of the aspects of the entity and its environment specified in paragraph 11 and of each of the internal control components specified in paragraphs 14-24; the sources of information from which the understanding was obtained; and the risk assessment procedures performed;

(c) The identified and assessed risks of material misstatement at the financial statement level and at the assertion level as required by paragraph 25; and

The risks identified, and related controls about which the auditor has obtained an understanding, as a result of the requirements in paragraphs 27-30. (Ref: Para.A131-A134)

STANDARD ON AUDITING (SA) 320: MATERIALITY IN PLANNING AND PERFORMING AN AUDIT

Introduction

Scope of this SA

1. This Standard on Auditing (SA) deals with the auditor's responsibility to apply the concept of materiality in planning and performing an audit of financial statements. SA 450, explains how materiality is applied in evaluating the effect of identified misstatements on the audit and of uncorrected misstatements, if any, on the financial statements.

Materiality in the Context of an Audit

2. Financial reporting frameworks often discuss the concept of materiality in the context of the preparation and presentation of financial statements. Although financial reporting frameworks may discuss materiality in different terms, they generally explain that:
   - Misstatements, including omissions, are considered to be material if they, individually or in the aggregate, could reasonably be expected to influence the economic decisions of users taken on the basis of the financial statements;
   - Judgments about materiality are made in the light of surrounding circumstances, and are affected by the size or nature of a misstatement, or a combination of both; and
   - Judgments about matters that are material to users of the financial statements are based on a consideration of the common financial information needs of users as a group.2 The possible effect of misstatements on specific individual users, whose needs may vary widely, is not considered.
3. Such a discussion, if present in the applicable financial reporting framework, provides a frame of reference to the auditor in determining materiality for the audit. If the applicable financial reporting framework does not include a discussion of the concept of materiality, the characteristics referred to in paragraph 2 provides the auditor with such a frame of reference.
4. **The auditor's determination of materiality is a matter of professional judgment, and is affected by the auditor's perception of the financial information needs of users of the financial statements. In this context, it is reasonable for the auditor to assume that users:**

(a) Have a reasonable knowledge of business and economic activities and accounting and a willingness to study the information in the financial statements with reasonable diligence;

(b) Understand that financial statements are prepared, presented and audited to levels of materiality;

(c) Recognize the uncertainties inherent in the measurement of amounts based on the use of estimates, judgment and the consideration of future events; and

(d) Make reasonable economic decisions on the basis of the information in the financial statements.

5. The concept of materiality is applied by the auditor both in planning and performing the audit, and in evaluating the effect of identified misstatements on the audit and of uncorrected misstatements, if any, on the financial statements and in forming the opinion in the auditor's report. (Ref: Para.A1)

6. In planning the audit, the auditor makes judgments about the size of misstatements that will be considered material. These judgments provide a basis for:

(a) Determining the nature, timing and extent of risk assessment procedures;

(b) Identifying and assessing the risks of material misstatement; and

(c) Determining the nature, timing and extent of further audit procedures.

The materiality determined when planning the audit does not necessarily establish an amount below which uncorrected misstatements, individually or in aggregate, will always be evaluated as immaterial. The circumstances related to some misstatements may cause the auditor to evaluate them as material even if they are below materiality. Although, it is not practicable to design audit procedures to detect misstatements that could be material solely because of their nature, the auditor considers not only the size but also the nature of uncorrected misstatements, and the particular circumstances of their occurrence, when evaluating their effect on the financial statements.3

Effective Date

7. This SA is effective for audits of financial statements for periods beginning on or after April 1, 2010.

Objective

8. The objective of the auditor is to apply the concept of materiality appropriately in planning and performing the audit.

Definition

9. For purposes of the SAs, performance materiality means the amount or amounts set by the auditor at less than materiality for the financial statements as a whole to reduce to an appropriately low level the probability that the aggregate of uncorrected and undetected misstatements exceeds materiality for

the financial statements as a whole. If applicable, performance materiality also refers to the amount or amounts set by the auditor at less than the materiality level or levels for particular classes of transactions, account balances or disclosures.

Requirements

Determining Materiality and Performance Materiality when Planning the Audit

10. When establishing the overall audit strategy, the auditor shall determine materiality for the financial statements as a whole. If, in the specific circumstances of the entity, there is one or more particular classes of transactions, account balances or disclosures for which misstatements of lesser amounts than the materiality for the financial statements as a whole could reasonably be expected to influence the economic decisions of users taken on the basis of the financial statements, the auditor shall also determine the materiality level or levels to be applied to those particular classes of transactions, account balances or disclosures. (Ref:Para. A2-A11).

11. The auditor shall determine performance materiality for purposes of assessing the risks of material misstatement and determining the nature, timing and extent of further audit procedures. (Ref: Para. A12).

Revision as the Audit Progresses

12. The auditor shall revise materiality for the financial statements as a whole (and, if applicable, the materiality level or levels for particular classes of transactions, account balances or disclosures) in the event of becoming aware of information during the audit that would have caused the auditor to have determined a different amount (or amounts) initially. (Ref: Para.A13)

13. If the auditor concludes that a lower materiality for the financial statements as a whole (and, if applicable, materiality level or levels for particular classes of transactions, account balances or disclosures) than that initially determined is appropriate, the auditor shall determine whether it is necessary to revise performance materiality, and whether the nature, timing and extent of the further audit procedures remain appropriate.

Documentation

14. The audit documentation shall include the following amounts and the factors considered in their determination:
    (a) Materiality for the financial statements as a whole (see paragraph10);
    (b) If applicable, the materiality level or levels for particular classes of transactions, account balances or disclosures (see paragraph10);
    (c) Performance materiality (see paragraph 11); and
    (d) Any revision of (a)-(c) as the audit progressed (see paragraphs12-13)

STANDARD ON AUDITING (SA) 330: THE AUDITOR'S RESPONSES TO ASSESSED RISKS

Introduction

Scope of this SA

1. This Standard on Auditing (SA) deals with the auditor's responsibility to design and implement responses to the risks of material misstatement identified and assessed by the auditor in accordance with SA 315, "Identifying and Assessing Risks of Material Misstatement Through Understanding the Entity and Its Environment" in a financial statement audit.

Effective Date

2. This SA is effective for audits of financial statements for periods beginning on or after April1, 2008.

Objective

3. The objective of the auditor is to obtain sufficient appropriate audit evidence about the assessed risks of material misstatement, through designing and implementing appropriate responses to those risks.

Definitions

4. For purposes of the SAs, the following terms have the meanings attributed below:
   (a) Substantive procedure–An audit procedure designed to detect material misstatements at the assertion level. Substantive procedures comprise:
      (i) Tests of details (of classes of transactions, account balances, and disclosures), and
      (ii) Substantive analytical procedures.
   (b) Test of controls – An audit procedure designed to evaluate the operating effectiveness of controls in preventing, or detecting and correcting, material misstatements at the assertion level.

Requirements Overall Responses

5. The auditor shall design and implement overall responses to address the assessed risks of material misstatement at the financial statement level. (Ref: Para.A1-A3)

Audit Procedures Responsive to the Assessed Risks of Material Misstatement at the Assertion Level

6. The auditor shall design and perform further audit procedures whose nature, timing and extent are based on and are responsive to the assessed risks of material misstatement at the assertion level. (Ref: Para.A4-A8)

7. **In designing the further audit procedures to be performed, the auditor shall:**

   (a) Consider the reasons for the assessment given to the risk of material misstatement at the assertion level for each class of transactions, account balance, and disclosure, including:

      (i) The likelihood of material misstatement due to the particular characteristics of the relevant class of transactions, account balance, or disclosure (i.e., the inherent risk); and

      (ii) Whether the risk assessment takes into account the relevant controls (i.e., the control risk), thereby requiring the auditor to obtain audit evidence to determine whether the controls are operating effectively (i.e., the auditor intends to rely on the operating effectiveness of controls in determining the nature, timing and extent of substantive procedures); and (Ref: Para.A9-A18)

   (b) Obtain more persuasive audit evidence the higher the auditor's assessment of risk. (Ref:Para.A19)

Tests of Controls

8. The auditor shall design and perform tests of controls to obtain sufficient appropriate audit evidence as to the operating effectiveness of relevant controls when:

   (a) The auditor's assessment of risks of material misstatement at the assertion level includes an expectation that the controls are operating effectively (i.e.,the auditor intends to rely on the operating effectiveness of controls in determining the nature, timing and extent of substantive procedures); or

   (b) Substantive procedures alone cannot provide sufficient appropriate audit evidence at the assertion level. (Ref: Para.A20-A24)

9. In designing and performing tests of controls, the auditor shall obtain more persuasive audit evidence the greater the reliance the auditor places on the effectiveness of a control. (Ref: Para.A25)

Nature and Extent of Tests of Controls

10. In designing and performing tests of controls, the auditor shall:

   (a) Perform other audit procedures in combination with inquiry to obtain audit evidence about the operating effectiveness of the controls, including:

      (i) How the controls were applied at relevant times during the period under audit.

      (ii) The consistency with which they were applied.

      (iii) By whom or by what means they were applied. (Ref: Para.A26-A29)

(b) Determine whether the controls to be tested depend upon other controls (indirect controls), and if so, whether it is necessary to obtain audit evidence supporting the effective operation of those indirect controls. (Ref: Para.A30-A31)

Timing of Tests of Controls

11. The auditor shall test controls for the particular time, or throughout the period, for which the auditor intends to rely on those controls, subject to paragraphs 12 and 15 below, in order to provide an appropriate basis for the auditor's intended reliance. (Ref: Para.A32)

Using audit evidence obtained during an interim period

12. When the auditor obtains audit evidence about the operating effectiveness of controls during an interim period, the auditor shall:
   (a) Obtain audit evidence about significant changes to those controls subsequent to the interim period; and
   (b) Determine the additional audit evidence to be obtained for the remaining period. (Ref: Para.A33-A34)

Using audit evidence obtained in previous audits

13. In determining whether it is appropriate to use audit evidence about the operating effectiveness of controls obtained in previous audits, and, if so, the length of the time period that may elapse before retesting a control, the auditor shall consider the following:
   (a) The effectiveness of other elements of internal control, including the control environment, the entity's monitoring of controls, and the entity's risk assessment process;
   (b) The risks arising from the characteristics of the control, including whether it is manual or automated;
   (c) The effectiveness of general IT-controls;
   (d) The effectiveness of the control and its application by the entity, including the nature and extent of deviations in the application of the control noted in previous audits, and whether there have been personnel changes that significantly affect the application of the control;
   (e) Whether the lack of a change in a particular control poses a risk due to changing circumstances; and
   (f) The risks of material misstatement and the extent of reliance on the control. (Ref:Para.A35)

14. If the auditor plans to use audit evidence from a previous audit about the operating effectiveness of specific controls, the auditor shall establish the continuing relevance of that evidence by obtaining audit evidence about whether significant changes in those controls have occurred subsequent to the previous audit. The auditor shall obtain this evidence by performing inquiry combined with observation or inspection, to confirm the understanding of those specific controls, and:

(a) If there have been changes that affect the continuing relevance of the audit evidence from the previous audit, the auditor shall test the controls in the current audit. (Ref: Para.A36)

(b) If there have not been such changes, the auditor shall test the controls at least once in every third audit, and shall test some controls each audit to avoid the possibility of testing all the controls on which the auditor intends to rely in a single audit period with no testing of controls in the subsequent two audit periods. (Ref: Para.A37-A39)

Controls over significant risks

15. When the auditor plans to rely on controls over a risk the auditor has determined to be a significant risk, the auditor shall test those controls in the current period.

Evaluating the Operating Effectiveness of Controls

16. When evaluating the operating effectiveness of relevant controls, the auditor shall evaluate whether misstatements that have been detected by substantive procedures indicate that controls are not operating effectively. The absence of misstatements detected by substantive procedures, however, does not provide audit evidence that controls related to the assertion being tested are effective. (Ref: Para.A40)

17. When deviations from controls upon which the audit or intends to rely are detected, the auditor shall make specific inquiries to understand these matters and their potential consequences, and shall determine whether:

    (a) The tests of controls that have been performed provide an appropriate basis for reliance on the controls;

    (b) Additional tests of controls are necessary; or

    (c) The potential risks of misstatement need to be addressed using substantive procedures. (Ref: Para. A41)

Substantive Procedures

18. Irrespective of the assessed risks of material misstatement, the auditor shall design and perform substantive procedures for each material class of transactions, account balance, and disclosure. (Ref: Para. A42-A47)

19. The auditor shall consider whether external confirmation procedures are to be performed as substantive audit procedures. (Ref: Para.A48-A51)

Substantive Procedures Related to the Financial Statement Closing Process

20. The auditor's substantive procedures shall include the following audit procedures related to the financial statement closing process:

    (a) Agreeing or reconciling the financial statements with the underlying accounting records; and

    (b) Examining material journal entries and other adjustments made during the course of preparing the financial statements. (Ref: Para.A52)

Substantive Procedures Responsive to Significant Risks

21. When the auditor has determined that an assessed risk of material misstatement at the assertion level is a significant risk, the auditor shall perform substantive procedures that are specifically responsive to that risk. When the approach to a significant risk consists only of substantive procedures, those procedures shall include tests of details. (Ref: Para.A53)

Timing of Substantive Procedures (Ref: Para.A54)

22. When substantive procedures are performed at an interim date, the auditor shall cover the remaining period by performing:

    (a) substantive procedures, combined with tests of controls for the intervening period; or

    (b) if the auditor determines that it is sufficient, further substantive procedures only;

    That provides a reasonable basis for extending the audit conclusions from the interim date to the period end. (Ref: Para. A55-A57)

23. If misstatements that the auditor did not expect when assessing the risks of material misstatement are detected at an interim date, the auditor shall evaluate whether the related assessment of risk and the planned nature, timing, or extent of substantive procedures covering the remaining period need to be modified. (Ref: Para.A58)

Adequacy of Presentation and Disclosure

24. The auditor shall perform audit procedures to evaluate whether the overall presentation of the financial statements, including the related disclosures, is in accordance with the applicable financial reporting framework. (Ref: Para.A59)

Evaluating the Sufficiency and Appropriateness of Audit Evidence

25. Based on the audit procedures performed and the audit evidence obtained, the auditor shall evaluate before the conclusion of the audit whether the assessments of the risks of material misstatement at the assertion level remain appropriate. (Ref: Para.A60-A61)

26. The auditor shall conclude whether sufficient appropriate audit evidence has been obtained. In forming an opinion, the auditor shall consider all relevant audit evidence, regardless of whether it appears to corroborate or to contradict the assertions in the financial statements. (Ref: Para.A62)

27. If the auditor has not obtained sufficient appropriate audit evidence as to a material financial statement assertion, the auditor shall attempt to obtain further audit evidence. If the auditor is unable to obtain sufficient appropriate audit evidence, the auditor shall express a qualified opinion or a disclaimer of opinion.

Documentation

28. The auditor shall document:

(a) The overall responses to address the assessed risks of material misstatement at the financial statement level, and the nature, timing and extent of the further audit procedures performed;

(b) The linkage of those procedures with the assessed risks at the assertion level; and

(c) The results of the audit procedures, including the conclusions where these are not otherwise clear. (Ref: Para.A63)

29. If the auditor plans to use audit evidences about the operating effectiveness of controls obtained in previous audits, the auditor shall document the conclusions reached about relying on such controls that were tested in a previous audit.

30. The auditors' documentation shall demonstrate that the financial statements agree or reconcile with the underlying accounting records

STANDARD ON AUDITING (SA) 402: AUDIT CONSIDERATIONS RELATING TO AN ENTITY USING SERVICE ORGANIZATION

Introduction

Scope of this SA

1. This Standard on Auditing (SA) deals with the user auditor's responsibility to obtain sufficient appropriate audit evidence when a user entity uses the services of one or more service organisations. Specifically, it expands on how the user auditor applies SA 315 and SA 330 in obtaining an understanding of the user entity, including internal control relevant to the audit, sufficient to identify and assess the risks of material misstatement and in designing and performing further audit procedures responsive to those risks.

2. Many entities outsource aspects of their business to organizations that provide services ranging from performing a specific task under the direction of an entity to replacing an entity's entire business units or functions, such as the tax compliance function. Many of the services provided by such organizations are integral to the entity's business operations; however, not all those services are relevant to the audit.

3. Services provided by a service organisation are relevant to the audit of a user entity's financial statements when those services, and the controls over them, are part of the user entity's information system, including related business processes, relevant to financial reporting. Although most controls at the service organisation are likely to relate to financial reporting, there may be other controls that may also be relevant to the audit, such as controls over the safeguarding of assets. A service organization's services are part of a user entity's information system, including related business processes, relevant to financial reporting if these services affect any of the following:

(a) The classes of transactions in the user entity's operations that are significant to the user entity's financial statements;

(b) The procedures, within both information technology (IT) and manual systems, by which the user entity's transactions are initiated, recorded, processed, corrected as necessary, transferred to the general ledger and reported in the financial statements;

(c) The related accounting records, either in electronic or manual form, supporting information and specific accounts in the user entity's financial statements that are used to initiate, record, process and report the user entity's transactions; this includes the correction of incorrect information and how information is transferred to the general ledger;

(d) How the user entity's information system captures events and conditions, other than transactions, that are significant to the financial statements;

(e) The financial reporting process used to prepare the user entity's financial statements, including significant accounting estimates and disclosures; and

(f) Controls surrounding journal entries, including non-standard journal entries used to record non- recurring, unusual transactions or adjustments.

4. The nature and extent of work to be performed by the user auditor regarding the services provided by a service organization depend on the nature and significance of those services to the user entity and the relevance of those services to the audit.

5. This SA does not apply to services provided by financial institutions that are limited to processing, for an entity's account held at the financial institution, transactions that are specifically authorized by the entity, such as the processing of checking account transactions by a bank or the processing of securities transactions by a broker. In addition, this SA does not apply to the audit of transactions arising from proprietary financial interests in other entities, such as partnerships, corporations and joint ventures, when proprietary interests are accounted for and reported to interest holders.

Effective Date

6. This SA is effective for audits of financial statements for periods beginning on or after April1, 2010.

Objectives

7. The objectives of the user auditor, when the user entity uses the services of a service organization, are:

(a) To obtain an understanding of the nature and significance of the services provided by the service organization and their effect on the user entity's internal control relevant to the audit, sufficient to identify and assess the risks of material misstatement; and

(b) To design and perform audit procedures responsive to those risks.

Definitions

8. For purposes of the SAs, the following terms have the meanings attributed below:

   (a) *Complementary user entity controls* – Controls that the service organization assumes, in the design of its service, will be implemented by user entities, and which, if necessary to achieve control objectives, are identified in the description of its system.

   (b) *Report on the description and design of controls at a service organization (referred to in this SA as a Type 1 report)* – A report that comprises:

      (i) A description, prepared by management of the service organization, of the service organization's system, control objectives and related controls that have been designed and implemented as at a specified date; and

      (ii) A report by the service auditor with the objective of conveying reasonable assurance that includes the service auditor's opinion on the description of the service organization's system, control objectives and related controls and the suitability of the design of the controls to achieve the specified control objectives.

   (c) Report on the description, design, and operating effectiveness of controls at a service organization (referred to in this SA as a Type 2 report) – A report that comprises:

      (i) A description, prepared by management of the service organization, of the service organization's system, control objectives and related controls, their design and implementation as at a specified date or throughout a specified period and, in some cases, their operating effectiveness throughout a specified period; and

      (ii) A report by the service auditor with the objective of conveying reasonable assurance that includes:

         (a) The service auditor's opinion on the description of the service organization's system, control objectives and related controls, the suitability of the design of the controls to achieve the specified control objectives, and the operating effectiveness of the controls; and

         (b) A description of the service auditor's tests of the controls and the results thereof.

   (d) *Service auditor* – An auditor who, at the request of the service organization, provides an assurance report on the controls of a service organisation.

   (e) *Service organization* – A third-party organization (or segment of a third-party organization) that provides services to user entities that are part of those entities' information systems relevant to financial reporting.

(f) *Service organization's system* – The policies and procedures designed, implemented and maintained by the service organization to provide user entities with the services covered by the service auditor's report.

(g) *Subservice organization* – A service organization used by another service organization to perform some of the services provided to user entities that are part of those user entities' information systems relevant to financial reporting.

(h) *User auditor* – An auditor who audits and reports on the financial statements of a user entity.

(i) *User entity* – An entity that uses a service organization and whose financial statements are being audited.

Requirements

Obtaining an Understanding of the Services Provided by a Service Organization, Including Internal Control

9. When obtaining an understanding of the user entity in accordance with SA 315,3 the user auditor shall obtain an understanding of how a user entity uses the services of a service organization in the user entity's operations, including: (Ref: Para.A1-A2)

   (a) The nature of the services provided by the service organization and the significance of those services to the user entity, including the effect thereof on the user entity's internal control; (Ref: Para.A3-A5)

   (b) The nature and materiality of the transactions processed or accounts or financial reporting processes affected by the service organization; (Ref: Para.A6)

   (c) The degree of interaction between the activities of the service organization and those of the user entity; and (Ref: Para.A7)

   (d) The nature of the relationship between the user entity and the service organization, including the relevant contractual terms for the activities under taken by the service organisation. (Ref: Para.A8-A11)

10. When obtaining an understanding of internal control relevant to the audit in accordance with SA 315,4 the user auditor shall evaluate the design and implementation of relevant controls at the user entity that relate to the services provided by the service organization, including those that are applied to the transactions processed by the service organization. (Ref: Para.A12-A14)

11. The user auditor shall determine whether a sufficient understanding of the nature and significance of the services provided by the service organization and their effect on the user entity's internal control relevant to the audit has been obtained to provide a basis for the identification and assessment of risks of material misstatement.

12. If the user auditor is unable to obtain a sufficient understanding from the user entity, the user auditor shall obtain that understanding from one or more of the following procedures: (Ref: Para. A15-A20)

(a) Obtaining a Type 1 or Type 2 report, if available;

(b) Contacting the service organization, through the user entity, to obtain specific information;

(c) Visiting the service organization and performing procedures that will provide the necessary information about the relevant controls at the service organisation; or

(d) Using another auditor to perform procedures that will provide the necessary information about the relevant controls at the service organisation.

Using a Type 1 or Type 2 Report to Support the User Auditor's Understanding of the Service Organisation

13. In determining the sufficiency and appropriateness of the audit evidence provided by a Type 1 or Type 2 report, the user auditor shall be satisfied as to: (Ref: Para.A21)

    (a) The service auditor's professional competence (except where the service auditor is a member of the Institute of Chartered Accountants of India) and independence from the service organisation; and

    (b) The adequacy of the standards under which the Type 1 or Type 2 report was issued.

14. If the user auditor plans to use a Type 1 or Type 2 report as audit evidence to support the user auditor's understanding about the design and implementation of controls at the service organization, the user auditor shall: (Ref: Para.A22-A23)

    (a) Evaluate whether the description and design of controls at the service organization is at a date or for a period that is appropriate for the user auditor's purposes;

    (b) Evaluate the sufficiency and appropriateness of the evidence provided by the report for the understanding of the user entity's internal control relevant to the audit; and

    (c) Determine whether complementary user entity controls identified by the service organization are relevant to the user entity and, if so, obtain an understanding of whether the user entity has designed and implemented such controls.

Responding to the Assessed Risks of Material Misstatement

15. In responding to assessed risks in accordance with SA 330, the user auditor shall: (Ref: Para. A24- A28)

    (a) Determine whether sufficient appropriate audit evidence concerning the relevant financial statement assertions is available from records held at the user entity; and, if not,

(b) Perform further audit procedures to obtain sufficient appropriate audit evidence or use another auditor to perform those procedures at the service organisation on the user auditor's behalf.

Tests of Controls

16. When the user auditor's risk assessment includes an expectation that controls at the service organization are operating effectively, the user auditor shall obtain audit evidence about the operating effectiveness of those controls from one or more of the following procedures: (Ref: Para. A29-A30)

(a) Obtaining a Type 2 report, if available;

(b) Performing appropriate tests of controls at the service organisation; or

(c) Using another auditor to perform tests of controls at the service organization on behalf of the user auditor.

Using a Type 2 Report as Audit Evidence that Controls at the Service Organization Are Operating Effectively

17. If, in accordance with paragraph 16(a), the user auditor plans to use a Type 2 report as audit evidence that controls at the service organization are operating effectively, the user auditor shall determine whether the service auditor's report provides sufficient appropriate audit evidence about the effectiveness of the controls to support the user auditor's risk assessment by:(Ref:Para.A31-A39)

(a) Evaluating whether the description, design and operating effectiveness of controls at the service organisation is at a date or for a period that is appropriate for the user auditor's purposes;

(b) Determining whether complementary user entity controls identified by the service organization are relevant to the user entity and, if so, obtaining an understanding of whether the user entity has designed and implemented such controls and, if so, testing their operating effectiveness;

(c) Evaluating the adequacy of the time period covered by the tests of controls and the time elapsed since the performance of the tests of controls; and

(d) Evaluating whether the tests of controls performed by the service auditor and the results thereof, as described in the service auditor's report, are relevant to the assertions in the user entity's financial statements and provide sufficient appropriate audit evidence to support the user auditor's risk assessment.

Type 1 and Type 2 Reports that Exclude the Services of a Subservice Organization

18. If the user auditor plans to use a Type 1 or a Type 2 report that excludes the services provided by a subservice organization and those services are relevant to the audit of the user entity's financial statements, the user auditor shall apply the requirements of this SA with respect to the services provided by the subservice organization. (Ref: Para.A40)

Fraud, Non-Compliance with Laws and Regulations and Uncorrected Misstatements in Relation to Activities at the Service Organisation

19. The user auditor shall inquire of management of the user entity whether the service organisation has reported to the user entity, or whether the user entity is otherwise aware of, any fraud, non - compliance with laws and regulations or uncorrected misstatements affecting the financial statements of the user entity. The user auditor shall evaluate how such matters affect the nature, timing and extent of the user auditor's further audit procedures, including the effect on the user auditor's conclusions and user auditor's report. (Ref: Para.A41)

Reporting by the User Auditor

20. The user auditor shall modify the opinion in the user auditor's report in accordance with SA 7055 if the user auditor is unable to obtain sufficient appropriate audit evidence regarding the services provided by the service organisation relevant to the audit of the user entity's financial statements. (Ref: Para.A42)
21. The user auditor shall not refer to the work of a service auditor in the user auditor's report containing an unmodified opinion unless required by law or regulation to do so. If such reference is required by law or regulation, the user auditor's report shall indicate that the reference does not diminish the user auditor's responsibility for the audit opinion. (Ref: Para.A43)
22. If reference to the work of a service auditor is relevant to an understanding of a modification to the user auditor's opinion, the user auditor's report shall indicate that such reference does not diminish the user auditor's responsibility for that opinion. (Ref: Para.A44)

STANDARD ON AUDITING (SA) 450: EVALUATION OF MISSTATEMENTS IDENTIFIED DURING THE AUDIT

Introduction

Scope of this SA

1. This Standard on Auditing (SA) deals with the auditor's responsibility to evaluate the effect of identified misstatements on the audit and of uncorrected misstatements, if any, on the financial statements. SA 700 (Revised) deals with the auditor's responsibility, in forming an opinion on the financial statements, to conclude whether reasonable assurance has been obtained about whether the financial statements as a whole are free from material misstatement. The auditor's conclusion required by SA 700 (Revised) takes into account the auditor's evaluation of uncorrected misstatements, if any, on the financial statements, in accordance with this SA. SA 3202 deals with the auditor's responsibility to apply the concept of materiality appropriately in planning and performing an audit of financial statements.

Effective Date

2. This SA is effective for audits of financial statements for periods beginning on or after April1, 2010.

Objective

3. The objective of the auditor is to evaluate:
   (a) The effect of identified misstatements on the audit; and
   (b) The effect of uncorrected misstatements, if any, on the financial statements.

Definitions

4. For purposes of the SAs, the following terms have the meanings attributed below:
   (a) Misstatement – A difference between the amounts, classification, presentation, or disclosure of a reported financial statement item and the amount, classification, presentation, or disclosure that is required for the item to be in accordance with the applicable financial reporting framework. Misstatements can arise from error or fraud. (Ref: Para.A1)
   (b) When the auditor expresses an opinion on whether the financial statements give a true and fair view or are presented fairly, in all material respects, misstatements also include those adjustments of amounts, classifications, presentation, or disclosures that, in the auditor's judgment, are necessary for the financial statements to give a true and fair view or present fairly, in all material respects. Uncorrected misstatements – Misstatements that the auditor has accumulated during the audit and that have not been corrected.

Requirements

Accumulation of Identified Misstatements

5. The auditor shall accumulate misstatements identified during the audit, other than those that are clearly trivial. (Ref: Para.A2-A3)

Consideration of Identified Misstatements as the Audit Progresses

6. The auditor shall determine whether the overall audit strategy and audit planned to be revised if:
   (a) The nature of identified misstatements and the circumstances of their occurrence indicate that other misstatements may exist that, when aggregated with misstatements accumulated during the audit, could be material; or (Ref: Para.A4)
   (b) The aggregate of misstatements accumulated during the audit approaches materiality determined in accordance with SA 320. (Ref: Para.A5)

7. If, at the auditor's request, management has examined a class of transactions, account balance or disclosure and corrected misstatements that were detected, the auditor shall perform additional audit procedures to determine whether misstatements remain. (Ref: Para.A6)

Communication and Correction of Misstatements

8. The auditor shall communicate on a timely basis all misstatements accumulated during the audit with the appropriate level of management, unless prohibited by law or regulation 3.The auditor shall request management to correct those misstatements .(Ref: Para.A7-A9)

9. If management refuses to correct some or all of the misstatements communicated by the auditor, the auditor shall obtain an understanding of management's reasons for not making the correct ions and shall take that understanding into account when evaluating whether the financial statements as a whole are free from material misstatement.(Ref:Para.A10)

Evaluating the Effect of Uncorrected Misstatements

10. Prior to evaluating the effect of uncorrected misstatements, the auditor shall reassess materiality determined in accordance with SA 320 to confirm whether it remains appropriate in the context of the entity's actual financial results. (Ref: Para.A11-A12)

11. The auditor shall determine whether uncorrected misstatements are material, individually or in aggregate. In making this determination, the auditor shall consider:

    (a) The size and nature of the misstatements, both in relation to particular classes of transactions, account balances or disclosures and the financial statements as a whole, and the particular circumstances of their occurrence; and (Ref: Para. A13-A17, A19-A20)

    (b) The effect of uncorrected misstatements related to prior periods on the relevant classes of transactions, account balances or disclosures, and the financial statements as a whole. (Ref: Para.A18)

Communication with Those Charged with Governance

12. The auditor shall communicate with those charged with governance4 uncorrected misstatements and the effect that they, individually or in aggregate, may have on the opinion in the auditor's report, unless prohibited by law or regulation. The auditor's communication shall identify material uncorrected misstatements individually. The auditor shall request that uncorrected misstatements be corrected. (Ref: Para.A21-A23)

13. The auditor shall also communicate with those charged with governance the effect of uncorrected misstatements related to prior periods on the relevant classes of transactions, account balances or disclosures, and the financial statements as a whole.

Written Representation

14. The auditor shall request a written representation from management and, where appropriate, those charged with governance whether they believe the effects of uncorrected misstatements are immaterial, individually and in aggregate, to the financial statements as a whole. A summary of such items shall be included in or attached to the written representation. (Ref: Para.A24)

Documentation

15. The audit documentation shall include: (Ref: Para.A25)

   (a) The amount below which misstatements would be regarded as clearly trivial (paragraph 5);

   (b) All misstatements accumulated during the audit and whether they have been corrected (paragraphs 5, 8 and 12);and

The auditor's conclusion as to whether uncorrected misstatements are material, individually or in aggregate, and the basis for that conclusion. (paragraph11)

STANDARD ON AUDITING (SA) 500: AUDIT EVIDENCE

Introduction

Scope of this SA

1. This Standard on Auditing (SA) explains what constitutes audit evidence in an audit of financial statements, and deals with the auditor's responsibility to design and perform audit procedures to obtain sufficient appropriate audit evidence to be able to draw reasonable conclusions on which to base the auditor's opinion.
2. This SA is applicable to all the audit evidence obtained during the course of the audit. Other SAs deal with specific aspects of the audit (for example, SA 3151), the audit evidence to be obtained in relation to a particular topic (for example, SA 5702), specific procedures to obtain audit evidence (for example, SA 5203), and the evaluation of whether sufficient appropriate audit evidence has been obtained (SA 200 and SA3304).

Effective Date

3. This SA is effective for audits of financial statements for periods beginning on or after April1, 2009.

Objective

4. The objective of the auditor is to design and perform audit procedures in such a way as to enable the auditor to obtain sufficient appropriate audit evidence to be able to draw reasonable conclusions on which to base the auditor's opinion.

Definitions

5. For purposes of the SAs, the following terms have the meanings attributed below:

   (a) Accounting records – The records of initial accounting entries and supporting records, such as checks and records of electronic fund transfers; invoices; contracts; the general and subsidiary ledgers, journal entries and other adjustments to the financial statements that are not reflected in journal entries; and records such as work sheets and spreadsheets supporting cost allocations, computations, reconciliations and disclosures.

   (b) Appropriateness (of audit evidence) – The measure of the quality of audit evidence; that is, its relevance and its reliability in providing support for the conclusions on which the auditor's opinion is based.

   (c) Audit evidence – Information used by the auditor in arriving at the conclusions on which the auditor's opinion is based. Audit evidence includes both information contained in the accounting records underlying the financial statements and other information.

   (d) Management's expert – An individual or organisation possessing expertise in a field other than accounting or auditing, whose work in that field is used by the entity to assist the entity in preparing the financial statements.

   (e) Sufficiency (of audit evidence) – The measure of the quantity of audit evidence. The quantity of the audit evidence needed is affected by the auditor's assessment of the risks of material misstatement and also by the quality of such audit evidence.

Requirements

Sufficient Appropriate Audit Evidence

6. The auditor shall design and perform audit procedures that are appropriate in the circumstances for the purpose of obtaining sufficient appropriate audit evidence. *(Ref: Para.A1-A25)*

Information to Be Used as Audit Evidence

7. When designing and performing audit procedures, the auditor shall consider the relevance and reliability of the information to be used as audit evidence. *(Ref: Para.A26-A33)*

8. When information to be used as audit evidence has been prepared using the work of a management's expert, the auditor shall, to the extent necessary, having regard to the significance of that expert's work for the auditor's purposes,: *(Ref: Para.A34-A36)*

   (a) Evaluate the competence, capabilities and objectivity of that expert; *(Ref: Para.A37-A43)*

(b) Obtain an understanding of the work of that expert; and *(Ref: Para.A44-A47)*

(c) Evaluate the appropriateness of that expert's work as audit evidence for the relevant assertion. *(Ref: Para.A48)*

9. When using information produced by the entity, the auditor shall evaluate whether the information is sufficiently reliable for the auditor's purposes, including as necessary in the circumstances:

(a) Obtaining audit evidence about the accuracy and completeness of the information; and *(Ref: Para. A49-A50)*

(b) Evaluating whether the information is sufficiently precise and detailed for the auditor's purposes. *(Ref: Para.A51)*

Selecting Items for Testing to Obtain Audit Evidence

10. When designing tests of controls and tests of details, the auditor shall determine means of selecting items for testing that are effective in meeting the purpose of the audit procedure. *(Ref: Para.A52-A56)*

Inconsistency in, or Doubts over Reliability of, Audit Evidence

11. If:

(a) audit evidence obtained from one source is inconsistent with that obtained from another; or

(b) the auditor has doubts over the reliability of information to be used as audit evidence,

The auditor shall determine what modifications or additions to audit procedures are necessary to resolve the matter, and shall consider the effect of the matter, if any, on other aspects of the audit. (Ref: Para. A57*)*

STANDARD ON AUDITING (SA) 501: AUDIT EVIDENCE—SPECIFIC CONSIDERATIONS FOR SELECTED ITEMS

Introduction

Scope of this SA

1. This Standard on Auditing (SA) deals with specific considerations by the auditor in obtaining sufficient appropriate audit evidence in accordance with SA 330, SA 500 and other relevant SAs, with respect to certain aspects of inventory, litigation and claims involving the entity, and segment information in an audit of financial statements.

Effective Date

2. This SA is effective for audits of financial statements for periods beginning on or after April1, 2010.

Objective

3. The objective of the auditor is to obtain sufficient appropriate audit evidence regarding the:
   (a) Existence and condition of inventory;
   (b) Completeness of litigation and claims involving the entity; and
   (c) Presentation and disclosure of segment in formation in accordance with the applicable financial reporting framework.

Requirements Inventory

4. When inventory is material to the financial statements, the auditor shall obtain sufficient appropriate audit evidence regarding the existence and condition of inventory by:
   (a) Attendance at physical inventory counting, unless impracticable, to: (Ref: Para. A1-A3)
      (i) Evaluate management's instructions and procedures for recording and controlling the results of the entity's physical inventory counting; (Ref: Para.A4)
      (ii) Observe the performance of management's count procedures; (Ref:Para.A5)
      (iii) Inspect the inventory; and (Ref: Para.A6)
      (iv) Perform test counts; and (Ref: Para.A7-A8)
   (b) Performing audit procedures over the entity's final inventory records to determine whether they accurately reflect actual inventory count results
5. If physical inventory counting is conducted at a date other than the date of the financial statements, the auditor shall, in addition to the procedures required by paragraph 4, perform audit procedures to obtain audit evidence about whether changes in inventory between the count date and the date of the financial statements are properly recorded. (Ref: Para. A9-A11)
6. If the auditor is unable to attend physical inventory counting due to unforeseen circumstances, the auditor shall make or observe some physical counts on an alternative date, and perform audit procedures on intervening transactions.
7. If attendance at physical inventory counting is impracticable, the auditor shall perform alternative audit procedures to obtain sufficient appropriate audit evidence regarding the existence and condition of inventory. If it is not possible to do so, the auditor shall modify the opinion in the auditor's report in accordance with SA 7053. (Ref: Para.A12-A14)
8. When inventory under the custody and control of a third party is material to the financial statements, the auditor shall obtain sufficient appropriate audit evidence regarding the existence and condition of that inventory by performing one or both of the following:
   (a) Request confirmation from the third party as to the quantities and condition of inventory held on behalf of the entity. (Ref: Para.A15)

(b) Perform in section or other audit procedures appropriate in the circumstances. (Ref: Para.A16)

Litigation and Claims

9. The auditor shall design and perform audit procedures in order to identify litigation and claims involving the entity which may give rise to a risk of material misstatement, including: (Ref: Para. A17-A19)

   (a) Inquiry of management and, where applicable, others within the entity, including in-house legal counsel;

   (b) Reviewing minutes of meetings of those charged with governance and correspondence between the entity and its external legal counsel; and

   (c) Reviewing legal expense accounts. (Ref: Para.A20)

10. If the auditor assesses a risk of material misstatement regarding litigation or claims that have been identified, or when audit procedures performed indicate that other material litigation or claims may exist, the auditor shall, in addition to the procedures required by other SAs, seek direct communication with the entity's external legal counsel. The auditor shall do so through a letter of inquiry, prepared by management and sent by the auditor, requesting the entity's external legal counsel to communicate directly with the auditor. If law, regulation or the respective legal professional body prohibits the entity's external legal counsel from communicating directly with the auditor, the auditor shall perform alternative audit procedures. (Ref: Para. A21-A25)

11. If:

   (a) management refuses to give the auditor permission to communicate or meet with the entity's external legal counsel, or the entity's external legal counsel refuses to respond appropriately to the letter of inquiry, or is prohibited from responding; and

   (b) the auditor is unable to obtain sufficient appropriate audit evidence by performing alternative audit procedures, the auditor shall modify the opinion in the auditor's report in accordance with SA 705.

Written Representations

12. The auditor shall request management and, where appropriate, those charged with governance to provide written representations that all known actual or possible litigation and claims whose effects should be considered when preparing the financial statements have been disclosed to the auditor and appropriately accounted for and disclosed in accordance with the applicable financial reporting framework.

Segment Information

13. The auditor shall obtain sufficient appropriate audit evidence regarding the presentation and disclosure of segment information in accordance with the applicable financial reporting framework by: (Ref: Para. A26)

(a) Obtaining an understanding of the methods used by management in determining segment information, and: (Ref: Para.A27)

  (i) Evaluating whether such methods are likely to result in disclosure in accordance with the applicable financial reporting framework; and

  (ii) Where appropriate, testing the application of such methods; and

(b) Performing analytical procedures or other audit procedures appropriate in the circumstances.

STANDARD ON AUDITING (SA) 505: EXTERNAL CONFIRMATIONS

Introduction

Scope of this SA

1. This standard on Auditing (SA) deals with the auditor's use of external confirmation procedures to obtain audit evidence in accordance with the requirements of SA 3301 and SA 5002. It does not address inquiries regarding litigation and claims. SA 5013 deals with obtaining sufficient appropriate audit evidence from such inquiries.

External Confirmation Procedures to Obtain Audit Evidence

2. SA 500 indicates that the reliability of audit evidence is influenced by its source and by its nature, and is dependent on the individual circumstances under which it is obtained4. That SA also includes the following generalisations applicable to audit evidence5:

   - Audit evidence is more reliable when it is obtained from independent sources outside the entity.
   - Audit evidence obtained directly by the auditor is more reliable than audit evidence obtained indirectly or by inference.
   - Audit evidence is more reliable when it exists in documentary form, whether paper, electronic or other medium.

   Accordingly, depending on the circumstances of the audit, audit evidence in the form of external confirmations received directly by the auditor from confirming parties may be more reliable than evidence generated internally by the entity. This SA is intended to assist the auditor in designing and performing external confirmations procedures to obtain relevant and reliable audit evidence.

3. Other SAs recognise the importance of external confirmations as audit evidence, for example:

   SA 330 discusses the auditor's responsibility to design and implement overall responses to address the assessed risks of material misstatement at the financial statement level, and to design and perform further audit procedures whose nature, timing and extent are based on, and are responsive to, the assessed risks of material misstatement at the assertion level6. In addition, SA330 requires that, irrespective of the assessed risks of material misstatement, the auditor designs and performs substantive procedures for each material class of transactions, account balance, and disclosure. The auditor is also required to consider whether external confirmation procedures are to be performed as substantive audit procedures.

- SA 330 requires that the auditor obtain more persuasive audit evidence the higher the auditor's assessment of risk8. To do this, the auditor may increase the quantity of the evidence or obtain evidence that is more relevant or reliable, or both. For example, the auditor may place more emphasis on obtaining evidence directly from third parties or obtaining corroborating evidence from a number of independent sources. SA 330 also indicates that external confirmation procedures may assist the auditor in obtaining audit evidence with the high level of reliability that the auditor requires to respond to significant risks of material misstatement, whether due to fraud or error9.
- SA 240 indicates that the auditor may design confirmation requests to obtain additional corroborative information as a response to address the assessed risks of material misstatement, whether due to fraud at the assertion level10.
- SA 500 indicates that corroborating information obtained from a source independent of the entity, such as external confirmations, may increase the assurance the auditor obtains from evidence existing within the accounting records or from the representations made by the management11.

Effective Date

4. This SA is effective for audit of financial statements for period beginning on or after April 1, 2010

Objective

5. The objective of the auditor, when using external confirmation procedures, is to design and perform such procedures to obtain relevant and reliable audit evidence.

Definitions

6. For purposes of the SAs, the following terms have the meanings attributed below:

   (a) External confirmation – Audit evidence obtained as a direct written response to the auditor from a third party (the confirming party), in paper form, or by electronic or other medium.

   (b) Positive confirmation request – A request that the confirming party respond directly to the auditor indicating whether the confirming party agrees or disagrees with the information in the request, or providing the requested information.

(c) Negative confirmation request – A request that the confirming party respond directly to the auditor only if the confirming party disagrees with the information provided in the request.

(d) Non-response – A failure of the confirming party to respond, or fully respond, to a positive confirmation request, or a confirmation request returned undelivered.

(e) Exception – A response that indicates a difference between information requested to be confirmed, or contained in the entity's records, and information provided by the confirming party.

Requirements

External Confirmation Procedures

7. When using external confirmation procedures, the auditor shall maintain control over external confirmation requests, including:

   (a) Determining the information to be confirmed or requested; (Ref: Para.A1)

   (b) Selecting the appropriate confirming party; (Ref: Para.A2)

   (c) Designing the confirmation requests, including determining that requests are properly addressed and contain return information for responses to be sent directly to the auditor; and (Ref: Para. A3-A6)

   (d) Sending the requests, including follow-up requests when applicable, to the confirming party. (Ref: Para. A7)

Management's Refusal to Allow the Auditor to Send a Confirmation Request

8. If management refuses to allow the auditor to send a confirmation request, the auditor shall:

   (a) Inquire as to management's reasons for the refusal, and seek audit evidence as to their validity and reasonableness; (Ref: Para.A8)

   (b) Evaluate the implications of management's refusal on the auditor's assessment of the relevant risks of material misstatement, including the risk of fraud, and on the nature, timing and extent of other audit procedures; and (Ref: Para.A9)

   (c) Perform alternative audit procedures designed to obtain relevant and reliable audit evidence. (Ref: Para.A10)

9. If the auditor concludes that management's refusal to allow the auditor to send a confirmation request is unreasonable, or the auditor is unable to obtain relevant and reliable audit evidence from alternative audit procedures, the auditor shall communicate with those charged with governance in accordance with SA 260. The auditor also shall determine the implications for the audit and the auditor's opinion in accordance with SA705.

Results of the External Confirmation Procedures

Reliability of Responses to Confirmation Requests

10. If the auditor identifies factors that give rise to doubts about the reliability of the response to a confirmation request, the auditor shall obtain further audit evidence to resolve those doubts. (Ref: Para. A11- A16)

11. If the auditor determines that a response to a confirmation request is not reliable, the auditor shall evaluate the implications on the assessment of the relevant risks of material misstatement, including the risk of fraud, and on the related nature, timing and extent of other audit procedures. (Ref: Para.A17)

Non-Responses

12. In the case of each non-response, the auditor shall perform alternative audit procedures to obtain relevant and reliable audit evidence. (Ref: ParaA18-A19)

    When a Response to a Positive Confirmation Request is Necessary to Obtain Sufficient Appropriate Audit Evidence

13. If the auditor has determined that a response to a positive confirmation request is necessary to obtain sufficient appropriate audit evidence, alternative audit procedures will not provide the audit evidence the auditor requires. If the auditor does not obtain such confirmation, the auditor shall determine the implications for the audit and the auditor's opinion in accordance with SA 705. (Ref: ParaA20)

Exceptions

14. The auditor shall investigate exceptions to determine whether or not they are indicative of misstatements. (Ref: Para.A21-A22)

Negative Confirmations

15. Negative confirmations provide less persuasive audit evidence than positive confirmations. Accordingly, the auditor shall not use negative confirmation requests as the sole substantive audit procedure to address an assessed risk of material misstatement at the assertion level unless all of the following are present: (Ref: Para.A23)

    (a) The auditor has assessed the risk of material misstatement as low and has obtained sufficient appropriate audit evidence regarding the operating effectiveness of controls relevant to the assertion;

    (b) The population of items subject to negative confirmation procedures comprises a large number of small, homogeneous, account balances, transactions or conditions;

    (c) A very low exception rate is expected ;and

    (d) The auditor is not aware of circumstances or conditions that would cause recipients of negative confirmation requests to disregard such requests.

Evaluating the Evidence Obtained

16. The auditor shall evaluate whether the results of the external confirmation procedures provide relevant and reliable audit evidence, or whether performing further audit procedures is necessary. (Ref: Para A24- A25)

STANDARD ON AUDITING (SA) 510: INITIAL AUDIT ENGAGEMENTS—OPENING BALANCES

Introduction

Scope of this SA

1. This Standard on Auditing (SA) deals with the auditor's responsibilities relating to opening balances when conducting an initial audit engagement. In addition to financial statement amounts, opening balances include matters requiring disclosure that existed at the beginning of the period, such as contingencies and commitments. When the financial statements include comparative financial information, the requirements and guidance in SA 7103 also apply. SA 300 includes additional requirements and guidance regarding activities prior to starting an initial audit..

Effective Date

2. This SA is effective for audits of financial statements for periods beginning on or after April 1, 2010.

Objective

3. In conducting an initial audit engagement, the objective of the auditor with respect to opening balances is to obtain sufficient appropriate audit evidence about whether:
   (a) Opening balances contain misstatements that materially affect the current period's financial statements; and
   (b) Appropriate accounting policies reflected in the opening balances have been consistently applied in the current period's financial statements, or changes thereto are properly accounted for and adequately presented and disclosed in accordance with the applicable financial reporting framework.

Definitions

4. For the purposes of the SAs, the following terms have the meanings attributed below:
   (a) Initial audit engagement – An engagement in which either:
      (i) The financial statements for the prior period were not audited; or
      (ii) The financial statements for the prior period were audited by a predecessor auditor.

(b) Opening balances – Those account balances that exist at the beginning of the period. Opening balances are based upon the closing balances of the prior period and reflect the effects of transactions and events of prior periods and accounting policies applied in the prior period. Opening balances also include matters requiring disclosure that existed at the beginning of the period, such as contingencies and commitments.

(c) Predecessor auditor – The auditor from a different audit firm, who audited the financial statements of an entity in the prior period and who has been replaced by the current auditor.

Requirements Audit Procedures *Opening Balances*

5. The auditor shall read the most recent financial statements, if any and the predecessor auditor's report thereon, if any, for information relevant to opening balances, including disclosures.

6. The auditor shall obtain sufficient appropriate audit evidence about whether the opening balances contain misstatements that materially affect the current period's financial statements by:

   (a) Determining whether the prior period's closing balances have been correctly brought forward to the current period or, when appropriate, any adjustments have been disclosed as prior period items in the current year's Statement of Profit and Loss3;

   (b) Determining whether the opening balances reflect the application of appropriate accounting policies; and

   (c) Performing one or more of the following: (Ref: Para.A1–A4)

      (i) Where the prior year financial statements were audited, perusing the copies of the audited financial statements including the other relevant documents relating to the prior period financial statements;

      (ii) Evaluating whether audit procedures performed in the current period provide evidence relevant to the opening balances; or

      (iii) Performing specific audit procedures to obtain evidence regarding the opening balances.

7. If the auditor obtains audit evidence that the opening balances contain misstatements that could materially affect the current period's financial statements, the auditor shall perform such additional audit procedures as are appropriate in the circumstances to determine the effect on the current period's financial statements. If the auditor concludes that such misstatements exist in the current period's financial statements, the auditor shall communicate the misstatements with the appropriate level of management and those charged with governance in accordance with SA450.

Consistency of Accounting Policies

8. The auditor shall obtain sufficient appropriate audit evidence about whether the accounting policies reflected in the opening balances have been consistently

applied in the current period's financial statements, and whether changes in the accounting policies have been properly accounted for and adequately presented and disclosed in accordance with the applicable financial reporting framework.

Relevant Information in the Predecessor Auditor's Report

9. If the prior period's financial statements were audited by a predecessor auditor and there was a modification to the opinion, the auditor shall evaluate the effect of the matter giving rise to the modification in assessing the risks of material misstatement in the current period's financial statements in accordance with SA 315.

Audit Conclusions and Reporting

Opening Balances

10. If the auditor is unable to obtain sufficient appropriate audit evidence regarding the opening balances, the auditor shall express a qualified opinion or a disclaimer of opinion, as appropriate, in accordance with SA 705. (Ref: Para. A5)

11. If the auditor concludes that the opening balances contain a misstatement that materially affects the current period's financial statements, and the effect of the misstatement is not properly accounted for or not adequately presented or disclosed, the auditor shall express a qualified opinion or an adverse opinion, as appropriate, in accordance with SA705.

Consistency of Accounting Policies

12. If the auditor concludes that:

    (a) the current period's accounting policies are not consistently applied in relation to opening balances in accordance with the applicable financial reporting framework; or

    (b) a change in accounting policies is not properly accounted for or not adequately presented or disclosed in accordance with the applicable financial reporting framework,

    The auditor shall express a qualified opinion or an adverse opinion as appropriate in accordance with SA 705.

Modification to the Opinion in the Predecessor Auditor's Report

13. If the predecessor auditor's opinion regarding the prior period's financial statements included a modification to the auditor's opinion that remains relevant and material to the current period's financial statements, the auditor shall modify the auditor's opinion on the current period's financial statements in accordance with SA 705 and SA 710. (Ref: Para.A6)

STANDARD ON AUDITING (SA) 520: ANALYTICAL PROCEDURES

Introduction

Scope of this SA

1. This Standard on Auditing (SA) deals with the auditor's use of analytical procedures as substantive procedures ("substantive analytical procedures"), and as procedures near the end of the audit that assist the auditor when forming an overall conclusion on the financial statements. The use of analytical procedures as risk assessment procedures is dealt with in SA 315. SA 330 includes requirements and guidance regarding the nature, timing and extent of audit procedures in response to assessed risks; these audit procedures may include substantive analytical procedures.

Effective Date

2. This SA is effective for audits of financial statements for periods beginning on or after April 1, 2010.

Objectives

3. The objectives of the auditor are:
   (a) To obtain relevant and reliable audit evidence when using substantive analytical procedures; and
   (b) To design and perform analytical procedures near the end of the audit that assist the auditor when forming an overall conclusion as to whether the financial statements are consistent with the auditor understands of the entity.

Definition

4. For the purposes of the SAs, the term "analytical procedures" means evaluations of financial information through analysis of plausible relationships among both financial and non-financial data. Analytical procedures also encompass such investigation as is necessary of identified fluctuations or relationships that are inconsistent with other relevant information or that differ from expected values by a significant amount. The auditor's choice of procedures, methods and level of application is a matter of professional judgment. (Ref: Para.A1-A3)

Requirements

Substantive Analytical Procedures

5. When designing and performing substantive analytical procedures, either alone or in combination with tests of details, as substantive procedures in accordance with SA 330, the auditor shall: (Ref: Para. A4-A5)
   (a) Determine the suitability of particular substantive analytical procedures for given assertions, taking account of the assessed risks of material

misstatement and tests of details, if any, for these assertions; (Ref: Para.A6-A11)

(b) Evaluate the reliability of data from which the auditor's expectation of recorded amounts or ratios is developed, taking account of source, comparability, and nature and relevance of information available, and controls over preparation; (Ref: Para.A12-A14)

(c) Develop an expectation of recorded amounts or ratios and evaluate whether the expectation is sufficiently precise to identify a misstatement that, individually or when aggregated with other misstatements, may cause the financial statements to be materially misstated; and (Ref: Para. A15)

(d) Determine the amount of any difference of recorded amounts from expected values that is acceptable without further investigation as required by paragraph 7. (Ref: Para.A16)

Analytical Procedures that Assist When Forming an Overall Conclusion

6. The auditor shall design and perform analytical procedures near the end of the audit that assist the auditor when forming an overall conclusion as to whether the financial statements are consistent with the auditor's understanding of the entity. (Ref: Para.A17-A19)

Investigating Results of Analytical Procedures

7. If analytical procedures performed in accordance with this SA identify fluctuations or relationships that are inconsistent with other relevant information or that differ from expected values by a significant amount, the auditor shall investigate such differences by:

   (a) Inquiring of management and obtaining appropriate audit evidence relevant to management's responses; and

   (b) Performing other audit procedures as necessary in the circumstances. (Ref: Para.A20-A21)

STANDARD ON AUDITING (SA) 530: AUDIT SAMPLING

Introduction

Scope of this SA

1. This Standard on Auditing (SA) applies when the auditor has decided to use audit sampling in performing audit procedures. It deals with the auditor's use of statistical and non-statistical sampling when designing and selecting the audit sample, performing tests of controls and tests of details, and evaluating the results from the sample.

2. This SA complements SA 5001, which deals with the auditor's responsibility to design and perform audit procedures to obtain sufficient appropriate audit evidence to be able to draw reasonable conclusions on which to base the audit

opinion. SA 500 provides guidance on the means available to the auditor for selecting items for testing, of which audit sampling is one means.

Effective Date

3. This SA is effective for audits of financial statements for periods beginning on or after April 1, 2009.

Objective

4. The objective of the auditor when using audit sampling is to provide a reasonable basis for the auditor to draw conclusions about the population from which the sample is selected.

Definitions

5. For purposes of the SAs, the following terms have the meanings attributed below:

   (a) Audit sampling (sampling) – The application of audit procedures to less than 100% of items within a population of audit relevance such that all sampling units have a chance of selection in order to provide the auditor with a reasonable basis on which to draw conclusions about the entire population.

   (b) Population – The entire set of data from which a sample is selected and about which the auditor wishes to draw conclusions.

   (c) Sampling risk – The risk that the auditor's conclusion based on a sample may be different from the conclusion if the entire population were subjected to the same audit procedure. Sampling risk can lead to two types of erroneous conclusions:

      (i) In the case of a test of controls, that controls are more effective than they actually are, or in the case of a test of details, that a material misstatement does not exist when in fact it does. The auditor is primarily concerned with this type of erroneous conclusion because it affects audit effectiveness and is more likely to lead to an inappropriate audit opinion.

      (ii) In the case of a test of controls, that controls are less effective than they actually are, or in the case of a test of details, that a material misstatement exists when in fact it does not. This type of erroneous conclusion affects audit efficiency as it would usually lead to additional work to establish that initial conclusions were incorrect.

   (d) Non-sampling risk – The risk that the auditor reaches an erroneous conclusion for any reason not related to sampling risk. (*Ref: ParaA1*)

   (e) Anomaly – A misstatement or deviation that is demonstrably not representative of misstatements or deviations in population.

   (f) Sampling unit – The individual items constituting a population. (*Ref: Para A2*)

(g) Statistical sampling – An approach to sampling that has the following characteristics:

(i) Random selection of the sample items; and

(ii) The use of probability theory to evaluate sample results, including measurement of sampling risk.

A sampling approach that does not have characteristics (I) and (ii) is considered non-statistical sampling.

(h) Stratification – The process of dividing a population into sub-populations, each of which is a group of sampling units which have similar characteristics (often monetary value).

(i) Tolerable misstatement – A monetary amount set by the auditor in respect of which the auditor seeks to obtain an appropriate level of assurance that the monetary amount set by the auditor is not exceeded by the actual misstatement in the population. *(Ref: Para.A3)*

(j) Tolerable rate of deviation – A rate of deviation from prescribed internal control procedures set by the auditor in respect of which the auditor seeks to obtain an appropriate level of assurance that the rate of deviation set by the auditor is not exceeded by the actual rate of deviation in the population.

Requirements

Sample Design, Size and Selection of Items for Testing

6. When designing an audit sample, the auditor shall consider the purpose of the audit procedure and the characteristics of the population from which the sample will be drawn. *(Ref: Para.A4-A9)*

7. The auditor shall determine a sample size sufficient to reduce sampling risk to an acceptably low level. *(Ref: Para. A10-A11)*

8. The auditor shall select items for the sample in such a way that each sampling unit in the population has a chance of selection. *(Ref: Para. A12-A13)*

Performing Audit Procedures

9. The auditor shall perform audit procedures, appropriate to the purpose, on each item selected.

10. If the audit procedure is not applicable to the selected item, the auditor shall perform the procedure on a replacement item. *(Ref: Para.A14)*

11. If the auditor is unable to apply the designed audit procedures, or suitable alternative procedures, to a selected item, the auditor shall treat that item as a deviation from the prescribed control, in the case of tests of controls, or a misstatement, in the case of tests of details. *(Ref: Para.A15-A16)*

Nature and Cause of Deviations and Misstatements

12. The auditor shall investigate the nature and cause of any deviations or misstatements identified, and evaluate their possible effect on the purpose of the audit procedure and on other areas of the audit. *(Ref: Para.A17)*
13. In the extremely rare circumstances when the auditor considers a misstatement or deviation discovered in a sample to be an anomaly, the auditor shall obtain a high degree of certainty that such misstatement or deviation is not representative of the population. The auditor shall obtain this degree of certainty by performing additional audit procedures to obtain sufficient appropriate audit evidence that the misstatement or deviation does not affect the remainder of the population.

Projecting Misstatements

14. For tests of details, the auditor shall project misstatements found in the sample to the population. *(Ref: Para.A18-A20)*

Evaluating Results of Audit Sampling

15. The auditor shall evaluate:
    (a) The results of the sample; and *(Ref: Para.A21-A22)*
    (b) Whether the use of audit sampling has provided a reasonable basis for conclusions about the population that has been tested. *(Ref: Para.A23)*

STANDARD ON AUDITING (SA) 540: AUDITING ACCOUNTING ESTIMATES, INCLUDING FAIR VALUE ACCOUNTING ESTIMATES, AND RELATED DISCLOSURES

Introduction

Scope of this SA

1. This Standard on Auditing (SA) deals with the auditor's responsibilities regarding accounting estimates, including fair value accounting estimates, and related disclosures in an audit of financial statements. Specifically, it expands on how SA 315 and SA 330 and other relevant SAs are to be applied in relation to accounting estimates. It also includes requirements and guidance on misstatements of individual accounting estimates, and indicators of possible management bias.

Nature of Accounting Estimates

2. Some financial statement items cannot be measured precisely, but can only be estimated. For purposes of this SA, such financial statement items are referred to as accounting estimates. The nature and reliability of information available to management to support the making of an accounting estimate varies widely, which thereby affects the degree of estimation uncertainty associated with accounting estimates. The degree of estimation uncertainty affects, in turn, the

risks of material misstatement of accounting estimates, including their susceptibility to unintentional or intentional management bias. *(Ref: Para.A1-A11)*

3. The measurement objective of accounting estimates can vary depending on the applicable financial reporting framework and the financial item being reported. The measurement objective for some accounting estimates is to forecast the outcome of one or more transactions, events or conditions giving rise to the need for the accounting estimate. For other accounting estimates, including many fair value accounting estimates, the measurement objective is different, and is expressed in terms of the value of a current transaction or financial statement item based on conditions prevalent at the measurement date, such as estimated market price for a particular type of asset or liability. For example, the applicable financial reporting framework may require fair value measurement based on an assumed hypothetical current transaction between knowledgeable, willing parties (sometimes referred to as "marketplace participants" or equivalent) in an arm's length transaction, rather than the settlement of a transaction at some past or future date.

4. A difference between the outcome of an accounting estimate and the amount originally recognised or disclosed in the financial statements does not necessarily represent a misstatement of the financial statements. This is particularly the case for fair value accounting estimates, as any observed outcome is invariably affected by events or conditions subsequent to the date at which the measurement is estimated for purposes of the financial statements.

Effective Date

5. This SA is effective for audits of financial statements for periods beginning on or after April1, 2009.

Objective

6. The objective of the auditor is to obtain sufficient appropriate audit evidence whether in the context of the applicable financial reporting framework:
   (a) accounting estimates, including fair value accounting estimates, in the financial statements, whether recognised or disclosed, are reasonable; and
   (b) related disclosures in the financial statements are adequate.

Definitions

7. For purposes of the SAs, the following terms have the meanings attributed below:
   (a) ***Accounting estimate*** – An approximation of a monetary amount in the absence of a precise means of measurement. This term is used for an amount measured at fair value where there is estimation uncertainty, as well as for other amounts that require estimation. Where this SA addresses only accounting estimates involving measurement at fair value, the term "fair value accounting estimates" issued.

(b) ***Auditor's point estimate or auditor's range*** – The amount, or range of amounts, respectively, derived from audit evidence for use in evaluating management's point estimate.

(c) ***Estimation uncertainty*** – The susceptibility of an accounting estimate and related disclosures to an inherent lack of precision in its measurement.

(d) ***Management bias*** – A lack of neutrality by management in the preparation and presentation of information.

(e) ***Management's point estimate*** – The amount selected by management for recognition or disclosure in the financial statements as an accounting estimate.

(f) ***Outcome of an accounting estimate*** –The actual monetary amount which results from the resolution of the underlying transaction(s), event(s) or condition(s) addressed by the accounting estimate.

Requirements

Risk Assessment Procedures and Related Activities

8. When performing risk assessment procedures and related activities to obtain an understanding of the entity and its environment, including the entity's internal control, as required by SA 315,4 the auditor shall obtain an understanding of the following in order to provide a basis for the identification and assessment of the risks of material misstatement for accounting estimates: *(Ref: Para.A12)*

(a) The requirements of the applicable financial reporting framework relevant to accounting estimates, including related disclosures. *(Ref: Para.A13-A15)*

(b) How management identifies those transactions, events and conditions that may give rise to the need for accounting estimates to be recognised or disclosed in the financial statements. In obtaining this understanding, the auditor shall make inquiries of management about changes in circumstances that may give rise to new, or the need to revise existing, accounting estimates. (Ref: Para. A16-A21)

(c) How management makes the accounting estimates, and an understanding of the data on which they are based, including: *(Ref: Para. A22-A23)*

(i) The method, including where applicable the model, used in making the accounting estimate; (*Ref: Para.A24-A26*)

(ii) Relevant controls; (*Ref: Para.A27-A28*)

(iii) Whether management has used an expert; (*Ref: Para.A29-A30*)

(iv) The assumptions underlying the accounting estimates; (*Ref: Para.A31-A36*)

(v) Whether there has been or ought to have been a change from the prior period in the methods for making the accounting estimates, and if so, why; and (*Ref: Para.A37*)

(vi) Whether and, if so, how management has assessed the effect of estimation uncertainty. (*Ref: Para. A38*)

9. The auditor shall review the outcome of accounting estimates included in the prior period financial statements, or, where applicable, their subsequent re-estimation for the purpose of the current period. The nature and extent of the auditor's review takes account of the nature of the accounting estimates, and whether the information obtained from the review would be relevant to identifying and assessing risks of material misstatement of accounting estimates made in the current period financial statements. However, the review is not intended to call into question the judgments made in the prior periods that were based on information available at that time. *(Ref: Para. A39-A44)*

Identifying and Assessing the Risks of Material Misstatement

10. In identifying and assessing the risks of material misstatement, as required by SA 315, the auditor shall evaluate the degree of estimation uncertainty associated with an accounting estimate. *(Ref: Para. A45- A46)*

11. The auditor shall determine whether, in the auditor's judgment, any of those accounting estimates that have been identified as having high estimation uncertainty give rise to significant risks. (Ref: Para. A47-A51)

Responses to the Assessed Risks of Material Misstatement

12. Based on the assessed risks of material misstatement, the auditor shall determine: *(Ref:Para.A52)*

(a) Whether management has appropriately applied the requirements of the applicable financial reporting framework relevant to the accounting estimate; and *(Ref: Para.A53-A56)*

(b) Whether the methods for making the accounting estimates are appropriate and have been applied consistently, and whether changes, if any, in accounting estimates or in the method for making them from the prior period are appropriate in the circumstances. *(Ref: Para.A57-A58)*

13. In responding to the assessed risks of material misstatement, as required by SA 330,6 the auditor shall undertake one or more of the following, taking account of the nature of the accounting estimate: *(Ref: Para. A59-A61)*

(a) Determine whether events occurring up to the date of the auditor's report provide audit evidence regarding the accounting estimate. *(Ref: Para.A62-A67)*

(b) Test how management made the accounting estimate and the data on which it is based. In doing so, the auditor shall evaluate whether: (Ref: Para. A68-A70)

(i) The method of measurement used is appropriate in the circumstances; and (*Ref: Para. A71-A76*)

(ii) The assumptions used by management are reasonable in light of the measurement objectives of the applicable financial reporting framework. (*Ref: Para.A77-A83*)

(c) Test the operating effectiveness of the controls over how management made the accounting estimate, together with appropriate substantive procedures. (Ref: Para. A84-A86)

(d) Develop a point estimate or a range to evaluate management's point estimate. For this purpose: (Ref: Para.A87-A91)

(i) When the auditor uses assumptions or methods that differ from management's, the auditor shall obtain an understanding of management's assumptions or methods sufficient to establish that the auditor's point estimate or range takes into account relevant variables and to evaluate any significant differences from management's point estimate. (Ref: Para.A92)

(ii) When the auditor concludes that it is appropriate to use a range, the auditor shall narrow the range, based on audit evidence available, until all outcomes within the range are considered reasonable. (Ref: Para.A93-A95)

14. In determining the matters identified in paragraph 12 or in responding to the assessed risks of material misstatement in accordance with paragraph 13, the auditor shall consider whether specialised skills or knowledge in relation to one or more aspects of the accounting estimates are required in order to obtain sufficient appropriate audit evidence. *(Ref: Para.A96-A101)*

Further Substantive Procedures to Respond to Significant Risks

Estimation Uncertainty

15. For accounting estimates that give rise to significant risks, in addition to other substantive procedures performed to meet the requirements of SA 330,7 the auditor shall evaluate the following: *(Ref: Para.A102)*

(a) How management has considered alternative assumptions or outcomes, and why it has rejected them, or how management has otherwise addressed estimation uncertainty in making the accounting estimate. *(Ref: Para.A103-A106)*

(b) Whether the significant assumptions used by management are reasonable. *(Ref: ParaA107-A109)*

(c) Where relevant to the reasonableness of the significant assumptions used by management or the appropriate application of the applicable financial reporting framework, management's intent to carry out specific courses of action and its ability to do so. *(Ref: Para.A110)*

16. If, in the auditor's judgment, management has not adequately addressed the effects of estimation uncertainty on the accounting estimates that give rise to significant risks, the auditor shall, if considered necessary, develop a range with which to evaluate the reasonableness of the accounting estimate. *(Ref: Para.A111-A112)*

Recognition and Measurement Criteria

17. For accounting estimates that give rise to significant risks, the auditor shall obtain sufficient appropriate audit evidence whether the following are in accordance with the requirements of the applicable financial reporting framework:
    (a) management's decision to recognise, or to not recognise, the accounting estimates in the financial statements; and *(Ref: Para. A113-A114)*
    (b) the selected measurement basis for the accounting estimates. *(Ref: Para.A115)*

Evaluating the Reasonableness of the Accounting Estimates, and Determining Misstatements

18. The auditor shall evaluate, based on the audit evidence, whether the accounting estimates in the financial statements are either reasonable in the context of the applicable financial reporting framework, or are misstated. *(Ref: Para.A116-A119)*

Disclosures Related to Accounting Estimates

19. The auditor shall obtain sufficient appropriate audit evidence about whether the disclosures in the financial statements related to accounting estimates are in accordance with the requirements of the applicable financial reporting framework. *(Ref: Para.A120-A121)*

21. For accounting estimates that give rise to significant risks, the auditor shall also evaluate the adequacy of the disclosure of their estimation uncertainty in the financial statements in the context of the applicable financial reporting framework. *(Ref: Para. A122-A123)*

Indicators of Possible Management Bias

22. The auditor shall review the judgments and decisions made by management in the making of accounting estimates to identify whether there are indicators of possible management bias. Indicators of possible management bias do not themselves constitute misstatements for the purposes of drawing conclusions on the reasonableness of individual accounting estimates. *(Ref: Para.A124-A125)*

Written Representations

23. The auditor shall obtain written representations from management and, where appropriate, those charged with governance whether they believe significant assumptions used in making accounting estimates are reasonable. *(Ref: Para.A126-A127)*

Documentation

24. The audit documentation shall include:

(a) The basis for the auditor's conclusions about the reasonableness of accounting estimates and their disclosure that give rise to significant risks; and

(b) Indicators of possible management bias, if any. *(Ref: Para.A128)*

STANDARD ON AUDITING (SA) 550: RELATED PARTIES

Introduction

Scope of this SA

1. This Standard on Auditing (SA) deals with the auditor's responsibilities regarding related party relationships and transactions when performing an audit of financial statements. Specifically, it expands on how SA 315, SA 330 and SA 240 are to be applied in relation to risks of material misstatement associated with related party relationships and transactions.

Nature of Related Party Relationships and Transactions

2. Many related party transactions are in the normal course of business. In such circumstances, they may carry no higher risk of material misstatement of the financial statements than similar transactions with unrelated parties. However, the nature of related party relationships and transactions may, in some circumstances, give rise to higher risks of material misstatement of the financial statements than transactions with unrelated parties. For example:
   - Related parties may operate through an extensive and complex range of relationships and structures, with a corresponding increase in the complexity of related party transactions.
   - Information systems may be ineffective at identifying or summarizing transactions and outstanding balances between an entity and its related parties.
   - Related party transactions may not be conducted under normal market terms and conditions; for example, some related party transactions may be conducted with no exchange of consideration.

Responsibilities of the Auditor

3. Because related parties are not independent of each other, many financial reporting frameworks establish specific accounting and disclosure requirements for related party relationships, transactions and balances to enable users of the financial statements to understand their nature and actual or potential effects on the financial statements. Where the applicable financial reporting framework establishes such requirements, the auditor has a responsibility to perform audit procedures to identify, assess and respond to the risks of material misstatement arising from the entity's failure to appropriately account for or disclose related party relationships, transactions or balances in accordance with the requirements of the framework.

4. **Even if the applicable financial reporting framework establishes minimal or no related party requirements, the auditor nevertheless needs to obtain an understanding of the entity's related party relationships and transactions sufficient to be able to conclude whether the financial statements, insofar as they are affected by those relationships and transactions: (Ref: Para. A1)**
   (a) Achieve a true and fair presentation (for fair presentation frameworks); or (*Ref: Para.A2*)
   (b) Are not misleading (for compliance frameworks). (*Ref: Para.A3*)
5. In addition, an understanding of the entity's related party relationships and transactions is relevant to the auditor's evaluation of whether one or more fraud risk factors are present as required by SA 240 because fraud may be more easily committed through related parties.
6. Owing to the inherent limitations of an audit, there is an unavoidable risk that some material misstatements of the financial statements may not be detected, even though the audit is properly planned and performed in accordance with the SAs. In the context of related parties, the potential effects of inherent limitations on the auditor's ability to detect material misstatements are greater for such reasons as the following:
   - Management may be unaware of the existence of all related party relationships and transactions, particularly if the applicable financial reporting framework does not establish related party requirements.
   - Related party relationships may present a greater opportunity for collusion, concealment or manipulation by management.
7. Planning and performing the audit with professional skepticism as required by SA 200 is therefore particularly important in this context, given the potential for undisclosed related party relationships and transactions. The requirements in this SA are designed to assist the auditor in identifying and assessing the risks of material misstatement associated with related party relationships and transactions, and in designing audit procedures to respond to the assessed risks.

Effective Date

8. This SA is effective for audits of financial statements for periods beginning on or after April 1, 2010.

Objectives

9. The objectives of the auditor are:
   (a) Irrespective of whether the applicable financial reporting framework establishes related party requirements, to obtain an understanding of related party relationships and transactions sufficient to be able:
      (i) To recognize fraud risk factors, if any , Arising from related party relationships and transactions that are relevant to the identification and assessment of the risks of material misstatement due to fraud; and

(ii) To conclude whether the financial statements, insofar as they are affected by those relationships and transactions:

(a) Achieve a true and fair presentation (for fair presentation frameworks); or

(b) Are not misleading (for compliance frameworks); and

(b) In addition, where the applicable financial reporting framework establishes related party requirements, to obtain sufficient appropriate audit evidence about whether related party relationships and transactions have been appropriately identified, accounted for and disclosed in the financial statements in accordance with the framework.

Definitions

10. For purposes of the SAs, the following terms have the meanings attributed below:

(a) Arm's length transaction–A transaction conducted on such terms and conditions as between a willing buyer and a willing seller who are unrelated and are acting independently of each other and pursuing their own best interests.

(b) Related party – A party that is either: *(Ref: Para.A4-A7)*

(i) A related party as defined in the applicable financial reporting framework; or

(ii) Where the applicable financial reporting framework establishes minimal or no related party requirements:

(a) A person or other entity that has control or significant influence, directly or indirectly through one or more intermediaries, over the reporting entity;

(b) Another entity over which the reporting entity has control or significant influence, directly or indirectly through one or more intermediaries; or

(c) Another entity that is under common control with the reporting entity through having:

(i) Common controlling ownership;

(ii) Owners who are close family members; or

(iii) Common key management.

However, entities that are under common control by a state (i.e., a national, regional or local government) are not considered related unless they engage in significant transactions or share resources to a significant extent with one another.

Requirements

Risk Assessment Procedures and Related Activities

11. As part of the risk assessment procedures and related activities that SA 315 and SA 240 require the auditor to perform during the audit, 8 the auditor shall perform the audit procedures and related activities set out in paragraphs 12-17 to obtain information relevant to identifying the risks of material misstatement associated with related party relationships and transactions. *(Ref: Para.A8)*

Understanding the Entity's Related Party Relationships and Transactions

12. The engagement team discussion that SA 315 and SA 240 require9 shall include specific consideration of the susceptibility of the financial statements to material misstatement due to fraud or error that could result from the entity's related party relationships and transactions. *(Ref: Para.A9-A10)*

13. The auditor shall inquire of management regarding:

    (a) The identity of the entity's related parties, including changes from the prior period; *(Ref: Para. A11- A14)*

    (b) The nature of the relationships between the entity and these related parties; and

    (c) Whether the entity entered into any transactions with these related parties during the period and, if so, the type and purpose of the transactions.

14. The auditor shall inquire of management and others within the entity, and perform other risk assessment procedures considered appropriate, to obtain an understanding of the controls, if any, that management has established to: *(Ref: Para.A15-A20)*

    (a) Identify, account for, and disclose related party relationships and transactions in accordance with the applicable financial reporting framework;

    (b) Authorize and approve significant transactions and arrangements with related parties; and *(Ref: Para. A21)*

    (c) Authorize and approve significant transactions and arrangements outside the normal course of business.

Maintaining Alertness for Related Party Information When Reviewing Records or Documents

15. During the audit, the auditor shall remain alert, when inspecting records or documents, for arrangements or other information that may indicate the existence of related party relationships or transactions that management has not previously identified or disclosed to the auditor. (Ref: Para. A22-A23)

    In particular, the auditor shall inspect the following for indications of the existence of related party relationships or transactions that management has not previously identified or disclosed to the auditor:

(a) Bank, legal and third party confirmations obtained as part of the auditor's procedures;

(b) Minutes of meetings of shareholders and of those charged with governance; and

(c) Such other records or documents as the auditor considers necessary in the circumstances of the entity.

16. If the auditor identifies significant transactions outside the entity's normal course of business when performing the audit procedures required by paragraph 15 or through other audit procedures, the auditor shall inquire of management about: *(Ref: Para.A24-A25)*

(a) The nature of these transactions; and *(Ref: Para.A26)*

(b) Whether related parties could be involved. *(Ref: Para.A27)*

Sharing Related Party Information with the Engagement Team

17. The auditor shall share relevant information obtained about the entity's related parties with the other members of the engagement team. *(Ref: Para.A28)*

Identification and Assessment of the Risks of Material Misstatement Associated with Related Party Relationships and Transactions

18. In meeting the SA 315 requirement to identify and assess the risks of material misstatement, 10 the auditor shall identify and assess the risks of material misstatement associated with related party relationships and transactions and determine whether any of those risks are significant risks. In making this determination, the auditor shall treat identified significant related party transactions outside the entity's normal course of business as giving rise to significant risks.

19. **If the auditor identifies fraud risk factors (including circumstances relating to the existence of a related party with dominant influence) when performing the risk assessment procedures and related activities in connection with related parties, the auditor shall consider such information when identifying and assessing the risks of material misstatement due to fraud in accordance with SA 240. *(Ref: Para. A6 and A29-A30)***

Responses to the Risks of Material Misstatement Associated with Related Party Relationships and Transactions

20. As part of the SA 330 requirement that the auditor respond to assessed risks, the auditor designs and performs further audit procedures to obtain sufficient appropriate audit evidence about the assessed risks of material misstatement associated with related party relationships and transactions. These audit procedures shall include those required by paragraphs 21-24. *(Ref: Para.A31-A34)*

Identification of Previously Unidentified or Undisclosed Related Parties or Significant Related Party Transactions

21. If the auditor identifies arrangements or information that suggests the existence of related party relationships or transactions that management has not previously identified or disclosed to the auditor, the auditor shall determine whether the underlying circumstances confirm the existence of those relationships or transactions.

22. If the auditor identifies related parties or significant related party transactions that management has not previously identified or disclosed to the auditor, the auditor shall:
    - (a) Promptly communicate the relevant information to the other members of the engagement team; *(Ref: Para.A35)*
    - (b) Where the applicable financial reporting framework establishes related party requirements:
        - (i) Request management to identify all transactions with the newly identified related parties for the auditor's further evaluation; and
        - (ii) Inquire as to why the entity's controls over related party relationships and transactions failed to enable the identification or disclosure of the related party relationships or transactions;
    - (c) Perform appropriate substantive audit procedures relating to such newly identified related parties or significant related party transactions; *(Ref: Para.A36)*
    - (d) Reconsider the risk that other related parties or significant related party transactions may exist that management has not previously identified or disclosed to the auditor, and perform additional audit procedures as necessary; and
    - (e) If the non-disclosure by management appears intentional (and therefore indicative of a risk of material misstatement due to fraud), evaluate the implications for the audit. *(Ref: Para.A37)*

Identified Significant Related Party Transactions outside the Entity's Normal Course of Business

23. For identified significant related party transactions outside the entity's normal course of business, the auditor shall:
    - (a) Inspect the underlying contracts or agreements, if any, and evaluate whether:
        - (i) The business rationale (or lack thereof) of the transactions suggests that they may have been entered into to engage in fraudulent financial reporting or to conceal misappropriation of assets; *(Ref: Para.A38-A39)*
        - (ii) The terms of the transactions are consistent with management's explanations; and

(iii) The transactions have been appropriately accounted for and disclosed in accordance with the applicable financial reporting framework; and

(b) Obtain audit evidence that the transactions have been appropriately authorized and approved. *(Ref: Para.A40-A41)*

Assertions That Related Party Transactions Were Conducted on Terms Equivalent to Those Prevailing in an Arm's Length Transaction

24. When management has made an assertion in the financial statements to the effect that a related party transaction was conducted on terms equivalent to those prevailing in an arm's length transaction, the auditor shall obtain sufficient appropriate audit evidence about the assertion. *(Ref: Para.A42-A45)*

Evaluation of the Accounting for and Disclosure of Identified Related Party Relationships and Transactions

25. In forming an opinion on the financial statements in accordance with SA 700, the auditor shall evaluate: *(Ref: Para.A46)*

(a) Whether the identified related party relationships and transactions have been appropriately accounted for and disclosed in accordance with the applicable financial reporting framework; and *(Ref: Para.A47)*

(b) Whether the effects of the related party relationships and transactions:

(i) Prevent the financial statements from achieving true and fair presentation (for fair presentation frameworks);or

(ii) Cause the financial statements to be misleading (for compliance frameworks).

Written Representations

26. Where the applicable financial reporting framework establishes related party requirements, the auditor shall obtain written representations from management and, where appropriate, those charged with governance that: *(Ref: Para.A48-A49)*

(a) They have disclosed to the auditor the identity of the entity's related parties and all the related party relationships and transactions of which they are aware; and

(b) They have appropriately accounted for and disclosed such relationships and transactions in accordance with the requirements of the framework.

Communication with Those Charged with Governance

27. Unless all of those charged with governance are involved in managing the entity14, the auditor shall communicate with those charged with governance significant matters arising during the audit in connection with the entity's related parties. *(Ref: Para.A50)*

Documentation

28. In meeting the documentation requirements of SA 230 and other SAs, the auditor shall include in the audit documentation the names of the identified related parties and the nature of the related party relationships.

STANDARD ON AUDITING (SA) 560: SUBSEQUENT EVENTS

Introduction

Scope of this SA

1. This Standard on Auditing (SA) deals with the auditor's responsibilities relating to subsequent events in an audit of financial statements. *(Ref: Para.A1)*

2. Financial statements may be affected by certain events that occur after the date of the financial statements. Many financial reporting frameworks1 specifically refer to such events. Such financial reporting frameworks ordinarily identify two types of events:

   (a) Those that provide evidence of conditions that existed at the date of the financial statements; and

   (b) Those that provide evidence of conditions that arose after the date of the financial statements.

   SA 700 explains that the date of the auditor's report informs the reader that the auditor has considered the effect of events and transactions of which the auditor becomes aware and that occurred up to that date.

Effective Date

3. This SA is effective for audits of financial statements for periods beginning on or after April 1, 2009.

Objectives

4. The objectives of the auditor are to:

   (a) Obtain sufficient appropriate audit evidence about whether events occurring between the date of the financial statements and the date of the auditor's report that require adjustment of, or disclosure in, the financial statements are appropriately reflected in those financial statements; and

   (b) Respond appropriately to facts that become known to the auditor after the date of the auditor's report, that, had they been known to the auditor at that date, may have caused the auditor to amend the auditor's report.

Definitions

5. For purposes of the SAs, the following terms have the meanings attributed below:

(a) Date of the financial statements – The date of the end of the latest period covered by the financial statements.

(b) Date of approval of the financial statements – The date on which all the statements that comprise the financial statements, including the related notes, have been prepared and those with the recognised authority have asserted that they have taken responsibility for those financial statements. (*Ref: Para. A2*)

(c) Date of the auditor's report – The date the auditor dates the report on the financial statements in accordance with SA 700. (*Ref: Para. A3*)

(d) Date the financial statements are issued – The date that the auditor's report and audited financial statements are made available to third parties. (*Ref: Para. A4-A5*)

(e) Subsequent events – Events occurring between the date of the financial statements and the date of the auditor's report, and facts that become known to the auditor after the date of the auditor's report.

Requirements

Events Occurring Between the Date of the Financial Statements and the Date of the Auditor's Report

6. The auditor shall perform audit procedures designed to obtain sufficient appropriate audit evidence that all events occurring between the date of the financial statements and the date of the auditor's report that require adjustment of, or disclosure in, the financial statements have been identified. The auditor is not, however, expected to perform additional audit procedures on matters to which previously applied audit procedures have provided satisfactory conclusions. *(Ref: Para.A6)*

7. The auditor shall perform the procedures required by paragraph 6 so that they cover the period from the date of the financial statements to the date of the auditor's report, or as near as practicable thereto. The auditor shall take into account the auditor's risk assessment in determining the nature and extent of such audit procedures, which shall include the following: *(Ref: Para.A7-A8)*

   (a) Obtaining an understanding of any procedures management has established to ensure that subsequent events are identified.

   (b) Inquiring of management and, where appropriate, those charged with governance as to whether any subsequent events have occurred which might affect the financial statements. *(Ref: Para.A9)*

   (c) Reading minutes, if any, of the meetings, of the entity's owners, management and those charged with governance, that have been held after the date of the financial statements and inquiring about matters discussed at any such meetings for which minutes are not yet available. (Ref: Para.A10)

   (d) Reading the entity's latest subsequent interim financial statements, if any.

8. When, as a result of the procedures performed as required by paragraphs 6 and 7, the auditor identifies events that require adjustment of, or disclosure in, the financial statements, the auditor shall determine whether each such event is appropriately reflected in those financial statements.

Written Representations

9. The auditor shall request management and, where appropriate, those charged with governance, to provide a written representation in accordance with SA 580, "Written Representations" that all events occurring subsequent to the date of the financial statements and for which the applicable financial reporting framework requires adjustment or disclosure have been adjusted or disclosed.

Facts Which Become Known to the Auditor after the Date of the Auditor's Report but Before the Date the

Financial Statements are Issued

10. The auditor has no obligation to perform any audit procedures regarding the financial statements after the date of the auditor's report. However, when, after the date of the auditor's report but before the date the financial statements are issued, a fact becomes known to the auditor that, had it been known to the auditor at the date of the auditor's report, may have caused the auditor to amend the auditor's report, the auditor shall: *(Ref: Para.A11)*
    (a) Discuss the matter with management and, where appropriate, those charged with governance.
    (b) Determine whether the financial statements need amendment and, if so,
    (c) Inquire how management intends to address the matter in the financial statements.

11. If management amends the financial statements, the auditor shall:
    (a) Carry out the audit procedures necessary in the circumstances on the amendment.
    (b) Unless the circumstances in paragraph 12 apply:
        (i) Extend the audit procedures referred to in paragraphs 6 and 7 to the date of the new auditor's report; and
        (ii) Provide a new auditor's report on the amended financial statements. The new auditor's report shall not be dated earlier than the date of approval of the amended financial statements.

12. When law, regulation or the financial reporting framework does not prohibit management from restricting the amendment of the financial statements to the effects of the subsequent events or events causing that amendments and those responsible for approving the financial statements are not prohibited from restricting their approval to that amendment, the auditor is permitted to restrict the audit procedures on subsequent events required in paragraph 11(b)(i) to that amendment. In such cases, the auditor shall either:

(a) Amend the auditor's report to include an additional date restricted to that amendment that thereby indicates that the auditor's procedures on subsequent events are restricted solely to the amendment of the financial statements described in the relevant note to the financial statements; or (Ref: Para. A12)

(b) Provide a new or amended auditor's report that includes a statement in an Emphasis of Matter paragraph or Other Matter(s) paragraph3 that conveys that auditor's procedures on subsequent events are restricted solely to the amendment of the financial statements as described in the relevant note to the financial statements.

13. In some entities, management may not be required by the applicable law, regulation or the financial reporting framework to issue amended financial statements and, accordingly, the auditor need not provide an amended or new auditor's report. However, when management does not amend the financial statements in circumstances where the auditor believes they need to be amended, then: *(Ref: Para.A13-A14)*

(a) If the auditor's report has not yet been provided to the entity, the auditor shall modify the opinion as required by SA 7054 and then provide the auditor's report; or

(b) If the auditor's report has already been provided to the entity, the auditor shall notify management and, unless all of those charged with governance are involved in managing the entity, those charged with governance, not to issue the financial statements to third parties before the necessary amendments have been made. If the financial statements are nevertheless subsequently issued without the necessary amendments, the auditor shall take appropriate action, to seek to prevent reliance on the auditor's report. *(Ref: Para.A15-A16)*

Facts Which Become Known to the Auditor after the Financial Statements have been Issued

14. After the financial statements have been issued, the auditor has no obligation to perform any audit procedures regarding such financial statements. However, when, after the financial statements have been issued, a fact becomes known to the auditor that, had it been known to the auditor at the date of the auditor's report, may have caused the auditor to amend the auditor's report, the auditor shall:

(a) Discuss the matter with management and, where appropriate, those charged with governance.

(b) Determine whether the financial statements need amendment and, if so,

(c) Inquire how management intends to address the matter in the financial statements.

15. If the management amends the financial statements, the auditor shall: *(Ref: Para.A17)*

(a) Carry out the audit procedures necessary in the circumstances on the amendment.

(b) Review the steps taken by management to ensure that anyone in receipt of the previously issued financial statements together with the auditor's report thereon is informed of the situation.

(c) Unless the circumstances in paragraph 12apply:

(i) Extend the audit procedures referred to in paragraphs 6 and 7 to the date of the new auditor's report, and the date the new auditor's report no earlier than the date of approval of the amended financial statements; and

(ii) Provide a new auditor's report on the amended financial statements.

(d) When the circumstances in paragraph 12 apply, amend the auditor's report, or provide a new auditor's report as required by paragraph12.

16. The auditor shall include in the new or amended auditor's report an Emphasis of Matter paragraph or Other Matter(s) paragraph referring to a note to the financial statements that more extensively discusses the reason for the amendment of the previously issued financial statements and to the earlier report provided by the auditor.

17. If management does not take the necessary steps to ensure that anyone in receipt of the previously issued financial statements is informed of the situation and does not amend the financial statements in circumstances where the auditor believes they need to be amended, the auditor shall notify management and, unless all of those charged with governance5 are involved in managing the entity, those charged with governance, that the auditor will seek to prevent future reliance on the auditor's report. If, despite such notification, management or those charged with governance do not take these necessary steps, the auditor shall take appropriate action to seek to prevent reliance on the auditor's report. *(Ref: Para.A18)*

STANDARD ON AUDITING (SA) 570: GOING CONCERN

Introduction

Scope of this SA

1. This Standard on Auditing (SA) deals with the auditor's responsibilities in the audit of financial statements relating to going concern and the implications for the auditor's report. (Ref: Para.A1)

Going Concern Basis of Accounting

2. Under the going concern basis of accounting, the financial statements are prepared on the assumption that the entity is a going concern and will continue its operations for the foreseeable future. General purpose financial statements are prepared using the going concern basis of accounting, unless management

either intends to liquidate the entity or to cease operations, or has no realistic alternative but to do so. Special purpose financial statements may or may not be prepared in accordance with a financial reporting framework for which the going concern basis of accounting is relevant (e.g., the going concern basis of accounting is not relevant for some financial statements prepared on a tax basis). When the use of the going concern basis of accounting is appropriate, assets and liabilities are recorded on the basis that the entity will be able to realize its assets and discharge its liabilities in the normal course of business. (Ref: Para.A2)

Responsibility for Assessment of the Entity's Ability to Continue as a Going Concern

3. Some financial reporting frameworks contain an explicit requirement for management to make a specific assessment of the entity's ability to continue as a going concern, and standards regarding matters to be considered and disclosures to be made in connection with going concern. The detailed requirements regarding management's responsibility to assess the entity's ability to continue as a going concern and related financial statement disclosures may also be set out in law or regulation.

4. In other financial reporting frameworks, there may be no explicit requirement for management to make a specific assessment of the entity's ability to continue as a going concern. Nevertheless, where the going concern basis of accounting is a fundamental principle in the preparation of financial statements as discussed in paragraph 2, the preparation of the financial statements requires management to assess the entity's ability to continue as a going concern even if the financial reporting framework does not include an explicit requirement to do so.

5. Management's assessment of the entity's ability to continue as a going concern involves making a judgment, at a particular point in time, about inherently uncertain future outcomes of events or conditions. The following factors are relevant to that judgment:

- The degree of uncertainty associated with the outcome of an event or condition increases significantly the further into the future an event or condition or the outcome occurs. For that reason, most financial reporting frameworks that require an explicit management assessment specify the period for which management is required to take into account all available information. The size and complexity of the entity, the nature and condition of its business and the degree to which itisaffectedbyexternalfactorsaffectthejudgmentregardingtheoutcomeofev entsorconditions.
- Any judgment about the future is based on information available at the time at which the judgment is made. Subsequent events may result in outcomes that are inconsistent with judgments that were reasonable at the time they were made.

Responsibilities of the Auditor

6. The auditor's responsibilities are to obtain sufficient appropriate audit evidence regarding, and conclude on, the appropriateness of management's use of the going concern basis of accounting in the preparation of the financial statements, and to conclude, based on the audit evidence obtained, whether a material uncertainty exists about the entity's ability to continue as a going concern. These responsibilities exist even if the financial reporting framework used in the preparation of the financial statements does not include an explicit requirement for management to make a specific assessment of the entity's ability to continue as a going concern.

7. However, as described in SA 200, 1 the potential effects of inherent limitations on the auditor's ability to detect material misstatements are greater for future events or conditions that may cause an entity to cease to continue as a going concern. The auditor cannot predict such future events or conditions. Accordingly, the absence of any reference to a material uncertainty about the entity's ability to continue as a going concern in an auditor's report cannot be viewed as a guarantee as to the entity's ability to continue as a going concern.

Effective Date

8. This SA is effective for audits of financial statements for periods beginning on or after April 1, 2017.

Objectives

9. The objectives of the auditor are:
   (a) To obtain sufficient appropriate audit evidence regarding, and conclude on, the appropriateness of management's use of the going concern basis of accounting in the preparation of the financial statements;
   (b) To conclude, based on the audit evidence obtained, whether a material uncertainty exists related to events or conditions that may cast significant doubt on the entity's ability to continue as a going concern; and
   (c) To report in accordance with this.

Requirements

Risk Assessment Procedures and Related Activities

10. When performing risk assessment procedures as required by SA 315, 2 the auditor shall consider whether events or conditions exist that may cast significant doubt on the entity's ability to continue as a going concern. In so doing, the auditor shall determine whether management has already performed a preliminary assessment of the entity's ability to continue as a going concern, and: (Ref: Para.A3–A6)
    (a) If If such an assessment has been performed, the auditor shall discuss the assessment with management and determine whether management has identified events or conditions that, individually or collectively, may

cast significant doubt on the entity's ability to continue as a going concern and, if so, management's plans to address them;

(b) If such an assessment has not yet been performed, the auditor shall discuss with management the basis for the intended use of the going concern basis of accounting, and inquire of management whether events or conditions exist that, individually or collectively, may cast significant doubt on the entity's ability to continue as a going concern.

11. The auditor shall remain alert throughout the audit for audit evidence of events or conditions that may cast significant doubt on the entity's ability to continue as a going concern. (Ref: Para.A7)

Evaluating Management's Assessment

12. The auditor shall evaluate management's assessment of the entity's ability to continue as a going concern. (Ref: Para. A8–A10, A12–A13)

13. In evaluating management's assessment of the entity's ability to continue as a going concern, the auditor shall cover the same period as that used by management to make its assessment as required by the applicable financial reporting framework, or by law or regulation if it specifies a longer period. If management's assessment of the entity's ability to continue as a going concern covers less than twelve months from the date of the financial statements as defined in SA 560,3 the auditor shall request management to extend its assessment period to at least twelve months from that date. (Ref: Para. A11–A13)

14. In evaluating management's assessment, the auditor shall consider whether management's assessment includes all relevant information of which the auditor is aware as a result of the audit.

Period beyond Management's Assessment

15. The auditor shall inquire of management as to its knowledge of events or conditions beyond the period of management's assessment that may cast significant doubt on the entity's ability to continue as a going concern. (Ref: Para.A14–A15)

Additional Audit Procedures When Events or Conditions Are Identified

16. If events or conditions have been identified that may cast significant doubt on the entity's ability to continue as a going concern, the auditor shall obtain sufficient appropriate audit evidence to determine whether or not a material uncertainty exists related to events or conditions that may cast significant doubt on the entity's ability to continue as a going concern (hereinafter referred to as "material uncertainty") through performing additional audit procedures, including consideration of mitigating factors. These procedures shall include: (Ref: Para.A16)

    (a) Where management has not yet performed an assessment of the entity's ability to continue as a going concern, requesting management to make its assessment.

(b) Evaluating management's plans for future actions in relation to its going concern assessment, whether the outcome of these plans is likely to improve the situation and whether management's plans are feasible in the circumstances. (Ref: Para.A17)

(c) Where the entity has prepared a cash flow forecast, and analysis of the forecast is a significant factor in considering the future outcome of events or conditions in the evaluation of management's plans for future actions: (Ref: Para.A18–A19)

  (i) Evaluating the reliability of the underlying data generated to prepare the forecast; and

  (ii) Determining whether there is adequate support for the assumptions underlying the forecast.

(d) Considering whether any additional facts or information have become available since the date on which management made its assessment.

(e) Requesting written representations from management and, where appropriate, those charged with governance, regarding their plans for future actions and the feasibility of these plans. (Ref: Para. A20)

Auditor Conclusions

17. The auditor shall evaluate whether sufficient appropriate audit evidence has been obtained regarding, and shall conclude on, the appropriateness of management's use of the going concern basis of accounting in the preparation of the financial statements.

18. Based on the audit evidence obtained, the auditor shall conclude whether, in the auditor's judgment, a material uncertainty exists related to events or conditions that, individually or collectively, may cast significant doubt on the entity's ability to continue as a going concern. A material uncertainty exists when the magnitude of its potential impact and likelihood of occurrence is such that, in the auditor's judgment, appropriate disclosure of the nature and implications of the uncertainty is necessary for: (Ref: Para.A21–A22)

(a) In the case of a fair presentation financial reporting framework, the fair presentation of the financial statements, or

(b) In the case of a compliance framework, the financial statements not to be misleading.

Adequacy of Disclosures When Events or Conditions Have Been Identified and a Material Uncertainty Exists

19. If the auditor concludes that management's use of the going concern basis of accounting is appropriate in the circumstances but a material uncertainty exists, the auditor shall determine whether the financial statements: (Ref: Para.A22–A23)

(a) Adequately disclose the principal events or conditions that may cast significant doubt on the entity's ability to continue as a going concern and management's plans to deal with these events or conditions; and

(b) Disclose clearly that there is a material uncertainty related to events or conditions that may cast significant doubt on the entity's ability to continue as a going concern and, therefore, that it may be unable to realize its assets and discharge its liabilities in the normal course of business.

Adequacy of Disclosures When Events or Conditions Have Been Identified but No Material Uncertainty Exists

20. If events or conditions have been identified that may cast significant doubt on the entity's ability to continue as a going concern but, based on the audit evidence obtained the auditor concludes that no material uncertainty exists, the auditor shall evaluate whether, in view of the requirements of the applicable financial reporting framework, the financial statements provide adequate disclosures about these events or conditions. (Ref: Para.A24–A25)

Implications for the Auditor's Report

Use of Going Concern Basis of Accounting Is Inappropriate

21. If the financial statements have been prepared using the going concern basis of accounting but, in the auditor's judgment, management's use of the going concern basis of accounting in the preparation of the financial statements is inappropriate, the auditor shall express an adverse opinion. (Ref: Para. A26–A27)

Use of Going Concern Basis of Accounting Is Appropriate but a Material Uncertainty Exists

Adequate Disclosure of a Material Uncertainty Is Made in the Financial Statements

22. If adequate disclosure about the material uncertainty is made in the financial statements, the auditor shall express an unmodified opinion and the auditor's report shall include a separate section under the heading "Material Uncertainty Related to Going Concern" to: (Ref: Para. A28–A31, A34)

(a) Draw attention to the note in the financial statements that discloses the matters set out in paragraph 19;and

(b) State that these events or conditions indicate that a material uncertainty exists that may cast significant doubt on the entity's ability to continue as a going concern and that the auditor's opinion is not modified in respect of the matter.

Adequate Disclosure of a Material Uncertainty Is Not Made in the Financial Statements

23. If adequate disclosure about the material uncertainty is not made in the financial statements, the auditor shall: (Ref: Para.A32–A34)

(a) Express a qualified opinion or adverse opinion, as appropriate, in accordance with SA 705 (Revised)4; and

(b) In the Basis for Qualified (Adverse) Opinion section of the auditor's report, state that a material uncertainty exists that may cast significant doubt on the entity's ability to continue as a going concern and that the financial statements do not adequately disclose this matter.

Management Unwilling to Make or Extend Its Assessment

24. If management is unwilling to make or extend its assessment when requested to do so by the auditor, the auditor shall consider the implications for the auditor's report. (Ref: Para.A35)

Communication with Those Charged with Governance

25. Unless all those charged with governance are involved in managing the entity, 5 the auditor shall communicate with those charged with governance events or conditions identified that may cast significant doubt on the entity's ability to continue as a going concern. Such communication with those charged with governance shall include the following:

(a) Whether the events or conditions constitute a material uncertainty;

(b) Whether management's use of the going concern basis of accounting is appropriate in the preparation of the financial statements;

(c) The adequacy of related disclosures in the financial statements; and

(d) Where applicable, the implications for the auditor's report.

Significant Delay in the Approval of Financial Statements

26. If there is significant delay in the approval of the financial statements by management or those charged with governance after the date of the financial statements, the auditor shall inquire as to the reasons for the delay. If the auditor believes that the delay could be related to events or conditions relating to the going concern assessment, the auditor shall perform those additional audit procedures necessary, as described in paragraph 16, as well as consider the effect on the auditor's conclusion regarding the existence of a material uncertainty, as described in paragraph18.

STANDARD ON AUDITING (SA) 580: WRITTEN REPRESENTATIONS

Introduction

Scope of this SA

1. This Standard on Auditing (SA) deals with the auditor's responsibility to obtain written representations from management and, where appropriate, those charged with governance.

Written Representations as Audit Evidence

2. Audit evidence is all the information used by the auditor in arriving at the conclusions on which the audit opinion is based. written representations are necessary information that the auditor requires in connection with the audit of

the entity's financial statements. Accordingly, similar to responses to inquiries, written representations are audit evidence. *(Ref: Para.A1)*

3. Although written representations provide necessary audit evidence, they do not provide sufficient appropriate audit evidence on their own about any of the matters with which they deal. Furthermore, the fact that management has provided reliable written representations does not affect the nature or extent of other audit evidence that the auditor obtains about the fulfillment of management's responsibilities, or about specific assertions.

Effective Date

4. This SA is effective for audits of financial statements for periods beginning on or after 1st April, 2009

Objectives

5. The objectives of the auditor are:
   (a) To obtain written representations from management and, where appropriate, those charged with governance that they believe that they have fulfilled their responsibility for the preparation of the financial statements and for the completeness of the information provided to the auditor;
   (b) To support other audit evidence relevant to the financial statements or specific assertions in the financial statements by means of written representations, if determined necessary by the auditor or required by other SAs; and
   (c) To respond appropriately to written representations provided by management and, where appropriate, those charged with governance, or if management or, where appropriate, those charged with governance do not provide the written representations requested by the auditor.

Definition

6. For purposes of the SAs, the following term has the meaning attributed below

   Written representations – A written statement by management provided to the auditor to confirm certain matters or to support other audit evidence. Written representations in this context do not include financial statements, the assertions therein, or supporting books and records.

7. For purposes of this SA, references to "management" should be read as "management and, where appropriate, those charged with governance." Furthermore, in the case of a fair presentation framework, management is responsible for the preparation and fair presentation of the financial statements in accordance with the applicable financial reporting framework; or the preparation of financial statements that give a true and fair view in accordance with the applicable financial reporting framework.

Requirements

Management from Whom Written Representations Requested

8. The auditor shall request written representations from management with appropriate responsibilities for the financial statements and knowledge of the matters concerned. *(Ref: Para.A2-A6)*

Written Representations about Management's Responsibilities

Preparation of the Financial Statements

9. The auditor shall request management to provide a written representation that it has fulfilled its responsibility for the preparation of the financial statements in accordance with the applicable financial reporting framework, including where relevant their fair presentation, as set out in the terms of the audit engagement. *(Ref: Para. A7-A9, A14, A22)*

Information Provided and Completeness of Transactions

10. The auditor shall request management to provide a written representation that:
    (a) It has provided the auditor with all relevant information and access as agreed in the terms of the audit engagement, and
    (b) All transactions have been recorded and are reflected in the financial statements. *(Ref: Para. A7-A9, A14, A22)*

Description of Management's Responsibilities in the Written Representations

11. Management's responsibilities shall be described in the written representations required by paragraphs 9 and 10 in the manner in which these responsibilities are described in the terms of the audit engagement.

Other Written Representations

12. Other SAs require the auditor to request written representations. If, in addition to such required representations, the auditor determines that it is necessary to obtain one or more written representations to support other audit evidence relevant to the financial statements or one or more specific assertions in the financial statements, the auditor shall request such other written representations. *(Ref: Para. A10-A13, A14, A22)*

Date of and Period(s) Covered by Written Representations

13. The date of the written representations shall be as near as practicable to, but not after, the date of the auditor's report on the financial statements. The written representations shall be for all financial statements and period(s) referred to in the auditor's report. *(Ref: Para.A15-A18)*

Form of Written Representations

14. The written representations shall be in the form of a representation letter addressed to the auditor. If law or regulation requires management to make

written public statements about its responsibilities, and the auditor determines that such statements provide some or all of the representations required by paragraphs 9 or 10, the relevant matters covered by such statements need not be included in the representation letter. *(Ref: Para. A19-A21)*

Doubt as to the Reliability of Written Representations and Requested Written Representations Not Provided

Doubt as to the Reliability of Written Representations

15. If the auditor has concerns about the competence, integrity, ethical values or diligence of management, or about its commitment to or enforcement of these, the auditor shall determine the effect that such concerns may have on the reliability of representations (oral or written) and audit evidence in general. *(Ref: Para.A24-A25)*

16. In particular, if written representations are inconsistent with other audit evidence, the auditor shall perform audit procedures to attempt to resolve the matter. If the matter remains unresolved, the auditor shall reconsider the assessment of the competence, integrity, ethical values or diligence of management, or of its commitment to or enforcement of these, and shall determine the effect that this may have on the reliability of representations (oral or written) and audit evidence in general. *(Ref: Para. A23)*

17. If the auditor concludes that the written representations are not reliable, the auditor shall take appropriate actions, including determining the possible effect on the opinion in the auditor's report in accordance with SA 7054, having regard to the requirement in paragraph 19 of this.

Requested Written Representations Not Provided

18. If management does not provide one or more of the requested written representations, the auditor shall:
    (a) Discuss the matter with management;
    (b) Re-evaluate the integrity of management and evaluate the effect that this may have on the reliability of representations (oral or written) and audit evidence in general; and
    (c) Take appropriate actions, including determining the possible effect on the opinion in the auditor's report in accordance with SA 705, having regard to the requirement in paragraph 19 of this SA.

Written Representations about Management's Responsibilities

19. The auditor shall disclaim an opinion on the financial statements in accordance with SA 705 if: *(Ref: Para.A26-A27)*
    (a) The auditor concludes that there is sufficient doubt about the integrity of management such that the written representations required by paragraphs 9 and 10 are not reliable; or
    (b) Management does not provide the written representations required by paragraphs 9 and10

STANDARD ON AUDITING (SA) 600: USING THE WORK OF ANOTHER AUDITOR

Introduction

1. The Standard on Auditing (SA) 200, " Basic Principles Governing an Audit", states (paragraph 9):

"When the auditor delegates work to assistants or uses work performed by other auditors and experts, he will continue to be responsible for forming and expressing his opinion on the financial information. However, he will be entitled to rely on work performed by others, provided he exercises adequate skill and care and is not aware of any reason to believe that he should not have so relied. In the case of any independent statutory appointment to perform the work on which the auditor has to rely in forming his opinion, such as in the case of the work of branch auditors appointed under the Companies Act, 1956 the auditor's report should expressly state the fact of such reliance."

2. The purpose of this Standard on Auditing (SA) is to establish standards to be applied in situations where an auditor (referred to herein as the 'principal auditor'), reporting on the financial information of an entity, uses the work of another auditor (referred to herein as the 'other auditor') with respect to the financial information of one or more components included in the financial information of the entity. This Standard also discusses the principal auditor's responsibility in relation to his use of the work of the other auditor. In this Standard, the term 'financial information' encompasses 'financial statements'.
3. This Standard does not deal with those instances where two or more auditors are appointed as joint auditors1 nor does it deal with the auditor's relationship with a predecessor auditor.
4. When the principal auditor concludes that the financial information of a component is immaterial, the procedures outlined in this Statement do not apply. When several components, immaterial in themselves, are together material in relation to the financial information of the entity as a whole, the procedures outlined in this Statement should be considered.
5. When the principal auditor uses the work of another auditor, the principal auditor should determine how the work of the other auditor will affect the audit.
6. "Principal auditor" means the auditor with responsibility for reporting on the financial information of an entity when that financial information includes the financial information of one or more components audited by another auditor.
7. "Other auditor" means an auditor, other than the principal auditor, with responsibility for reporting on the financial information of a component which is included in the financial information audited by the principal auditor.
8. "Component" means a division, branch, subsidiary, joint venture, associated enterprises or other entity whose financial information is included in the financial information audited by the principal auditor.

Acceptance as Principal Auditor

9. The auditor should consider whether the auditor's own participation is sufficient to be able to act as the principal auditor. For this purpose the auditor would consider:
   (a) the materiality of the portion of the financial information which the principal auditor audits;
   (b) the principal auditor's degree of knowledge regarding the business of the components;
   (c) the risk of material misstatements in the financial information of the components audited by the other auditor; and
   (d) the performance of additional procedures as set out in this SA regarding the components audited by other auditor resulting in the principal auditor having significant participation in such audit.

The Principal Auditor's Procedures

10. In certain situations, the statute governing the entity may confer a right on the principal auditor to visit a component and examine the books of account and other records of the said component, if he thinks it necessary to do so. Where another auditor has been appointed for the component, the principal auditor would normally be entitled to rely upon the work of such auditor unless there are special circumstances to make it essential for him to visit the component and/or to examine the books of account and other records of the said component.

11. When planning to use the work of another auditor, the principal auditor should consider the professional competence of the other auditor in the context of specific assignment if the other auditor is not a member of the Institute of Chartered Accountants of India.

12. The principal auditor should perform procedures to obtain sufficient appropriate audit evidence, that the work of the other auditor is adequate **for** the principal auditor's purposes, in the context of the specific assignment. When using the work of another auditor, the principal auditor should ordinarily perform the following procedures:
    (a) Advise the other auditor of the use that is to be made of the other auditor's work and report and make sufficient arrangements for co-ordination of their efforts at the planning stage of the audit. The principal auditor would inform the other auditor of matters such as areas requiring special consideration, procedures for the identification of inter-component transactions that may require disclosure and the time-table for completion of audit; and
    (b) Advise the other auditor of the significant accounting, auditing and reporting requirements and obtain representation as to compliance with them.

13. The principal auditor might discuss with the other auditor the audit procedures applied or review a written summary of the other auditor's procedures and

findings which may be in the form of a completed questionnaire or check-list. The principal auditor may also wish to visit the other auditor. The nature, timing and extent of procedures will depend on the circumstances of the engagement and the principal auditor's knowledge of the professional competence of the other auditor. This knowledge may have been enhanced from the review of the previous audit work of the other auditor.

14. The principal auditor may conclude that it is not necessary to apply procedures such as those described in paragraph 13 because sufficient appropriate audit evidence previously obtained that acceptable quality control policies and procedures are complied with in the conduct of other auditor's practice

15. The principal auditor should consider the significant findings of the other auditor.

16. The principal auditor may consider it appropriate to discuss with the other auditor and the management of the component, the audit findings or other matters affecting the financial information of the components. He may also decide that supplemental tests of the records or the financial statements of the component are necessary. Such tests may, depending upon the circumstances, be performed by the principal auditor or the other auditor.

17. In certain circumstances, the other auditor may happen to be a person other than a professionally qualified auditor. This may happen, for instance, where a component is situated in a foreign country and the applicable laws permit a person other than a professionally qualified auditor to audit the financial statements of such component. In such circumstances, the procedures outlined in paragraphs 10 to 16 assume added importance.

18. The principal auditor should document in his working papers the components whose financial information was audited by other auditors; their significance to the financial information of the entity as a whole; the names of the other auditors; and any conclusions reached that individual components are not material. The principal auditor should also document the procedures performed and the conclusions reached. For example, the auditor would document the results of discussions with the other auditor and review of the written summary of the other auditor's procedures. However, the principal auditor need not document the reasons for limiting the procedures in the circumstances described at 14 above, provided those reasons are summarized elsewhere in the documentation maintained by the principal auditor. Where the other auditor's report is other than unmodified, the principal auditor should also document how he has dealt with the qualifications or adverse remarks contained in the other auditor's report in framing his own report.

Co-ordination between Auditors

19. There should be sufficient liaison between the principal auditor and the other auditor. For this purpose, the principal auditor may find it necessary to issue written communication(s) to the other auditor.

20. The other auditor, knowing the context in which his work is to be used by the principal auditor, should co-ordinate with the principal auditor. For example, by

bringing to the principal auditor's immediate attention any significant findings requiring to be dealt with at entity level, adhering to the time-table for audit of the component, etc. He should ensure compliance with the relevant statutory requirements. Similarly, the principal auditor should advise the other auditor of any matters that come to his attention that he thinks may have an important bearing on the other auditor's work.

21. When considered necessary by him, the principal auditor may require the other auditor to answer a detailed questionnaire regarding matters on which the principal auditor requires information for discharging his duties. The other auditor should respond to such questionnaire on a timely basis.

Reporting Considerations

22. When the principal auditor concludes, based on his procedures, that the work of the other auditor cannot be used and the principal auditor has not been able to perform sufficient additional procedures regarding the financial information of the component audited by the other auditor, the principal auditor should express a qualified opinion or disclaimer of opinion because there is a limitation on the scope of audit.

23. In all circumstances, if the other auditor issues, or intends to issue, a modified auditor's report, the principal auditor should consider whether the subject of the modification is of such nature and significance, in relation to the financial information of the entity on which the principal auditor is reporting that it requires a modification of the principal auditor's report.

Division of Responsibility

24. The principal auditor would not be responsible in respect of the work entrusted to the other auditors, except in circumstances which should have aroused his suspicion about the reliability of the work performed by the other auditors.

25. When the principal auditor has to base his opinion on the financial information of the entity as a whole relying upon the statements and reports of the other auditors, his report should state clearly the division of responsibility for the financial information of the entity by indicating the extent to which the financial information of components audited by the other auditors have been included in the financial information of the entity, e.g., the number of divisions/branches/subsidiaries or other components audited by other auditors.

Effective Date

26. This Standard on Auditing becomes operative for all audits relating to accounting periods beginning on or after April 1, 2002.

Compatibility with International Standard on Auditing (ISA) 600

The auditing standards established in this Standard on Auditing (SA) are generally consistent, in all material respects, with those set out in ISA 600 "Using the Work of another Auditor".

STANDARD ON AUDITING (SA) 610: USING THE WORK OF INTERNAL AUDITORS

Introduction

Scope of this SA

1. This Standard on Auditing (SA) deals with the external auditor's responsibilities if using the work of internal auditors. This includes (a) using the work of the internal audit function in obtaining audit evidence and (b) using internal auditors to provide direct assistance under the direction, supervision and review of the external auditor.
2. This SA does not apply if the entity does not have an internal audit function. (Ref: Para.A2)
3. If the entity has an internal audit function, the requirements in this SA relating to using the work of that function do not apply if:
   (a) The responsibilities and activities of the function are not relevant to the auditor
   (b) Based on the auditor's preliminary understanding of the function obtained as a result of procedures performed under

   SA 315, 1 the external auditor does not expect to use the work of the function in obtaining audit evidence.

   Nothing in this SA requires the external auditor to use the work of the internal audit function to modify the nature or timing, or reduce the extent, of audit procedures to be performed directly by the external auditor; it remains a decision of the external auditor in establishing the overall audit strategy.
4. Furthermore, the requirements in this SA relating to direct assistance do not apply if the external auditor does not plan to use internal auditors to provide direct assistance.
5. In some cases, the external auditor may be prohibited, or restricted to some extent, by law or regulation from using the work of the internal audit function or using internal auditors to provide direct assistance. The SAs do not override laws or regulations that govern an audit of financial statements. Such prohibitions or restrictions will therefore not prevent the external auditor from complying with the SAs. (Ref: Para.A31)

Relationship between SA 315 and SA 610 (Revised)

6. Many entities establish internal audit functions as part of their internal control and governance structures. The objectives and scope of an internal audit function, the nature of its responsibilities and its organizational status, including the function's authority and accountability, vary widely and depend on the size and structure of the entity and the requirements of management and, where applicable, those charged with governance.

7. SA 315 addresses how the knowledge and experience of the internal audit function can inform the external auditor's understanding of the entity and its environment and identification and assessment of risks of material misstatement. SA 315 also explains how effective communication between the internal and external auditors also creates an environment in which the external auditor can be informed of significant matters that may affect the external auditor's work.

8. Depending on whether the internal audit function's organizational status and relevant policies and procedures adequately support the objectivity of the internal auditors, the level of competency of the internal audit function, and whether the function applies a systematic and disciplined approach, the external auditor may also be able to use the work of the internal audit function in a constructive and complementary manner. This SA addresses the external auditor's responsibilities when, based on the external auditor's preliminary understanding of the internal audit function obtained as a result of procedures performed under SA 315, the external auditor expects to use the work of the internal audit function as part of the audit evidence obtained4. Such use of that work modifies the nature or timing, or reduces the extent, of audit procedures to be performed directly by the external auditor.

9. In addition, this SA also addresses the external auditor's responsibilities if considering using internal auditors to provide direct assistance under the direction, supervision and review of the external auditor

10. There may be individuals in an entity that perform procedures similar to those performed by an internal audit function. However, unless performed by an objective and competent function that applies a systematic and disciplined approach, including quality control, such procedures would be considered internal controls and obtaining evidence regarding the effectiveness of such controls would be part of the auditor's responses to assessed risks in accordance with SA330.

The External Auditor's Responsibility for the Audit

11. The external auditor has sole responsibility for the audit opinion expressed, and that responsibility is not reduced by the external auditor's use of the work of the internal audit function or internal auditors to provide direct assistance on the engagement. Although they may perform audit procedures similar to those performed by the external auditor, neither the internal audit function nor the internal auditors are independent of the entity as is required of the external auditor in an audit of financial statements in accordance with SA 2006. This SA, therefore, defines the conditions that are necessary for the external auditor to be able to use the work of internal auditors. It also defines the necessary work effort to obtain sufficient appropriate evidence that the work of the internal audit function, or internal auditors providing direct assistance, is adequate for the purposes of the audit. The requirements are designed to provide a framework for the external auditor's judgments regarding the use of the work of internal auditors to prevent over or undue use of such work.

Effective Date

12. This SA is effective for audits of financial statements for periods beginning on or after 01st April, 2016.

Objectives

13. The objectives of the external auditor, where the entity has an internal audit function and the external auditor expects to use the work of the function to modify the nature or timing, or reduce the extent, of audit procedures to be performed directly by the external auditor, or to use internal auditors to provide direct assistance, are:
    (a) To determine whether the work of the internal audit function or direct assistance from internal auditors can be used, and if so, in which areas and to what extent; and having made that determination:
    (b) If using the work of the internal audit function, to determine whether that work is adequate for purposes of the audit; and
    (c) If using internal auditors to provide direct assistance, to appropriately direct, supervise and review their work.

Definitions

14. For purposes of the SAs, the following terms have the meanings attributed below:
    (a) Internal audit function – A function of an entity that performs assurance and consulting activities designed to evaluate and improve the effectiveness of the entity's governance, risk management and internal control processes. (Ref: Para.A1–A4)
    (b) Direct assistance – The use of internal auditors to perform audit procedures under the direction, supervision and review of the external auditor.

Requirements

Determining Whether, in Which Areas, and to What Extent the Work of the Internal Audit Function Can Be Used

Evaluating the Internal Audit Function

15. The external auditor shall determine whether the work of the internal audit function can be used for purposes of the audit by evaluating the following:
    (a) The extent to which the internal audit function's organizational status and relevant policies and procedures support the objectivity of the internal auditors; (Ref: Para.A5–A9)
    (b) The level of competence of the internal audit function; and (Ref: Para.A5–A9)
    (c) Whether the internal audit function applies a systematic and disciplined approach, including quality control. (Ref: Para. A10–A11)

16. The external auditor shall not use the work of the internal audit function if the external auditor determines that:
    (a) The function's organizational status and relevant policies and procedures do not adequately support the objectivity of internal auditors;
    (b) The function lacks sufficient competence; or
    (c) The function does not apply a systematic and disciplined approach, including quality control. (Ref: Para.A12–A14)

Determining the Nature and Extent of Work of the Internal Audit Function that Can Be Used

17. As a basis for determining the areas and the extent to which the work of the internal audit function can be used, the external auditor shall consider the nature and scope of the work that has been performed, or is planned to be performed, by the internal audit function and its relevance to the external auditor's overall audit strategy and audit plan. (Ref: Para.A15–A17)
18. The external auditor shall make all significant judgments in the audit engagement and, to prevent undue use of the work of the internal audit function, shall plan to use less of the work of the function and perform more of the work directly: (Ref: Para.A15–A17)
    (a) The more judgment is involved in:
        (i) Planning and performing relevant audit procedures; and
        (ii) Evaluating the audit evidence gathered; (Ref: Para.A18–A19)
    (b) The higher the assessed risk of material misstatement at the assertion level, with special consideration given to risks identified as significant; (Ref: Para.A20–A22)
    (c) The less the internal audit function's organizational status and relevant policies and procedures adequately support the objectivity of the internal auditors; and
    (d) The lower the level of competence of the internal audit functions.
19. The external auditor shall also evaluate whether, in aggregate, using the work of the internal audit function to the extent planned would still result in the external auditor being sufficiently involved in the audit, given the external auditor's sole responsibility for the audit opinion expressed. (Ref: Para. A15–A22)
20. The external auditor shall, in communicating with those charged with governance an overview of the planned scope and timing of the audit in accordance with SA 260, communicate how the external auditor has planned to use the work of the internal audit function. (Ref: Para.A23)

Using the Work of the Internal Audit Function

21. If the external auditor plans to use the work of the internal audit function, the external auditor shall discuss the planned use of its work with the function as a basis for coordinating their respective activities. (Ref: Para.A24–A26)

22. The external auditor shall read the reports of the internal audit function relating to the work of the function that the external auditor plans to use to obtain an understanding of the nature and extent of audit procedures it performed and the related findings.

23. The external auditor shall perform sufficient audit procedures on the body of work of the internal audit function as a whole that the external auditor plans to use to determine its adequacy for purposes of the audit, including evaluating whether

    (a) The work of the function had been properly planned, performed, supervised, reviewed and documented;

    (b) Sufficient appropriate evidence had been obtained to enable the function to draw reasonable conclusions; and

    (c) Conclusions reached are appropriate in the circumstances and the reports prepared by the function are consistent with the results of the work performed. (Ref: Para. A27–A30)

24. The nature and extent of the external auditor's audit procedures shall be responsive to the external auditor's evaluation of:

    (a) The amount of judgment involved;

    (b) The assessed risk of material misstatement;

    (c) The extent to which the internal audit function's organizational status and relevant policies and procedures support the objectivity of the internal auditors; and

    (d) The level of competence of the function; (Ref: Para. A27–A29) and shall include re-performance of some of the work. (Ref: Para.A30)

25. The external auditor shall also evaluate whether the external auditor's conclusions regarding the internal audit function in paragraph 15 of this SA and the determination of the nature and extent of use of the work of the function for purposes of the audit in paragraphs 18–19 of this SA remain appropriate.

Determining Whether, in Which Areas, and to What Extent Internal Auditors Can Be Used to Provide Direct Assistance

Determining Whether Internal Auditors Can Be Used to Provide Direct Assistance for Purposes of the Audit

26. The external auditor may be prohibited by law or regulation from obtaining direct assistance from internal auditors. If so, paragraphs 27–35 and 37 do not apply. (Ref: Para.A31)

27. If using internal auditors to provide direct assistance is not prohibited by law or regulation, and the external auditor plans to use internal auditors to provide direct assistance on the audit, the external auditor shall evaluate the existence and significance of threats to objectivity and the level of competence of the internal auditors who will be providing such assistance. The external auditor's evaluation of the existence and significance of threats to the internal auditors'

objectivity shall include inquiry of the internal auditors regarding interests and relationships that may create a threat to their objectivity. (Ref: Para. A32–A34)

28. The external auditor shall not use an internal auditor to provide direct assistance if:
    (a) There are significant threats to the objectivity of the internal auditor; or
    (b) The internal auditor lacks sufficient competence to perform the proposed work. (Ref: Para.A32–A34)

Determining the Nature and Extent of Work that Can Be Assigned to Internal Auditors Providing Direct Assistance

29. In determining the nature and extent of work that may be assigned to internal auditors and the nature, timing and extent of direction, supervision and review that is appropriate in the circumstances, the external auditor shall consider:
    (a) The amount of judgment involved in:
        (i) Planning and performing relevant audit procedures; and
        (ii) Evaluating the audit evidence gathered;
    (b) The assessed risk of material misstatement; and
    (c) The external auditor's evaluation of the existence and significance of threats to the objectivity and level of competence of the internal auditors who will be providing such assistance. (Ref: Para. A35–A39)

30. The external auditor shall not use internal auditors to provide direct assistance to perform procedures that:
    (a) Involve making significant judgments in the audit; (Ref: Para.A19)
    (b) Relate to higher assessed risks of material misstatement where the judgment required in performing the relevant audit procedures or evaluating the audit evidence gathered is more than limited; (Ref: Para.A38)
    (c) Relate to work with which the internal auditors have been involved and which has already been, or will be, reported to management or those charged with governance by the internal audit function; or
    (d) Relate to decisions the external auditor makes in accordance with this SA regarding the internal audit function and the use of its work or direct assistance. (Ref: Para.A35–A39)

31. Having appropriately evaluated whether and, if so, to what extent internal auditors can be used to provide direct assistance on the audit, the external auditor shall, in communicating with those charged with governance an overview of the planned scope and timing of the audit in accordance with SA 260,9 communicate the nature and extent of the planned use of internal auditors to provide direct assistance so as to reach a mutual understanding that such use is not excessive in the circumstances of the engagement. (Ref: Para.A39)

32. The external auditor shall evaluate whether, in aggregate, using internal auditors to provide direct assistance to the extent planned, together with the planned use of the work of the internal audit function, would still result in the

external auditor being sufficiently involved in the audit, given the external auditor's sole responsibility for the audit opinion expressed.

Using Internal Auditors to Provide Direct Assistance

33. Prior to using internal auditors to provide direct assistance for purposes of the audit, the external auditor shall:
    - (a) Obtain written agreement from an authorized representative of the entity that the internal auditors will be allowed to follow the external auditor's instructions, and that the entity will not intervene in the work the internal auditor performs for the external auditor; and
    - (b) Obtain written agreement from the internal auditors that they will keep confidential specific matters as instructed by the external auditor and inform the external auditor of any threat to their objectivity.
34. The external auditor shall direct, supervise and review the work performed by internal auditors on the engagement in accordance with SA 220. In so doing:
    - (a) The nature, timing and extent of direction, supervision, and review shall recognize that the internal auditors are not independent of the entity and be responsive to the outcome of the evaluation of the factors in paragraph 29 of this SA; and
    - (b) The review procedures shall include the external auditor checking back to the underlying audit evidence for some of the work performed by the internal auditors.

    The direction, supervision and review by the external auditor of the work performed by the internal auditors shall be sufficient in order for the external auditor to be satisfied that the internal auditors have obtained sufficient appropriate audit evidence to support the conclusions based on that work. (Ref: Para. A40–A41)
35. In directing, supervising and reviewing the work performed by internal auditors, the external auditor shall remain alert for indications that the external auditor's evaluations in paragraph 27 are no longer appropriate.

Documentation

36. If the external auditor uses the work of the internal audit function, the external auditor shall include in the audit documentation:
    - (a) The evaluation of:
        - (i) Whether the function's organizational status and relevant policies and procedures adequately support the objectivity of the internal auditors;
        - (ii) The level of competence of the function; and
        - (iii) Whether the function applies a systematic and disciplined approach, including quality control;
    - (b) The nature and extent of the work used and the basis for that decision; and

(c) The audit procedures performed by the external auditor to evaluate the adequacy of the work used.

37. If the external auditor uses internal auditors to provide direct assistance on the audit, the external auditor shall include in the audit documentation:

(a) The evaluation of the existence and significance of threats to the objectivity of the internal auditors, and the level of competence of the internal auditors used to provide direct assistance;

(b) The basis for the decision regarding the nature and extent of the work performed by the internal auditors;

(c) Who reviewed the work performed and the date and extent of that review in accordance with SA 230;

(d) The written agreements obtained from an authorized representative of the entity and the internal auditors under paragraph 33 of this SA; and

(e) The working papers prepared by the internal auditors who provided direct assistance on the audit engagement.

STANDARD ON AUDITING (SA) 620: USING THE WORK OF AN AUDITOR'S EXPERT

Introduction

Scope of this

1. This Standard on Auditing (SA) deals with the auditor's responsibilities regarding the use of an individual or organization's work in a field of expertise other than accounting or auditing, when that work is used to assist the auditor in obtaining sufficient appropriate audit evidence.

2. This SA does not deal with:

(a) Situations where the engagement team includes a member with expertise in specialized area of accounting or auditing, which is dealt with in SA 2201;or

(b) The auditor's use of the work of an individual or organization possessing expertise in a field other than accounting or auditing, whose work in that field is used by the entity to assist the entity in preparing the financial statements(a management's expert), which is dealt with in SA5002.

The Auditor's Responsibility for the Audit Opinion

3. The auditor has sole responsibility for the audit opinion expressed, and that responsibility is not reduced by the auditor's use of the work of an auditor's expert. Nonetheless, if the auditor using the work of an auditor's expert, having followed this SA, concludes that the work of that expert is adequate for the auditor's purposes, the auditor may accept that expert's findings or conclusions in the expert's field as appropriate audit evidence.

Effective Date

4. This SA is effective for audits of financial statements for periods beginning on or after April 1, 2010.

Objectives

5. The objectives of the auditor are:
   (a) To determine whether to use the work of an auditor's expert; and
   (b) If using the work of an auditor's expert, to determine whether that work is adequate for the auditor's purposes.

Definitions

6. For purposes of the SAs, the following terms have the meanings attributed below:
   (a) Auditor's expert – An individual or organization possessing expertise in a field other than accounting or auditing, whose work in that field is used by the auditor to assist the auditor in obtaining sufficient appropriate audit evidence. An auditor's expert may be either an auditor's internal expert (who is a partner or staff, including temporary staff, of the auditor's firm or a network firm), or an auditor's external expert. (Ref: Para.A1-A3)
   (b) Expertise – Skills, knowledge and experience in a particular field.
   (c) Management's expert – An individual or organization possessing expertise in a field other than accounting or auditing, whose work in that field is used by the entity to assist the entity in preparing the financial statements.

Requirements

Determining the Need for an Auditor's Expert

7. If expertise in a field other than accounting or auditing is necessary to obtain sufficient appropriate audit evidence, the auditor shall determine whether to use the work of an auditor's expert. (Ref: Para. A4- A9)

Nature, Timing and Extent of Audit Procedures

8. The nature, timing and extent of the auditor's procedures with respect to the requirements in paragraphs 9-13 of this SA will vary depending on the circumstances. In determining the nature, timing and extent of those procedures, the auditor shall consider matters including: (Ref: Para.A10)
   (a) The nature of the matter to which that expert's work relates;
   (b) The risks of material misstatement in the matter to which that expert's work relates;
   (c) The significance of that expert's work in the context of the audit;
   (d) The auditor's knowledge of and experience with previous work performed by that expert; and

(e) Whether that expert is subject to the auditor's firm's quality control policies and procedures. (Ref: Para. A11-A13)

The Competence, Capabilities and Objectivity of the Auditor's Expert

9. The auditor shall evaluate whether the auditor's expert has the necessary competence, capabilities and objectivity for the auditor's purposes. In the case of an auditor's external expert, the evaluation of objectivity shall include inquiry regarding interests and relationships that may create a threat to that expert's objectivity. (Ref: Para.A14-A20)

Obtaining an Understanding of the Field of Expertise of the Auditor's Expert

10. The auditor shall obtain a sufficient understanding of the field of expertise of the auditor's expert to enable the auditor to: (Ref: Para.A21-A22)
    (a) Determine the nature, scope and objectives of that expert's work for the auditor's purposes; and
    (b) Evaluate the adequacy of that work for the auditor's purposes.

Agreement with the Auditor's Expert

11. The auditor shall agree, in writing when appropriate, on the following matters with the auditor's expert: (Ref: Para.A23-A26)
    (a) The nature, scope and objectives of that expert's work; (Ref: Para.A27)
    (b) The respective roles and responsibilities of the auditor and that expert; (Ref: Para.A28-A29)
    (c) The nature, timing and extent of communication between the auditor and that expert, including the form of any report to be provided by that expert; and (Ref: Para.A30)
    (d) The need for the auditor's expert to observe confidentiality requirements. (Ref: Para.A31)

Evaluating the Adequacy of the Auditor's Expert's Work

12. The auditor shall evaluate the adequacy of the auditor's expert's work for the auditor's purposes, including: (Ref: Para. A32)
    (a) The relevance and reasonableness of that expert's findings or conclusions, and their consistency with other audit evidence; (Ref: Para.A33-A34)
    (b) If that expert's work involves use of significant assumptions and methods, the relevance and reasonableness of those assumptions and methods in the circumstances; and (Ref: Para. A35-A37)
    (c) If that expert's work involves the use of source data that is significant to that expert's work, the relevance, completeness, and accuracy of that source data. (Ref: Para.A38-A39)
13. If the auditor determines that the work of the auditor's expert is not adequate for the auditor's purposes, the auditor shall: (Ref: Para.A40)

(a) Agree with that expert on the nature and extent of further work to be performed by that expert; or

(b) Perform further audit procedures appropriate to the circumstances.

Reference to the Auditor's Expert in the Auditor's Report

14. The auditor shall not refer to the work of an auditor's expert in an auditor's report containing an unmodified opinion unless required by law or regulation to do so. If such reference is required by law or regulation, the auditor shall indicate in the auditor's report that the reference does not reduce the auditor's responsibility for the audit opinion. (Ref: Para.A41)

15. If the auditor makes reference to the work of an auditor's expert in the auditor's report because such reference is relevant to an understanding of a modification to the auditor's opinion, the auditor shall indicate in the auditor's report that such reference does not reduce the auditor's responsibility for that opinion. (Ref: Para.A42)

STANDARD ON AUDITING (SA) 700: FORMING AN OPINION AND REPORTING ON FINANCIAL STATEMENTS

Introduction

Scope of this SA

1. This Standard on Auditing (SA) deals with the auditor's responsibility to form an opinion on the financial statements. It also deals with the form and content of the auditor's report issued as a result of an audit of financial statements.

2. SA 701 deals with the auditor's responsibility to communicate key audit matters in the auditor's report. SA 705 (Revised) and SA 706 (Revised) deal with how the form and content of the auditor's report are affected when the auditor expresses a modified opinion or includes an Emphasis of Matter paragraph or an Other Matter paragraph in the auditor's report. Other SAs also contain reporting requirements that are applicable when issuing an auditor's report.

3. This SA applies to an audit of a complete set of general purpose financial statements and is written in that context. SA 800 deals with special considerations when financial statements are prepared in accordance with a special purpose framework. SA 805 deals with special considerations relevant to an audit of a single financial statement or of a specific element, account or item of a financial statement. This SA also applies to audits for which SA 800 or SA 805 apply.

4. The requirements of this SA are aimed at addressing an appropriate balance between the need for consistency and comparability in auditor reporting globally and the need to increase the value of auditor reporting by making the information provided in the auditor's report more relevant to users. This SA promotes consistency in the auditor's report, but recognizes the need for

flexibility to accommodate particular circumstances of individual jurisdictions. Consistency in the auditor's report, when the audit has been conducted in accordance with SAs, promotes credibility in the global marketplace by making more readily identifiable those audits that have been conducted in accordance with globally recognized standards. It also helps to promote the user's understanding and to identify unusual circumstances when they occur.

Effective Date

5. This SA is effective for audits of financial statements for periods beginning on or after April 1, 2018.

Objectives

6. The objectives of the auditor are:

(a) To form an opinion on the financial statements based on an evaluation of the conclusions drawn from the audit evidence obtained; and

(b) To express clearly that opinion through a written report.

Definitions

7. For purposes of the SAs, the following terms have the meanings attributed below:

(a) General purpose financial statements – Financial statements prepared in accordance with a general purpose framework.

(b) General purpose framework – A financial reporting framework designed to meet the common financial information needs of a wide range of users. The financial reporting framework may be a fair presentation framework or a compliance framework.

The term "fair presentation framework" is used to refer to a financial reporting framework that requires compliance with the requirements of the framework and:

(i) Acknowledges explicitly or implicitly that, to achieve fair presentation of the financial statements, it may be necessary for management to provide disclosures beyond those specifically required by the framework; or

(ii) Acknowledges explicitly that it may be necessary for management to depart from a requirement of the framework to achieve fair presentation of the financial statements. Such departures are expected to be necessary only in extremely rare circumstances.

The term "compliance framework" is used to refer to a financial reporting framework that requires compliance with the requirements of the framework, but does not contain the acknowledgements in (i) or (ii) above.

(c) Unmodified opinion – The opinion expressed by the auditor when the auditor concludes that the financial statements are prepared, in all material respects, in accordance with the applicable financial reporting framework.

8. Reference to "financial statements" in this SA means "a complete set of general purpose financial statements, including the related notes." The related notes ordinarily comprise a summary of significant accounting policies and other explanatory information and any other information required to be included as part of the financial statements by the laws and regulations governing the entity. The requirements of the applicable financial reporting framework determine the form and content of the financial statements, and what constitutes a complete set of financial statements.

9. Reference to "Accounting Standards" in this SA includes:
   - The Accounting Standards issued by the Institute of Chartered Accountants of India (ICAI); or The Standards of Accounting notified by the Central Government in pursuance of section 133 of the Companies Act, 2013 and the Rules there under; or
   - The International Financial Reporting Standards (IFRSs); or
   - The International Public Sector Accounting Standards (IPSASs) issued by the International Public Sector Accounting Standards Board;

   As may be applicable to the entity.

Requirements

Forming an Opinion on the Financial Statements

10. The auditor shall form an opinion on whether the financial statements are prepared, in all material respects, in accordance with the applicable financial reporting framework.

11. In order to form that opinion, the auditor shall conclude as to whether the auditor has obtained reasonable assurance about whether the financial statements as a whole are free from material misstatement, whether due to fraud or error. That conclusion shall take into account:
    (a) The auditor's conclusion, in accordance with SA 330, whether sufficient appropriate audit evidence has been obtained;
    (b) The auditor's conclusion, in accordance with SA 450, whether uncorrected misstatements are material, individually or in aggregate; and
    (c) The evaluations required by paragraphs12–15.

12. The auditor shall evaluate whether the financial statements are prepared, in all material respects, in accordance with the requirements of the applicable financial reporting framework. This evaluation shall include consideration of the qualitative aspects of the entity's accounting practices, including indicators of possible bias in management's judgments. (Ref: Para.A1–A3)

13. In particular, the auditor shall evaluate whether, in view of the requirements of the applicable financial reporting framework:
    (a) The financial statements adequately disclose the significant accounting policies selected and applied;

(b) The accounting policies selected and applied are consistent with the applicable financial reporting framework and are appropriate;

(c) The accounting estimates made by management are reasonable;

(d) The information presented in the financial statements is relevant, reliable, comparable, and understandable;

(e) The financial statements provide adequate disclosures to enable the intended users to understand the effect of material transactions and events on the information conveyed in the financial statements; and (Ref: Para.A4)

(f) The terminology used in the financial statements, including the title of each financial statement, is appropriate.

14. When the financial statements are prepared in accordance with a fair presentation framework, the evaluation required by paragraphs 12–13 shall also include whether the financial statements achieve fair presentation. The auditor's evaluation as to whether the financial statements achieve fair presentation shall include consideration of:

(a) The overall presentation, structure and content of the financial statements; and

(b) Whether the financial statements, including the related notes, represent the underlying transactions and events in a manner that achieves fair presentation.

15. The auditor shall evaluate whether the financial statements adequately refer to or describe the applicable financial reporting framework. (Ref: Para.A5–A10)

Form of Opinion

16. The auditor shall express an unmodified opinion when the auditor concludes that the financial statements are prepared, in all material respects, in accordance with the applicable financial reporting framework.

17. If the auditor:

(a) concludes that, based on the audit evidence obtained, the financial statements as a whole are not free from material misstatement; or

(b) is unable to obtain sufficient appropriate audit evidence to conclude that the financial statements as a whole are free from material misstatement,

The auditor shall modify the opinion in the auditor's report in accordance with SA 705 (Revised).

18. If financial statements prepared in accordance with the requirements of a fair presentation framework do not achieve fair presentation, the auditor shall discuss the matter with management and, depending on the requirements of the applicable financial reporting framework and how the matter is resolved, shall determine whether it is necessary to modify the opinion in the auditor's report in accordance with SA 705 (Revised). (Ref: Para.A11)

19. When the financial statements are prepared in accordance with a compliance framework, the auditor is not required to evaluate whether the financial

statements achieve fair presentation. However, if in extremely rare circumstances the auditor concludes that such financial statements are misleading; the auditor shall discuss the matter with management and, depending on how it is resolved, shall determine whether, and how, to communicate it in the auditor's report. (Ref: Para.A12)

Auditor's Report

20. The auditor's report shall be in writing. (Ref: Para.A13–A14)

Auditor's Report for Audits Conducted in Accordance with Standards on Auditing

Title

21. The auditor's report shall have a title that clearly indicates that it is the report of an independent auditor. (Ref: Para.A15)

Addressee

22. The auditor's report shall be addressed, as appropriate, based on the circumstances of the engagement. (Ref: Para.A16)

Auditor's Opinion

23. The first section of the auditor's report shall include the auditor's opinion, and shall have the heading "Opinion".

24. The Opinion section of the auditor's report shall also:

    (a) Identify the entity whose financial statements have been audited;

    (b) State that the financial statements have been audited;

    (c) Identify the title of each statement comprising the financial statements;

    (d) Refer to the notes, including the summary of significant accounting policies; and

    (e) Specify the date of, or period covered by, each financial statement comprising the financial statements. (Ref: Para.A17–A18)

25. When expressing an unmodified opinion on financial statements prepared in accordance with a fair presentation framework, the auditor's opinion shall, unless otherwise required by law or regulation, use one of the following phrases, which are regarded as being equivalent:

    (a) In our opinion, the accompanying financial statements present fairly, in all material respects, [...] in accordance with [the applicable financial reporting framework]; or

    (b) In our opinion, the accompanying financial statements give a true and fair view of [...] in accordance with [the applicable financial reporting framework]. (Ref: Para.A19–A26)

26. When expressing an unmodified opinion on financial statements prepared in accordance with a compliance framework, the auditor's opinion shall be that the accompanying financial statements are prepared, in all material respects, in accordance with [the applicable financial reporting framework]. (Ref: Para.A21–A26)

27. If the reference to the applicable financial reporting framework in the auditor's opinion is not to Accounting Standards referred to in paragraph 9, the auditor's opinion shall identify the origin of such other framework.

Basis for Opinion

28 The auditor's report shall include a section, directly following the Opinion section, with the heading "Basis for Opinion", that: (Ref: Para. A27)

(a) States that the audit was conducted in accordance with Standards on Auditing; (Ref: Para.A28)

(b) Refers to the section of the auditor's report that describes the auditor's responsibilities under the SAs;

(c) Includes a statement that the auditor is independent of the entity in accordance with the relevant ethical requirements relating to the audit, and has fulfilled the auditor's other ethical responsibilities in accordance with these requirements. The statement shall refer to the *Code of Ethics issued by ICAI* (Ref: Para.A29–A34)

(d) States whether the auditor believes that the audit evidence the auditor has obtained is sufficient and appropriate to provide a basis for the auditor's opinion.

Going Concern

29. Where applicable, the auditor shall report in accordance with SA 570 (Revised).

Key Audit Matters

30. For audits of complete sets of general purpose financial statements of listed entities, the auditor shall communicate key audit matters in the auditor's report in accordance with SA701.

31. When the auditor is otherwise required by law or regulation or decides to communicate key audit matters in the auditor's report, the auditor shall do so in accordance with SA 701. (Ref: Para. A35– A38)

Responsibilities for the Financial Statements

32. The auditor's report shall include a section with a heading "Responsibilities of Management for the Financial Statements." The auditor's report shall use the term that is appropriate in the context of the legal framework applicable to the entity and need not refer specifically to "management". In some entities, the appropriate reference may be to those charged with governance. (Ref: Para.A39)

33. This section of the auditor's report shall describe management's responsibility for: (Ref: Para. A40– A43)

(a) Preparing the financial statements in accordance with the applicable financial reporting framework, and for such internal control as management determines is necessary to enable the preparation of financial statements that are free from material misstatement, whether due to fraud or error; and

(b) Assessing the entity's ability to continue as a going concern14 and whether the use of the going concern basis of accounting is appropriate as well as disclosing, if applicable, matters relating to going concern. The explanation of management's responsibility for this assessment shall include a description of when the use of the going concern basis of accounting is appropriate. (Ref: Para.A43)

34. This section of the auditor's report shall also identify those responsible for the oversight of the financial reporting process, when those responsible for such oversight are different from those who fulfill the responsibilities described in paragraph 33 above. In this case, the heading of this section shall also refer to "Those Charged with Governance" or such term that is appropriate in the context of the legal framework applicable to entity. (Ref: Para.A44)

35. When the financial statements are prepared in accordance with a fair presentation framework, the description of responsibilities for the financial statements in the auditor's report shall refer to "the preparation and fair presentation of these financial statements" or "the preparation of financial statements that give a true and fair view," as appropriate in the circumstances.

Auditor's Responsibilities for the Audit of the Financial Statements

36. The auditor's report shall include a section with the heading "Auditor's Responsibilities for the Audit of the Financial Statements."

37. This section of the auditor's report shall: (Ref: Para.A45)

(a) State that the objectives of the auditor are to:

(i) Obtain reasonable assurance about whether the financial statements as a whole are free from material misstatement, whether due to fraud or error; and

(ii) Issue an auditor's report that includes the auditor's opinion. (Ref: Para.A46)

(b) State that reasonable assurance is a high level of assurance, but is not a guarantee that an audit conducted in accordance with SAs will always detect a material misstatement when it exists; and

(c) State that misstatements can arise from fraud or error, and either:

(i) Describe that they are considered material if, individually or in the aggregate, they could reasonably be expected to influence the economic decisions of users taken on the basis of these Financial statements; or

(ii) Provide a definition or description of materiality in accordance with the applicable financial reporting framework. (Ref: Para. A47)

38. The Auditor's Responsibilities for the Audit of the Financial Statements section of the auditor's report shall further: (Ref: Para.A45)

(a) State that, as part of an audit in accordance with SAs, the auditor exercises professional judgment and maintains professional skepticism throughout the audit; and

(b) Describe an audit by stating that the auditor's responsibilities are:

(i) To identify and assess the risks of material misstatement of the financial statements, whether due to fraud or error; to design and perform audit procedures responsive to those risks; and to obtain audit evidence that is sufficient and appropriate to provide a basis for the auditor's opinion. The risk of not detecting a material misstatement resulting from fraud is higher than for one resulting from error, as fraud may involve collusion, forgery, intentional omissions, misrepresentations, or the override of internal control.

(ii) To obtain an understanding of internal control relevant to the audit in order to design audit procedures that are appropriate in the circumstances, but not for the purpose of expressing an opinion on the effectiveness of the entity's internal control. In circumstances when the auditor also has a responsibility to express an opinion on the effectiveness of internal control in conjunction with the audit of the financial statements, the auditor shall omit the phrase that the auditor's consideration of internal control is not for the purpose of expressing an opinion on the effectiveness of the entity's internal control.

(iii) To evaluate the appropriateness of accounting policies used and the reasonableness of accounting estimates and related disclosures made by management.

(iv) To conclude on the appropriateness of management's use of the going concern basis of accounting and, based on the audit evidence obtained, whether a material uncertainty exists related to events or conditions that may cast significant doubt on the entity's ability to continue as a going concern. If the auditor concludes that a material uncertainty exists, the auditor is required to draw attention in the auditor's report to the related disclosures in the financial statements or, if such disclosures are inadequate, to modify the opinion. The auditor's conclusions are based on the audit evidence obtained up to the date of the auditor's report. However, future events or conditions may cause an entity to cease to continue as a going concern.

(v) When the financial statements are prepared in accordance with a fair presentation framework, to evaluate the overall presentation, structure and content of the financial statements, including the disclosures, and whether the financial statements represent the underlying transactions and events in a manner that achieves fair presentation.

(c) When SA 600 applies, further describe the auditor's responsibilities in a group audit engagement by stating:

The division of responsibility for the financial information of the entity by indicating the extent to which the financial information of components is audited by the other auditors has been included in the financial information of the entity, e.g., the number of divisions/branches/subsidiaries or other components audited by other auditors

39. The Auditor's Responsibilities for the Audit of the Financial Statements section of the auditor's report also shall: (Ref: Para.A45)

(a) State that the auditor communicates with those charged with governance regarding, among other matters, the planned scope and timing of the audit and significant audit findings, including any significant deficiencies in internal control that the auditor identifies during the audit;

(b) State that the auditor provides those charged with governance with a statement that the auditor has complied with relevant ethical requirements regarding independence and communicate with them all relationships and other matters that may reasonably be thought to bear on the auditor's independence, and where applicable, related safeguards; and

(c) For audits of financial statements of all such entities for which key audit matters are communicated in accordance with SA 701, state that, from the matters communicated with those charged with governance, the auditor determines those matters that were of most significance in the audit of the financial statements of the current period and are therefore the key audit matters. In accordance with the requirements of SA 701, the auditor describes these matters in the auditor's report unless law or regulation precludes public disclosure about the matter or when, in extremely rare circumstances, the auditor determines that a matter should not be communicated in the auditor's report because the adverse consequences of doing so would reasonably be expected to outweigh the public interest benefits of such communication. (Ref: Para.A48)

Location of the description of the auditor's responsibilities for the audit of the financial statements

40. The description of the auditor's responsibilities for the audit of the financial statements required by paragraphs 38–39 shall be included: (Ref: Para.A49)

(a) Within the body of the auditor's report;

(b) Within an appendix to the auditor's report, in which case the auditor's report shall include a reference to the location of the appendix; or (Ref: Para.A49–A50)

(c) By a specific reference within the auditor's report to the location of such a description on a website of an appropriate authority, where law, regulation or the auditing standards expressly permit the auditor to do so. (Ref: Para. A49, A51–A52)

41. When the auditor refers to a description of the auditor's responsibilities on a website of an appropriate authority, the auditor shall determine that such description addresses, and is not inconsistent with, the requirements in paragraphs 38–39 of this SA. (Ref: Para.A51)

Other Reporting Responsibilities

42. If the auditor addresses other reporting responsibilities in the auditor's report on the financial statements that are in addition to the auditor's responsibilities under the SAs, these other reporting responsibilities shall be addressed in a separate section in the auditor's report with a heading titled "Report on Other Legal and Regulatory Requirements" or otherwise as appropriate to the content of the section, unless these other reporting responsibilities address the same topics as those presented under the reporting responsibilities required by the SAs in which case the other reporting responsibilities may be presented in the same section as the related report elements required by the SAs. (Ref: Para.A53–A55)

43. If other reporting responsibilities are presented in the same section as the related report elements required by the SAs, the auditor's report shall clearly differentiate the other reporting responsibilities from the reporting that is required by the SAs. (Ref: Para.A55)

44. If the auditor's report contains a separate section that addresses other reporting responsibilities, the requirements of paragraphs 20–39 of this SA shall be included under a section with a heading "Report on the Audit of the Financial Statements." The "Report on Other Legal and Regulatory Requirements" shall follow the "Report on the Audit of the Financial Statements." (Ref: Para.A55)

Signature of the Auditor

45. The auditor's report shall be signed. The report is signed by the auditor (i.e. the engagement partner) in his personal name. Where the firm is appointed as the auditor, the report is signed in the personal name of the auditor and in the name of the audit firm. The partner/proprietor signing the audit report also needs to mention the membership number assigned by the Institute of Chartered Accountants of India. They also include the registration number of the firm, wherever applicable, as allotted by ICAI, in the audit reports signed by them17. (Ref: Para.A56-A57)

Place of Signature

46. The auditor's report shall name specific location, which is ordinarily the city where the audit report is signed.

Date of the Auditor's Report

47. The auditor's report shall be dated no earlier than the date on which the auditor has obtained sufficient appropriate audit evidence on which to base the auditor's opinion on the financial statements, including evidence that: (Ref: Para.A58–A61)

    (a) All the statements that comprise the financial statements, including the related notes, have been prepared; and

    (b) Those with the recognized authority have asserted that they have taken responsibility for those financial statements.

Auditor's Report Prescribed by Law or Regulation

48. If the auditor is required by law or regulation applicable to the entity to use a specific layout, or wording of the auditor's report, the auditor's report shall refer to Standards on Auditing only if the auditor's report includes, at a minimum, each of the following elements: (Ref: Para. A62–A63)

(a) A title.

(b) An addressee, as required by the circumstances of the engagement.

(c) An Opinion section containing an expression of opinion on the financial statements and a reference to the applicable financial reporting framework used to prepare the financial statements (see paragraph 27).

(d) An identification of the entity's financial statements that have been audited.

(e) A statement that the auditor is independent of the entity in accordance with the relevant ethical requirements relating to the audit, and has fulfilled the auditor's other ethical responsibilities in accordance with these requirements. The statement shall refer to the Code of Ethics issued by ICAI.

(f) Where applicable, a Basis for Qualified (or Adverse) Opinion section that addresses, and is not inconsistent with, the reporting requirements in paragraph 23 of SA 570(Revised).

(g) Where applicable, a section that includes the information required by SA 701, or additional information about the audit that is prescribed by law or regulation and that addresses, and is not inconsistent with, the reporting requirements in that SA. (Ref: Para.A63–A64)

(h) A description of management's responsibilities for the preparation of the financial statements and an identification of those responsible for the oversight of the financial reporting process that addresses, and is not inconsistent with, the requirements in paragraphs32–35.

(i) A reference to Standards on Auditing and the law or regulation, and a description of the auditor's responsibilities for an audit of the financial statements that addresses, and is not inconsistent with, the requirements in paragraphs 36–39. (Ref: Para.A49–A50)

(j) The auditor's signature.

(k) The Place of signature

(l) The date of the auditor's report.

Auditor's Report for Audits Conducted in Accordance with Both Standards on Auditing Issued by ICAI and International Standards on Auditing or Auditing Standards of Any Other Jurisdiction

49. An auditor may be required to conduct an audit in accordance with, in addition to the Standards on Auditing issued by ICAI, the International Standards on Auditing or auditing standards of any other jurisdiction. If this is the case, the auditor's report may refer to Standards on Auditing in addition to the International Standards on Auditing or auditing standards of such other jurisdiction, but the auditor shall do so only if: (Ref: Para. A68–A69)

(a) There is no conflict between the requirements in the ISAs or such auditing standards of other jurisdiction and those in SAs that would lead the auditor (i) to form a different opinion, or (ii) not to include an Emphasis of Matter paragraph or Other Matter paragraph that, in the particular circumstances, is required by SAs; and

(b) The auditor's report includes, at a minimum, each of the elements set out in paragraphs 48(a)–(m) above when the auditor uses the layout or wording specified by the Standards on Auditing. However, reference to "law or regulation" in paragraph 48(j) shall be read as reference to the Standards on Auditing. The auditor's report shall thereby identify such Standards on Auditing.

50. When the auditor's report refers to both the ISAs or the auditing standards of a specific jurisdiction and the Standards on Auditing issued by ICAI, the auditor's report shall clearly identify the same including the jurisdiction of origin of the other auditing standards.

Supplementary Information Presented with the Financial Statements (Ref: Para. A70–A76)

51. If supplementary information that is not required by the applicable financial reporting framework is presented with the audited financial statements, the auditor shall evaluate whether, in the auditor's professional judgment, supplementary information is nevertheless an integral part of the financial statements due to its nature or how it is presented. When it is an integral part of the financial statements, the supplementary information shall be covered by the auditor's opinion.

52. If supplementary information that is not required by the applicable financial reporting framework is not considered an integral part of the audited financial statements, the auditor shall evaluate whether such supplementary information is presented in a way that sufficiently and clearly differentiates it from the audited financial statements. If this is not the case, then the auditor shall ask management to change how the unaudited supplementary information is presented. If management refuses to do so, the auditor shall identify the unaudited supplementary information and explain in the auditor's report that such supplementary information has not been audited.

STANDARD ON AUDITING (SA) 701: COMMUNICATING KEY AUDIT MATTERS IN THE INDEPENDENT AUDITOR'S REPORT

Introduction

Scope of this SA

1. This Standard on Auditing (SA) deals with the auditor's responsibility to communicate key audit matters in the auditor's report. It is intended to address both the auditor's judgment as to what to communicate in the auditor's report and the form and content of such communication.

2. The purpose of communicating key audit matters is to enhance the communicative value of the auditor's report by providing greater transparency about the audit that was performed. Communicating key audit matters provides additional information to intended users of the financial statements ("intended users") to assist them in understanding those matters that, in the auditor's professional judgment, were of most significance in the audit of the financial statements of the current period. Communicating key audit matters may also assist intended users in understanding the entity and areas of significant management judgment in the audited financial statements. (Ref: Para.A1–A4)
3. The communication of key audit matters in the auditor's report may also provide intended users a basis to further engage with management and those charged with governance about certain matters relating to the entity, the audited financial statements, or the audit that was performed.
4. Communicating key audit matters in the auditor's report is in the context of the auditor having formed an opinion on the financial statements as a whole. Communicating key audit matters in the auditor's report is not:
   (a) A substitute for disclosures in the financial statements that the applicable financial reporting framework requires management to make, or that are otherwise necessary to achieve fair presentation;
   (b) A substitute for the auditor expressing a modified opinion when required by the circumstances of a specific audit engagement in accordance with SA 705(Revised);
   (c) A substitute for reporting in accordance with SA 570 (Revised)2 when a material uncertainty exists relating to events or conditions that may cast significant doubt on an entity's ability to continue as a going concern; or
   (d) A separate opinion on individual matters. (Ref: Para.A5–A8)
5. **This SA applies to audits of complete sets of general purpose financial statements of listed entities and circumstances when the auditor otherwise decides to communicate key audit matters in the auditor's report. ThisSAalsoplieswhentheauditorisrequiredbylaworregulationtocommuni catekeyauditmattersin**

   The auditor's report.3 However, SA 705 (Revised) prohibits the auditor from communicating key audit matters when the auditor disclaims an opinion on the financial statements, unless such reporting is required by law or regulation.

Effective Date

6. This SA is effective for audits of financial statements for periods beginning on or after April 1, 2018.

Objectives

7. The objectives of the auditor are to determine key audit matters and, having formed an opinion on the financial statements, communicate those matters by describing them in the auditor's report.

Definition

8. For purposes of the SAs, the following term has the meaning attributed below:

   Key audit matters— Those matters that, in the auditor's professional judgment, were of most significance in the audit of the financial statements of the current period. Key audit matters are selected from matters communicated with those charged with governance.

Requirements

Determining Key Audit Matters

9. The auditor shall determine, from the matters communicated with those charged with governance, those matters that required significant auditor attention in performing the audit. In making this determination, the auditor shall take into account the following: (Ref: Para.A9–A18)
   (a) Areas of higher assessed risk of material misstatement, or significant risks identified in accordance with SA 315.5 (Ref: Para.A19–A22)
   (b) Significant auditor judgments relating to areas in the financial statements that involved significant management judgment, including accounting estimates that have been identified as having high estimation uncertainty. (Ref: Para.A23–A24)
   (c) The effect on the audit of significant events or transactions that occurred during the period. (Ref: Para. A25–A26)

10. The auditor shall determine which of the matters determined in accordance with paragraph 9 were of most significance in the audit of the financial statements of the current period and therefore are the key audit matters. (Ref: Para. A9–A11, A27–A30)

Communicating Key Audit Matters

11. The auditor shall describe each key audit matter, using an appropriate subheading, in a separate section of the auditor's report under the heading "Key Audit Matters," unless the circumstances in paragraphs 14 or 15 apply. The introductory language in this section of the auditor's report shall state that:
   (a) Key audit matters are those matters that, in the auditor's professional judgment, were of most significance in the audit of the financial statements [of the current period]; and
   (b) These matters were addressed in the context of the audit of the financial statements as a whole, and in forming the auditor's opinion thereon, and the auditor does not provide a separate opinion on these matters. (Ref: Para.A31–A33)

Key Audit Matters Not a Substitute for Expressing a Modified Opinion

12. The auditor shall not communicate a matter in the Key Audit Matters section of the auditor's report when the auditor would be required to modify the opinion in accordance with SA 705 (Revised) as a result of the matter. (Ref: Para.A5)

Descriptions of Individual Key Audit Matters

13. The description of each key audit matter in the Key Audit Matters section of the auditor's report shall include a reference to the related disclosure(s), if any, in the financial statements and shall address: (Ref: Para.A34–A41)

(a) Why the matter was considered to be one of most significance in the audit and therefore determined to be a key audit matter; and (Ref: Para.A42–A45)

(b) How the matter was addressed in the audit. (Ref: Para.A46–A51)

Circumstances in Which a Matter Determined to Be a Key Audit Matter Is Not Communicated in the Auditor's Report

14. The auditor shall describe each key audit matter in the auditor's report unless: (Ref: Para. A53–A56)

(a) Law or regulation precludes public disclosure about the matter; or (Ref: Para.A52)

(b) In extremely rare circumstances, the auditor determines that the matter should not be communicated in the auditor's report because the adverse consequences of doing so would reasonably be expected to outweigh the public interest benefits of such communication. This shall not apply if the entity has publicly disclosed information about the matter.

Interaction between Descriptions of Key Audit Matters and Other Elements Required to Be Included in the Auditor's Report

15. A matter giving rise to a modified opinion in accordance with SA 705 (Revised), or a material uncertainty related to events or conditions that may cast significant doubt on the entity's ability to continue as a going concern in accordance with SA 570 (Revised), are by their nature key audit matters. However, in such circumstances, these matters shall not be described in the Key Audit Matters section of the auditor's report and the requirements in paragraphs 13–14 do not apply. Rather, the auditor shall:

(a) Report on these matter(s) in accordance with the applicable SA(s); and

(b) Include a reference to the Basis for Qualified (Adverse) Opinion or the Material Uncertainty Related to Going Concern section(s) in the Key Audit Matters section. (Ref: Para.A6–A7)

Form and Content of the Key Audit Matters Section in Other Circumstances

16. If the auditor determines, depending on the facts and circumstances of the entity and the audit, that there are no key audit matters to communicate or that the only key audit matters communicated are those matters addressed by paragraph 15, the auditor shall include a statement to this effect in a separate section of the auditor's report under the heading "Key Audit Matters." (Ref: Para. A57–A59)

Communication with Those Charged with Governance

17. The auditor shall communicate with those charged with governance:

(a) Those matters the auditor has determined to be the key audit matters; or

(b) If applicable, depending on the facts and circumstances of the entity and the audit, the auditor's determination that there are no key audit matters to communicate in the auditor's report. (Ref: Para. A60–A63)

Documentation

18. The auditor shall include in the audit documentation: (Ref: Para.A64)

(a) The matters that required significant auditor attention as determined in accordance with paragraph 9, and the rationale for the auditor's determination as to whether or not each of these matters is a key audit matter in accordance with paragraph 10;

(b) Where applicable, the rationale for the auditor's determination that there are no key audit matters to communicate in the auditor's report or that the only key audit matters to communicate are those matters addressed by paragraph 15;and

(c) Where applicable, the rationale for the auditor's determination not to communicate in the auditor's report a matter determined to be a key audit matter.

STANDARD ON AUDITING (SA) 705: MODIFICATIONS TO THE OPINION IN THE INDEPENDENT AUDITOR'S REPORT

Introduction

Scope of this SA

1. This Standard on Auditing (SA) deals with the auditor's responsibility to issue an appropriate report in circumstances when, in forming an opinion in accordance with SA 700 (Revised),1 the auditor concludes that a modification to the auditor's opinion on the financial statements is necessary. This SA also deals with how the form and content of the auditor's report is affected when the auditor expresses a modified opinion. In all cases, the reporting requirements in SA 700 (Revised) apply, and are not repeated in this SA unless they are explicitly addressed or amended by the requirements of this SA.

Types of Modified Opinions

2. This SA establishes three types of modified opinions, namely, a qualified opinion, an adverse opinion, and a disclaimer of opinion. The decision regarding which type of modified opinion is appropriate depends upon:

(a) The nature of the matter giving rise to the modification, that is, whether the financial statements are materially misstated or, in the case of an inability to obtain sufficient appropriate audit evidence, may be materially misstated; and

(b) The auditor's judgment about the pervasiveness of the effects or possible effects of the matter on the financial statements. (Ref: Para.A1)

Effective Date

3. This SA is effective for audits of financial statements for periods beginning on or after April 1, 2018.

Objective

4. The objective of the auditor is to express clearly an appropriately modified opinion on the financial statements that is necessary when:
   (a) The auditor concludes, based on the audit evidence obtained, that the financial statements as a whole are not free from material misstatement; or
   (b) The auditor is unable to obtain sufficient appropriate audit evidence to conclude that the financial statements as a whole are free from material misstatement.

Definitions

5. For purposes of the SAs, the following terms have the meanings attributed below:
   (a) Pervasive – A term used, in the context of misstatements, to describe the effects on the financial statements of misstatements or the possible effects on the financial statements of misstatements, if any, that are undetected due to an inability to obtain sufficient appropriate audit evidence. Pervasive effects on the financial statements are those that, in the auditor's judgment:
      (i) Are not confined to specific elements, accounts or items of the financial statements;
      (ii) If so confined, represent or could represent a substantial proportion of the financial statements; or
      (iii) In relation to disclosures, are fundamental to users' understanding of the financial statements.
   (b) Modified opinion – A qualified opinion, an adverse opinion or a disclaimer of opinion on the financial statements.

Requirements

Circumstances When a Modification to the Auditor's Opinion is required

6. The auditor shall modify the opinion in the auditor's report when:
   (a) The auditor concludes that, based on the audit evidence obtained, the financial statements as a whole are not free from material misstatement; or (Ref: Para.A2–A7)
   (b) The auditor is unable to obtain sufficient appropriate audit evidence to conclude that the financial statements as a whole are free from material misstatement. (Ref: Para. A8–A12)

Determining the Type of Modification to the Auditor's Opinion

Qualified Opinion

7. The auditor shall express a qualified opinion when:
   (a) The auditor, having obtained sufficient appropriate audit evidence, concludes that misstatements, individually or in the aggregate, are material, but not pervasive, to the financial statements; or
   (b) The auditor is unable to obtain sufficient appropriate audit evidence on which to base the opinion, but the auditor concludes that the possible effects on the financial statements of undetected misstatements, if any, could be material but not pervasive.

Adverse Opinion

8. The auditor shall express an adverse opinion when the auditor, having obtained sufficient appropriate audit evidence, concludes that misstatements, individually or in the aggregate, are both material and pervasive to the financial statements.

Disclaimer of Opinion

9. The auditor shall disclaim an opinion when the auditor is unable to obtain sufficient appropriate audit evidence on which to base the opinion, and the auditor concludes that the possible effects on the financial statements of undetected misstatements, if any, could be both material and pervasive.

10. The auditor shall disclaim an opinion when, in extremely rare circumstances involving multiple uncertainties, the auditor concludes that, notwithstanding having obtained sufficient appropriate audit evidence regarding each of the individual uncertainties, it is not possible to form an opinion on the financial statements due to the potential interaction of the uncertainties and their possible cumulative effect on the financial statements.

Consequence of an Inability to Obtain Sufficient Appropriate Audit Evidence Due to a Management-Imposed Limitation after the Auditor Has Accepted the Engagement

11. If, after accepting the engagement, the auditor becomes aware that management has imposed a limitation on the scope of the audit that the auditor considers likely to result in the need to express a qualified opinion or to disclaim an opinion on the financial statements, the auditor shall request that management remove the limitation.

12. If management refuses to remove the limitation referred to in paragraph 11 of this SA, the auditor shall communicate the matter to those charged with governance, unless all of those charged with governance are involved in managing the entity, and determine whether it is possible to perform alternative procedures to obtain sufficient appropriate audit evidence.

13. If the auditor is unable to obtain sufficient appropriate audit evidence, the auditor shall determine the implications as follows:
   (a) If the auditor concludes that the possible effects on the financial statements of undetected misstatements, if any, could be material but not pervasive, the auditor shall qualify the opinion; or
   (b) If the auditor concludes that the possible effects on the financial statements of undetected misstatements, if any, could be both material

and pervasive so that a qualification of the opinion would be inadequate to communicate the gravity of the situation, the auditor shall:

(i) Withdraw from the audit, where practicable and possible under applicable law or regulation; or (Ref: Para.A13)

(ii) If withdrawal from the audit before issuing the auditor's report is not practicable or possible, disclaim an opinion on the financial statements. (Ref. Para.A14)

14. If the auditor withdraws as contemplated by paragraph 13(b) (i), before withdrawing, the auditor shall communicate to those charged with governance any matters regarding misstatements identified during the audit that would have given rise to a modification of the opinion. (Ref: Para.A15)

Other Considerations Relating to an Adverse Opinion or Disclaimer of Opinion

15. When the auditor considers it necessary to express an adverse opinion or disclaim an opinion on the financial statements as a whole, the auditor's report shall not also include an unmodified opinion with respect to the same financial reporting framework on a single financial statement or one or more specific elements, accounts or items of a financial statement. To include such an unmodified opinion in the same report3 in these circumstances would contradict the auditor's adverse opinion or disclaimer of opinion on the financial statements as a whole. (Ref: Para. A16)

Form and Content of the Auditor's Report When the Opinion is Modified

Auditor's Opinion

16. When the auditor modifies the audit opinion, the auditor shall use the heading "Qualified Opinion," "Adverse Opinion," or "Disclaimer of Opinion," as appropriate, for the Opinion section. (Ref:Para.A17–A19)

Qualified Opinion

17. When the auditor expresses a qualified opinion due to a material misstatement in the financial statements, the auditor shall state that, in the auditor's opinion, except for the effects of the matter(s) described in the Basis for Qualified Opinion section:

(a) When reporting in accordance with a fair presentation framework, the accompanying financial statements present fairly, in all material respects (or give a true and fair view of) [...] in accordance with [the applicable financial reporting framework];or

(b) When reporting in accordance with a compliance framework, the accompanying financial statements have been prepared, in all material respects, in accordance with [the applicable financial reporting framework].

When the modification arises from an inability to obtain sufficient appropriate audit evidence, the auditor shall use the corresponding phrase "except for the possible effects of the matter(s) ..." for the modified opinion. (Ref: Para.A20)

Adverse Opinion

18. When the auditor expresses an adverse opinion, the auditor shall state that, in the auditor's opinion, because of the significance of the matter(s) described in the Basis for Adverse Opinion section:
    (a) When reporting in accordance with a fair presentation framework, the accompanying financial statements do not present fairly (or give a true and fair view of) […] in accordance with [the applicable financial reporting framework];or
    (b) When reporting in accordance with a compliance framework, the accompanying financial statements have not been prepared, in all material respects, in accordance with [the applicable financial reporting framework].

Disclaimer of Opinion

19. When the auditor disclaims an opinion due to an inability to obtain sufficient appropriate audit evidence, the auditor shall:
    (a) State that the auditor does not express an opinion on the accompanying financial statements;
    (b) State that, because of the significance of the matter(s) described in the Basis for Disclaimer of Opinion section, the auditor has not been able to obtain sufficient appropriate audit evidence to provide a basis for an audit opinion on the financial statements; and
    (c) Amend the statement required by paragraph 24(b) of SA 700 (Revised), which indicates that the financial statements have been audited, to state that the auditor was engaged to audit the financial statements.

Basis for Opinion

20. When the auditor modifies the opinion on the financial statements, the auditor shall, in addition to the specific elements required by SA 700 (Revised): (Ref: Para.A21)
    (a) Amend the heading "Basis for Opinion" required by paragraph 28 of SA 700 (Revised) to "Basis for Qualified Opinion," "Basis for Adverse Opinion," or "Basis for Disclaimer of Opinion," as appropriate; and
    (b) Within this section, include a description of the matter giving rise to the modification.

21. If there is a material misstatement of the financial statements that relates to specific amounts in the financial statements (including quantitative disclosures in the notes to the financial statements), the auditor shall include in the Basis for Opinion section a description and quantification of the financial effects of the misstatement, unless impracticable. If it is not practicable to quantify the financial effects, the auditor shall so state in this section. (Ref: Para. A22)

22. If there is a material misstatement of the financial statements that relates to narrative disclosures, the auditor shall include in the Basis for Opinion section an explanation of how the disclosures are misstated.

23. If there is a material misstatement of the financial statements that relates to the non-disclosure of information required to be disclosed, the auditor shall:

    (a) Discuss the non-disclosure with those charged with governance;

    (b) Describe in the Basis for Opinion section the nature of the omitted information; and

    (c) Unless prohibited by law or regulation, include the omitted disclosures, provided it is practicable to do so and the auditor has obtained sufficient appropriate audit evidence about the omitted information. (Ref: Para.A23)

24. If the modification results from an inability to obtain sufficient appropriate audit evidence, the auditor shall include in the Basis for Opinion section the reasons for that inability.

25. When the auditor expresses a qualified or adverse opinion, the auditor shall amend the statement about whether the audit evidence obtained is sufficient and appropriate to provide a basis for the auditor's opinion required by paragraph 28(d) of SA 700 (Revised) to include the word "qualified" or "adverse", as appropriate.

26. When the auditor disclaims an opinion on the financial statements, the auditor's report shall not include the elements required by paragraphs 28(b) and 28(d) of SA 700 (Revised). Those elements are:

    (a) A reference to the section of the auditor's report where the auditor's responsibilities are described; and

    (b) A statement about whether the audit evidence obtained is sufficient and appropriate to provide a basis for the auditor's opinion.

27. Even if the auditor has expressed an adverse opinion or disclaimed an opinion on the financial statements, the auditor shall describe in the Basis for Opinion section the reasons for any other matters of which the auditor is aware that would have required a modification to the opinion, and the effects thereof. (Ref: Para.A24)

Description of Auditor's Responsibilities for the Audit of the Financial Statements When the Auditor Disclaims an Opinion on the Financial Statements

28. When the auditor disclaims an opinion on the financial statements due to an inability to obtain sufficient appropriate audit evidence, the auditor shall amend the description of the auditor's responsibilities required by paragraphs 38–40 of SA 700 (Revised) to include only the following: (Ref: Para.A25)

    (a) A statement that the auditor's responsibility is to conduct an audit of the entity's financial statements in accordance with Standards on Auditing and to issue an auditor's report;

    (b) A statement that, however, because of the matter(s) described in the Basis for Disclaimer of Opinion section, the auditor was not able to obtain sufficient appropriate audit evidence to provide a basis for an audit opinion on the financial statements; and

(c) The statement about auditor independence and other ethical responsibilities required by paragraph 28(c) of SA 700 (Revised).

Considerations When the Auditor Disclaims an Opinion on the Financial Statements

- Unless required by law or regulation, when the auditor disclaims an opinion on the financial statements, the auditor's report shall not include a Key Audit Matters section in accordance with SA 701.4 (Ref: Para.A26

Communication with Those Charged with Governance

- When the auditor expects to modify the opinion in the auditor's report, the auditor shall communicate with those charged with governance the circumstances that led to the expected modification and the wording of the modification. (Ref: Para. A27)

STANDARD ON AUDITING (SA) 706: EMPHASIS OF MATTER PARAGRAPHS AND OTHER MATTER PARAGRAPHS IN THE INDEPENDENT AUDITOR'S REPORT

Introduction

Scope of this SA

1. This Standard on Auditing (SA) deals with additional communication in the auditor's report when the auditor considers it necessary to:

   (a) Draw users' attention to a matter or matters presented or disclosed in the financial statements that are of such importance that they are fundamental to users' understanding of the financial statements; or

   (b) Draw users' attention to any matter or matters other than those presented or disclosed in the financial statements that are relevant to users' understanding of the audit, the auditor's responsibilities or the auditor's report.

2. SA 7011 establishes requirements and provides guidance when the auditor determines key audit matters and communicates them in the auditor's report. When the auditor includes a Key Audit Matters section in the auditor's report, this SA addresses the relationship between key audit matters and any additional communication in the auditor's report in accordance with this SA. (Ref: Para.A1–A3)

3. SA 570 (Revised) 2 establishes requirements and provides guidance about communication in the auditor's report relating to going concern.

4. Appendices 1 and 2 identify SAs that contain specific requirements for the auditor to include Emphasis of Matter paragraphs or Other Matter paragraphs in the auditor's report. In those circumstances, the requirements in this SA regarding the form of such paragraphs apply. (Ref: Para.A4)

Effective Date

5. This SA is effective for audits of financial statements for periods beginning on or after April 1, 2018.

Objective

7. The objective of the auditor, having formed an opinion on the financial statements, is to draw users' attention, when in the auditor's judgment it is necessary to do so, by way of clear additional communication in the auditor's report, to:
   (a) A matter, although appropriately presented or disclosed in the financial statements, that is of such importance that it is fundamental to users' understanding of the financial statements; or
   (b) As appropriate, any other matter that is relevant to users' understanding of the audit, the auditor's responsibilities or the auditor's report.

Definitions

7. For purposes of the SAs, the following terms have the meanings attributed below:
   (a) Emphasis of Matter paragraph – A paragraph included in the auditor's report that refers to a matter appropriately presented or disclosed in the financial statements that, in the auditor's judgment, is of such importance that it is fundamental to users' understanding of the financial statements.
   (b) Other Matter paragraph – A paragraph included in the auditor's report that refers to a matter other than those presented or disclosed in the financial statements that, in the auditor's judgment, is relevant to users' understanding of the audit, the auditor's responsibilities or the auditor's report.

Requirements

Emphasis of Matter Paragraphs in the Auditor's Report

8. If the auditor considers it necessary to draw users' attention to a matter presented or disclosed in the financial statements that, in the auditor's judgment, is of such importance that it is fundamental to users' understanding of the financial statements, the auditor shall include an Emphasis of Matter paragraph in the auditor's report provided: (Ref: Para.A5–A6)
   (a) The auditor would not be required to modify the opinion in accordance with SA 705 (Revised)3 as a result of the matter; and
   (b) When SA 701 applies, the matter has not been determined to be a key audit matter to be communicated in the auditor's report. (Ref: Para.A1–A3)
9. When the auditor includes an Emphasis of Matter paragraph in the auditor's report, the auditor shall:

(a) Include the paragraph within a separate section of the auditor's report with an appropriate heading that includes the term "Emphasis of Matter";

(b) Include in the paragraph a clear reference to the matter being emphasized and to where relevant disclosures that fully describe the matter can be found in the financial statements. The paragraph shall refer only to information presented or disclosed in the financial statements; and

(c) Indicate that the auditor's opinion is not modified in respect of the matter emphasized. (Ref: Para. A7– A8, A16–A17)

Other Matter Paragraphs in the Auditor's Report

10. If the auditor considers it necessary to communicate a matter other than those that are presented or disclosed in the financial statements that, in the auditor's judgment, is relevant to users' understanding of the audit, the auditor's responsibilities or the auditor's report, the auditor shall include an Other Matter paragraph in the auditor's report, provided:

(a) This is not prohibited by law or regulation; and

(b) When SA 701 applies, the matter has not been determined to be a key audit matter to be communicated in the auditor's report. (Ref: Para.A9–A14)

11. When the auditor includes an Other Matter paragraph in the auditor's report, the auditor shall include the paragraph within a separate section with the heading "Other Matter," or other appropriate heading. (Ref: Para.A15–A17)

Communication with Those Charged with Governance

12. If the audit or expects to include an Emphasis of Matter or an Other Matter paragraph in the auditor's report, the auditor shall communicate with those charged with governance regarding this expectation and the wording of this paragraph. (Ref: Para. A18)

STANDARD ON AUDITING (SA) 710: COMPARATIVE INFORMATION—CORRESPONDING FIGURES AND COMPARATIVE FINANCIAL STATEMENTS

Introduction

Scope of this SA

1. This Standard on Auditing (SA) deals with the auditor's responsibilities regarding comparative information in an audit of financial statements. When the financial statements of the prior period have been

Audited by a predecessor auditor or were not audited, the requirements and guidance in SA 5101 regarding opening balances also apply.

The Nature of Comparative Information

2. The nature of the comparative information that is presented in an entity's financial statements depends on the requirements of the applicable financial reporting framework. There are two different broad approaches to the auditor's reporting responsibilities in respect of such comparative information: Corresponding figures[2] and comparative financial statements. The approach to be adopted is often specified by law or regulation but may also be specified in the terms of engagement.

3. The essential audit reporting differences between the approaches are:
   (a) For corresponding figures, the auditor's opinion on the financial statements refers to the current period only; whereas
   (b) For comparative financial statements, the auditor's opinion refers to each period for which financial statements are presented.

   This SA addresses separately the auditor's reporting requirements for each approach.

Effective Date

4. This SA is effective for audits of financial statements for periods beginning on or after April 1, 2011.

Objectives

5. The objectives of the auditor are:
   (a) To obtain sufficient appropriate audit evidence about whether the comparative information included in the financial statements has been presented, in all material respects, in accordance with the requirements for comparative information in the applicable financial reporting framework; and
   (b) To report in accordance with the auditor's reporting responsibilities.

Definitions

6. For purposes of the SAs, the following terms have the meanings attributed below:
   (a) Comparative information – The amounts and disclosures included in the financial statements in respect of one or more prior periods in accordance with the applicable financial reporting framework.
   (b) Corresponding figures – Comparative information where amounts and other disclosures for the prior period are included as an integral part of the current period financial statements, and are intended to be read only in relation to the amounts and other disclosures relating to the current period (referred to as "current period figures"). The level of detail presented in the corresponding amounts and disclosures is dictated primarily by its relevance to the current period figures.

(c) Comparative financial statements – Comparative information where amounts and other disclosures for the prior period are included for comparison with the financial statements of the current period but, if audited, are referred to in the auditor's opinion. The level of information included in those comparative financial statements is comparable with that of the financial statements of the current period.

For purposes of this SA, references to "prior period" should be read as "prior periods" when the comparative information includes amounts and disclosures for more than one period.

Requirements Audit Procedures

7. The auditor shall determine whether the financial statements include the comparative information required by the applicable financial reporting framework and whether such information is appropriately classified. For this purpose, the auditor shall evaluate whether:

   (a) The comparative information agrees with the amounts and other disclosures presented in the prior period; and

   (b) The accounting policies reflected in the comparative information are consistent with those applied in the current period or, if there have been changes in accounting policies, whether those changes have been properly accounted for and adequately presented and disclosed.

8. If the auditor becomes aware of a possible material misstatement in the comparative information while performing the current period audit, the auditor shall perform such additional audit procedures as are necessary in the circumstances to obtain sufficient appropriate audit evidence to determine whether a material misstatement exists. If the auditor had audited the prior period's financial statements, the auditor shall also follow the relevant requirements of SA5603.

9. As required by SA 5804, the auditor shall request written representations for all periods referred to in the auditor's opinion. The auditor shall also obtain a specific written representation regarding any prior period item that is separately disclosed in the current year's statement of profit and loss.(Ref: Para.A1)

Audit Reporting

Corresponding Figures

10. When corresponding figures are presented, the auditor's opinion shall not refer to the corresponding figures except in the circumstances described in paragraphs 11, 12, and 14. (Ref: Para.A2)

11. If the auditor's report on the prior period, as previously issued, included a qualified opinion, a disclaimer of opinion, or an adverse opinion and the matter which gave rise to the modification is unresolved, the auditor shall modify the auditor's opinion on the current period's financial statements. In the Basis for Modification paragraph in the auditor's report, the auditor shall either:

(a) Refer to both the current period's figures and the corresponding figures in the description of the matter giving rise to the modification when the effects or possible effects of the matter on the current period's figures are material; or

(b) In other cases, explain that the audit opinion has been modified because of the effects or possible effects of the unresolved matter on the comparability of the current period's figures and the corresponding figures. (Ref: Para.A3-A5)

12. If the auditor obtains audit evidence that a material misstatement exists in the prior period financial statements on which an unmodified opinion has been previously issued, the auditor shall verify whether the misstatement has been dealt with as required under the applicable financial reporting framework and, if that is not the case, the auditor shall express a qualified opinion or an adverse opinion in the auditor's report on the current period financial statements, modified with respect to the corresponding figures included therein. (Ref: Para.A6)

Prior Period Financial Statements Audited by a Predecessor Auditor

13. If the financial statements of the prior period were audited by a predecessor auditor and the auditor is permitted by law or regulation to refer to the predecessor auditor's report on the corresponding figures and decides to do so, the auditor shall state in an Other Matter paragraph in the auditor's report:

(a) That the financial statements of the prior period were audited by the predecessor auditor;

(b) The type of opinion expressed by the predecessor auditor and, if the opinion was modified, the reasons therefore; and

(c) The date of that report. (Ref: Para.A7)

Prior Period Financial Statements Not Audited

14. If the prior period financial statements were not audited, the auditor shall state in an Other Matter paragraph in the auditor's report that the corresponding figures are unaudited. Such a statement does not, however, relieve the auditor of the requirement to obtain sufficient appropriate audit evidence that the opening balances do not contain misstatements that materially affect the current period's financial statements5. (Ref: Para.A7a)

Comparative Financial Statements

15. When comparative financial statements are presented, the auditor's opinion shall refer to each period for which financial statements are presented and on which an audit opinion is expressed. (Ref:Para.A8-A9)

16. When reporting on prior period financial statements in connection with the current period's audit, if the auditor's opinion on such prior period financial statements differs from the opinion the auditor previously expressed, the auditor shall disclose the substantive reasons for the different opinion in an Other Matter paragraph in accordance with SA 706. (Ref: Para.A10)

Prior Period Financial Statements Audited by a Predecessor Auditor

17. If the financial statements of the prior period were audited by a predecessor auditor, in addition to expressing an opinion on the current period's financial statements, the auditor shall state in an Other Matter paragraph

(a) That the financial statements of the prior period were audited by a predecessor auditor;

(b) The type of opinion expressed by the predecessor auditor and, if the opinion was modified, the reasons therefore; and

(c) The date of that report,

unless the predecessor auditor's report on the prior period's financial statements is revised with the financial statements.

18. If the auditor concludes that a material misstatement exists that affects the prior period financial statements on which the predecessor auditor had previously reported without modification, the auditor shall communicate the misstatement with the appropriate level of management and those charged with governance and request that the predecessor auditor be informed. If the prior period financial statements are amended, and the predecessor auditor agrees to issue a new auditor's report on the amended financial statements of the prior period, the auditor shall report only on the current period. (Ref: Para.A11)

Prior Period Financial Statements Not Audited

19. If the prior period financial statements were not audited, the auditor shall state in an Other Matter paragraph that the comparative financial statements are unaudited. Such a statement does not, however, relieve the auditor of the requirement to obtain sufficient appropriate audit evidence that the opening balances do not contain misstatements that materially affect the current period's financial statements

STANDARD ON AUDITING (SA) 720: THE AUDITOR'S RESPONSIBILITY IN RELATION TO OTHER INFORMATION IN DOCUMENTS CONTAINING AUDITED FINANCIAL STATEMENTS

Introduction

Scope of this SA

1. This Standard on Auditing (SA) deals with the auditor's responsibility in relation to other information in documents containing audited financial statements and the auditor's report thereon. In the absence of any separate requirement in the particular circumstances of the engagement, the auditor's opinion does not cover other information and the auditor has no specific responsibility for determining whether or not other information is properly stated. However, the auditor reads the other information because the credibility of the audited financial statements may be undermined by material inconsistencies between the audited financial statements and other information. *(Ref: Para.A1)*

2. In this SA "documents containing audited financial statements" refers to annual reports (or similar documents), that are issued to owners (or similar stakeholders), containing audited financial statements and the auditor's report thereon. This SA may also be applied, adapted as necessary in the circumstances, to other documents containing audited financial statements. *(Ref: Para.A2-A4)*

Effective Date

3. This SA is effective for audits of financial statements for periods beginning on or after April 1, 2010.

Objective

4. The objective of the auditor is to respond appropriately when documents containing audited financial statements and the auditor's report thereon include other information that could undermine the credibility of those financial statements and the auditor's report.

Definitions

5. For purposes of the SAs the following terms have the meanings attributed below:
   - (a) Other information – Financial and non-financial information (other than the financial statements and the auditor's report thereon) which is included, either by law, regulation or custom, in a document containing audited financial statements and the auditor's report thereon.
   - (b) Inconsistency – Other information that contradicts information contained in the audited financial statements. A material inconsistency may raise doubt about the audit conclusions drawn from audit evidence previously obtained and, possibly, about the basis for the auditor's opinion on the financial statements.
   - (c) Misstatement of fact – Other information that is unrelated to matters appearing in the audited financial statements that is incorrectly stated or presented. A material misstatement of fact may undermine the credibility of the document containing audited financial statements.

Requirements

Reading Other Information

6. The auditor shall read the other information to identify material inconsistencies, if any, with the audited financial statements.
7. The auditor shall make appropriate arrangements with management or those charged with governance to obtain the other information prior to the date of the auditor's report. If it is not possible to obtain all the other information prior to the date of the auditor's report, the auditor shall read such other information as soon as practicable. *(Ref: Para.A5)*

Material Inconsistencies

8. If, on reading the other information, the auditor identifies a material inconsistency, the auditor shall determine whether the audited financial statements or the other information needs to be revised.

Material Inconsistencies Identified in Other Information Obtained Prior to the Date of the Auditor's Report

9. When revision of the audited financial statements is necessary and management refuses to make the revision, the auditor shall modify the opinion in accordance with SA705.

10. When revision of the other information is necessary and management refuses to make the revision, the auditor shall communicate this matter to those charged with governance; and
    (a) Include in the auditor's report an Other Matter(s) paragraph describing the material inconsistency in accordance with SA 706; or
    (b) Where withdrawal is legally permitted, withdraw from the engagement. *(Ref: Para. A6-A7)*

Material Inconsistencies Identified in Other Information Obtained Subsequent to the Date of the Auditor's Report

11. When revision of the audited financial statements is necessary, the auditor shall follow the relevant requirements in SA560.3

12. When revision of the other information is necessary and management agrees to make the revision, the auditor shall carry out the procedures necessary under the circumstances. *(Ref: Para.A8)*

13. When revision of the other information is necessary, but management refuses to make the revision, the auditor shall notify those charged with governance of the auditor's concern regarding the other information and take any further appropriate action. *(Ref: Para.A9)*

Material Misstatements of Fact

14. If, on reading the other information for the purpose of identifying material inconsistencies, the auditor becomes aware of an apparent material misstatement of fact, the auditor shall discuss the matter with management. *(Ref: Para.A10)*

15. When, following such discussions, the auditor still considers that there is an apparent material misstatement of fact, the auditor shall request management to consult with a qualified third party, such as the entity's legal counsel, and the auditor shall consider the advice received.

16. When the auditor concludes that there is a material misstatement of fact in the other information which management refuses to correct, the auditor shall notify those charged with governance of the auditor's concern regarding the other information and take any further appropriate action. *(Ref: Para.A11)*

STANDARD ON AUDITING (SA) 800: SPECIAL CONSIDERATIONS—AUDITS OF FINANCIAL STATEMENTS PREPARED IN ACCORDANCE WITH SPECIAL PURPOSE FRAMEWORKS

Introduction

Scope of this SA

1. The Standards on Auditing (SAs) in the 100-700 series apply to an audit of financial statements. This SA deals with special considerations in the application of those SAs to an audit of financial statements prepared in accordance with a special purpose framework.
2. This SA is written in the context of a complete set of financial statements prepared in accordance with a special purpose framework. SA 8051, deals with special considerations relevant to an audit of a single financial statement or of a specific element, account or item of a financial statement.
3. This SA does not override the requirements of the other SAs; nor does it purport to deal with all special considerations that may be relevant in the circumstances of the engagement.

Effective Date

4. This SA is effective for audits of financial statements for periods beginning on or after April 1, 2011.

Objective

5. The objective of the auditor, when applying SAs in an audit of financial statements prepared in accordance with a special purpose framework, is to address appropriately the special considerations that are relevant to:
   (a) The acceptance of the engagement;
   (b) The planning and performance of that engagement; and
   (c) Forming an opinion and reporting on the financial statements.

Definitions

6. For purposes of the SAs, the following terms have the meanings attributed below:
   (a) Special purpose financial statements – Financial statements prepared in accordance with a special purpose framework. (Ref: Para. A4)
   (b) Special purpose framework – A financial reporting framework designed to meet the financial information needs of specific users. The financial reporting framework may be a fair presentation framework or a compliance framework2. (Ref: Para. A1-A4)
7. The related notes ordinarily comprise a summary of significant accounting policies and other explanatory information. The requirements of the applicable

financial reporting framework determine the form and content of the financial statements, and what constitutes a complete set of financial statements.

Requirements

Considerations When Accepting the Engagement

Acceptability of the Financial Reporting Framework

8. SA 210 requires the auditor to determine the acceptability of the financial reporting framework applied in the preparation of the financial statements3. In an audit of special purpose financial statements, the auditor shall obtain an understanding of: (Ref: Para.A5-A8)
   (a) The purpose for which the financial statements are prepared;
   (b) The intended users; and
   (c) The steps taken by management to determine that the applicable financial reporting framework is acceptable in the circumstances.

Considerations When Planning and Performing the Audit

9. SA 200 requires the auditor to comply with all SAs relevant to the audit4. In planning and performing an audit of special purpose financial statements, the auditor shall determine whether application of the SAs requires special consideration in the circumstances of the engagement. (Ref: Para.A9-A12)

10. SA 315 requires the auditor to obtain an understanding of the entity's selection and application of accounting policies5. In the case of financial statements prepared in accordance with the provisions of a contract, the auditor shall obtain an understanding of any significant interpretations of the contract that management made in the preparation of those financial statements. An interpretation is significant when adoption of another reasonable interpretation would have produced a material difference in the information presented in the financial statements.

Forming an Opinion and Reporting Considerations

11. When forming an opinion and reporting on special purpose financial statements, the auditor shall apply the requirements in SA 700 (Revised). (Ref: Para.A13)

Description of the Applicable Financial Reporting Framework

12. SA 700 (Revised) requires the auditor to evaluate whether the financial statements adequately refer to or describe the applicable financial reporting framework7. In the case of financial statements prepared in accordance with the provisions of a contract, the auditor shall evaluate whether the financial statements adequately describe any significant interpretations of the contract on which the financial statements are based.

13. SA 700 (Revised) deals with the form and content of the auditor's report. In the case of an auditor's report on special purpose financial statements:

(a) The auditor's report shall also describe the purpose for which the financial statements are prepared and, if necessary, the intended users, or refer to a note in the special purpose financial statements that contains that information; and

(b) If management has a choice of financial reporting frameworks in the preparation of such financial statements, the explanation of management's responsibility for the financial statements shall also make reference to its responsibility for determining that the applicable financial reporting framework is acceptable in the circumstances.

Alerting Readers that the Financial Statements Are Prepared in Accordance with a Special Purpose Framework

14. **The auditor's report on special purpose financial statements shall include an Emphasis of Matter paragraph alerting users of the auditor's report that the financial statements are prepared in accordance with a special purpose framework and that, as a result, the financial statements may not be suitable for another purpose. The auditor shall include this paragraph under an appropriate heading. (Ref: Para.A14-A15)**

STANDARD ON AUDITING (SA) 805: SPECIAL CONSIDERATIONS—AUDITS OF SINGLE FINANCIAL STATEMENTS AND SPECIFIC ELEMENTS, ACCOUNTS OR ITEMS OF A FINANCIAL STATEMENT

Introduction

Scope of this SA

1. The Standards on Auditing (SAs) in the 100-700 series apply to an audit of financial statements and are to be adapted as necessary in the circumstances when applied to audits of other historical financial information. This SA deals with special considerations in the application of those SAs to an audit of a single financial statement or of a specific element, account or item of a financial statement. The single financial statement or the specific element, account or item of a financial statement may be prepared in accordance with a general or special purpose framework. If prepared in accordance with a special purpose framework, SA 800 also applies to the audit. (Ref: Para.A1-A4)

2. This SA does not apply to the report of a component auditor, issued as a result of work performed on the financial information of a component at the request of a group engagement team for purposes of an audit of group financial statements (see Proposed Revised SA 600).

3. This SA does not override the requirements of the other SAs; nor does it purport to deal with all special considerations that may be relevant in the circumstances of the engagement.

Effective Date

4. This SA is effective for audits of single financial statements or of specific elements, accounts or items for periods beginning on or after April 1, 2011. In the case of audits of single financial statements or of specific elements, accounts or items of a financial statement prepared as at a specific date, this SA is effective for audits of such information prepared as at a date on or after April 1, 2011.

Objective

5. The objective of the auditor, when applying SAs in an audit of a single financial statement or of a specific element, account or item of a financial statement, is to address appropriately the special considerations that are relevant to:
   (a) The acceptance of the engagement;
   (b) The planning and performance of that engagement; and
   (c) Forming an opinion and reporting on the single financial statement or on the specific element, account or item of a financial statement.

Definitions

6. For purposes of this SA, reference to:
   (a) "Element of a financial statement" or "element" means an "element, account or item of a financial statement";
   (b) "Financial Reporting Standards" means the Accounting Standards issued by the Institute of Chartered Accountants of India (ICAI) or Accounting Standards, notified by the Central Government by publishing the same as the Companies (Accounting Standards) Rules, 2006, or the Accounting Standards for Local Bodies issued by the Institute of Chartered Accountants of India, as may be applicable; and
   (c) A single financial statement (for example, a cash flow statement) or to a specific element of a financial statement (for example, cash and bank balances) includes the related notes. The related notes ordinarily comprise a summary of significant accounting policies and other explanatory information relevant to the financial statement or to the element.

Requirements

Considerations When Accepting the Engagement

Application of SAs

7. SA 200 requires the auditor to comply with all SAs relevant to the audit3. In the case of an audit of a single financial statement or of a specific element of a financial statement, this requirement applies irrespective of whether the auditor is also engaged to audit the entity's complete set of financial statements. If the auditor is not also engaged to audit the entity's complete set of financial statements, the auditor shall determine whether the audit of a single financial

statement or of a specific element of those financial statements in accordance with SAs is practicable. (Ref: Para.A5-A6)

Acceptability of the Financial Reporting Framework

8. SA 210 requires the auditor to determine the acceptability of the financial reporting framework applied in the preparation of the financial statements4. In the case of an audit of a single financial statement or of a specific element of a financial statement, this shall include whether application of the financial reporting framework will result in a presentation that provides adequate disclosures to enable the intended users to understand the information conveyed in the financial statement or the element, and the effect of material transactions and events on the information conveyed in the financial statement or the element. (Ref: Para. A7)

Form of Opinion

9. SA 210 requires that the agreed terms of the audit engagement include the expected form of any reports to be issued by the auditor5. In the case of an audit of a single financial statement or of a specific element of a financial statement, the auditor shall consider whether the expected form of opinion is appropriate in the circumstances. (Ref: Para. A8-A9)

Considerations When Planning and Performing the Audit

10. SA 200 states that SAs are written in the context of an audit of financial statements; they are to be adapted as necessary in the circumstances when applied to audits of other historical financial information.6 7In planning and performing the audit of a single financial statement or of a specific element of a financial statement, the auditor shall adapt all SAs relevant to the audit as necessary in the circumstances of the engagement. (Ref: Para.A10-A14)

Forming an Opinion and Reporting Considerations

11. When forming an opinion and reporting on a single financial statement or on a specific element of a financial statement, the auditor shall apply the requirements in SA 700 (Revised), adapted as necessary in the circumstances of the engagement. (Ref: Para.A15-A16)

Reporting on the Entity's Complete Set of Financial Statements and on a Single Financial Statement or on a Specific Element of Those Financial Statements

12. If the auditor undertakes an engagement to report on a single financial statement or on a specific element of a financial statement in conjunction with an engagement to audit the entity's complete set of financial statements, the auditor shall express a separate opinion for each engagement.

13. An audited single financial statement or an audited specific element of a financial statement may be published together with the entity's audited complete set of financial statements. If the auditor concludes that the presentation of the single financial statement or of the specific element of a financial statement does not differentiate it sufficiently from the complete set of financial statements, the auditor shall ask management to rectify the situation.

Subject to paragraphs 15 and 16, the auditor shall also differentiate the opinion on the single financial statement or on the specific element of a financial statement from the opinion on the complete set of financial statements. The auditor shall not issue the auditor's report containing the opinion on the single financial statement or on the specific element of a financial statement until satisfied with the differentiation.

Modified Opinion, Emphasis of Matter Paragraph or Other Matter Paragraph in the Auditor's Report on the Entity's Complete Set of Financial Statements

14. If the opinion in the auditor's report on an entity's complete set of financial statements is modified, or that report includes an Emphasis of Matter paragraph or an Other Matter paragraph, the auditor shall determine the effect that this may have on the auditor's report on a single financial statement or on a specific element of those financial statements. When deemed appropriate, the auditor shall modify the opinion on the single financial statement or on the specific element of a financial statement, or include an Emphasis of Matter paragraph or an Other Matter paragraph in the auditor's report, accordingly. (Ref: Para.A17)

15. If the auditor concludes that it is necessary to express an adverse opinion or disclaim an opinion on the entity's complete set of financial statements as a whole, SA 705 does not permit the auditor to include in the same auditor's report an unmodified opinion on a single financial statement that forms part of those financial statements or on a specific element that forms part of those financial statements9. This is because such an unmodified opinion would contradict the adverse opinion or disclaimer of opinion on the entity's complete set of financial statements as a whole. (Ref: Para.A18)

16. If the auditor concludes that it is necessary to express an adverse opinion or disclaim an opinion on the entity's complete set of financial statements as a whole but, in the context of a separate audit of a specific element that is included in those financial statements, the auditor nevertheless considers it appropriate to express an unmodified opinion on that element, the auditor shall only do so if:

(a) The auditor is not prohibited by law or regulation from doing so;

(b) That opinion is expressed in an auditor's report that is not published together with the auditor's report containing the adverse opinion or disclaimer of opinion; and

(c) The specific element does not constitute a major portion of the entity's complete set of financial statements.

17. The auditor shall not express an unmodified opinion on a single financial statement of a complete set of financial statements if the auditor has expressed an adverse opinion or disclaimed an opinion on the complete set of financial statements as a whole. This is the case even if the auditor's report on the single financial statement is not published together with the auditor's report containing the adverse opinion or disclaimer of opinion. This is because a single financial statement is deemed to constitute a major portion of those financial statements.

STANDARD ON AUDITING (SA) 810: ENGAGEMENTS TO REPORT ON SUMMARY FINANCIAL STATEMENTS

Introduction

Scope of this SA

1. This Standard on Auditing (SA) deals with the auditor's responsibilities when undertaking an engagement to report on summary financial statements derived from financial statements audited in accordance with SAs by that same auditor.

Effective Date

2. This SA is effective for engagements for periods beginning on or after April 1, 2011.

Objectives

3. The objectives of the auditor are to:
   - (a) Determine whether it is appropriate to accept the engagement to report on summary financial statements;
   - (b) Form an opinion on the summary financial statements based on an evaluation of the conclusions drawn from the evidence obtained; and
   - (c) Express clearly that opinion through a written report that also describes the basis for that opinion.

Definitions

4. For purposes of this SA, the following terms have the meanings attributed below:
   - (a) Applied criteria – The criteria applied by management in the preparation of the summary financial statements.
   - (b) Audited financial statements – Financial statements1 audited by the auditor in accordance with SAs, and from which the summary financial statements are derived.
   - **(c) Summary financial statements– Historical financial information that is derived from financial statements but that contains less detail than the financial statements, while still providing a structured representation consistent with that provided by the financial statements of the entity's economic resources or obligations at a point in time or the changes therein for a period of time. Different jurisdictions may use different terminology to describe such historical financial information**

Requirements Engagement Acceptance

5. The auditor shall, ordinarily, accept an engagement to report on summary financial statements in accordance with this SA only when the auditor has been

engaged to conduct an audit in accordance with SAs of the financial statements from which the summary financial statements are derived. (Ref: Para. A1)

6. Before accepting an engagement to report on summary financial statements, the auditor shall: (Ref: Para.A2)

   (a) Determine whether the applied criteria are acceptable; (Ref: Para.A3-A7)

   (b) Obtain the agreement of management that it acknowledges and understands its responsibility:

      (i) For the preparation of the summary financial statements in accordance with the applied criteria;

      (ii) To make the audited financial statements available to the intended users of the summary financial statements without undue difficulty (or, if law or regulation provides that the audited financial statements need not be made available to the intended users of the summary financial statements and establishes the criteria for the preparation of the summary financial statements, to describe that law or regulation in the summary financial statements); and

      (iii) To include the auditor's report on the summary financial statements in any document that contains the summary financial statements and that indicates that the auditor has reported on them.

   (c) Agree with management the form of opinion to be expressed on the summary financial statements (see paragraphs9-11).

7. If the auditor concludes that the applied criteria are unacceptable or is unable to obtain the agreement of management set out in paragraph 6(b), the auditor shall not accept the engagement to report on the summary financial statements, unless required by law or regulation to do so. An engagement conducted in accordance with such law or regulation does not comply with this SA. Accordingly, the auditor's report on the summary financial statements shall not indicate that the engagement was conducted in accordance with this SA. The auditor shall include appropriate reference to this fact in the terms of the engagement. The auditor shall also determine the effect that this may have on the engagement to audit the financial statements from which the summary financial statements are derived.

Nature of Procedures

8. The auditor shall perform the following procedures, and any other procedures that the auditor may consider necessary, as the basis for the auditor's opinion on the summary financial statements:

   (a) Evaluate whether the summary financial statements adequately disclose their summarized nature and identify the audited financial statements.

   (b) When summary financial statements are not accompanied by the audited financial statements, evaluate whether they describe clearly:

(i) From whom or where the audited financial statements are available; or

(ii) The law or regulation that specifies that the audited financial statements need not be made available to the intended users of the summary financial statements and establishes the criteria for the preparation of the summary financial statements.

(c) Evaluate whether the summary financial statements adequately disclose the applied criteria.

(d) Compare the summary financial statements with the related information in the audited financial statements to determine whether the summary financial statements agree with or can be re-calculated from the related information in the audited financial statements.

(e) Evaluate whether the summary financial statements are prepared in accordance with the applied criteria.

(f) Evaluate, in view of the purpose of the summary financial statements, whether the summary financial statements contain the information necessary, and are at an appropriate level of aggregation, so as not to be misleading in the circumstances.

(g) Evaluate whether the audited financial statements are available to the intended users of the summary financial statements without undue difficulty, unless law or regulation provides that they need not be made available and establishes the criteria for the preparation of the summary financial statements. (Ref: Para.A8)

Form of Opinion

9. When the auditor has concluded that an unmodified opinion on the summary financial statements is appropriate, the auditor's opinion shall, unless otherwise required by law or regulation, use one of the following phrases: (Ref: Para.A9)

(a) The summary financial statements are consistent, in all material respects, with the audited financial statements, in accordance with [the applied criteria]; or

(b) The summary financial statements are a fair summary of the audited financial statements, in accordance with [the applied criteria].

10. If law or regulation prescribes the wording of the opinion on summary financial statements in terms that are different from those described in paragraph 9, the auditor shall:

(a) Apply the procedures described in paragraph 8 and any further procedures necessary to enable the auditor to express the prescribed opinion; and

(b) Evaluate whether users of the summary financial statements might misunderstand the auditor's opinion on the summary financial statements and, if so, whether additional explanation in the auditor's report on the summary financial statements can mitigate possible misunderstanding.

11. If, in the case of paragraph 10(b), the auditor concludes that additional explanation in the auditor's report on the summary financial statements cannot mitigate possible misunderstanding, the auditor shall not accept the engagement, unless required by law or regulation to do so. An engagement conducted in accordance with such law or regulation does not comply with this SA. Accordingly, the auditor's report on the summary financial statements shall not indicate that the engagement was conducted in accordance with this SA.

Timing of Work and Events Subsequent to the Date of the Auditor's Report on the Audited Financial Statements

12. The auditor's report on the summary financial statements may be dated later than the date of the auditor's report on the audited financial statements. In such cases, the auditor's report on the summary

    Financial statements shall state that the summary financial statements and audited financial statements do not reflect the effects of events that occurred subsequent to the date of the auditor's report on the audited financial statements that may require adjustment of, or disclosure in, the audited financial statements. (Ref: Para.A10)

13. The auditor may become aware of facts that existed at the date of the auditor's report on the audited financial statements, but of which the auditor previously was unaware. In such cases, the auditor shall not issue the auditor's report on the summary financial statements until the auditor's consideration of such facts in relation to the audited financial statements in accordance with SA 5604 has been completed.

Auditor's Report on Summary Financial Statements

Elements of the Auditor's Report

14. The auditor's report on summary financial statements shall include the following elements5: (Ref: Para. A15)
    (a) A title clearly indicating it as the report of an independent auditor. (Ref: Para.A11)
    (b) An addressee. (Ref: Para.A12)
    (c) An introductory paragraph that:
        (i) Identifies the summary financial statements on which the auditor is reporting, including the title of each statement included in the summary financial statements; (Ref: Para.A13)
        (ii) Identifies the audited financial statements;
        (iii) Refers to the auditor's report on the audited financial statements, the date of that report, and, subject to paragraphs 17-18, the fact that an unmodified opinion is expressed on the audited financial statements;
        (iv) If the date of the auditor's report on the summary financial statements is later than the date of the auditor's report on the audited financial statements, states that the summary financial

statements and the audited financial statements do not reflect the effects of events that occurred subsequent to the date of the auditor's report on the audited financial statements; and

(v) A statement indicating that the summary financial statements do not contain all the disclosures required by the financial reporting framework applied in the preparation of the audited financial statements, and that reading the summary financial statements is not a substitute for reading the audited financial statements.

(d) A description of management's responsibility for the summary financial statements, explaining that management is responsible for the preparation of the summary financial statements in accordance with the applied criteria.

(e) A statement that the auditor is responsible for expressing an opinion on the summary financial statements based on the procedures required by this SA.

(f) A paragraph clearly expressing an opinion. (see paragraphs9-11)

(g) The auditor's signature along with the firm registration number, wherever applicable, and the membership number assigned by the Institute of Chartered Accountants of India (ICAI).

(h) The date of the auditor's report. (Ref: Para.A14)

(i) The place of signature.

15. If the addressee of the summary financial statements is not the same as the addressee of the auditor's report on the audited financial statements, the auditor shall evaluate the appropriateness of using a different addressee. (Ref: Para.A12)

16. The auditor shall date the auditor's report on the summary financial statements no earlier than: (Ref: Para.A14)

(a) The date on which the auditor has obtained sufficient appropriate evidence on which to base the opinion, including evidence that the summary financial statements have been prepared and those with the recognized authority have asserted that they have taken responsibility for them; and

(b) The date of the auditor's report on the audited financial statements.

Modifications to the Opinion, Emphasis of Matter Paragraph or Other Matter Paragraph in the Auditor's Report on the Audited Financial Statements (Ref: Para. A15)

17. When the auditor's report on the audited financial statements contains a qualified opinion, an Emphasis of Matter paragraph, or an Other Matter paragraph, but the auditor is satisfied that the summary financial statements are consistent, in all material respects, with or are a fair summary of the audited financial statements, in accordance with the applied criteria, the auditor's report on the summary financial statements shall, in addition to the elements in paragraph14:

(a) State that the auditor's report on the audited financial statements contains a qualified opinion, an Emphasis of Matter paragraph, or an Other Matter paragraph; and

(b) Describe:

(i) The basis for the qualified opinion on the audited financial statements, and that qualified opinion; or the Emphasis of Matter or the Other Matter paragraph in the auditor's report on the audited financial statements; and

(ii) The effect thereof on the summary financial statements, if any.

18. When the auditor's report on the audited financial statements contains an adverse opinion or a disclaimer of opinion, the auditor's report on the summary financial statements shall, in addition to the elements in paragraph 14:

(a) State that the auditor's report on the audited financial statements contains an adverse opinion or disclaimer of opinion;

(b) Describe the basis for that adverse opinion or disclaimer of opinion; and

(c) State that, as a result of the adverse opinion or disclaimer of opinion, it is inappropriate to express an opinion on the summary financial statements.

Modified Opinion on the Summary Financial Statements

19. If the summary financial statements are not consistent, in all material respects, with or are not a fair summary of the audited financial statements, in accordance with the applied criteria, and management does not agree to make the necessary changes, the auditor shall express an adverse opinion on the summary financial statements. (Ref: Para.A15)

Restriction on Distribution or Use or Alerting Readers to the Basis of Accounting

20. When distribution or use of the auditor's report on the audited financial statements is restricted, or the auditor's report on the audited financial statements alerts readers that the audited financial statements are prepared in accordance with a special purpose framework, the auditor shall include a similar restriction or alert in the auditor's report on the summary financial statements.

Comparatives

21. If the audited financial statements contain comparatives, but the summary financial statements do not, the auditor shall determine whether such omission is reasonable in the circumstances of the engagement. The auditor shall determine the effect of an unreasonable omission on the auditor's report on the summary financial statements. (Ref: Para.A16)

22. If the summary financial statements contain comparatives that were reported on by another auditor, the auditor's report on the summary financial statements shall also contain the matters that SA 710 requires the auditor to include in the auditor's report on the audited financial statements6. (Ref: Para.A17)

Unaudited Supplementary Information Presented with Summary Financial Statements

23. The auditor shall evaluate whether any unaudited supplementary information presented with the summary financial statements is clearly differentiated from the summary financial statements. If the auditor concludes that the entity's presentation of the unaudited supplementary information is not clearly differentiated from the summary financial statements, the auditor shall ask management to change the presentation of the unaudited supplementary information. If management refuses to do so, the auditor shall explain in the auditor's report on the summary financial statements that such information is not covered by that report. (Ref: Para.A18)

Other Information in Documents Containing Summary Financial Statements

24. The auditor shall read other information included in a document containing the summary financial statements and related auditor's report to identify material inconsistencies, if any, with the summary financial statements. If, on reading the other information, the auditor identifies a material inconsistency, the auditor shall determine whether the summary financial statements or the other information needs to be revised. If, on reading the other information, the auditor becomes aware of an apparent material misstatement of fact, the auditor shall discuss the matter with management. (Ref: Para.A19)

Auditor Association

25. If the auditor becomes aware that the entity plans to state that the auditor has reported on summary financial statements in a document containing the summary financial statements, but does not plan to include the related auditor's report, the auditor shall request management to include the auditor's report in the document. If management does not do so, the auditor shall determine and carry out other appropriate actions designed to prevent management from inappropriately associating the auditor with the summary financial statements in that document. (Ref: Para.A20)

26. The auditor may be engaged to report on the financial statements of an entity, while not engaged to report on the summary financial statements. If, in this case, the auditor becomes aware that the entity plans to make a statement in a document that refers to the auditor and the fact that summary financial statements are derived from the financial statements audited by the auditor, the auditor shall be satisfied that:

    (a) The reference to the auditor is made in the context of the auditor's report on the audited financial statements; and

    (b) The statement does not give the impression that the auditor has reported on the summary financial statements.

    If (a) or (b) are not met, the auditor shall request management to change the statement to meet them, or not to refer to the auditor in the document. Alternatively, the entity may engage the auditor to report on the summary financial statements and include the related auditor's report in the

document. If management does not change the statement, delete the reference to the auditor, or include an auditor's report on the summary financial statements in the document containing the summary financial statements, the auditor shall advise management that the auditor disagrees with the reference to the auditor, and the auditor shall determine and carry out other appropriate actions designed to prevent management from inappropriately referring to the auditor. (Ref: Para. A20)

STANDARD ON REVIEW ENGAGEMENTS (SRE) 2400: ENGAGEMENTS TO REVIEW HISTORICAL FINANCIAL STATEMENTS

Introduction Scope of this SRE

1. This Standard on Review Engagements (SRE) deals with: (Ref: Para.A1)
   (a) The practitioner's responsibilities when engaged to perform a review of historical financial statements, when the practitioner is not the auditor of the entity's financial statements; and
   (b) The form and content of the practitioner's report on the financial statements.
2. This SRE does not address a review of an entity's financial statements or interim financial information performed by a practitioner who is the independent auditor of the entity's financial statements. (Ref: Para. A2)
3. This SRE is to be applied, adapted as necessary, to reviews of other historical financial information.

Relationship with SQC 1

4. Quality control systems, policies and procedures are the responsibility of the firm. SQC 1 applies to firms of professional accountants in respect of a firm's engagements to review financial statements. The provisions of this SRE regarding quality control at the level of individual review engagements are premised on the basis that the firm is subject to SQC 1. (Ref: Para.A3-A4)

The Engagement to Review Historical Financial Statements

5. The review of historical financial statements is a limited assurance engagement, as described in the Framework for Assurance Engagements. (Ref: Para.A5-A6)
6. In a review of financial statements, the practitioner expresses a conclusion that is designed to enhance the degree of confidence of intended users regarding the preparation of an entity's financial statements in accordance with an applicable financial reporting framework. The practitioner's conclusion is based on the practitioner obtaining limited assurance. The practitioner's report includes a description of the nature of a review engagement as context for the readers of the report to be able to understand the conclusion.

7. The practitioner performs primarily inquiry and analytical procedures to obtain sufficient appropriate evidence as the basis for a conclusion on the financial statements as a whole, expressed in accordance with the requirements of this SRE.

8. If the practitioner becomes aware of a matter that causes the practitioner to believe the financial statements may be materially misstated, the practitioner designs and performs additional procedures, as the practitioner considers necessary in the circumstances, to be able to conclude on the financial statements in accordance with this SRE.

Authority of this SRE

9. This SRE contains the objectives of the practitioner in following the SRE which provide the context in which the requirements of this SRE are set, and are intended to assist the practitioner in understanding what needs to be accomplished in a review engagement.

10. The SRE contains requirements, expressed using "shall," that are designed to enable the practitioner to meet the stated objectives.

11. In addition, this SRE contains introductory material, definitions, and application and other explanatory material, that provide context relevant to a proper understanding of the SRE.

12. The application and other explanatory material provides further explanation of the requirements and guidance for carrying them out. While such guidance does not itself impose a requirement, it is relevant to the proper application of the requirements. The application and other explanatory material may also provide background information on matters addressed in this SRE that assists in the application of the requirements

Effective Date

13. This SRE is effective for reviews of financial statements for periods beginning on or after April 1, 2016.

Objectives

14. The practitioner's objectives in a review of financial statements under this SRE are to:

    (a) Obtain limited assurance, primarily by performing inquiry and analytical procedures, about whether the financial statements as a whole are free from material misstatement, thereby enabling the practitioner to express a conclusion on whether anything has come to the practitioner's attention that causes the practitioner to believe the financial statements are not prepared, in all material respects, in accordance with an applicable financial reporting framework; and

    (b) Report on the financial statements as a whole and communicate, as required by this SRE.

15. In all cases when limited assurance cannot be obtained and a qualified conclusion in the practitioner's report is insufficient in the circumstances, this SRE requires that the practitioner either disclaim a conclusion in the report

issued for the engagement or, where appropriate, withdraw from the engagement if withdrawal is possible under applicable law or regulation. (Ref. Para. A7-A9, A114-A115)

Definitions

16. The Glossary of Terms issued by the ICAI ("the Glossary") includes the terms defined in this SRE as well as descriptions of other terms used in this SRE, to assist in consistent application and interpretation. For example, the terms "management" and "those charged with governance" used throughout this SRE are as defined in the Glossary. (Ref: Para. A10-A11)

17. For purposes of this SRE, the following terms have the meanings attributed below:

    (a) Analytical procedures — Evaluations of financial information through analysis of plausible relationships among both financial and non-financial data. Analytical procedures also encompass such investigation as is necessary of identified fluctuations or relationships that are inconsistent with other relevant information or that differ from expected values by a significant amount.

    (b) Engagement risk — The risk that the practitioner expresses an in appropriate conclusion when the financial statements are materially misstated.

    (c) General purpose financial statements — Financial statements prepared in accordance with a general purpose framework.

    (d) General purpose framework — A financial reporting framework designed to meet the common financial information needs of a wide range of users. The financial reporting framework may be a fair presentation framework or a compliance framework.

    (e) Inquiry — Inquiry consists of seeking information of knowledgeable persons, financial and non- financial, within the entity or outside the entity.

    (f) Limited assurance — The level of assurance obtained where engagement risk is reduced to a level that is acceptable in the circumstances of the engagement, but where that risk is greater than for a reasonable assurance engagement, as the basis for expressing a conclusion in accordance with this SRE. The combination of the nature, timing and extent of evidence gathering procedures is at least sufficient for the practitioner to obtain a meaningful level of assurance. To be meaningful, the level of assurance obtained by the practitioner is likely to enhance the intended users' confidence about the financial statements. (Ref: Para.A12)

    (g) Practitioner — A professional accountant in public practice. The term includes the engagement partner or other members of the engagement team, or, as applicable, the firm. Where this SRE expressly intends that a requirement or responsibility be fulfilled by the engagement partner, the term "engagement partner" rather than "practitioner" is used.

    (h) Professional judgment — The application of relevant training, knowledge and experience, within the context provided by assurance, accounting and ethical standards, in making informed decisions about the courses of action that are appropriate in the circumstances of the review engagement.

(i) Relevant ethical requirements — Ethical requirements to which the engagement team is subject, which ordinarily comprise the Code of Ethics issued by the Institute of Chartered Accountants of India (ICAI) together with other relevant pronouncements issued by the ICAI.

(j) Special purpose financial statements — Financial statements prepared in accordance with a special purpose framework.

(k) Special purpose framework — A financial reporting framework designed to meet the financial information needs of specific users. The financial reporting framework may be a fair presentation framework or a compliance framework.

Requirements

Conduct of a Review Engagement in Accordance with this SRE

18. The practitioner shall have an understanding of the entire text of this SRE, including its application and other explanatory material, to understand its objectives and to apply its requirements properly. (Ref: Para. A13)

Complying with Relevant Requirements

19. The practitioner shall comply with each requirement of this SRE, unless a requirement is not relevant to the review engagement. A requirement is relevant to the review engagement when the circumstances addressed by the requirement exist.

20. **The practitioner shall not represent compliance with this SRE in the practitioner's report unless the practitioner has complied with all the requirements of this SRE relevant to the review engagement.**

Ethical Requirements

21. The practitioner shall comply with relevant ethical requirements, including those pertaining to independence. (Ref: Para.A14-A15)

Professional Skepticism and Professional Judgment

22. The practitioner shall plan and perform the engagement with professional skepticism recognizing that circumstances may exist that cause the financial statements to be materially misstated. (Ref: Para. A16-A19)

23. The practitioner shall exercise professional judgment in conducting a review engagement. (Ref: Para. A20-A24)

Engagement Level Quality Control

24. The engagement partner shall possess competence in assurance skills and techniques, and competence in financial reporting, appropriate to the engagement circumstances. (Ref: Para.A25)

25. The engagement partner shall take responsibility for: (Ref: Para.A26-A29)

(a) The overall quality of each review engagement to which that partner is assigned;

(b) The direction, supervision, planning and performance of the review engagement in compliance with professional standards and applicable legal and regulatory requirements; (Ref: Para.A30)

(c) The practitioner's report being appropriate in the circumstances; and

(d) The engagement being performed in accordance with the firm's quality control policies, including the following:

  (i) Being satisfied that appropriate procedures regarding the acceptance and continuance of client relationships and engagements have been followed, and that conclusions reached are appropriate, including considering whether there is information that would lead the engagement partner to conclude that management lacks integrity; (Ref: Para.A31-A32)

  (ii) Being satisfied that the engagement team collectively has the appropriate competence and capabilities, including assurance skills and techniques and expertise in financial reporting, to:

    (a) Perform the review engagement in accordance with professional standards and applicable legal and regulatory requirements; and

    (b) Enable a report that is appropriate in the circumstances to be issued; and

  (iii) Taking responsibility for appropriate engagement documentation being maintained.

Relevant Considerations after Engagement Acceptance

26. If the engagement partner obtains information that would have caused the firm to decline the engagement had that information been available earlier, the engagement partner shall communicate that information promptly to the firm, so that the firm and the engagement partner can take the necessary action.

Compliance with Relevant Ethical Requirements

27. Throughout the engagement, the engagement partner shall remain alert, through observation and making inquiries as necessary, for evidence of non-compliance with relevant ethical requirements by members of the engagement team. If matters come to the engagement partner's attention through the firm's system of quality control or otherwise that indicate that members of the engagement team have not complied with relevant ethical requirements, the engagement partner, in consultation with others in the firm, shall determine the appropriate action

Monitoring

28. An effective system of quality control for a firm includes a monitoring process designed to provide the firm with reasonable assurance that the firm's policies and procedures relating to the system of quality control are relevant, adequate and operate effectively. The engagement partner shall consider the results of

the firm's monitoring process as evidenced in the latest information circulated by the firm and, if applicable, other network firms and whether deficiencies noted in that information may affect the reviewing agreement.

Acceptance and Continuance of Client Relationships and Review Engagements

Factors Affecting Acceptance and Continuance of Client Relationships and Review Engagements

29. Unless required by law or regulation, the practitioner shall not accept a review engagement if: (Ref: Para.A33-A34)
    - (a) The practitioner is not satisfied:
        - (i) That there is a rational purpose for the engagement; or (Ref: Para.A35)
        - (ii) That a review engagement would be appropriate in the circumstances; (Ref: Para.A36)
    - (b) The practitioner has reason to believe that relevant ethical requirements, including independence, will not be satisfied;
    - (c) The practitioner's preliminary understanding of the engagement circumstances indicates that information needed to perform the review engagement is likely to be unavailable or unreliable; (Ref: Para.A37)
    - (d) The practitioner has cause to doubt management's integrity such that it is likely to affect proper performance of the review; or (Ref: Para.A36)
    - (e) Management or those charged with governance impose a limitation on the scope of the practitioner's work in the terms of a proposed review engagement such that the practitioner believes the limitation will result in the practitioner disclaiming a conclusion on the financial statements.

Preconditions for Accepting a Review Engagement

30. Prior to accepting a review engagement, the practitioner shall: (Ref: Para.A38)
    - (a) Determine whether the financial reporting framework applied in the preparation of the financial statements is acceptable including, in the case of special purpose financial statements, obtaining an understanding of the purpose for which the financial statements are prepared and of the intended users; and (Ref: Para.A39-A45)
    - (b) Obtain the agreement of management that it acknowledges and understands its responsibilities: (Ref: Para.A46-A49)
        - (i) For preparation of the financial statements in accordance with the applicable financial reporting framework, including, where relevant, their fair presentation;
        - (ii) For such internal control as management determines is necessary to enable the preparation of financial statements that are free from material misstatement, whether due to fraud or error; and
        - (iii) To provide the practitioner with:
            - (a) Access to all information of which management is aware that is relevant to the preparation of the financial statements, such as records, documentation and other matters;

(b) Additional information that the practitioner may request from management for the purpose of the review; and

(c) Unrestricted access to persons within the entity from whom the practitioner determines it necessary to obtain evidence.

31. If the practitioner is not satisfied as to any of the matters set out above as preconditions for accepting a review engagement, the practitioner shall discuss the matter with management or those charged with governance. If changes cannot be made to satisfy the practitioner as to those matters, the practitioner shall not accept the proposed engagement unless required by law or regulation to do so. However, an engagement conducted under such circumstances does not comply with this SRE. Accordingly, the practitioner shall not include any reference within the practitioner's report to the review having been conducted in accordance with this SRE.

32. If it is discovered after the engagement has been accepted that the practitioner is not satisfied as to any of the above preconditions, the practitioner shall discuss the matter with management or those charged with governance, and shall determine:

(a) Whether the matter can be resolved;

(b) Whether it is appropriate to continue with the engagement; and

(c) Whether and, if so, how to communicate the matter in the practitioner's report.

Additional Considerations When the Wording of the Practitioner's Report Is Prescribed by Law or Regulation

33. The practitioner's report issued for the review engagement shall refer to this SRE only if the report complies with the requirements of paragraph 86.

34. In some cases, when the review is performed pursuant to the specific law or regulation applicable to the entity, such law or regulation may prescribe the layout or wording of the practitioner's report in a form or in terms that are significantly different from the requirements of this SRE. In those circumstances, the practitioner shall evaluate whether users might misunderstand the assurance obtained from the review of the financial statements and, if so, whether additional explanation in the practitioner's report can mitigate possible misunderstanding. (Ref: Para. A50, A141)

35. If the practitioner concludes that additional explanation in the practitioner's report cannot mitigate possible misunderstanding, the practitioner shall not accept the review engagement unless required by law or regulation to do so. A review conducted in accordance with such law or regulation does not comply with this SRE. Accordingly, the practitioner shall not include any reference within the practitioner's report to the review having been conducted in accordance with this SRE. (Ref: Para. A50, A141)

Agreeing the Terms of Engagement

36. The practitioner shall agree the terms of the engagement with management or those charged with governance, as appropriate, prior to performing the engagement.

37. The agreed terms of engagement shall be recorded in an engagement letter or other suitable form of written agreement, and shall include: (Ref: Para. A51-A53, A55)

    (a) The intended use and distribution of the financial statements, and any restrictions on use or distribution where applicable;

    (b) Identification of the applicable financial reporting framework;

    (c) The objective and scope of the review engagement;

    (d) The responsibilities of the practitioner;

    (e) The responsibilities of management, including those in paragraph 30(b); (Ref: Para. A46-A49, A54)

    (f) A statement that the engagement is not an audit, and that the practitioner will not express an audit opinion on the financial statements; and

    (g) Reference to the expected form and content of the report to be issued by the practitioner, and a statement that there may be circumstances in which the report may differ from its expected form and content.

Recurring Engagements

38. On recurring review engagements, the practitioner shall evaluate whether circumstances, including changes in the engagement acceptance considerations, require the terms of engagement to be revised and whether there is a need to remind management or those charged with governance, as appropriate, of the existing terms of engagement. (Ref: Para.A56)

Acceptance of a Change in the Terms of the Review Engagement

39. The practitioner shall not agree to a change in the terms of the engagement where there is no reasonable justification for doing so. (Ref: Para.A57-A59)

40. If, prior to completing the review engagement, the practitioner is requested to change the engagement to an engagement for which no assurance is obtained, the practitioner shall determine whether there is reasonable justification for doing so. (Ref: Para.A60-A61)

41. If the terms of engagement are changed during the course of the engagement, the practitioner and management or those charged with governance, as appropriate, shall agree on and record the new terms of the engagement in an engagement letter or other suitable form of written agreement.

Communication with Management and Those Charged with Governance

42. The practitioner shall communicate with management or those charged with governance, as appropriate, on a timely basis during the course of the review engagement, all matters concerning the review engagement that, in the practitioner's professional judgment, are of sufficient importance to merit the

attention of management or those charged with governance, as appropriate. (Ref: Para.A62-A68)

Performing the Engagement

Materiality in a Review of Financial Statements

43. The practitioner shall determine materiality for the financial statements as a whole, and apply this materiality in designing the procedures and in evaluating the results obtained from those procedures. (Ref: Para.A69-A72)

44. The practitioner shall revise materiality for the financial statements as a whole in the event of becoming aware of information during the review that would have caused the practitioner to have determined a different amount initially. (Ref. Para.A73)

The Practitioner's Understanding

45. The practitioner shall obtain an understanding of the entity and its environment, and the applicable financial reporting framework, to identify areas in the financial statements where material misstatements are likely to arise and thereby provide a basis for designing procedures to address those areas. (Ref: Para. A74- A76)

46. The practitioner's understanding shall include the following: (Ref: Para. A77, A86, A88)
    - (a) Relevant industry, regulatory, and other external factors including the applicable financial reporting framework;
    - (b) The nature of the entity, including:
        - (i) Its operations;
        - (ii) Its ownership and governance structure;
        - **(iii) The types of investments that the entity is making and plans to make;**
        - (iv) The way that the entity is structured and how it is financed; and
        - (v) The entity's objectives and strategies;
    - (c) The entity's accounting systems and accounting records; and
    - (d) The entity's selection and application of accounting policies.

Designing and Performing Procedures

47. In obtaining sufficient appropriate evidence as the basis for a conclusion on the financial statements as a whole, the practitioner shall design and perform inquiry and analytical procedures: (Ref: Para. A78-A82, A86, A88)
    - (a) To address all material items in the financial statements, including disclosures; and
    - (b) To focus on addressing areas in the financial statements where material misstatements are likely to arise.

48. The practitioner's inquiries of management and others within the entity, as appropriate, shall include the following: (Ref: Para.A83-A86)

(a) How management makes the significant accounting estimates required under the applicable financial reporting framework;

(b) The identification of related parties and related party transactions, including the purpose of those transactions;

(c) Whether there are significant, unusual or complex transactions, events or matters that have affected or may affect the entity's financial statements, including:

(i) Significant changes in the entity's business activities or operations;

(ii) Significant changes to the terms of contracts that materially affect the entity's financial statements, including terms of finance and debt contracts or covenants;

(iii) Significant journal entries or other adjustments to the financial statements;

(iv) Significant transactions occurring or recognized near the end of the reporting period;

(v) The status of any uncorrected misstatements identified during previous engagements; and

(vi) Effects or possible implications for the entity of transactions or relationships with related parties;

(d) The existence of any actual, suspected or alleged:

(i) Fraud or illegal acts affecting the entity; and

(ii) Non-compliance with provisions of laws and regulations that are generally recognized to have a direct effect on the determination of material amounts and disclosures in the financial statements, such as tax and pension laws and regulations;

(e) Whether management has identified and addressed events occurring between the date of the financial statements and the date of the practitioner's report that require adjustment of, or disclosure in, the financial statements;

(f) The basis for management's assessment of the entity's ability to continue as a going concern; (Ref: Para.A87)

(g) Whether there are events or conditions that appear to cast doubt on the entity's ability to continue as a going concern;

(h) Material commitments, contractual obligations or contingencies that have affected or may affect the entity's financial statements, including disclosures; and

(i) Material non-monetary transactions or transactions for no consideration in the financial reporting period under consideration.

49. In designing analytical procedures, the practitioner shall consider whether the data from the entity's accounting system and accounting records are adequate for the purpose of performing the analytical procedures. (Ref: Para.A88-A90)

Procedures to Address Specific Circumstances

Related Parties 6

50. During the review, the practitioner shall remain alert for arrangements or information that may indicate the existence of related party relationships or transactions that management has not previously identified or disclosed to the practitioner.

51. If the practitioner identifies significant transactions outside the entity's normal course of business in the course of performing the review, the practitioner shall inquire of management about:

 (a) The nature of those transactions;

 (b) Whether related parties could be involved; and

 (c) The business rationale (or lack thereof) of those transactions. Fraud and non-compliance with laws or regulations

52. When there is an indication that fraud or non-compliance with laws or regulations, or suspected fraud or non-compliance with laws or regulations, has occurred in the entity, the practitioner shall:

 (a) Communicate that matter to the appropriate level of senior management or those charged with governance as appropriate;

 (b) Request management's assessment of the effect(s), if any, on the financial statements;

 (c) Consider the effect, if any, of management's assessment of the effects of fraud or non-compliance with laws or regulations communicated to the practitioner on the practitioner's conclusion on the financial statements and on the practitioner's report; and

 (d) Determine whether there is a responsibility to report the occurrence or suspicion of fraud or illegal acts to a party outside the entity. (Ref: Para.A91)

Going concern

53. A review of financial statements includes consideration of the entity's ability to continue as a going concern. In considering management's assessment of the entity's ability to continue as a going concern, the practitioner shall cover the same period as that used by management to make its assessment as required by the applicable financial reporting framework, or by law or regulation where a longer period is specified.

54. If, during the performance of the review, the practitioner becomes aware of events or conditions that may cast significant doubt about the entity's ability to continue as a going concern, the practitioner shall: (Ref: Para.A92)

 (a) Inquire of management about plans for future actions affecting the entity's ability to continue as a going concern and about the feasibility of those plans, and also whether management believes the outcome of those plans will improve the situation regarding the entity's ability to continue as a going concern;

 (b) Evaluate the results of those inquiries, to consider whether management's responses provide a sufficient basis to:

Appendix 10: Abstracts of guidance notes on terms used in financial statements issued by the Institute of Chartered Accountants of India

Introduction

(1) The objective of this guidance note is to facilitate a broad and basic understanding of the various terms as well as to promote consistency and uniformity in their usage. As such it does not purport to provide a comprehensive or rigid dictionary.

(2) The basic considerations to be borne in mind when selecting terms for use in the financial statements are clarity, significance and consistency.

(3) This guidance note does not primarily cover the terms used in a specific sense by certain specialised institutions, e.g., banks, insurance companies, financial institutions or electricity companies. However, it is possible that some of the terms defined here may have common application for such institutions.

(4) Many of the terms have, over a period of time, acquired a worldwide usage and recognition. Therefore, while formulating this guidance note, the Accounting Standards Board has taken into consideration the terminologies in use in various countries as formulated by their respective professional bodies.

(5) The terms have been defined in this note, keeping in view their usage in the preparation and presentation of the financial statements. Some of these terms may have different meanings when used in the context of certain special enactments.

(6) The definitions of the terms in this guidance note do not spell out the accounting procedure and are not prescriptive of a course of action.

General Definitions

1. **Absorption Costing**

   A method whereby the cost is determined so as to include the appropriate share of both *variable* and *fixed costs*.

2. **Acceptance**

   The drawee's signed assent on bill of exchange, to the order of the drawer. This term is also used to describe a bill of exchange that has been accepted.

3. **Account Receivable**

   See sundry debtor

4. **Accounting Policies**

   The specific accounting principles and the methods of applying those principles adopted by an enterprise in the preparation and presentation of financial statements.

5. **Accrual**

Recognition of revenues and costs as they are earned or incurred (and not as money is received or paid). It includes recognition of trans-actions relating to assets and liabilities as they occur irrespective of the actual receipts or payments.

6. **Accrual Basis of Accounting**

The method of recording transactions by which revenues, costs, assets and liabilities are reflected in the accounts in the period in which they accrue. The 'accrual basis of accounting' includes considerations relating to deferrals, allocations, depreciation and amortisation. This basis is also referred to as mercantile basis of accounting.

7. **Accrued Asset**

A developing but not yet enforceable claim against another person which accumulates with the passage of time or the rendering of service or otherwise. It may arise from the rendering of services (including the use of money) which at the date of accounting have been partly performed, and are not yet billable.

8. **Accrued Expense**

An expense which has been incurred in an accounting period but for which no enforceable claim has become due in that period against the enterprise. It may arise from the purchase of services (including the use of money) which at the date of accounting have been only partly performed, and are not yet billable.

9. **Accrued Liability**

A developing but not yet enforceable claim by another person which accumulates with the passage of time or the receipt of service or otherwise. It may arise from the purchase of services (including the use of money) which at the date of accounting have been only partly performed, and are not yet billable.

10. **Accrued Revenue**

Revenue which has been earned in an accounting period but in respect of which no enforceable claim has become due in that period by the enterprise. It may arise from the rendering of services (including the use of money) which at the date of accounting have been partly performed, and are not yet billable.

11. **Accumulated Depletion**

The total to date of the periodic *depletion* charges on *wasting assets*.

12. **Accumulated Depreciation**

The total to date of the periodic *depreciation* charges on *depreciable assets*.

13. **Actual Cost**

See **cost**

14. Ad-valorem

A method of levying tax or duty on goods by using their assessable value as the tax base.

15. Added Value

See value added

16. Added Value Statement

See Value added statement

17. Advance

Payment made on account of, but before completion of, a contract, or before acquisition of goods or receipt of services.

18. Amortisable Amount

See amortization

19. Amortisation

The gradual and systematic writing off of an *asset* or an account over an appropriate period. The amount on which *amortisation* is provided is referred to as *amortisable amount. Depreciation* accounting is a form of amortisation applied to *depreciable assets. Depletion* accounting is another form of amortisation applied to *wasting assets*. Amortisation also refers to gradual extinction or *provision* for extinction of a debt by gradual *redemption* or *sinking fund* payments or the gradual writing off to *revenue* of miscellaneous expenditure carried forward, e.g., *share issue expenses, preliminary expenses*, etc.

20. Amortised Value

The *amortisable amount* less any portion already provided by way of *amortisation.*

21. Annual Report

The information provided annually by the management of an enterprise to the owners and other interested persons concerning its operations and financial position. It includes the information statutorily required, e.g., in the case of a company, the *balance sheet, profit and loss statement* and notes on accounts, the *auditor's report* thereon, and the report of the Board of Directors. It also includes other information voluntarily provided e.g., *value added statement*, graphs, charts, etc.

22. Appropriation Account

An account sometimes included as a separate section of the *profit and loss statement* showing application of *profits* towards *dividends, reserves*, etc.

23. Assets

Tangible objects or intangible rights owned by an enterprise and carrying probable future benefits.

24. Auditor's Report

The formal expression of opinion by an independent external auditor on the financial statements of an enterprise including such reservations, qualifications and negations as may be called for and incorporating, where appropriate, such statutory affirmations as may be prescribed.

25. Authorised Share Capital

The number and par value, of each class of shares that an enterprise may issue in accordance with its instrument of incorporation. This is sometimes referred to as **nominal share capital.**

26. Average Cost

The *cost* of an item at a point of time as determined by applying an average of the cost of all items of the same nature over a period. When weightages are also applied in the computation, it is termed as weighted average cost.

27. Bad Debts

Debts owed to an enterprise which are considered to be irrecoverable.

28. Balance Sheet

A statement of the financial position of an enterprise as at a given date, which exhibits its *assets, liabilities, capital, reserves* and other account balances at their respective *book values*.

29. Bill of Exchange

An instrument in writing containing an unconditional order, signed by the maker, directing a certain person to pay a certain sum of money only, to or to the order of a certain person or to the bearer of the instrument.

30. Bond

See debenture

31. Bonus Shares

Shares allotted by captalisation of the *reserves* or *surplus* of a corporate enterprise.

32. Book Value

The amount at which an item appears in the books of account or financial statements. It does not refer to any particular basis on which the amount is determined e.g, *cost*, replacement value, etc.

33. Call

A demand pursuant to terms of issue to pay a part or whole of the balance remaining payable on shares or debentures after allotment.

34. Called-up Share Capital

That part of the *subscribed share capital* which shareholders have been required to pay.

35. Capital

Generally refers to the amount invested in an enterprise by its owners e.g. *paid-up share capital* in a corporate enterprise. It is also used to refer to the interest of owners in the assets of an enterprise.

36. Capital Assets

Assets, including *investments* not held for sale, conversion or consumption in the ordinary course of business.

37. Capital Commitment

Future liability for capital expenditure in respect of which contracts have been made.

38. Capital Employed

The finances deployed by an enterprise in its *net fixed assets, investments* and working *capital.* Capital employed in an operation may, however, exclude *investments* made outside that operation.

39. Capital Loss

See capital **profit**

40. Capital Profit

Excess of the proceeds realised from the sale, transfer, or exchange of the whole or a part of a *capital asset* over its *cost.* When the result of of this computation is negative, it is referred to as **capital loss**.

41. Capital Redemption Reserve

A reserve created on *redemption* of the *redeemable preference shares* of a corporate enterprise out of its *profits* which would otherwise have been available for distribution as *dividend.*

42. Capital Reserve

A reserve of a corporate enterprise which is not available for distribution as *dividend.*

43. Capital Work-in-progress

Expenditure on *capital, assets* which are in the process of construction or completion.

44. Cash Basis of Accounting

The method of recording transactions by which *revenues* and *costs* and *assets* and *liabilities* are reflected in the accounts in the period in which actual receipts or actual payments are made.

45. Cash Discount

A reduction granted by a supplier from the invoiced price in consideration of immediate payment or payment within a stipulated period.

46. Cash Profit

The *net profit* as increased by non-cash costs, such as *depreciation*, amortisation, etc. When the result of the computation is negative, it is termed as cash loss.

47. Changes in Financial Position, Statement of

A financial statement which summarises, for the period covered by it, the changes in the financial position including the sources from which funds were obtained by the enterprise and the specific uses to which such funds were applied. This is also called the **funds flow statement.**

48. Charge

An encumbrance on an *asset* to secure an indebtedness or other obligations. It may be fixed or floating.

49. Cheque

A *bill of exchange* drawn upon a specified banker and not expressed to be payable otherwise than on demand.

50. Collateral Security

Security which is given in addition to the principal security against the same *liability* or obligation.

51. Contingency

A condition or situation, the ultimate outcome of which, *gain* or *loss*, will be known or determined only on the occurrence or non-occurrence of one or more uncertain future events.

52. Contingent Asset

An *asset* the existence, ownership or value of which may be known or determined only on the occurrence or non-occurrence of one or more un-certain future events.

53. Contingent Liability

An obligation relating to an existing condition orsitualion which may arise in future depending on the occurrence, or non-occurrence of one or more uncertain future events.

54. Contra Account

One or two or more accounts which partially or wholly off-set another or other accounts.

55. Cost

The amount of *expenditure* incurred on or attributable to a specified article, product or activity.

56. Cost of Purchase

The purchase price including duties and taxes, freight inwards and other expenditure directly attributable to acquisition, less*trade discounts* rebates, duty drawbacks, and subsidies in respect of such purchase.

57. Cost-plus Contract

A contract under which the contractor is reimbursed for allowable or otherwise denned *costs* as increased by a percentage of such *costs* or an agreed fee.

58. Cost of Goods Sold

The cost of goods sold during an accounting period. In manufacturing operations, it includes (i) cost of materials; (ii) labour and factory overheads; selling and administrative expenses are normally excluded.

59. Cost of Sales

Cost of goods sold plus selling and administrative expenses.

60. Conversion Cost

Cost incurred to convert raw materials or components into finished or semi-finished products. This normally includes *costs* which are specifically attributable to units of production, i.e, direct labour, direct expenses and subcontracted work, and production overheads as applicable in accordance with either the *direct cost or absorption costing method.* Production overheads exclude expenses which relate to general administration, finance. selling and distribution.

61. Convertible Bond

See **convertible** Debenture

62. Convertible Debenture

A **debenture** which gives the holder a right to its conversion, wholly or partly, in shares in accordance with the terms of issue.

63. Creditor

See **sundry** creditor

64. Cumulative Dividend

A dividend *payable* on *cumulative preference shares*, which, if unpaid, accumulates as a claim against the earnings of a corporate enterprise, before any distribution is made to the other shareholders.

65. Cumulative Preference Shares

A class of preference shares entitled to payment of *cumulative dividends*. Preference shares are always deemed to be cumulative, unless they are expressly made non-cumulative.

66. Current Assets

Cash and other *assets* that are expected to be converted into cash or consumed in the production of goods or rendering of services in the normal course of business.

67. Current Liability

Liability including loans, deposits and bank overdraft which falls due for payment in a relatively short period, normally not more than twelve months.

68. Debenture

A formal document constituting acknowledgement of a debt by an enterprise, usually given under its common seal and normally containing provisions regarding payment of interest, repayment of principal and security, if any. It is transferable in the appropriate manner.

69. Debenture Redemption Reserve

A reserve created for the *redemption* of *debentures* at a future date.

70. Debtor

See sundry **debtor**

71. Deferral

Postponement of recognition of a revenue or expense after its related receipt or payment (or incurrence of a *liability*) to a subsequent period to which it applies. Common examples of deferrals include pre-paid rent and taxes, unearned subscriptions received in advance by newspapers and magazine selling companies, etc.

72. Deferred Expenditure

Expenditure for which payment has been made or *a liability* incurred but which is carried forward on the presumption that it will be of benefit over a subsequent period or periods. This is also referred to as **deferred revenue expenditure.**

73. Deferred Revenue

Revenue or income received or recorded before it is earned and carried forward to a subsequent period or periods to which it relates.

74. Deferred Revenue Expenditure

See deferred expenditure

75. Deficiency

The excess of *liabilities* over *assets* of an enterprise at a given date. The debit balance in the *profit and loss statement.*

76. Deficit

The debit balance in the profit and loss statement.

77. Depletion

A measure of exhaustion of a *wasting asset* represented by periodic write off of *cost* or other substituted value.

78. Depreciable Amount

The historical cost, or other amount substituted for historical cost of a depreciable *asset* in the finincial statements, less the estimated residual value.

79. Depreciable Asset

Asset which is expected to be used during more than one accounting period, has a limited *useful life*, and is held by an enterprise for use in the production or supply of goods, and services, for rental to others, or for administrative purposes and not for the purpose of sale in the ordinary course of business.

80. Depreciation

A measure of the wearing out, consumption or other loss of value of a *depreciable asset* arising from use, effluxion of time or *obsolescence* through technology and market changes. It is allocated so as to charge a fair proportion in each accounting period during the *useful life* of the *asset.* It includes *amortisation* of *assets* whose *useful life* is predetermined and *depletion of wasting assets.*

81. Depreciation Method

Any method of calculating *depreciation* for an accounting period.

82. Depreciation Rate

A percentage applied to the historical cost or the substituted amount of a *depreciable asset* (or in case of *diminishing balance method,* the historical cost or the substituted amount less accumulated *depredation*).

83. Development Allowance Reserve

A *reserve* created in compliance with one of the conditions for claiming *development* allowance under the Income-tax Act, 1961.

84. Development Rebate Reserve

A *reserve* created in compliance with one of the conditions for claiming development rebate under the Income-tax Act, 1961.

85. Diminishing Balance Method

A method under which the periodic charge for *depreciation* of an *asset* is computed by applying a fixed percentage to its historical cost or substituted amount less *accumulated depreciation* (net book value). This is also referred to as written down value method.

86. Direct Cost

An item of *cost* that can be reasonably identified with a specific unit of product or with a specific operation or other cost céntre.

87. Direct Costing

A method whereby the *cost* is determined so as to include the appropriate share of *variable costs* only, all *fixed costs* being charged against *revenue* in the period in which they are incurred.

88. Discount

A reduction from a list price, quoted price or invoiced price. It also refers to the price for *obtaining* payment on a bill before its maturity.

89. Dividend

A distribution to shareholders out of *profits or reserves* available for this *purpose*.

90. Dividend Equalisation Reserve

A *reserve* created to maintain the rate of *dividend* in future years.

91. Earnings per Share

The earnings in monetary terms attributable to each *equity share*, based on the *net profit* for the period, before taking into account *prior period items, extraordinary items* and adjustments resulting from changes in *accounting policies* but after deducting tax appropriate thereto and preference *dividends*, divided by the number of equity shares issued and ranking for dividend in respect of that period.

92. Entity Concept

The view of the relationship between the accounting entity and its owners which regards the entity as a separate person, distinct and apart from its owners.

93. Equity Share

A share which is not a preference share. Also sometimes called, **ordinary** *share***.**

94. Expenditure

Incurring a *liability*, disbursement of cash or transfer of property for the purpose of *obtaining* assets, goods or services.

95. Expense

A cost relating to the operations of an accounting period or to the *revenue* earned *during* the period or the benefits of which do not extend beyond that period.

96. Expired Cost

That portion of an *expenditure* from which no further benefit is expected. Also termed *as* expense.

97. Extraordinary Item

Gain or loss which arises from events or transactions that are distinct from ordinary *activities* of the enterprise and which are both material and expected not to recur frequently or regularly. This would also include material adjustments necessitated by circumstances, which, though related to previous periods, are determined in the current period.

98. Fair Market Value

The price that would be agreed to in an open and unrestricted market between knowledgeable and willing parties dealing at arm's length who are fully informed *and* not under any compulsion to transact. Arm's length is a term applied to any transaction on the assumption that the parties to the transaction would act without being influenced by each other or by any other person.

99. Fictitious Asset

Item grouped under *assets* in a *balance sheet* which has no real value (e.g. the debit balance of the *profit and* loss statement).

100. First Charge

A *charge* having priority over other charges.

101. First In, First Out (FIFO)

Computation or the cost ofi items sold or consumed during a period is though they were sold or consumed in order of their acquisition.

102. Fixed Asset

Asset held for the purpose of providing or producing goods or services and *that* is not held for resale in the normal course of business.

103. Fixed Cost

That cost of production which by its very nature remains relatively unaffected in a defined period of time by variations in the volume of production.

104. Fixed Deposit

Deposit for a *specified* period and at specified rate of interest.

105. Fixed or Specific Charge

A charge which attaches to a particular *asset* which is identified when the charge is *created*, and the identity of the *asset* does not change during the subsistence of the *charge.*

106. Fleating Charge

A general *charge* on some or all *assets* of an enterprise which are not attached to specific assets and are given as security against a debt.

107. Foreign Currency, Translation of

The process of expressing amounts stated in a foreign currency into equivalent *amounts* in local currency by using an exchange rate between the two currencies.

108. Foreign Currency Conversion

The process of expressing amounts stated in a foreign currency into equivalent *amounts* in local currency by using the exchange rate at which the foreign currency is bought or sold.

109. Forfeited Share

A share to which title is lost by a member for non-payment of call money or default in fulfilling any engagement between members or expulsion of members *where* the articles specifically provide therefor.

110. Free Reserve

A reserve the utilisation of which is not restricted in any manner.

111. Functional Classification

A system of classification of *expenses* and *revenues* and the *corresponding assets* and *liabilities* to each function or activity, rather than by reference to their nature.

112. Fund

An account usually of the nature of a *reserve* or a *provision* which is represented by specifically earmarked *assets*.

113. Fundamental Accounting Assumptions

Basic accounting assumptions which underlie the preparation and presentation of financial statements. They *are going concern*, consistency. and *accrual*. *Usually*, they are not specifically stated because their acceptance and use are assumed. Disclosure is necessary if they are not followed.

114. Funds Flow Statement

See changes in financial position, statementof

115. Gain

A monetary benefit, *profit* or advantage resulting from a transaction or group of transactions.

116. General Reserve

A revenue *reserve* which is not earmarked for a specific purpose.

117. Going Concern Assumption

An accounting assumption according to which an enterprise is viewed as continuing in operation for the foreseeable future. It is assumed that the *enterprise* has neither the intention nor the necessity of liquidation or of curtailing materially the scale of its operations.

118. Goodwill

An intangible *asset* arising from business connections or trade name or reputation *of* an enterprise.

119. Gross Margin or Gross Profit

The excess of the proceeds of goods sold and services rendered during a period over their *cost*, before taking into account administration, selling, *distribution* and financing expenses. When the result of this computation is negative it is referred to as **gross loss.**

120. Gross Sales

See sales turnover

121. Gross Turnover

See sales turnover

122. Income

See revenue

123. Income and Expenditure Statement

A financial statement, often prepared by non-profit making enterprises like clubs, *associations* etc. to present their revenues and expenses for an accounting period and to show the excess of revenues over expenses (or *vice versa*) for that period. It is similar to profit and loss statement and is also called **revenue and expense statement.**

124. Intangible Asset

Asset which does not have a physical identity e.g. *goodwill*, patents, *copyright* etc.

125. Internal Audit

An independent appraisal activity within an enterprise whether by the staff of the enterprise or by a firm of accountants appointed for that purpose, for the review of accounting, financial and other operations and controls as a basis for service to management. It involves a specialised application of the techniques of auditing.

126. Internal Check

A system of allocation of responsibility, division of work, and methods of recording transactions, whereby the work of an employee or group of employees is checked continuously by correlating it with the work of others. An essential feature is that no one employee or group of employees has exclusive control over any *transaction* or group of transactions.

127. Internal Control

The entire system of controls, financial and otherwise, established by the management in order to carry on the business of the enterprise in an orderly and efficient *manner*, ensure adherence to management policies, safeguard the assets and secure as far as possible the accuracy and completeness of the records.

128. Interim Report

The information provided with reference to a date before the close of the accounting period by the management of an enterprise to owners or other interested *persons* concerning its operations or financial position.

129. Inventory

Tangible property held for sale in the ordinary course of business, or in the process of production for such sale, or for consumption in the production of goods on services for sale, including maintenance supplies and consumables other than machinery spares.

130. Investment

Expenditure on *assets* held to earn interest, *income, profit* or other *benefits*.

131. Investments

Assets held not for operational purposes or for rendering services i.e. assets other thw*fixed assets* or *current assets* (e.g. securities, shares, *debentures*, immovable properties)

132. Investment Allowance Reserve

A reserve created in compliance with one of the conditions for claiming *investment* allowance under the Income-tax Act, 1961.

133. Issned Share Capital

That portion of the *authorised share capital* which has actually been offered *for* subscription. This includes any bonus shares allotted by the corporate enterprise.

134. Last in. First Out (LIFO)

Computation of the *cost* of items sold or consumed during a period on the basis that the items last acquired were sold or consumed first.

135. Liability

The financial obligation of an enterprise other than owners' funds.

136. Lien

Right of one person to satisfy a claim against another by holding or retaining possession of that other's *assets*/property.

137. Long-term Liability

Liability which does not fall due for payment in a relatively short period, i.e., normally a period not more than twelve months.

138. Loss

See profit

139. Materiality

An accounting concept according to which all relatively important and relevant items, i.e., items th; knowledge of which might influence the decisions of the user *of* the financial statements are disclosed in the financial statements.

140. Mercantile Basis of Accounting

See accrual basis of accounting

141. Mortgage

A transfer of interest in specific immovable property for the purpose of securing a loan advanced, or to be advanced, an existing or future debt or the performance of an engagement which may give rise to a pecuniary *liability*. The security is redeemed when the loan is repaid or the debt discharged or the obligations performed.

142. Net Assets

The excess of the book value of assets (other than *fictitious assets*) of an enterprise over its *liabilities*. This is also referred to as net worth or shareholders' funds.

143. Net Fixed Assets

Fixed *assets less accumulated depreciation* thereon up-to-date

144. Net Loss

See net profit

145. Net Profit

The excess of *revenue* over *expenses* during a particular accounting period. When the result of this computation is negative, it is referred to as net loss. The net profit may be shown before or after tax.

146. Net Realisable Value

The actual/estimated selling price of an *asset* in the ordinary course of the business less cost of completion and cost necessarily to be incurred in order to make the *sale*.

147. Net Sales

See sales turnover

148. Net Turnover

See sales turnover

149. Net Worth

See net assets

150. Nominal Share Capital

See authorised share capital

151. Obsolescence

Diminution in the value of an *asset* by reason of its becoming out-of-date or less useful due to technological changes, improvement in production methods, change in *market* demand for the product or service output of the *asset*, or legal or other restrictions.

152. Operating Profit

The *net profit* arising from the normal operations and activities of an enterprise without taking account of extraneous transactions and expenses of a purely *financial* nature.

153. Paid-up Share Capital

That part of the *subscribed share capital* for which consideration in cash or otherwise has been received. This includes *bonus shares* allotted by the corporate enterprise.

154. Pari Passu Charge

Charge created by an enterprise on its *assets* in favour of more than one person on *the* condition that each such person has equal rights of realisation out of the assets as the other(s).

155. Pledge

Deposit of goods by one person (pledger or pawnor) to another person (pledgee or pawnee) as a security for payment of a debt or performance of a promise. The pledgee has a special *lien*/right on the property in the pledged goods with a right to sell the same after notice if the pledger fails to discharge the debt or perform his promise on the stipulated date.

156. Preference Share Capital

That part of the *share capital* of a corporate enterprise which enjoys preferential rights in respect of payments of fixed *dividend* and repayment of *capital*. *Preference* shares may also have full or partial participating rights in surplus profits or surplus capital.

157. Preferential Payment

Payment which in a winding up or insolvency has to be made in priority to all other *debts* as per statute.

158. Preliminary Expenses

Expenses relating to the formation of an enterprise. These include legal, accounting and share issue expenses incurred for formation of the enterprise.

159. Pre-paid Expense

Payment for expense in an accounting period, the benefit for which will accrue in the subsequent accounting period(s).

160. Prime Cost

The total *cost* of direct materials, direct wages and other direct production expenses.

161. Prior Period Item

A material charge or credit which arises in the current period as a result of errors or omissions in the preparation of the financial statements of one or more prior periods.

162. Profit

A general term for the excess *of revenue* over related *cost.* When the result of this computation is negative it is referred to as loss. Also see gross profit, operating profit, net profit.

163. Profit and Loss Statement

A financial statement which presents the *revenues* and *expense.of* an enterprise for an accounting period and shows the excess of *revenues* over expenses (or *vice versa*). It is also known as profit and loss account.

164. Promissory Note

An instrument in writing (not being a bank note or currency note) containing an unconditional undertaking, signed by the maker, 10 pay a certain sum of money only to, or to the order of, a certain person or to the bearer of the instrument.

165. Propriety Concept

A concept of evaluating performance or specific transactions of an enterprise with reference to the tests of commonly accepted norms. customs and standards of conduct including those based on considerations of public interest.

166. Provision

An amount written off or retained by way of providing for *depreciation* or diminution in value of *assets* or retained by way of providing for any known *liability* the amount of which cannot be determined with substantial accuracy.

167. Provision for Doubtful Debts

A provision made for debts considered doubtful of recovery.

168. Prudence

A concept of care and caution used in accounting according to which (in view of the uncertainty attached to future events) *profits* are not anticipated, but recognised only when realised, though not necessarily in cash. Under this concept, provision is made for all known *liabilities* and losses, even though the amount cannot be determined with certainty and represents only a best estimate in the light of available information.

169. Public Deposits

Fixed *deposits* accepted by an enterprise from the public in accordance with the prevailing Rules made in this behalf.

170. Redeemable Preference Share

The preference share that is repayable eilher after a fixed or deter-minable period or at any time decided by the management (by giving due notice), under certain conditions prescribed by the instrument of incorporation or the terms of issue.

171. Redemption

Repayment as per given terms normally used in connection with preference shares and *debentures*.

172. Reduction of Capital

The extinguishment or reduction of shareholders' liability on any of the shares of a corporate enterprise in respect of the *share capital* not fully paid up or the cancellation *of paid-up share capital* of a company which is not represented by available *assets*. It also refers to the return of any *paid-up share capital* in excess of requirements.

173. Reserve

The portion of earnings, receipts or other surplus of an enterprise (whether capital or revenue) appropriated by the management for a general or a specific purpose other than a *provision* for *depreciation* or diminution in the value of *assets* or for a known *liability*. The reserves are primarily of two types : *capital reserves* and *revenue reserves*.

174. Revaluation Reserve

A reserve created on the revaluation of *assets or net assets* of an enterprise represented by the surplus of the estimated replacement cost or estimated market values over the *book values* thereof.

175. Revenue

The gross inflow of cash, receivables or other consideration arising in the course of the ordinary activities of an enterprise from the sale of goods, from the rendering of services, and from the use by others of enterprise resources yielding interest, royalties and *dividends*. Revenue is measured by the charges made to customers or clients for goods supplied and services rendered to them and by the charges and rewards arising from the use of resources by them. It excludes amounts collected on behalf of third parties such as certain taxes. In an agency relationship, the revenue is the amount of commission and not the gross inflow of cash, receivables or other consideration.

176. Revenue and Expense Statement

See income and expenditure statement

177. Revenue Reserve

Any *reserve* other than a *capital reserve*.

178. Right Share

An allotment of shares on the issue of fresh *capital* by a corporate enterprise to which a shareholder is entitled on payment, by virtue of his holding certain shares in the enterprise in proportion to the number of shares already held by him. (Shares allotted to certain categories of *debenture* holders pursuant to the rights enjoyed by them arc sometimes called right shares)

179. Sales Turnover

The aggregate amount for which sales are effected or services rendered by an enterprise. The terms gross turnover and net turnover (or gross sales and net sales) are sometimes used to distinguish the sales aggregate before and after deduction of returns and trade discounts.

180. Secured Loan

Loan secured wholly or partly against an *asset.*

181. Self-Insurance

The assumption by an enterprise of a risk which is not covered by an external insurance agency and for which internal allocations or *provisions* have been made.

182. Share Capital

Aggregate amount of money paid or credited as paid on the snares and/of stocks of a corporate enterprise.

183. Share Discount

The excess of the face value of shares over their issue price.

184. Shareholders' Equity

The interest of the shareholders in the *net assets* of a corporate enterprise. However, in the case of liquidation it is represented by the residual *assets* after meeting prior claims.

185. Shareholders' Funds

See net assets

186. Share Issue Expenses

Costs incurred in connection with the issue and allotment of shares. These include legal and professional fees, advertising expenses, printing costs, underwriting commission, brokerage, and also expenses in connection with the issue of prospectus and allotment of shares.

187. Share Premium

The excess of the issue price of shares over their face value.

188. Short-term Liability

See current liability

189. Sinking Fund

A fund created for the repayment of a *liability* or for the replacement of an asset.

190. Social Cost Benefit Analysis

The identification, measurement and reporting of *social costs* and *benefits* related to a project or an enterprise.

191. Social Cost

The cost or the loss to society resulting from the operations of an enterprise in its particular circumstances. Such costs are often not readily measurable in monetary terms. This term is also used in a specific sense to denote the costs incurred by an enterprise in providing social amenities.

192. Social Benefit

The benefits or income to society resulting from operations of an enterprise in its particular circumstances. Such benefits are often not readily measurable in monetary terms.

193. Standard Cost

A pre-determined *cost* of an activity, operation, process or product, established as a basis for control and reporting.

194. Straight Line Method

The method under which the periodic charge for *depreciation* is computed by dividing the *depreciable amount* of a *depreciable asset* by the estimated number of years of its useful life.

195. Subscribed Share Capital

That portion of the *issued share capital* which has actually been subscribed and allotted. This includes any *bonus shares* allotted by the corporate enterprise.

196. Substance over Form

An accounting concept according to which the substance and not merely the legal form of transactions and events governs their accounting treatment and presentation in financial statements.

197. Sundry Creditor

Amount owed by an enterprise on account of goods purchased or services received or in respect of contractual obligations. Also termed as trade creditor or account payable.

198. Sundry Debtor

Person from whom amounts are due for goods sold or services rendered or in respect of contractual obligations. Also termed as debtor, trade debtor, account receivable.

199. Surplus

Credit balance in the *profit and loss statement* after providing for proposed appropriations, e.g., *dividend or reserves.*

200. Test Check

Examination of representative items selected from an account or record for the purpose of arriving at an opinion on the entire account or record.

201. Trade Creditor

See sundry creditor

202. Trade Debtor

See sundry debtor

203. Trade Discount

A reduction granted by a supplier from the list price of goods or services on business considerations other than for prompt payment.

204. Transfer Price

The price charged (or valus assigned) to a product or service which is transferred within an enterprise from one segment/division to another.

205. Unclaimed Dividend

Dividend which has been declared by a corporate enterprise and a warrant or a cheque in respect whereof has been despatched but has not been encashed by the shareholder concerned.

206. Unexpired Cost

That portion of an *expenditure* whose benefit has not yet been exhausted.

207. Unissued Share Capital

That portion of the *authorised share capital* for which shares have not been offered for subscription.

208. Unpaid Dividend

Dividend which has been declared by a corporate enterprise but has not been paid, or the warrant or *cheque* in respect whereof has not been despatched within the prescribed period.

209. Useful Life

Life which is either (1) the period over which a *depreciable asset* is expected to be used by the enterprise; or (ii) the number of production or similar units expected to be obtained from the use of the *asset* by the enterprise.

210. Value Added

The increase in value of a product or service resulting from an alteration in the form, location or availability excluding the cost of bought-out materials or services. This is also referred to as added value.

211. Value Added Statement

A statement of the value added that an enterprise hasbeen able to generate and its distribution a nong those contributing to its generation. This is also referred to as addedvalue statement.

212. Variable Cost

That cost which varies directly, or nearly directly, with the volume of activity.

213. Wasting Asset

Natural resource which is subject to *depletion* through the process of extraction or use e.g. mines, quarries.

214. Weighted Average Cost

See average cost

215. Working Capital

The funds available for conducting day-to-day operations of an enterprise. Also represented by the excess of *current assets* over *current liabilities* including short-term loans.

216. Work in Process

Work in Process includes all materials which, have undergone manufacturing or processing operations, but upon which further operations are necessary before the product is ready for sale.

217. Written Down Value Method (W.D.V.)

See diminishing balance method

Appendix 11: Abstracts of guidance note on audit reports and certificates for special purposes of ICAI

(1) Introduction: The purpose of this Guidance Note is to provide guidance on engagements which require a 'professional accountant in public practice' (hitherto known as "practitioner") to issue reports other than those which are issued in audits or reviews of historical financial information. The reports which are issued pursuant to audits or reviews of historical financial information are dealt with in Standards on Auditing (SAs) and Standards on Review Engagements (SREs), respectively, issued by the Institute of Chartered Accountants of India (ICAI).

(2) In some cases, Government and other authorities under various statutes or notifications require reports or certificates from practitioners in support of statements or other information provided by an entity. Such reports or certificates can also be required to be issued to fulfill a contractual reporting obligation or may be required by the management or those charged with governance of an entity for its own special purposes.

(3) Sometimes, the applicable law and regulation or a contractual arrangement that an entity might have entered into, prescribe the wording of report or certificates. The wording often requires the use of word or phrase like "certify" or "true and correct" to indicate absolute level of assurance expected to be provided by the practitioner on the subject matter. Absolute assurance indicates that a practitioner has performed procedures as considered appropriate to reduce the engagement risk 3 to zero.

(4) A practitioner is expected to provide either a reasonable assurance (about whether the subject matter of examination is materially misstated) or a limited assurance (stating that nothing has come to the practitioner's attention that causes the Practitioner to believe that the subject matter is materially misstated). A practitioner is not expected to reduce the engagement risk to zero. This is because there are inherent limitations attached to the procedures which a practitioner may perform in relation to issuance of a report or certificate, as the case may be. The inherent limitations arise from:

   (a) the nature of financial reporting;

   (b) the use of selective testing;

   (c) the inherent limitations of internal controls;

   (d) the fact that much of the evidence4 available to the practitioner is persuasive rather than conclusive;

   (e) the nature of procedures to be performed in a specific situation;

   (f) the use of professional judgment5 in gathering and evaluating evidence and forming conclusions based on that evidence;

   (g) in some cases, the characteristics of the underlying subject matter6 when evaluated or measured against the criteria7; and

(h) the need for the engagement to be conducted within a reasonable period of time and at a reasonable cost.

(5) In view of the above, depending upon the nature, timing and extent of procedures that can be performed based upon the facts and circumstances of the case, a report or certificate issued by a practitioner can provide either reasonable or limited level of assurance. Therefore, whenever a practitioner is required to give a "certificate" or a "report" for special purpose, the practitioner needs to undertake a careful evaluation of the scope of the engagement, i.e., whether the practitioner would be able to provide reasonable assurance or limited assurance on the subject matter.

(6) The word 'certificate' as described in the laws and regulations or even in the contracts that an entity might have entered into can normally be associated with reasonable assurance. However, depending upon the circumstances and based upon the nature, timing and extent of the procedures which a practitioner can perform, the practitioner can conclude that a reasonable assurance cannot be expressed on the subject matter of the "certificate" and only limited assurance conclusion can be given. The practitioner's procedures in case where reasonable assurance is to be expressed would be substantially different (and more extensive) from circumstances where limited assurance is to be expressed. The Guidance Note, at relevant places, lists the different procedures to be performed in a reasonable assurance engagement vis a vis limited assurance engagement. Accordingly, for the purpose of this Guidance Note, the terms, "report"/"certificate" indicates an "assurance report" issued in compliance with this Guidance Note.

(7) Assurance engagements include both assertion based engagements[8], in which a party other than the practitioner measures or evaluates the underlying subject matter against the criteria, and direct reporting engagements[9], in which the practitioner measures or evaluates the underlying subject matter against the criteria. To be meaningful, the level of assurance obtained by the practitioner is likely to enhance the intended users'[10] confidence about the subject matter information11 to a degree that is clearly more than in consequential.

Chartered Accountants of India (ICAI). Appendix 1 to the Guidance Note contains a glossary of certain important terms used in the Guidance Note and is an integral part of the Guidance Note. Further, for the purposes of this Guidance Note, reference to "appropriate party(ies)" should be read hereafter as "the responsible party, the measurer or the evaluator, or the engaging party, as appropriate."

Scope

(8) This Guidance Note covers assurance engagements other than audits or reviews of historical financial information, as described in the Framework for Assurance Engagements (Assurance Framework) issued by the ICAI. This Guidance Note does not apply to assurance engagements for which subject specific Standards on Assurance Engagements have been issued by the ICAI.

(9) Not all engagements performed by the practitioners are assurance engagements. Some frequently performed engagements that are not assurance engagements, and therefore not covered by the Guidance Note, include:

(a) Engagements covered by Standards on Related Services (SRS), such as agreed-upon procedures and compilation engagements;

(b) The preparation of tax returns where no assurance opinion/conclusion is expressed; and

(c) Consulting (or advisory) engagements, such as management and tax consulting.

(10) This Guidance Note can also be applied on the reports or certificates related to historical non-financial information that a practitioner may be called upon to issue from time to time. ICAI, from time to time, issues specific Guidance Notes to provide guidance on certain assurance engagements. While complying with the requirements of those specific Guidance Notes, a practitioner may also draw guidance from the principles enunciated in this Guidance Note.

Objectives

(11) In conducting an assurance engagement, the objectives of the practitioner are:

(a) To obtain either reasonable assurance or limited assurance, as appropriate, about whether the subject matter information is free from material misstatement;

(b) To express an opinion (in a reasonable assurance engagement)/a conclusion (in a limited assurance engagement) regarding the outcome of the measurement or evaluation of the underlying subject matter through a written report. The report also describes the basis for the conclusion;

(c) Where the subject matter information is made up of a number of aspects, separate opinion/conclusion may be provided on each aspect. All such separate opinions/conclusions do not need to relate to the same level of assurance. Rather, each opinion/conclusion is expressed in the form that is appropriate to either a reasonable assurance engagement or a limited assurance engagement. References in this Guidance Note to the opinion/conclusion in the assurance report include each opinion/conclusion when separate opinions/conclusions are provided;

(d) To communicate further as required by this Guidance Note.

(12) In all cases when reasonable assurance or limited assurance, as appropriate, cannot be obtained and a qualified opinion/conclusion in the practitioner's assurance report is insufficient in the circumstances for the purposes of reporting to the intended users, this Guidance Note requires that the practitioner disclaim an opinion/a conclusion or withdraw (or resign) from the engagement, where withdrawal is possible under applicable law or regulation.

(13) The roles played by the responsible party, the measurer or evaluator, and the engaging party can vary. The management and governance structures vary by jurisdiction and by entity, reflecting influences such as different cultural and

legal backgrounds, and size and ownership characteristics. Such diversity means that it is not possible for the Guidance Note to specify for all engagements, the person(s) with whom the practitioner is to inquire of, request representations from, or otherwise communicate with in all circumstances. In some cases, for example, when the appropriate party(ies) is(are) only part of a complete legal entity, identifying the appropriate management personnel or those charged with governance with whom to communicate, will require the exercise of professional judgment to determine which person(s) have the appropriate responsibilities for, and knowledge of, the matters concerned.

Conduct of an Assurance Engagement in Accordance with Guidance Note

(14) The Guidance Note aims to bring out the procedural differences between a limited assurance engagement vis a vis a reasonable assurance engagement. In this Guidance Note, guidance that applies to only limited assurance or reasonable assurance engagements have been presented in a columnar format with the letter "L" (limited assurance) or "R"(reasonable assurance) after the paragraph number. Although some procedures are required only for reasonable assurance engagements, these may nonetheless be appropriate in some limited assurance engagements.

Inability to Achieve an Objective

(15) If any of the objectives enumerated in this Guidance Note (refer paragraphs 12 to 14) cannot be achieved, the practitioner should evaluate whether this requires the practitioner to modify the practitioner's opinion/conclusion or withdraw from the engagement (where withdrawal is possible under applicable law or regulation). In case the practitioner is unable to achieve an objective, it represents a significant matter requiring documentation in accordance with paragraph 92 of this Guidance Note.

Ethical and Quality Control Requirements

(16) A practitioner who performs assurance engagements covered under this Guidance Note is governed by the same ethical and quality control requirements as are described in paragraphs 4 and 5 of the Framework for Assurance Engagements.

Engagement Acceptance and Continuance

(17) The practitioner needs to be satisfied that appropriate procedures regarding the acceptance and continuance of client relationships and assurance engagements have been followed, and should determine that conclusions reached in this regard are appropriate.

(18) The practitioner should accept or continue an assurance engagement only when:

(a) The practitioner has no reason to believe that relevant ethical requirements, including independence, will not be satisfied;

(b) The practitioner is satisfied that those persons who are to perform the engagement collectively (the engagement team) have the appropriate competence and capabilities; and

(c) The basis upon which the engagement is to be performed has been agreed, through:

(i) Establishing that the preconditions for an assurance engagement are present (see also paragraphs 21-22); and

(ii) Confirming that there is a common understanding between the practitioner and the engaging party of the terms of the engagement, including the practitioner's reporting responsibilities.

(19) If the practitioner obtains information that would have caused the practitioner to decline the engagement had that information been available earlier, the practitioner should take necessary action promptly. In case of a firm, the practitioner (i.e., the engagement partner) should communicate that information promptly to the firm, so that the firm and the engagement partner can take the necessary action.

Preconditions for the Assurance Engagement

(20) In order to establish whether the preconditions for an assurance engagement are present, the practitioner should, on the basis of a preliminary knowledge of the engagement circumstances and discussion with the appropriate party(s), determine whether:

(a) The roles and responsibilities of the appropriate parties are suitable in the circumstances; and

(b) The engagement exhibits all of the following characteristics:

(i) The underlying subject matter is appropriate;

(ii) The criteria that the practitioner expects to be applied in the preparation of the subject matter information are suitable for the engagement circumstances, including that these exhibit the following characteristics as described in paragraph 35 of the Framework for Assurance Engagements:

(a) Relevance.

(b) Completeness.

(c) Reliability.

(d) Neutrality.

(e) Understandability.

(iii) The criteria that the practitioner expects to be applied in the preparation of the subject matter information will be available to the intended users.

(iv) The practitioner expects to be able to obtain the evidence needed to support the member's conclusion;

(v) The practitioner's opinion/conclusion, in the form appropriate to either a reasonable assurance engagement or a limited assurance engagement, is to be contained in a written report; and

(vi) A rational purpose including, in the case of a limited assurance engagement that the practitioner expects to be able to obtain a meaningful level of assurance.

(21) If the preconditions for an assurance engagement are not present, the practitioner should discuss the matter with the engaging party. If changes cannot be made to meet the preconditions, the practitioner would be well advised not to accept the engagement as an assurance engagement, unless required by law or regulation to do so.

Limitation on Scope Prior to Acceptance of the Engagement

(22) If the engaging party imposes a limitation on the scope of the practitioner's work in the terms of a proposed assurance engagement, such that the practitioner believes the limitation will result in the practitioner disclaiming an opinion/a conclusion on the subject matter information, the practitioner should not accept such an engagement as an assurance engagement, unless required by law or regulation to do so.

Agreeing on the Terms of the Engagement

(23) The practitioner should agree the terms of the engagement with the engaging party. The agreed terms of the engagement should be specified in sufficient detail in an engagement letter or other suitable form of written agreement, written confirmation, or in law or regulation. It is in the interests of both, the engaging party and the practitioner, that the practitioner communicates in writing the agreed terms of the engagement before the commencement of the engagement to help avoid misunderstandings. The terms of engagement, at a minimum, should include the following:

(a) the objective and scope of engagement;

(b) the responsibilities of the practitioner;

(c) the responsibilities of engaging party;

(d) the responsibilities of the responsible party (if different from the engaging party);

(e) identification of the suitable criteria to be used;

(f) identification of the subject matter including reference to the law or regulation or the contracts;

(g) Unrestricted access to whatever records, documentation and other information requested in connection with the engagement;

(h) The fact that the engagement cannot be relied upon to disclose errors, illegal acts or other irregularities, for example, fraud or defalcations that may exist;

(i) reference to the expected form and content of report to be issued by the practitioner ;and

(j) a statement that there may be circumstances in which a report may differ from its expected form and content.

(24) The agreed terms of engagement can also include other general terms of engagement so long as those terms are not inconsistent with the applicable laws and regulations.

(25) The form and content of the written agreement or contract will vary with the engagement circumstances. For example, if law or regulation prescribes in sufficient detail the terms of the engagement, the practitioner need not record them in a written agreement, except for the fact that such law or regulation applies and that the appropriate party acknowledges and understands its responsibilities under such law or regulation. Law or regulation, particularly in the public sector, may mandate the appointment of a practitioner and set out specific powers, such as the power to access appropriate party(s) records and other information, and responsibilities, such as requiring the practitioner to report directly to an authority, the legislature or the public, in case appropriate party(s) attempt to limit the scope of the engagement.

(26) On recurring engagements, the practitioner should assess whether the circumstances require the terms of the engagement to be revised and whether there is a need to remind the engaging party of the existing terms of the engagement

Acceptance of a Change in the Terms of the Engagement

(27) The practitioner should not agree to a change in the terms of the engagement where there is no reasonable justification for doing so. If such a change is made, the practitioner should not disregard evidence that was obtained prior to the change. A change in circumstances that affects the intended users' requirements, or a misunderstanding concerning the nature of the engagement, may justify a request for a change in the engagement, for example, from an assurance engagement to a non-assurance engagement, or from a reasonable assurance engagement to a limited assurance engagement. An inability to obtain sufficient appropriate evidence to form a reasonable assurance opinion/conclusion is not an acceptable reason to change from a reasonable assurance engagement to a limited assurance engagement

Assurance Report Prescribed by Law or Regulation

(28) In some cases, law or regulation prescribes the layout or wording of the assurance report. In these circumstances, the practitioner would need to evaluate:

(a) Whether intended users might misunderstand the assurance conclusion; and

(b) If so, whether additional explanation in the assurance report can mitigate possible misunderstanding.

(29) If the practitioner concludes that additional explanation in the assurance report cannot mitigate possible misunderstanding, as the law or regulation does not allow the practitioner to provide such additional explanation in the assurance

report to mitigate the risk of users misunderstanding of the assurance conclusion, the practitioner should not accept the engagement, unless required by law or regulation to do so.

(30) In case the practitioner is required to issue an assurance report under the applicable laws or regulations, the practitioner should discuss the matter with the engaging party. The practitioner should provide a draft of the assurance report to be issued that duly incorporates the essential elements thereof as prescribed in paragraph 80 of the Guidance Note to the layout or the wordings so prescribed. Both, the practitioner and the engaging party, should agree on the resulting modifications to the layout or wording prescribed under the laws or regulations. The agreement on layout or wording of the assurance report should be duly documented in the engagement letter. The practitioner should then accept and perform the engagement and issue the final assurance report duly incorporating therein the essential elements prescribed in the Guidance Note. If the engaging party does not agree to this approach, the practitioner should consider whether it would be appropriate to accept the engagement.

(31) It may also happen that the concerned authorities reject the aforesaid assurance report issued by the practitioner on account of the modifications made to the prescribed layout or wording. In such circumstances, the practitioner should obtain the evidence of rejection of the assurance report by the concerned authorities and make it a part of the engagement documentation. The practitioner, in such a case, may issue the assurance report in the format prescribed under the law or regulation since the practitioner would have complied with the requirements of this Guidance Note while issuing the certificate in the first instance. The practitioner can also consider enclosing a statement containing essential elements of an assurance report as prescribed in paragraph 80 of this Guidance Note to the format prescribed under the law or regulation. The enclosure should also state the fact that a report issued earlier in accordance with this Guidance Note had been rejected by the concerned authorities.

32A. It is recognised that rejections of assurance reports or certificates issued might have also occurred in the past or there could be a situation where the concerned regulator has expressly indicated that any modification to the layout or the wording of the format is not acceptable and if time period available to follow the process in paragraphs 31 and 32 is not sufficient, the practitioner may issue the assurance report in the format prescribed under the law or regulation. If the practitioner has complied with all the requirements of this Guidance Note, the practitioner should also enclose a statement containing essential elements of an assurance report as prescribed in paragraph 80 of this Guidance Note, to the format prescribed under the law or regulation by giving suitable reference of the statement in the format. (e.g. "in terms of our statement of even date" or "to be read with the enclosed statement of even date" etc.)

(32) Similarly, the practitioner may conclude, that even where permitted by the law/regulation or it is otherwise accepted by the concerned regulatory bodies to provide additional information/ explanation in the assurance report, doing the

same will not mitigate the risk of users' misunderstanding of the assurance conclusion expressed. In such circumstance, the practitioner should mention the circumstances not allowing the practitioner to bring down the risk of users' misunderstanding in the report being issued by the practitioner. The practitioner should also include such matters in the scope of work documented in the engagement letter

Professional Skepticism, Professional Judgment, and Assurance Skills and Techniques

(33) The practitioner would need to plan and perform an engagement with professional skepticism, recognizing that circumstances may exist that may cause the subject matter information to be materiality misstated.

(34) The practitioner needs to exercise professional judgment in planning and performing an assurance engagement, including determining the nature, timing and extent of procedures.

(35) The practitioner should also apply assurance skills and techniques as part of an iterative, systematic engagement process.

Planning

(36) The practitioner should plan the engagement so that it will be performed in an effective manner, including setting the scope, timing and direction of the engagement, and determining the nature, timing and extent of planned procedures that are required to be carried out in order to achieve the objective of the engagement.

(37) The practitioner should determine whether the criteria are suitable for the engagement circumstances, including that they exhibit the characteristics identified in paragraph 21(b) (ii).

(38) If it is discovered after the engagement has been accepted that one or more preconditions for an assurance engagement is not present, the practitioner should discuss the matter with the appropriate party(s), and determine:

- (a) Whether the matter can be resolved to the practitioner's satisfaction;
- (b) Whether it is appropriate to continue with the engagement; and
- (c) Whether and, if so, how to communicate the matter in the assurance report.

(39) If it is discovered after the engagement has been accepted that some or all of the applicable criteria are unsuitable or some or all of the underlying subject matter is not appropriate for an assurance engagement, the practitioner would need to consider withdrawing from the engagement, if withdrawal is possible under applicable law or regulation. If the practitioner continues with the engagement, the practitioner should express a qualified or adverse opinion/conclusion, or disclaimer of opinion/conclusion, as appropriate in the circumstances

Materiality

(40) The practitioner would consider materiality when:

(a) Planning and performing the assurance engagement, including when determining the nature, timing and extent of procedures; and

(b) Evaluating whether the subject matter information is free from material misstatement.

(41) Professional judgments about materiality are made in light of surrounding circumstances, but are not affected by the level of assurance, that is, for the same intended users and purpose, materiality for a reasonable assurance engagement is the same as for a limited assurance engagement because materiality is based on the information needs of intended users.

(42) The applicable criteria may discuss the concept of materiality in the context of the preparation and presentation of the subject matter information and thereby provide a frame of reference for the practitioner in considering materiality for the engagement. Although applicable criteria may discuss materiality in different terms, the concept of materiality generally includes the matters discussed in paragraphs 42-50. If the applicable criteria do not include a discussion of the concept of materiality, these paragraphs provide the practitioner with a frame of reference.

(43) Misstatements, including omissions, are considered to be material if they, individually or in the aggregate, could reasonably be expected to influence relevant decisions of intended users taken on the basis of the subject matter information. The practitioner's consideration of materiality is a matter of professional judgment, and is affected by the practitioner's perception of the common information needs of intended users as a group. In this context, it is reasonable for the practitioner to assume that intended users:

(a) Have a reasonable knowledge of the underlying subject matter, and a willingness to study the subject matter information with reasonable diligence;

(b) Understand that the subject matter information is prepared and assured to appropriate levels of materiality, and have an understanding of any materiality concepts included in the applicable criteria;

(c) Understand any inherent uncertainties involved in the measuring or evaluating the underlying subject matter; and

(d) Make reasonable decisions on the basis of the subject matter information taken as a whole.

Unless the engagement has been designed to meet the particular information needs of specific users, the possible effect of misstatements on specific users, whose information needs may vary widely, is not ordinarily considered.

(44) Materiality is considered in the context of qualitative factors and, when applicable, quantitative factors. The relative importance of qualitative factors and quantitative factors when considering materiality in a particular engagement is a matter for the practitioner's professional judgment.

(45) Qualitative factors may include such things as:

(a) The number of persons or entities affected by the subject matter.

(b) The interaction between, and relative importance of, various components of the subject matter information when it is made up of multiple components, such as a report that includes numerous performance indicators.

(c) The wording chosen with respect to subject matter information that is expressed in narrative form.

(d) The characteristics of the presentation adopted for the subject matter information when the applicable criteria allow for variations in that presentation.

(e) The nature of a misstatement, for example, the nature of observed deviations from a control when the subject matter information is a statement that the control is effective.

(f) Whether a misstatement affects compliance with law or regulation.

(g) In the case of periodic reporting on an underlying subject matter, the effect of an adjustment that affects past or current subject matter information or is likely to affect future subject matter information.

(h) Whether a misstatement is the result of an intentional act or is unintentional

(i) Whether a misstatement relates to the relationship between the responsible party, the measurer or evaluator, or the engaging party or their relationship with other parties.

(j) When a threshold or benchmark value has been identified, whether the result of the procedure deviates from that value.

(k) When the underlying subject matter is a governmental program or public sector entity, whether a particular aspect of the program or entity is significant with regard to the nature, visibility and sensitivity of the program or entity.

(l) When the subject matter information relates to a conclusion on compliance with law or regulation, the seriousness of the consequences of non-compliance.

(46) Quantitative factors relate to the magnitude of misstatements relative to reported amounts for those aspects of the subject matter information, if any, that are:

(a) Expressed numerically; or

(b) Otherwise related to numerical values (for example, the number of observed deviations from a control may be a relevant quantitative factor when the subject matter information is a statement that the control is effective).

(47) When quantitative factors are applicable, planning the engagement solely to detect individually material misstatements overlooks the fact that the aggregate of uncorrected and undetected individually immaterial misstatements may cause the subject matter information to be materially misstated. It may therefore be appropriate when planning the nature, timing and extent of

procedures for the practitioner to determine a quantity less than materiality as a basis for determining the nature, timing and extent of procedures.

(48) Materiality relates to the information covered by the assurance report. Therefore, when the engagement covers some, but not all, aspects of the information communicated about an underlying subject matter, materiality is considered in relation to only that portion that is covered by the engagement.

(49) Concluding on the materiality of the misstatements identified as a result of the procedures performed requires professional judgment. For example, in a compliance engagement, the entity may have complied with nine provisions of the relevant law or regulation, but did not comply with one provision. Professional judgment is needed to conclude whether the entity complied with the relevant law or regulation as a whole. For example, the practitioner may consider the significance of the provision with which the entity did not comply, as well as the relationship of that provision to the remaining provisions of the relevant law or regulation

Understanding the Underlying Subject Matter and Other Engagement Circumstances

(50) The practitioner should make inquiries of the appropriate party(s) regarding:

(a) Whether they have knowledge of any actual, suspected or alleged intentional misstatement or non-compliance with laws and regulations affecting the subject matter information;

(b) Whether the responsible party has an internal audit function and, if so, make further inquiries to obtain an understanding of the activities and main findings of the internal audit function with respect to the subject matter information; and

(c) Whether the responsible party has used any experts in the preparation of the subject matter information

Limited Assurance	Reasonable Assurance
52L. The practitioner should obtain an understanding of the underlying subject matter and other engagement circumstances sufficient to:	52R. The practitioner should obtain an understanding of the underlying subject matter and other engagement circumstances sufficient to:
(a) Enable the practitioner to identify areas where a material misstatement of the subject matter information is likely to arise; and	(a) Enable the practitioner to identify and assess the risks of material misstatement in the subject matter information; and
(b) Thereby, provide a basis for designing and performing procedures to address the areas identified in paragraph	(b) Thereby, provide a basis for designing and performing procedures to respond to the assessed risks and to obtain reasonable assurance to support the practitioner's opinion.

Limited Assurance	Reasonable Assurance
52L (a) and to obtain limited assurance to support the practitioner's conclusion.	
53L.obtaining an	53R. In obtaining an understanding of the underlying
Understanding of the underlying subject matter and other engagement circumstances under paragraph 52L, the practitioner should consider consider the process used to prepare the subject matter information.	**Engagement circumstances** Under paragraph 52R, the practitioner should obtain an understanding of internal control over the preparation of the subject matter information relevant to the engagement. This includes evaluating the design of those controls relevant to the engagement and determining whether they have been implemented by addition to the inquiry of the personnel responsible for the subject matter information.

Obtaining Evidence

Risk Consideration and Responses to Risks

Limited Assurance	Reasonable Assurance
54L. Based on the practitioner's understanding (see paragraph 52L), the practitioner should: (a) Identify areas where a material misstatement of the subject matter information is likely to arise; (b) Design and perform procedures to address the areas identified in paragraph 54L (a) and to obtain limited assurance to support the practitioner's conclusion.	54R. Based on the practitioner's understanding (see paragraph 52R) the practitioner should: (a) Identify and assess the risks of material misstatement in the subject matter information; and (b) Design and perform procedures to respond to the assessed risks and to obtain reasonable assurance to support the practitioner's opinion. In addition to any other procedures on the subject matter information that are appropriate in the engagement circumstances, the practitioner's procedures would include obtaining sufficient appropriate evidence as to the operating effectiveness of relevant controls

Limited Assurance	Reasonable Assurance
	over the subject matter information when: (i) The practitioner's assessment of the risks of material misstatement includes an expectation that controls are operating effectively, , or (ii) Procedures other than testing of controls cannot alone provide sufficient appropriate evidence.
Determining Whether Additional Procedures are necessary in a Limited Assurance Engagement	Revision of Risk Assessment in a Reasonable Assurance Engagement
55L. If the practitioner becomes aware of a matter(s) that causes the practitioner to believe that the subject matter information may be materially misstated, the practitioner should design and perform additional procedures to obtain further evidence until the practitioner is able to: (a) Conclude that the matter is not likely to cause the subject matter information to be materially misstated; or (b) Determine that the matter(s) causes the subject matter information to be materially misstated.	55R. The practitioner's assessment of the risks of material misstatement in the subject matter information may change during the course of the engagement as additional evidence is obtained. In circumstances where the practitioner obtains evidence which is inconsistent with the evidence on which the practitioner originally based the assessment of the risks of material misstatement, the practitioner should revise the assessment and modify the planned procedures accordingly.

(51) When designing and performing procedures, the practitioner would also need to consider the relevance and reliability of the information to be used as evidence. If:

(a) Evidence obtained from one source is inconsistent with that obtained from another; or

(b) The practitioner has doubts about the reliability of information to be used as an evidence, the practitioner should determine what changes or additions to the procedures are necessary to resolve the matter, and should consider the effect of the matter, if any, on other aspects of the engagement.

(52) The practitioner should accumulate uncorrected misstatements identified during the engagement other than those that are clearly trivial and determine the effect of the misstatement on the assurance report.

Work Performed by a Practitioner's Expert

(53) When the work of a practitioner's expert is to be used, the practitioner should also:

(a) Evaluate whether the practitioner's expert has the necessary competence, capabilities and objectivity for the practitioner's purposes. In the case of a practitioner's external expert, the evaluation of objectivity should include inquiry regarding interests and relationships that may create a threat to that expert's objectivity;

(b) Obtain a sufficient understanding of the field of expertise of the practitioner's expert;

(c) Agree with the practitioner's expert on the nature, scope and objectives of that expert's work; and

(d) Evaluate the adequacy of the practitioner's expert's work for the practitioner's purposes.

Work Performed by Another Practitioner, a Responsible Party's or Measurer's or Evaluator's Expert, or an Internal Auditor

(54) When the work of another practitioner is to be used, the practitioner should evaluate whether that work is adequate for the practitioner's purposes.

(55) If information to be used as evidence has been prepared using the work of a responsible party's or a measurer's or evaluator's expert, the practitioner should, to the extent necessary having regard to the significance of that expert's work for the practitioner's purposes:

(a) Evaluate the competence, capabilities and objectivity of that expert;

(b) Obtain an understanding of the work of that expert; and

(c) Evaluate the appropriateness of that expert's work as evidence.

(56) If the practitioner plans to use the work of the internal audit function, the practitioner should evaluate the following:

(a) The extent to which the internal audit function's organizational status and relevant policies and procedures support the objectivity of the internal auditors;

(b) The level of competence of the internal audit function;

(c) Whether the internal audit function applies a systematic and disciplined approach, including quality control; and

(d) Whether the work of the internal audit function is adequate for the purposes of the engagement.

Written Representations

(57) The practitioner should request from the appropriate party(s) a written representation:

(a) That it has provided the practitioner with all information of which the appropriate party(s) is aware that is relevant to the engagement.

(b) Confirming the measurement or evaluation of the underlying subject matter against the applicable criteria, including that all relevant matters are reflected in the subject matter information.

(58) If, in addition to required representations, the practitioner determines that it is necessary to obtain one or more written representations to support other evidence relevant to the subject matter information, the practitioner should request such other written representations.

(59) When written representations relate to matters that are material to the subject matter information, the practitioner should:

(a) Evaluate their reasonableness and consistency with other evidence obtained, including other representations (oral or written);and

(b) Consider whether those making the representations can be expected to be well-informed on the particular matters.

(60) The date of the written representations should be as near as practicable to, but not after, the date of the assurance report.

Requested Written Representations Not Provided or Not Reliable

(61) If one or more of the requested written representations are not provided or the practitioner concludes that there is sufficient doubt about the competence, integrity, ethical values, or diligence of those providing the written representations, or that the written representations are otherwise not reliable, the practitioner should:

(a) Discuss the matter with the appropriate party(s);

(b) Re-evaluate the integrity of those from whom the representations were requested or received and evaluate the effect that this may have on the reliability of representations (oral or written) and evidence in general; and

(c) Take appropriate actions, including determining the possible effect on the conclusion in the assurance report.

Subsequent Events

(62) When relevant to the engagement, the practitioner should consider the effect on the subject matter information and on the assurance report of events up to the date of the assurance report and should respond appropriately to the facts that become known to the practitioner after the date of the assurance report, that, had they been known to the practitioner at that date, may have caused the practitioner to amend the assurance report. The extent of consideration of subsequent events depends on the potential for such events to affect the subject matter information and to affect the appropriateness of the practitioner's conclusion. However, the practitioner has no responsibility to perform any procedures regarding the subject matter information after the date of the assurance report

Other Information

(63) When documents containing the subject matter information and the assurance report thereon include other information, the practitioner should read that other information to identify material inconsistencies, if any, with the subject matter information or the assurance report and, if on reading that other information, the practitioner:

(a) Identifies a material inconsistency between that other information and the subject matter information or the assurance report; or

(b) Becomes aware of a material misstatement of fact in that other information that is unrelated to matters appearing in the subject matter information or the assurance report,

The practitioner should discuss the matter with the appropriate party(s) and take further action as appropriate.

Description of Applicable Criteria

(64) The practitioner would need to evaluate whether the subject matter information adequately refers to or describes the applicable criteria. The description of the applicable criteria advises intended users of the framework on which the subject matter information is based, and is particularly important when there are significant differences between various criteria regarding how particular matters may be treated in the subject matter information.

(65) A description that the subject matter information is prepared in accordance with particular applicable criteria is appropriate only if the subject matter information complies with all relevant requirements of those applicable criteria that are effective. A description of the applicable criteria that contains imprecise qualifying or limiting language (for example, "the subject matter information is in substantial compliance with the requirements of XYZ") is not an adequate description as it may mislead users of the subject matter information.

Forming the Assurance Opinion/Conclusion

(66) The practitioner should evaluate the sufficiency and appropriateness of the evidence obtained in the context of the engagement and, if necessary in the circumstances, attempt to obtain further evidence. The practitioner should consider all relevant evidence, regardless of whether it appears to corroborate or to contradict the measurement or evaluation of the underlying subject matter against the applicable criteria. If the practitioner is unable to obtain necessary further evidence, the practitioner should consider the implications for the practitioner's opinion/conclusion in paragraph 72.

(67) The practitioner should form an opinion/a conclusion about whether the subject matter information is free of material misstatement. In forming that opinion/conclusion, the practitioner should consider the practitioner's conclusion in paragraph 71 regarding the sufficiency and appropriateness of evidence obtained and an evaluation of whether uncorrected misstatements are material, individually or in the aggregate.

(68) Evidence is necessary to support the practitioner's opinion/conclusion and assurance report. It is cumulative in nature and is primarily obtained from procedures performed during the course of the engagement. It may, however, also include information obtained from other sources, such as previous engagements (provided the practitioner has determined whether changes have occurred since the previous engagement that may affect its relevance to the current engagement) or the quality control procedures for client acceptance and continuance. Evidence may come from sources inside and outside the appropriate party(s). Also, information that may be used as evidence may have been prepared by an expert employed or engaged by the appropriate party(s). Evidence comprises both information that supports and corroborates aspects of the subject matter information, and any information that contradicts aspects of the subject matter information. In addition, in some cases, the absence of information (for example, refusal by the appropriate party(s) to provide a requested representation) is used by the practitioner, and therefore, also constitutes evidence. Most of the practitioner's work in forming the assurance opinion/conclusion consists of obtaining and evaluating evidence.

(69) If the practitioner is unable to obtain sufficient appropriate evidence, a scope limitation exists and the practitioner should express a qualified opinion/conclusion or disclaim an opinion/conclusion, or withdraw from the engagement, where withdrawal is possible under applicable law or regulation, as appropriate.

Preparing the Assurance Report

(70) The assurance report should be in writing and should contain a clear expression of the practitioner's opinion/conclusion about the subject matter information. Where the subject matter information is made up of a number of aspects, separate opinions/conclusions may be provided on each aspect. All such separate opinions/conclusions do not need to relate to the same level of assurance. Rather, each conclusion is expressed in the form that is appropriate to either a reasonable assurance engagement or a limited assurance engagement. References in this Guidance Note to the opinion/conclusion in the assurance report include each opinion/conclusion when separate opinions/conclusions are provided.

(71) The practitioner's opinion/conclusion should be clearly separated from information or explanations that are not intended to affect the practitioner's opinion/conclusion, including any Emphasis of Matter, Other Matter, findings related to particular aspects of the engagements, recommendations or additional information included in the assurance report. The wording used should make it clear that an Emphasis of Matter, Other Matter, findings, recommendations or additional information is not intended to detract from the practitioner's opinion/conclusion.

(72) Oral and other forms of expressing conclusions can be misunderstood without the support of a written report. For this reason, the practitioner shall not report orally without providing a written assurance report.

(73) This Guidance Note does not require a standardized format for reporting on all assurance engagements. Instead, it identifies the basic elements the assurance report is to include. Assurance reports are tailored to the specific engagement circumstances. The practitioner may use headings, paragraph numbers, typographical devices, for example the bolding of text and other mechanisms to enhance the clarity and readability of the assurance report.

(74) The practitioner may choose a "short form" or "long form" style of reporting to facilitate effective communication to the intended users. "Short-form" reports ordinarily include only the basic elements. "Long-form" reports include other information and explanations that are not intended to affect the practitioner's conclusion. In addition to the basic elements, long-form reports may describe in detail the terms of the engagement, the applicable criteria being used, findings relating to particular aspects of the engagement, details of the qualifications and experience of the practitioner and others involved with the engagement, disclosure of materiality levels, and, in some cases, recommendations. The practitioner may find it helpful to consider the significance of providing such information to the information needs of the intended users. As required by paragraph 76, additional information is clearly separated from the practitioner's conclusion and phrased in such a manner so as make it clear that it is not intended to detract from that conclusion.

Assurance Report Content

(75) In order to assert compliance with this Guidance Note, among other things, the assurance report should include at a minimum the following basic elements:

(a) A *title* that clearly indicates the report is an independent assurance report. An appropriate title helps to identify the nature of the assurance report, and to distinguish it from reports issued by others, such as those who do not have to comply with the same ethical requirements as the practitioner. In case, the applicable law or regulation or the contractual arrangement entered by the entity specifies a title or phrases to identify the assurance report, the practitioner may use the title or phrases so prescribed.

(b) An *addressee*. An addressee identifies the party or parties to whom the assurance report is directed. The assurance report is ordinarily addressed to the engaging party, but in some cases there may be other intended users.

(c) An *identification or description of the level of assurance obtained by the practitioner, the subject matter information and, when appropriate, the underlying subject matter*. When the practitioner's conclusion is phrased in terms of a statement made by the appropriate party, that statement should accompany the assurance report, be reproduced in the assurance report or be referenced therein to a source that is available to the intended users. Identification and description of the subject matter information and, when appropriate, the underlying subject matter may include, for example:

- The point in time or period of time to which the measurement or evaluation of the underlying subject matter relates.
- Where applicable, the name of the responsible party or component of the responsible party to which the underlying subject matter relates.
- An explanation of those characteristics of the underlying subject matter or the subject matter information of which the intended users should be aware, and how such characteristics may influence the precision of the measurement or evaluation of the underlying subject matter against the applicable criteria, or the persuasiveness of available evidence. For example:
- The degree to which the subject matter information is qualitative versus quantitative, objective versus subjective, or historical versus prospective.
- Changes in the underlying subject matter or other engagement circumstances that affect the comparability of the subject matter information from one period to the next.

(d) *Identification of the applicable criteria*. The assurance report identifies the applicable criteria against which the underlying subject matter was measured or evaluated so that the intended users can understand the basis for the practitioner's opinion/conclusion. The assurance report may include the applicable criteria, or refer to them if they are included in the subject matter information or if they are otherwise available from a readily accessible source. It may be relevant in the circumstances, to disclose:

- The source of the applicable criteria, and whether or not the applicable criteria are embodied in law or regulation, or issued by authorized or recognized bodies of experts that follow a transparent due process, that is, whether they are established criteria in the context of the underlying subject matter (and if they are not, a description of why they are considered suitable).
- Measurement or evaluation methods used when the applicable criteria allows for choice between a number of methods.
- Any significant interpretations made in applying the applicable criteria in the engagement circumstances.
- Whether there have been any changes in the measurement or evaluation methods used.

(e) Where appropriate, a description of any significant inherent limitations associated with the measurement or evaluation of the underlying subject matter against the applicable criteria. While in some cases, inherent limitations can be expected to be well-understood by the intended users of an assurance report, in other cases it may be appropriate to make explicit reference to them in the assurance report. For example, in an assurance report related to the effectiveness of internal control, it may be appropriate to note that the historic evaluation of effectiveness is not relevant to future periods due to the risk that internal control may become inadequate because of changes in conditions, or that the degree of compliance with policies or procedures may deteriorate.

(f) When the applicable criteria are designed for a specific purpose, a statement alerting readers to this fact and that, as a result, the subject matter information may not be suitable for another purpose. In some cases the applicable criteria used to measure or evaluate the underlying subject matter may be designed for a specific purpose. For example, a regulator may require certain entities to use particular applicable criteria designed for regulatory purposes. To avoid misunderstandings, the practitioner alerts readers of the assurance report to this fact and that therefore, the subject matter information may not be suitable for another purpose.

(g) In addition to the alert as required in the preceding paragraph, the practitioner may consider it appropriate to indicate that the assurance report is intended solely for specific users. Depending on the engagement circumstances, for example, the law or regulation of the particular jurisdiction, this may be achieved by restricting the distribution or use of the assurance report. While an assurance report may be restricted in this way, the absence of a restriction regarding a particular user or purpose does not itself indicate that a legal responsibility is owed by the practitioner in relation to that user or for that purpose. Whether a legal responsibility is owed will depend on the legal circumstances of each case and the relevant jurisdiction.

(h) A statement to identify the responsible party and the measurer or evaluator if different, and to describe their responsibilities and the practitioner's responsibilities. Identifying relative responsibilities informs the intended users that the responsible party is responsible for the underlying subject matter, that the measurer or evaluator is responsible for the measurement or evaluation of the underlying subject matter against the applicable criteria, and that the Practitioner's role is to independently express an opinion/conclusion about the subject matter information

(i) A statement that the engagement was performed in accordance with this Guidance Note.

(j) A statement that the firm, of which the practitioner is a partner has applied SQC 1, Quality Control for Firms that Perform Audits and Reviews of Historical Financial Information, and Other Assurance and Related Services Engagements.

(k) A statement that the practitioner complies with the independence and other ethical requirements of the Code of Ethics issued by the Institute of Chartered Accountants of India. The following is an illustration of a statement in the assurance report regarding compliance with ethical requirements:

"We conducted our engagement in accordance with the Guidance Note on Reports or Certificates for Special Purposes issued by the Institute of Chartered Accountants of India. That Guidance Note requires that we comply with the ethical requirements of the Code of Ethics issued by the Institute of Chartered Accountants of India."

(l) *An informative summary of the work performed* as the basis for the practitioner's opinion/conclusion. In the case of a limited assurance engagement, an appreciation of the nature, timing, and extent of procedures performed is essential to understanding the practitioner's opinion/conclusion. In a limited assurance engagement, the summary of the work performed should state that:

(i) The procedures performed in a limited assurance engagement vary in nature and timing from, and are less in extent than for, a reasonable assurance engagement; and

(ii) Consequently, the level of assurance obtained in a limited assurance engagement is substantially lower than the assurance that would have been obtained had a reasonable assurance engagement been performed.

It is important that the summary be written in an objective way that allows intended users to understand the work done as the basis for the practitioner's opinion/conclusion. In most cases, this will not involve detailing the entire work plan, but on the other hand it is important for it not to be so summarized as to be ambiguous, nor written in a way that is overstated or embellished.

(m) The practitioner's opinion/conclusion:

(i) When appropriate, the opinion/conclusion should inform the intended users of the context in which the practitioner's opinion/conclusion is to be read.

It may be appropriate to inform the intended users of the context in which the practitioner's opinion/conclusion is to be read when the assurance report includes an explanation of particular characteristics of the underlying subject matter of which the intended users should be aware. The practitioner's opinion/conclusion may, for example, include wording such as: "This opinion/conclusion has been formed on the basis of the matters outlined elsewhere in this independent assurance report."

(ii) In a reasonable assurance engagement, the opinion is expressed in a positive form. Examples of opinion expressed in a form appropriate for a reasonable assurance engagement include:

- When expressed in terms of the underlying subject matter and the applicable criteria, "In our opinion, the entity has complied, in all material respects, with XYZ law";

- When expressed in terms of the subject matter information and the applicable criteria, "In our opinion, the Statement of Net Worth is properly prepared, in all material respects, based on XYZ criteria"; or
- When expressed in terms of a statement made by the appropriate party, "In our opinion, the [appropriate party's] statement that the entity has complied with XYZ law is, in all material respects, fairly stated," or "In our opinion, the [appropriate party's] statement that the key performance indicators are presented in accordance with XYZ criteria is, in all material respects, fairly stated".

(iii) In a limited assurance engagement, the conclusion is expressed in a form that conveys whether, based on the procedures performed and evidence obtained, a matter(s) has come to the practitioner's attention to cause the practitioner to believe that the subject matter information is materially misstated. Examples of conclusions expressed in a form appropriate for a limited assurance engagement include:

- When expressed in terms of the underlying subject matter and the applicable criteria, "Based on the procedures performed and evidence obtained, nothing has come to our attention that causes us to believe that [the entity] has not complied, in all material respects, with XYZ law."
- When expressed in terms of the subject matter information and the applicable criteria, "Based on the procedures performed and evidence obtained, we are not aware of any material amendments that need to be made to the assessment of key performance indicators for them to be in accordance with XYZ criteria";or
- When expressed in terms of a statement made by the appropriate party, "Based on the procedures performed and evidence obtained, nothing has come to our attention that causes us to believe that the [appropriate party's] statement that [the entity] has complied with XYZ law, is not, in all material respects, fairly stated."

(iv) The opinion/conclusion in (ii) or (iii) should be phrased using appropriate words for the underlying subject matter and applicable criteria given the engagement circumstances and need to be phrased in terms of:

(a) The underlying subject matter and the applicable criteria;

(b) The subject matter information and the applicable criteria; or

(c) A statement made by the appropriate party.

Forms of expression which may be useful for underlying subject matters include, for example, one, or a combination of, the following:

- For compliance engagements—"in compliance with" or "in accordance with."
- For engagements when the applicable criteria describe a process or methodology for the preparation or presentation of the subject matter information—"properly prepared."
- For engagement when the principles of fair presentation are embodied in the applicable criteria—"fairly stated."

(v) When the practitioner expresses a modified opinion/conclusion, the assurance report should contain:

(a) A section that provides a description of the matter(s) giving rise to the modification; and

(b) A section that contains the practitioner's modified opinion/conclusion

(n) The practitioner's signature. The assurance report is signed by the practitioner in his personal name. Where a Firm is appointed to carry out the engagement, there port is signed in the personal name of the practitioner and in the name of the audit firm. The partner/proprietor signing the assurance report also needs to mention the membership number assigned by the ICAI. They also include the registration number of the Firm, wherever applicable, as allotted by ICAI, in the assurance reports signed by them.

(o) The date of the assurance report. The assurance report should be dated no earlier than the date on which the practitioner has obtained the evidence on which the practitioner's opinion/conclusion is based, including evidence that those with the recognized authority have asserted that they have taken responsibility for the subject matter information.

(p) The place of signature.

Reference to the Practitioner's Expert in the Assurance Report

(76) If the practitioner refers to the work of a practitioner's expert in the assurance report, the wording of that report should not imply that the practitioner's responsibility for the opinion/conclusion expressed in that report is reduced because of the involvement of that expert.

Assurance Report Prescribed by Law or Regulation

(77) If the practitioner is required by law or regulation to use a specific layout or wording of the assurance report, the assurance report should refer to this Guidance Note, only if the assurance report includes, at a minimum, each of the elements identified in paragraph 80.

Unmodified and Modified Opinions/Conclusions

(78) The practitioner should express an unmodified opinion/conclusion when the practitioner concludes:

(a) In the case of a reasonable assurance engagement, that the subject matter information is prepared, in all material respects, in accordance with the applicable criteria; or

(b) In the case of a limited assurance engagement, that, based on the procedures performed and evidence obtained, no matter(s) has come to the attention of the practitioner that causes the practitioner to believe that the subject matter information is not prepared, in all material respects, in accordance with the applicable criteria.

(79) If the practitioner considers it necessary to:

(a) Draw intended users' attention to a matter presented or disclosed in the subject matter information that, in the practitioner's judgment, is of such importance that it is fundamental to intended users' understanding of the subject matter information (an Emphasis of Matter paragraph);or

(b) Communicate a matter other than those that are presented or disclosed in the subject matter information that, in the practitioner's judgment, is relevant to intended users' understanding of the engagement, the practitioner's responsibilities or the assurance report (an Other Matter paragraph),

and this is not prohibited by law or regulation, the practitioner may do so in a paragraph in the assurance report, with an appropriate heading, that clearly indicates the practitioner's opinion/conclusion is not modified in respect of the matter/s. In the case of an Emphasis of Matter paragraph, such a paragraph should refer only to the information presented or disclosed in the subject matter information.

(80) The practitioner would need to express a modified opinion/conclusion in the following circumstances:

(a) When, in the practitioner's professional judgment, a scope limitation exists and the effect of the matter could be material. In such cases, the practitioner should express a qualified opinion/conclusion or a disclaimer of opinion/conclusion.

(b) When, in the practitioner's professional judgment, the subject matter information is materially misstated. In such cases, the practitioner should express a qualified opinion/conclusion or adverse opinion/conclusion.

Examples of qualified and adverse opinions/conclusions and a disclaimer of opinions/conclusion are:

- Qualified conclusion (an example for limited assurance engagements with a material misstatement) – "Based on the procedures performed and the evidence obtained, except for the effect of the matter described in the Basis for Qualified Conclusion section of our report, nothing has come to our attention that causes us to believe that the [appropriate party's] statement does not present fairly, in all material respects, the entity's compliance with XYZ law."

- Adverse opinion (an example for a material and pervasive misstatement for both reasonable assurance and limited assurance engagements) – "Because of the significance of the matter described in the Basis for Adverse Opinion/Conclusion section of our report, the [appropriate party's] statement does not present fairly the entity's compliance with XYZ law."
- Disclaimer of conclusion (an example for a material and pervasive limitation of scope for both reasonable assurance and limited assurance engagements) – "Because of the significance of the matter described in the Basis for Disclaimer of Opinion/Conclusion section of our report, we have not been able to obtain sufficient appropriate evidence to form an opinion/ conclusion on the [appropriate party's] statement. Accordingly, we do not express an opinion/ conclusion on that statement."

(81) The practitioner should express a qualified opinion/conclusion when, in the practitioner's professional judgment, the effects, or possible effects, of a matter are not so material and pervasive as to require an adverse opinion/conclusion or a disclaimer of opinion/conclusion. A qualified opinion/conclusion should be expressed as being "except for" the effects, or possible effects, of the matter to which the qualification relates

(82) The term 'pervasive' describes the effects on the subject matter information of misstatements or the possible effects on the subject matter information of misstatements, if any, that are undetected due to an inability to obtain sufficient appropriate evidence. Pervasive effects on the subject matter information are those that, in the practitioner's professional judgment:

(a) Are not confined to specific aspects of the subject matter information;

(b) If so confined, represent or could represent a substantial proportion of the subject matter information; or

(c) In relation to disclosures, are fundamental to the intended users' understanding of the subject matter information.

(d) The nature of the matter, and the practitioner's judgment about the pervasiveness of the effects or possible effects on the subject matter information, affects the type of conclusion to be expressed.

(83) If the practitioner expresses a modified opinion/conclusion because of a scope limitation but is also aware of a matter(s) that causes the subject matter information to be materially misstated, the practitioner should include in the assurance report a clear description of both the scope limitation and the matter(s) that causes the subject matter information to be materially misstated.

(84) When the statement made by the appropriate party has identified and properly described that the subject matter information is materially misstated, the practitioner should either:

(a) Express a qualified opinion/conclusion or adverse opinion/conclusion phrased in terms of the underlying subject matter and the applicable criteria; or

(b) If specifically required by the terms of the engagement to phrase the opinion/conclusion in terms of a statement made by the appropriate party, express an unqualified opinion/conclusion but include an Emphasis of Matter paragraph in the assurance report, referring to the statement made by the appropriate party that identifies and properly describes that the subject matter information is materially misstated. In some cases, the measurer or evaluator may identify and properly describe that the subject matter information is materially misstated. For example, in a compliance engagement the measurer or evaluator may correctly describe the instances of non- compliance. In such circumstances, paragraph 88 requires the practitioner to draw the intended users' attention to the description of the material misstatement, by either expressing a qualified or adverse opinion/conclusion or by expressing an unqualified opinion/conclusion but emphasizing the matter by specifically referring to it in the assurance report.

(85) **Appendix 2** to the Guidance Note contains illustrative formats of Reports/Certificates.

Other Communication Responsibilities

(86) The practitioner should consider whether, pursuant to the terms of the engagement and other engagement circumstances, any matter has come to the attention of the practitioner that is to be communicated with the responsible party, the measurer or evaluator, the engaging party, those charged with governance or others.

Documentation

(87) The practitioner should prepare on a timely basis engagement documentation that provides a record of the basis for the assurance report that is sufficient and appropriate to enable an experienced practitioner, having no previous connection with the engagement, to understand:

(a) The nature, timing and extent of the procedures performed to comply with the Guidance Note and applicable legal and regulatory requirements;

(b) The results of the procedures performed, and the evidence obtained; and Significant matters arising during the engagement, the conclusions reached thereon, and significant professional judgments made in reaching those conclusions

(88) If the practitioner identifies information that is inconsistent with the practitioner's final opinion/conclusion regarding a significant matter, the practitioner should document how the practitioner addressed the inconsistency.

(89) The practitioner should assemble the engagement documentation in an engagement file and complete the administrative process of assembling the

final engagement file on a timely basis after the date of the assurance report. SQC 1 requires establishment of policies and procedures for the timely completion of the assembly of engagement files. An appropriate time limit within which to complete the assembly of the final engagement file is ordinarily not more than 60 days after the date of the assurance report.

(90) The completion of the assembly of the final engagement file after the date of the assurance report is an administrative process that does not involve the performance of new procedures or the drawing of new opinion/conclusions. Changes may, however, be made to the documentation during the final assembly process if they are administrative in nature. Examples of such changes include:

- Deleting or discarding superseded documentation.
- Sorting, collating and cross-referencing working papers.
- Signing off on completion checklists relating to the file assembly process.
- Documenting evidence that the practitioner has obtained, discussed and agreed with the relevant practitioners of the engagement team before the date of the assurance report.

(91) After the assembly of the final engagement file has been completed, the practitioner should not delete or discard engagement documentation of any nature before the end of its retention period. The retention period for assurance engagements ordinarily is no shorter than seven years from the date of assurancereport.[34]

(92) If the practitioner finds it necessary to amend existing engagement documentation or add new engagement documentation after the assembly of the final engagement file has been completed the practitioner should, regardless of the nature of the amendments or additions, document:

(a) The specific reasons for making the amendments or additions; and

(b) When, and by whom, they were made and reviewed.

Glossary of Terms Used in the Guidance Note

For purposes of this Guidance Note, the following terms have the meanings attributed below.

Assurance engagement—An engagement in which a practitioner aims to obtain sufficient appropriate evidence in order to express an opinion/conclusion, designed to enhance the degree of confidence of the intended users, other than the responsible party about the subject matter information (that is, the outcome of the measurement or evaluation of an underlying subject matter against criteria). Each assurance engagement is classified on two dimensions:

Either a reasonable assurance engagement or a limited assurance engagement:

- *Reasonable assurance engagement*—An assurance engagement in which the practitioner reduces engagement risk to an acceptably low level in the circumstances of the engagement, as the basis for the practitioner's opinion. The practitioner's opinion is expressed in a form that conveys the practitioner's opinion on the outcome of the measurement or evaluation of the underlying subject matter against the criteria.

- *Limited assurance engagement*—An assurance engagement in which the practitioner reduces engagement risk to a level that is acceptable in the circumstances of the engagement but where that risk is greater than for a reasonable assurance engagement, as the basis for expressing a conclusion in a form that conveys whether, based on the procedures performed and evidence obtained, a matter(s) has(have) come to the practitioner's attention to cause the practitioner to believe that the subject matter information is materially misstated. The nature, timing, and extent of procedures performed in a limited assurance engagement is limited compared with that necessary in a reasonable assurance engagement but is planned to obtain a level of assurance that is, in the practitioner's professional judgment, meaningful.

Either assertion based engagement or a direct reporting engagement:

- *Assertion based engagement*—An assurance engagement in which a party other than the practitioner measures or evaluates the underlying subject matter against the criteria. A party other than the practitioner also often presents the resulting subject matter information in a report or statement. In some cases, however, the subject matter information may be presented by the practitioner in the assurance report. In an attestation engagement, the practitioner's conclusion addresses whether the subject matter information is free from material misstatement. The practitioner's conclusion may be phrased in terms of:
  - (i) The underlying subject matter and the applicable criteria;
  - (ii) The subject matter information and the applicable criteria; or
  - (iii) A statement made by the appropriate party.
- *Direct reporting engagement*—An assurance engagement in which the practitioner measures or evaluates the underlying subject matter against the applicable criteria and the practitioner presents the resulting subject matter information as part of, or accompanying, the assurance report. In a direct engagement, the practitioner's conclusion addresses the reported outcome of the measurement or evaluation of the underlying subject matter against the criteria.

2. Assurance skills and techniques—Those planning, evidence gathering, evidence evaluation, communication and reporting skills and techniques demonstrated by an assurance practitioner that are distinct from expertise in the underlying subject matter of any particular assurance engagement or its measurement or evaluation. Assurance skill and techniques include:
   - Application of professional skepticism and professional judgment;
   - Planning and performing an assurance engagement, including obtaining and evaluating evidence;

- Understanding information systems and the role and limitations of internal control;
- Linking the consideration of materiality and engagement risks to the nature, timing and extent of procedures;
- Applying procedures as appropriate to the engagement (which may include inquiry, inspection, re-calculation, re-performance, observation, confirmation, and analytical procedures); and
- Systematic documentation practices and assurance report- writing skills.

3. Criteria—The benchmarks used to measure or evaluate the underlying subject matter. The "applicable criteria" are the criteria used for the particular engagement. Suitable criteria are required for reasonably consistent measurement or evaluation of an underlying subject matter within the context of professional judgment. Without the frame of reference provided by suitable criteria, any conclusion is open to individual interpretation and misunderstanding. The suitability of criteria is context-sensitive, that is, it is determined in the context of the engagement circumstances. Even for the same underlying subject matter here can be different criteria, which will yield a different measurement or evaluation. For example, a measurer or evaluator might select, as one of the criteria for the underlying subject matter of customer satisfaction, the number of customer complaints resolved to the acknowledged satisfaction of the customer; another measurer or evaluator might select the number of repeat purchases in the three months following the initial purchase. The suitability of criteria is not affected by the level of assurance, that is, if criteria are unsuitable for a reasonable assurance engagement, they are also unsuitable for a limited assurance engagement, and vice versa. Suitable criteria include, when relevant, criteria for presentation and disclosure.

4. Engagement circumstances — The broad context defining the particular engagement, which includes the terms of the engagement; whether it is a reasonable assurance engagement or a limited assurance engagement, the characteristics of the underlying subject matter; the measurement or evaluation criteria; the information needs of the intended users; relevant characteristics of the responsible party, the measurer or evaluator, and the engaging party and their environment; and other matters, for example events, transactions, conditions and practices, that may have a significant effect on the engagement.

5. Engagement partner — The partner or other person in the firm who is a member of the Institute of Chartered Accountants of India and is in full time practice and is responsible for the engagement and its performance, and for the assurance report that is issued on behalf of the firm, and who, where required, has the appropriate authority from a professional, legal or regulatory body.

6. Engagement risk — The risk that the practitioner expresses an inappropriate conclusion when the subject matter information is materiallymisstated[35].

7. Engaging party—The party(s) that engages the practitioner to perform the assurance engagement. The engaging party may be under different circumstances, management or those charged with governance of the

responsible party, a legislature, the intended users, the measurer or evaluator, or a different third party

8. Engagement team — All personnel performing an engagement, including any experts contracted by the firm in connection with that engagement.
9. Evidence — Information used by the practitioner in arriving at the practitioner's conclusion. Evidence includes both, information contained in relevant information systems, if any, and other information
10. Firm — A sole practitioner/proprietor, partnership or any such entity of professional accountants, as may be permitted by law.
11. Historical financial information — Information expressed in financial terms in relation to a particular entity, derived primarily from that entity's accounting system, about economic events occurring in past time periods or about economic conditions or circumstances at points in time in the past.
12. Internal audit function – A function of an entity that performs assurance and consulting activities, designed to evaluate and improve the effectiveness of the entity's governance, risk management and internal control processes.
13. Intended users — The individual(s) or organization(s), or group(s) thereof that the practitioner expects will use the assurance report.

    In some cases there may be intended users other than those to whom the assurance report is addressed. The practitioner may not be able to identify all those who will read the assurance report, particularly, where a large number of people have access to it. In such cases, particularly where possible, users are likely to have a broad range of interests in the underlying subject matter, intended users may be limited to major stakeholders with significant and common interests. Intended users may be identified in different ways, for example, by agreement between the practitioner and the responsible party or engaging party, or by law or regulation.

    Intended users or their representatives may be directly involved with the practitioner and the responsible party (and the engaging party, if different) in determining the requirements of the engagement. Regardless of the involvement of others however, and unlike an agreed-upon procedures engagement (which involves reporting factual findings based upon procedures agreed with the engaging party and any appropriate third parties, rather than a conclusion):

    (a) The practitioner is responsible for determining the nature, timing and extent of procedures; and

    (b) The practitioner may need to perform additional procedures, if information comes to the practitioner's attention that differs significantly from that on which the determination of planned procedures was based.

In some cases, intended users (for example, bankers and regulators) impose a requirement on, or request the appropriate party(s) to arrange for an assurance engagement to be performed for a specific purpose. When engagements use criteria that are designed for a specific purpose, paragraph 80 requires a statement alerting readers to this fact. In addition, the practitioner may consider it appropriate to indicate that the assurance report is intended solely for specific users. Depending on the engagement circumstances, this may be achieved by restricting the distribution or use of the assurance report.

14. Measurer or evaluator — The party(s) who measures or evaluates the underlying subject matter against the criteria. The measurer or evaluator possesses expertise in the underlying subject matter. In many attestation engagements, the responsible party may also be the measurer or evaluator, and the engaging party. The measurer or evaluator is responsible for having a reasonable basis for the subject matter information. What constitutes a reasonable basis will depend on the nature of the underlying subject matter and other engagement circumstances. In some cases, a formal process with extensive internal controls may be needed to provide the measurer or evaluator with a reasonable basis that the subject matter information is free from material misstatement. The fact that the practitioner will report on the subject matter information is not a substitute for the measurer or evaluator's own processes to have a reasonable basis for the subject matter information.

15. Misstatement — A difference between the subject matter information and the appropriate measurement or evaluation of the underlying subject matter in accordance with the criteria. Misstatements can be intentional or unintentional, qualitative or quantitative, and include omissions.

16. Misstatement of fact (with respect to other information) — Other information that is unrelated to matters appearing in the subject matter information or the assurance report that is incorrectly stated or presented. A material misstatement of fact may undermine the credibility of the document containing the subject matter information.

17. Other information — Information (other than the subject matter information and the assurance report thereon) which is included, either by law, regulation or custom, in a document containing the subject matter information and the assurance report thereon.

18. Practitioner's expert — An individual or organization possessing expertise in a field other than assurance, whose work in that field is used by the practitioner to assist the practitioner in obtaining sufficient appropriate evidence. A practitioner's expert may be either a practitioner's internal expert (who is a partner or staff, including temporary staff, of the practitioner's firm or a network firm), or a practitioner's external expert.

19. Professional judgment —The application of relevant training, knowledge and experience, within the context provided by assurance and ethical standards, in making informed decisions about the courses of action that are appropriate in the circumstances of the engagement.

20. Professional skepticism — An attitude that includes a questioning mind, being alert to conditions which may indicate possible misstatement, and a critical assessment of evidence.

21. Responsible party — The party(s) responsible for the underlying subject matter. All assurance engagements have at least three parties: the responsible party, the practitioner, and the intended users. In many attestation engagements, the responsible party may also be the measurer or evaluator, and the engaging party.
22. Risk of material misstatement — The risk that the subject matter information is materially misstated prior to the engagement.
23. Subject matter information — The outcome of the measurement or evaluation of the underlying subject matter against the criteria, i.e., the information that results from applying the criteria to the underlying subject matter. In some cases, the subject matter information may be a statement that evaluates an aspect of a process, or of performance or compliance, in relation to the criteria. For example, "ABC's governance structure conformed with XYZ criteria during the period…"
24. Underlying subject matter—The phenomenon that is measured or evaluated by applying criteria.

Appendix 12: Provisions relating to misconduct under the Chartered Accountants Act, 1949

CHAPTER V
MISCONDUCT

21. Disciplinary Directorate

(1) The Council shall, by notification, establish a Disciplinary Directorate headed by an officer of the Institute designated as Director (Discipline) and such other employees for making investigations in respect of any information or complaint received by it.

(2) On receipt of any information or complaint along with the prescribed fee, the Director (Discipline) shall arrive at a prima facie opinion on the occurrence of the alleged misconduct.

(3) Where the Director (Discipline) is of the opinion that a member is guilty of any professional or other misconduct mentioned in the First Schedule, he shall place the matter before the Board of Discipline and where the Director (Discipline) is of the opinion that a member is guilty of any professional or other misconduct mentioned in the Second Schedule or in both the Schedules, he shall place the matter before the Disciplinary Committee.

(4) In order to make investigations under the provisions of this Act, the Disciplinary Directorate shall follow such procedure as may be specified.

(5) Where a complainant withdraws the complaint, the Director (Discipline) shall place such withdrawal before the Board of Discipline or, as the case may be, the Disciplinary Committee, and the said Board or Committee may, if it is of the view that the circumstances so warrant, permit the withdrawal at any stage.

21A. Board of Discipline

(1) The Council shall constitute a Board of Discipline consisting of–

(a) a person with experience in law and having knowledge of disciplinary matters and the profession, to be its presiding officer;

(b) two members one of whom shall be a member of the Council elected by the Council and the other member shall be nominated by the Central Government from amongst the persons of eminence having experience in the field of law, economics, business, finance or accountancy

(c) the Director (Discipline) shall function as the Secretary of the Board.

(2) The Board of Discipline shall follow summary disposal procedure in dealing with all cases before it.

(3) Where the Board of Discipline is of the opinion that a member is guilty of a professional or other misconduct mentioned in the First Schedule, it shall afford to the member an opportunity of being heard before making any order against him and may thereafter take any one or more of the following actions, namely:–

(a) reprimand the member;

(b) remove the name of the member from the Register up to a period of three months;

(c) impose such fine as it may think fit which may extend to rupees one lakh.

(4) The Director (Discipline) shall submit before the Board of Discipline all information and complaints where he is of the opinion that there is no prima facie case and the Board of Discipline may, if it agrees with the opinion of the Director (Discipline), close the matter or in case of disagreement, may advise the Director (Discipline) to further investigate the matter.

21B. Disciplinary Committee

(1) The Council shall constitute a Disciplinary Committee consisting of the President or the Vice-President of the Council as the Presiding Officer and two members to be elected from amongst the members of the Council and two members to be nominated by the Central Government from amongst the persons of eminence having experience in the field of law, economics, business, finance or accountancy:

Provided that the Council may constitute more Disciplinary Committees as and when it considers necessary.

(2) The Disciplinary Committee, while considering the cases placed before it shall follow such procedure as may be specified

(3) Where the Disciplinary Committee is of the opinion that a member is guilty of a professional or other misconduct mentioned in the Second Schedule or both the First Schedule and the Second Schedule, it shall afford to the member an opportunity of being heard before making any order against him and may thereafter take any one or more of the following actions, namely :–

(a) reprimand the member;

(b) remove the name of the member from the Register permanently or for such period, as it thinks fit;

(c) impose such fine as it may think fit, which may extend to rupees five lakhs.

(4) The allowances payable to the members nominated by the Central Government shall be such as may be specified

22. Professional or other misconduct defined

For the purposes of this Act, the expression "professional or other misconduct" shall be deemed to include any act or omission provided in any of the Schedules, but nothing in this Section shall be construed to limit or abridge in any way the power conferred or duty cast on the Director (Discipline) under sub-section (1) of Section 21 to inquire into the conduct of any member of the Institute under any other circumstances

Appendix 13: First and Second Schedule Chartered Accountant Act, 1949

THE FIRST SCHEDULE

***See* Sections 21(3), 21A(3) and 22**

Part I:

Professional misconduct in relation to chartered accountants in practice A chartered accountant in practice shall be deemed to be guilty of professional misconduct, if he – allows any person to practice in his name as a chartered accountant unless such person is also a chartered accountant in practice and is in partnership with or employed by him;

(1) pays or allows or agrees to pay or allow, directly or indirectly, any share, commission or brokerage in the fees or profits of his professional business, to any person other than a member of the Institute or a partner or a retired partner or the legal representative of a deceased partner, or a member of any other professional body or with such other persons having such qualifications as may be prescribed, for the purpose of rendering such professional services from time to time in or outside India.

Explanation – In this item, "partner" includes a person residing outside India with whom a chartered accountant in practice has entered into partnership which is not in contravention of item (4) of this Part;

(2) accepts or agrees to accept any part of the profits of the professional work of a person who is not a member of the Institute:

Provided that nothing herein contained shall be construed as prohibiting a member from entering into profit sharing or other similar arrangements, including receiving any share commission or brokerage in the fees, with a member of such professional body or other person having qualifications, as is referred to in item (2) of this Part

(3) enters into partnership, in or outside India, with any person other than a chartered accountant in practice or such other person who is a member of any other professional body having such qualifications as may be prescribed, including a resident who but for his residence abroad would be entitled to be registered as a member under clause (v) of sub-section (1) of Section 4 or whose qualifications are recognised by the Central Government or the Council for the purpose of permitting such partnerships;

(4) secures, either through the services of a person who is not an employee of such chartered accountant or who is not his partner or by means which are not open to a chartered accountant, any professional business:

Provided that nothing herein contained shall be construed as prohibiting any arrangement permitted in terms of items (2), (3) and (4) of this Part;

(5) solicits clients or professional work either directly or indirectly by circular, advertisement, personal communication or interview or by any other means:

Provided that nothing herein contained shall be construed as preventing or prohibiting–

(i) any chartered accountant from applying or requesting for or inviting or securing professional work from another chartered accountant in practice; or

(ii) a member from responding to tenders or enquiries issued by various users of professional services or organisations from time to time and securing professional work as a consequence;

(6) advertises his professional attainments or services, or uses any designation or expressions other than chartered accountant on professional documents, visiting cards, letter heads or sign boards, unless it be a degree of a University established by law in India or recognised by the Central Government or a title indicating membership of the Institute of Chartered Accountants of India or of any other institution that has been recognised by the Central Government or may be recognised by the Council:

Provided that a member in practice may advertise through a write up setting out the services provided by him or his firm and particulars of his firm subject to such guidelines2 as may be issued by the Council;

(7) accepts a position as auditor previously held by another chartered accountant or a certified auditor who has been issued certificate under the Restricted Certificate Rules, 1932 without first communicating with him in writing;

(8) accepts an appointment as auditor of a company without first ascertaining from it whether the requirements of Section 225 of the Companies Act, 1956* in respect of such appointment have been duly complied with;

(9) charges or offers to charge, accepts or offers to accept in respect of any professional employment, fees which are based on a percentage of profits or which are contingent upon the findings, or results of such employment, except as permitted under any regulation made under this Act;

(10) engages in any business or occupation other than the profession of chartered accountant unless permitted by the Council so to engage:

Provided that nothing contained herein shall disentitle a chartered accountant from being a director of a company (not being a managing director or a whole time director) unless he or any of his partners is interested in such company as an auditor;

(11) allows a person not being a member of the Institute in practice, or a member not being his partner to sign on his behalf or on behalf of his firm, any balance-sheet, profit and loss account, report or financial statements.

Part II: Professional misconduct in relation to members of the Institute in service

A member of the Institute (other than a member in practice) shall be deemed to be guilty of professional misconduct, if he being an employee of any company, firm or person–

(1) pays or allows or agrees to pay directly or indirectly to any person any share in the emoluments of the employment undertaken by him;

(2) accepts or agrees to accept any part of fees, profits or gains from a lawyer, a chartered accountant or broker engaged by such company, firm or person or agent or customer of such company, firm or person by way of commission or gratification.

Part III: Professional misconduct in relation to members of the Institute generally

A member of the Institute, whether in practice or not, shall be deemed to be guilty of professional misconduct, if he–

(1) not being a fellow of the Institute, acts as a fellow of the Institute;

(2) does not supply the information called for, or does not comply with the requirements asked for, by the Institute, Council or any of its Committees, Director (Discipline), Board of Discipline, Disciplinary Committee, Quality Review Board or the Appellate Authority;

(3) while inviting professional work from another chartered accountant or while responding to tenders or enquiries or while advertising through a write up, or anything as provided for in items (6) and (7) of Part I of this Schedule, gives information knowing it to be false.

Part IV: Other misconduct in relation to members of the Institute generally

A member of the Institute, whether in practice or not, shall be deemed to be guilty of other misconduct, if he–

(1) is held guilty by any civil or criminal court for an offence which is punishable with imprisonment for a term not exceeding six months;

(2) in the opinion of the Council, brings disrepute to the profession or the Institute as a result of his action whether or not related to his professional work.

The Second Schedule

[See Sections 21(3), 21B (3) and 22]

Part I: Professional misconduct in relation to chartered accountants in practice

A chartered accountant in practice shall be deemed to be guilty of professional misconduct, if he–

(1) discloses information acquired in the course of his professional engagement to any person other than his client so engaging him, without the consent of his client or otherwise than as required by any law for the time being in force;

(2) certifies or submits in his name, or in the name of his firm, a report of an examination of financial statements unless the examination of such statements and the related records has been made by him or by a partner or an employee in his firm or by another chartered accountant in practice;

(3) permits his name or the name of his firm to be used in connection with an estimate of earnings contingent upon future transactions in a manner which may lead to the belief that he vouches for the accuracy of the forecast;

(4) expresses his opinion on financial statements of any business or enterprise in which he, his firm, or a partner in his firm has a substantial interest;

(5) fails to disclose a material fact known to him which is not disclosed in a financial statement, but disclosure of which is necessary in making such financial statement where he is concerned with that financial statement in a professional capacity;

(6) fails to report a material misstatement known to him to appear in a financial statement with which he is concerned in a professional capacity;

(7) does not exercise due diligence, or is grossly negligent in the conduct of his professional duties;

(8) fails to obtain sufficient information which is necessary for expression of an opinion or its exceptions are sufficiently material to negate the expression of an opinion;

(9) fails to invite attention to any material departure from the generally accepted procedure of audit applicable to the circumstances;

(10) fails to keep moneys of his client other than fees or remuneration or money meant to be expended in a separate banking account or to use such moneys for purposes for which they are intended within a reasonable time.

Part II: Professional misconduct in relation to members of the Institute generally

A member of the Institute, whether in practice or not, shall be deemed to be guilty of professional misconduct, if he–

(1) contravenes any of the provisions of this Act or the regulations made thereunder or any guidelines issued by the Council;

(2) being an employee of any company, firm or person, discloses confidential information acquired in the course of his employment except as and when required by any law for the time being in force or except as permitted by the employer;

(3) includes in any information, statement, return or form to be submitted to the Institute, Council or any of its Committees, Director (Discipline), Board of Discipline, Disciplinary Committee, Quality Review Board or the Appellate Authority any particulars knowing them to be false;

(4) defalcates or embezzles moneys received in his professional capacity.

Part III: Other misconduct in relation to members of the Institute generally

A member of the Institute, whether in practice or not, shall be deemed to be guilty of other misconduct, if he is held guilty by any civil or criminal court for an offence which is punishable with imprisonment for a term exceeding six months

Appendix 14: First and Second Schedule to the Cost and Works Accountants Act, 1959

'The First Schedule

[See sections 21(4) and 22]

Part I: Professional misconduct in relation to Cost Accountants in Practice

A cost accountant in practice shall be deemed to be guilty of professional misconduct, if he—

(1) allows any person to practice in his name as a cost accountant unless such person is also a cost accountant in practice and is in partnership with or employed by himself;

(2) pays or allows or agrees to pay or allow, directly or indirectly, any share, commission or brokerage in the fees or profits of his professional work, to any person other than a member of the Institute or a partner or a retired partner or the legal representative of a deceased partner.

Explanation: In this item, "partner" includes a person residing outside India with whom a cost accountant in practice has entered into partnership which is not in contravention of item (4) of this part;

(3) accepts or agrees to accept any part of the profits of the professional work of a lawyer, auctioneer, broker or other agent who is not a member of the Institute;

(4) enters into partnership with any person other than a cost accountant in practice or a person resident without India who but for his residence abroad would be entitled to be registered as a member of the Institute under clause (iv) of sub-section (1) of section 4 or whose qualifications are recognised by the Central Government or the Council for the purpose of permitting such partnerships, provided that the cost accountant shares in the fees or profits of the professional work of the partnership both within and without India;

(5) secures, either through the services of a person not qualified to be his partner or by means which are not open to a cost accountant, any professional work;

(6) solicits clients or professional work either directly or indirectly, by circular, advertisement, personal communication or interview or by any other means;

(7) advertises his professional attainments or services, or uses any designation or expression other than cost accountant on professional documents, visiting cards, letter-heads or sign boards, unless it be a degree of a University established by law in India or recognised by the Central Government or a title indicating membership of the Institute of Cost and Works Accountants of India or of any other institution that has been recognised by the Central Government or may be recognised by the Council;

(8) accepts a position as cost accountant previously held by another cost accountant in practice without first communicating with him in writing;

(9) charges or offers to charge, accepts or offers to accept in respect of any professional employment fees which are based on a percentage of profits or

which arc contingent upon the findings or results of such employment, except in cases which are permitted under any regulations made under this Act;

(10) engages in any business or occupation other than the profession of cost accountant unless permitted by the Council so to engage :

Provided that nothing contained herein shall disentitle a cost accountant from being a director of a company unless he or any of his partners is interested in such company as accountant;

(11) allows a person not being a member of the Institute in practice or a member not being his partner to sign on his behalf or on behalf of his firm, any cost or pricing statements or any other statements related thereto.

Part II: Professional Misconduct in relation to Members of the Institute in Service

A member of the Institute (other than a member in practice) shall be deemed to be guilty of professional misconduct, if he being an employee of any company, firm or person—

(1) pays or allows or agrees to pay directly or indirectly, to any person any share in the emoluments of the employment undertaken by the member;

(2) accepts or agrees to accept any part of fees, profits or gains from a lawyer, a cost accountant or broker engaged by such company, firm or person or agent or customer of such company, firm or person by way of commission or gratification;

Part III: Professional Misconduct in relation to Members of the Institute Generally

A member of the Institute whether in practice or not shall be deemed to be guilty of professional misconduct, if he—

(1) not being a fellow of the Institute acts as a fellow of the Institute;

(2) does not supply the information called for, or does not comply with the requirements asked for by the Institute, Council or any of its Committees, Director (Discipline), Board of Discipline, Disciplinary Committee, Quality Review Board or the Appellate Authority;

(3) while inviting professional work from another cost accountant or while responding to tenders or enquiries or while advertising through a write up, or anything as provided for in items (6) and (7) of Part I of this Schedule, gives information knowing it to be false

Part IV: Other Misconduct in relation to members of the Institute Generally

A member of the institute, whether in practice or not, shall be deemed to be guilty of other misconduct, if—

(1) he is held guilty by any civil or criminal court for an offence which is punishable with imprisonment for a term not exceeding six months;

(2) in the opinion of the Council he brings disrepute to the profession or the institute as a result of his action whether or not related to his professional work.

The Second Schedule

[See sections 21(5) and 22]

Part I: Professional Misconduct in relation to Cost Accountants in Practice

A cost accountant in practice shall be deemed to be guilty of professional misconduct, if he—

(1) discloses information acquired in the course of his professional engagement to any person other than the client so engaging him, without the consent of such client, or otherwise than as required by any law for the time being in force;

(2) certifies or submits in his name or in the name of his firm a report of an examination of cost accounting and related statements, unless the examination of such statements has been made by him or by a partner or an employee in his firm or by another cost accountant in practice;

(3) permits his name or the name of his firm to be used in connection with an estimate of cost or earnings contingent upon future transactions in a manner which may lead to the belief that he vouches for the accuracy of the forecast;

(4) expresses his opinion on cost or pricing statements of any business or any enterprise in which he, his firm or a partner in his firm has a substantial interest, unless he discloses the interest also in his report;

(5) fails to disclose in a cost or pricing statement a material fact known to him, which is not disclosed in a cost or pricing statement, but disclosure of which is necessary to make such statement not misleading;

(6) fails to report a material mis-statement known to him to appear in a cost or pricing statement with which he is concerned in a professional capacity;

(7) is grossly negligent in the conduct of his professional duties;

(8) fails to obtain sufficient information to warrant the expression of an opinion or makes exceptions which are sufficiently material to negate the expression of an opinion;

(9) fails to invite attention to any material departure from the generally accepted procedure of costing and pricing applicable to the circumstances;

(10) fails to keep moneys of his client in a separate banking account or to use such moneys for purposes for which they are intended.

Part II: Professional Misconduct in relation to Members of the Institute Generally

A member of the Institute, whether in practice or not, shall be deemed to be guilty of professional misconduct, if he—

(1) contravenes any of the provisions of this Act or the regulations made thereunder;

(2) being an employee of any company, firm or person, discloses confidential information acquired in the course of his employment, except as and when required by any law for the time being in force or except as permitted by the employer

(3) includes in any information, statement, return or form to be submitted to the Institute, Council or any of its Committees, Director (Discipline), Board of Discipline, Disciplinary Committee, Quality Review Board or the Appellate Authority any particulars knowing them to be false

(4) defalcates or embezzles moneys received in his professional capacity

Other Misconduct in relation to Members of the Institute Generally

A member of the Institute, whether in practice or not, shall be deemed to be guilty of other misconduct, if he is held guilty by any civil or criminal court for an offence which is punishable with imprisonment for a term exceeding six months.

Appendix 15: GST Audit Engagement Letter

Strictly Private and Confidential

Date ____________

To,

____

____

____

Dear Sir,

Proposal for Certification under Section 44(2) of the CGST Act, 2017 for the financial year ended March 31, 2018 – Form GSTR-9C

Following your request seeking for our proposal for certification of Form GSTR-9C under Section44 (2) of the CGST Act, 2018 for the financial year 2017-18, we are pleased to provide our proposal for certification of Form GSTR-9C.

1. Scope and Objective

1.1 The objective is to certify the reconciliation statement as provided in Form GSTR-9C, based on the Annual Return prepared by the Management as required under Section 35(5) and 44 of the CGST Act, 2017, with the Audited Financial Statement.

1.2 GST law requires the management to maintain prescribed documents and other accounting records provided under Section 35(1) of the CGST Act, 2017. Further the Company is also required to furnish Annual Return under Section 44 of the CGST Act, 2017 in the prescribed format. Maintenance of the books of accounts, records under the GST laws and the financial statements are the responsibility of the registered person. Our responsibility is only to certify the details as required in Form GSTR-9C.

1.3 The management is responsible for making available to us, as and when required by us, all the accounting records and all other records and related information, providing us all explanations that we may require from time to time which to the best of its knowledge and belief, are necessary for the purposes of our certification. The management is also responsible to provide us with unrestricted access to persons within the entity from whom we determine it necessary to obtain details. This includes our entitlement to require from the officers of the Company such information and explanations as we may think necessary for execution of our work.

1.6 The responsibility for prevention and detection of fraud, irregularities and error rests with the Company's management. Your internal accounting control structure should provide you with reasonable assurance, though not necessarily absolute assurance, against the possibility of fraud, irregularities and errors.

1.7 We understand that all the records, documentation, and information we request in connection with our certification will be made available to us. Management's co-operation in providing us with records, documentation and information and agreed upon assistance on a timely basis is an important factor in our being able to issue the report by that date.

2. Fees

2.1 Our fees are based on the level of effort of our people and the skills and experience of the personnel assigned to the work.

Scope of Services	**Amount in Rs.**
Certification of Form GSTR-9C -20 States	

2.2 Our fee does not include GST on professional services rendered. This will be recovered on actual basis.

2.3 Expenses necessarily incurred while engaged on this assignment will be billed to you at cost. If we expect additional time costs to be incurred as a result of any change in the scope of work, or difficulties in obtaining information and which caused additional work, we will discuss the matter of incremental fees with you promptly.

2.4 Our invoices are payable on demand in full upon presentation.

3. Time Frame

The estimated time frame for completion of the Services would be mutually agreed. This estimate is based on the assumption that information and assistance necessary to conduct the Services is provided to us on a timely basis.

4. Confidentiality of information

4.1 We understand the confidential nature of the engagement and will hold in strict confidence all information obtained from you. Subject to paragraph 4.2, 4.3, 4.4 and 4.5 below, we will not disclose such information to others or use such information except in connection with the performance of the services agreed in this proposal.

4.2 We may share information relating to you, to our relationship with you, and to the Services, including Confidential Information, privately and in confidence, with our partners, members, directors, employees and associated persons and other parties, in each case who are required to implement safeguards to protect confidentiality, in order to support certification work, facilitate the administration of our engagement or support the maintenance of quality and standards in our work.

4.3 This clause shall not prohibit our disclosure of Confidential Information where we are required by law or a competent regulatory authority to disclose or where we wish to disclose it to our professional indemnity insurers or advisers, in which event we may do so in confidence only.

4.4 We may disclose in our external communication the fact that we have rendered services to your company by identifying the name of your company, reproducing your logo and/or indicating only the general nature of services rendered by us including such details as have properly entered the public domain.

4.5 We may be requested to make certain work papers available to the ICAI, PCAOB, SEBI or any other regulatory body (local or international) pursuant to authority given to it by law or regulation. If requested, access to such work papers will be provided under the supervision of our personnel. Furthermore, upon request, we may provide photocopies of selected work papers to the regulatory body which may intend, or decide, to distribute the photocopies or information contained therein to others. You hereby waive, to the fullest extent permissible under applicable Indian law, the rights provided under any applicable laws, regulations, professional standards, or other provisions that might restrict the ability of the firm, or associated person, to comply with requests by a regulatory body for production of documents or information in the firm's or associated person's possession, custody or control that was obtained in the conduct of audit services by such firm or person, and consent, to the fullest extent permissible under applicable law, to action taken in furtherance of the foregoing by the firm or associated person.

5. Limitation of Liability

We shall not be responsible for any consequential, incidental, special or punitive damages, nor for direct compensatory damages in excess of the fees actually received by us for the performance of Services hereunder.

We shall use our judgement in resolving issues where the tax law may be unclear, or where there are conflicts between taxing authorities' interpretation of law and other supportable positions. You will appreciate that tax advice of the applicable standard is based on interpretation of the law and experience with the revenue authorities. Therefore, the conclusions reached and views expressed are often matters of opinion rather than certainty. Furthermore, tax regulations, its judicial interpretation and the policies of the tax authorities are subject to change from time to time, which may adversely affect advice that we have given. Therefore, we shall not be responsible for any penalty or interest imposed by tax authorities on the Company.

6. Other matters

6.1 We may communicate with you by electronic mail on the basis that in consenting to this method of communication you accept the inherent risks (including the security risks of interception of or unauthorised access to such communications, the risks of corruption of such communications and the risks of viruses or other harmful devices) and that you shall perform virus checks.

6.2 We may be required to connect the firm's computers to your network during this engagement. You hereby provide your consent to this. While the firm takes reasonable steps to protect its computers using system hardening and anti-virus utilities, we are not responsible for any damage it may inadvertently cause to your computer and networks.

7. Acknowledgement and Acceptance

If the scope and terms of the Engagement are acceptable, please acknowledge your acceptance by signing the confirmation attached, returning the enclosed copy of this Letter to us at the above address.

Yours sincerely,

for ________________________

For____________

Appendix 16: GST Audit Acceptance Letter

To

Date:__________

The Board of Directors

XYZ & Co. Ltd.

Sub: Acceptance of GST Audit

Ref: This is with reference to your letter dated ………………..,..

Dear Sir/ Madam,

You have requested that we conduct the Goods and services tax audit for the financial year _____ on quarterly basis/of your organisation.

We are pleased to confirm our acceptance and our understanding of this engagement by means of this letter. Our audit will be in accordance with the principles laid down by the Auditing Assurance Standards issued by the ICAI from time to time as applicable to Goods and service tax provisions and relevant notifications and circulars issued there under, with the objective of expressing our opinion on internal control system and compliance with the law and procedure relating to Goods and Services.

In forming our opinion on the internal control system and procedure, we will perform sufficient tests to obtain reasonable assurance as to whether the information contained in the records and other source data is reliable and sufficient. We enclose the draft Goods and services audit program, which is indicative of the areas normally covered. Our audit assignment would cover the following areas:

(a) Nature of business

(b) Organisation Structure and Instruction Manual

(c) Supply

(d) Records and Returns

(e) Job work

(f) Valuation

(g) Reconciliation and analysis

We would curtail/extend the procedures depending on the periodic review as the audit progresses.

Because of the test nature and other inherent limitations of an audit, together with the inherent limitations of any system of internal control, there is an unavoidable risk that even some material misstatement may remain undiscovered.

May we remind you that the responsibility for the preparation of various reconciliations between GST returns/reports/intimations submitted and other records is that of the management of the company.

We look forward to full cooperation from you staff and we trust that they will make available to us whatever records, documentation and other information requested in connection with our audit.

Our fees, which will be billed as work progresses, based on the time required by the individuals assigned to the engagement plus direct out-of-pocket expenses. Individual hourly rates vary according to the degree of responsibility involved and the experience and skill required.

This letter will be effective for future years unless it is terminated, amended or superseded.

Please sign and return a copy of this letter to indicate that it is in accordance with your understanding of the arrangements for our audit of the financial statements.

Yours faithfully

Appendix 17: List of important publications of the Institute of Chartered Accountants of India, ICAI, New Delhi

INDIRECT TAXES COMMITTEE – idtc@icai.in

1. **Representation/Input to Government- GST**
2. **Representation/Input to Government-Budget memorandum**
3. **GST Publications**
4. **E-learning on UAE VAT**
5. **E-learning on Customs Duty**
6. **E-Handbook on Classification under GST (30.07.2018)**
7. **E-publication on E-way bill under GST (July, 2018)**
8. **E-Handbook on Job work under GST-June, 2018**
9. **E-Handbook on GST Amendments (08.06.2018)**
10. **Background material on GST Acts and Rules, 2017- May, 2018**
    a. **Volume-I**
    b. **Volume-II**
    c. **Addendum to Background Material on GST Acts and Rules**
11. **Compliances of Service tax/GST in Banking Sector**
12. **FAQs & MCQs on GST (August, 2018)**
13. **Background Material on Exempted Services under GST (03.01.2018)**
14. **Hand Book on GST for Service Providers (31.10.17)**
15. **Booklet on-Seamless Credit - language edited (17.10.17)**
16. **Simplified GST Guide for Manufacturer (25.08.17)**
17. **Study Paper on Taxation of E-Commerce under GST (02.08.2017)**
18. **E-Book on How to Get Registered under GST (01.08.17)**
19. **The Constitution (One Hundred and First Amendment) Act, 2016 (21.09.16)**
20. **Impact of GST on Jammu & Kashmir Taxation System — Study Report (20.01.16)**

PROFESSIONAL PUBLICATIONS/ ACT & REGULATIONS

1. The Chartered Accountants Act, 1949 (Edn. 2013)
2. The Chartered Accountants Regulations, 1988 (Edn. 2013)
3. ICAI Rules made by Central Government (2014)
4. Frequently Asked Questions on Members & Firms

ETHICAL STANDARDS:

1. Recent Decisions of Ethical Standards Board
2. Short notes on High Court Decisions

3. Draft Code of Ethics (Edn.2017)
4. Frequently Asked Questions on Ethical Issues (Edn.2012)
5. Guidance Note on Independence of Auditors (Edn.2005)
6. Disciplinary Cases Vol I to IX

FISCAL LAW COMMITTEE:

1. Technical Guide on Income Computation and Disclosure Standards (Edn'2017)
2. Guidance Note on Audit of Public Charitable Institutions Under the Income-Tax Act, 1961
3. Taxation of Charitable Trusts and Institutions - A Study
4. Guidance Note on Report on International Transactions under Section 92E of the Income-Tax Act, 1961 (Transfer Pricing)- (Revised-2016)
5. Taxation of Non-Residents
6. State-level VAT in India - A Study
7. Guidance Note on Tax Audit under Section 44AB of the Income-Tax Act (Edn 2005)
8. Aspects of International Taxation - A Study
9. Study of Financial Records and Understanding of Audit Techniques

TECHNICAL DIRECTORATE

1. Compendium of Opinions containing opinions finalised by the Expert Advisory Committee upto February 11, 2016 as contained in Volume I to Volume XXXV of the Compendium of Opinion
2. Guidance Note on Accounting for Oil and Gas Producing Activities (Ind AS)
3. Guidance Note on Combined and Carve–Out Financial Statements (September 2016)
4. Guidance Note on Accounting for Depreciation in companies in the context of Schedule II to the Companies Act, 2013
5. Guidance Note on Accounting for Derivative contracts (Issued 2015)
6. Guidance Note on Accounting for Expenditure on Corporate Social Responsibility Activities (Issued May 15, 2015)
7. Guidance Note on Accounting for Oil and Gas Producing Activities (revised 2013)
8. Guidance Note on Accounting for Corporate Dividend Tax
9. Guidance Note on Accounting for Employee Share-based Payments
10. Guidance Note on Accounting for State-level Value Added Tax
11. Guidance Note on Accounting by Schools
12. Guidance Note on Accounting for Credit Available in Respect of Minimum Alternative Tax under the Income-tax Act, 1961
13. Guidance Note on Accounting for Real Estate Transactions (Revised 2012)
14. Guidance Note on Measurement of Income Tax for Interim Financial Reporting in the context of AS 25.

15. Guidance Note on Accounting Treatment for MODVAT/CENVAT
16. Guidance Note on Applicability of AS 25 to Interim Financial Results
17. Guidance Note on Turnover in case of Contractors
18. Guidance Note on Accounting for Rate Regulated Activities
19. Guidance Note on Accounting for Self-generated Certified Emission Reductions (CERs) (Issued 2012)
20. Guidance Note on Accounting and Auditing of Political Parties
21. Guidance Note on Terms Used in Financial Statements
22. Guidance Note on Accrual Basis of Accounting
23. Guidance Note on Accounting by Dot-Com Companies
24. Guidance Note on Accounting Treatment for Excise Duty (Revised 2000)
25. Preface to the Statement of Accounting Standards (Revised 2004)
26. AS - 1 Disclosure of Accounting Policies (Issued 1979)
27. AS - 2 Valuation of Inventories (Revised 1999)
28. AS - 3 Cash Flow Statements (Revised 1997)
29. AS - 4 Contingencies and Events Occurring After the Balance Sheet Date (Revised 1995)
30. AS - 5 Net Profit or Loss for the Period, Prior Period Items and Changes in Accounting Policies (Revised 1997)
31. AS - 6 Depreciation Accounting (Revised 1994)
32. AS - 7 Construction Contracts (Revised 2002)
33. AS - 8 Accounting for Research And Development (Issued 1985)
34. AS - 9 Revenue Recognition (Issued 1985)
35. AS - 10 Accounting for Fixed Assets (Issued 1985)
36. AS - 11 The Effects of Changes in Foreign Exchange Rates (Revised 2003)
37. AS - 12 Accounting for Government Grants (Issued 1991)
38. AS - 13 Accounting for Investments (Issued 1993)
39. AS - 14 Accounting for Amalgamations (Issued 1994)
40. AS - 15 Accounting for Retirement Benefits in the Financial Statements of Employers (Issued 1995)
41. AS - 16 Borrowing Costs (Issued 2000)
42. AS - 17 Segment Reporting (Issued 2000)
43. AS - 18 Related Party Disclosures (Issued 2000)
44. AS - 19 Leases (Issued 2001)
45. AS - 20 Earnings Per Share (Issued 2001)
46. AS - 21 Consolidated Financial Statements (Issued 2001)
47. AS - 22 Accounting for Taxes on Income (Issued 2001)
48. AS - 23 Accounting for Investments in Associates in Consolidated Financial Statements (Issued 2001)
49. AS - 24 Discounting Operations (Issued 2002)

50. AS - 25 Interim Financial Reporting (Issued 2002)
51. AS - 26 Intangible Assets (Issued 2002)
52. AS - 27 Financial Reporting of Interests in Joint Ventures (Issued 2002)
53. AS - 28 Impairment of Assets (Issued 2002)
54. AS - 29 Provisions, Contingent Liabilities and Contingent Assets (Issued - 2003)
55. Study on Unconventional Methods in Special Audits and Investigations
56. Technical Guide on Review and Certification of Investment Risk Management Systems and Processes of Insurance Companies (2013)
57. Technical Guide on Internal & Concurrent Audit of Investment Functions of Insurance Companies (2013).
58. Checklist for Disclosures under Accounting Standards
59. Companies (Accounting Standards) Amendment Rules, 2018

AUDITING AND ASSURANCE STANDARD BOARD:

1. Guidance Note on Audit of Consolidated Financial Statements (Revised 2016)
2. Guidance Note on Reports or Certificates for Special Purposes (Revised 2016)
3. Guidance Note on Reports in Company Prospectuses (Revised 2016)
4. Guidance Note on Audit of Internal Financial Controls over Financial Reporting issued by Auditing and Assurance Standards Board.
5. Revised Guidance Note on Reporting on Fraud under Section 143(12) of the Companies Act, 2013 released by Auditing and Assurance Standards Board
6. AASB releases Guidance Note on Reporting under Section 143 (3)(f) and (h) of the Companies Act, 2013.
7. Guidance Note on the Companies (Auditor's Report) Order, 2016 issued by Auditing and Assurance Standards Board
8. Guidance Note on Audit of Property, Plant and Equipment
9. Guidance Note on Certification of XBRL Financial Statements
10. Guidance Note on Audit of Accounts of Non-Corporate Entities (Bank Borrowers)
11. Guidance Note on Audit of Cash and Bank Balances
12. Guidance Note on Audit of Debtors, Loans and Advances
13. Guidance Note on Audit of Expenses
14. Guidance Note on Audit of Inventories
15. Guidance Note on Audit of Investments
16. Guidance Note on Audit of Liabilities
17. Guidance Note on Audit of Miscellaneous Expenditure (Revised)
18. Guidance Note on Audit of Payment of Dividend
19. Guidance Note on Audit of Revenue
20. Guidance Note on Auditing of Accounts of Liquidators
21. Guidance Note on Capital and Reserves

22. Guidance Note on Certificate on Corporate Governance (Revised)
23. Guidance Note on Certificate to be Issued by the Auditor of a Company Pursuant to Companies (Acceptance of Deposits) Rules, 1975
24. Guidance Note on Certification of Documents for Registration of Charges
25. Guidance Note on Computer Assisted Audit Techniques (CAATs)
26. Duty Cast on the Auditors under Section 45-MA of the Reserve Bank of India Act, 1934
27. Independence of Auditors (Revised)
28. Preparation of Financial Statements on Letterheads and Stationery of Auditors
29. Provision for Proposed Dividend
30. Section 227(3) (e) and (f) of the Companies Act, 1956 (Revised)
31. Section 293 A of the Companies Act and the Auditor
32. SA 200, Overall Objectives of the Independent Auditor and the Conduct of an Audit in Accordance with Standards on Auditing
33. SA 210, Agreeing the Terms of Audit Engagements
34. SA 230, Audit Documentation
35. SA 240, The Auditor's Responsibilities Relating to Fraud in an Audit of Financial Statements
36. Revised SA 260, Communication with Those Charged with Governance
37. SA 265, Communicating Deficiencies in Internal Control to Those Charged with Governance and Management
38. SA 299, Responsibility of Joint Auditors
39. Revised SA 299, Joint Audit of Financial Statements
40. SA 300, Planning an Audit of Financial Statements
41. SA 315, Identifying and Assessing the Risks of Material Misstatement Through Understanding the Entity and Its Environment
42. SA 320, Materiality in Planning and Performing an Audit
43. SA 330, The Auditor's Responses to Assessed Risks
44. SA 402, Audit Considerations Relating to an Entity Using a Service Organisation
45. SA 450, Evaluation of Misstatements Identified During the Audit
46. SA 500, Audit Evidence
47. SA 501, Audit Evidence-Specific Considerations for Selected Items
48. SA 505, External Confirmations
49. SA 510, Initial Audit Engagements – Opening Balances
50. SA 520, Analytical Procedures
51. SA 530, Audit Sampling
52. SA 540, Auditing Accounting Estimates, Including Fair Value Accounting Estimates, and Related Disclosures
53. SA 550, Related Parties

54. SA 560, Subsequent Events
55. Revised SA 570, Going Concern
56. SA 580, Written Representations
57. SA 600, Using the Work of Another Auditor
58. Revised SA 610, Using the Work of Internal Auditors
59. SA 620, Using the Work of an Auditor's Expert
60. SA 700, Forming an Opinion and Reporting on Financial Statements
61. SA 800, Special Considerations—Audits of Financial Statements Prepared in Accordance with Special Purpose Frameworks
62. SA 805, Special Considerations—Audits of Single Financial Statements and Specific Elements, Accounts or Items of a Financial Statement
63. SA 810 , Engagements to Report on Summary Financial Statements
64. SRE 2400 (Revised), Engagements to Review Historical Financial Statements
65. SRE 2410 "Review of Interim Financial Information Performed by the Independent Auditor of the Entity"

CORPORATE LAWS & CORPORATE GOVERNANCE COMMITTEE

1. Guidance Note on Schedule III to the Companies Act 2013
2. Technical Guide on Valuation-(Edn'18)
3. Guidance Note on Certification of Documents for Registration of Charges (Edn'05)
4. Guidance Note on Section 293A of The Companies Act and The Auditor (Edn'76)
5. Bulletins of the Corporate Laws & Corporate Governance
6. A Study on the Companies (Acceptance of Deposit) Rules, 1975 (Edn'77)
7. Statement on the Amendments to Schedule VI to the Companies Act, 1956
8. A Study on Succession, Wills, Family Arrangements & HUF Partitions
9. Reference on Foreign Exchange Management, 1999
10. A Study on Registration of Charges Under the Companies Act, 1956
11. A Study on Consumer Protection Act, 1986
12. A Study on the Industries (Development and Regulation) Act, 1951

CONTINUING PROFESSIONAL EDUCATION COMMITTEE

1. Concept Paper - Goods & Services Tax in India & Role of Chartered Accountants

INTERNAL AUDIT STANDARDS BOARD

1. Knowledge Booklet I - Enhancing Governance through Internal Audit
2. Knowledge Booklet II - A New Era in Internal Audit-Companies Act, 2013
3. Preface to the Standards on Internal Audit
4. Standard on Internal Audit (SIA) 1-Planning an Internal Audit

5. Standard on Internal Audit (SIA) 2 - Basic Principles Governing Internal Audit
6. Standard on Internal Audit (SIA) 3 – Documentation
7. Standard on Internal Audit (SIA) 4, Reporting
8. Standard on Internal Audit (SIA) 5, Sampling
9. Standard on Internal Audit (SIA) 6, Analytical Procedures
10. Standard on Internal Audit (SIA) 7, Quality Assurance in Internal Audit
11. Standard on Internal Audit (SIA) 8, Terms of Internal Audit Engagement
12. Standard on Internal Audit (SIA) 9, Communication with Management
13. Standard on Internal Audit (SIA) 10, Internal Audit Evidence
14. Standard on Internal Audit (SIA) 11, Consideration of Fraud in an Internal Audit
15. Standard on Internal Audit (SIA) 12, Internal Control Evaluation
16. Standard on Internal Audit (SIA) 13, Enterprise Risk Management
17. Standard on Internal Audit (SIA) 14, Internal Audit in an Information Technology Environment
18. Standard on Internal Audit (SIA) 15, Knowledge of the Entity and its Environment
19. Standard on Internal Audit (SIA) 16, Using the Work of an Expert
20. Standard on Internal Audit (SIA) 17, Consideration of Laws and Regulations in an Internal Audit
21. Standard on Internal Audit (SIA) 18, Related Parties

IND AS IMPLEMENTATION COMMITTEE

1. Indian Accounting Standards (Ind AS): An Overview (Revised 2017)
2. Educational Material on Ind AS 16, Property, Plant and Equipment
3. Educational Material on Indian Accounting Standard (Ind AS) 1, Presentation of Financial Statements (Revised 2016)
4. Educational Material on Indian Accounting Standard (Ind AS) 2, Inventories (Revised 2016)
5. Educational Material on Indian Accounting Standard (Ind AS) 7, Statement of Cash Flows (Revised 2016)
6. Educational Material on Indian Accounting Standard (Ind AS) 37, Provisions, Contingent Liabilities and Contingent Assets (Revised 2016)
7. Educational Material on Indian Accounting Standard (Ind AS) 101, First-time Adoption of Indian Accounting Standards
8. Educational Material on Indian Accounting Standard (Ind AS) 10, Events after the Reporting Period
9. Educational Material on Indian Accounting Standards (Ind AS) 18 Revenue
10. Educational Material on Indian Accounting Standard (Ind AS) 108 Operating Segment

Appendix 18: List of publications of the Institute of Cost & Works Accountants of India

A. GUIDELINES & OTHER PUBLICATIONS

1. Guidelines on Certification of Cash
2. Compensatory Support
3. Compendium-Fields for Practicing
4. Cost Accountants (Ed. 96)
5. Fields for Practicing Cost Accountants (Abridged) (Ed. 96)
6. Guidelines on Inventory Valuation
7. Guidelines on Activity Based Costing
8. Guidance Notes on Valuation Audit under Excise Law
9. Guidelines on Cost Audit 3rd revised edition
10. Cost Audit Social Objectives
11. Cost Audit (Report) Rules, 1996
12. Guidance Note on Cost Management in Higher Education
13. Guidance Note on Cost Management in Healthcare Sector
14. Guidance Note on Anti Profiteering.

B. RESEARCH PUBLICATIONS

1. Financing Assets Replacement
2. Inflation Accounting As a Tool to Fight Inflation
3. Inflation Accounting Tools and Techniques
4. Management Accounting Problems in Small Scale Industries
5. Glossary of Management Accounting Terms
6. Corporate Capital Structure and Cost of Capital
7. Cost and Quality Control
8. Management Information Reports for Operating Managers
9. Cost Accounting in Commercial Banking Industry
10. Farm Management Accounting and Control
11. Management Accountant and the Computer
12. An Introduction to Cost Accounting in Commercial Banking Industry
13. Management and Accounting for Research and Development - The Indian Praxis
14. Research Bulletin (Biannual each issue)
15. Guidelines on Capacity Determination (Revised)
16. Profit Planning (ed. 96)
17. Mutual Funds in India (ed. 96)
18. Human Resource Accounting (ed.96)

19. Performance Enablers for MSMEs- 3P Model, Performance, Productivity And Profitability.

C. INDUSTRY PUBLICATIONS

1. Cost Accounting Records Rules and Cost Audit (Report) Rules
2. Cycle Industry
3. Cement Industry
4. Electric Lamp
5. Electric Motor
6. Automobile Battery Industry
7. Caustic Soda
8. Tyre and Tube Industry
9. Tractor Industry
10. Motor Vehicles Industry
11. Room Air-Conditioner Industry
12. Refrigerator Industry
13. Electric Fan Industry
14. Aluminium Industry
15. Dyes
16. Vanaspati Industry
17. Industrial Alcohol
18. Sugar Industry
19. Paper Industry
20. Nylon
21. Cotton Textile Industry
22. Soda Ash Industry
23. Jute Industry
24. Rayon Industry
25. Dry Cell Battery Industry
26. Power Driven Pump Industry
27. Cables and Conductors Industry
28. Infant Milk Food Industry
29. Sulphuric Acid Industry
30. Steel Tubes & Pipes Industry
31. Formulation Industry
32. Mini Steel Plant Industry
33. Fertilizer Industry
34. Insecticides (Tech Grade) Industry
35. Bulk Drugs (revised)

Appendix 19: Statutory provisions in Customs law relating to Customs Audit

CUSTOMS ACT, 1962

SECTION 99A - Audit

The proper officer may carry out the audit of assessment of imported goods or export goods or of an auditee under this Act either in his office or in the premises of the auditee in such manner as may be prescribed.

Explanation— For the purposes of this section, "auditee" means a person who is subject to an audit under this section and includes an importer or exporter or custodian approved under section 45 or licensee of a warehouse and any other person concerned directly or indirectly in clearing, forwarding, stocking, carrying, selling or purchasing of imported goods or export goods or dutiable goods.

(Chapter XIIA inserted by section 90 of the Finance Act, 2018 (13 of 2018) w.e.f. 29.03.2018.)

SECTION 45 - Restrictions on custody and removal of imported goods

(1) Save as otherwise provided in any law for the time being in force, all imported goods unloaded in a customs area shall remain in the custody of such person as may be approved by the Principal Commissioner of Customs or Commissioner of Customs until they are cleared for home consumption or are warehoused or are transhipped in accordance with the provisions of Chapter VIII.

(2) The person having custody of any imported goods in a customs area, whether under the provisions of sub-section (1) or under any law for the time being in force,

(a) shall keep a record of such goods and send a copy thereof to the proper officer;

(b) shall not permit such goods to be removed from the customs area or otherwise dealt with, except under and in accordance with the permission in writing of the proper officer or in such manner as may be prescribed.

(3) Notwithstanding anything contained in any law for the time being in force, if any imported goods are pilferred after unloading thereof in a customs area while in the custody of a person referred to in sub-section (1), that person shall be liable to pay duty on such goods at the rate prevailing on the date of delivery of an 4[arrival manifest or import manifest] or, as the case may be, an import report to the proper officer under section 30 for the arrival of the conveyance in which the said goods were carried.

CUSTOMS AUDIT REGULATIONS, 2018

Notification No. 45/2018-Customs (N.T.) dated 24th May, 2018

G.S.R.484(E). - In exercise of the powers conferred by clause (k) of section 157, read with section 99A and clause (ii) of sub-section (2) of section 158, of the Customs Act, 1962 (52 of 1962) and in supersession of the On-site Post Clearance Audit at the Premises of Importers and Exporters Regulation, 2011, except as respect things done or omitted to be done before such supersession, the Central Board of Indirect Taxes and Customs hereby makes the following regulations, namely: -

1. Short title and commencement.

(1) These regulations may be called the Customs Audit Regulations, 2018.

(2) They shall come into force on the date of their publication in the Official Gazette.

2. Definitions.

In these regulations, unless the context otherwise requires, -

(a) **"Act"** means the Customs Act, 1962 (52 of 1962);

(b) **"audit"** includes examination or verification of declaration, record, entry, document, import or export licence, authorisation, scrip, certificate, permission etc., books of account, test or analysis reports, and any other document relating to imported goods or export goods or dutiable goods, and may include inspection of sample and goods, if such sample or goods are available and where necessary, drawl of samples;

(c) **"auditee"** means a person who is subject to an audit under section 99A of the Act and includes an importer or exporter or custodian approved under section 45 or licensee of a warehouse and any other person concerned directly or indirectly in clearing, forwarding, stocking, carrying, selling or purchasing of imported goods or export goods or dutiable goods;

(d) **"audit report"** includes the audit findings in the report prepared after the audit containing details about objections raised by the proper officer and explanation given by the auditee, if any;

(e) **"books of account"** includes ledgers, day-books, cash books, account-books, other accounts related record whether kept in written or printed form or stored electronically;

(f) **"electronic records"** means data or record stored in any form and manner relevant for the purpose of Audit under section 99A of the Act;

(g) **"premises"** includes the registered office, branch office, warehouse, factory, or any other premises at which, imported goods or export goods or dutiable goods or books of account or records of transaction or other related documents, in relation to the said goods are ordinarily kept, for any purpose by an auditee.

(h) Words and expressions used and not defined herein but defined in the Act, shall have the same meaning respectively, assigned to them in the Act.

3. Auditee to preserve and make available relevant documents

(1) The auditee shall preserve and on request by the proper officer make available in a timely manner, for the purposes of audit, true and correct information, records including electronic records, documents or accounts maintained in compliance of the provisions of the Act, rule or regulations, made there under or any other law for the time being in force, maintained for a minimum period of five years in relation to imported goods or export goods or dutiable goods.

(2) The auditee shall render assistance to the proper officer and his team of officers in the discharge of their official duty and shall in no case refuse or obstruct the proper officer or his team of officers in discharge of their official duty.

4. Selection for Audit

The selection of auditee or the selection of import declarations or export declarations, as the case may be, for the purposes of audit shall primarily be based on risk evaluation through appropriate selectivity criteria.

5. Manner of conducting audit

(1) The proper officer may conduct audit either in his office or in certain cases at the premises of an auditee.

(2) The proper officer may, where considered necessary, request the auditee to furnish documents, information or record including electronic record, as may be relevant to audit.

(3) The proper officer shall give not less than fifteen days advance notice to the auditee to conduct audit at the premises of the auditee.

(4) The proper officer may, where considered necessary, inspect the imported goods or export goods or dutiable goods at the premises of the auditee or request the auditee to produce sample, if available, with him.

(5) The proper officer shall inform the auditee of the objections, if any, before preparing the audit report to provide him an opportunity to offer clarifications with supporting documents.

(6) Where the auditee is in agreement with the audit findings, he may make voluntary payments of duty, interest or other sums, due, if any, in part or in full and the proper officer shall record the same in the audit report.

(7) Where the proper office has asked the auditee to furnish information, document, record or sample for the purposes of audit, it shall be mandatory for the proper officer to inform outcome of such audit to the auditee.

(8) The proper officer shall complete audit in cases where it is conducted at the premises of the auditee within thirty days from the date of starting of the audit.

Provided that the jurisdictional Commissioner of Customs may extend the period of completion of audit from thirty days to sixty days, by an order in writing.

6. Assistance of professionals

(1) If the proper officer, having regard to the nature and complexity of the audit, is of the opinion that the audit has to be done with the assistance of a professional like Chartered Accountant, Cost Accountant, an expert in the field of computer

sciences or information technology etc., may do so, with the previous approval of the Principal Commissioner/Commissioner of Customs.

7. Penalty

Any auditee, who contravenes any provision of these regulations or abets such contravention or fails to comply with any provision of these regulations with which it was his duty to comply, shall be liable to a penalty which may extend to fifty thousand Indian rupees.

Appendix 20: Annual Returns in Form 9 and 9A

Form GSTR - 9[1] [2]

[*See rule 80*]

Annual Return

Pt. I	Basic Details					
1	Financial Year					
2	GSTIN					
3A	Legal Name					
3B	Trade Name (if any)					
Pt. II	Details of Outward and inward supplies made during the financial year					
			(Amount in INR in all tables)			
	Nature of Supplies	Taxable Value	Central Tax	State Tax / UT Tax	Integrated Tax	Cess
	1	2	3	4	5	6
4	Details of advances, inward and outward supplies made during the financial year on which tax is payable					
A	Supplies made to un-registered persons (B2C)					
B	Supplies made to registered persons (B2B)					
C	Zero rated supply (Export) on payment of tax (except supplies to SEZs)					
D	Supply to SEZs on payment of tax					
E	Deemed Exports					
F	Advances on which tax has been paid but invoice has not been issued (not covered under (A) to (E) above)					
G	Inward supplies on which tax is to be paid on reverse charge basis					

1 Inserted vide Notf no. 39/2018-CT dt. 04.09.2018

2 Substituted vide Notf no. 74/2018-CT dt 31.12.2018

H	Sub-total (A to G above)					
I	Credit Notes issued in respect of transactions specified in (B) to (E) above (-)					
J	Debit Notes issued in respect of transactions specified in (B) to (E) above (+)					
K	Supplies / tax declared through Amendments (+)					
L	Supplies / tax reduced through Amendments (-)					
M	Sub-total (I to L above)					
N	Supplies and advances on which tax is to be paid (H + M) above					
5	Details of Outward supplies made during the financial year on which tax is not payable					
A	Zero rated supply (Export) without payment of tax					
B	Supply to SEZs without payment of tax					
C	Supplies on which tax is to be paid by the recipient on reverse charge basis					
D	Exempted					
E	Nil Rated					
F	Non-GST supply (includes ‘no supply’)					
G	Sub-total (A to F above)					
H	Credit Notes issued in respect of transactions specified in A to F above (-)					
I	Debit Notes issued in respect of transactions specified in A to F above (+)					
J	Supplies declared through Amendments (+)					
K	Supplies reduced through Amendments (-)					
L	Sub-Total (H to K above)					
M	Turnover on which tax is not to be paid (G + L above)					
N	Total Turnover (including advances) (4N + 5M - 4G above)					

Pt. III	Details of ITC for the financial year					
	Description	Type	Central Tax	State Tax / UT Tax	Integrat ed Tax	Cess
	1	2	3	4	5	6
6	Details of ITC availed during the financial year					
A	Total amount of input tax credit availed through FORM GSTR-3B (sum total of Table 4A of FORM GSTR-3B)		<Auto>	<Auto>	<Auto>	<Auto>
B	Inward supplies (other than imports and inward supplies liable to reverse charge but includes services received from SEZs)	Inputs				
		Capital Goods				
		Input Services				
C	Inward supplies received from unregistered persons liable to reverse charge (other than B above) on which tax is paid & ITC availed	Inputs				
		Capital Goods				
		Input Services				
D	Inward supplies received from	Inputs				
	registered persons liable to reverse charge (other than B above) on which tax is paid and ITC availed	Capital Goods				
		Input Services				
E	Import of goods (including supplies from SEZs)	Inputs				
		Capital Goods				
F	Import of services (excluding inward supplies from SEZs)					
G	Input Tax credit received from ISD					
H	Amount of ITC reclaimed (other than B above) under the provisions of the Act					
I	Sub-total (B to H above)					
J	Difference (I - A above)					
K	Transition Credit through TRAN-I (including revisions if any)					
L	Transition Credit through TRAN-II					
M	Any other ITC availed but not specified above					
N	Sub-total (K to M above)					
O	Total ITC availed (I + N above)					
7	Details of ITC Reversed and Ineligible ITC for the financial year					
A	As per Rule 37					
B	As per Rule 39					

C	As per Rule 42						
D	As per Rule 43						
E	As per section 17(5)						
F	Reversal of TRAN-I credit						
G	Reversal of TRAN-II credit						
H	Other reversals (pl. specify)						
I	Total ITC Reversed (Sum of A to H above)						
J	Net ITC Available for Utilization (6O - 7I)						
8	Other ITC related information						
A	ITC as per GSTR-2A (Table 3 & 5 thereof)			<Auto>	<Auto>	<Auto>	<Auto>
B	ITC as per sum total of 6(B) and 6(H) above			<Auto>			
C	ITC on inward supplies (other than imports and inward supplies liable to reverse charge but includes services received from SEZs) received during 2017-18 but availed during April to September, 2018						
D	Difference [A-(B+C)]						
E	ITC available but not availed						
F	ITC available but ineligible						
G	IGST paid on import of goods (including supplies from SEZ)						
H	IGST credit availed on import of goods (as per 6(E) above)			<Auto>			
I	Difference (G-H)						
J	ITC available but not availed on import of goods (Equal to I)						
K	Total ITC to be lapsed in current financial year (E + F + J)			<Auto>	<Auto>	<Auto>	<Auto>
Pt. IV	**Details of tax paid as declared in returns filed during the financial year**						
9	Description	Tax Payable	Paid through cash	Paid through ITC			
				Centra l Tax	State Tax / UT Tax	Integrated Tax	Cess
	1	2	3	4	5	6	7
	Integrated Tax						
	Central Tax						
	State/UT Tax						
	Cess						

	Interest						
	Late fee						
	Penalty						
	Other						

Pt. V	**Particulars of the transactions for the previous FY declared in returns of April to September of current FY or upto date of filing of annual return of previous FY whichever is earlier**					
	Description	Taxable Value	Centra l Tax	State Tax / UT Tax	Integrated Tax	Cess
	1	2	3	4	5	6
10	Supplies / tax declared through Amendments (+) (net of debit notes)					
11	Supplies / tax reduced through Amendments (-) (net of credit notes)					
12	Reversal of ITC availed during previous financial year					
13	ITC availed for the previous financial year					

14	Differential tax paid on account of declaration in 10 & 11 above		
	Description	Payable	Paid
	1	2	3
	Integrated Tax		
	Central Tax		
	State/UT Tax		
	Cess		
	Interest		

Pt. VI 15	**Other Information Particulars of Demands and Refunds**							
	Details	Central Tax	State Tax/ UT Tax	Integrated Tax	Cess	Interest	Penalty	Late Fee / Others
	1	2	3	4	5			
A	Total Refund claimed							

B	Total Refund sanctioned							
C	Total Refund Rejected							
D	Total Refund Pending							
E	Total demand of taxes							
F	Total taxes paid in respect of E above							
G	Total demands pending out of E above							
Information on supplies received from composition taxpayers, deemed supply under section 143 and goods sent on approval basis								
	Details			Taxable Value	Centra l Tax	State Tax / UT Tax	Integrat ed Tax	Cess
	1			2	3	4	5	6
A	Supplies received from Composition taxpayers							
B	Deemed supply under Section 143							
	Goods sent on approval basis but not returned							
17	HSN Wise Summary of outward supplies							
HSN Code	UQC	Total Quant ity	Taxable Value	Rate of Tax	Central Tax	State Tax/ UT Tax	Integrated Tax	Cess
1	2	3	4	5	6	7	8	9
18	HSN Wise Summary of Inward supplies							
HSN Code	UQC	Total Quant ity	Taxable Value	Rate of Tax	Central Tax	State Tax/ UT Tax	Integrated Tax	Cess
1	2	3	4	5	6	7	8	9

19	Late fee payable and paid		
	Description	Payable	Paid
	1	2	3
A	Central Tax		
B	State Tax		

Verification:

I hereby solemnly affirm and declare that the information given herein above is true and correct to the best of my knowledge and belief and nothing has been concealed there from and in case of any reduction in output tax liability the benefit thereof has been/will be passed on to the recipient of supply.

Signature

Place — Name of Authorised Signatory

Date — Designation/Status

Instructions: -

1. Terms used:
   a. GSTIN: Goods and Services Tax Identification Number
   b. UQC: Unit Quantity Code
   c. HSN: Harmonized System of Nomenclature Code
2. It is mandatory to file all your **FORM GSTR-1** and **FORM GSTR-3B** for the FY 201718 before filing this return. The details for the period between July 2017 to March 2018 are to be provided in this return.
3. It may be noted that additional liability for the FY 2017-18 not declared in **FORM GSTR-1** and **FORM GSTR-3B** may be declared in this return. However, taxpayers cannot claim input tax credit unclaimed during FY 2017-18 through this return.
4. Part II consists of the details of all outward supplies & advances received during the financial year for which the annual return is filed. It may be noted that all the supplies for which payment has been made through **FORM GSTR-3B** between July 2017 to March 2018 shall be declared in this part. The instructions to fill Part II are as follows:

Table No.	Instructions
4A	Aggregate value of supplies made to consumers and unregistered persons on which tax has been paid shall be declared here. These will include details of supplies made through E-Commerce operators and are to be declared as net of credit notes or debit notes issued in this regard. Table 5, Table 7 along with respective amendments in Table 9 and Table 10 of **FORM GSTR-1** may be used for filling up these details.
4B	Aggregate value of supplies made to registered persons (including supplies made to UINs) on which tax has been paid shall be declared

Table No.	Instructions
	here. These will include supplies made through E-Commerce operators but shall not include supplies on which tax is to be paid by the recipient on reverse charge basis. Details of debit and credit notes are to be mentioned separately. Table 4A and Table 4C of **FORM GSTR-1** may be used for filling up these details.
4C	Aggregate value of exports (except supplies to SEZs) on which tax has been paid shall be declared here. Table 6A of **FORM GSTR-1** may be used for filling up these details.
4D	Aggregate value of supplies to SEZs on which tax has been paid shall be declared here. Table 6B of GSTR-1 may be used for filling up these details.
4E	Aggregate value of supplies in the nature of deemed exports on which tax has been paid shall be declared here. Table 6C of **FORM GSTR-1** may be used for filling up these details.
4F	Details of all unadjusted advances i.e. advance has been received and tax has been paid but invoice has not been issued in the current year shall be declared here. Table 11A of **FORM GSTR-1** may be used for filling up these details.
4G	Aggregate value of all inward supplies (including advances and net of credit and debit notes) on which tax is to be paid by the recipient (i.e.by the person filing the annual return) on reverse charge basis. This shall include supplies received from registered persons, unregistered persons on which tax is levied on reverse charge basis. This shall also include aggregate value of all import of services. Table 3.1(d) of **FORM GSTR-3B** may be used for filling up these details.
4I	Aggregate value of credit notes issued in respect of B to B supplies (4B), exports (4C), supplies to SEZs (4D) and deemed exports (4E) shall be declared here. Table 9B of **FORM GSTR-1** may be used for filling up these details.
4J	Aggregate value of debit notes issued in respect of B to B supplies (4B), exports (4C), supplies to SEZs (4D) and deemed exports (4E) shall be declared here. Table 9B of **FORM GSTR-1** may be used for filling up these details.
4K & 4L	Details of amendments made to B to B supplies (4B), exports (4C), supplies to SEZs (4D) and deemed exports (4E), credit notes (4I), debit notes (4J) and refund vouchers shall be declared here. Table 9A and Table 9C of **FORM GSTR-1** may be used for filling up these details.
5A	Aggregate value of exports (except supplies to SEZs) on which tax has not been paid shall be declared here. Table 6A of **FORM GSTR-1** may be used for filling up these details.

Table No.	Instructions
5B	Aggregate value of supplies to SEZs on which tax has not been paid shall be declared here. Table 6B of GSTR-1 may be used for filling up these details.
5C	Aggregate value of supplies made to registered persons on which tax is payable by the recipient on reverse charge basis. Details of debit and credit notes are to be mentioned separately. Table 4B of FORM GSTR-1 may be used for filling up these details.
5D,5E and 5F	Aggregate value of exempted, Nil Rated and Non-GST supplies shall be declared here. Table 8 of FORM GSTR-1 may be used for filling up these details. The value of "no supply" shall be declared under Non-GST supply (5F).
5H	Aggregate value of credit notes issued in respect of supplies declared in 5A, 5B, 5C, 5D, 5E and 5F shall be declared here. Table 9B of FORM GSTR-1 may be used for filling up these details.
5I	Aggregate value of debit notes issued in respect of supplies declared in 5A, 5B, 5C, 5D, 5E and 5F shall be declared here. Table 9B of FORM GSTR-1 may be used for filling up these details.
5J & 5K	Details of amendments made to exports (except supplies to SEZs) and supplies to SEZs on which tax has not been paid shall be declared here. Table 9A and Table 9C of FORM GSTR-1 may be used for filling up these details.
5N	Total turnover including the sum of all the supplies (with additional supplies and amendments) on which tax is payable and tax is not payable shall be declared here. This shall also include amount of advances on which tax is paid but invoices have not been issued in the current year. However, this shall not include the aggregate value of inward supplies on which tax is paid by the recipient (i.e. by the person filing the annual return) on reverse charge basis.

5. Part III consists of the details of all input tax credit availed and reversed in the financial year for which the annual return is filed. The instructions to fill Part III are as follows:

Table No.	Instructions
6A	Total input tax credit availed in Table 4A of **FORM GSTR-3B** for the taxpayer would be auto-populated here.
6B	Aggregate value of input tax credit availed on all inward supplies except those on which tax is payable on reverse charge basis but includes supply of services received from SEZs shall be declared here. It may be noted that the total ITC availed is to be classified as ITC on inputs, capital goods and input services. Table 4(A)(5) of **FORM GSTR-3B** may be used for filling up these details. This shall not include ITC which was availed, reversed and then reclaimed in the ITC ledger. This is to be declared separately under 6(H) below.

Table No.	Instructions
6C	Aggregate value of input tax credit availed on all inward supplies received from unregistered persons (other than import of services) on which tax is payable on reverse charge basis shall be declared here. It may be noted that the total ITC availed is to be classified as ITC on inputs, capital goods and input services. Table 4(A)(3) of **FORM GSTR-3B** may be used for filling up these details.
6D	Aggregate value of input tax credit availed on all inward supplies received from registered persons on which tax is payable on reverse charge basis shall be declared here. It may be noted that the total ITC availed is to be classified as ITC on inputs, capital goods and input services. Table 4(A)(3) of **FORM GSTR-3B** may be used for filling up these details.
6E	Details of input tax credit availed on import of goods including supply of goods received from SEZs shall be declared here. It may be noted that the total ITC availed is to be classified as ITC on inputs and capital goods. Table 4(A)(1) of **FORM GSTR-3B** may be used for filling up these details.
6F	Details of input tax credit availed on import of services (excluding inward supplies from SEZs) shall be declared here. Table 4(A)(2) of **FORM GSTR- 3B** may be used for filling up these details.
6G	Aggregate value of input tax credit received from input service distributor shall be declared here. Table 4(A)(4) of FORM GSTR-3B may be used for filling up these details.
6H	Aggregate value of input tax credit availed, reversed and reclaimed under the provisions of the Act shall be declared here.
6J	The difference between the total amount of input tax credit availed through **FORM GSTR-3B** and input tax credit declared in row B to H shall be declared here. Ideally, this amount should be zero.
6K	Details of transition credit received in the electronic credit ledger on filing of **FORM GST TRAN-I** including revision of TRAN-I (whether upwards or downwards), if any shall be declared here.
6L	Details of transition credit received in the electronic credit ledger after filing of **FORM GST TRAN-II** shall be declared here.
6M	Details of ITC availed but not covered in any of heads specified under 6B to 6L above shall be declared here. Details of ITC availed through **FORM ITC- 01** and **FORM ITC-02** in the financial year shall be declared here.
7E, 7F, 7G and 7H	This column should also contain details of any input tax credit reversed under section 17(5) of the CGST Act, 2017 and details of ineligible transition credit claimed under FORM GST TRAN-I or FORM GST TRAN-II and then subsequently reversed. Table 4(B) of FORM GSTR-

Table No.	Instructions
	3B may be used for filling up these details. Any ITC reversed through FORM ITC -03 shall be declared in 7H. If the amount stated in Table 4D of FORM GSTR-3B was not included in table 4A of FORM GSTR-3B, then no entry should be made in table 7E of FORM GSTR-9. However, if amount mentioned in table 4D of FORM GSTR-3B was included in table 4A of FORM GSTR-3B, then entry will come in 7E of FORM GSTR-9.
8A	The total credit available for inwards supplies (other than imports and inwards supplies liable to reverse charge but includes services received from SEZs) pertaining to FY 2017-18 and reflected in FORM GSTR-2A (table 3 & 5 only) shall be auto-populated in this table. This would be the aggregate of all the input tax credit that has been declared by the corresponding suppliers in their FORM GSTR-1.
8B	The input tax credit as declared in Table 6B and 6H shall be auto-populated here.
8C	Aggregate value of input tax credit availed on all inward supplies (except those on which tax is payable on reverse charge basis but includes supply of services received from SEZs) received during July 2017 to March 2018 but credit on which was availed between April to September 2018 shall be declared here. Table 4(A)(5) of FORM GSTR-3B may be used for filling up these details.
8D	Aggregate value of the input tax credit which was available in FORM GSTR- 2A (table 3 & 5 only) but not availed in FORM GSTR-3B returns shall be computed based on values of 8A, 8B and 8C. However, there may be circumstances where the credit availed in FORM GSTR-3B was greater than the credit available in FORM GSTR-2A. In such cases, the value in row 8D shall be negative.
8E & 8F	The credit which was available and not availed in FORM GSTR-3B and the credit was not availed in FORM GSTR-3B as the same was ineligible shall be declared here. Ideally, if 8D is positive, the sum of 8E and 8F shall be equal to 8D.
8G	Aggregate value of IGST paid at the time of imports (including imports from SEZs) during the financial year shall be declared here.
8H	The input tax credit as declared in Table 6E shall be auto-populated here.
8K	The total input tax credit which shall lapse for the current financial year shall be computed in this row.

6. Part IV is the actual tax paid during the financial year. Payment of tax under Table 6.1 of **FORM GSTR-3B** may be used for filling up these details.
7. Part V consists of particulars of transactions for the previous financial year but paid in the **FORM GSTR-3B** of April to September of current FY or date of filing of Annual Return for previous financial year (for example in the annual return for the FY 2017-18, the transactions declared in April to September 2018

for the FY 2017-18 shall be declared), whichever is earlier. The instructions to fill Part V are as follows:

Table No.	Instructions
10 & 11	Details of additions or amendments to any of the supplies already declared in the returns of the previous financial year but such amendments were furnished in Table 9A, Table 9B and Table 9C of **FORM GSTR-1** of April to September of the current financial year or date of filing of Annual Return for the previous financial year, whichever is earlier shall be declared here.
12	Aggregate value of reversal of ITC which was availed in the previous financial year but reversed in returns filed for the months of April to September of the current financial year or date of filing of Annual Return for previous financial year , whichever is earlier shall be declared here. Table 4(B) of **FORM GSTR-3B** may be used for filling up these details.
13	Details of ITC for goods or services received in the previous financial year but ITC for the same was availed in returns filed for the months of April to September of the current financial year or date of filing of Annual Return for the previous financial year whichever is earlier shall be declared here. Table 4(A) of **FORM GSTR-3B** may be used for filling up these details. However, any ITC which was reversed in the FY 2017-18 as per second proviso to subsection (2) of section 16 but was reclaimed in FY 2018-19, the details of such ITC reclaimed shall be furnished in the annual return for FY 2018-19.

8. Part VI consists of details of other information. The instructions to fill Part VI are as follows:

Table No.	Instructions
15A, 15B, 15C and 15D	Aggregate value of refunds claimed, sanctioned, rejected and pending for processing shall be declared here. Refund claimed will be the aggregate value of all the refund claims filed in the financial year and will include refunds which have been sanctioned, rejected or are pending for processing. Refund sanctioned means the aggregate value of all refund sanction orders. Refund pending will be the aggregate amount in all refund application for which acknowledgement has been received and will exclude provisional refunds received. These will not include details of non-GST refund claims.
15E, 15F and 15G	Aggregate value of demands of taxes for which an order confirming the demand has been issued by the adjudicating authority shall be declared here. Aggregate value of taxes paid out of the total value of confirmed demand as declared in 15E above shall be declared here. Aggregate value of demands pending recovery out of 15E above shall be declared here.
16A	Aggregate value of supplies received from composition taxpayers shall be declared here. Table 5 of FORM GSTR-3B may be used for filling up

Table No.	Instructions
	these details.
16B	Aggregate value of all deemed supplies from the principal to the job-worker in terms of sub-section (3) and sub-section (4) of Section 143 of the CGST Act shall be declared here.
16C	Aggregate value of all deemed supplies for goods which were sent on approval basis but were not returned to the principal supplier within one eighty days of such supply shall be declared here.
17 & 18	Summary of supplies effected and received against a particular HSN code to be reported only in this table. It will be optional for taxpayers having annual turnover upto ? 1.50 Cr. It will be mandatory to report HSN code at two digits level for taxpayers having annual turnover in the preceding year above ? 1.50 Cr but upto ? 5.00 Cr and at four digits' level for taxpayers having annual turnover above ? 5.00 Cr. UQC details to be furnished only for supply of goods. Quantity is to be reported net of returns. Table 12 of FORM GSTR- 1 may be used for filling up details in Table 17. It may be noted that this summary details are required to be declared only for those inward supplies which in value independently account for 10 % or more of the total value of inward supplies.
19	Late fee will be payable if annual return is filed after the due date.

9. Towards the end of the return, taxpayers shall be given an option to pay any additional liability declared in this form, through **FORM DRC-03**. Taxpayers shall select "Annual Return" in the drop down provided in **FORM DRC-03**. It may be noted that such liability can be paid through electronic cash ledger only

Form GSTR - 9A[3] [4]

[*See rule 80*]

Annual Return (For Composition Taxpayer)

Pt. I	**Basic Details**						
1	Financial Year						
2	GSTIN						
3A	Legal Name	<Auto>					
3B	Trade Name (if any)	<Auto>					
4	Period of composition scheme during the year (From — To —)						
5	Aggregate Turnover of Previous Financial Year						
	(Amount in ? in all tables)						
Pt. II	**Details of outward and inward supplies made during the financial year**						
	Description	Turnover	Rate of Tax	Central Tax	State / UT Tax	Integrated tax	Cess
	1	2	3	4	5	6	7
6	Details of Outward supplies made during the financial year						
A	Taxable						
B	Exempted, Nil-rated						
C	Total						
7	Details of inward	supplies on which tax is payable on reverse charge basis (net of debit/credit notes) for the financial year					
	Description	Taxable Value	Central Tax		State Tax / UT Tax	Integrated Tax	Cess
	1	2	3		4	5	6
A	Inward supplies liable to reverse charge received from registered persons						
B	Inward supplies liable to reverse charge received from unregistered persons						
C	Import of services						
D	Net Tax Payable on (A), (B) and (C) above						
8	Details of other inward supplies for the financial year						
A	Inward supplies from registered persons (other than 7A above)						

3 Inserted vide Notf no. 39/2018-CT dt. 04.09.2018

4 Substituted vide Notf no. 74/2018-CT dt 31.12.2018

B	Import of Goods					
Pt. III	**Details of tax paid as declared in returns filed during the financial year**					
9	Description	Total tax payable	Paid			
	1	2	3			
	Integrated Tax					
	Central Tax					
	State/UT Tax					
	Cess					
	Interest					
	Late fee					
	Penalty					
Pt. IV	**Particulars of the transactions for the previous FY declared in returns of April to September of current FY or upto date of filing of annual return of previous FY whichever is earlier**					
	Description	Turnover	Central Tax	State Tax / UT Tax	Integrated Tax	Cess
	1	2	3	4	5	6
10	Supplies / tax (outward) declared through Amendments (+) (net of debit notes)					
11	Inward supplies liable to reverse charge declared through Amendments (+) (net of debit notes)					
12	Supplies / tax (outward) reduced through Amendments (-) (net of credit notes)					
13	Inward supplies liable to reverse charge reduced through Amendments (-) (net of credit notes)					
14	Differential tax paid on account of declaration made in 10, 11, 12 & 13 above					
	Description	Payable	Paid			
	1	2	3			
	Integrated Tax					
	Central Tax					
	State/UT Tax					
	Cess					
	Interest					

Pt. V 15	**Other Information Particulars of Demands and Refunds**							
	Description	Central Tax	State Tax / UT Tax	Integrated Tax	Cess	Interest	Penalty	Late Fee/ Others
	1	2	3	4	5	6	7	8
A	Total Refund claimed							

B	Total Refund sanctioned							
C	Total Refund Rejected							
D	Total Refund Pending							
E	Total demand of taxes							
F	Total taxes paid in respect of E above							
G	Total demands pending out of E above							

16	Details of credit reversed or availed				
	Description	Central Tax	State Tax/ UT Tax	Integrated Tax	Cess
	1	2	3	4	5
A	Credit reversed on opting in the composition scheme (-)				
B	Credit availed on opting out of the composition scheme (+)				

17	Late fee payable and paid		
	Description	Payable	Paid
	1	2	3
A	Central Tax		
B	State Tax		

Verification:

I hereby solemnly affirm and declare that the information given herein above is true and correct to the best of my knowledge and belief and nothing has been concealed there from and in case of any reduction in output tax liability the benefit thereof has been/will be passed on to the recipient of supply.

Signature

Name of Authorised Signatory

Place

Date

Designation / Status

Instructions: -

1. It is mandatory to file all your **FORM GSTR-4** for the FY 2017-18 before filing this return. The details for the period between July 2017 to March 2018 shall be provided in this return.
2. It may be noted that additional liability for the FY 2017-18 not declared in **FORM GSTR-4** may be declared in this return.
3. Part I consists of basic details of taxpayer. The instructions to fill Part I are as follows:

Table No.	Instructions
5	Aggregate turnover for the previous financial year is the turnover of the financial year previous to the year for which the return is being filed. For example for the annual return for FY 2017-18, the aggregate turnover of FY 2016-17 shall be entered into this table. It is the sum total of turnover of all taxpayers registered on the same PAN.

4. Part II consists of the details of all outward and inward supplies in the financial year for which the annual return is filed. The instructions to fill Part II are as follows:

Table No.	Instructions
6A	Aggregate value of all outward supplies net of debit notes / credit notes, net of advances and net of goods returned for the entire financial year shall be declared here. Table 6 and Table 7 of **FORM GSTR-4** may be used for filling up these details.
6B	Aggregate value of exempted, Nil Rated and Non-GST supplies shall be declared here.
7A	Aggregate value of all inward supplies received from registered persons on which tax is payable on reverse charge basis shall be declared here. Table 4B, Table 5 and Table 8A of **FORM GSTR-4** may be used for filling up these details.
7B	Aggregate value of all inward supplies received from unregistered persons (other than import of services) on which tax is payable on reverse charge basis shall be declared here. Table 4C, Table 5 and Table 8A of **FORM GSTR-4** may be used for filling up these details.
7C	Aggregate value of all services imported during the financial year shall be declared here. Table 4D and Table 5 of **FORM GSTR-4** may be used for filling up these details.
8A	Aggregate value of all inward supplies received from registered persons on which tax is payable by the supplier shall be declared here. Table 4A and Table 5 of **FORM GSTR-4** may be used for filling up these details.
8B	Aggregate value of all goods imported during the financial year shall be declared here.

5. Part IV consists of the details of amendments made for the supplies of the previous financial year in the returns of April to September of the current FY or

date of filing of Annual Return for previous financial year (for example in the annual return for the FY 2017-18, the transactions declared in April to September 2018 for the FY 2017-18 shall be declared), whichever is earlier. The instructions to fill Part V are as follows:

Table No.	Instructions
10,11,12,13 and 14	Details of additions or amendments to any of the supplies already declared in the returns of the previous financial year but such amendments were furnished in Table 5 (relating to inward suppiies) or Table 7 (relating to outward supplies) of **FORM GSTR- 4** of April to September of the current financial year or upto the date of filing of Annual Return for the previous financial year, whichever is earlier shall be declared here.

6. Part V consists of details of other information. The instruction to fill Part V are as follows

Table No.	Instructions
15A, 15B, 15C and 15D	Aggregate value of refunds claimed, sanctioned, rejected and pending for processing shall be declared here. Refund claimed will be the aggregate value of all the refund claims filed in the financial year and will include refunds which have been sanctioned, rejected or are pending for processing. Refund sanctioned means the aggregate value of all refund sanction orders. Refund pending will be the aggregate amount in all refund application for which acknowledgement has been received and will exclude provisional refunds received. These will not include details of non-GST refund claims.
15E, 15F and 15G	Aggregate value of demands of taxes for which an order confirming the demand has been issued by the adjudicating authority has been issued shall be declared here. Aggregate value of taxes paid out of the total value of confirmed demand in 15E above shall be declared here. Aggregate value of demands pending recovery out of 15E above shall be declared here.
16A	Aggregate value of all credit reversed when a person opts to pay tax under the composition scheme shall be declared here. The details furnished in **FORM ITC-03** may be used for filling up these details.
16B	Aggregate value of all the credit availed when a registered person opts out of the composition scheme shall be declared here. The details furnished in **FORM ITC-01** may be used for filling up these details.
17	Late fee will be payable if annual return is filed after the due date.”;

7. Towards the end of the return, taxpayers shall be given an option to pay any additional liability declared in this form, through **FORM DRC-03**. Taxpayers shall select “Annual Return” in the drop down provided in **FORM DRC-03**. It may be noted that such liability shall be paid through electronic cash ledger only.

Appendix 21: Reconciliation Statement and Certification in Form 9C

Form GSTR-9C[5] [6]

See rule 80(3)

PART - A - Reconciliation Statement

Pt. I	**Basic Details**		
1	Financial Year		
2	GSTIN		
3A	Legal Name	<Auto>	
3B	Trade Name (if any)	<Auto>	
4	Are you liable to audit under any Act? <<Please specify>>		
	(Amount in ? in all tables)		
Pt. II	**Reconciliation of turnover declared in audited Annual Financial Statement with turnover declared in Annual Return (GSTR9)**		
5	Reconciliation of Gross Turnover		
A	Turnover (including exports) as per audited financial statements for the State / UT (For multi-GSTIN units under same PAN the turnover shall be derived from the audited Annual Financial Statement)		
B	Unbilled revenue at the beginning of Financial Year	(+)	
C	Unadjusted advances at the end of the Financial Year	(+)	
D	Deemed Supply under Schedule I	(+)	
E	Credit Notes issued after the end of the financial year but reflected in the annual return	(-)	
F	Trade Discounts accounted for in the audited Annual Financial Statement but are not permissible under GST	(+)	
G	Turnover from April 2017 to June 2017	(-)	
H	Unbilled revenue at the end of Financial Year	(-)	
I	Unadjusted Advances at the beginning of the Financial Year	(-)	
J	Credit notes accounted for in the audited Annual Financial Statement but are not permissible under GST	(+)	
K	Adjustments on account of supply of goods by SEZ units to DTA Units	(-)	
L	Turnover for the period under composition scheme	(-)	
M	Adjustments in turnover under section 15 and rules thereunder	(+/-)	

5 Inserted vide Notf no. 49/2018-CT dt 13.09.2018

6 Substituted vide Notf no. 74/2018-CT dt 31.12.2018

N	Adjustments in turnover due to foreign exchange fluctuations	(+/-)	
O	Adjustments in turnover due to reasons not listed above	(+/-)	
P	Annual turnover after adjustments as above		<Auto>
Q	Turnover as declared in Annual Return (GSTR9)		
R	Un-Reconciled turnover (Q - P)		AT1
6	Reasons for Un - Reconciled difference in Annual Gross Turnover		
A	Reason 1	<<Text>>	
B	Reason 2	<<Text>>	
C	Reason 3	<<Text>>	
7	Reconciliation of Taxable Turnover		
A	Annual turnover after adjustments (from 5P above)		<Auto>
B	Value of Exempted, Nil Rated, Non-GST supplies, No-Supply turnover		
C	Zero rated supplies without payment of tax		
D	Supplies on which tax is to be paid by the recipient on reverse charge basis		
E	Taxable turnover as per adjustments above (A-B-C-D)		<Auto>
F	Taxable turnover as per liability declared in Annual Return (GSTR9)		
G	Unreconciled taxable turnover (F-E)		AT 2
8	Reasons for Un - Reconciled difference in taxable turnover		
A	Reason 1	<<Text>>	
B	Reason 2	<<Text>>	
C	Reason 3	<<Text>>	

Pt. III	**Reconciliation of tax paid**					
9	Reconciliation of rate wise liability and amount payable thereon					
	Tax payable					
	Description	Taxable Value	Central tax	State tax/ UT tax	Integrated Tax	Cess, if applicable
	1	2	3	4	5	6
A	5%					
B	5% (RC)					
C	12%					
D	12% (RC)					
E	18%					
F	18% (RC)					
G	28%					
H	28% (RC)					
I	3%					
J	0.25%					
K	0.10%					

L	Interest				
M	Late Fee				
N	Penalty				
O	Others				
P	Total amount to be paid as per tables above	<Auto>	<Auto>	<Auto>	<Auto>
Q	Total amount paid as declared in Annual Return (GSTR 9)				
R	Unreconciled payment of amount (PT1)				
10	Reasons for un-reconciled payment of amount				
A	Reason 1	<<Text>>			
B	Reason 2	<<Text>>			
C	Reason 3	<<Text>>			
11	Additional amount payable but not paid (due to reasons specified under Tables 6,8 and 10 above)				

			To be paid through Cash			
	Description	Taxable Value	Central tax	State tax / UT tax	Integrated tax	Cess, if applicable
	1	2	3	4	5	6
	5%					
	12%					
	18%					
	28%					
	3%					
	0.25%					
	0.10%					
	Interest					
	Late Fee					
	Penalty					
	Others (please specify)					

Pt. IV	**Reconciliation of Input Tax Credit (ITC)**	
12	Reconciliation of Net Input Tax Credit (ITC)	
A	ITC availed as per audited Annual Financial Statement for the State/ UT (For multi-GSTIN units under same PAN this should be derived from books of accounts)	

B	ITC booked in earlier Financial Years claimed in current Financial Year	(+)	
C	ITC booked in current Financial Year to be claimed in subsequent Financial Years	(-)	
D	ITC availed as per audited financial statements or books of account		<Auto>
E	ITC claimed in Annual Return (GSTR9)		
F	Un-reconciled ITC		ITC 1
13	Reasons for un-reconciled difference in ITC		
A	Reason 1	<<Text>>	
B	Reason 2	<<Text>>	
C	Reason 3	<<Text>>	

14	Reconciliation of ITC declared in Annual Return (GSTR9) with ITC availed on expenses as per audited Annual Financial Statement or books of account			
	Description	Value	Amount of Total ITC	Amount of eligible ITC availed
	1	2	3	4
A	Purchases			
B	Freight/Carriage			
C	Power and Fuel			
D	Imported goods (Including received from SEZs)			
E	Rent and Insurance			
F	Goods lost, stolen, destroyed, written off or disposed of by way of gift or free samples			
G	Royalties			
H	Employees' Cost (Salaries, wages, Bonus etc.)			
I	Conveyance charges			
J	Bank Charges			
K	Entertainment charges			
L	Stationery Expenses (including postage etc.)			
M	Repair and Maintenance			
N	Other Miscellaneous expenses			
O	Capital goods			
P	Any other expense 1			
Q	Any other expense 2			
R	Total amount of eligible ITC availed			<<Auto>>
S	ITC claimed in Annual Return (GSTR9)			

T	Un-reconciled ITC (ITC 2)			
15	Reasons for un - reconciled difference in ITC			
A	Reason 1	<<Text>>		
B	Reason 2	<<Text>>		
C	Reason 3	<<Text>>		
16	Tax payable on un-reconciled difference in ITC (due to reasons specified in 13 and 15 above)			
	Description	Amount Payable		
	Central Tax			
	State/UT Tax			
	Integrated Tax			
	Cess			
	Interest			
	Penalty			

Pt. V	**Auditor's recommendation on additional Liability due to non-reconciliation**					
		To be paid through Cash				
	Description	Value	Central tax	State tax/ UT tax	Integrated tax	Cess, if applicable
	1	2	3	4	5	6
	5%					
	12%					
	18%					
	28%					
	3%					
	0.25%					
	0.10%					
	Input Tax Credit					
	Interest					
	Late Fee					
	Penalty					
	Any other amount paid for supplies not included in Annual					
	Return (GSTR 9)					
	Erroneous refund to be paid back					
	Outstanding demands to be settled					
	Other (Pl. specify)					

Verification:

I hereby solemnly affirm and declare that the information given herein above is true and correct to the best of my knowledge and belief and nothing has been concealed there from.

**(Signature and stamp/Seal of the Auditor)

Place:
Name of the signatory
Membership No
Date:
Full address
Verification of registered person:
I hereby solemnly affirm and declare that I am uploading the reconciliation statement in FORM GSTR-9C prepared and duly signed by the Auditor and nothing has been tampered or altered by me in the statement. I am also uploading other statements, as applicable, including financial statement, profit and loss account and balance sheet etc.

Signature

Place:
Date:

Name of Authorized Signatory Designation/status

Instructions: -

1. Terms used:
   (a) GSTIN: Goods and Services Tax Identification Number
2. It is mandatory to file all your FORM GSTR-1, FORM GSTR-3B and FORM GSTR -9 for the FY 2017-18 before filing this return. The details for the period between July 2017 to March 2018 are to be provided in this statement for the financial year 2017-18. The reconciliation statement is to be filed for every GSTIN separately.
3. The reference to current financial year in this statement is the financial year for which the reconciliation statement is being filed for.
4. Part II consists of reconciliation of the annual turnover declared in the audited Annual Financial Statement with the turnover as declared in the Annual Return furnished in FORM GSTR-9 for this GSTIN. The instructions to fill this part are as follows :-

Table No.	Instructions
5A	The turnover as per the audited Annual Financial Statement shall be declared here. There may be cases where multiple GSTINs (State-wise) registrations exist on the same PAN. This is common for persons / entities with presence over multiple States. Such persons / entities, will have to internally derive their GSTIN wise turnover and declare the same here. This shall include export turnover (if any). It may be noted that reference to audited Annual Financial Statement includes reference to books of accounts in case of persons / entities having presence over multiple States.

Table No.	Instructions
5B	Unbilled revenue which was recorded in the books of accounts on the basis of accrual system of accounting in the last financial year and was carried forward to the current financial year shall be declared here. In other words, when GST is payable during the financial year on such revenue (which was recognized earlier), the value of such revenue shall be declared here. (For example, if rupees Ten Crores of unbilled revenue existed for the financial year 2016-17, and during the current financial year, GST was paid on rupees Four Crores of such revenue, then value of rupees Four Crores rupees shall be declared here)
5C	Value of all advances for which GST has been paid but the same has not been recognized as revenue in the audited Annual Financial Statement shall be declared here.
5D	Aggregate value of deemed supplies under Schedule I of the CGST Act, 2017 shall be declared here. Any deemed supply which is already part of the turnover in the audited Annual Financial Statement is not required to be included here.
5E	Aggregate value of credit notes which were issued after 31st of March for any supply accounted in the current financial year but such credit notes were reflected in the annual return (GSTR-9) shall be declared here.
5F	Trade discounts which are accounted for in the audited Annual Financial Statement but on which GST was leviable (being not permissible) shall be declared here.
5G	Turnover included in the audited Annual Financial Statement for April 2017 to June 2017 shall be declared here.
5H	Unbilled revenue which was recorded in the books of accounts on the basis of accrual system of accounting during the current financial year but GST was not payable on such revenue in the same financial year shall be declared here.
5I	Value of all advances for which GST has not been paid but the same has been recognized as revenue in the audited Annual Financial Statement shall be declared here.
5J	Aggregate value of credit notes which have been accounted for in the audited Annual Financial Statement but were not admissible under Section 34 of the CGST Act shall be declared here.
5K	Aggregate value of all goods supplied by SEZs to DTA units for which the DTA units have filed bill of entry shall be declared here.
5L	There may be cases where registered persons might have opted out of the composition scheme during the current financial year. Their turnover as per the audited Annual Financial Statement would include turnover both

Table No.	Instructions
	as composition taxpayer as well as normal taxpayer. Therefore, the turnover for which GST was paid under the composition scheme shall be declared here.
5M	There may be cases where the taxable value and the invoice value differ due to valuation principles under section 15 of the CGST Act, 2017 and rules thereunder. Therefore, any difference between the turnover reported in the Annual Return (GSTR 9) and turnover reported in the audited Annual Financial Statement due to difference in valuation of supplies shall be declared here.
5N	Any difference between the turnover reported in the Annual Return (GSTR9) and turnover reported in the audited Annual Financial Statement due to foreign exchange fluctuations shall be declared here.
5O	Any difference between the turnover reported in the Annual Return (GSTR9) and turnover reported in the audited Annual Financial Statement due to reasons not listed above shall be declared here.
5Q	Annual turnover as declared in the Annual Return (GSTR 9) shall be declared here. This turnover may be derived from Sr. No. 5N, 10 and 11 of Annual Return (GSTR 9).
6	Reasons for non-reconciliation between the annual turnover declared in the audited Annual Financial Statement and turnover as declared in the Annual Return (GSTR 9) shall be specified here.
7	The table provides for reconciliation of taxable turnover from the audited annual turnover after adjustments with the taxable turnover declared in annual return (GSTR-9).
7A	Annual turnover as derived in Table 5P above would be auto-populated here.
7B	Value of exempted, nil rated, non-GST and no-supply turnover shall be declared here. This shall be reported net of credit notes, debit notes and amendments if any.
7C	Value of zero rated supplies (including supplies to SEZs) on which tax is not paid shall be declared here. This shall be reported net of credit notes, debit notes and amendments if any.
7D	Value of reverse charge supplies on which tax is to be paid by the recipient shall be declared here. This shall be reported net of credit notes, debit notes and amendments if any.
7E	The taxable turnover is derived as the difference between the annual turnover after adjustments declared in Table 7A above and the sum of all supplies (exempted, non- GST, reverse charge etc.) declared in Table 7B, 7C and 7D above.
7F	Taxable turnover as declared in Table (4N - 4G) + (10-11) of the Annual

Table No.	Instructions
	Return (GSTR9) shall be declared here.
8	Reasons for non-reconciliation between adjusted annual taxable turnover as derived from Table 7E above and the taxable turnover declared in Table 7F shall be specified here.

5. Part III consists of reconciliation of the tax payable as per declaration in the reconciliation statement and the actual tax paid as declared in Annual Return (GSTR9). The instructions to fill this part are as follows:-

Table No.	Instructions
9	The table provides for reconciliation of tax paid as per reconciliation statement and
	amount of tax paid as declared in Annual Return (GSTR 9). Under the head labelled "RC", supplies where tax was paid on reverse charge basis by the recipient (i.e. the person for whom reconciliation statement has been prepared) shall be declared.
9P	The total amount to be paid as per liability declared in Table 9A to 9O is auto populated here.
9Q	The amount payable as declared in Table 9 of the Annual Return (GSTR9) shall be declared here. It should also contain any differential tax paid on Table 10 or 11 of the Annual Return (GSTR9).
10	Reasons for non-reconciliation between payable / liability declared in Table 9P above and the amount payable in Table 9Q shall be specified here.
11	Any amount which is payable due to reasons specified under Table 6, 8 and 10 above shall be declared here.

6. Part IV consists of reconciliation of Input Tax Credit (ITC). The instructions to fill Part IV are as under:-

Table No.	Instructions
12A	ITC availed (after reversals) as per the audited Annual Financial Statement shall be declared here. There may be cases where multiple GSTINs (State-wise) registrations exist on the same PAN. This is common for persons / entities with presence over multiple States. Such persons / entities, will have to internally derive their ITC for each individual GSTIN and declare the same here. It may be noted that reference to audited Annual Financial Statement includes reference to books of accounts in case of persons / entities having presence over multiple States.
12B	Any ITC which was booked in the audited Annual Financial Statement of earlier financial year(s) but availed in the ITC ledger in the financial year for which the reconciliation statement is being filed for shall be declared

Table No.	Instructions
	here. This shall include transitional credit which was booked in earlier years but availed during Financial Year 2017-18.
12C	Any ITC which has been booked in the audited Annual Financial Statement of the current financial year but the same has not been credited to the ITC ledger for the said financial year shall be declared here.
12D	ITC availed as per audited Annual Financial Statement or books of accounts as derived from values declared in Table 12A, 12B and 12C above will be autopopulated here.
12E	Net ITC available for utilization as declared in Table 7J of Annual Return (GSTR9) shall be declared here.
13	Reasons for non-reconciliation of ITC as per audited Annual Financial Statement or books of account (Table 12D) and the net ITC (Table12E) availed in the Annual Return (GSTR9) shall be specified here.
14	This table is for reconciliation of ITC declared in the Annual Return (GSTR9) against the expenses booked in the audited Annual Financial Statement or books of account. The various sub-heads specified under this table are general expenses in the audited Annual Financial Statement or books of account on which ITC may or may not be available. Further, this is only an indicative list of heads under which expenses are generally booked. Taxpayers may add or delete any of these heads but all heads of expenses on which GST has been paid / was payable are to be declared here.
14R	Total ITC declared in Table 14A to 14Q above shall be auto populated here.
14S	Net ITC availed as declared in the Annual Return (GSTR9) shall be declared here.
	Table 7J of the Annual Return (GSTR9) may be used for filing this Table.
15	Reasons for non-reconciliation between ITC availed on the various expenses declared in Table 14R and ITC declared in Table 14S shall be specified here.
16	Any amount which is payable due to reasons specified in Table 13 and 15 above shall be declared here.

7. Part V consists of the auditor's recommendation on the additional liability to be discharged by the taxpayer due to non-reconciliation of turnover or non-reconciliation of input tax credit. The auditor shall also recommend if there is any other amount to be paid for supplies not included in the Annual Return. Any refund which has been erroneously taken and shall be paid back to the Government shall also be declared in this table. Lastly, any other outstanding demands which is recommended to be settled by the auditor shall be declared in this Table.

8. Towards the end of the return, taxpayers shall be given an option to pay any additional liability declared in this form, through FORM DRC-03. Taxpayers shall select "Reconciliation Statement" in the drop down provided in FORM DRC-03. It may be noted that such liability shall be paid through electronic cash ledger only.

PART - B- CERTIFICATION

I. Certification in cases where the reconciliation statement (FORM GSTR-9C) is drawn up by the person who had conducted the audit:

* I/we have examined the—

(a) balance sheet as on ____________

(b) the profit and loss account/income and expenditure account for the period beginning from _________ to ending on__________, and

(c) the cash flow statement for the period beginning from _________ to ending on, __________ –attached herewith, of

M/s _________ (Name), ___________ (Address), _________ (GSTIN).

2. Based on our audit I/we report that the said registered person—

*has maintained the books of accounts, records and documents as required by the IGST/CGST/<<>>GST Act, 2017 and the rules/notifications made/issued thereunder

*has not maintained the following accounts/records/documents as required by the IGST/CGST/<<>>GST Act, 2017 and the rules/notifications made/issued thereunder:

1.

2.

3.

3. (a) *I/we report the following observations/ comments / discrepancies / inconsistencies; if any:

3. (b) *I/we further report that, -

(A) *I/we have obtained all the information and explanations which, to the best of *my/our knowledge and belief, were necessary for the purpose of the audit/ information and explanations which, to the best of *my/our knowledge and belief, were necessary for the purpose of the audit were not provided/partially provided to us.

(B) In *my/our opinion, proper books of account *have/have not been kept by the registered person so far as appears from*my/ our examination of the books.

(C) I/we certify that the balance sheet, the *profit and loss/income and expenditure account and the cash flow Statement are *in agreement/not in agreement with the books of account maintained at the Principal place of business at ___________and ** __________________additional place of business within the State.

4. The documents required to be furnished under section 35 (5) of the CGST Act / SGST Act and Reconciliation Statement required to be furnished under section 44(2) of the CGST Act / SGST Act is annexed herewith in Form No. GSTR-9C.
5. In *my/our opinion and to the best of *my/our information and according to explanations given to *me/us, the particulars given in the said Form No.GSTR-9C are true and correct subject to following observations/qualifications, if any:
   (a) ______________________________
   (b) ______________________________
   (c) ______________________________

**(Signature and stamp/Seal of the Auditor)

Place: ___________

Name of the signatory ___________

Membership No ___________

Date: ___________

Full address ___________

II. Certification in cases where the reconciliation statement (FORM GSTR-9C) is drawn up by a person other than the person who had conducted the audit of the accounts:

*I/we report that the audit of the books of accounts and the financial statements of M/s. ______________________ (Name and address of the assessee with GSTIN) was conducted by M/s ______________(full name and address of auditor along with status), bearing membership number in pursuance of the provisions of the ______________ Act, and *I/we annex hereto a copy of their audit report dated ______________ along with a copy of each of :-

(a) balance sheet as on

(b) the *profit and loss account/income and expenditure account for the period beginning from ______________ to ending on ______________,

(c) the cash flow statement for the period beginning from ___________to ending on ______________, and

(d) documents declared by the said Act to be part of, or annexed to, the *profit and loss account/income and expenditure account and balance sheet.

2. I/we report that the said registered person—

*has maintained the books of accounts, records and documents as required by the IGST/CGST/<>GST Act, 2017 and the rules/notifications made/issued thereunder

*has not maintained the following accounts/records/documents as required by the IGST/CGST/<>GST Act, 2017 and the rules/notifications made/issued thereunder:

1.

2.
3.

3. The documents required to be furnished under section 35 (5) of the CGST Act / SGST Act and Reconciliation Statement required to be furnished under section 44(2) of the CGST Act / SGST Act is annexed herewith in Form No.GSTR-9C.
4. In *my/our opinion and to the best of *my/our information and according to examination of books of account including other relevant documents and explanations given to *me/us, the particulars given in the said Form No.9C are true and correct subject to the following observations/qualifications, if any:
   (a) ____________
   (b) ____________
   (c) ____________

____

**(Signature and stamp/Seal of the Auditor)
Place: ____________
Name of the signatory ____________
Membership No ____________
Date: ____________
Full address ____________

Appendix 22: Draft – Ethical issues and guidance for audit under Section 35(5) of CGST Act, 2017[7]

[By Ethical Standard Board]

INTRODUCTION

1.1 The members of ICAI are entitled, vide Section 35(5) of CGST Act, 2017 to render Audit under this Act. Section 2(1)(b) of the Chartered Accountants Act, 1949 enables members of ICAI to engage, inter alia, in the services involving auditing. Accordingly, as in other Audits, the members of the Institute in practice, either individually, or in partnership with other chartered accountants, may engage in Audit under the CGST Act, 2017.

1.2 Audit being an attest function, members are not permitted to engage in other occupation or business while doing Audit, with the exception of activities mentioned in the Resolution of Council made at its 242nd Meeting held in May, 2004. The said Resolution forms part of Appendix (9) to The Chartered Accountants Regulations, 1988.

1.3 Members of the Institute are required to comply with various ethical provisions, while rendering Audit under the CGST Act, 2017. Non-compliance with the same may make them liable for professional misconduct.

PROFESSIONAL MISCONDUCT

1.4 As per Section 22 of The Chartered Accountants Act, 1949, the expression "Professional or other misconduct" shall be deemed to include any act or omission provided in any of the Schedules to the Act, but nothing in this section shall be construed to limit or abridge in any way the power conferred or duty cast on the Director (Discipline) under sub-section (1) of section 21 to enquire into conduct of any member of the Institute under any other circumstances.

1.5 A member is liable for disciplinary action under Section 21 of the Chartered Accountants Act if he is found guilty of any professional or "other misconduct". This provision empowers the Director (Discipline) to enquire into any conduct of a member under any other circumstance. This is considered necessary because a Chartered Accountant is expected to maintain the highest standards and integrity even in his/her personal affairs and any deviation from these standards, would expose him/ her to disciplinary action.

---

7 The Institute of Chartered Accountant of India (ICAI) has started working on the guidance note on ethical standards in conduct of the reconciliation statement and its certification, which touches on the basic principles to be followed, precautions to be taken in assignment including the important ethical standards to be considered during GST audit assignment.

COMPLIANCE WITH CODE OF ETHICS

1.6 A chartered accountant in practice shall be deemed to be guilty of professional misconduct, if he contravenes any of the provisions of Chartered Accountants Act, 1949 or the regulations made thereunder or any guidelines issued by the Council.

1.7 The Part-A of Code of Ethics, 2009, which is based on provisions of International Ethics Standards Board of Accountants (IESBA) Code of Ethics, has been issued as a Guideline of the Council. The provisions of Part-B of Code of Ethics are based on the domestic provisions, including Chartered Accountants Act, 1949, Chartered Accountants Regulations, 1988, Guidelines of the Council, Case law, etc. Accordingly, the non-compliance of provisions of the Code may result in professional misconduct.

1.8 Some of the relevant provisions of the Code of Ethics are being reproduced here. For detailed guidance, Code of Ethics may be referred by the members.

FUNDAMENTAL PRINCIPLES

1.9 The Code of Ethics lists out the Fundamental principles to be followed by the members:-

(a) Integrity

A chartered accountant should be straightforward and honest in all professional and business relationships.

(b) Objectivity

A chartered accountant should not allow bias, conflict of interest or undue influence of others to override professional judgments.

(c) Professional Competence and Due Care

A chartered accountant has a continuing duty to maintain professional knowledge and skill at the level required to ensure that a client or employer receives competent professional service based on current developments in practice, legislation, and techniques. A chartered accountant should act diligently and in accordance with applicable technical and professional standards while providing professional services.

(d) Confidentiality

A chartered accountant should respect the confidentiality of information acquired as a result of professional and employment relationships and should not disclose any such information to third parties without proper and specific authority unless there is a legal or professional right or duty to disclose. Confidential information acquired as a result of professional and employment relationships should not be used for the personal advantage of the chartered accountant or third parties.

(e) Professional Behaviour

A chartered accountant should comply with relevant laws and regulations and should avoid any action that discredits the profession.

CONCEPTUAL FRAMEWORK APPROACH

1.10 The Code of Ethics describes the Conceptual Framework Approach. The circumstances in which chartered accountants operate may give rise to specific threats to compliance with the fundamental principles. It is impossible to define every situation that creates such threats and specify the appropriate mitigating action. In addition, the nature of engagements and work assignments may differ and consequently different threats may exist requiring the application of different safeguards. A conceptual framework that requires a chartered accountant to identify, evaluate and address threats to compliance with the fundamental principles, rather than merely comply with a set of specific rules which may be arbitrary, is, therefore, in the public interest. This Code provides a framework to assist a chartered accountant to identify, evaluate and respond to threats to compliance with the fundamental principles. If identified threats are other than clearly insignificant, a chartered accountant should, where appropriate, apply safeguards to eliminate the threats or reduce them to an acceptable level, such that compliance with the fundamental principles is not compromised.

1.11 A chartered accountant has an obligation to evaluate any threats to compliance with the fundamental principles when the chartered accountant knows, or could reasonably be expected to know, of circumstances or relationships that may compromise compliance with the fundamental principles.

1.12 A chartered accountant should take qualitative as well as quantitative factors into account when considering the significance of a threat. If a chartered accountant cannot implement appropriate safeguards, the chartered accountant should decline or discontinue the specific professional service involved, or where necessary resign from the client.

THREATS AND SAFEGUARDS

1.13 Compliance with the fundamental principles may potentially be threatened by a broad range of circumstances. Many threats fall into the following categories:

(a) Self-interest threats, which may occur as a result of the financial or other interests of a chartered accountant or of a relative;

(b) Self-review threats, which may occur when a previous judgment needs to be re- evaluated by the chartered accountant responsible for that judgment;

(c) Advocacy threats, which may occur when a chartered accountant promotes a position or opinion to the point that subsequent objectivity may be compromised;

(d) Familiarity threats, which may occur when, because of a relationship, a chartered accountant becomes too sympathetic to the interests of others; and

(e) Intimidation threats, which may occur when a chartered accountant may be deterred from acting objectively by threats, actual or perceived.

1.14 Safeguards that may eliminate or reduce such threats to an acceptable level fall into two broad categories:

(a) Safeguards created by the profession, legislation or regulation; and

(b) Safeguards in the work environment.

1.15 Safeguards created by the profession, legislation or regulation include, but are not restricted to:

- Educational, training and experience requirements for entry into the profession.
- Continuing professional development requirements.
- Corporate governance regulations.
- Professional standards.
- Professional or regulatory monitoring and disciplinary procedures.
- External review by a legally empowered third party of the reports, returns, communications or information produced by a chartered accountant.

1.16 The nature of the safeguards to be applied will vary depending on the circumstances. In exercising professional judgment, a chartered accountant should consider what a reasonable and informed third party, having knowledge of all relevant information, including the significance of the threat and the safeguards applied, would conclude to be unacceptable.

1.17 In evaluating compliance with the fundamental principles, a chartered accountant may be required to resolve a conflict in the application of fundamental principles.

1.18 When initiating either a formal or informal conflict resolution process, a chartered accountant should consider the following, either individually or together with others, as part of the resolution process:

(a) Relevant facts;

(b) Ethical issues involved;

(c) Fundamental principles related to the matter in question;

(d) Established internal procedures; and

(e) Alternative courses of action.

Having considered these issues, a chartered accountant should determine the appropriate course of action that is consistent with the fundamental principles identified. The chartered accountant should also weigh the consequences of each possible course of action. If the matter remains unresolved, the chartered accountant should consult with other appropriate persons within the firm or employing organization for help in obtaining resolution.

Where a matter involves a conflict with, or within, an organization, a chartered accountant should also consider consulting with those charged with governance of the organization, such as the board of directors or the audit committee.

1.19 It may be in the best interests of the chartered accountant to document the substance of the issue and details of any discussions held or decisions taken, concerning that issue.

1.20 If a significant conflict cannot be resolved, a chartered accountant may wish to obtain professional advice from the relevant professional body or legal advisors, and thereby obtain guidance on ethical issues without breaching confidentiality. For example, a chartered accountant may have encountered a fraud, the reporting of which could breach the chartered accountant's responsibility to respect confidentiality. The chartered accountant should consider obtaining legal advice to determine whether there is a requirement to report.

1.21 If, after exhausting all relevant possibilities, the ethical conflict remains unresolved, a chartered accountant should, where possible, refuse to remain associated with the matter creating the conflict. The chartered accountant may determine that, in the circumstances, it is appropriate to withdraw from the engagement team or specific assignment, or to resign altogether from the engagement or the firm .

1.22 A chartered accountant in practice may also find the specific circumstances give rise to unique threats to compliance with one or more of the fundamental principles. Such unique threats obviously cannot be categorized. In either professional or employment relationships, a chartered accountant in practice should always be on the alert for such circumstances and threats.

1.23 Safeguards that may eliminate or reduce threats to an acceptable level fall into two broad categories:

(a) Safeguards created by the profession, legislation or regulation; and

(b) Safeguards in the work environment.

1.24 In the work environment, the relevant safeguards will vary depending on the circumstances. Work environment safeguards comprise firm-wide safeguards and engagement specific safeguards.

CLIENT ACCEPTANCE

1.25 Before accepting a new client relationship, a chartered accountant in practice should consider whether acceptance would create any threats to compliance with the fundamental principles. Potential threats to integrity or professional behaviour may be created from, for example, questionable issues associated with the client (its owners, management and activities).

1.26 Members are required to comply with the ICAI Know Your Client (KYC) Norms, while accepting an assignment of GST Audit. The Council has formulated the Know Your Client (KYC) norms at its 356th Meeting held on 29th, 30th June and 1st July, 2016. The norms are mandatory in nature and shall apply to all assignments pertaining to attest functions. These have come into effect for the assignments done on or after 1.1.2017.

CONFLICT OF INTEREST

1.27 A chartered accountant in practice should take reasonable steps to identify circumstances that could pose a conflict of interest. Such circumstances may give rise to threats to compliance with the fundamental principles. For example, a threat to objectivity may be created when a chartered accountant in practice competes directly with a client or has a joint venture or similar arrangement with major competitor of a client. A threat to objectivity or confidentiality may also be created when a chartered accountant in practice performs services for clients whose interests are in conflict or the clients are in dispute with each other in relation to the matter or transaction in question.

1.28 A chartered accountant in practice should evaluate the significance of any threats. Evaluation includes considering, before accepting or continuing a client relationship or specific engagement, whether the chartered accountant in practice has any business interests, or relationships with the client or a third party that could give rise to threats. If threats are other than clearly significant, safeguards should be considered and applied as necessary to eliminate them or reduce them to an acceptable level.

1.29 Depending upon the circumstances giving rise to the conflict, safeguards should ordinarily include the chartered accountant in practice:

(a) Notifying the client of the firm's business interest or activities that may represent a conflict of interest, and obtaining their consent to act in such circumstances; or

(b) Notifying all known relevant parties that the chartered accountant in practice is acting for two or more parties in respect of a matter where their respective interests are in conflict, and obtaining their consent to so act; or

(c) Notifying the client that the chartered accountant in practice does not act exclusively for any one client in the provision of proposed services (for example, in a particular market sector or with respect to a specific service) and obtaining their consent to so act.

1.30 The following additional safeguards should also be considered:

(a) The use of separate engagement teams; and

(b) Procedures to prevent access to information (e.g., strict physical separation of such teams, confidential and secure data filing); and

(c) Clear guidelines for members of the engagement team on issues of security and confidentiality; and

(d) The use of confidentiality agreements signed by employees and partners of the firm; and

(e) Regular review of the application of safeguards by a senior individual not involved with relevant client engagements.

1.31 Where a conflict of interest poses a threat to one or more of the fundamental principles, including objectivity, confidentiality or professional behaviour, that cannot be eliminated or reduced to an acceptable level through the application of safeguards, the chartered accountant in practice should conclude that it is not appropriate to accept a specific engagement or that resignation from one or more conflicting engagements is required.

1.32 Where a chartered accountant in practice has requested consent from a client to act for another party (which may or may not be an existing client) in respect of a matter where the respective interests are in conflict and that consent has been refused by the client, then they must not continue to act for one of the parties in the matter giving rise to the conflict of interest.

INDEPENDENCE

1.33 In the case of an assurance engagement it is in the public interest and, therefore, required by this Code of Ethics, that members of assurance teams, firms and, when applicable, network firms be independent of assurance clients.

1.34 Independence requires:

The state of mind that permits the expression of a conclusion without being affected by influences that compromise professional judgment, allowing an individual to act with integrity, and exercise objectivity and professional skepticism.

The avoidance of facts and circumstances that are so significant that a reasonable and informed third party, having knowledge of all relevant information, including safeguards applied, would reasonably conclude a firm's, or a member of the assurance team's, integrity, objectivity or professional skepticism had been compromised.

1.35 The use of the word "independence" on its own may create misunderstandings. Standing alone, the word may lead observers to suppose that a person exercising professional judgment ought to be free from all economic, financial and other relationships. This is impossible, as every member of society has relationships with others. Therefore, the significance of economic, financial and other relationships should also be evaluated in the light of what a reasonable and informed third party having knowledge of all relevant information would reasonably conclude to be unacceptable.

1.36 Many different circumstances, or combination of circumstances, may be relevant and accordingly it is impossible to define every situation that creates threats to independence and specify the appropriate mitigating action that should be taken. In addition, the nature of assurance engagements may differ and consequently different threats may exist, requiring the application of different safeguards. A conceptual framework that requires firms and members of assurance teams to identify, evaluate and address threats to independence, rather than merely comply with a set of specific rules which may be arbitrary, is, therefore, in the public interest.

FINANCIAL INTERESTS

1.37 A financial interest in an assurance client may create a self-interest threat. In evaluating the significance of the threat, and the appropriate safeguards to be applied to eliminate the threat or reduce it to an acceptable level, it is necessary to examine the nature of the financial interest. This includes an evaluation of the role of the person holding the financial interest, the materiality of the financial interest and the type of financial interest (direct or indirect).

1.38 If a member of the assurance team, or his relative has a direct financial interest, or a material indirect financial interest in the assurance client, the self-interest threat created would be so significant the only safeguards available to eliminate the threat or reduce it to an acceptable level would be to:

(a) Dispose of the direct financial interest prior to the individual becoming a member of the assurance team;

(b) Dispose of the indirect financial interest in total or dispose of a sufficient amount of it so that the remaining interest is no longer material prior to the individual becoming a member of the assurance team; or

(c) Remove the member of the assurance team from the assurance engagement.

CLOSE BUSINESS RELATIONSHIPS

1.39 A close business relationship between a firm or a member of the assurance team and the assurance client or its management, or between the firm, a network firm and a financial statement audit client, will involve a commercial or common financial interest and may create self-interest and intimidation threats. The following are examples of such relationships:

- Having a material financial interest in a joint venture with the assurance client or a controlling owner, director, officer or other individual who performs senior managerial functions for that client.
- Arrangements to combine one or more services or products of the firm with one or more services or products of the assurance client and to market the package with reference to both parties.

In the case of a financial statement audit client, unless the financial interest is immaterial and the relationship is clearly insignificant to the firm, the network firm and the audit client, no safeguards could reduce the threat to an acceptable level. In the case of an assurance client that is not a financial statement audit client, unless the financial interest is immaterial and the relationship is clearly insignificant to the firm and the assurance client, no safeguards could reduce the threat to an acceptable level. Consequently, in both these circumstances the only possible courses of action are to:

(a) Terminate the business relationship;

(b) Reduce the magnitude of the relationship so that the financial interest is immaterial and the relationship is clearly insignificant; or

(c) Refuse to perform the assurance engagement.

Unless any such financial interest is immaterial and the relationship is clearly insignificant to the member of the assurance team, the only appropriate safeguard would be to remove the individual from the assurance team.

PERSONAL RELATIONSHIPS

1.40 Relationships between a member of the assurance team and a director, an officer or certain employees, depending on their role, of the assurance client, may create self-interest, familiarity or intimidation threats. It is impracticable to attempt to describe in detail the significance of the threats that such relationships may create. The significance will depend upon a number of factors including the individual's responsibilities on the assurance engagement, the relationship and role of the relative or other individual within the assurance client. Consequently, there is a wide spectrum of circumstances that will need to be evaluated and safeguards to be applied to reduce the threat to an acceptable level.

EMPLOYMENT WITH THE CLIENT

1.41 A firm or a member of the assurance team's independence may be threatened if a director, an officer or an employee of the assurance client in a position to exert direct and significant influence over the subject matter information of the assurance engagement has been a member of the assurance team or partner of the firm. Such circumstances may create self-interest, familiarity and intimidation threats particularly when significant connections remain between the individual and his or her former firm. Similarly, a member of the assurance team's independence may be threatened when an individual participates in the assurance engagement knowing, or having reason to believe, that he or she is to, or may, join the assurance client sometime in the future.

RECENT SERVICE WITH THE CLIENT

1.42 To have a former officer, director or employee of the assurance client serve as a member of the assurance team may create self-interest, self-review and familiarity threats. This would be particularly true when a member of the assurance team has to report on, for example, subject matter information he or she had prepared or elements of the financial statements he or she had valued while with the assurance client.

NO OFFICER OR EMPLOYEE OF THE CLIENT TO BE AUDITOR

1.43 No person who is an officer or employee of an entity shall be qualified for appointment as auditor of that entity.

PROVISION OF NON-ASSURANCE SERVICES TO THE CLIENT

1.44 Firms have traditionally provided to their assurance clients a range of non-assurance services that are consistent with their skills and expertise. Assurance clients value the benefits that derive from having these firms, which have a good understanding of the business, bring their knowledge and skill to bear in other areas. Furthermore, the provision of such non-assurance services will often result in the assurance team obtaining information regarding the assurance client's business and operations that is helpful in relation to the assurance engagement. The greater the knowledge of the assurance client's business, the better the assurance team will understand the assurance client's procedures and controls, and the business and financial risks that it faces. The provision of non-assurance services may, however, create threats to the independence of the firm, a network firm or the members of the assurance team, particularly with respect to perceived threats to independence. Consequently, it is necessary to evaluate the significance of any threat created by the provision of such services. In some cases it may be possible to eliminate or reduce the threat created by application of safeguards. In other cases no safeguards are available to reduce the threat to an acceptable level.

WRITING BOOKS OF ACCOUNT

1.45 Members are not permitted to write the books of account of their auditee clients. Attention is invited to "Guidance Note on Independence of Auditors" in this regard.

AUDIT UNDER COMPANIES ACT, 2013

1.46 The Audit under the Companies Act, 2013 and the Audit under the CGST Act, 2017 may be undertaken simultaneously.

TAX AUDIT UNDER INCOME TAX ACT,1961

1.47 The Audit under Income Tax Act, 1961 and the Audit under the CGST Act, 2017 may be undertaken simultaneously.

ADVISORY SERVICES

1.48 Advisory services, as mentioned under ICAI Guidelines for Management Consultancy and other Services, and Regulation 191 of the Chartered Accountants Regulations, 1988, may be rendered along with Audit under the CGST Act, 2017 .

FEES OVERDUE

1.49 A self-interest threat may be created if fees due from an assurance client for professional services remain unpaid for a long time, especially if a significant part is not paid before the issue of the assurance report for the following year.

Generally the payment of such fees should be required before the report is issued. The following safeguards may be applicable:

- Discussing the level of outstanding fees with the audit committee, or others charged with governance.
- Involving an additional chartered accountant who did not take part in the assurance engagement to provide advice or review the work performed.

The firm should also consider whether the overdue fees might be regarded as being equivalent to a loan to the client and whether, because of the significance of the overdue fees, it is appropriate for the firm to be re-appointed.

- Discussing the level of outstanding fees with the audit committee, or others charged with governance.
- Involving an additional chartered accountant who did not take part in the assurance engagement to provide advice or review the work performed.

The firm should also consider whether the overdue fees might be regarded as being equivalent to a loan to the client and whether, because of the significance of the overdue fees, it is appropriate for the firm to be re-appointed.

PRICING

1.50 When a firm obtains an assurance engagement at a significantly lower fee level than that charged by the predecessor firm, or quoted by other firms, the self-interest threat created will not be reduced to an acceptable level unless:

(a) The firm is able to demonstrate that appropriate time and qualified staff are assigned to the task; and

(b) All applicable assurance standards, guidelines and quality control procedures are being complied with.

RESTRICTION ON FEES

1.51 The fees which are based on a percentage of profits or which are contingent upon the findings, or results of such work, is not allowed except in cases which are permitted under Regulation 192 of The Chartered Accountants Regulations, 1988.

GIFTS AND HOSPITALITY

1.52 Accepting gifts or hospitality from an assurance client may create self-interest and familiarity threats. When a firm or a member of the assurance team accepts gifts or hospitality, unless the value is clearly insignificant, the threats to independence cannot be reduced to an acceptable level by the application of any safeguard. Consequently, a firm or a member of the assurance team should not accept such gifts or hospitality.

PROFESSIONAL MISCONDUCT AND TWO SCHEDULES TO THE CHARTERED ACCOUNTANTS ACT, 1949

Persons to be allowed practice in own name

1.53 A Chartered accountant shall be deemed to be guilty of professional misconduct if he allows any person to practice in his name as a chartered accountant unless such person is also a chartered accountant in practice and is in partnership with or employed by him;

Bar on paying or receiving share with others

1.54 A Chartered accountant shall be deemed to be guilty of professional misconduct if he pays or allows or agrees to pay or allow, directly or indirectly, any share, commission or brokerage in the fees or profits of his professional business, to any person other than a member of the Institute or a partner or a retired partner or the legal representative of a deceased partner, or a member of any other professional body or with such other persons having such qualifications as may be prescribed, for the purpose of rendering such professional services from time to time in or outside India.

1.55 A Chartered accountant shall be deemed to be guilty of professional misconduct if he accepts or agrees to accept any part of the profits of the professional work of a person who is not a member of the Institute. However, nothing herein contained shall be construed as prohibiting a member from entering into profit sharing or other similar arrangements, including receiving any share commission or brokerage in the fees, with a member of such professional body or other person having qualifications as may be prescribed.

Partnership to be only among members in practice

1.56 A Chartered accountant shall be deemed to be guilty of professional misconduct if he enters into partnership, in or outside India, with any person other than a chartered accountant in practice or such other person who is a member of any other professional body having such qualifications as may be prescribed, including a resident who but for his residence abroad would be entitled to be registered as a member under clause (v) of sub-section (1) of Section 4 or whose qualifications are recognised by the Central Government or the Council for the purpose of permitting such partnerships;

Restriction on categories from whom services may be secured

1.57 A Chartered accountant shall be deemed to be guilty of professional misconduct if he secures, either through the services of a person who is not an employee of such chartered accountant or who is not his partner or by means which are not open to a chartered accountant, any professional business. However, nothing herein contained shall be construed as prohibiting any arrangement permitted in the items (2), (3) and (4) of Part-I of First Schedule to The Chartered Accountants Act, 1949;

Bar on solicitation

1.58 A Chartered accountant shall be deemed to be guilty of professional misconduct if he solicits clients or professional work either directly or indirectly by circular, advertisement, personal communication or interview or by any other means. However, nothing herein contained shall be construed as preventing or prohibiting—

(i) any chartered accountant from applying or requesting for or inviting or securing professional work from another chartered accountant in practice;

(ii) a member from responding to tenders or enquiries issued by various users of professional services or organisations from time to time and securing professional work as a consequence;

1.59 The government departments, government Companies/ corporations, courts, co-operative societies and banks and other similar institutions prepare panels of Chartered Accountants for allotment of audit and other professional work. Where the existence of such a panel is within the knowledge of a member, he is free to write to the concerned organization with a request to place his name on the panel. However, it would not be proper for the Chartered Accountant to make roving enquiries by applying to any such organization for having his name included in any such panel. It is permissible to quote fees on enquiries being received or respond to tenders from the organizations requiring professional services, which maintain such panel.

1.60 It is not permissible for a member to address letters or circulars to persons who are likely to require services of a Chartered Accountant since it would tantamount to advertisement.

Bar on advertisement of services except as may be allowed

1.61 A Chartered accountant shall be deemed to be guilty of professional misconduct if he advertises his professional attainments or services, or uses any designation or expressions other than chartered accountant on professional documents, visiting cards, letter heads or sign boards, unless it be a degree of a University established by law in India or recognised by the Central Government or a title indicating membership of the Institute of Chartered Accountants of India or of any other institution that has been recognized by the Central Government or may be recognised by the Council. However, a member in practice may advertise through a write up, setting out the services provided by him or his firm and particulars of his firm subject to such guidelines as may be issued by the Council.

1.62 The Council has issued Advertisement Guidelines No. 1-CA(7)/Council Guidelines/01/2008 dt. 14.5.2008, vide which the members may advertise through a write up setting out their particulars or of their firms and services provided by them subject to the Guidelines, which must be presented in such a manner as to maintain the profession's good reputation, dignity and its ability to serve the public interest. The Member(s)/Firm(s) should ensure that the contents of the Write up are true to the best of their knowledge and belief and are in conformity with these Guidelines and be aware that the Institute of Chartered Accountants of India does not own any responsibility whatsoever for such contents or claims by the Writer Member(s)/ Firm(s).

Mandatory communication with previous Auditor

1.63 A Chartered accountant shall be deemed to be guilty of professional misconduct if he accepts a position as auditor previously held by another chartered accountant or a certified auditor who has been issued certificate under the Restricted Certificate Rules, 1932 without first communicating with him in writing.

1.64 The requirement for communicating with the previous auditor being a Chartered Accountant in practice would apply to all types of audit , and accordingly applies to Audit under the CGST Act, 2017 as well .

1.65 The existence of a dispute as regards the fees may be root cause of an auditor being changed. This would not constitute valid professional reason on account of which an audit should not be accepted by the member to whom it is offered. However, in the case of an undisputed audit fees for carrying out the statutory audit under the CGST Act, 2017 having not been paid, the incoming auditor should not accept the appointment unless such fees are paid. In respect of other dues, the incoming auditor should in appropriate circumstances use his influence in favour of his predecessor to have the dispute as regards the fees settled. In this connection, attention of members is invited to the Council Guidelines No. 1-CA/(7)/02/2008 dated 08.08.08. In the said guidelines, Council has explained that the provision for audit fee in accounts signed by both the auditee and the auditor shall be considered as " undisputed" audit fee and "sick unit" shall mean where the net worth is negative.

1.66 Existence of qualified report by the Previous Auditor is a valid professional reason for non-acceptance of the Audit assignment. However, in this case , he may accept the audit if he is satisfied that the attitude of the retiring auditor was not proper and justified. If, on the other hand, he feels that the retiring auditor had qualified the report for good and valid reasons, he should refuse to accept the audit. There is no rule, written or unwritten, which would prevent an auditor from accepting the appointment offered to him in these circumstances. However, before accepting the audit, he should ascertain the full facts of the case. For nothing will bring the profession to disrepute so much as the knowledge amongst the public that if an auditor is found to be "inconvenient" by the client, he could readily be replaced by another who would not displease the client and this point cannot be too over-emphasised.

1.67 Members should communicate with a retiring auditor in such a manner as to retain in their hands positive evidence of the delivery of the communication to the addressee. In the opinion of the Council, communication by a letter sent "Registered Acknowledgement due" or by hand against a written acknowledgement would in the normal course provide such evidence.

1.68 A Chartered accountant shall be deemed to be guilty of professional misconduct if he charges or offers to charge, accepts or offers to accept in respect of any professional employment, fees which are based on a percentage of profits or which are contingent upon the findings, or results of such employment, except as permitted under any regulation made under this Act.

The Council has , vide the authority granted as above , framed Regulation 192 which exempts members from this rule in certain professional services.

AUDITOR NOT TO ENGAGE IN OTHER BUSINESS/OCCUPATION

1.69 A Chartered accountant shall be deemed to be guilty of professional misconduct if he engages in any business or occupation other than the profession of chartered accountants unless permitted by the Council so to engage. However, nothing contained herein shall disentitle a chartered accountant from being a director of a Company, (not being a managing director or a whole time director), unless he or any of his partners is interested in such company as an auditor.

1.70 The Council has formulated Regulations 190A & 191 , specifying the activities with which a member in practice can associate himself with or without the permission of the Council.

1.71 However, as mentioned in para 1.2 of this Guidance Note , the members in practice engaged in activities enlisted in Regulation 191 are deemed to be in part-time practice, and shall not be eligible to engage in Audit, with the exception of activities mentioned in the Resolution of Council made at its 242nd Meeting held in May, 2004.

NOT TO DISCLOSE CLIENT INFORMATION

1.72 A Chartered accountant shall be deemed to be guilty of professional misconduct if he discloses information acquired in the course of his professional engagement to any person other than his client so engaging him, without the consent of his client or otherwise than as required by any law for the time being in force.

AUDITOR NOT TO HAVE SUBSTANTIAL INTEREST

1.73 A chartered accountant in practice shall be deemed to be guilty of professional misconduct, if he expresses his opinion on financial statements of any business or enterprise in which he, his firm or a partner in his firm has a substantial interest. In this context, "substantial interest" shall have the same meaning as assigned to it in the Appendix (9) to The Chartered Accountants Regulations, 1988.

DUTY TO EXERCISE DUE DILIGENCE

1.74 A chartered accountant in practice shall be deemed to be guilty of professional misconduct, if he does not exercise due diligence, or is grossly negligent in the conduct of his professional duties.

FEES FOR OTHER ASSIGNMENT NOT TO EXCEED AUDIT FEES IN CERTAIN CLIENTS

1.75 As per Chapter IX of Council General Guidelines, 2008, a member of the Institute in practice shall not accept the appointment as statutory auditor of Public Sector Undertaking(s)/Government Company(ies)/Listed Company(ies) and other Public Company(ies) having turnover of Rs. 50 crores or more in a year where he accepts any other work(s) or assignment(s) or service(s) in regard to the same Undertaking(s)/ Company(ies) on a remuneration which in total exceeds the fee payable for carrying out the statutory audit of the same Undertaking/company.

INDEBTEDNESS

1.76 As per Chapter X of Council General Guidelines, 2008, a member of the Institute in practice or a partner of a firm in practice or a firm shall not accept appointment as auditor of a concern while indebted to the concern or given any guarantee or provided any security in connection with the indebtedness of any third person to the concern, for limits fixed in the statute and in other cases for amount exceeding Rs. 10,000/-.

UNJUSTIFIED REMOVAL OF AUDITORS

1.77 If the member engaged in Audit under CGST Act, 2017 feels that he has been unjustifiably removed by the client, he may file a complaint before the Ethical Standards Board, and the Ethical Standards Board can intervene in such cases. No other chartered accountant should accept the audit assignment if the removal of his predecessor is not on valid grounds.

GENERALLY ACCEPTED AUDIT PROCEDURE

1.78 The Clause (9) of Part-I of Second Schedule to The Chartered Accountants Act, 1949 treats it as professional misconduct to fail to invite attention to any material departure from the generally accepted procedure of audit applicable to the circumstances. What constitutes "generally accepted audit procedure" would depend upon the facts and circumstances of each case, but guidance is available from the various pronouncements of the Institute issued from time to time by way of quality control and engagement standards, statements, general clarifications, guidance notes and technical guides, practice manuals, studies and other papers.

Note: *The Institute of Chartered Accountants of India has come out with Technical guide on filing annual return and GST audit certification in the Month of October 2018 which could be referred by professionals. The Guidance Note of ICAI [which would have recommendatory status would be issued only after the due process of framing a Guidance Note is completed maybe in 2019.]*

Bibliography/Webliography/ References

1. Classification & Exemption- GST - December 2017 CA Madhukar N Hiregange & CA Vasant Bhat - Bharat Law House, New Delhi
2. GST Tariff –October 2018 – CA Madhukar N Hiregange, CA Rajesh Kumar TR & CA Sudhir VS - Bharat Law House, New Delhi
3. Compendium of Issues and Solution in GST – March 2018, May 2019 – CA Madhukar N Hiregange & Adv. Naveen Kumar K S- Wolter Kluwer, New Delhi
4. Background Material of GST – May 2018, April 2019 – Institute of Chartered Accountants of India – Indirect Tax Committee
5. Technical guide on Annual return & GST Audit – 2018 Institute of Chartered Accountants of India- Indirect Tax Committee
6. ICAI website – www.icai.org.in
7. ICAI SA 230- Audit documentation
8. ICAI SA 250 – Considerations of law and regulations
9. ICAI SA 265: Communicating Deficiencies to those charged with governance (see Appendix)
10. ICAI SA 260: Communication to those charged with governance (see Appendix)
11. ICAI SA 210: agreeing to the terms of Audit engagement
12. ICAI SA 230: Audit documentation
13. ICAI SA 260: Communication with those charged with governance
14. ICAI SA 300: Planning an audit of financial statements
15. ICAI SA 315: Identifying and assessing the risk of material misstatement through understanding the entity and its environment
16. ICAI SA 320: Materiality in planning and performing the audit
17. ICAI SA 330: Auditors responses to assessed risks
18. Standards on Internal Auditing (SIA) 15: Obtaining Information from the tax payer

19. Excise Audit Manual, 2002 – Adv.Ravishankar K S & CA Madhukar N Hiregange- Centax Publications
20. Practical guide to service tax – CA Madhukar N Hiregange, CA Rajesh Kumar T R & CA Sudhir VS - Bharat Law House
21. Central Excise Made Simple-2017 – CA Madhukar N Hiregange & CA Rajesh Kumar TR - Bharat Law House
22. https://pcaobus.org/Standards/Auditing/Pages/Auditing_Standard_3.aspx
23. https://pcaobus.org/Standards/Archived/Pages/AU339A.aspx
24. http://www.accaglobal.com/in/en/student/exam-support-resources/fundamentals-exams-study-resources/f8/technical-articles/effective-audit-service.html : ACCA/Audit Working Papers
25. SA 299: Responsibilities of Joint Auditors
26. SA 520: Analytical procedures
27. SA 530: Audit sampling
28. Audit material of ICAI
29. Annual return and Audit under GST – Swastik Publications
30. AS 1– Disclosure of Accounting Policies (Ind AS 1)
31. AS 2 – Valuation of Inventories (Ind AS 2)
32. AS3 – Cash Flow Statements (Ind AS 7)
33. AS 4 – Contingencies and Events occurring after the Balance Sheet date (Ind AS 10)
34. AS 5 – Net profit or Loss for the Period, Prior Period Items and Changes in Accounting Policies (Ind AS 8)
35. AS 7 – Accounting for Construction Contracts (Ind AS 11)
36. AS 9 – Revenue Recognition (Ind AS 18)
37. AS 10 – Property, Plant and Equipment (Ind AS 16)
38. AS 11 – The effects of changes in foreign exchange rates (Ind AS 21)
39. AS 12 – Accounting for Government Grants (Ind AS 20)
40. AS 18 – Related Party Disclosures (Ind AS 24)
41. AS 29 – Provisions contingent liabilities and assets (Ind AS 37)
42. AS 24 – Discontinuing operations (Ind AS 105)
43. Ind AS – Icai.org/ in